Mammon and Manon in Early New Orleans

THE FIRST SLAVE SOCIETY IN THE DEEP SOUTH, 1718–1819

D0937818

Thomas N. Ingersoll

The University of Tennessee Press / Knoxville

The paper used in this book meets the minimum requirements of
ANSI/NISO Z39.48-1992 (R 1997) (Permanence of Paper). The binding materials
have been chosen for strength and durability. Printed on recycled paper.

Library of Congress Cataloging-in-Publication Data
Ingersoll, Thomas N.
Mammon and Manon in early New Orleans : the first slave society
in the Deep South, 1718–1819 / Thomas N. Ingersoll. — 1st ed.
          p. cm.
Includes bibliographical references (p.) and index.
ISBN 1-57233-023-6 (cl.: alk. paper)
ISBN 1-57233-024-4 (pbk.: alk. paper)
1. New Orleans (La.)—History—18th century. 2. New Orleans
(La.)—History—19th century. 3. New Orleans (La.)—Race relations.
4. New Orleans (La.)—Social conditions. 5. Slavery—Louisiana—New
Orleans—History—18th century. 6. Slavery—Louisiana—New
Orleans—History—19th century. I. Title.
F379.N557 I54 1999
976.3'35—ddc21   98-25313

To N. Neil Ingersoll
&
Jean Lavonne Ingersoll

Contents

Illustrations

FIGURES

MAPS

TABLES

Acknowledgments

In a work of this kind, one relies on the help of many people, and this book received the kind assistance of experts and friends from many walks of life.

Archivists, librarians, and other staff members of various institutions were very generous with their time. These institutions include: The Historic New Orleans Collection, the Louisiana State Museum, the New Orleans Public Library, the several departments of Howard-Tilton Memorial Library at Tulane University, the several departments of the Earl K. Long Library of the University of New Orleans, the Special Collections Department of Xavier University Library, the Archives of the Archdiocese of New Orleans, the Notarial Archives of New Orleans, the Archives Nationales (Paris), the Archivo Histórico Nacional, the Biblioteca Nacional (Madrid), the Archives Nationales (Montreal), the National Archives (Ottawa), the National Archives (Washington), the Newberry Library, the Special Collections of the University of Texas at Austin, and the Louisiana Division of the University of Southwestern Louisiana Library.

Several other university libraries—including those of the University of California at Los Angeles, Berkeley, and Santa Barbara; McGill University; the University of Ottawa; the University of Montreal; Concordia University; Stanford University, Georgetown University, and the University of North Carolina at Chapel Hill—generously allowed me free access.

I owe special debts to archivists Alfred E. Lemmon, Charles E. Nolan, Edward F. Haas, Wilbur E. Meneray, and Colin Hamer.

I am indebted to the CRSH for funding a research trip to European archives.

Several journals published articles in which discussions of certain topics scattered here among various chapters were brought together and documented in greater detail than is possible here; namely, the *William and Mary Quarterly*, *Law and History Review*, and *Louisiana History*, to the editors of which I am very obliged.

Several people read either the entire manuscript or substantial portions of it at various stages in its development, especially Joyce Appleby, Geoffrey Symcox, Claudia Mitchell-Kernan, and Kathleen Brown in its first form as a doctoral dissertation. Two anonymous readers for the University of Tennessee Press devoted many hours of conscientious effort to persuading me to clarify difficult passages.

Others critiqued one or more individual chapters: Morris S. Arnold, Gilbert C. Din, (the late) Samuel Wilson Jr., Jaquelyn Pope Warshaw, and the several members of the Early American Thesis Seminar of Pacific Palisades.

Colleagues who offered invaluable advice at the outset include Willard Rollings, Patricia K. Galloway, and Joseph Logsdon. I discussed key issues with Warren Billings, John A. Dickinson, Arlette Gautier, Eugene D. Genovese, Gwendolyn Midlo Hall, Kimberly S. Hanger, Louis Lavallée, Claude Morin, Judith K. Schafer, Paul Lachance, Ann Patton Malone, Joseph Zitomersky, and (the late) Jack D. L. Holmes.

For awakening my interest in the early South, I am grateful to John E. Tricamo and Jerald A. Combs.

No one put more effort into this project than Gary B. Nash, who encouraged me to pursue the research and who read version after version of every chapter of the original dissertation, a heroic effort beyond the call of duty.

Finally, I owe thanks to research assistants Christian Alcindor, Julio Bustamante, Daviken Studnicki-Gizbert, Viviane Bouchard, and Yves Otis. Edward Shapiro worked hard on several difficult photographs. Librarian Rose Lambert was particularly kind to me at the Louisiana State Museum.

Introduction

This is the story of a community built by slaveowners and slaves and how it grew during its first century. Unlike books about southern colonies, counties, or small towns, this book's aim is to describe social and political continuity and change in a large urban-rural community over a long period. New Orleans was from its origin a slave society with a black majority. Moreover, it combined the kind of labor and social relations associated with both an urban setting *and* plantations—plantations that began immediately at the borders of what long remained a villagelike town center, encircling it in compact fashion. Only at the end of the eighteenth century did the town center fill with people and begin to expand into a true city with suburbs. Although historians have written numerous accounts of either slavery or slaveowners, this is the history of all the people in the slave society of one community and its gradual transformation from a plantation-dominated parish into a booming city. Everybody in this community was shaped by his or her color, class, and gender, and this story focuses on how individuals struggled to either maintain or undo those categories and the hierarchical structure they formed, a structure ruled by a class of rich white people, particularly men.

Research for this work was guided by the conviction that development in early America was less about European cultural institutions than about social "structural arrangements that did not strictly govern most human interaction but set the boundaries for it . . . within the context of a triracial society."[1] The most important factor in molding this society was color: in a slave society, all relations are determined by a legally defined "race" of slaves. This view builds on previous studies of slavery in colonial America, such as Peter H. Wood's

Black Majority.[2] In both Wood's coastal South Carolina and New Orleans a black majority was not just instrumental in the building of a colony but also the key to the foundation of a conscious, organized planter class. Wood devoted little space to exploring the lives of white people and their personal relations with slaves and free blacks because his object was to describe the slaves themselves, their contributions to the development of the colony, and their struggle against the supremacy of the slaveowners. By contrast, the focus here is on the interaction of individual blacks and whites in molding the society of New Orleans. This approach also differs from Alan Kulikoff's in *Tobacco and Slaves,* which is concerned with masters and slaves but treats them on a topical and statistical basis and includes the geographically dispersed people of several large, rural Chesapeake counties, each of which was "far too vast a territory to constitute a single community."[3] By contrast, this study reveals the actual relations of power among a few thousand people who formed a true, compact community within a rather small residential area. It is the story of real individuals and families of all colors and conditions, over a period of several generations, all struggling to create order despite the basic moral lawlessness of slavery.

Class was the second factor that made New Orleans what it was, although there was only one true class, that of the planters. The evidence from New Orleans helps to sharpen our understanding of the basic chemistry of relations between masters and slaves in the formation of the planter class. When historians first began studying slavery in earnest, they exaggerated the power of masters, but in the 1960s and 1970s, "there was an equally noticeable tendency to exaggerate the power of the slaves."[4] This book seeks to make a contribution to the present trend toward a more refined evaluation of what powers masters and slaves had and how they negotiated with one another. The deeper one penetrates the archives, the more impressed one is by the inability of either group to maintain solidarity consistently. The slaveholders had many advantages, being a vulnerable minority with a compelling need to unify under an ideological banner to protect their interest, and enjoying the support of a major imperial military force and a common European cultural heritage.[5] Their class was, nevertheless, weakened by the extremely independent behavior of individual masters, who often pursued their own particular interests in open defiance of the dictates of their class. They were united only by fear of the black majority, which was, however, too divided to exploit to the utmost the fissures in the regime. Although blacks always outnumbered whites, they lacked allies, and their variety of interests and cultural backgrounds impaired their ability to form a class.

Gender makes almost any generalization about masters and slaves subject to qualification, because both white and black women's experience with the slave regime was different from that of men. This subject has been quite literally buried in a heap of myths because historians and popular writers have established as queen of New Orleans the figure of the sultry temptress, "Manon," or the enduring popular image of New Orleans as a place where women of both colors gave themselves up to illicit sex with men, whenever the latter were not indulging in other vices or crimes. It will be argued throughout this book that this notion deserves not modification but retirement. Domestic relations in New Orleans were as regular as they were in Charleston, until the nineteenth century, when the peculiar geographic position of the town and its transformation into a large and anonymous city made it, among other things, the capital of the sex trade in the South. In fact, Mammon ruled in New Orleans, and although he was responsible for the horrible disorder of the founding, he required a semblance of order and respectability to attract immigrants and capital to satisfy his devotees' ambition. So Manon was effectively suppressed by 1731. She tried to rise again at the end of the eighteenth century, in the form of the supposed black "Jezebel" whose charms, it was believed, "would inevitably result in the disappearance of the 'pure' Caucasian," but she was held down by the collective force exerted especially by white women in defense of their own threatened status.[6]

In simpler terms, the overarching argument is that over the course of its first century, this community's development was marked by order, contrary to the prevailing interpretation of early New Orleans as an anarchy, a kind of paradise for "thieves, vagabonds, and prostitutes."[7] The evidence provided in the chapters to follow shows very clearly that the streets and plantations of New Orleans were not an exotic domain of vice and crime and that the town was, in fact, as morally orderly as the closest neighboring towns, Charleston and Savannah. Yet it was "order" only in a comparative sense, for any slave society is by definition disorderly, based on bad faith.

The planter class and the slaves created a community remarkably similar to other slave societies found in continental North America. The province of Louisiana was governed by the metropolitan powers of Bourbon France, Bourbon Spain, and then Napoleonic France before the lower part of the colony became the state of Louisiana in the United States. (The basic political changes are presented schematically below.) It will be argued in the chapters to follow, however, that the social development of New Orleans was marked by a remarkable degree of continuity over time. Slave society is basically conservative: its social organization does not permit much deviation from a standard regime so long as slaves form the majority, and the political administrations altered conditions only indirectly and slightly.

Debate about the character of slave society in a comparative context still turns on the argument by Frank Tannenbaum in his book, *Slave and Citizen,* published in 1947.[8] He asserts that legal protections of slaves in Spanish or Portuguese colonies and religious attitudes in all Catholic colonies prevented masters from completely dehumanizing their chattels, whereas they were most dehumanized in Anglo-American colonies, and somewhere in between these two extremes in French colonies.

Despite much criticism, Tannenbaum's book is still widely read. Because New Orleans developed under the rule of successive French and Spanish regimes and then came under American republican institutions after 1803, it presents an opportunity to test Tannenbaum's thesis. If he was right about the effect of law and religion, the story of the town's planter class should reveal that slaves were somewhat dehumanized by masters under French laws and clergy, then less so under Spanish institutions, and then more than ever after American rule began in 1803.

The evidence shows, however, that laws or religion had little or no influence on either the planter class or the condition of black slaves or free blacks. The basic character of society was the same in New Orleans as in Wood's South Carolina, Kulikoff's Prince George's County, or anywhere else where the labor of black slaves was the mainstay of the economy. New Orleans was distinctive in some ways. Every slave society was unique because of variations in the size of the slave population, the supply of slaves, the slaves' ethnic origins, the local crop regime, the rate of manumission, or the settlement pattern. These specific conditions could make a big difference to some people. Moreover, communities can be classified according to these conditions, especially according to the local demographic profile. Fundamental cultural distinctions between slave societies are not to be found, however, for regardless of minor variations, a basic, large degree of dehumanization was required to define a group of people as a race and keep them legally degraded. Slave society had to be organized to prevent the strivings of blacks to assert a moral claim to freedom (an ideological claim by the end of the eighteenth century), to limit the number and social status of those who were manumitted, and to protect but also police the individual master who was lord on his plantation and regarded the rules of his class as designed to restrain everyone but him.

The slave societies of North America form a natural family, therefore, somewhat different from those of the Caribbean, particularly on account of demography. While New Orleans is the most distinctive slave society in North America because of its exceptional geographic isolation, it will be seen that it was indisputably North American in character, not Caribbean. The demographic character of the town was not at all like that of the major French West Indian societies, and very few of the settlers or slaves came from the West Indies until the very end of the colonial period, long after the town's essential patterns had been shaped by the original settlers and Africans. The social development of New Orleans was much like that of other slave societies in colonial North America, which is why it was incorporated so easily into the United States after 1803 without major cultural conflicts.

If the specific European legal regime in New Orleans had little effect on the character of its development, the laws were, nevertheless, essential tendons in the articulation of the social structure. This is all the more true, from the standpoint of the historian, because judicial records form one of the major archives of colonial Louisiana. Many other kinds of evidence familiar to historians of English colonies do not exist for Louisiana. Since colonists did not have representative institutions, they did not vote and left no electoral or legislative records. They never had to pay property taxes and left no cadastral records. Since their limited personal correspondence was almost entirely with French people in their home towns—in every corner of France and New France—few of their letters have been collected or published. They had no newspapers until the end of the colonial era. This study relies on rich imperial reports and eyewitness accounts to retrieve the town's history, but also on judicial records. Dependence on the latter is not excessive: I have studied or at least briefly examined all records of every sort concerning New Orleans, but court proceedings are the major means of entry into the lives of these people.

The dangers of using judicial records are well known: they tend to overemphasize disorder, overrepresent the possessing classes, and overemphasize the role of specific individuals. In fact, in this case the judicial records serve to revise the prevailing view that the town's social life was chaotic: after the early years, for example, judges confronted few white criminals in the courtroom. Moreover, although the records as a whole are dominated by the planter class, the focus is not on the planters but on social relations between all elements of the community, and the role of the individual is constantly juxtaposed against the power of structural forces. What follows is not a legal history but a social history that by necessity often rests on evidence extracted in bits and pieces from the records of trials, suits, and to some extent from the laws themselves.

"Plantations in a town?" the reader will ask. Yes: defining the contours of this community proved to be problematic. Trained by a historian of colonial American towns, I began with the conventional concept of urban community that excluded plantations but soon discovered that the people of New Orleans did not share that limited concept.[9] Their definition of the town is carefully laid out in chapter 1, but it can be encapsulated here: the subject of this study was a tiny seaport on a bend in the Mississippi River together with the plantations that clustered snugly around it. This community was a town in the eighteenth century, but only a minority of its denizens actually lived in the urban space marked out on the map as "New Orleans." It did not begin to become a city with suburbs, street lamps, numerous hostelries, and the other marks of true urban life until the end of the eighteenth century. In the last section of the book, the town center will become fully urbanized, meaning that the streets with townhouses and shops will spread beyond the original boundaries: faubourgs will appropriate the commons and plantations that lay directly on the borders of the town center, so the distinction between city and country will become more refined. Real travel time between plantation and port was always short, and people moved back and forth between periphery and center frequently. The reader should be prepared to move as readily around this community as the inhabitants did in the eighteenth century, from the handful of buildings huddled at the riverbend where people socialized, to the indigo fields, cypress swamps, and slave quarters of Tchoupitoulas, Bayou St. Jean, or the Lower Coast, where the majority worked and slept.

It is necessary to emphasize that this book is not about the colony of Louisiana that stretched beyond Cannes Bruslées, a subject that cries out for synthesis. A recent outpouring of books about the Old Southwest is promising, and it is to be hoped that interest in the region will continue to grow. Gwendolyn Midlo Hall, Paul Lachance, and others have written about African Americans in the colony at large; the Native Americans of the region have received the attention of Daniel Usner and Patricia Galloway, yet the difficult task of describing the enormous colony is far from finished. Many of the conclusions presented in this book about New Orleans are not true of the rest of Louisiana. Communities such as those of Illinois or Pointe Coupée were quite unlike New Orleans.

Since the political history of Louisiana is the source of confusion, it is useful to specify that this book is concerned only with the last four of the seven periods in the following summary overview of the early history of the lower Mississippi Valley:

1. Sixteenth century. Spanish explorers periodically searched the region for gold.

2. Seventeenth century. French Canadian explorers gradually pushed down the Mississippi River and claimed Louisiana for France in 1682.

3. Eighteenth century: 1699–1718. Jacques and Jean-Baptiste Le Moyne ("Iberville" and "Bienville") led a small expedition of their fellow Canadians to the region to establish small settlements. The founders had ambitious plans to roll back the British colonies of the Atlantic seaboard, but the crown was content to secure the strategic back door to Canada and tap the Indians' fur supply. The number of settlers, soldiers, and slaves in Louisiana was never more than a few hundred at any time in this period.

4. Eighteenth century: 1718–31. New Orleans was founded by the regency government of the duke of Orléans, perhaps the largest state-sponsored settlement of the European colonial era, involving up to twenty thousand people. Of these, only about one-fourth actually arrived, survived, and remained in the New Orleans region by 1731, with a few colonists and soldiers scattered among posts in the interior. The "Mississippi" stock bubble of 1720 ruined Louisiana's reputation, and if the slaveowning minority had not had such promising investments in New Orleans, and if Louis XV had not taken over administration of Louisiana from the Company of the Indies in 1731, most settlers would have abandoned the place.

5. Eighteenth century: 1731–69. Louisiana's population continued to grow slowly, augmented by few immigrants. The colonists were just strong enough to drive back but not defeat Indian enemies in the 1730s and to develop a diversified, modest export economy. When Louis XV lost New France to the British in 1760, he gave New Orleans and Louisiana west of the Mississippi River to Charles III of Spain. The Spanish king sent a governor to New Orleans, but he was unable to take control of the colony, and several clumsy moves by the Spanish provoked

a bloodless insurrection in 1768, as a result of which the colonists forced the governor to flee Louisiana.

6. Eighteenth century: 1769–1803. Charles III sent a powerful general and a small army to reorganize the colony by force. The general tried and executed the leaders of the revolt and introduced Spanish rule over the stunned colonists. Despite this episode, the remaining whites subsequently benefited from liberalized trade privileges within the Spanish empire, the unofficial toleration of illegal trade with British and American merchants, reasonably efficient civil and military administration, exemption from taxation, and the encouragement of voluntary white and involuntary black immigration. The people of New Orleans supported Governor Bernardo Gálvez's expedition of 1779–81 during the American Revolution, which led to the rapid seizure of West Florida from the English. But the Spanish monarchy became so weak after the death of Charles III that in a complex exchange Spain gave Louisiana back to France in 1800. The French did not actually take possession of the colony, however, until just days before an American governor took over from them in December 1803, for Napoleon sold the colony to the Americans.

7. Nineteenth century: 1803–19. The colony was subsequently integrated into the Republic without major incidents, and the town experienced rapid economic development, rising in one generation to become one of the richest plantation societies and seaports in the United States. Immigration by people of every description transformed the town into a city. The slaveholding class was so strong and so conservative, so able to minimize the effects of ethnic diversity, that the town became the economic capital of the Deep South over night with a remarkably small degree of social strife.

This is a work of synthesis, not a monograph but an attempt to describe social development over a long period of time. It will be obvious to the reader by now that the locus of power will be found in the competing ambitions of the slaveholders, the blacks, and the few Indians who were always part of the community. The ambitions of slaveowners led them into delusion and bad faith, and some into ruthless exploitation and cruelty. By "delusion" I mean, for example, their conviction that they alone built and controlled the destiny of New Orleans, whereas when blacks looked at New Orleans in 1819 they could see only buildings they had built, fields that flourished because of their expertise, levees they had maintained to keep out the implacable river, a society they had shaped by resistance. The planters' principal delusion, in fact, was that while most individual masters imagined themselves both superior to and loved unconditionally by their own slaves, collectively their success was limited by resentful blacks. The planters arranged their own political life to suppress debilitating conflict among themselves, and in 1803 they finally shook off the annoyance of metropolitan power, but the potential political power of their slaves (so terrifyingly demonstrated in Saint Domingue in the 1790s) remained a threat to their supremacy and self-image, and it informed all their social relations with blacks.

The various social groups, rather than politics, will command our attention, but the thread of the town's political life is woven into the story. In part 1, chapter 1 offers an explanation of why France undertook the unprecedented colonizing scheme of founding New Orleans, and a description of the mass migration itself. Chapter 2 describes the creation of a social structure by the founding generation of colonists, and chapter 3 outlines the origin of the black community. Chapter 4 treats whites and blacks together in a slave society, with emphasis on the effect of creolization in the second generation. (The word "creole" and its derivatives in this book always mean, simply, "born in America.")[10] In chapter 5, the comparative analysis begins, focused here on showing that New Orleans was not a French Caribbean colonial society.

In part 2, chapters 6, 7, and 8 imitate the basic pattern of part 1 by covering whites, blacks, and the comparative analysis respectively during the Spanish regime.

Part 3 follows the same pattern of analysis: chapters 9, 10, and 11 on whites, blacks, and the comparative context, in which both the uniqueness of New Orleans and its essential similarity to other slave societies in the Deep South are described. The book ends amid the Missouri crisis resulting from the Louisiana Purchase, and a capitalist shock reminiscent of the one that marked the founding of New Orleans: the crash of 1819. It proved to be but a momentary inconvenience to the final triumph of the planter class.

A NOTE ON THE TEXT

All French names have been simplified and reduced to original spellings when possible, shorn of the "de" and seigneurial tags wherever possible, except in those cases in which historical figures like Bienville are better known by their manorial names. The variety of names and spellings in the record is a historian's nightmare. A person of substance might be referred to by the honorific "sieur" followed by a family name or manorial title. A brother or nephew might suddenly inherit a manorial title and thereby lay a snare for the unwary researcher. A woman might be referred to by either her maiden family name or the name of her husband or former husband. Common French people, both men and women, were in fact typically known by their colorful nicknames, which I avoid in the interest of uniformity. Some immigrants changed their surnames. Most French people had at least two Christian names, and Marie-Catherine might be known by that name, or by Marie, Catherine, or a diminutive. The same was true of slaves, who usually had French Christian names, but they might also be referred to by a variety of diminutives, nicknames, African names, or a combination of all four.

Monetary amounts in part 1 are in livres, the French *livre tournois* being the equivalent of just under one and a half English shillings at the beginning of the eighteenth century. In parts 2 and 3, the "$" sign or "dollar" refers to the Spanish *peso* (*piastre* in French, dollar in English), the equivalent of five livres.

A NOTE ON ARCHIVAL SOURCES

Research for this work was conducted in most documentary collections containing material on early New Orleans found in Louisiana, France, Spain, and Canada. As a result, footnotes contain many different kinds of citations. While most of these are familiar to historians of North America, certain clarifications are in order.

A reference to a file in the Louisiana Historical Collection at the Louisiana Historical Center of the Louisiana State Museum, New Orleans, is by principals and date of a specific judicial case. A cataloguing effort was never finished, and files are retrieved most easily by citations of the kind I provide. I have taken one exceptional liberty in order to simplify citations to this important source. Since its inception, the Louisiana Historical Collection has had only one major manuscript collection, the colonial judicial records, broken into two sections, the "Records of the Superior Council" of the French regime and the "Spanish Judicial Records" of the Spanish regime, the entire mass being filed in a continuous row of Hollinger boxes in chronological order. Rather than cluttering footnotes by repeating RSC or SJR in every citation to the many cases I explore, upon the first citation of this collection in each chapter the reader is alerted that all cases in that chapter will refer to one or the other of these sections, but only LHC will be cited thereafter, since no other documents in LHC are cited in this book.

Citations of series of unpublished imperial reports always give folio numbers. The most frequently cited collection of this kind is the series of reports made by officials to the French Ministry of Marine and other authorities in France, known as Archives Nationales, Archives Coloniales, series C13 A, B, and C, "Correspondance à l'arrivée en provenance de la Louisiane," 1678–1807. Moreover, each subseries is organized into a number of registers, typically having rough chronological integrity, within which the folios are numbered. Thus a citation of this kind will be presented as follows: Bienville to Maurepas, 25 July 1733, AN [for the National Archives of France], AC [for the colonial section], C13A [for the subseries], 16:265–65v [the register number and folio numbers for that specific part of the document containing the relevant evidence]. Since folios are numbered only on the obverse, it is standard practice to employ "v" for "verso" to indicate the other side of a given numbered folio. Since archivists are capable of making occasional mistakes like everyone else, when they accidentally used the same folio numbers twice, it is indicated by "bis" if the second folio of the same number is cited. While I have used microfilm copies of this particular collection (in the Archives Nationales of France, the Historic New Orleans Collection, and the National Archives of Canada) because the originals are closed to the public, reel numbers are of no help in locating documents.

In every case, original documents are cited unless these no longer exist or are inaccessible. Thus, for example, citations to the records of the deliberations of the cabildo refer not to the commonly cited but unreliable translations nor to the originals, which are closed to the public, but to the transcriptions in the vault of New Orleans Public Library.

I have translated titles of offices and the like in the interest of clarity, except in those cases where no exact translation is possible, as in the case of *commissaire ordonnateur,* who was the colony's chief judge and a kind of *intendant* but with less power.

PART I.
THE FRENCH REGIME,
1718–1769

"Fatal Golden Dreams": I

The Founding of New Orleans, 1718–1731

It is inconceivable to those who were witnesses of the horrors of those times,
and who look back upon them now as on a dream, that a sudden revolution did
not break out—that Law and the regent did not perish by a tragical death.

—Charles Pinot Duclos on the Mississippi bubble, 1720

Little girl, would you like to come to Mississippi? We'll give you a treasury
official for a husband, a man richer than your weight in gold.

—Mississippi Bandoliers to Marguerite Jobart, 1720

It is here [in New Orleans] that one loves without self-interest, without
jealousy, without inconstancy. Our fellow countrymen came here to search for
gold, they do not conceive that we have found here a far richer treasure.

—Chevalier Des Grieux in *Manon Lescaut*, 1731

The founding of New Orleans was chaotic, a fatal experience for many participants because of bad judgment in Paris. The regency government of the duke of Orléans attempted to create an entire, complex society based on both free and slave labor by transporting an enormous number of people to Louisiana in the space of a few years, a project without precedent in colonial America, and the result was a staggering loss of life. Colonists struggled to compensate for poor initial planning and the subsequent attempt by metropolitan bureaucrats to govern the settlement's economic development from afar.

For all of the suffering and confusion, by 1731 a small but profit-making slave society had been established on the banks of the Mississippi River, dominated by a still loosely knit and volatile slaveholding class. The planters were just strong enough to stave off attempts by Indians and African slaves to destroy their power. They were barely able to weather continuing bad policy decisions made in France. The planters' strength arose from their crude but effective unity of purpose as a class, a unity forged to an important degree by their leader, Jean-Baptiste Bienville, who made the colony's new capital one of the most geographically cohesive plantation societies in the Americas. A few wealthy founders established large estates in the interior, far from the capital, but most failed quickly, leaving the small knot of plantations at New Orleans. The town survived because of its exceptional consolidation, which enabled colonists to maximize the advantages of their common interests against their enemies. The settlement's reputation was doomed by 1731, however, a remote place with no instant riches that was thought to be inhabited by a dissolute mob of outcasts from the Old World, a reputation that severely limited its future growth.

The choice of the site for New Orleans was a strategic decision based on nearly two centuries of exploration in the region. The Spanish were the first Europeans to claim and explore the lower Mississippi Valley in the 1540s, but the only mark they left was a bitter memory among the local Native Americans of Hernando de Soto's brutal quest for gold.[1] Partly because they found no treasure, partly because early Spanish ships could not navigate interior waterways, European colonization did not occur until much later, after French explorers from Canada paddled down the Mississippi River to its mouth. The French were interested in the region from the earliest settlement of New France, but it was only on April 9, 1682, that an obsessive visionary named Robert La Salle and his Italian friend Henri de Tonti claimed the interior of North America and named it Louisiana in honor of Louis XIV.[2] They forged friendly relations with Indian nations who were still angry about the Spaniards' violence one and a half centuries earlier.[3] They were followed in 1699 by a group of Canadians from New France led by Pierre Le Moyne, Sieur d'Iberville, who built forts on the Biloxi and Mobile Rivers, east of the Mississippi.

The French planned to gain control of the region above the Gulf of Mexico and then expand French control northward along the Atlantic coast, which they claimed by right of prior discovery. Iberville hoped to drive the English from North America.[4] During those two decades following 1699, however, only a small number of colonists and soldiers held down the French claim. Iberville secured allies among local Indian nations and seduced down the river a few other members of the Canadian gentry plus some *coureurs de bois* and *voyageurs* of western Canada.[5] But Iberville succumbed to fever in Cuba in 1706, just before his projected attack on South Carolina during the War of the Spanish Succession. He was replaced in the role of Louisiana's guiding spirit by his younger brother, Jean-Baptiste Le Moyne, Sieur de Bienville.[6] Bienville would live nearly forty years in the colony, serve often as its governor, and retire to France with a fortune in 1743. In 1706, however, only his intrepid personality sustained him, for he was young and officially disfavored, his brother having died leaving unsatisfactory accounts of the king's property. In those first two decades, Bienville's motley flock of young men and a few French women could not establish anything resembling European society, surrounded as they were by many thousands of Native Americans. More than once the colonists were forced to winter with friendly Indians to keep from starving, and it was all Bienville could do to keep his charges from being assimilated into those Indian towns.

The Le Moynes' dream of a Louisiana empire was ill fated because Louis XIV "was always more excited by one fortress in Flanders or the Palatinate than by all of India, Canada and Louisiana put together."[7] If the crown of France had done anything to facilitate settlement, the French could have filled the rich valleys of the North American interior with colonists. But in 1718 French Louisiana barely existed.[8] No plan had been developed and little effort made to turn it into a true agricultural colony of settlement.[9] The king had regarded the outpost as such a nuisance during the war that in 1712 he leased it to a wealthy commoner, Antoine Crozat, who was mainly interested in the peltry trade. Crozat milked that source for its easy profits, invested little in the colony, saddled it with a cranky governor who demoralized the settlers, and finally, in 1717, declared it to be of little value and yielded it back to the crown.[10]

When Crozat pulled out of Louisiana, he left a population that struck a newly arrived French official as a riotous mob of libertines under the rule of neither law nor religion.[11] Constantly threatening to become a group of mixed-race peoples (métis) who would abandon their European heritage, numbering about four hundred, this unique society has been described in detail by Marcel Giraud.[12] The early pioneers had played an important role for the French nation at a time when the English would have seized an unoccupied lower Mississippi Valley, but thereafter these settlers and their descendants mostly lived in the Mobile River Valley and other settlements far from New Orleans.

Their society was no model for the one now projected, which had been so long advocated by the Le Moynes: a slave society supported by a hinterland full of farmers that would not only rival Virginia and South Carolina economically but also provide a base for overwhelming the English in those colonies.

From the beginning, Iberville and Bienville had recognized the significance of a particular site, one of the many turns in the sinuous river that flowed into the Gulf of Mexico one hundred miles below.[13] Those treacherous miles of muddy water south of the river bend would discourage enemy intrusion. That particular crescent in the shoreline was the origin of an old Indian portage to a series of huge lakes that provided an eastern, backdoor route to the gulf. That Indian trail was the key to control of the entire Mississippi River delta on the underbelly of North America, a region that contained some of the richest soil in the world.[14] Besides, it was impossible to establish a settlement on the river closer to the coast, for "a little below New Orleans the soil begins to be very shallow on both sides the Mississippi."[15] Moreover, the whole region lying between the lakes and the river was protected by a natural levee bordering the river that could be reinforced. After decades of neglect by the absolute monarch, Bienville could survey the miles of rich riverine deposits and cypress forest stretched behind the riverbend and envision a colonial capital there.

The key to the change in Louisiana's fortunes lay in the extraordinary situation in Paris. For some restless nobles were in an expansive mood following the Sun King's death, and, under the rule of the duke of Orléans during the childhood of Louis XV, they acted on Bienville's advice. They chose the crescent to be the focal point of a grand design, the largest colonial settlement ever undertaken by a European government. It was a scheme to link Canada, Louisiana, and the Antilles in a strong economic cordon. Unfortunately, that object was combined with an improbable plan to induce a fiscally naive aristocracy enervated by royal absolutism to adapt overnight to a new world of commercial capital.

Orléans attempted a radical break with the past by an elaborate system promoted by John Law, a Scots financial dreamer and the regent's personal friend. Law convinced Orléans to create France's first national bank and then to link it with a joint-stock company enjoying a royal monopoly on overseas trade. This company would launch a tobacco colony in Louisiana that would end France's increasing dependence upon Virginia for tobacco. The strategy was to overcome French aristocratic prejudices against commercial investment and stocks, for according to the antibourgeois feudal ethos, such things were unworthy of the noble warriors aristocrats claimed to be. To overcome their resistance, leading peers would simply be given large blocks of "Mississippi" stock in the crown-controlled joint-stock company; so other lords and the general public would buy shares to emulate them and share in the profits. Capital raised from stock sales would finance the settlement of Louisiana by the company. Colonists would pay off the costs of settlement by tobacco production with slave labor and by mining the "immense treasures" of gold or silver that must exist, it was believed, somewhere in such a huge territory.[16] Royal import fees on tobacco would produce a revenue of four million livres.[17]

Law's plan was well suited to a society moving from a war to a peace economy. Instead of serving in huge armies, ordinary French people would be strategically positioned as settlers in the contest with Great Britain and Spain to control mainland North America, and capital would be created instead of wasted on war. Both goals might have been within reach, for England had shown the way by stabilizing financial corporations and exchange mechanisms with a national bank in the 1690s. France had an enormous population (about twenty million) from which to cull settlers to support an expanded colonial trade network. The "honest adventurer" Law and Orléans convinced many key members of the upper classes to subscribe to their plan. By 1719, what was eventually called the Compagnie des Indes became an all-inclusive trade monopoly, the company of all companies, based on publicly traded shares, capitalized at the fabulous level of one hundred million livres.[18] The company attracted rich concessionaires, who would develop land grants with indentured servants and deported whites laboring alongside African slaves advanced by the company. Law also orchestrated a promotional campaign to convince ambitious common people to emigrate voluntarily to a paradise where they would be greeted by complaisant Indians.[19] The one magic ingredient required to make the scheme work was public confidence in the stock. That was not to be, however, because Law's undoubted brilliance was fatally undercut by his recklessness. His media campaign was too successful, for in 1720 the shares of stock in Louisiana's future, which promised only 5 percent annual interest, lured the greedy gamblers of the upper classes into a frenzy of speculation. Moreover, Law had a naive notion that the government could and should print unlimited quantities of paper money. In the Paris stock exchange in Rue Quincampoix, investors created a bubble that soon burst in a moment of panic: suddenly the stock was worthless because no one would buy it.[20]

The episode showed that the French, passionately fond of gambling, were still far from a normal course toward capitalist development.[21] Louis XIV had so reduced the Second Estate to the feudal concerns of manor, benefice, and royal favor that aristocrats could bring to the world of stock investments little more than fascination with the sudden wealth of a lotto or buried treasure.[22] When excited shareholders ignorant of conditions in America forced the prices of the company shares to celestial heights in 1720 and Louisiana did not produce riches capable of sustaining shares at 2,000 percent over par, Law could not prevent the stock from collapsing, and he fled into exile. Angry mobs surged through Paris looking for him, and a man whose lackeys' livery merely resembled Law's was nearly torn to pieces.[23] Not only was the country's colonizing spirit wounded, but the new Banque Royale was a casualty of the collapse. France was thereafter inhibited from developing institutions of higher finance, and the financial crisis that precipitated the French Revolution in 1789 can be traced in part to the events of 1720.[24]

New Orleans was "the theatre of the fatal golden dreams of Law's speculation," and its development was stunted by the event for many decades.[25] Before Law's downfall, the Company of the Indies spent over nine million livres on Louisiana and transported up to seven thousand white people to the colony. The company also carried nineteen hundred African slaves before the bubble burst in 1720 and was to bring in roughly thirty-five hundred more before its exclusive tenure ended a decade later.[26] Regardless of the planning and expense, the company did not deliver enough provisions to keep so many people alive. Moreover, war broke out between Spain and France in 1718, forcing the colonists into a costly campaign to seize Spanish Pensacola in West Florida. They gained the post, lost it, regained it, and burned it in 1719, a huge waste of energies, depleting provisions and creating great confusion just before the main body of immigrants arrived.[27]

According to the colonist Dumont de Montigny, so many people arrived so suddenly in 1719 that Bienville had to disperse many "soldiers, workmen, and even officers" to live with the Biloxi and Pascagoula Indians, "who received them with great pleasure."[28] But the crowding worsened despite Bienville's urgent warnings to moderate the flow of newcomers. The immigrants who waited at staging areas on the Gulf of Mexico were already dying from fevers at terrible rates. (Biloxi was the center of activity in the colony until 1723, when New Orleans was sufficiently developed to become the seat of government and primary port.) When the bubble burst late in 1720, thousands of settlers and slaves were already under sailing orders, and many were unloaded in Louisiana that following summer. The group contained some white convicts or social deviants who were forcibly recruited from prisons or street corners, and Louisiana authorities were callous toward them. By the time of the bubble, a specially appointed crew of recruiters called "the Mississippi Bandoliers" roamed the kingdom in search of vulnerable young people to deport, like sixteen-year-old Marguerite Jobart (noted in this chapter's second epigraph), who was seized violently by the bandoliers when she refused their extravagant offer. By 1721, communities throughout France had watched tumbrils filled with unfortunate outcasts rolling toward seaports for exile in Louisiana. Many of these people were simply dumped on the beach at Biloxi following their long transatlantic voyage and provided with no farming supplies or guns. Some rich planters produced crops immediately and were able to relieve some distress, but the crops were too few, and hungry colonists devoured the livestock intended to breed herds and flocks. Some people died "from eating herbs they did not know . . . others from eating oysters."[29] Many died from diseases caused by the strange pathogens their fellow passengers carried with them from various regions.[30] Some just starved. This event was not really more murderous than the prolonged agony of Virginia's founding generations nor so awful as the French resettlement of Guiana in the 1760s, but more people died with more shocking rapidity than in early Virginia, and the Guiana episode still lay in the future.[31]

Surviving Louisiana colonists reaped the hostility of a metropolitan elite that was paralyzed by the consequences of its own folly. The company's engineers laid out New Orleans and surveyed land grants for thousands, but few voluntary immigrants came after that: common French people had a horror of the place. The few settlers who did arrive in the years after 1721 were independent people with connections in France who could acquire land and slaves on credit in Louisiana. After some colonists provoked a devastating attack by one of the local Indian nations in 1729, described below, the Company of the Indies was thoroughly discredited, and the company's directors abandoned the colony to the king in 1731.[32] Thus, the stock bubble proved to be the first step in an inversion of the public image of "Mississippi" from paradise to purgatory. The disinclination of most French people to emigrate to North America was reinforced by dread of Louisiana as a barren land of folly, a wilderness infested with deported thugs and harlots, bloodthirsty Indians, and horrid wild animals.[33]

The colony's image in France was perfected in that same year of 1731, when New Orleans became the supposed destination of the "wretched exiles," Chevalier Des Grieux and his corrupt lover in Abbé Prévost's popular melodrama, *Manon Lescaut*. Hounded from polite society in France, they take refuge in Louisiana only to run afoul of local authorities, so they flee to the desert, where Manon dies. Prévost's voluptuous Manon came to serve not only as a general eighteenth-century metaphor for the unimproved and degenerative Western Hemisphere but also as a symbol of deprivation, vice, and tyranny in New Orleans. Des Grieux might be satisfied with the "far richer treasure" of pure love to be had in a hellish wasteland, but for most French people that was an insufficient reward to move to New Orleans. The colony was a condemned terrain of exile ruled by Mammon, the god of avarice, but forever haunted by the restless spirit of Manon.[34] Thus, as reported home by Ursuline Sister Marie Madeleine Hachard upon arrival in New Orleans in 1727, after the worst mortality of the founding years was over, she was surprised to meet mostly nice people rather than the ugly mob she expected: most of the white exiles who might have formed a mob were gone by then.[35] But after 1731 not even contrary reports by a nun could retire the image of Manon in France. After 1721, French immigration to Louisiana was minimal, less than one thousand before the end of the French regime.

Now let us examine the settlers more carefully. Most of the white founders and a sizable number of the black ones arrived between 1718 and 1721. They are listed in table 1 in rough order of status.[36] Superficially this group may appear to reflect French society: a small number of people of means and privilege on one side and a large category of common people, including slaves, on the other. But the founding population did not resemble that of the Old World, not at all.

The two white groups were much closer to one another than they were in France for four reasons. First, no representatives of the upper echelons of the first two estates were included: no great lords or bishops ever settled in Louisiana. The original plans for production in the Mississippi scheme emphasized the central role of a group of large land grants to magnates in France who promised to develop these concessions. The Company of the Indies provided investors with both forced and voluntary indentured French settlers and enslaved Africans on credit, who would produce a staple for export. Concessionaires kept the profits of their plantations and promised not to engage privately in trade, and the Company of the Indies provided transport and

TABLE I

ARRIVALS IN LOUISIANA, 1718–21

Settler	N	%
Officers (military and administrative)	122	1.4
Concessionaires or their agents	119	1.4
Company clerks and employees	43	0.5
Company laborers (artisans)	302	3.3
Indentured (unskilled and skilled)	2,462	27.6
White women	1,215	13.6
White children	502	5.6
Deportees (farmers and indigents)	1,278	14.3
Soldiers	977	11.0
African slaves	1,901	21.3
Total	8,921	100.0

profited by its monopoly of the colony's trade with the outside world.[37] This arrangement was in accord with the old theory of colonial mercantilism by which the *exclusif* was maintained for select merchants of the mother country.[38]

Since the magnate investors had no intention of going to America, they hired directors for their Louisiana property, most of them drawn from the lower French and French Canadian gentry, although the concession normally carried the magnate's name. One of these is described as having one hundred whites, forty-six black slaves, and two Indian slaves in 1721, producing rice and other provisions.[39] Because the initial master plan was overly ambitious and underfunded, however, most of the large concessions proved to be too far from New Orleans for their lonely inhabitants to be either happy or secure, and in any case the white laborers soon died or earned their freedom after serving out their term of indenture. After the bubble, few concessionaires were willing or able to invest any more money in their Louisiana properties, and most of the magnate-owned concessions collapsed.[40]

The result of the disintegration of the large concessions was that by 1731 the majority of permanent planters were locals, free and independent settlers of relatively low rank who had acquired a few slaves and henceforth formed the solid core of the planter class.[41] Only a few original Louisianians even hailed from the French gentry: a majority of those who settled permanently were of the Canadian gentry, such as the Le Moynes. These people usually had common or even very common ancestry, like the "gentry" of Virginia, who might even soil their hands working their plantations. While those of Louisiana were no more democratically minded than the planters of Virginia, like them they could not separate themselves so far or so disdainfully from those settlers who lacked manorial titles as they would have done in France.

A second reason New Orleans society could not be described as European was that after the early years there remained relatively few settlers derived directly from the peasantry, the people who comprised the vast majority of the population of France. The disease debacle produced by the mass migration to Louisiana disproportionately affected the poorest and most vulnerable. Above all, early New Orleans society was not composed of disreputable people who had to leave France. For the actual criminals and "libertines" who arrived in Louisiana, life was short, and ultimately they played a small part in the colony's history. The deportees numbered 1,278, only 21 percent of the 6,043 French immigrants listed in table 1. Many were unsuited to the purpose for which they were transported. The criminals comprised smugglers of untaxed salt or tobacco, the homeless, and libertines, including the minority of persons who were actually guilty of crimes against property or persons. It is true that the deportees had a wide variety of skills. The *Maréchal d'Estrées* out of La Rochelle in 1719, for example, transported 70 men convicted of tobacco smuggling, ranging in age from ten to seventy years, and included hemp-dressers, tailors, a silversmith, cook, paper-maker, mason, and surgeon. Even the lowest class—deserters, vagabonds, and libertines—included shoemakers, silk workers, and a founder, button maker, tailor, surgeon, and tapestry maker.[42] But there was little immediate demand for many of these skills in Louisiana and most of these people were supposed to do heavy manual labor, for which they were not trained.

Another group of the deportees were those cast out of bourgeois or artisan families, usually for "irreligion" and generally called *libertines*, meaning anyone not sufficiently obedient to authority.[43] One Charles, twenty-two years old, had gone to Paris to study theology. Falling into debt instead, his parents turned him over to the authorities with a small pension that would help him survive in America.[44] Some parents were in danger of being ruined by their daughters or battered by their sons. The parents of Aymée, forty, begged authorities to send her to Mississippi because she was an incorrigible "notorious libertine."[45] A fifteen-year-old boy named Pierre was condemned by his parents as a libertine who had beaten his mother. But the warden of Bicêtre Prison decided that he was too young and refused the request to remove him from France.[46] On the other hand, another teenager barely missed a trip to Louisiana only because her mother saved her. Widow Picard petitioned in 1723 for the release of her Perette, who had been arrested for debauchery in 1718 and was actually included in a group of 150 chained women on their way to the prison ship, when she escaped with the help of some soldiers, only to be reincarcerated.[47]

If unfortunates like these who landed in Louisiana had survived the founding years, they would receive more attention here, but the vast majority of ordinary people, like Charles, Aymée, or Perette, either died of some disease within a short time or were assigned to one of the lonely outposts that dotted the interior. Louisiana authorities complained bitterly about the burden of deportees, who were unequipped to be good colonists, and the crown soon responded to these complaints, arresting the press gangs' activities after the first shipments of convicts. In the mid-1730s the ministry did deport a few more people to Louisiana, but only in small groups of about two dozen at a time according to Bienville's occasional request, which also always specified salt smugglers, presumed to be sturdy farmers. Altogether, no more than one hundred deportees were sent out from France in the decades following the founding era.[48]

The exiles who arrived before 1731 were unwanted, unmotivated, and most of them soon dead, and the early complaints about them by early administrators and priests have been unduly emphasized by historians as applying to the entire colonial era.[49] Louisiana was never a penal colony. The authorities stopped complaining about supposed criminal elements by the end of the 1720s because they had all but disappeared. So those who did survive the early years were mostly "respectable" people, and this was one key to the essential character of the social order that developed in New Orleans.[50]

The lower end of the social structure was also not occupied by the German recruits. About four thousand German settlers (not found in table 1) were destined for the colony, but after suffering appalling mortality while waiting in French ports for transport, during the passage over, and after they arrived, the Germans were reduced to less than two hundred by 1725.[51] They founded Côte des Allemands, the German Coast, the only farming village in lower Louisiana, about thirty miles above New Orleans.[52]

The lowest class of white society was dominated, in fact, by one particular order of whites below all of those so far discussed, who lived at the boundary between white and black status: the soldiers. In the Bienville era about two hundred of them (more in time of war) were stationed in or near New Orleans. Their basic penury can be weighed from the budget in table 2.[53] By the end of the French regime the crown was obligated for nearly one million livres annually, and the extreme disproportion between the top officers and the others, as revealed in this early budget, remained unchanged. At less than two livres per month, common soldiers could not live decently even though they were supplied with basic necessities.[54] An angry mob of soldiers had terrified Ordonnateur Hubert in 1717, and after the founding of New Orleans they verged on mutiny on two other occasions when superiors tried to cut their income.[55] The first major popular action in New Orleans resulted from the Company of the Indies' determination to reduce wages in 1723, when troops and workers threatened rebellion together and the Superior Council was forced to back down.[56] Just after Governor Vaudreuil's arrival a bread mutiny was barely averted.[57] Soldiers grumbled and schemed to desert to the Spanish or the Indians in desperation.[58] They never staged a successful revolt because they were never openly oppressed long and hard enough, but also because the government had a policy of dividing them ethnically by maintaining a regiment of mercenary Swiss troops in New Orleans, who were treated by their colonel as his personal property. The Swiss contingent ranged up to half of the New Orleans garrison and was specifically intended to divide mutinous spirit at the capital.[59]

The usual cause of soldiers' real distress was their officers' use of recruits for their personal enrichment. There is some indication that authorities in France had a policy to recruit men for Louisiana who had skills useful in the colony's economy, fully aware that they were expected to supplement their income and that of their officers by their labor out of uniform. In a study of 245 recruits sent out between 1727 and 1730, those trained in woodworking and related construction trades (a key sector in the town's economy) were clearly dominant, and those associated with the more refined artisanry of early industrial France formed a distinct minority (see table 3).[60] Like the civil immigrants, the soldiers came from a great variety of provinces, but residents from the maritime region predominated: no less than 47 percent of this sample came from Brittany. These men could be expected to work and to suffer abuse because of their poverty, their relative youth (most of them in their late teens

TABLE 2

MILITARY BUDGET FOR A FORCE OF 819 IN LOUISIANA
IN 1731, IN LIVRES

Officers, Troops, and Support	Livres
Major officers (26)	42,940
Minor officers (121)	41,056
Troops (672)	12,096
Indians	20,000
Internal navigation	23,000
Improvements	10,000
Forts	5,750
Hospital	5,000
Total	159,842

NOTE: The budget does not include subsistence for the troops.

or early twenties), their illiteracy (about 6 out of 10 could not write their own names), and their low-status skills. Several methods of exploitation were possible, including the manipulation of rations, outright cash milking in officer-owned canteens, and the command of soldiers' labor to officers' personal advantage. As Governor Cadillac had warned back in 1716, if he "allowed the majority of the officers to have their way they would treat the soldiers like slaves."[61] The extent of this exploitation depended upon the greed or conscience of the individual officer, as well as upon the example set by the governor commandant.

Troops seem to have been comparatively well treated in the Bienville era. As he pointed out frankly to the ministry in 1733, "An officer who has a family cannot support himself with his salary alone" and so was likely to resort to "an open and usurious commerce," including the exploitation of his troops. The best the governor could do was to suppress the worst "avidity," even if that meant that "three fourths [of the officers] are obliged to drink water [instead of wine] which impairs the health considerably in hot climates."[62] In the end, Bienville was able to restrain his officers well enough that he never had to report a case of mutiny by the soldiers during his exclusive tenure.

Except for one ugly exception in the late 1740s, the townspeople do not

TABLE 3

OCCUPATION BY ECONOMIC SECTOR, LITERACY, AND AGE OF 245
RECRUITS FROM FRANCE POSTED TO LOUISIANA, 1727–30

Sector	N	Illiterate	% Illiterate	Literate	Educated	Average Age
No metier	85	44	52	23	18	24.0
Construction	59	33	56	21	5	23.2
Miscellaneous artisans	22	7	32	8	7	23.2
Leather workers	19	14	74	5	0	21.2
Clothiers	18	10	55	6	2	21.1
Agricultural workers	18	16	88	2	0	21.8
Food processors	17	11	64	5	1	24.9
Smiths	7	6	86	1	0	21.1
Total	245	141	58	71	33	23.1

appear to have clashed with the soldiers, who were never quartered upon the citizenry, an arrangement that caused bitterness in English colonies such as New York. Unlikely to meet young white women of their class who might marry and domesticate them, most soldiers frittered away their lives in drink and billiards when they were not on active duty or working hired out for wages. Common labor of all types was performed either by slaves or by soldiers. Here was the small reserve of white labor that must have played an important part in the town's parallel economy over the years.[63] Subject to harsh corporal discipline by military authority, the individual soldier was a threat to the public peace only when amok on the cheap guildive sold in officers' canteens. Over the years, only a few settled down and augmented the civilian population, because few could create families and credit: most returned to France at the end of their service.[64]

When colonial authorities convinced the crown to stop the flow of convicts to Louisiana, the most important result was that the dignity and security of all white labor was improved by the more exclusive definition of free labor. Those few deportees who survived the early disease screening were probably bitter about their transportation to the colonies and became the outlaws against whom the attorney general soon (1724) lodged the complaint that they "debauch and drag down the servants, the lazy, savages and negroes and induce them to steal from their masters."[65] This remonstrance must have been a tirade aimed at a handful, and public disorder by the deportees ceased to be a problem after that time because so few remained. The common people still alive in 1733 were permitted to leave if they wished, according to a kind of general amnesty, and Bienville and Salmon worried that the colony might be deserted— but it was not.[66]

The few indentured who survived to gain freedom and settle in the colony had little hope of social mobility and were usually found "drinking whatever they earned" on Sundays.[67] As they became free, however, they contributed to the class of nonslaveholders who made up about two-fifths of the white population by the end of the French regime. They did not form a dangerous class. "Police" of the white population meant a stroll on Sunday during mass by officials to arrest scofflaws who did not close taverns and shops.[68] Because of the catastrophic winnowing of the common white immigrants, the class structure of New Orleans underwent a dramatic contraction, and what remained was a slave society.

The third and most important way New Orleans looked different from towns in France was that it was a society in which the slaves formed such an overwhelming proportion of the population that the organization of social relations was basically shaped to maintain the dangerously inequitable distribution of wealth and power in whites' favor. Whites' status as a numerical minority created a spirit of racial solidarity because their number was so small and declined without respite at first. White immigration was reduced to a trickle after 1721, but Africans continued to arrive over the following decade. Thus, as seen in table 4, at the end of the first phase of the colony's history, in 1731, 1,629 Europeans and 4,112 Africans remained in lower Louisiana.[69] More than half of the colony's Europeans and nearly 90 percent of its blacks lived in the close confines of New Orleans Parish. The black population, composed mainly of young adults upon arrival, aged quickly and actually seems to have declined at first. The only population estimate for the middle period (1746) states that there were only 1,500 whites and 3,000 blacks "à la Nouvelle Orléans."[70] (Since the estimate is for military purposes, it is possible that it excludes small children.) And the gross disproportion between slave and free in the parish would be moderated in time because the stream of white immigrants after the early 1730s, albeit weak, was more substantial and steady than the trickle of black slaves who arrived. Nonetheless, beginning in the 1740s the whole population of Louisiana grew at a respectable rate, peculiar by comparison to other

North American colonies only in the sense that no less than 57 percent of the colony's population lived in New Orleans Parish.[71] This geographical concentration of the population was an important advantage for a town situated on the fringe of a vast hinterland filled with Native Americans. And this was the fourth reason why New Orleans could not be compared to towns in France: it was set down in a sea of potentially hostile Indians.

Native Americans had occupied the Mississippi Valley for hundreds of generations, and as many as 150,000 of them inhabited Louisiana in 1699, although probably less than half that would remain in 1763 after disease and war took their toll.[72] Meanwhile, they retained sovereignty over most of the territory. Those who lived closest to New Orleans would exert an important influence on its development, especially because they produced many goods and services the colonists needed.[73]

Some colonists took over lands previously cleared and worked by Indians and took up their local crop complex of corn, beans, pumpkins, and tobacco and bought the Indians' surplus too. One planter, Bénard de La Harpe, moved directly into an old Acolapissa cabin near New Orleans and bought a Chitimacha slave woman, who promptly demonstrated her skill at killing threatening alligators. Nonetheless, La Harpe went on to confess that "if we could have done well without [Indians], I could have wished to have been rid of them forever—

TABLE 4

CENSUS OF THE LOWER MISSISSIPPI VALLEY IN 1731, EXCLUDING INDIANS

| | Europeans | | Africans | |
	New Orleans	Other	New Orleans	Other
Men	110	123	2,211	276
Soldiers	400	200	0	0
Indentured men	78	113	0	0
Women	100	102	948	117
Children	217	186	500	60
Total	905	724	3,659	453

but we had neither a flesh nor a fish market," which explained part of the problem.[74] The dependency went far beyond the provisions they supplied the French, like the venison and fish furnished by the nearby Acolapissa and Tchoupitoulas. The Indians of the entire region gathered enormous numbers of furs and skins to sell to the French, a crucial source of foreign exchange for the colony. Planters were likely to buy corn from Indians to nourish slaves. When the Superior Council heard in 1724 that a large slave shipment was expected, it resolved not to be unprepared as in the past and purchased four hundred barrels of corn from the Tunicas and Natchez.[75] This was an example of the growing importance of what Daniel H. Usner Jr. calls the "frontier exchange economy," which dominated Louisiana beyond New Orleans' borders and to which Indians also contributed as guides, interpreters, craftsmen, and sometimes doctors.[76] Finally, colonists bought a few Indian slaves from their local Indian captors, and these slaves provided the beginning of a small but permanent feature of the town's population.

The Indians represented a serious threat to the colonists because both the Indians and the colonists claimed the soil, and because in those thousands of Indian towns and villages social relations were in most ways antithetical to those in a slave society. In the former, production was oriented to preserve the community as a whole, whereas in New Orleans production was organized to enrich a specific class. Hierarchy existed in Indian societies, and some of them, such as that of the Natchez, were highly stratified. But stratification of the Natchez was based much more on the consensual estimation of personal character and not, as in New Orleans, on legally defined racial or class status at birth over which individuals had little or no control. All of this was embodied in differing attitudes toward land. The Natchez had a highly developed concept of property in land, as did all Indians: they *owned* their part of the Mississippi Valley because they farmed, hunted, and defended it. Their division of the land, farming techniques, and distribution of its fruits, however, were determined by the interest of the Natchez Nation rather than that of a particular class. This value-system was not just different from that of the Europeans, its communitarian basis was a distinct threat to the values of the class that dominated French society on principles rooted in inequality. The planters had seen abundant examples of these dangers. Ever since 1699, many French settlers who lived for a time in Indian society had shown a troubling inclination to remain there. Whites had easily taken to eating sagamité, sleeping on animal skins, and cohabiting with Indian women.[77] Even more crucial after 1718 was the danger that Indians would welcome and harbor black slaves who ran away from their masters.

The Indians' threat to the colonists because of their values and political power were demonstrated to the utmost in the terrible year of 1729, when the Natchez and some black slaves added the finishing touches to the colony's bad reputation in France. Three major nations dominated the lower Mississippi Valley: the Choctaws, Chickasaws, and Natchez. Whites could cultivate allies among them because of their anti-Spanish bias, the anti-English policy of the Choctaws, and the rivalry among these three nations that led them to seek allies. In the early years, Iberville established a good reputation for the French with the Choctaws and Natchez because he was neither a Spaniard nor an English ally of the Choctaws' enemies the Chickasaws.

By the time Bienville replaced his brother, he had shown that he understood New World peoples, respecting their memory of insults and learning to speak their languages.[78] The French especially valued the locals' hateful historical memory of Hernando de Soto two centuries after his death, and Bienville aimed to avoid any injustice that might overshadow De Soto's villainy.[79] He employed many strategies to compensate for French weakness. He hoped to convert Indians to Christianity. He took many pains about image, advising the ministry to send no priests who were not robust lest the Indians sneer at them, and he induced the king to invite Indians to Paris to impress them with French might.[80] The French placed out orphan boys in Indian villages, thereby providing the colony with a number of important bilingual go-betweens (enfants de langue).[81] Bienville's policy was based on high-minded standards of justice backed by a ruthless discipline of those Indians who threatened the French; yet he also relished the role of dispassionate judge in criminal matters involving colonists and Indians.[82] He was careful to visit the various nations regularly, carrying presents and good will, instead of permitting the chiefs to descend en masse upon New Orleans, where they could measure the numerical weakness of the French. As it was, a large variety of Indian warriors frequented the capital on errands through the years, but they were usually convivial and welcome. The promotion of interracial domestic relations played no part in Bienville's policy: the seventeenth-century experiment with a policy of intermarriage between the colonists of New France and the Indians had been a failure.[83]

There was no trace of romanticism in Bienville's behavior: his Indian policy grew out of the basic numerical inferiority of the French and his self-interested respect for Indians' expectations.[84] Bienville's policy was well summarized by an early settler named André-Joseph Pénicaut, a young Rochellais indentured *(engagé)* carpenter who left an important account of the colony. "God Wills," he wrote, "that Frenchmen live in this country in order to spread the Catholic religion to His glory and at the same time to found a second French empire to the glory of His Most Christian Majesty."[85] To accomplish this, Bienville knew that he must raise stout barriers between the Native Americans and the people of New Orleans.

Pénicaut's solemn piety takes for granted the grim imperial war between England and France, fought in southern continental America mainly by the Indian allies of the Louisianians and Carolinians. Each side paid its Indians to bring in scalps of the other side's allies, and that spelled the Indians' ruin.[86] The French commanders were always at a disadvantage in this contest because for various reasons the English were better able to maintain the Indians' trade connections to Europe.[87] The brutality with which the Superior Council decided upon a policy of encouraging the mutual extermination of the Choctaws and Chickasaws beginning in 1723 illustrates the colony's vulnerable position.[88] But French policy contained no element of contempt at first. When Bienville was recalled to France in 1725, however, his successors, Étienne Périer and Jacques Delachaise, scrapped his code, which had won the Indians' respect, with disastrous results.

Since the traditional enmity of the Chickasaws for the Choctaws strongly inclined the latter to ally with the French, the Natchez were the most immediate potential enemies of the colonists, and Bienville had pursued a careful policy in regard to that proud and sensitive people.[89] The Natchez were the smallest of the local nations, but also one of the most warlike. Bienville had carried out small police actions against disruptive Natchez bands in 1714 and 1723 (styled the First and Second Natchez Wars) but he had maintained an alliance with the nation. The French even established a small settlement with some slave plantations very near the main Natchez town, many days journey upriver from New Orleans.

Governor Étienne Périer arrived to replace Bienville in 1727. An inexperienced and bumptious administrator assisted by the arrogant ordonnateur Jacques Delachaise, he had a low regard for Indians. For example, he invited Choctaw chiefs to parlay at New Orleans instead of traveling to see them, oblivious to the danger.[90] He could not control his post commandants.[91] One of them, Major Chépart, on his own account or in league with Périer, provoked the Natchez by seizing some of the Indians' finest lands. Unwilling to submit to this, accustomed to yield land only by formal agreements, the Natchez organized a conspiracy against the French in 1729. It worked perfectly at the Natchez post, where the Indians took advantage of whites' dependence on them by filtering into the fort at dawn to borrow the colonists' guns for the ostensible purpose of hunting meat. They then suddenly slew about 250 people, gave Major Chépart a dishonorable death at the hands of an outcast executioner, and carried away many women and slaves.[92] Most unnervingly for the French, some of the Natchez colonists' black slaves cooperated with their captors in attacking whites, hoping to enslave for themselves those white women and children who were spared.[93] Périer's terrified reports and those of other officials strongly suggest that this disaster was the governor's fault.[94] It also may have been true, however, as Périer reported, that the various Indian nations, instigated by the English, plotted to destroy the French everywhere in the colony.[95]

According to the observer Father Le Petit, Périer and the French at New Orleans were in a "panic terror" of the Indians.[96] When surgeon Brosset's Negress told him there was a slave plot in New Orleans itself, Périer summarily executed the supposed leaders and then made a desperate and crude attempt to sour relations between local blacks and Indians and to comfort white settlers, offering freedom to some black slaves for slaughtering the peaceful remnant of the Chawashas tribe near New Orleans.[97] He sent out a force of five hundred Choctaws and French soldiers plus the recently freed blacks, who fell upon the Natchez and killed or captured about 150 Indians, mostly women and other noncombatants, and recovered most of the white women and children and up to 50 black slaves.[98] He then ruined the credit of this victory by disgusting his Indian allies when he burned at the stake in New Orleans a woman, the captive wife of a Natchez chief.[99] Périer lacked the will to extirpate the approximately 200 surviving warriors, who now joined the Chickasaw Nation. Some, or perhaps all, of these Natchez men would one day join the Cherokees, and, finally, the Creeks, among whom their descendants were found early in the nineteenth century.[100]

The exasperated Company of the Indies angrily condemned Périer and abandoned the colony to the king, who reappointed Bienville as commandant general.[101] When he returned to the colony in 1733, he was faced with the necessity of punishing the combined force of Chickasaws and Natchez.[102] "As long as the Chickasaws exist," he reported, "we shall always have to fear that they will entice away the others from us in favor of the English."[103] By the rules of Bienville's own policy, the offending Indians had to be annihilated, reluctant though he was to rely so heavily on the alliance with the internally divided Choctaws. Much of the governor's time in the 1730s was given over to mounting and leading two major expeditions against the Chickasaws and Natchez. Both wars were considered costly failures by contemporaries because no decisive battles were fought to establish the colonists' superiority, but the enemy Indians were reduced and intimidated by the effort. By the end of his service in 1743, Bienville had restored alliances with at least the major, pro-French faction of the Choctaws and had impressed the South Carolinians with his ability to marshall large forces in the interior.[104]

The Natchez disaster reveals one basic problem that beset the colony: the unwillingness of authorities in France to trust the empire's best servants. Versailles divided executive power in the colony in order to weaken it vis-à-vis the crown, and when Governor Bienville demonstrated an ability to overcome built-in impediments to his effective authority in the 1720s, he was recalled and replaced by a neophyte who had never shown the capacity to govern a new colony. Events at Natchez serve to introduce the colony's most serious problem, that of metropolitan domination of Louisiana's government.

Interference by authorities in France was also evident in the realm of production and commerce. Important pieces of the colony's export economy were in place in 1718, especially skins and furs supplied by Indian hunters.[105] The profits from that trade tended to run in old channels that terminated in Mobile, however, and only a select few were enriched by it. The need of the Caribbean sugar islands for wood of every description, from lumber to shingles and house frames, provided New Orleans with its most important reliable export in its first half-century, but the proportion of the bulk of these products to their value was low.[106] According to the Law scheme, New Orleans was founded to anchor a huge tobacco colony resembling Virginia in the center of North America.[107] Unlike most Europeans, the French took to smoking only gradually because people thought it dangerous, but demand began to grow rapidly after 1700.[108] Law's plan to import nothing but tobacco after October 1, 1721, was the main "gold mine" sensible stock purchasers banked upon in 1718. As it turned out, Virginia-quality tobacco was not suited to New Orleans' wet soils, although small quantities were successfully grown on the high ground at Natchez and later at Pointe Coupée after the Natchez settlement was destroyed, but Virginians remained the main suppliers to France.[109]

Indigo was the most attractive crop to colonists in search of a freightable product since it did well in New Orleans and could be reduced to highly compact forms for easy shipment: it became the mainstay of the settlement's export economy. Blue die had been extracted from the indigo plant since ancient times, and it became increasingly important with the growing trade in woolens and cottons. French cloth makers needed a lot of it.[110] A crucial contribution to the economy was made by the Africans, who introduced rice from West Africa. Peter Wood tentatively concludes that Africans introduced the crop to South Carolina, but the evidence is clear in the case of Louisiana. The slavers with the first commissions to take cargoes to New Orleans in 1719 were specifically ordered to acquire both Africans with experience growing the crop and the seed supply they would need to introduce it to America. As in South Carolina, it became an important crop, and even planters had to eat rice flour when wheat flour was not to be had.[111] In general, the most successful planters in the early period specialized in indigo but employed their slaves in the production of wood products as well. Some experimented with several other high-return staples, such as silk or myrtleberry wax candles.[112] Although New Orleans' economic development was never very impressive, it rapidly became a functional, profit-making slave society, as well as the commercial hub of a province with a viable, self-sustaining economy, one not unlike those of the English colonies on the Atlantic seaboard like South Carolina.

Before the middle of the French regime, the planters and farmers of the parish were making "a great profit . . . [of] generally cent. per cent. in returns" by carrying to the West Indies lumber, bricks, tiles, corn, rice, and peas, in exchange for sugar, coffee, rum ("which the negroes consume in drink") and other luxuries.[113] In this variety, the slaveholders resembled less those in single-crop societies like Virginia than those with the flexible deployment of labor found in early South Carolina.[114] The port was also visited occasionally by traders working the routes between Central America and Spain, who introduced campeachy and Brazil wood, cocoa, cochineal, tortoise shell, leather, indigo, sarsparilla, snuff, vanilla, and other goods, carrying away local produce. Direct trade between New Orleans merchants and Spanish colonies was cloaked to avoid attracting unwanted attention by authorities in Madrid, but over time this trade was substantial.[115]

New Orleans suffered from the fact that the Company of the Indies succeeded in warding off foreign traders at first. The crown opened up the town to all legitimate French merchants after 1731, except those carrying slaves, which were still a company monopoly, but most merchants from France avoided the place.[116] Once there, a captain had to strike a bargain because he could not sail on to some neighboring port for a better deal, as he could in the West Indies. A merchant could not be assured of a return cargo or even suitable bills of exchange, partly on account of competition with Spanish merchants who visited the port. An economic historian may be impressed by the energy with which the Ministry of Marine promoted trade to New Orleans, but more decisive were the factors that repelled merchants: arbitrary changes in policy regarding bounties and other technicalities, uncertain price supports for colonial produce, and a generally more restrictive mercantilist mentality than that of the English, all of which discouraged private initiative, especially when a port was associated with the Company of the Indies.[117]

The colony's comparatively slow rate of growth resulted from a combina-

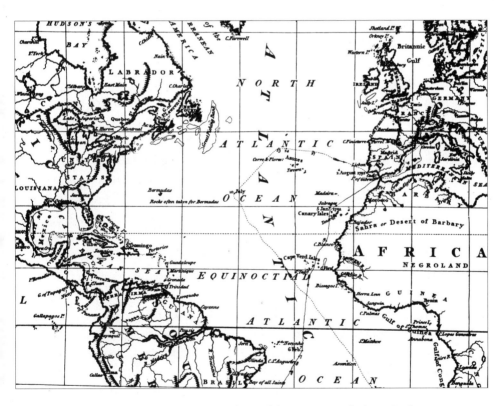

Map 1. New Orleans in the Atlantic world. Detail from a map in Charles P. C. Fleurieu, *A Voyage Round the World, 1790–1792, Performed by Étienne Marchand*, 2 vols. (1797; reprint, New York: Da Capo Press, 1969).

tion of Bourbon absolutism that denied the colonists the right to make their own basic decisions, weak local consumer demand in a slave-based economy, plus the geographic position of the colony. The settlement had the misfortune to be situated well to the rear of the screen of the West Indian islands. A key to both the demography and economics of the colony was its remote geographic position. The closest French port was Le Cap François on the northern coast of Saint Domingue.[118] That made trading to New Orleans very risky. Even though Le Cap may appear close to New Orleans on a map, it could take a vessel as long to sail from one to the other, on a winding path through the Gulf of Mexico and up the Mississippi, as it took to travel from Africa across the Atlantic to Saint Domingue, four to eight weeks for a ship, although a light, expertly handled craft might make it in much less. The mouth of the Mississippi was hard to find, full of hull-smashing giant tree trunks shooting down the river, and separated from the gulf by a dangerous bar.[119] The one-hundred-mile ascent to New Orleans could be exasperatingly long because the walls of virgin forest blocked winds required by sailing vessels, and at the last turn before a ship came up to New Orleans the direction of the wind current reversed, requiring towing.[120] The complete voyage from France to New Orleans could take over three months.[121] So through decades of French rule the colony received inadequate service by French ships because their masters favored the easily accessible, rich ports of the West Indies.[122] Above all, Saint Domingue drained the African slave supply that might have cheapened labor in Louisiana and stimulated planters to increase production. Coasting vessels usually had to obtain such necessities for New Orleans as wine, coffee, and sugar in Saint Domingue in return for Louisiana lumber, bricks, or dry legumes.[123]

The main problem was not geography, however, but the fundamental failing of a crown that discouraged its subjects from exercising initiative. It was the crown that had delegated authority to a jealous company, and both tried to determine the colony's economic development on the basis of demand in France with little attention to conditions in Louisiana.[124] It was from the royal council that the colonists received orders that they "must not think of sugar plantations," although much later the region would prove to be suited to sugar cane.[125] When the colonists tried and failed to grow tobacco as originally planned they turned to indigo with a will, but in 1727 metropolitan authorities abruptly tried to force them to grow tobacco again, until the early 1730s, when the revival of indigo was permitted.[126] Indigo production remained far below its potential, however, for want of an adequate supply of labor.[127] It was the crown that failed to provide bounties to slavers to sail to Louisiana. The father and son succession of Jérome and Jean-Frédéric Phélypeaux (Counts of Ponchartrain and Maurepas respectively) at the Ministry of Marine represented the best leadership the old regime bureaucracy had to offer the nation, but it was not enough to compensate for the structural weaknesses of absolutism in the imperial struggle for North America.[128] Perhaps the basic problem for Louisiana was the same as in other French colonies: France was a remarkably traditional society with an inelastic work force, which discouraged both industrialization and emigration.[129]

By 1731, Louisiana had only one town composed of a cluster of plantations centered around a small knot of government buildings rather than the mixed-labor extensive province envisioned by John Law. Except for the tiny German village, some anomalous Illinois settlements that were actually offshoots of New France, and a handful of tiny military posts in the hinterland, "Louisiana" remained little more than an expression, for the only real "colony" was the New Orleans plantation region that began at Cannes Bruslées. The geographical remoteness of New Orleans across a stormy gulf and up a treacherous river made the place unattractive to settlers and merchants alike. Immigrants from France had better prospects in the West Indies. Such a society in a distant corner of the colonial world could not have grown without a degree of state-subsidized immigration and commerce, a small expense that was well within the means of Louis XV.

Nonetheless, because of the stubborn determination of the slaveholders, the new "colony" did survive. But this "town"—New Orleans Parish—is not easy to describe because a traditional distinction between urban and rural space does not serve the purpose. The subject of this book is a *community* as it was defined by the people who lived in it, and that requires the historian to ignore those cartographers who marked a little spot on a bend in the Mississippi as "New Orleans." That spot was laid out neatly as a simple rectangular grid, eleven blocks (or *"îles"*) along the river and six blocks deep, partly enclosed by a small moat, a grid not unlike those to be found at Mobile and Bienville's native Montreal.[130] While this looked impressive on paper, however, only about half of those sixty-six blocks were actually developed in the French colonial period. Even in the 1760s this town center consisted of a string of government buildings and shops together with modest town houses of the planters. This was an overgrown village with a few large buildings of a type usually not found in a village: it was not a true urban space until much later, toward the end of the Spanish colonial period.

Bienville emphasized the small scale of the town center when he redesigned its central space in the 1730s. The center square on the rectangle's side fronting the river was the Place d'Armes, a plaza presided over by a barbette of cannon on the levee and St. Louis Church facing the river from the other side of the square. This was the central focus of authority in the colony. The gathering place for anything from religious festivals to judicial executions, the plaza was also just behind the stretch of levee where members of all groups paraded to socialize. When the original army barracks on the town's periphery collapsed, Bienville built new ones on opposite sides of the plaza, with officers' quarters at their head near the levee. He explained that in case of attack, the barracks together with the church could be barricaded off and defended like a fort with an escape route on the river. Moreover, he argued, these public works would make the town center look more impressive. His description serves to reveal how pathetic the town center really was. Bienville concentrated all the true buildings in one place as a kind of facade to disguise the tiny population in the seat of government.[131]

The true population of New Orleans was much larger, comprising both the few hundred people in the town center and the remaining majority of the community's inhabitants, who lived in the plantation region lying close by. The parish or town of New Orleans included the two "coasts" as they were then called, upper and lower from the town center, including Cannes Brulées and Tchoupitoulas above the town, and the Lower Coasts stretching below the town in the direction of the Gulf of Mexico. Cannes Bruslées was more heavily settled in the early days, but it was so far from the town center that it declined in importance relative to Tchoupitoulas. This is roughly the same area as that of today's metropolis of Orleans Parish, although it also included the parishes (today's Jefferson and St. Bernard Parishes) that were pieced off in the nineteenth century.

This definition of New Orleans rests on several kinds of evidence, but especially the settlers' own definition of the community. When colonists went into the courtroom they typically defined themselves as "residents of New Orleans" even if they lived as far away as Tchoupitoulas, where neither court, church, nor any other institution existed. Tchoupitoulas was just a populous neighborhood of New Orleans. Only by this definition can the demographic growth of this community be measured with any accuracy. Both quotidian and seasonal mobility between plantation and town center was frequent because it was easy. Many families were divided, living partly in the town center and partly on the plantation, and spouses married freely between neighborhoods. The original intent of the founders to concentrate the capital's population and restrict dispersal was effective; the town became increasingly more densely populated over the century rather than spreading geographically. The census takers were dutifully analytical in tabulating separately the town center and the strips of settlement above, below, and across from it on the west bank, but that did not mean they regarded those places as separate communities. These were neighborhoods of a town that was strongly knit together by its focus upon the center. This community is the subject of this book, not the small, odd collection of inhabitants the census men found at home in the center.[132]

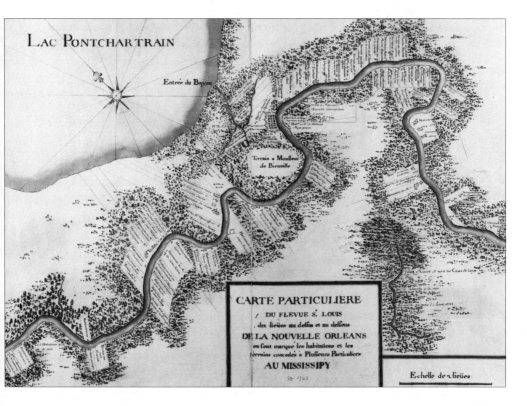

Map 2. New Orleans Parish and part of the Parish of Côte des Allemands *(left)*. From *Carte Particulière du Fleuve St. Louis dix lieües au dessus et au dessous de la Nouvelle-Orléans*, c. 1723. Courtesy of the Edward E. Ayer Collection, the Newberry Library, Chicago.

Social life was concentrated in the town center according to plan. Of great importance were Bienville's policies of distributing land so as to create as compact a community as possible and requiring slaveowners to establish townhouses. The anti-Bienvillite Chevalier de Pradel roosted in his mansion on the other side of the river for years, but his wife did live in the town center, and all the evidence together suggests that planters spent as much time there as they could. Most whites and many blacks were from towns in the Old World, and free people of all colors went to the town center often for marketing, socializing, or worship on Sundays. Community life had fluctuating seasonal patterns: in winter, everyone who could afford it gravitated to the town center for at least part of the many weeks of festivities between harvest and planting.

In addition to the social reasons for concentrating the population in one small area was the factor of natural necessity: water was a prime determinant of the town's layout. First, most of the parish, which stretched one hundred miles below the town center, was either uninhabitable swamp or poor soil subject to flooding and fit only for free-ranging livestock. Second, the natural levee on the left bank was very short and expensive to build up and maintain: the plantations *had* to huddle behind it close to the town center. This infrastructure had to be surveyed anxiously by the whole community and repaired on a regular or emergency basis with the help of neighbors' slaves, for everyone could lose their property to a break in the levee.[133] Third, the town was naturally knit together by the exceptionally complex system of navigable waterways within which it was situated. The site accommodated centuries of Indian custom and it also served the geopolitical considerations discussed earlier: the town had to be built athwart the old Indian portage between the big lakes and the river, the trail that now terminated as Rue de l'Hôpital. It was only a few hours to the Gulf of Mexico by the river, or one and a half miles above the town center was Bayou St. Jean, and schooners that drew no more than six feet of water could take the back way from this river through Lakes Pontchartrain and Borgne to the gulf in two days or less. Bienville could distribute land in such a way that all plantations had a generous helping of arable and cypress forest, with direct access to the gulf by the river or Lake Pontchartrain, and yet be situated close (in real travel time) to the town center.

The plantation regions not only began directly at the termini of the longitudinal streets of the center, they were laid out in narrow strips so that they were highly concentrated. The town center itself could be reached by the Mississippi from Tchoupitoulas in just minutes. While most plantations were just out of shouting distance from one another, geography was no obstacle to socializing. Where water routes did not serve the purpose, roads connected the plantations. No healthy resident would have required so much as four and a half hours even to walk from the most distant plantation to the town center, which is what a mounted William Byrd II required to get to Williamsburg from his plantation in 1710.[134]

The environment in which this community was situated was an exceptionally rich one, although it included many dangers and inconveniences, which affected the look of the town. Throughout the colonial period the town consisted mainly of wooden buildings, constructed of the ubiquitous cypress, although some public buildings were mainly brick by midcentury, including several large ones, such as the convent.[135] The use of wood meant that buildings were subject to rapid decay by the action of the humidity and swarming insects. The supreme example of disorder in the town was caused by the dampness of the place: the dead would not stay buried, for the ooze was likely to thrust them up into the daylight in all states of decomposition. Many died in the frequent epidemics of the early years; disease seems to have remained a serious problem until the early 1730s. Colonists appear to have had access to a number of doctors, for what their expertise was worth.[136] For survivors, the climate was mixed, with a long season of delightfully balmy days, plus four or five very hot and humid months and two cold ones with frosts. During the annual hurricane season at least some planters were likely to suffer.

Finally, people must have been terribly plagued by strange pests like vipers and alligators but above all by the mosquitoes, which could be repelled only by smoky wood fires. Countervailing these agents of unhealthfulness was the fact that the area teemed with edible subtropical flora and fauna, and the alluvial soils would richly favor the least effort to sow and reap if the farmer was lucky with weather. Most European and American outsiders marveled at the fecundity of the soil, and most people could probably eat well after the early years, although obtaining a good diet probably cost slaves much of their free work time.[137] But those who survived the disease barrier, free and slave, had reason to hope they would live to old age in the lush environment.

In such a dangerous and lonely place, however, socializing with neighbors was often a person's chief solace, and that made the town center especially important. Above all, the town center was the main point of contact with the outside world. The grid was situated right on the river, so that ships could land goods directly at the quay near the markets in the area of the plaza. The streets were directly accessible from the surrounding neighborhoods, for the town center was never protected by more than a mere fence and some sentry boxes behind a ditch, an illustration of the people's fatalistic sense that the town was basically indefensible in case of a concerted military attack. They had the good luck, however, never to be attacked until 1815, one of the few seaports in North America or the Caribbean that could make such a claim. Thus, the town center gave the inhabitants a sense of security, order, and social cohesion.

The Place d'Armes was the focal point of the community, dominated by St. Louis Church.[138] The church was flanked by the presbytery on one side and by the prison and guardhouse on the other.[139] The presbytery was the Capuchins' principal establishment, which was decrepit along with the other religious and military buildings by the 1740s. The jail was the first all-brick building (1730) and had four "cells" on the ground floor and four "rooms" upstairs, probably meant for blacks and whites, respectively. The jail was never imposing or secure, but as will be seen, it was the ultimate demarcation between the good and the bad and the final abode for those who were led to the gallows in the main square.

The Ursulines' large complex terminated the left tier of buildings radiating from the church, which was commanded by the King's storehouses. Beyond the lower quay was the brickery, the centerpiece of the plantation and workshop complex belonging originally to the company and later to a succession of leading families, beginning with Chevalier De Morand. Beyond that were plantations that eventually stretched, on both sides of the river, to English Turn, where there was a small advance redoubt and garrison.[140]

The right tier above the plaza included the buildings of the company and principal officers and, by midcentury, the governor's house, which took up two squares bounded by Levee, Bienville, Royal, and Iberville Streets. At first, however, Bienville lived on his plantation directly above the town center next to the huge terrain he divided between himself and the Jesuits. The priests were outside the town center because they were Bienville's interlopers against the royally designated spiritual fathers of the town, the Capuchins, but their plantation was a model enterprise to inspire anyone traveling between the town center and Tchoupitoulas. This was the neighborhood where the ablest of the early Canadians and French gentry established their plantations.

Across the river from the town center was the slave depot and plantation of the Company of the Indies, the personal property of the king after 1731.[141]

Located on the right bank originally to serve as a quarantine station before introducing newly arrived slaves into the general population, it was, nonetheless, one of the primary institutions of the town and effectively part of the town center. In other words, all of the institutions of government, church, and military were concentrated on or near the plaza and were closely flanked by the planters on all sides. The planter was far enough away from the town center to be lord or lady of a princely domain, and all but supreme there, but close enough to the official rendezvous of the slaveholding class to maximize all of its advantages. The slaveowners' collective power was enhanced by this geographic coherence, as compared with the more dispersed settlement of many slave societies like that of William Byrd's Virginia Tidewater. Moreover, the military heart of this bold, continuous front was professional career soldiery, in contrast to the citizen militia in British colonies. This geographical concentration and militarization of power was directed outward, intended to impress the outside world to which the colonists were connected by the river. But it was also directed inward at a biracial society in which order could never be taken for granted because the black majority was uneasily maintained in captivity; and it was aimed at a hinterland full of native peoples the colonists feared, on a distant frontier where the nearest friendly Europeans were far away.

Formation of the Planter Class and a Stable Order 2

Louisiane might lack inhabitants
but soon'll be full of residents
    Perhaps in a hundred years or so.
And mistresses there'll have to be
With favors granted you shall see
    Just like here at home.
                  —From a satirical French song, c. 1720

The *habitants* [are] gracious and polite[,] . . . very well-disposed,
and have a very lively spirit, and penetrating; they lack only the
means to cultivate [their lands] better.
                —Captain Vaugine de Nuisement on New Orleans, 1752

What were the French Settlers about 40 or 50 Years ago? Most of
them disbanded Soldiers, and People of little or no Property; yet
they have not only reared up large Families of Children, but are
now many of them Masters of 20, 40, or 60 Negroes, have built
elegant Houses, and have every Thing they can wish for in Plenty
upon their flourishing Plantations.
                —Anonymous British merchant in New Orleans, 1773

Early New Orleans has a reputation as "the wickedest city in the world," a
myth nourished by some grim facts about the town after it became part of the
United States: it became the prostitution and gambling capital of the South in

the nineteenth century.[1] The town was terribly scarred by the Civil War and Reconstruction: it was occupied by an army longer than any community in the history of the country, a violent interregnum that confirmed a chaotic image of the place. Yet historians have embraced the myth that the town was *always* wracked by vice, corruption, and violence, a Wild West outpost where life was "hedonistic" and "short."[2] According to this view, "the pervasive colonial permissiveness" was imported by the Canadian settlers and "sustained by the limited influence and worldliness of the Catholic clergy."[3]

In another version, the "chaos" of the French period resulted from the "extreme . . . brutality and corruption" of the colony's officials.[4] The leading historian of the founding era of New Orleans, Marcel Giraud, encapsulates the classic explanation for "looseness of morals": it was the natural result of the deportation of criminals to the colony.[5] But Charles Gayarré is the original source for the enduring story of New Orleans during the French regime as a "chaos of iniquities."[6] This theme was popularized by George W. Cable in the post–Civil War period.[7] Contrary to this ruling interpretation, after 1731 French New Orleans was at least as orderly as any other eighteenth-century slave society because Mammon, not Manon, ruled. The planters formed family dynasties and a remarkably inclusive and self-assured class in a stable structure.

The confusion of the founding era was soon quelled. The people who might have been the most troublesome elements in the new society either never came, like the privileged lords of France, or soon died, namely the great majority of the luckless deportees. What remained was a small group of colonists derived from a rather narrow band from the middle of the spectrum of eighteenth-century society. Some were by their birth and breeding "common," the rest had some claim to respectability, but these two groups were not separated by a social chasm. Moreover, in the dangerous racial situation so tragically highlighted by the Natchez War of 1729, these two groups had a compelling common interest that bound them together.

A second important factor that made order possible was the way the land was distributed. Bienville concentrated New Orleans methodically by clustering planters on the best lands surrounding the town center.[8] Plantations were measured by a number of linear arpents (192 feet) of river frontage with its alluvial soil by a typical depth of 40 arpents back into the cypress swamps, or about 680 English acres for a plantation of 20 x 40 arpents, the size the crown specified as the largest allowable. Bienville's grants to individuals tended to be smaller than that.[9] On the Tchoupitoulas coast adjoining the town center on the river's left bank, and on the present-day Algiers coast (right bank), thirty-six representative settlers received 249 arpents frontage in grants ranging from 3 to 12 arpents frontage. Bienville's grants were closely packed for common defense and social cohesion, but all of them were big enough to be slave plantations. The land was so rich and the grants so generous that complaints and disputes about land were rare.

A third reason that domestic stability was not difficult to achieve was the ethnic profile of the founding generation: it was a potentially volatile mixture that was solidified by a hard core of American-born creoles from New France. The cultural variety of the founding generation can hardly be exaggerated: colonists arrived from every corner of France. On the list of twenty-seven settlers for the Semonville-Canet concession who embarked on the *Philippe* in 1719, the twenty-two whose origins are listed represent twelve different regions and seventeen different towns and villages in the four corners of France.[10] The various regions of the mother country were still quite distinctive early in the eighteenth century, and only a few gross generalizations about eighteenth-century "French" culture are possible.[11]

Quite different from all the French immigrants was the hard nucleus of middling planters formed by the Canadians who developed the Tchoupitoulas coast *quartier*. Dominated by the numerous Chauvin clan, this neighborhood provided a sheet anchor for the town: their social role was out of all proportion to their numbers because they had a commitment to the future settlement of their descendants in the colony. At the opposite end of town, at English Turn (where Bienville had "turned" back English invaders in the era of the War of the Spanish Succession), another group of Canadians also tried to build up estates, but they were less successful and in time persisted there only in small numbers.[12] The Canadian heart of the New Orleans community set its tone, an inclusive American sensibility that overrode cultural instability introduced by other immigrants.

Religious heterodoxy was another potential source of unrest, but it was artificially quieted by the strict establishment of Roman Catholicism. Louis XIV had harried France's Protestants out of the land in 1685, which gained points with the pope even though it "disturbed, divided and impoverished the kingdom and strengthened all its enemies."[13] It was the crown's policy to keep Protestants, Jews, and Jansenists out of the colonies, although a few settled there anyway. Crypto-Protestants still existed in most parts of France after the 1680s, especially in the far western regions from which so many Louisiana immigrants hailed, and the crown was willing to tolerate discreet heretics in Louisiana despite hand wringing by local Catholic priests.[14] Protestants may have contributed 10 percent of Louisiana's founding population.[15] So New Orleans was religiously various from the beginning, if certainly not pluralist, and even some Jews joined the colony in the 1750s.[16] But the non-Catholics were content not to worship publicly and Roman orthodoxy was never challenged. The only way a Protestant could marry was to recant, like the Swiss immigrant Marianne Bernardin, who renounced her religion in 1727 to marry Joseph Dauphin.[17]

Added to the creole Canadian leaven and the balm of Catholic conformity was the rootedness of those settlers who survived and persisted, a fourth and crucial factor making for a stable order. To some extent this was achieved only by force in the early days, because many people would have fled New Orleans after 1729 if they had not been actively prevented from doing so by authorities. But after Bienville's return a majority did stay, and the same was true of most later immigrants: if they arrived in Louisiana with the ambition to retire to France, few did so in the end. Louisiana planters could see a vast expanse of rich soil along the river, a patrimony for landed dynasties—yet it is also true that few struck it rich enough to retire in style to France.

One man in particular anchored the settlement and encouraged by example the commitment of those who stayed: Claude Villars Dubreuil. Although no great lords settled in Louisiana, it was a peculiarity of the planter class in New Orleans that Dubreuil far outstripped the others by his great wealth. This singularly rich and industrious great planter, who bore one of the most distinguished family names in France, sailed to Louisiana from La Rochelle, the old Protestant port, in 1719. He brought a group of artisans and settled in Tchoupitoulas, later acquiring a second plantation closer to the town center. He engaged in a remarkable variety of economic pursuits, constructing some of the town center's major buildings, importing slaves, and later promoting sugarcane cultivation on a limited scale. Because of his breeding and energy he set a high local standard, validated entrepreneurial values, and encouraged local pride: that such a rich man was willing to remain in such an unpromising location gave heart to lesser landowners. He died in the colony in 1757, never converting his American wealth into a more exalted French title and comfortable retirement in France. He was typical of planters in New Orleans in that respect, as in other mainland North American slave colonies.[18] After Louisiana became a royal colony in 1731, most slaveowners were committed, like Dubreuil, to their patrimony in the colony.

A fifth factor that helped create order in the fledgling settlement, which must be neither overlooked nor exaggerated, was the introduction of French laws, which were the basic codes in Louisiana as in New France. The crown ordained that the ancient Customs of Paris, or civil laws, together with Louis XIV's own recent criminal code of 1670 and the Code Noir of 1724 were the law of the land. The entire judicial administration was assigned to the Superior Council, first established in 1712, composed of crown-appointed locals or men who soon became local residents and slaveholders. The decision of the superior councillors when they sat as a court in either civil or criminal cases could be appealed to royal courts in Paris, but that was rarely done. Post commandants may have held petty courts for the smallest offenses, but the power of the court at New Orleans, the *commissaire ordonnateur* at its head, was undivided.[19] It is certainly true that its authority was projected outward, to circulate throughout the peculiar distended colonial settlement network in the vast colony of Louisiana.[20] But the councillors were above all the primary local officers in New Orleans. They acted as municipal councillors for the town as well as administrators and justices for the entire colony. New Orleans lacked a separate municipal government before 1769.

The council suffered no popular interference with its power to enforce the councillors' political and economic domination of society, using European class assumptions and methods of rule, albeit under surveillance by the crown. In fact, the extent of their domination was unknown in Old World towns, where an array of local ruling-class corporations had to share local power.[21] Members of the council combined duties of administration and justice that were normally kept separate, making them magistrates of the highest order. Lawyers were few in the colony because French justice never involved juries. An injured party merely petitioned the judges of the bench, who regarded their first duty in civil or criminal complaints to discover the true facts and to do so as quickly as possible. By contrast with the English, judges did not allow litigants to appeal to customary precedents and legal technicalities. No judge could act alone, for three judges sat in civil matters and five in criminal cases, according to the company's instructions of 1719. The leading historian of judicial practice in the colony is generally admiring.[22]

The Superior Council's administrative deliberations were not always harmonious because of political factionalism, even though political life had a very limited framework within which to develop, as planned by the absolutist regime in France. Power was divided between the governor, who was a military commandant, the commissaire ordonnateur, who was a civil administrator, and the rest of the Superior Council members. Factionalism typically involved an adversarial relationship between governor and ordonnateur. The governor had the highest local authority, but the ordonnateur's judicial role gave him considerable prestige. These two officers were often at odds because the boundary between their jurisdictions was deliberately left vaguely defined. Competition between them created factions in the early period, roughly pro-Bienvillite and anti-Bienvillite.[23] During the last phase of his service, Bienville was lucky to have a cooperative ordonnateur (Edme Salmon), and there was virtually no factionalism in the 1730s and early 1740s. Bienville was not one of the most successful colonial administrators, but neither was he one of the least successful. His campaigns against Indians in the 1730s were expensive and far from being triumphs, but the fact that New Orleans was not destroyed by Indians or ever attacked was the result of his dedication.[24]

Bienville was replaced by another Canadian, Pierre-François Vaudreuil, who was far less competent.[25] Besides his clumsy handling of the alliance with the Choctaws, Vaudreuil formed a league with the major of the garrison in New Orleans, Jean-Baptiste Membrède, in an attempt to force everyone to drink in taverns controlled by Membrède. Through a combination of passive resistance by the general public, some scandalous violent incidents involving soldiers, and formal protests to the Ministry of Marine by Vaudreuil's ordonnateur, Michel, the major was dismissed and finally sent to France early in 1754.

Vaudreuil was replaced by Governor Louis Billouart Kerlérec in 1753, and it was during his tenure that the colonists of all classes engaged briefly in something like modern political behavior. During the Seven Years' War (or French and Indian War), the governor ordered that merchant ships flying any flag be admitted to the remote and merchandise-starved port. While Kerlérec was on a diplomatic junket in Mobile, his ordonnateur, one Gaston Rochemore, seized the huge cargo of a Jew from Jamaica in an attempt to force him to pay Rochemore a bribe.[26] This caused a furious backlash by the townspeople. Encouraged by Kerlérec, they signed petitions to Paris, held meetings, and generally behaved in ways feared by Louis XV on principle.[27] Both officials were recalled to fight out the sordid affair before officials in Paris during many years in the 1760s.[28] This incident demonstrates that the New Orleanians, like colonists everywhere, chafed under mercantilist restrictions and had the potential to organize a direct challenge to metropolitan authority, demonstrated most vividly in the insurrection of 1768, as described in a later chapter.

The sixth, supreme factor that compelled colonists to create a settled order rather than the saturnalia painted by Gayarré was that this was a slave society. Slaveholding counteracted disruptive forces in two ways. First, the need for a white minority to keep blacks degraded enforced order among white people: the rabble of settlers that emerges from histories of the province could not have created a slave society. Second, the institution of slavery was "popularized." The great mortality of the initial decade reduced the founding white population to such a small group, and the low rate of immigration to the colony did so little to expand it, that common white workers soon came to constitute, as Bienville put it, the "bourgeoisie," intermediate between the slaveowners and the soldiers and slaves.[29] From their ranks a slaveholder might not be too proud to select a spouse if no better was to be had from among the trickle of newcomers that did arrive from France after 1731. From the ranks of that bourgeoisie one might rise, and quickly.

Up to a point, membership in the planter class was predetermined: men and women of a certain level of birth would not have gone to the colony without assurance that they would acquire slaves on credit. Thus, in the beginning, the distribution of slaves was guided by considerations having nothing to do with fairness or the demonstrable capabilities of particular individuals and everything to do with favoritism and connections.[30] The company's standing policy was to advance blacks to those best able to pay, although its own officials also brazenly appropriated as many slaves to their own use as possible. The explanation by Périer and Delachaise as to why they had to withhold extra Africans from recent shipments for their own plantations was laughably flimsy.[31] In fact, competition among qualified settlers to obtain as many slaves as they could was bitter during the first generation, although specific allotments and abuses are impossible to determine.

Several conditions promoted entry into the slaveholding class from the nonslaveholding "bourgeoisie." Because so few immigrants arrived after 1731, the town's white population intermarried across the barriers of social status that discouraged such marriages in France. When combined with the rules of inheritance that tended to divide estates, that meant that the slave population was reapportioned among a large number of slaveholders. Table 5 demon-

TABLE 5
CLASS STRUCTURE OF THE CIVILIAN POPULATION
OF NEW ORLEANS IN 1766

	Households (N)	Slaves (N)	Class
Nonslaveholding households	241	0	X
Slaveholding households (Slaves per household)			
1	57	57	A
2	62	124	A
3	32	96	A
4	35	140	A
5	26	130	A
6	26	156	A
7	26	168	A
8	14	112	A
9–12	25	259	AA
13–16	18	253	AA
17–20	15	270	AA
21–30	20	522	AA
31–40	10	365	AA
41–50	5	226	AA
51–60	5	285	AAA
61–70	3	201	AAA
71–80	1	74	AAA
81–90	2	177	AAA
91–151	3	362	AAA
Total	626	3,977	

NOTE: X = nonslaveholders; A = small slaveholders (983 slaves, or 24 percent of all slaves); AA = middling slaveholders (1,895 slaves, or 48 percent of all slaves); AAA = large slaveholders (1,099 slaves, or 28 percent of all slaves).

strates that while the essential class division in New Orleans was the same as in any slave society (one was either in or not in the slaveholding class), the ownership of slaves became remarkably prevalent. The total wealth of the slaveholders' class was limited by the number of slaves available for sale, but the low rate of immigration meant that the slaveholding class grew to include a remarkable 61 percent of all households by the end of the French regime.[32]

As shown graphically in fig. 1, middle-level slaveholders (those owning from 9 to 50 slaves) were dominant, owning almost half of all slaves, and large slaveholders were few: a mere fourteen owned over 50 slaves. Only two were large enough to be regarded as very large slaveholders, the Church (the Ursulines and Capuchins owning in four separate groups a total of 123 slaves) and the Destréhan family, purchasers of the main portion of the Dubreuil plantation, with 151. This great extent of the slaveholding class must have served to bind the white colonists together very tightly and to mitigate social strife among them.

The extremely low rate of immigration to the colony after 1731 meant that those promising colonists from the lowest ranks who survived faced bet-

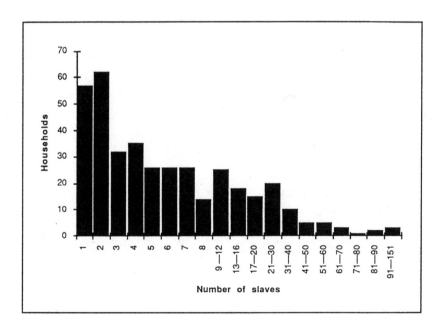

Fig. 1. Distribution of slaveholding households, New Orleans, 1766.

ter prospects than they might have expected. Marie-Louise Ste. Hermine was a humble example of this phenomenon. Deported to the colony by a *lettre de cachet* at the founding, she became a pious spinster and dispenser of charity, and died a slaveowner, freeing a mulatto boy upon her deathbed.[33] Entry into the slaveholding class remained easiest, however, for well-connected men from France, favored by many locals as spouses for their marriageable girls. Military officers from France were particularly well positioned. Jean-Charles Pradel arrived in the colony with his name, a minor military commission, and a small family loan, and rose to become one of the richest planters by the 1750s.[34]

Having emphasized the remarkable inclusiveness of the slaveholding class, it is important to note that several factors not only made competition to gain slaves intense in the early years but made ranking *within* the planter class very volatile. New Orleans was founded by a highly heterogeneous group of white people who were mostly strangers to one another without settled local networks, and the lack of personal commitments to one another must have weakened normal restraints on greed at first. Competition was intensified in the early years by the fact that so many slaveholders had minor manorial tags (from France and New France) behind their family names, which made them comparable and sensitive to insults. The regency government of the duke of Orléans established a policy at the outset in 1718 not to create provincial titles attached to lands in the new colony, a reflection of the general French aristocratic reaction against an inflation of titles.[35] Thus, since most planters had the right to be addressed as "sieur" on the basis of petty titles in France or New France, and the crown would not create new manorial property in Louisiana, one's status was determined by how many slaves one could acquire.[36] In one sense, slavery made the social structure vastly more simple than it was in France, where twelve or more "classes" could be discerned by contemporaries.[37]

The process of constituting the slaveowning class can be followed in the story of family formation by the founders, presided over by the Superior Council in its role as a court, where the men of the town had all the typical resources available during the mature old regime. When the entire corpus of cases in that court is taken into account, it is truly remarkable how little trouble was caused by the first phase of family formation by people who were mostly strangers to one another. Ethnic friction appears to have been nonexistent. Canadians and the French intermarried; French people from widely diverging provinces intermarried; and, although French immigrants looked down upon most Germans because they were peasants, they would marry notables like the Darensbourgs (who were actually Swiss), and these links tied the German Coast to the town.[38] Angry confrontations in court between the planters were rare, usually inspired by debts.[39] Duels were rare.[40] Status competition was acted out in the jostling over seating in church, the stage upon which similar dramas were played out in English colonies.[41]

The individual man was nearly an absolute master in his own domain, whatever his status in relation to other men. The "government of the family" at the beginning of the eighteenth century was still mostly unchanged from its medieval form, and had been strongly reasserted in the course of the Counter-Reformation. Man ruled as lord over wife and child, according to the social historian Jean-Louis Flandrin, because Judeo-Christian monotheism and patriarchal authority went hand in hand, and because patriarchy was promoted by absolutist kings, for the authority of the father legitimized their authority. According to the ideal, the family was a set of reciprocal relationships between the father and his wife, children, and servants, in which they would serve their master as if serving God, and in return he would respect his wife, educate his children, and be a father to his servants. He was expected by authorities to maintain domestic peace, by corporal punishment if necessary, a mere continuation of the ancient institution of slavery according to Flandrin.[42] A weak husband suffered the public's humiliating charivari, or denunciation of his misrule. French traditions could not be perpetuated entire in New Orleans, however, because the sex distribution among the founders was imbalanced and it remained so, though less marked after the first generation.[43] Because of that imbalance, women enjoyed more potential power in the town's early social structure than they did in the Old World.

As Flandrin summarizes the condition of women in France: revival of Roman law in the thirteenth century substantially increased the importance of private property in all social relations. That lead to a deterioration of women's legal condition because of the new supremacy of the patrilinearity of descent arising from the need to preserve estates. That entailed a whole series of changes, such as the superior status accorded the patronymic surname, the exclusion of women from the throne of France by the Salic Law, and the various laws that excluded women from vassalage and other legal domains now made masculine preserves.[44]

Nevertheless, this negative trend for the status of women as a group was somewhat softened by new personal protections of individual wives by some laws. Courts began to protect their financial interests better, to protect them against extreme corporal discipline by husbands, and to grant separation more frequently. "In the daily life of the household," Flandrin argues, "the wife became gradually and partially emancipated from the tutelage of her husband." Moreover, by the seventeenth century the Church succeeded in abating concubinage in France, except among the nobility, a trend that added to the dignity of the wife.[45]

A rising male anxiety is detectable in France at this time about the improving status of wives, and since so many Europeans in Louisiana before 1760 were born and raised in France, conditions there are the starting point for measuring their condition in Louisiana. Late in seventeenth-century France, women's salons and a proto-feminist defense of women's rights to education appeared for the first time.[46] The reaction of opponents was extreme: they trumpeted the view that women's natural role was to please men and remain in the domestic sphere, a position later formalized by Jean-Jacques Rousseau.[47] In most areas of the country, the relations between men and women were troubled because women's inheritance rights and increasing economic involvement were countered by the antifeminist ideology that women were too weak to be responsible independent individuals. Male French settlers in Louisiana were likely to arrive with assumptions based upon the prevalent concern among men that wives had too much legal power in the family.[48]

Male anxiety must have been heightened in Louisiana in the early decades by the pronounced disparity between the male and female portions of the population. As can be seen in table 1 (chapter 1), only 13.6 percent of the major wave of white immigrants were women and teenaged girls, many of them disadvantaged by poverty or a bad reputation. Theoretically, that imbalance gave these women some negotiating power in domestic relations. Most men and women were in their twenties and thirties and marriageable. All but one of the sixteen women described as deported from Rochefort on *The Two Brothers,* for example, for whom ages were recorded, were twenty-one or older. This mixture created an artificial and bizarre marriage market in which women and girls—even deportees—were generally better able to exercise more control over their choice of partner because of high male demand for spouses. It was also attended with great risk in those early years: of the thirty-nine total women of all origins deported on *The Two Brothers,* only seven lived long enough to register their names in the New Orleans sacramental registers, most by marrying in the early 1720s, and none of them nor their spouses appear in the records again—none of the thirty-nine women recorded any descendants.[49] Thus, while a deported woman enjoyed the remote possibility of achieving a respectability that was impossible in France, those women most likely to appear in the sacramental registers, particularly as mothers and founders of lineages, were those respectable people who arrived in the colony already married.

The conditions of the marriage market continued to favor women throughout the French period, although to a declining degree, we suppose, as immigration declined.[50] Even so, the sex distribution of the civilian, marriageable population remained somewhat out of balance at 5.7 males to 4.2 females, which was comparable to other North American colonies.[51] Immigration picked up after the Seven Years' War, however, and the result is visible in the records of 176 marriages in the decade between 1759 and 1768. In the last years of the French regime, men born in New Orleans faced significant competition for brides with men born in Europe. While the number of locally born men and women was about the same, both locally born women and those born elsewhere (mostly in other parts of Louisiana) were almost twice as likely to marry immigrants from France as to marry locally born men (see table 6). The reasons for this are obscure but must have been cultural in part: either local young women favored men with the cachet of birth in "the mother country" or the parents of those women favored the resulting European socioeconomic connections, or, most probably, favoritism by both parents and daughters played a role.

TABLE 6

BIRTHPLACES OF WHITE BRIDES AND GROOMS MARRIED
IN ST. LOUIS CHURCH, 1759–68

| | Grooms | | | |
| | New World | | Old World | |
Brides	N	(%)	N	(%)
New Orleans	41	23.3	62	35.2
Elsewhere	25	14.2	48	27.3
Total	66	37.5	110	62.5

Since studies of French immigration have consistently shown that people of this nationality went to the New World in far fewer numbers than the English, usually when their status in France was under great pressure, we must assume that most immigrant men marrying local women had little more to offer than their names and origins, whereas brides offered dowries of land, slaves, or money. The result for about six out of ten New Orleans–born men in this period was that they had no hope of marrying locally, in part because the immigrant stream included almost no women. Many local men undoubtedly sought brides in the hinterland of Louisiana, some created illicit liaisons with black women, others went without domestic comforts and never married. But this appears to be a new situation in the 1760s: local men had faced less competition in the marriage market through much of the French period, when immigrants avoided "Mississippi," reputed to be a land of doomed outcasts.

The most important institutional advantage of women in Louisiana, by comparison with women in the English colonies, was that of community property. At marriage all property of both spouses, unless it was otherwise designated, fell into the community, to which a widow was always entitled to half. In very specific contracts, wives were guaranteed either this half, a fixed sum or dower, or *rente* instead, and a *preciput* or right to remove personal property (especially wardrobe) from the community without affecting the widow's share. Above all, she had the right to renounce the community and retreat with dowry and preciput in advance of creditors if the community was outweighed by her husband's debts.[52] There was one major exception, as in all the slave colonies: an original owner was empowered to seize slaves not paid for, in advance of the widow's community privileges from her marriage contract.[53] The importance of community property should not be exaggerated, because at bottom a wife could perform no legal act: husband was lord. And despite the French law of partible inheritance, shrewd men could nullify a widow's freedom of choice as her children's tutor by his donations inter vivos (i.e., gifts to selected children before he died) to maintain a modified form of primogeniture.[54]

If all New Orleans wives benefited from a surplus of potential spouses and from community property, a few independent women helped fill the town's great need for entrepreneurial talent. Common women worked much as they did elsewhere and in the early days played a greater variety of roles, such as peddling perishables, a function that would soon be monopolized by blacks. But some white women engaged in more sophisticated commercial behavior. When Widow Piquery lost her husband, the royal baker, she took over baking for the king's servants.[55] A Madame Goudeau appears to have been a wholesaler, known from the suit of a trader who thought she was too shrewd.[56] Elizabeth Bunel, separated from her husband because he was a ne'er-do-well, is found repeatedly in the record involved in various property transfers.[57]

The most intriguing woman of this period was Dame Delabrosse Azemard. She appeared in full colors only once, in 1763, when she angrily sued two planters. She had contracted for delivery of 414 ten-foot lengths of lumber to be delivered from the Laseigne and Flottmanville plantations, and when she took a work gang to raft them downriver to her sawmill, only about half the order was in acceptable condition. When contractor Flottmanville countersued to force her to pay up on the plantation she also rented from him, the court ordered him to deliver the logs he promised and to pay a substantial indemnity for loss of her mill time. Azemard composed some very colorful oratory in her demand for the deed to the plantation, complaining that she was "the butt of Flottmanville's chicanery."[58] This was an enterprising woman engaged in traditionally male activities like planting and milling. She was not afraid to run a large enterprise requiring the supervision of gangs of men, and she dared sue men who crossed her.[59] On the other hand, few women as ambitious as she are to be found in the record, perhaps because other Flottmanvilles foiled their enterprises.

Women's condition was affected in part by the rate of literacy among them. It is never easy to measure, and historians typically count the incidence of signatures and mere marks on marriage contracts or other documents. These indexes are often ambiguous and unrepresentative, but the best measure available for New Orleans is the incidence of signatures and marks of white sponsors of slave baptisms in the Louisiana records of the founding generation. For the three-year period between 1731 and 1733, it is possible to single out 225 slaves in the sacramental register for whom either signatures or marks of godparents are certainly identifiable, as shown in table 7.[60] The literacy rates for both sexes seem rather high, suggesting either that the sponsors were drawn disproportionately from the best-educated minority or that the permanent colonial population was fairly well educated, the former being most likely. While the literacy rate among women was distinctly lower than that for men, it was not so low as to account by itself for the much weaker representation of women than men in the town's commercial affairs.

Because of the special need to protect white women from falling under the influence of black men, slavery increased the motivation of the husband to

TABLE 7

SIGNATURE RATE OF SLAVES BAPTISMAL SPONSORS
IN SAINT LOUIS CHURCH, 1731–33 (N = 225)

Sponsors' Signatures	Baptisms (N)	Baptisms (%)
Male and female	125	55.6
Male only	65	28.9
Female only	5	2.2
Neither	30	13.3
Total	225	100.0
Total literate males	190	84.4 of males
Total literate females	130	57.8 of females

dominate his wife and daughters and for all men to discourage the operation of plantations by women. Still, their domination was undercut by other factors. The seat of the richest slaveowners, the big house, with its burden of servants for the sake of comfort and conspicuous display, imposed a significant managerial role on white women, an even greater role in the formative years. In New Orleans, moreover, the stolid prosperity of the Ursulines Nuns' establishment and their numerous civic activities must have raised both the status of women and the moral consciousness of the town in general. But the factor of numerical inferiority was probably most important in maintaining women's individual value and collective status.

Cases from the judicial record illustrate the issues of power between the sexes in the slaveholding class. A charge of breach of marital contract by Jean-Baptiste Gauvin against Marie-Louise Soulande summarizes key aspects of marital matching and the policy of the court in this new society. Gauvin kept an inn at the intersection of Bourbon and St. Ann Streets and had probably not been established long, when, in May 1740, he vigorously protested the banns published by Widow Soulande and Louis Cheval. The banns, or required publication of intent to marry, were designed in part for such a situation: to protect prior claims like Gauvin's. His evidence was incontestable:

several witnesses knew of their agreement, and she even wore Gauvin's ring. Yet she had dared to entertain a change of mind. If she had wanted to marry Cheval, she probably would have satisfied custom if she had merely returned the first suitor's property. Certainly there is no case of the court ever enforcing a marital match against a woman's will. At any rate, she married Gauvin, for that September they filed for her share of her recently deceased husband's property, totaling 38,208 livres.[61] In other words, she brought to the community with Gauvin a significant influx of capital for a rising young man.[62]

The fact that Gauvin's marriage was good for his career does not mean that the match was not affectionate. In fact, there may have been a better chance for affectionate rather than forced or arranged marriages in early provincial America than in Europe. Perhaps Marie-Louise was only playing a little game when she flirted with Cheval, but the evidence suggests a rich provincial widow putting her husband on notice that she had a mind and will of her own.[63]

A key indicator of the power relations between men and women was in the legal recourse a woman could pursue against spousal abuse. The worst manifestations of wife beating have been found in those Western societies in which courts fail to take action against it. Fathers were supposed to beat dependents to discipline them, which could lead to harsh treatment.[64] Separation of property and residence was possible only under unusual circumstances and complete divorce was out of the question, so only a handful of cases ever came before the court. The record of marital separation in New Orleans in the early colonial period is fairly complete, and it shows that women could count on the court for shelter from sadistic men, as if there was a special commitment to protect the colony's reputation in this regard so as to encourage French women to emigrate there.[65]

In the first scandalous separation case, Bienville's royal physician, Pierre Manadé, was charged by his wife of eight years, Louise, with seven and a half years of cruel treatment with a variety of weapons. When the court immediately took her under its protection upon her demand, Pierre sputtered indignantly that if Louise got away with it, all women would "seize some pretense to live at their husbands' expense," that is, to live apart on her portion of the community. The court awarded separation of property without hesitation because she provided witnesses that he had a gambling problem too. The doctor was allowed to save face, however, because Louise was not awarded separation of bed and board. So she took refuge with the Ursulines to make her point about the cruelty, and then she was awarded a pension of five hundred livres by the court. Commissaire Ordonnateur Delachaise (in his position as chief judge) disapproved of Manadé because he had married the rich widow in order to buy a plantation and "thinks only of his pleasures." So Delachaise got his commission revoked, but this was also one prong of his attack on Bienville's party, to which the doctor belonged. The court was reluctant to grant separation because the Company of the Indies had given him a lot of credit based on his wife's resources. This reach of the company deep into colonial domestic affairs is impressive.[66] But this case also reveals a dream success story of an upwardly mobile white man who very soon had it all—a rich wife, plantation, royal commission, and a life of pleasures.

Other domestic cases that came before the court in the early years illustrate the general guidelines of the judges' thinking. The court readily granted separation of property to a woman when her interests were threatened by the spouse's business ventures or vices, thereby putting others on notice that she was a privileged creditor of the community property. A woman had to be careful not to jeopardize the good will of the court, however, as did Marie-Louise Marganne Rossard. Her husband, royal notary Michel Rossard, was a gambler with a drinking problem that made his records difficult for historians to read and led Marie-Louise to separate her property from his. When he died in 1736, only six years after their marriage, she panicked and began trying to conceal effects of the estate, the bulk of which she had brought to the community, evidently fearful that other creditors would ruin her. The court was furious and stopped her in her tracks. The key here again, however, was that the principal creditor demanding a major share of the estate was the company, to which the couple was indebted for slaves.[67] As for virtual divorce (separation of property, bed, and board), the court was willing to allow it but cases were rare. One striking instance was the complete, amicable separation of Jean and Angélique Guillot, seemingly an annulment. Their contract specified that she was to have civil independence and that they might change their minds and rejoin in the future. It may or may not have been the result of an unusual difference between them: she could sign her name in good script but he was illiterate and could only make his mark.[68] It is significant that this kind of separation was allowed in early New Orleans—but this was perhaps the only example of it.

The position of women before the court appears to have deteriorated temporarily as the patriarchal regime became more settled and militant in the midcentury era of Governor Vaudreuil's administration. The court in this period was less responsive to battered wives. The most unseemly divorce case was that of Silvie Marné, widow Barbaut, who in 1743 sued her second husband of three years, Jean-Pierre Hardy. He went on trade expeditions to Illinois, she complained, leaving her nothing to live on, and beat her when she complained. The suit was accompanied by depositions in her favor, and the court summoned Hardy. His response was that she provoked him to beat her.[69] The court took no further action and stalled for several years. Only in 1748, when Hardy's wife and stepson beat him up in the street to convince him to settle, did the court finally grant full separation. This was the most scandalous and prolonged case of marital conflict in colonial New Orleans, and it was not representative of the way most marriages worked. This case does show, however, that judges in this period were reluctant to intervene.[70]

Unnecessary delays occurred in other domestic cases in these years, perhaps because councillors hesitated to meddle in the marriages of their male peers in such a small town now that everyone knew one another. One fine example of these cases adds unflattering touches to the portrait of Major Membrède, the same man found bullying the taverngoers of the town later in his career. In 1745 he was sued by his battered wife Françoise, who claimed he also threatened the property of her children. The court ordered the convent to take her in and demanded an accounting from Membrède, who blustered that she was a liar. The court denied Françoise's petition for separation, and when she petitioned a few months later, the court was again swayed by a lengthy protest by the major that he had only the tenderest affection for his family.[71]

The record of domestic relations among white people definitely does not reveal a condition of moral chaos.[72] Few couples lived without the Christian sacrament of marriage. There was a low rate of prenuptial conceptions. Of 127 unions with issue for whom the condition of the bride can be determined from 1759 to 1768, a mere 9 brides (or 7 percent) were pregnant when they married, and the only case of bigamy on record caused an immense scandal, a perfect example of how rarely domestic irregularity occurred.[73] One Louis-René-François de Manne passed as a gentleman of Saint Domingue in 1733, exciting the town with a scheme to carry Louisiana produce to Martinique and import African slaves. He promptly married a widow of means. Soon thereafter he was identified as a previously married Frenchman, and he absconded to Carolina, taking with him several of his illegal wife's slaves. The outrage occasioned by this episode can scarcely be exaggerated, and local officials were careful to fill their reports with every detail of this unique event.[74]

Finally, a few people did exist who would not marry and contributed a kernel of truth to the myth of a moral abyss. But the rare occasion upon which hand-wringing officials were specific about their number was when Périer and Delachaise reported at the end of the town's first eight years that "many" strumpets had produced a total of "five or six" illegitimate children, not an impressive figure.[75] A number of white men remained lifelong bachelors, but only one denunciation of a resident's homosexuality is found in the priests' reports.[76] The Ursuline Sister Marie-Madeleine reported in 1727 that she saw mainly "virtuous people."[77] Father Raphael's complaint about interracial concubinage in New Orleans in 1726, referred to with great emphasis by some historians, is, in fact, quite vague. The priest specifically noted that the problem was declining rapidly, and he did not repeat the charge during the many years this severe critic served in the town. He was more concerned about the prevailing lax attitude toward the Sabbath.[78] The governor and ordonnateur reported in 1732 that the "several" remaining dissolute women were being driven out, and secular administrators never discussed the issue again.[79] In sum, domestic relations among the colonists were marked by a low number of marital separations and an extreme rarity of gross immorality like bigamy, concubinage, or incest. Traditional marriage was the rule, and marriage bonds were usually broken by death. All of this implied a wholesome environment in which to raise children.

The patriarch's second class of dependents, children, were virtual chattels increasingly under parents' social domination after the sixteenth century, but Flandrin also sees children as the key to the detachment of the modern conjugal family from the old diffuse lineage of the house, kinfolk, domestic servants—the neighborhood or band.[80] A correspondence between increasingly sentimental, less brutal domestic relations and a growing emphasis on parental duty to children, "may have developed in the parents both the sense of the responsibilities that they were assuming in procreating children, and the desire to avoid them by not procreating [many] children."[81] The effect was to bring down family size among property-owning classes to the smaller scale of peasants' families. This improved the status and treatment of children by reducing the tendency to "put out" all but the first-born male child, which had embroiled families in bitter conflicts.[82]

The key factor shaping the lives of children in New Orleans was that they were so few in the founding generation. Because their hands were always useful, especially for the most tedious labor, it was likely that poor children were welcome and better off as a group than they would have been in France, where they were more numerous and taken for granted. They were also more likely to be taken in by new Louisiana families from a class above the one into which they were born, and the practice of "putting out" was probably rare. It is also true that children must have suffered most when the colony was new. The early disaster of disease and poor provisioning was reported to have been especially hard on them.[83] Those orphans who lived were entitled to a ration from the company, however, which made them attractive to foster parents. The boys were soon taken in by families, and the girls went to the care of the nuns until they could be suitably married.[84]

The freedom of individual children to realize their aspirations was determined in part by the quality of their education, but evidence of the availability of schools in New Orleans is mixed. The Capuchins' Father Raphael reported in 1725 that he had established what he called a "little college" with fifteen promising scholars. The master of the school was a former Capuchin who had left the order "through a thoughtlessness of youth," whom the Capuchins hired to teach boys writing, mathematics, drawing, and singing. The priests rented a little house with three thousand livres advanced by "several" private persons. Raphael wrote enthusiastically of expanding it into a seminary to offer Latin and liberal arts. He soon discovered, however, that the inhabitants "are satisfied to have [students] taught to read and write and regard all the rest as useless," even though a few students tried other subjects.[85] Even more discouraging, the gentlemen who advanced the money grew nervous that the company would not reimburse them, and "because they do not wish to put themselves to an expense for the public," they threatened to renege.[86] At some point in the 1720s the school ceased to operate for several decades, and most people could not afford to send their children to France. Moreover, even those who could afford it feared to send their children to the mother country because they were likely to refuse to return to America except to collect their inheritances.[87] Entreaties by Bienville and Salmon for authorization of a new school were ignored by the crown, and the education of boys was apparently in the hands of Jesuits or secular teachers on a private basis.[88]

Girls may have had better access to basic education than did boys in the town. From the moment they arrived, the Ursuline Nuns were pleased to report that "from all sides they promised us boarding students," and the sisters immediately established their girls' school in 1727, the second oldest such institution in mainland North America after the Ursulines' establishment in New France (1639), and just before the first girls' school in Saint Domingue in 1731.[89] Although they taught a very limited curriculum, the nuns were a real boon to the small population in New Orleans. In the islands, by comparison, proportionately fewer nuns served the much larger population. In 1765, about as many sisters (less than one dozen) served New Orleans as served in all Saint Domingue.[90] Despite the industry of the local nuns, a rich family like the Pradels could obtain a polished education for their girls beyond the primary level only by sending them to schools in France.[91]

Another indicator of the position of white children was the generous policy exhibited by the Superior Council in granting emancipation from parents when petitioned.[92] Until the age of twenty-five, children and young adults lived under the legal domination of their parents or their official "tutors" if the parents were deceased. Yet very few petitioned for emancipation in New Orleans. The rarity of these requests indicates that young people had reasons to be optimistic in those early decades. For one thing, unlike parts of the older English colonies, where land became increasingly scarce in the eighteenth century, land remained plentiful and easy to obtain in the lower Mississippi Valley. Children were supposed to inherit equally, so the eldest son was not favored at the others' expense. Even though that law was full of loopholes, the abundance of available land must have moderated the urge to concentrate the estate in the hands of one son. Certain individual children were able to shoot from the lowest to the highest station in life in a land of opportunity. René-Auguste Chouteau was the child of a dysfunctional marriage of common people in New Orleans when he was informally adopted by a man and sent to upper Louisiana at the tender age of thirteen, entrusted with considerable responsibility. He oversaw the foundation of St. Louis and soon became one of the wealthiest and most powerful men in the colony.[93] On average, most children were better off from the point of view of socioeconomic opportunity than they were in France.

The institution of godparenting did limit parents' powers to a degree, for the implicit religious duty of godparents to keep one eye on parental behavior continued after Louis XIV secularized the institution, whereby godparents became baptismal "sponsors" and civil "tutors."[94] Agnès Fine has described the role of these secondary parents in detail. Not only did the godparent having the same sex as the godchild give that child his or her name at baptism, but also throughout life both godparents were expected to give the child gifts on holidays, provide spiritual or moral counsel, adopt the child if both parents died, and perhaps intervene actively to protect the child if parents became abusive.[95] White children always had two godparents at baptism in New Orleans, and most often those spiritual parents were not married, that is, they hailed from two different families, which would tend to maximize their protective role by giving a child a choice between two quite different appellant mediators in case of need. Nonetheless, almost nothing is recorded concerning the actual functioning of godparenting to protect children, except occasionally in their role as tutors after the death of parents.[96]

A case from 1743 illustrates how much could go wrong on occasions when tutorship did not work. It began with a fierce protest to the Superior Council by stepfather and tutor Louis Tixerant and wife Marie Arlut about her son by an earlier marriage, André Carrière. Twenty years old, he had engaged to marry a woman of thirty-two named St. Martin. His parents were bursting with indignation that this scandalous girl lived not with her mother but in her own rooms, where she received André and other young people.[97] This shows that provincial prudery marked New Orleans social life in the mid–eighteenth century as much as it did in the English colonies. The court took André's side when he demanded to be emancipated five years before the legal minimum, ordering an accounting of his inheritance. This led to an explosion of suits: his parents tried to cut André off without a sou, André demanded they pay compensation, and he himself was sued by an ally of his parents whom he beat savagely one night. In the light of conflicting evidence, the safest conclusion is that authorities appear to have favored early emancipation and would defend a son's choice of spouse, but parents, even a stepparent, retained great residual influence.[98]

In fact, there is little evidence in New Orleans of the tension about property in families found by some historians of France.[99] The record as a whole suggests that domestic conflict arose primarily from relations between husbands and wives. The partition of estates into precisely equal shares by the court in a region where land was virtually given away to young families meant that conflict between adults and children and between siblings was muted. Many successions were like Jacques Fazende's of 1760, in which three boys and three girls divided a net estate of 58,601 livres into exactly equal shares, and that was that.[100]

Having stressed the generally good conditions for children in New Orleans, it is now appropriate to emphasize that in one respect the second generation faced a peculiar situation. Those who were born creoles faced two problems: the young men faced a marriage market in which men from France had an advantage, and the increasing level of competition in the marriage market at the end of the French regime meant that a number of girls found themselves propelled into the marriage market at a tender age, often too early, which meant a decline in their independence and, presumably, their happiness. Parental prearrangement may also have played a role, but we have almost nothing to indicate this.[101] Again, we are forced to rely on data taken from a fraction of the total marriages made by members of the creole generations: incomplete records of the period between 1759 and 1768. The age at first marriage for sixty-two New Orleans–born brides can be determined for those years, and the overall average was 15.65 years. No less than thirty-three were younger than that, 12 to 15 years old.[102] Girls of this age are not really capable of exercising much free choice on the basis of rational evaluation of suitors, and there would appear to be a strong degree of parental control, at least over the marriage matches of daughters.

Jean-Charles Pradel hoped to find husbands for his girls in western France, for in his view only a few men in Louisiana were worthy of them, and these were likely to own "nothing more than a cape and a sword."[103] After Jean-Charles's death in 1764, control of the family passed to his long-estranged, strong-willed wife, Alexandrine Delachaise. She not only took over the two family plantations but also was immediately faced with the issue of marrying her daughter Jeanne-Henriette, twenty-four years old. This daughter had been virtually betrothed to one man in Louisiana, apparently her mother's choice, whom she had convinced to take the girl without a dowry. Now Jeanne-Henriette balked, "changed her mind," wishing to marry her first cousin in France, but Alexandrine angrily refused to approve, in the first instance because the man's mother was Spanish ("whose milk he sucked"), and also because he was ignorant and lazy. She threatened to disinherit Jeanne-Henriette.[104] Reading between the lines, it appears that Jeanne-Henriette had no say in the choice of her spouse from the beginning. When both Jeanne-Henriette and her sister, Marie-Louise (born 1744) disobeyed orders to come to Louisiana in 1766, where Alexandrine could better control them, she threatened to disinherit both of them.[105] Complaining bitterly that she had become an old spinster because of her mother's "mistreatment," Jeanne-Henriette finally yielded, returned home, married her first suitor, a French infantry captain's son named Charles D'Inguimbert, lost her inheritance to the state because of her mother's involvement with the New Orleans rebels of 1768, and died, probably miserable, in 1774. Marie-Louise married her deceased brother's brother-in-law in France, far from her mother's clutches, and died there in 1782.[106] If at all typical, the negative implications of this degree of parental control for a wholesome pattern of spousal relations—and especially for female mental health—are obvious.

In this review of the construction of the slaveowning class, not much has been said about relations among its members. This is explored in more detail in chapter 4, but some preliminary remarks are in order here. The constant need to draw together to control the black population welded them together as a class, although that should not be exaggerated. As lords of their domains they were not much on cooperating with one another as partners. Some did form venture partnerships like that between Louis Tixerant and Antoine Aufrère to produce tar and pitch on the other side of the lake.[107] Sieurs Pradel and Foucault agreed to keep livestock on the property they purchased from the Jesuits' auction in 1763, and Pradel's widow, Alexandrine, contracted with one William Martin to produce rum on her plantation in 1766.[108] These contracts appear to have caused few quarrels, but partnerships were not numerous. Consolidation of investment capital rarely occurred by this method because the role of plantation lordship made it hard for a man to render himself liable for the decisions of a partner.[109]

Not only was cooperative business activity little recorded, but locals did not behave in ways that would encourage outside investors to stay. Outsiders were liable to be plundered if they became vulnerable, as shown by the case of Paul Rasteau, scion of one of the rich crypto-Protestant mercantile houses in La Rochelle, whose father sent him to New Orleans early in the 1740s in response to a private contract by the crown in an attempt to stimulate the town's economy. He may have been the town's first real merchant capitalist with important transatlantic trade connections. He soon had very extensive business affairs throughout the Gulf region and loaned money to many people.[110] Then, shortly after he married a local girl of fifteen, Rasteau was drowned in Florida escaping a shipwreck. The council protected the widow's claims for her dowry but then permitted local creditors to ravage the outsider's estate in compensation for consignments that went down in Rasteau's ship. Local debtors of the deceased, by contrast, appear to have enjoyed a windfall moratorium, and all of this was at the expense of Rasteau's heirs in France. It was no way to encourage the French bourgeoisie to settle in the Mississippi Valley.[111]

While the planters might fleece outsiders, they generally did not prey upon one another. The vast majority of collections for debt, for example, were civilized affairs usually caused by inability to pay. Rarely does the record include a case of swindling, such as Sieur Boisclair's appropriation of the Widow Piquery's land and forest while she was busy with the royal bakery or Sieur Bobé's suit to recover the value of twenty-seven slaves sold to Sieur Duplanty, who tried to pay off in inferior peltry.[112] Henry P. Dart suggested that probate racketeering was a problem in early Louisiana, and there are a few cases in support of that thesis. Dart had the sordid Rasteau affair in mind. Settlement of the estate of Raymond D'Ausseville, who had mixed the property of vacant estates with his own in his official capacity, required twenty years (1745–65) to sort out.[113] But these were rare cases. Complaints by colonists against one another about land or estates were seldom long entailed in courts.[114]

Since New Orleans was a slave society from the beginning, the identity of the slaveholders and their role as a ruling class were clear from the outset, and this clarity must have been an advantage to them. In the French period, however, this was still "a class-in-itself, reacting to pressures on its objective position" by slaves, imperial administrators, Indians, or markets, and it would be prevented until after 1803 from becoming a truly free "class-for-itself, consciously striving to shape the world in its own image" through elaborate legislation based on a more explicitly developed ideology.[115] The slaveholders were united primarily by their common problem of keeping blacks enslaved, and were neither motivated nor able to develop an ideology of proslavery and a forceful strategy to promote it. They were not motivated ideologically because abolitionists did not threaten slavery. They were not able because they did not have full control of their local institutions. Like any colonists, and particularly French colonists by comparison with their English neighbors, they lacked independence from the metropole that would have permitted them to act as they saw fit—to develop sugar production for export, for example, or to seek out and import slaves as they pleased. This is not to say, however, that they were powerless to impose order on their society. Conflict among them was muted because their families were extensively intermarried by the 1760s: any disagreement could quickly reverberate throughout family networks in such a small society. By their enforcement of the laws and by the creation of an integrated class that could control the slave majority and command deference from white common people, they made their community as structured and intolerant of misbehavior (as defined by them) as any slave society in North America. For all of that, however, this was still an American society, which meant the lower orders of white people were not as deferential as they were in the Old World.

The distinction between gentlemen and common men in France traveled with the colonists on their transatlantic voyage, but the degree of subservience the latter owed the former was open to renegotiation in New Orleans. Because the highest and the lowest orders of French society were missing, the distance between the upper and lower halves of free society in the province was blurred. Situated just below the slaveowning class, the artisans of New Orleans began with an improved position in the New World, by providing crucial services. They were unlikely to expand as a group, however, for a slave system provided a weak market for their skills. They could demand high compensation, like their unskilled fellow workers who received high wages, good board, and expanded Old World privileges of St. Monday. Even so, in New Orleans it proved very difficult to retain either skilled or unskilled workers in any number.[116] Authorities ardently desired them, which helps explain why they had to back down in 1723, when they feared that soldiers and laborers might combine to fight a cut in their wages.[117] Despite all efforts, by the 1730s only a few skilled white laborers remained in the town, that is, the 78 indentured listed in the census of 1731 (who would soon be freedmen) and up to half of the 110 other male civilians (see table 3 in chapter 1), and immigration by artisans from France remained next to nil.[118]

The judicial record reveals artisans asserting themselves against the grain of their traditional status. When wronged, these men went straight to a sympathetic Superior Council. The last thing Louisiana needed was a reputation for injustice to skilled workingmen. John A. Dickinson finds in his study of judicial procedure in New France that the court served to maintain the hierarchy but court action was comparatively inexpensive and the rich did not receive favorable treatment: the same was true in New Orleans.[119] When a case of wage claims by four workers against a plantation director named Verteuil was decided in their favor and Verteuil stalled, the Attorney General was furious. He denounced the director for encouraging "this sort of pleading so dangerous to colonies." This was representative of the court's reaction to the mistreatment of free labor, which it sought to protect.[120]

A group of cases revolving around false accusations for theft also reveals the legal and social position of artisans in the courts. In one early case in July 1727, a literate house joiner named Étienne Bouet was falsely charged by Sieur and Madame Goublaye that he stole clothes and brandy from them while working on their house. He pleaded very specifically that as "a worker [*ouvrier*] obliged to gain his livelihood with the public" he could not let the insult pass. A sergeant had even searched his lodging. He wanted Madame (the accuser) to pay him a substantial indemnity and all court costs, to pay two thousand livres to the church and deserving poor, and to apologize to him publicly before the church after high mass. The court could not have granted such a demand, but its actual response is unknown.[121] Overall, the court's handling of this kind of case shows that it was anxious to insure that white labor was at least heard. A degree of deference was required, nonetheless. At the outset of Périer's administration, as Father Raphael reported disapprovingly, the lowly Mr. Pailla, "one of the good *habitants*," was condemned by the Superior Council to pay a fifty écus fine; make amends before the Church and council, and to be whipped and then banished for five years, for merely "injuring and insulting" Sieur Perrault.[122]

Despite judicial protection, the artisan class was hardly likely to grow naturally from within since slavery limited the prospects of its members. This can be seen in the record of apprenticeship. A few children were apprenticed by their parents, and occasionally a young person indentured himself, like Bernard Longueville, a fifteen year old from Bordeaux abandoned in Louisiana, who neatly signed his own four-year contract to tailor François Doyon.[123] But only thirty-nine contracts of indenture were recorded for this entire period between 1737 and 1769, when the phenomenon was at its height. Even if the rate of such contracts in years when the Superior Council records are complete were extrapolated, the estimated total would still be unimpressive. This was because of the paucity of white artisans, because "native-born blacks began to be put to trades," as the Rutmans have shown in Virginia, and because whites had higher ambitions to employ their sons in building up land into slave plantations.[124]

The meager record tells little about the indentured children themselves. Of the thirty-nine indentures, fathers apprenticed sons in eleven cases, stepfathers in eight, mothers in three, and the remainder were outright orphans apprenticed by other relatives or the state, except for three young men who contracted for themselves. Of the fifteen whose ages were noted, the range was twelve to twenty-three years old, engaged for three to five years. Only six signed their own contracts and masters were almost never required to teach their charges anything but the trade itself. The record of apprenticeship reveals that most white children were not put out of the family under strange masters. In a land where subsistence was relatively easy, and where social mobility was possible, the nonslaveholding family was able to operate more often as a unit throughout the lives of all members. That maximized their opportunity to become a slaveholding family.

Below the artisan level, there were virtually no white poor after the founding years, except for the troops. The indentured in the census of 1731 were soon free and few were replaced. Free, nonslaveholding landholders did not form a significant portion of the population as they did in early Virginia's Eastern Shore district, as described by James Perry, but their range of opportunities was similar: a period of indentured servitude, probably followed by sharecropping or overseership, then small holding.[125] Destitute white people appeared rarely in the record because they were few. Even though the distinction between slaveowners and non-slaveowners was a large one, the extremes of rich and poor found in France were not seen in early New Orleans. Settlers without slaves rarely had any other ambition than to join the slaveholding class. Carpenter Simon Rousset died in a plain cabin with a bark roof, but it was on his own lot, which sold for 330 livres.[126] Another carpenter at the other end of the period had only some personal effects and notes of indebtedness, but he owned a slave and so was not insolvent.[127] Some did well without slaves. One nonslaveholder, Jean Louis, began with nothing in New Orleans in the early days, and then left his substantial estate to build St. John Charity Hospital for the honest poor. He must have been guided more by piety than compelling necessity because only five people were admitted when it opened in 1737.[128]

Those found in poverty were most likely to be women. Widow Duranton had her husband's soldier uniform and gun, some clothes, and a chamber pot. She lived in a cabin on Dubreuil's land, and he even assigned her a slave to serve her at the end. A shocking, unusual case of white poverty in the record was that of Jacqueline Chaumont. She appealed to the court for protection because her soldier husband was long departed to another post, and the innkeeper LeGros had beaten her and ruined her only good eye, so her young son had to lead her through the streets to beg.[129] This was a rare case of a woman physically abused by a man to whom she was not married. Far more typical of distressed women was Marguerite LeJeune, who petitioned the court for permission to sell her house in New Orleans in 1753. She had to move to Pointe Coupée district (hardly as unfortunate as taking refuge in St. John Charity Hospital), because the town was too expensive for her. The white poor were never mentioned as a group, for it was relatively easy to escape poverty in Louisiana if one was white and capable of working three days a week.

These same conditions meant that major crimes by whites were rare.

Most of the handful of murders of white people by other whites took place outside New Orleans at the lonely outposts where life was hardest. The court rarely had to hand down capital sentences.[130] The most gruesome was that of Jacques Baude in November 1767, who went on drunken sprees of mayhem and had killed men in France, Cuba, and finally in Bourbon Street one night after curfew. The judges condemned him to be broken on the scaffold and mounted on a wheel to die. The executioner was ordered to strangle him one hour after he had been on the wheel.[131] Another exceptional murder case in New Orleans concerned Jean-Baptiste Gauvin, introduced earlier in his suit to hold Marie-Louise Soulande to her promise to marry him in the summer of 1740. One day in his tavern soon after his marriage, some soldiers quarreled over the position of a pool ball. In a wild moment, Jean-Baptiste stabbed to death an enraged soldier in self-defense. In this case of an accident, the contrite Gauvin was allowed to lie low, to be hanged only in effigy, pardoned by the king, and become a respectable citizen again.[132] Other kinds of criminal cases involving whites were rare. Nonfatal assault by whites upon other whites in the period between 1743 and 1769 led to only about a dozen prosecutions. They were mostly coarse situations, to which any society is subject.[133] Capital punishment and judicial torture of white people were almost unheard of because serious crimes were almost never committed by them.[134]

Theft by whites was also uncommon: the most serious crime committed by nonslaveholders was cattle rustling. At Cannes Brulées above Tchoupitoulas, Pierre-Joseph Delisle Dupart had a large cattle ranch. In the early 1750s he lost so many head that he armed his slaves to guard his lands. One day, they caught two white men butchering a cow or an ox and tried to arrest them, which touched off a melee. The white men were Dupart's neighbors and claimed in court that his cattle damaged their fields. They flatly denied everything of which they were accused by the slaves, arguing that slaves' honor was worthless. They noted the inherent danger to all whites in allowing a band of blacks to roam about armed. The council found the rustlers guilty but sentenced them only to light fines and stern warnings. The court did not order Dupart to disarm his slaves.[135]

In New Orleans, as in most colonies, white people were generally able to police themselves. It was quite possible for the whole town to participate in a twenty-four-hour celebration of the Peace of Paris that combined decorous military ceremonies and religious observances, a barbecue of some oxen, and then a frolic of the kind the people of New Orleans loved best. All "dined and danced throughout the night until 7 a. m. on the following morning."[136] This sort of highly structured communal festivity would have been impossible in a town given over to perpetual riot and orgy. The governor who sponsored this affair was fresh from France, an overstarched moralist who thought the colonists were lazy, but he did not picture a society in which there was no order. Otherwise the colony would not have developed. Even according to the rather fussy Ordonnateur Michel, "it is to tell the truth, my lord, the best land that there is in the world and the finest colony that the King could possess. His Majesty will have reason in the future to repent not having profited by [its] considerable advantages. . . . They are all asking for negroes and really cannot succeed without that. Things are moving along very well. The colony is growing everyday on its own. One need merely spur it on, so to speak."[137] The slaveowning class did have an important internal weakness by comparison to Virginia planters: they had no institutions independent of the royal Superior Council. "The most important imprimatur of status among the men of Middlesex," according to the Rutmans, was "the degree to which they served the public."[138] In New Orleans, aside from a handful of crown officers, public service was not encouraged by the crown. Even so, the evidence from New Orleans shows that a large degree of stability could be attained in a slave society even in the absence of an ethos of public service.

The town developed under a shadow: the conviction that the colonists had been rejected by their countrymen and neglected by the crown. Yet the planters organized immediately and effectively to create a class that was able to give the town the same orderly structure that was created in any successful colony. The old story about New Orleans as a sink of immorality in which elemental rules of eighteenth-century society were ignored is untrue, a myth that ignores the bedrock activities of family formation, conflict resolution, and labor management that gave the planters' society remarkable stability. That stability was essential because their success and even their very lives were hostage to the ever-present threat of rebellion by the black majority.

Black Majority: 3

Slaves and Free Blacks during the French Regime

The Masters think only of milking the profit from the labor of these poor wretches.

—Father Raphael de Luxembourg, 1725

A rumor had been disseminated here that the negroes were going to rise in revolt last Christmas Eve and that they would choose the time when we were at midnight mass. . . . Those who went to the midnight mass were armed like Don Quixote.

—Commissaire Ordonnateur Edmé Salmon, 1732

No man can serve two masters: for either he will hate the one, and love the other; or else he will hold to the one, and despise the other. Ye cannot serve God and mammon.

—Matthew 6:24

New Orleans was the first settlement in the New World to have a black majority from the beginning; unlike other slave societies, which developed gradually in regions where the labor force was at first dominated by indentured white servants, New Orleans began as a slave society.[1] Although John Law's scheme aimed to stock the colony with thousands of white farmers and laborers, that part of the plan failed. So slaves had to do most of the work: clearing swamps, building infrastructure, cultivating both staple crops and food crops. Born into a variety of socioeconomic groups in Africa, they were all confined to a legally degraded status in America on the basis of their color, and any aspiration to escape their status was defined as villainous. As a result of unrelenting labor and cultural fissures in the founding slave community, they had little time, energy, or motivation to create families and community, but somehow they did. They demonstrated the resilience of the human spirit by creating their own social structure from the very diverse elements that composed the founding generation. Some of them attacked the system itself at the risk of their lives.

Africans arrived in New Orleans with the vaguest and most fearful ideas about the intentions of their captors and limited knowledge of one another.[2] The transatlantic voyage was particularly bad for many of those bound for the Louisiana colony. The wait in prisons at African slave posts was horribly long even before one was locked in the hold of a slaver. The *Saint Louis* spent one entire year collecting slaves on the African coast before setting out on a seventeen-week voyage to Louisiana.[3] Many of those purchased in Africa never made it. The earliest small voyages to New Orleans showed mortality rates of 2 to 16 percent, which was within the norm or even low for the early eighteenth century. Then in 1728 the *Duc de Noailles* had a very bad voyage, although it took only about three months to reach New Orleans from Africa, under the average time of fourteen weeks on that leg of the trip, an average based on a range of seven to twenty-eight weeks to Louisiana.[4] Nonetheless, only 242 of 351 people in this cargo made it, and half of them were immediately hospitalized with scurvy, of which one-fourth soon died. The *Galathée* then lost 170 of a cargo of 400. Seven voyages between 1727 and 1731 for which the mortality was recorded lost 507 out of 2,528, or 20 percent. The fast voyage of *Vénus* in 1728 brought 341 Africans to New Orleans in only seven weeks, by not making the usual stop to refresh the cargo in Saint Domingue. Only 21 were lost along the way, but the rest were delivered deathly ill with scurvy.[5] One cargo never made it to Louisiana: the vessel caught fire 150 leagues out of the port of Juda, and all 260 slaves went down with the ship.[6]

When sold in New Orleans, the slaves were regarded as so many units or parts of a *pièce d'Inde*, a measurement meaning "prime adult laborer," a skilled farmer or craftsmen of an indelible color that could be defined as the mark of slaves.[7] Because masters regarded their personalities as a nuisance and seldom described them carefully, little is known about their painful adjustment to slavery after they arrived. They came with some experience of an institution historians call "slavery" in Africa, but it was not like the racial plantation slave regime of North America: it was a transient condition that was not based on race.[8] Those who had been slaves in Africa were far more unfree as slaves in the New World, and, by contrast with Africa, their descendants were required by law to remain in slavery. Slaves were members of the master's family in Africa, but this was only theoretically true in New Orleans.[9]

The task of creating a black community and local culture was complicated by several factors from the beginning. Most obviously, the French controlled all levers of power. They wrote and applied the law, had systems of communication that long remained imperfectly understood by the Africans, could forge alliances with huge neighboring Indian nations based on European trade goods, and created a transportation system that connected them with all other white people, who would come in force to protect their own kind in the event of a slave revolt. The slaves did not understand this in 1731, when some of them plotted to take over Louisiana, but after that it was clear that successful mass revolt was impossible. Up to that point, however, the central problem of what to do about their enslavement deeply divided them.

Ethnic variation divided slaves, more than it did the French, who at least shared a common king, religion, and language. Africans who were brought to New Orleans were from a variety of regions and a wide variety of nations. The majority were either Senegalese, Guineas, Bambaras, or Ibos. The provision of a majority of blacks from Senegalese markets was in accordance with French planters' tastes in supposed ethnic attributes and skills, but Senegambia's superficial cultural unity masked deep social divisions.[10] Moreover, regardless of masters' preferences they would buy slaves of any origin, so the population was very mixed.[11] It was divided by African historical traditions, in particular by the animosity between Sudanese speakers, including the Senegalese, and Bantu speakers, including the Congolese, and by linguistic and other variation that was found within Senegal or Angola.[12] Determining origins was relatively easy; most were readily identifiable in the slave quarter by the variety of distinctive scarification practiced by most West African nations.[13] If a person's skin was not marked in this fashion, then distinctive accents, vocabularies, or speech patterns betrayed one's origin.

One part of the slave force in New Orleans was composed of non-Africans: Indians from a variety of Louisiana nations who were purchased or captured in war. The colonists had hoped to exploit forced Indian labor on a large scale, but that proved as difficult in Louisiana as in other North American colonies. Indian slaves could too easily run away and obtain refuge with free

Indians, and the small population of colonists could not risk large-scale local recruitment of slaves in any case. So the colonists traded Indian slaves to the West Indies in return for Africans at the rate of two for one, as the English did, but never in significant numbers.[14] Over time, a few Indians accumulated in the local slave community, and from the Africans' point of view that was another uncertain and potentially divisive element in their midst.

Religion must have seriously undermined the unity of slaves at first. The majority of West Africans were polytheistic, but religious practice was extremely various.[15] Above all, religious particularity was a problem for the immigrant concerned that he or she lacked knowledge of countermeasures to the magic commanded by a member of another nation by drawing on the power of its deities.[16] Nothing could have been of greater importance in the making of the African American community than suppression of African magical practices in the interest of peace and solidarity. A rare bit of evidence of this is found in advice to prospective slaveholders by Antoine-Simon Le Page Du Pratz, who recommended that a planter not try to take away a newly arrived African's gris-gris, or amulets, because "the old negroes soon make them lose conceit of them."[17] This is important proof of the active suppression of African cultural practices in the slave quarter. One final religious division existed in the slave community: that between a Moslem minority and the non-Moslems. No direct evidence of Moslems in the early days of New Orleans has appeared, but the famous eighteenth-century Maryland slave Ayuba Suleiman Diallo came from the same region as many Louisiana slaves, Senegambia, and his master set him apart from other slaves by treating him with some consideration because he was a Islamic monotheist with knowledge of Jesus.[18]

Many West African nations were at war with one another in Africa, wars stimulated or at least partly sustained by the transatlantic slave trade itself, and the bitterness bred by these wars must have been carried in the slave ships to America.[19] In his description of Sierra Leone, for example, Jean Barbot describes the hatred between the two groups into which the region was divided.[20] In the interior, the Bambaras were immersed in chronic imperial warfare in the eighteenth century, which bred a hellish social atmosphere. Bambaras must have been generally hated by non-Bambaras. For example, one slave accused of murdering a white soldier in 1748 tried to exploit the Bambaras' supposed reputation as liars to shift suspicion from himself to one of them.[21]

National origins could be the cause of bitterness in other ways in the slave community. One of the most vivid examples in the early period is that of

Louis Congo. Slaves from the Congo formed a small group in early New Orleans, and it would appear that Louis, a capital offender, was reprieved on account of his minority ethnic origin (and an aptitude?) to be the public executioner to administer judicial sentences passed against blacks.[22] He was freed, given a small plot, and permitted to have his wife live there with him. As *executeur des hautes oeuvres*, Congo was to administer punishments: he could charge forty livres for the wheel or the stake, thirty for a hanging, ten for a whipping or branding, and five for fastening an iron collar.[23] This job, combined with the distinction of his origin, meant that he would be hated. Three runaway slaves broke into his house and tried to kill him in the summer of 1726.[24] Ten years later he was assaulted again by two runaways, who jumped him in broad daylight when he was hunting on the west bank.[25] Louis Congo lived in fear, a Central African with a scorned office in a community overwhelmingly dominated by people from West Africa.

Africans came from societies that were marked by hierarchy, and, while some people brought as slaves to the New World had been slaves at the bottom of the hierarchy in the Old World, others had been property owners. Even slaves from the same nation in Africa were at odds socially when they arrived in New Orleans. Jean Barbot described classes in Senegambia that were sharply demarcated by the clothing they wore. While common people seldom wore more than a loincloth, the nobility wore elaborate costumes of cotton and linen that were much decorated with gris-gris. The nobility was marked off from the commonalty in many other ways. Wealth was also measured by the ownership of slaves. While there is disagreement about the degree of similarity between African and American slave systems, historians agree that African slavery was not based on a concept of "race": it was not as strictly hereditary as it was in America, and individual slaves might achieve positions of trust and wealth unknown in America.[26] The fact remains that the social spectrum in Africa was complex, and we can well imagine Africans in America making distinctions based on status in "the old country."[27]

Nevertheless, these status positions in the Old World were denatured when removed from their native context, and, as Sidney W. Mintz agues persuasively, since complex African social structures could not be transferred to the New World in the slavers, "the capacity of isolated representatives of African societies to perpetuate or to recreate the cultural contents of the past [in America] was seriously impaired," however high the status of an individual in the Old World.[28] Thus, new distinctions of status were created by the production regime in Louisiana. All of the main exports from the colony required sophisticated management of every step in the process (described in chapter 5), and slaves with particular aptitudes might gain the special appreciation of the master and certain privileges. Some slaves might be raised above others because they were trusted to maximize production, especially at those times when the master or overseer could not be on the spot. Distinctions arose between the mass of low-status field hands and the minority of artisans, between the master's personal domestic servants and the rest. Status in the work place carried over into the quarter.

African nations also varied in the ways men and women interacted. According to Barbot, meals were sexually segregated among peoples living in the interior, whereas coastal peoples dined in sexually mixed family groups. In the Gold Coast region and many other areas, women completely dominated the domestic markets, although the buying and selling of slaves was controlled by men.[29] In some nations, but not others, it was common for girls to be taken as wives before puberty.[30] While most nations practiced male circumcision, some nations circumcised women while others did not.[31] A man's former status and national origin might also be marked in America by his number of former wives, as many West African societies were polygynous.[32]

What these variations meant in the New World is still not clear. Certainly, polygamy was reduced by conditions in America, especially by the masters' hostility to it and by the imbalance in the distribution of the sexes. The older view that this sexual imbalance was primarily the result of American planters' preference for male workers has given way to the new understanding that African suppliers were responsible for making far more men than women available to transatlantic traders because women were more highly valued by African masters. This was true because of "their sexuality [their value as wives], their slightly greater productivity in domestic labor under conditions of a restricted market for slave produce, and the difficulty of controlling men under African conditions."[33] This must have given women a greater degree of negotiating power with African men in America because they were few, upsetting if not destroying traditional patriarchal power.

Finally, slaves were divided by their distribution among white households. According to the census of 1766, the majority of slaves lived on plantations and in townhouses with small- to medium-sized slave forces, as seen in fig. 2, a graphic representation of the figures presented in table 5 (see chapter 2). The larger the concentrations of slaves on large plantations, the better the opportunity for building subcommunities well knit by family formation, and large plantations were few in New Orleans. Still, there was a fair prospect of family formation on the numerous plantations of twenty or more, but choices of spouses were sharply limited.

Slaves had to create a community out of the bare roots of traditional knowledge, with the institutions they knew in Africa confused by variety and subject to official repression in the New World. Countervailing the many divisions that divided them were ties that bound them together: slaves shared a degree of unity because of their legal status, their physical deprivation, and their uncertainty about the future. So they created a social structure in which kin relations, their own marks of status, and basic individual worth were respected, social relations that were, in time, clothed with local ways and traditions produced by creative self-expression. About the details practically nothing is known.

New Orleans slaves undoubtedly achieved a greater measure of social stability in their quarters than the slaves in, say, South Carolina, because the African slave trade to Louisiana all but ceased in 1733. This should not be

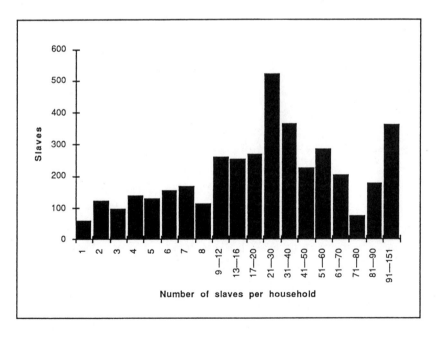

Fig. 2. Number of slaves per household, New Orleans, 1766.

exaggerated: even with relative stability in this period, they could create a separate structure that set only certain limits to the power of the planters, a cohesive class whose ability to dominate society steadily increased after 1731. Moreover, a major reshuffling of slave property beginning in the late 1750s and growth of the slave trade beginning in the 1760s would gravely weaken whatever autonomy and self-confidence had been achieved in the slave community. These conflicting tendencies—the ethnic and other divisions among the slaves and the compelling urge to create community in which some measure of independence from white control was possible—are well illustrated in the history of rebellion in Louisiana in the earlier period.[34]

Blacks' collective struggle for freedom began during the middle passage. In 1723, the crew of the *Courrier de Bourbon* mercilessly suppressed a conspiracy to take over the ship on its way to New Orleans.[35] A group of three hundred slaves nearly managed to take over the *Annibal* in a revolt just after the ship left Africa for New Orleans in 1729. Arming themselves with anything that was not tied down, they were stopped only by indiscriminate firing by the crew, who killed forty-five and wounded forty-seven more, including women and children. The leaders were hanged, but the group remained rebellious and the captain was much relieved to sell them in Saint Domingue rather than spend more weeks on the same vessel with them crossing the Gulf of Mexico to New Orleans.[36]

Rebellion on slavers might be explained away as the fault of slave traders, but what happened in the colony could not be blamed on outsiders. Brute force was the fundamental method by which slaves were controlled. The judicial record for the first decade of New Orleans' history is full of evidence of the most horrific bloodletting by whites in order to achieve mastery. The French demonstrated what would happen to a slave accused of the ultimate offense in 1722, when they burned one alive for killing a white man.[37] Besides sheer corporal discipline, the colonists also had to employ some cunning, especially by committing the Indian nations to the regime. Bienville had recognized the threat of Indian-African alliance as early as 1723, when it was an important clause in his treaty with the Natchez that "they bring in dead or alive a negro who has taken refuge among them for a long time and makes them seditious speeches against the French nation."[38] Périer had a policy before 1729 to award Indians in the hinterland huge bounties to bring in runaway slaves who escaped New Orleans. Not only would slaveowners retrieve their property, but it would supposedly kindle in blacks "a hatred for the savages so strong that the

French will have no fear of any intelligence between the two peoples."[39] The cooperation of some black slaves with Natchez warriors in 1729 in hopes of enslaving the white captives was deeply unsettling. In response to this threat of a general Indian-African conjunction, Périer devised a crude scheme to sour relations between them, as seen earlier, by offering freedom to some black slaves for slaughtering the Chawashas. It is instructive to compare two reports Périer wrote the same day about this disgusting action. In his letter to the Minister of Marine, he expressed the wish that he could order the slaves to destroy "all these little nations that are of no use to us and that might on the contrary incite our Negroes to rebellion," as was seen recently at Natchez.[40] In his letter to the Company of the Indies, however, he explains that he "has not dared to use all the Negro volunteers to destroy the other small nations on the banks of the river for fear of rendering these Negroes too bold and inclining them, perhaps, to revolt."[41] However ridiculous Périer appears, in his confusion he reveals the central dilemma of the white settlers. He now included the freed executioners of the Chawashas in the force of Choctaws and French soldiers he sent out to fall upon Natchez, and, according to one observer, the fifteen freed blacks "fought like heroes."[42] It was cold comfort in light of subsequent events.

The cooperation by some black slaves with the Natchez Indians in 1729 explains the almost fanatical effort the whites exerted to recover every single slave that either absconded with or was carried away by the hostile Natchez. This was not just about the restoration of property but about the dangerous policy of allowing blacks to be incorporated into the Indian community, which would corrode the wall that whites erected between the two groups and lead to increased slave marronage or worse.[43] Three of the black slaves who had cooperated with the Natchez were handed over to the Choctaws, who burned them alive, helping the French to create hatred between blacks and Indians.[44]

This episode was followed in 1731 by a substantial conspiracy by a specific group of slaves to end the French regime. The whites' reaction to the Natchez uprising undoubtedly contributed to stimulating this plot, assuming that it actually existed. According to one high-ranking official, however, there was a further explanation of the plot: in spite of the effort to recover slaves carried off by the Natchez as rapidly as possible, it had not been fast enough. The slaves had had time to discover that their Indian captors would not kill them and allowed them "liberty," permitting them to work or hunt when they saw fit, like the Indians.[45] This information they communicated to the other slaves of New Orleans when they were captured and returned, which led to the plot. In June 1731, the members of the Bambara nation allegedly organized to kill all whites. According to Major Beauchamp, they planned to make themselves masters of the other slaves, but no record exists of the trials so their side of the story is not known.[46] It would have been natural for the Bambaras to create a version of their own Old World society, which was based on an African type of slavery.[47] The accused leaders (five to twelve men and one woman) were sent to the wheel or the noose, and their bodies were left to rot on the Bayou Road.[48] The governor admitted cavalierly that "it was neither clear nor certain that the Negroes had formed this black intrigue," but since "all New Orleans was in an extravagant alarum," he had to set an example to soothe jangled nerves.[49] In order to carry out the executions, it was necessary "to put all the habitants under arms" to prevent a general revolt.[50] Another plot was rumored six months later, when the whites turned out armed "like Don Quixote" for Christmas Eve midnight mass, but according to Ordonnateur Edme Salmon, it was a false alarm.[51] In fact, this marked the end of concerted slave conspiracy in New Orleans in the French period.[52]

This turbulence illustrates several points about the nature of politics in the slave community, and, more generally, in slave society. First, the mere rumor of a general uprising was enough to terrify the colonists, demonstrating the great political potential of the slaves. It was all the more true in an era in which the Indians' revolt had shown, as Périer put it, that the one thing that could lead to the "complete loss" of the colony "would be a union of the Savage Nations and the Negro Slaves."[53] Second, it shows the ability of at least a portion of the slave community to unite to destroy the white regime, an illustration of the powerful cooperative forces arising out of their mutual sympathy for one another. Third, however, the incident also shows that the slaves were very vulnerable to betrayal, for the conspiracies in both 1729 and 1731 were revealed by slaves. Moreover, given the fragmentation of the slave community in the early days, it was an ethnic subgroup that was suspected of plotting in 1731, and these people did not aim to liberate a supposed black "race." Fourth, the sanguinary terribleness of a black uprising served to mitigate the potential for political discord in the white community: it bound them together more than ever in defense of black slavery and violent retribution. Events in New Orleans over the next century occurred in the shadow of memories of those years. As late as 1800, there were living whites and blacks who remembered the sound of bones breaking on the wheel and the cries of the victims as the sun slowly put them out of their misery high above the Bayou Road.

The fifth and most important conclusion to be drawn from these events is that, aside from the temporary setback in 1729, the colonists' alliance with the Indians was the key factor: control of the hinterland by Indians explains why North American slave societies achieved and maintained a level of stability that was eventually shattered in the Antilles by slave rebellion. The Choctaws' show of unity with the French and their brutal executions made a permanent impression on the blacks of New Orleans: the policy of preventing friendship between the two groups worked. By 1748, when some renegade Indians raided the German Coast to steal slaves, many of the settlers' slaves reportedly fought with their masters.[54] This capped what had become a tradition of some individual slaves' participation with the colonists in their wars against the Chickasaws beginning in 1730 and continuing through that decade.[55]

One further fracture was created in the black community by the masters, the creation of an anomalous subgroup of free blacks, although for many decades its small size meant that it was not a source of serious division. As noted earlier, Périer freed a small group of African men for their massacre of peaceful Indians in 1729. These accompanied the expeditions against the Chicakasaws and Natchez. Their leader, one Simon, probably the future stalwart of the free black community, Simon Calfat, earned a permanent place in southern hagiography by a daring sortie into the Chickasaws' camp to plunder their horses, escaping in a hail of the Indians' bullets.[56] These people joined a handful of free blacks who had actually participated in the founding. Marie, a domestic servant, and Jean-Baptiste César, a laborer, were the first recorded French free blacks, who arrived in 1719.[57] In 1724, the free and literate black Raphael Bernard had to petition the court to recover two hundred livres he had loaned the white man Cadot. (The petition was granted, with interest and costs on Cadot.) Much more serious was his suit against his employer Sieur Jean-Baptiste Faucon Dumanoir, a major concessionaire and agent for the company, whom he served with fidelity. Bernard wanted his wages, his trunk, and the liberty to return to France. Dumanoir refused for two years to pay and struck Raphael with his cane when petitioned. The court ordered Dumanoir to pay, although Raphael was not allowed to leave.[58] Finally, perhaps the most unusual Old World (voluntary?) immigrant of all was Simon Vanon, free Negro, born in Senegal.

Vanon signed sacramental registers in the 1720s both as a godparent and bride-groom in a perfectly correct European script, which he must have learned as a youth in Africa.[59]

Another figure of the early free black minority was John Mingo, a run-away slave from South Carolina who arrived naked and starving in New Orleans in 1726, the only known runaway to reach Louisiana from so far away. The best possible dream of the runaway was then fulfilled when Jonathas Darby, director of the Cantillon Concession, declared him free and permitted him to buy on installments Thérèse to be his wife, and to live on a small piece of land and hire out to work. Two years later the couple was managing the slaves of Chavannes' plantation. The planter's wording of the agreement indicated he hired skilled people, for planting was to be "as we decide together [to be] suitable, whether the cultivation of tobacco, cotton, and provisions, or lumbering enterprises." Although this contract provided that the couple's wages would go to Darby to complete the purchase of Thérèse, Mingo went to the court at the end of 1730 to complain that Darby still claimed Thérèse, even though she was paid for. The court decided that it was impossible to tell who was in the right about the amount of tobacco Mingo had paid, and merely ordered that the Mingos could not be separated.[60] In general, only a handful of slaves were permitted to use their skills for the purpose of earning the price of freedom.

The more typical emancipations resulted from many years of uninter-rupted domestic service by a slave. Bienville, for example, freed Jorgé and Marie for twenty-six years' service in 1735. Upon his departure in 1743, Bienville also freed their son Zacarie, or Jacob, according to an agreement whereby he would serve five more years in the colony, "after which he shall be perfectly free, enjoying the privileges of all free men, with due respect for his master and his descendants, whom he shall always consider as his protectors."[61] Jean-Charles Pradel freed St. Louis ("La Nuit") after many years service and made him his overseer. In 1765, Madame Pradel even entrusted him with the delicate task of traveling to France to fetch home her rebellious daughters.[62] Obviously these emancipations were the expansive gestures of rich gentlemen, who could afford to free the most favored among many others they left in bondage. The "privileges of all free men," supposedly granted to free blacks, was just a phrase, however, for in practice it meant the rights to hold property and enter into contracts, not to be socially equal to whites, as is clear from Bienville's caveat.

A spate of emancipations in wills were registered by officers in the 1730s, typified by that of Joseph Meunier. He freed the mulattress Marie, who was eleven years old, because of her services and her attachment to him. He had raised her and, "knowing not if he should return" from the campaign against the Chickasaws, he wished as a *"marque de tendresse"* to free her.[63] Another example from the same period looks exactly like Meunier's, but it illustrates that the route to freedom from French masters was seldom smooth, fair, or short. One St. Julien freed Marie-Charlotte and her daughter Louise before going off to battle, lodging them with the Ursulines as pensioners. Soon thereafter he died, and the Attorney for Vacant Estates Raymond D'Ausseville nullified the manumissions because St. Julien's estate was much indebted, and he had not asked the required consent by government to free the women. On this technicality, Marie-Charlotte and Louise were remanded to the convent, where they were forgotten until 1737, when the nuns demanded the huge bill of 450 livres for their upkeep. D'Ausseville paid and then sold them to recover the money. But Marie-Charlotte was not content with this injustice and pressed a case, and she was finally manumitted by the governor and *ordonnateur* at the end of 1743. Then she tried to sue D'Ausseville's estate for his concealment of her emancipation and for wages of 20 livres per month since she had been seized.[64] Moreover, some emancipations were so restricted as to be virtually meaningless. When François Trudeau freed his children's nurse, Jeanneton, after twenty-three years of service, it was only on the condition that she serve him so long as he lived.[65]

The distinction between slavery and freedom for blacks was paper thin: the privilege of not being slaves could be revoked. The Superior Council sold the freedman Jean-Baptiste back into slavery on account of his theft of clothes.[66] Clearly, free blacks were very imperfectly free if they could be plunged back into slavery at any time. New Orleans was not a fluid society with an ill-defined racial hierarchy; free blacks were "Negroes" who merely enjoyed the revocable privilege of not being slaves. In general, manumissions were rare in French Louisiana, and the attitude toward free blacks in New Orleans was the same as in neighboring English colonies.[67] They were isolated on the other side too; if not far removed from slavery, freedmen were set against slaves, especially because they were recruited to be drivers, overseers like Mingo, or hunters of runaway slaves.[68] At the same time, this should not be exaggerated: the free black community was so small—no more than two hundred by the end of the regime—and so poor that their social distance from slaves was less marked than it became in later years.[69]

Thus a combination of ethnic fragmentation, labor hierarchy, and emancipation reinforced the basic obstacle to family and community formation: no institution among slaves was sanctioned either by law or custom. The marriage of slaves "before the church" conferred no civil status on the spouses, so most of those who married and created families, the bedrock of their community, did so according to their own ceremonies. Assumptions about the eagerness of all people to marry, however, should be resisted. According to Arlette Gautier, women in Africa were in some ways better off than European women. Prenuptial sexual experimentation or even cohabitation was permissible, presumably allowing women greater choice of spouses. A woman's husband had to pay a bride price, which was not a purchase but a deposit in a contract with the woman's family. Wife beating was prohibited, and divorce was easy. In striking contrast to European women, a (non-Moslem) African woman monopolized all but the most prestigious economic transactions of the family and retained a part of her profits from the market for her own lineage. She also enjoyed the support of true female associations unknown in Europe. Nevertheless, polygyny was practiced by most groups, which degraded the status of women, and although a man could not beat a wife, he could have one killed or sold into slavery for misconduct. This power over wives reflected the exclusion of women from politics, although the wives of a chief might be influential.[70]

Focusing on French West Indian planters, who vacillated between policies of encouraging and discouraging slaves to marry, Gautier discounts the effect of masters' policies, believing that many black women renounced the institution of marriage to avoid subjecting themselves to African husbands who would concentrate all the "despotism" designed for many wives upon one in a monogamous household, a household in which her legal economic authority was nil.[71] The Company of the Indies may have made a special effort to provide Louisiana with a self-sustaining black population, for the proportion of males to females in the four earliest voyages for which distributions are known was rather low for the slave trade at seven to four, including 567 men and 148 boys, 304 women and 109 girls.[72] By the end of the first decade, slaves constituted from one-half to two-thirds of all baptisms in New Orleans.[73] This suggests that New Orleans planters encouraged slaves to marry informally and reproduce, particularly after the slave trade collapsed, but Gautier shows that individual women struggled to retain some degree of choice in this most personal of all relations.

Conditions in black slave families were anything but healthy at first. Because of the basic character of the slave trade, the slave population included no older adults, no grandparents for many years. Children were few at first as well. Then, when women began bearing children, the master would abridge their natural development at an early age by employing them in tedious labor that maddened adults, like seeding cotton. Although children of all races in the colonies were indulged to a "bizarre" degree by their mothers, according to one observer, black children first began to understand the system when they were struck by white children or overseers and discovered that their parents were powerless to protect them.[74] So it is important to be wary of the misconception that family life was a comfort and a structural beam of community merely if it was monogamous. Moreover, there are indications that monogamy did not become the norm among a clear majority of slaves for a long time. On the only significant plantation for which records exist for the early period, the D'Asfeld-Jonchère Concession sold to D'Aunoy and Assailly in 1738, rates of family formation appear almost normal. Of eighty-five adults, all but seventeen were listed as couples, although that is not to say they were formally married.[75] But the inventory of the mature Bienvenu plantation in 1753 shows thirty-six men, twenty women, and twenty-two children. There were only eighteen couples, that is, no less than half the men (most in their twenties and thirties) were shown as single. And when the Dubreuil plantation was auctioned in 1758, it included eighty-eight men, seventy-seven women, and forty children. This is a remarkably small number of children, and among the adults there were only thirty-six married couples, even though distribution of the sexes approached normal levels.[76]

Couples faced a major challenge because masters discouraged slaves from marrying off the plantation. The slave family had no independent existence because it was subsumed in the "family" of the patriarchal planter, who sought to govern his slaves' most personal behavior.[77] This is illustrated in detail in the advice to prospective slaveowners by the Louisiana planter Du Pratz, a Dutch-born French army officer. Du Pratz's policy was essentially therapeutic, aimed at maximizing the advantage to the planter of the new slave's fearfulness and shock. He advised that the master do everything possible to make slaves comfortable when they were introduced to the plantation. It was easiest to make them obedient "by doing them justice," by not overworking them, by encouraging them to entertain one another, and by encouraging them to marry and remain monogamous.[78]

Other aspects of Du Pratz's advice also would have affected the slave family. He advocated the task system as the most efficient, probably linked with his allotment of personal gardens to slaves. The drawings of Dumont and others show that slaves had both gardens in their quarters and plots of waste ground to work. Du Pratz may have reasoned that if granted limited autonomy, they would finish their tasks more industriously so they could get to their own fields, the better to nourish their families. The value of these plots is described at this time by John Martin Bolzius of Georgia: "They are given as much land as they can handle.... For if they do not work they make mischief and damage. (*Sed datur tertium, idque maxime necessarium*, namely, one should instruct them in the Christian religion according to Abraham's example, Genesis 18:19.) They sell their own crops and buy some necessary things."[79] Clearly, masters preferred to keep slaves working every day.

The degree to which Du Pratz's advice was heeded by other planters is unclear: policy must have varied from plantation to plantation. It could depend on whether or not the master or his overseer was present. D'Ausseville was warned by Doctor Manadé that his overseer, Jacques Charpentier, was "beating your negroes senseless" and that he might not like the doctor's bill.[80] Furious, D'Ausseville threatened Charpentier ("Le Roy") with legal action, warning him that "by your ferocity, you can but drive the negroes to revolt or to throw themselves in the river."[81] Pregnant women had miscarried because he punished them immoderately. This letter was ineffective, however, because in August D'Ausseville had to take the overseer to court because he forced the slaves to till land he rented, worked them long hours, fed them little, killed three by abuse, caused six miscarriages, and was guilty of "infamous and scandalous commerce ... openly in the field with the negresses."[82] The court was sufficiently impressed to hear testimony from Bizao how Charpentier had beaten her to punish her husband and how he finally beat her insubordinate husband to death.[83] Perhaps the slave's family life had been disrupted, perhaps he just could not face another summer in the indigo fields in the broiling sun.

Other cases show the many ways in which the family life of slaves was prevented, interrupted, or inconvenienced. A fifteen-month-old girl was reported to be dying of starvation in 1737 because her mother was hired to the Grandprés to nurse madame's child.[84] Since marriage between slaves was not allowed by the planters to have any legal or moral basis, it could rest on the thin reed of sexual fidelity. One senses the extreme frustration of François Baraca, whose wife, witnesses revealed, Baraca believed to be having a liaison with Mamouroux. They quarreled one night, and he beat her to death with a faggot or stave. He tried to appeal to the judges' masculine sympathy, claiming that he merely asked for his dinner when she started to abuse him and threatened to hit him, so he beat her and accidentally killed her. Unmoved, the court decided to make an example of this signal threat to valuable property (especially because he had fled the scene and mocked his pursuers) and had him hanged and exposed to view for twenty-four hours.[85] In a much more typical, less dramatic case, the deceased Joseph Chauvin's slave force was broken up into lots for rent during the minority of his heirs: they faced the uncertain regime of unknown masters and separation from their customary community.[86] Even in a geographically tight-knit community like New Orleans, where slave families could meet periodically if dispersed, this kind of wholesale arbitrary separation must have discouraged family formation and healthy domestic relations. More common was the transfer of individuals from master to master.

The central feature of the property relation of master to slave was the power to sell him or her, so sales records reveal important details about slaves' lives. The motives for masters to sell slaves ranged from financial necessity, to speculation upon the productive capacity of the slave, to retribution for wrongdoing by the slave, although motives were seldom stated explicitly. Transfers of slaves by sale were comparatively rare during the French regime, unsusceptible to reliable statistical analysis, for the weakness of the African slave trade meant masters avoided alienating slaves. The transactions that were recorded ranged from the simple and unexplained sale by one planter to another of Jasmin in 1736, warranted against epilepsy for only three months, to the cynical unloading of an incapacitated slave, like Angélique, who was half-blind, or like Hypolite because he had advanced venereal disease.[87] Another way a man might try to get rid of a decrepit slave was to trade. One of these exchanges left the surgeon major of New Orleans red-faced.[88] The king's commissary, François Roujot, bought an unnamed Negress from another planter, who claimed that Surgeon Jean Gueydon had examined her and declared her sound. Roujot soon approached Gueydon, explaining that he had bought the woman to send to his brother-in-law in Natchitoches, and that, since she did not want to go, Gueydon might give a slave who would go in exchange for the balky slave and five hundred livres. After all, a slave removed from New Orleans against her will was likely to run away, and Roujot would lose his entire investment. Gueydon agreed upon the assurance that the slave he was getting "had no fault other than that to wish not to go up to Natchitoches." That turned out to be a ruse, which Gueydon fell for because the exchange appeared to be hugely in his favor. Either he had never examined the slave and had lied about her originally, or he was not a very good doctor. At any rate, he soon discovered that she was "violently afflicted by venerian maladies" and not much good for labor. He did not like being tricked any more than Roujot—the Superior Council agreed and annulled the exchange. As for the slave, assuming it was true that she did not want to be removed to the extreme western limit of Louisiana, her mutinous stance serves as an introduction to the theme of everyday or nonviolent slave resistance.

Slaves struggled against impediments to the formation of family and community, against their masters' authority to exploit their labor and interfere in their personal lives. In refusing to accept authority unconditionally, slaves were only human and they had only to be human to be criminals in New Orleans. To obtain more food, better clothing, or, above all, more free time than allotted by the master was to resort to crime. Whites' personal crimes against blacks went largely unrecorded, but it is also true that much slave crime went unreported because culprits were either undetected or not prosecuted by judges. Masters were reluctant to charge their own slaves in the court, which meted out the harshest sentences: the executioner could permanently ruin a slave. Moreover, unlike in France, where society punished only the convicted criminal, the public jail and gibbet punished the master along with the slave in New Orleans by denying him the slave's labor, by revealing publicly his inability to control the slave, and by making him liable for court costs. Thus, masters were likely to punish slaves' offenses themselves rather than turning them over to authorities.

The ways in which masters tried to avoid the criminal court are illustrated in the remainder of Du Pratz's advice, in which there was less psychology and more sheer force. Whenever the master was sure of a slave's guilt, he should severely whip him or her but dress the wounds. One must never trust them. Place their cabins close enough to watch them, Du Pratz enjoined; do not let them sleep in your house at night, try to keep your children away from them, and keep them too busy to congregate. Even old people should be set to easy tasks like fishing to keep them busy.[89] Thus, the planters' main object should be to fill the slave's every hour to prevent "mischief," and the slave's main object was to gain as many hours and illicit comforts for himself as possible. Whenever his transgression was serious enough, especially when it harmed the interests of another master, the slave faced prosecution, and the judicial records contain important insights into the lives of slaves.

Chattels who owned nothing could be expected to take whatever was not tightly secured, yet slaves were rarely prosecuted for major theft of goods. Explaining this would take in many factors, beginning with the small size of New Orleans, where few secrets could be kept. In any slave society, the smallest display of wealth by a black aroused suspicion. The case of theft by Babette, who had been rented out away from her parents at age eleven, is instructive. A mere child, with the crudest concept of private property, she did what most children do if given half a chance: she took enough cash to buy what all children want, treats and clothes, which was soon noticed. To teach her that this was stealing, mere humiliation would not work: since Babette (and her parents) could not own property, only fear of extreme pain could teach her to respect other people's property. Thus, the court ordered twenty lashes for her. The whites who sold her things had to return the money, pay stiff fines, and listen to stern warnings about repeat offenses.[90] The remarkable case of Pierre Ferrand is quite different but illustrates the same point about the difficulty a slave faced in concealing stolen goods. Ferrand noticed a slave wearing a piece of lace he knew to be stolen from Chez Frédéric and demanded an explanation. The slave claimed it was purchased from a slave belonging to Nicholas Judice, so Ferrand confronted the latter, who informed him that the slave actually belonged to his brother, who had absolved the slave when the slave begged for it on his knees. Outraged, Ferrand retorted that Judice's brother was a "rascal" if he indulged such criminality. Convinced that his family had been insulted, Nicholas Judice waylaid Ferrand the next morning and caned him, a form of violence with class implications. This occasioned a big, nasty, unresolved suit for damages.[91]

As Philip J. Schwarz found in the court records of Virginia, slave crimes against property formed far and away the single largest category of crime, but the principal method of theft in any slave society was not to steal goods but labor from the master by running away.[92] Far and away the most common transgression was to run away briefly, called petit marronage by the French. Few complaints were filed, because it was usually a matter between master and slave, tolerated or lightly punished until it exceeded the limit of the former's tolerance, when he or she might then ask the court to punish the transgressor. This form of marronage was probably less common in New Orleans than outside the parish, for its settlement was so compact that friends and relatives could visit each other on a fairly regular basis without breaking customary rules. An individual's right to visit kin at times other than Sunday must have been relatively easy to establish because there was little loss to the master. Nevertheless, authorities saw not individual slaves but many of them moving too freely and too often beyond the boundaries of their plantations, and they repeatedly pronounced severe penalties for slaves who met in social groups on the domain of another master.

The attempt to run away for good was a much more serious crime. In New Orleans, the number of *grands marons* was insignificant by comparison with the French islands, and petty marronage within or beyond limits established by masters was the main form of running away.[93] Less than one hundred citations for marronage were collected during the French regime, including all of the major cases in the judicial records of the Louisiana Historical Collection. About three out of four times the cases concerned grand marronage by single slaves who escaped permanently, and the remainder concerned small roving bands of maroons.

White concern about maroons was out of proportion to the real threat, although their exactions from herds and henhouses could be a nuisance. In the summer of 1726, the attack by three runaways on Louis Congo prompted a thundering assault by the attorney general, who informed the Superior Council that a *grande bande* of maroons marauded on the outskirts of New Orleans with impunity. Even though the king by his *bonté paternelle* had outlawed capital punishment of slaves for simple desertion, armed maroons could and should be executed. This was undoubtedly the "gang" that was suppressed in the following year, the Natanpallé group, which was reported to have sixteen slaves in 1727, but no permanent maroon camps were reported after that date.[94]

Planters' anxieties about maroons after that time were shaped by dramatic events in the West Indies. The first local campaign to enforce the article of the Code Noir requiring planters to report marronage came in the mid-1730s in the wake of slave uprisings in Martinique and other islands. Planters came forward as ordered and filed their claims for missing slaves. Livet's Pierrot, twenty-two years old, was away nine months, was recaptured, and was now gone again, living in the woods near the plantation. Roquigny's Rencontre left at the age of twenty-one, five years earlier, but had been heard from only the first year, when he roamed freely up and down the river. Former governor Périer's Pierrot was reported as a maroon four years earlier at the age of twenty-seven, not heard of since; he could be recognized by Périer's brand on his right breast. A few months later this absentee planter's overseer hauled another offender to court, one Guela, who was a thirty-year-old, unbaptized West African who told all in French. He seemed almost glad for the opportunity to inform authorities that he ran away for fear of being beaten and because he was hungry, but he had done it only once before and returned on his own. The court made an example of him and ordered that both Guela's ears be cut, that he be branded with the fleur de lys on his right shoulder, and that he be threatened with whipping if he ran away again.[95]

The overall record of police enforcement suggests that marronage was not a serious problem: runaways established no permanent settlements and controlled no territory. Bienville contracted with some Indians for a maroon hunt in 1738 because Lower Coast planters complained of depredations on their cattle. Only one slave was caught—Lafleur, who had "long since" run away and who admitted only that he had encountered three other maroons; he denied killing livestock. His sentence was not recorded but undoubtedly entailed corporal punishment.[96] Like Guela, he would have claimed to live only upon vegetables filched from the plantation and wild plants, raccoons, and opossums found in the cypress swamp, for the killing of livestock was a capital offense. In fact, Lafleur implicated one Pierrot in a campaign to recruit slaves to establish a maroon stronghold, but the plan was not consummated. Jacques Livet also complained that Pierrot had recruited another of his slaves, Samson, to "pillage the plantation" on its border. Most runaways did not get far enough to join other runaways. Jacques Coustilhas's Pierrot (yet another Pierrot) died alone of hunger and the winter cold within eight days after deserting the overseer who managed for a deceased planter's heirs.[97]

In the Bienville era, the peak of concern about maroons was in the winter of 1740–41, when the town sent a king's lieutenant out with an expedition of free blacks and slaves to capture runaways. They caught two, who had lived in the swamps for months living on raccoon and opossum. Sieur Chaperon's *commandeur*, or driver, was accused of sheltering these and other maroons, even in his own cabin, and permitting them to work for rations, all of which he and other slaves of the plantation stoutly and believably denied. Probably the most telling moment was when it came out in the slaves' testimony that Madame Chaperon had indeed hired one of the runaways to do some wood chopping, revealing one of the most profound ironies of the slave system: some masters were willing to profit from the labor stolen from other masters. But in the Bienville era marronage did not remotely approach the dimensions it eventually achieved, briefly, in the early 1780s. It may have been bad enough that Attorney General Fleuriau suffered repeated loss of cattle to runaways, but he never proved that maroons, rather than Indians or his own slaves, were responsible.[98] Cattle rustling by maroons was the penultimate crime, only one short step from concerted rebellion itself, and reports of it were extremely unusual.

Group marronage, though rare, was taken very seriously by planters because that road led to insurrection. It typically involved only a few slaves, and none were able to remain free for long. Early in 1745 a group of slaves belonging to several masters briefly ranged up and down behind plantations on the other side of the river, burning a barn and attempting to burn down the plantation house of Raguet. He was the owner of a slave named Marianne, who almost sounds as if she was the leader of this group of at least four people.[99] In 1751 four men and a woman stole a large canoe and managed to remain free for a while, but they were hunted down and two of them were killed in the final capture.[100]

Only scraps remain of an important marronage case involving an innkeeper named Jean Gonzalle, who received a power of attorney from his departing brother, André, on June 7, 1739. André enjoined Jean to capture and discipline as he saw fit his mulatto slave Pierre Delapie, who had been "going from plantation to plantation along the river" for ten days. Jean soon discovered that Pierre hired himself out as a freeman to herd cattle for Joseph Chaperon, a tough downriver planter often found in the court's records, here found capitalizing on his neighbor's misfortune, just like Madame Chaperon in the case discussed above. Chaperon refused to give up Pierre, claiming that Bienville had granted permission to keep him. Bienville denied that, but Ordonnateur Salmon's court allowed Pierre to keep working as a free man until his master returned and proved ownership.[101]

Joseph Chaperon soon had reason to regret his opportunism at the expense of another slaveowner because in July he learned that Pierre had seduced away three of his slaves, the Bambara Antoine, his wife the Senegalese Fauchon, and another Bambara, Vulcain, who had been hamstrung, almost never mentioned in New Orleans. They stole André Gonzalle's loaded pirogue and shallope, which made Chaperon liable![102] Almost five years later, Chaperon was tipped off that these slaves had made it to the large colonial capital of Havana, where they lived as free people.[103] Not until 1747 was there any further news, when seventeen-year-old Delisle Dupart returned from Havana and told of several New Orleans maroons there.[104] The owners of all missing slaves pooled their resources and sent slave catchers to Cuba. They returned with only two, although these slaves reported that about one dozen local slaves lived on the Spanish island.[105] This is the only long-term "community" of New Orleans maroons, and they succeeded because they escaped the colony entirely. Their masters did not permit their success to go unchallenged, but the Cuban refuge could not have been very important because it was not mentioned in the records again.

Slaves continued to run away in the later generations of the French regime, and they continued to have no refuge in Louisiana to which to run where they could establish an alternative order. The judicial archives indicate that a new regime for runaways began in 1763 with the arrival of the new attorney general, Nicolas Lafrénière, a local from Tchoupitoulas who had spent several years in France. Lafrénière was proud, ambitious, eloquent, and perhaps cynical. He immediately embarked on a campaign to make himself popular by persecuting errant blacks, and five years later he would lead whites into an insurrection against Spain. Slavery in New Orleans in the decades before Lafrénière's appointment had acquired a mostly unrecorded set of informal rules. Passes for slaves who traveled off the plantation seem to have been rare: they were not an object of inquiry in court, as they would have been if they had been issued routinely. Masters hated to be pestered about passes, and moreover, passes were of imperfect utility and an embarrassment if a significant portion of the white population (especially soldiers) was illiterate.[106] Slave patrols were only sporadic, usually unnecessary because of the police function of the guard kept by the troops.

Lafrénière set himself against what he condemned as great disorder. Having stopped in Saint Domingue on the way home, he was undoubtedly impressed by the legacy of fear there stemming from the big slave conspiracy of the late 1750s. More to the point, news was already spreading throughout the Americas of the Berbice slave rebellion in Guiana, where approximately the same number of slaves found in New Orleans took over the colony for months in 1763 and visited bloody retribution on those masters they hated.[107] Lafrénière declared war against marronage. In fact, the whole number of culprits he prosecuted in this period is not impressive. Early in 1764, a group of fourteen slaves took the very unusual step of revolting on a plantation at Cannes Bruslées, at the extreme western edge of town. The testimony of the slaves and their overseer suggested that the latter was malicious, playing tricks like promising them a respite in their cabins on a freezing morning but furiously whipping them off to work. They took off as a group and lived on raccoon and alligator behind the plantation. When some went to New Orleans to represent their grievances, the whole group was locked up and sentenced to twenty-five lashes each. The group Leader, Sainbas, also had his ears cut and was branded to record his escape.[108] Another slave, Nicolas, caught killing a cow out of malice rather than hunger, was flogged and branded with a V (for *voleur*, "thief") on his cheek. The slave who had bought the cow's hide from him was condemned to be tortured, although this was to frighten him because he was only presented in the torture chamber and then released.[109]

This Cannes Bruslées case was unique, for Lafrénière's dragnet swept up mostly single runaways. Chantalou's François lasted seven weeks behind the Dubreuil plantation after Christmas 1763. A creole of Saint Domingue, he was probably an inveterate runaway sent to Louisiana for that reason, for his master there had cut his ears and branded him. This is the only definite report in the record of a master personally mutilating a slave as punishment, and it happened in Saint Domingue. Louisiana planters probably adhered to the Code Noir provision that all such punishments must be rendered judicially. In this case the attorney general argued that since milder punishments had not worked, François should have his right foreleg broken.[110] Desillets's cowherd Jeannot was too old to flog at the age of sixty-five years, but the court cut his ears and branded him for enjoying five months on his own. Another slave had nurtured Jeannot for a while, but his master caught him when he was reduced to open begging in the streets.[111] Sixteen additional complete cases in the years 1764 to 1767 taken as a group reveal one common characteristic. Of those fifteen accused whose origins were noted or deducible, ten were young outsiders, mostly field slaves: Africans, creoles of Saint Domingue, and one from Philadelphia. They were most likely to report that overseers had mistreated them by too much work, too little food, or brutal treatment. Since outsiders were a minority in the slave force, their two-to-one ratio to local creoles among all maroons indicates not only incomplete adaptation to slavery but also perhaps their low outsider status in the New Orleans slave community itself.[112]

Louis was a thirty-five-year-old Bambara runaway in New Orleans from Illinois, whose case illustrates the outsider phenomenon and the effect of brutality. He originally belonged to a New Orleans master who sold him to a Saint Domingue planter, probably as punishment for insubordination, who had in turn sold him to an Illinois farmer who put him in the mines. The slaves of the lead mines in Illinois were perhaps the most lonely people in

Louisiana. Just as in the antebellum era, when masters threatened to sell recalcitrant slaves down river to the Deep South, there was probably a threat by New Orleans masters to send slaves up river for a spell in the mines. Louis soon had enough and fled in a stolen pirogue to New Orleans, where he worked for himself, telling everyone he had permission. Unfortunately, he also stole goods from whites to trade for necessities like a gun. When he was finally caught and tried, he refused to confess, even after the slave he lived with and others testified that he was a notorious thief. He was tortured by three blows with a hammer, crude but effective, and he gave in. He was sentenced to be broken on the wheel and exposed on the Bayou Road. The court issued a merciful *retentum* that Louis was to be strangled before he was broken.[113] Of the sixteen prosecutions, one other slave was sentenced to torture and the wheel, Louis's friend Cézar. The court had no mercy and submitted him live to the wheel, for on two occasions Cézar had fired a gun at a white man.[114]

Of the total of twenty complete cases of single maroons prosecuted by Lafrénière, including three women, two were executed in the most gruesome manner just described; two were hanged and left exposed to the elements; two were flogged, branded, or hamstrung; five were flogged and branded; seven had both ears cut and a cheek or shoulder branded; one was sold away from her lover; and the fate of one is unknown.

The justification for Lafrénière's law-and-order campaign was complex. No doubt Lafrénière thought news of slave disturbances in Saint Domingue and Guiana had to be counteracted by a show of brutality.[115] But it was also welcomed by planters who thought it important to impress slaves with their continuing might despite the fact that their king had abandoned them by the cession of their colony to Spain, which was widely rumored by 1763. The whites revered their king and his humiliation of them helps explain why they lashed out at vulnerable blacks in these politically critical years.[116] Finally, another factor was that there was a sudden, dramatic wave of estate sales in the late 1750s and early 1760s (described in the next chapter) that disrupted slave subcommunities and meant a change of masters for many slaves, always a potential source of special tension.

Clearly, slaves would have established maroon villages if that had been possible, and it is well documented that a small number of them did establish a maroon village during the American War of Independence. But during the six decades prior to the early 1780s, one finds a mere jumble of runaway cases involving individuals and temporary small groups.[117] There is no hint in local authorities' voluminous reports that *grands marons* were numerous, formed communities, or posed a profound threat to the colonists.[118] Spanish administrators would have mentioned any serious threat in their reports in the 1760s, when they had every incentive to seize upon and magnify any sign of disorder in the colony, and one finds no reports of maroon communities by Antonio Ulloa or others: they did not exist. Most marronage was of the petit kind, much as Philip D. Morgan finds in studying South Carolina runaways.[119]

As a black majority, the slaves represented a formidable potential challenge to their masters, as they had demonstrated in the days of Périer. But the black community was deeply divided by social distinctions imposed by the masters (slave and free, skilled and unskilled), and by their own various and competing interests arising from individual status in Africa and diverse African cultures, a result of the slave trade. The struggle by individuals to find their own measure of dignity or "freedom" and to build community together within limits set by masters was a severe challenge. They overcame great obstacles, resisting the regime as stoutly as they could, and created a coherent, if ever-vulnerable, parallel community within slave society, one with its own rules that nurtured its members, but under the supreme authority of the law of slavery, which was never in any real danger of collapse after 1729.

Two Communities, One Creole Society: 4

The Interweaving of White and Black Lives

The negroes, especially the men who remain in the possession of the Crown, most of them very old and infirm, are very useful to the service and they are never underemployed. . . . The women likewise. . . . [And] they save the King throughout the colony at least 100,000 livres in wages of workmen and laborers.

—Governor Vaudreuil and
Commissaire Ordonnateur Michel to Rouillé, 1751

The Jansenists in lovingness,
And Jesuits in their lowliness,
    Will wax warm in partisanship.
The humble monks and prelates bold
Will take in sums of cash and gold,
    Their reward for preaching Jesus.

—From a satirical French song about Louisiana, c. 1720

In the broad middle period between the 1730s and the 1770s, New Orleans was a small town with an early curfew, so quiet that only a few soldiers stood guard at night. By day the seaport at the levee was a lively hub of trade, the only town in the lower Mississippi Valley, drawing people of all colors from the hinterland. On the surface, it was as well ordered as any town in colonial North America. The social structure became even more settled as the second, locally creolized generation of colonists and slaves grew up, soon becoming at least as numerous as those who had been born in the Old World or New France. The secular slaveholders dominated a society modeled on the patriarchal order of their king, and their power was streamlined and reinforced in 1763, when (on Louis XV's warrant) they eliminated an alternative local authority, the Jesuits and their plantation. As the historians of Maryland write of the colony after the early decades of European settlement, "creole family life was more stable than that of immigrants," and the same was true of New Orleans.[1] Beneath the surface of apparent serenity, however, were the boiling hot springs of emotion over which any slave society is built. The lives of the whites and blacks were so tightly entwined, so inseparable night and day, that, however much both groups tried to create separate communities and individuals tried to create their own identities, they were all reminded at every turning that this was impossible. Every action by a slave in search of some measure of autonomy reverberated in the master's household, and every decision or circumstance in the master's life disrupted life in the slaves' quarters. The composite culture they created together moderated but could not solve the basic problems of community building they faced, especially the slaves, epitomized by the sudden, massive reorganization of the slave community by sales and partitions of estates in the late 1750s and early 1760s.

The children of the European and African founders were creoles. The word meant simply "born in the New World," but creolization of a society was a complex process that is still little understood. The major elements of it were the diminishing importance of Old World mores, the acquisition of immunities to fatal epidemic diseases, and the adjustment to slavery. For whites, the cultural development was very subtle and not terribly disturbing, for most continued to think of themselves, at least in a general sense, as "French." By contrast, the adjustment for blacks is largely the story of the diminishing salience of African ways and history, on one hand, and, on the other, the emergence of African-American culture parallel to that of the whole local community, the latter being dominated by the French language, religion, and laws. About the early history of what is specifically African-American almost nothing is known. Blacks' partial adaptation of French ways is documented here and there. Christianity spread among slaves gradually as their children were baptized and received crude religious doctrination. These children grew up knowing little of Africa, and their elders' memories were refreshed only by small shipments of Africans after 1733. Children grew up speaking French, so, as is usually true of immigrants to America, linguistic differences would have separated the first and second generations: their parents spoke French imperfectly with African accents.[2] A handful of slaves were actually sent to France for training, which would have reinforced that tendency. Angélique, for example, an eighteen-year-old Negress, was taken to France by Cécile Le Blanc Bruslé in 1733 to learn a trade.[3] Thus, the children of both Europeans and Africans contributed to a common local culture as members of a single but polarized society. The documents suggest that the end result was more European than African, but since Africans wrote hardly any of the documents, they must be read with care to tell the story of creolization.

The most obvious turning point in relations between blacks and whites is that after 1731 the era of slave rebellion appears to have come to an abrupt end: not even rumors of slave plots troubled the town until many decades later. No more revolts occurred because relations between white and blacks became more routinized and predictable after 1731 for several reasons. Of greatest importance was family formation among slaves—not that it was now favored by planters for the first time, but that it continued to occur as it had prior to 1731. The importance of this factor in depressing the tendency toward outright slave rebellion can scarcely be exaggerated. When a majority of slave women became mothers and many men became fathers, they collectively wielded sufficient sway to discourage concerted violent resistance by others that would harm or terrify children, wreck families, even threaten the community with wholesale disruption. Since so many had families to care for by the 1730s, and since the whites had demonstrated superior reserve military power, which was further augmented by additional troops in 1733 and again in 1751, the majority view among slaves was that successful rebellion was impossible. Another thing that explains the end of the era of rebellion is the collapse of the African slave trade to the colony. This gave the black community a degree of stability, a structure in which moderate slave leaders could prevail.[4]

Planters' children grew up to their roles as slave masters in a settled society, their lives seldom ruffled by the intrusions of new immigrants and almost never by the arrival of new slaves. The growth rate of the white population—192 percent in thirty-five years—was much greater than that of blacks and must have been a source of self-confidence that made whites feel less defensive. Outnumbered by four to one in the parish and surrounding region in 1731, they were outnumbered by only about two to one by the end of the French period because the black population grew by a modest 36 percent in thirty-five years, as seen by comparing table 8 to table 4.[5] Moreover, this community was so small that most people recognized most other people or at least their rela-

TABLE 8

CENSUS OF THE LOWER MISSISSIPPI VALLEY IN 1766,
EXCLUDING INDIANS

| | Europeans | | Africans | |
	New Orleans	Other	New Orleans	Other
Men	574	484	0	0
Soldiers	200	400	0	0
Women	424	479	0	0
Children	1,200	1,596	0	0
Total	2,398	2,959	3,977	1,581

tionship to someone else: "so-and-so's wench," or "master so-and-so's son."
For example, when a young métis slave hanged himself in the jailyard before he
could be whipped for a minor theft ordered by his master, the *jailor* com-
mented indignantly that he had known the boy all his life and knew him to be
"serious and straight-walking," obviously crediting the slave's protest of innocence.[6] Customary habits and general knowledge of one another moderated
the regime during these middle decades of the century, when creoles came to
constitute the majority of the population. This was the major change: regard
for one another based on familiarity. Now, let us begin with a look at the many
ways the two groups were entangled and forced to know each other.

In its simplest form, the logic that wove together the lives of whites and
blacks was the legal status of blacks as property. Throughout the life cycle of
white people, the number and qualities of their human property defined their
wealth and status. Seemingly a straightforward relation, in fact slaves complicated and confused property relations and status among whites because they
were not mere objects, they were human individuals. The decisions of masters
in the pursuit of wealth and status were usually made without regard for the
needs and wishes of these individuals. In response, slaves could cope only by
seeking leverage—any influence at all on the conditions in which they lived—
and that profoundly complicated relations between them and white people
and between white individuals too. To compensate for the human qualities of
the slave, which the law of chattels could not annul, the master was compelled

to study the comportment and psychology of the slave with as much care as the slave was studying him for symptoms of weakness, signs of promise of some advantage. This mutual scrutiny had the paradoxical effect of forcing the two into a very personal and potentially explosive human relation.

Slaves were the single most important element in the two fundamental legal transactions a colonist was likely to engage in during his or her life cycle: marriage contracts and successions of estate. Frequently, slaves were the major donations of property made by spouses (or their parents) when contracting marriage. Contracts usually worked smoothly, but in the early period, when the Company of the Indies claimed most slaves until they were paid for, these contracts could give rise to lawsuits, especially when slaves sought a measure of autonomy.[7] One fascinating squabble between masters combines the problems of slave title in both marriage contracts and successions, plus the effort of a slave to form a family. In the early 1730s, an unnamed black slave belonging to Géneviève-Elizabeth Bunel (Widow Trépanier) fell in love with an unnamed female slave belonging to Marie-Françoise Gaspard. The slaves had what Bunel denounced as an "illicit marriage," meaning one between slaves of two different owners and without Bunel's permission, much less the Church's sanction.[8] The male slave, who happened to be the widow's slave driver, sought relentlessly to convince her to buy his wife and child from the Gaspards, which she did in 1735, despite the fact that she regarded their relationship as "vile and infamous."[9] Unfortunately, the sale was conducted by Marie-Françoise's husband, an impecunious tailor, and he acted over his wife's protest. The slaves had come to her by an earlier marriage and, according to the law, her community with her first husband, Louve, was the inheritance of the two children by that marriage, and the deeply indebted Gaspard intended to use the proceeds of the sale for his own purposes without regard for the interest of his stepchildren. Marie-Françoise even got a judgment against him in her capacity as legal tutor to the Louve children, and early in 1738 Gaspard was forced to appeal to the Superior Council to make Bunel take back her money and return the slaves. Bunel was furious, blaming the Gaspards for permitting the misbehavior of their slave in the first place, which now disrupted her domestic tranquillity a second time, brought scandal to her house, and made her look like a fool. The final act in this drama would be comical if the situation was not so tragic, for the Company of the Indies stepped in to rule that Marie-Françoise and her first husband had never paid much on what was owing for their slave, so on that account alone she should never have been sold and had to be returned to the Louve minors, who were liable to the company for her.[10] This story shows how deeply and inextricably entwined were the lives of blacks and whites because slaves were the real property that sealed the most important contracts the colonists signed, which were vulnerable to disputes, manipulation, or disruption by any of the parties involved.

Often revealing of slaves' strategies to achieve autonomy are those suits by masters against others for damaging the value of their slaves. An amazing variety of situations could produce this kind of suit, but particularly productive of friction was slave hiring. The renting or hiring of slaves was an important method of redistributing this scarce resource where the external slave supply was weak. A few people had slave artisans whose time they could not exploit to the fullest, so they rented them to others who required specialized labor, or an owner might hire a trusted slave to himself or herself: the slave charged what the market would bear, turned over a fixed sum to the master, and kept the rest. It is often difficult to tell in suits arising from these arrangements whether the slave was self-hired, for that was regarded as an illicit practice and masters had reason to disguise it. Direct hiring of slaves by one master to another was typical in the early years, but self-hire gradually became more common as society became more settled and masters and slaves came to know each other better. Still, the direct hire of slaves remained important, including whole groups of slaves belonging to a succession without heirs capable of managing slaves, and the hirer accepted important risks, such as the possibility of a slave's suicide.[11]

Nicolas Delisle Dupart leased a plantation and nine slaves to André Jung in 1750 on condition that the slaves remain on that plantation, "which should be governed and managed wisely [en bon père de famille]." Instead, Jung put the slaves to work where he pleased and one of them lost an eye because of Jung's negligence, for which Delisle Dupart demanded compensation.[12] L'Éveillé was temporarily "abandoned in a barge on Lake Pontchartrain" by the man to whom he was hired, and he panicked and drowned. His owner demanded either his value or his replacement by a man of similar value.[13] Surgeon Bernard-Alexandre Vielle leased fifteen slaves to Gérard Pery and one of the most valued of them, François, cut his own throat, presumably because of mistreatment, so Vielle demanded the full market value of twenty-five hundred livres.[14]

The outcome of these cases is unclear, perhaps because the judges warned both parties that liability would be difficult to determine and persuaded them to reach a settlement. What these cases have in common is that the slave in question is always definitely or probably exercising some degree of personal volition. The slave who lost an eye presumably could have avoided it if he had been more alert. L'Éveillé drowned because he was a rational but disoriented human being. François did the one thing no other property could do: he destroyed himself. The hirer in every case was ultimately responsible for these tragedies simply because he was exploiting slave labor, but the issue was whether the slaves had been unduly exploited to the point that their judgment was impaired. That forced judges to make nearly impossible determinations of facts before they could even imagine determining equity.

Another unusual case shows how the key problem in slave-hire suits was usually the slave's own volition. In the summer of 1752, Joseph, eighteen years old, who was rented from the Fazende Minors by their tutor, Étienne Layssard, insisted on going swimming in the Mississippi River. The Fazende boys, Antoine and Jacques, shouted at him from the shore to come in out of the treacherous current. (Layssard was not present.) Joseph was soon exhausted, and although both of his parents jumped in to try and save him, he drowned. His parents were so depressed that they were put under a suicide watch. Layssard refused to take responsibility for this accident: the river's dangers were notorious and Joseph directly disobeyed the orders of white people.[15] But in the slaveowner's view, there was virtually no such thing as a slave's independent will; a slave could be harmed only because of a lessee's negligence. Joseph could not be blamed because that was contrary to the logic of slavery. How could the court decide this kind of suit? The court was rarely presented with open-and-shut cases of negligence, as in the death of Coffy in 1763. The surgeon's report ruled that the cause was exhaustion from malnutrition, and the court-appointed arbitrators awarded his owner, Madame Delapommeraye, a claim of two thousand livres on the man to whom Coffy was hired.[16]

Suits arising from harm inflicted on slaves who were not hired out are even more interesting. Chevalier Charles De Morand, a leading resident, sent his cook, Scipio, to Pairoc's butcher shop one day. Scipio quarreled with Pairoc, perhaps about the quality of the meat, perhaps about the master's credit, and the butcher took one of the tools of his trade to the man and sliced into a finger, then chased him from the shop with a "fuck you and your master!"[17] This slave was a proxy or extension of his master and, as such, was vulnerable to the redirected violence that social hierarchy among whites could produce.

De Morand wanted to be compensated for the slave's resulting loss of labor time, although the tone of his petition is clearly aimed at letting Pairoc know that he was out of line speaking of a gentleman like that.

Other slaves also caused their masters trouble when acting as their proxies or when a master was not present. Widow Jeanne La Croix sent two slaves, Jean and Jean Louis, to the Piquery plantation one early evening in 1763. Apparently, the shortest route was an indirect one that involved trespassing on the land leased by the Dupré brothers, one of whom fired on the slaves, killing Jean and wounding Jean Louis. The widow wanted the value of the slaves and the costs of suing the Duprés.[18] Joseph Chaperon sued the master of a slave who beat nearly to death Chaperon's slave driver, Pierrot, who was carrying a written pass for another slave to travel between plantations.[19] This same Chaperon frequently demonstrated his own inclination to violence against slaves. In the year following the above incident, his neighbor Michel Brosset passed Chaperon's place on the levee road, in company with his slave Lafleur. The latter may have been involved in a recent plot of a group of slaves belonging to several masters who had hoped to escape to an island in the Gulf of Mexico.[20] Perhaps Lafleur had corrupted Chaperon's slaves. At any rate, Chaperon descended on Lafleur, yelling, "Under your former master you were an honest man but now you're a rascal like Brosset!" and caned him.[21] Naturally, Brosset had to sue, even if Lafleur was not badly hurt, because from his point of view it was he who had been humiliated—even if it was the slave who had embroiled him with his neighbor. The clergy's slaves do not appear to have enjoyed a protected status. For example, an elderly man belonging to the Capuchins incurred the wrath of Pierre Luquet by trying to pass the white man's house driving a wagon. For whatever reason, Luquet set upon him with a cane and broke his arm. While no criminal action was lodged—the Superior Council never brought a criminal indictment against a white man merely for hurting a slave—the assailant did have to pay 204 livres for the doctor's bill and lost labor time.[22]

A crime against another person's property by one's slave was an extremely serious matter, providing some of the best evidence of how tightly linked were master and slave and how impossible it was for masters to achieve the kind of absolute independence they craved. One example is the largest theft on record, that by slave Louis Jupiter Gamelle, twenty-five years old, a native African but baptized Catholic, who brazenly stole large sums from several of the most prominent planters, including Jean Prévost, resident agent of the Company of the Indies, in 1744. Louis was turned in by his master, Pradel, who caught him with large bills and abandoned him to the court to avoid liability, the only way a master could avoid paying damages in excess of the slave's value. Gamelle was desperate and wily, admitting to a small theft and leading the judges astray by falsely accusing one Alexandre. So one month following his indictment, the court had him tortured, probably by a hot iron, and he promptly confessed and was condemned to the gallows.[23] Torture was quite rare in New Orleans, employed only when the guilty black or common white refused to confess to a major crime.

Pradel's abandonment of Gamelle to the court highlights a major feature of slave society. The basic social contradiction in the master-slave relation made it impossible for a planter "to draw a sharp line between regulation of the institution according to law, appropriate to market settings, and regulation according to sentiment, appropriate to the plantation," as Mark Tushnet puts it.[24] The planter was trying to behave simultaneously as impersonal capitalist in a market society and as absolute master of human beings, the latter a relationship "engaging the full personalities of the slaveowner and the slave." Unlike the bourgeois entrepreneur, who is little concerned about the private lives of his replaceable wage laborers, "when a slaveowner purchases a slave, he or she acquires, not the use of the slave's labor power—not, that is, only part of the slave's activities—but the slave's labor: all the activities in which the slave engages."[25] The planter's basic concern was to keep the slave healthy and productive by striving to protect the slave from other slaves and masters or from self-destruction, to regard the slave first and foremost as a form of capital to be preserved. By virtue of that interest, however, the planter was forced to be responsible for everything that this human property did, and these conditions vexed his ambition to behave independently in the market with sheer capitalist interests at heart. It drove him relentlessly into human conflicts with slaves and with fellow slaveowners, the latter being contrary to the rules of neighborliness essential to the continuing supremacy of the planter class. In the ultimate contradictory situation, such as the one Pradel faced on account of Gamelle, he had to destroy his capital, the most uncapitalist act of all, on account of a human weakness, even though it had not diminished the productivity of the slave.

A clear pattern emerges from this group of cases: the slaves in question all exercised a high degree of independent decision making that illustrates two fundamental characteristics of slave society. On one hand, the slave system

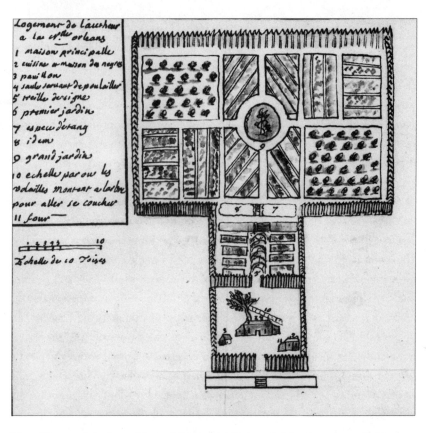

Fig. 3. House and gardens of François-Benjamin Dumont de Montigny, c. 1730, by Dumont de Montigny. Courtesy of the Edward E. Ayer Collection, the Newberry Library, Chicago.

Legend: 1. main house, 2. Negroes' kitchen and house, 3. pavilion, 4. willow serving as henhouse, 5. trellis for vines, 6. first garden, 7. a kind of pond, 8. another, 9. main garden, 10. ladder for the fowls to climb the tree to roost, 11. oven.

could not break the independent will of slaves: La Croix's slaves ignored the well-known law of trespass and took the shortcut, the Capuchins' slave persisted in some annoying behavior that drove Luquet to violence, Pierrot somehow provoked a beating, Lafleur did something to enrage Chaperon, and Gamelle stole. Second, this independence, combined with the fact that slaves were of necessity thrown into situations in which white people who were not their owners treated them as human beings rather than property, meant that the chattel relation made it inevitable that individual slaves could and would cause conflict between individual masters, in other words, dangerous social disorder of a kind that existed only in slave society.

The tendency of slaves to disrupt neighborliness among whites by their resistance was most obvious when a white person simply ignored the basic rules of slave society to serve his own interests by intriguing with slaves at their masters' expense. One day in 1753, Alexandre Bauré of the Cannes Bruslées quarter at the extreme upper limit of New Orleans Parish discovered that some of his slaves had stolen two hundred chickens and five quarters of rice. Upon investigation, he found that they had exchanged them for tafia (the crudest rum) supplied by his neighbor, Joseph Fossier, a trade that "has induced the Negroes to steal from their masters for a long time." Bauré whipped one of his slaves until he confessed, the slave then broke free, stole a gun, and fled to Fossier's to trade that for drink. Other planters and overseers testified they had long suspected Fossier, so he was convicted and had to pay a large fine and an indemnity to Bauré. He was warned of more severe punishment if caught again. Nothing was more threatening to the system than this kind of cooperation between whites and blacks.[26]

Nonetheless, the gemeinschaft character of the New Orleans community explains the rarity of collusion between slaves and nonslaveholders. Poor whites who associated with slaves and "demoralized" them, as planters put it euphemistically, were a problem in the earliest days before most marginal white people had died or had been turned out of town. Thus, in 1724, the attorney general presented a thumping remonstrance to the Superior Council that most deportees lived "a libertine life" and must be transported to distant posts, for they "debauch and demoralize the servants, the lazy, savages, and negroes, and induce them to steal from their masters."[27] Significantly, almost nothing is heard about this problem after the early years except for a handful of scattered cases, of which the Degoute case of 1765 is a notable example. The butcher Pierre Degoute, two white associates, and the Delachaises' slave Jacob were charged with cattle rustling, marketing the meat, and fencing the hides through a glover. This gang was probably responsible for most of the rustling complained of in the parish in these years, rather than the slave maroons who were suspected by the attorney general. Degoute and Jacob were interrogated under torture, but neither admitted guilt. Pierre's white partner, who had fled, was convicted and hanged in absentia, and Jacob got a whipping just for admitting that he had helped the man find some stray cattle.[28] This is a very unusual case: scheming between whites and slaves was not a class issue after the early 1730s because the nonslaveholding population had been whittled down to a respectable core, in which the Degoutes were few. On the other hand, it is true that slaves were "corrupted" in the marketplace by a general scofflaw attitude prevalent in the white community in regard to the domestic economy, as is clear from the police code of 1751.

Slave law in Louisiana is a very complex subject, and historians have put too much emphasis on the famous royal Code Noir of 1724. In a detailed discussion of that code in the next chapter, it will be seen that while it certainly governed the legal disposition of slaves as chattels, its few provisions concerning slave treatment do not reveal much about the actual state of slave relations in New Orleans. As in all slave societies, planters established their own rules on their estates, and the only way these can be discovered is through the record of judicial practice (the cases cited throughout this book) and through the local police regulations written by the planter class.

The New Orleans code "Regulations of Police" of 1751 was passed in the wake of the Membrède affair, a political scandal that also involved the effort of New Orleans' chief military and police officer (Major Membrède, acting in the name of the governor) to profit from the sale of alcohol to slaves. The resulting public outcry forced Governor Vaudreuil and Commissaire Ordonnateur Michel to decree in the name of the king the code of 1751, the first systematic police code in the colony. A number of its provisions were concerned with regulating taverns for the whole town, others were concerned specifically with the behavior of slaves.

At the heart of the Regulations of 1751, however, are several articles that provide insight into local conditions after three decades of slavery. Article 19 set out with classic simplicity the contradiction between the need of the individual planter to protect his valuable property from the rigor of the law against the slave's body for social transgressions and the interest of the slave-owning class to preserve order by the strict policing of all blacks:

> It having always been the intention of his Majesty that every individual, on his plantation or elsewhere, should punish his Negroes with moderation, as a kind father would correct his children; and most of the inhabitants of this colony having misunderstood the king's wishes on this subject, and overlooking in their slaves such faults as are too important not to be repressed, we cannot recommend too much to the owners of slaves, to be more energetic in checking their disorders, and to chastise without passion on all proper occasions. We give them notice that, if we discover any undue laxity in the exercise of the authority herein mentioned,

we shall cause the slaves whom they treat with too much lenity, to be seized and punished with exemplary severity.[29]

Masters were especially forbidden, as in the past, to allow their slaves to attend or host general dance parties, and free people must not purchase "any object whatever" from slaves, and the penalty for a second offense was henceforth to be the royal galleys for life.[30] The problems and the solutions were typical.

In groups, slaves could concert plots of all kinds to undermine the system. According to the angry language of the code's Article 26, many masters allowed slaves too much liberty at night, "in order to assemble with those of the country, who come prowling through the town, to commit every kind of malfeasances, and to be drinking at the taverns."[31] Masters were sternly enjoined to keep slaves in after sundown rather than to rely upon public vigilance. No single piece of evidence better captures the tone of race relations in New Orleans in 1751. In a small settlement where everyone came to know everyone else upon sight, the natural propensity of human beings to socialize was a strong challenge to the regime of the slaveholding class. Some poor tavern keepers served blacks, and some ordinary nonslaveholding whites evidently would drink with them under the same roof. This is why the code was aimed at whites and blacks, not at masters and slaves. The rules of race subordination had to be inculcated in ordinary white people to counter natural human tendencies.

Some articles of the code were directed at slaves themselves, such as that promising fifty lashes and a brand, "in order to make known, in case of need, the nature of his crime," for any slave failing to show "the respect and submission which he owes to white people." But the main thrust of the remaining articles was to commit all whites, including the lowliest nonslaveholders, to uphold the slave regime by active surveillance of all black people. The central matter was addressed in Article 24, which stated that "any Negro" abroad in public could and should be "stopped by any white person" and denounced to the authorities if he or she could not show a pass.[32] Any white person should seize any cane or stick carried by "any Negro" and beat him or her with it, and since "Negroes break down all the horses of the colony" by stealing and riding them hard, any white was authorized to shoot any mounted black who failed to halt upon demand.[33]

The second problem was independent production and marketing by slaves.

According to conventional wisdom, the purchase of anything from slaves without written permission promoted the initiative of slaves to steal from their masters and sell the goods to other whites. The real problem was the temptation to steal labor time from the master, either by outright subterfuge or by expanding by some artful means the privilege of free time. Most masters thought it was to their advantage to allow slaves to exploit their limited free time to improve their living conditions, and it was obviously to their advantage to purchase whatever slaves offered for sale, usually the produce of their own labor. In all slave societies this behavior of masters undermined the system and was repeatedly legislated or decreed against in urgent terms. Planters remained, nonetheless, on the honor system no matter how piously they might endorse a police code. New Orleans masters were never penalized for their slaves' behavior except when one's unruly slave damaged the interest of another master.

Of greatest interest about the Regulations of 1751 are the measures designed to regulate the local market to prevent its takeover by blacks in general and slaves in particular. Articles 13 and 14 set a very high fine of two hundred livres for anyone who forestalls the market by buying from hinterland farmers or anyone who sells to a resident of New Orleans before reaching the market. But Article 15 reveals that forestalling was probably the work of entrepreneurial blacks on Sundays: the master is made liable for the fine when his slave is guilty of either buying from a trader or selling to another Negro, and in default of payment both Negro buyer and seller are to receive thirteen lashes in the marketplace. Those slaves who were permitted by masters to carry guns to hunt game for the New Orleans market collectively posed a serious problem as early as 1744, as indicated in an angrily worded ordinance.[34]

This code suggests that conditions in New Orleans in 1751 were open to an unusual degree of negotiation by slaves. It was decreed in an age when the founding African generation began to give way to a creolized second generation. Although it is by no means a reliable guide to slave treatment, the code suggests that New Orleans, where most of the colony's slaves remained concentrated, was such a small community (about 6,200 people in 1766) and so little disrupted by the African slave trade, European immigration, or booming transatlantic commerce, that the day-to-day regime might have been slightly relaxed in this middle period. The increasing creolization of black society led whites to issue the code to impress a new generation of slaves who were too young to remember Périer's terrifying executions. Above all, the human regard that developed over time between individual blacks and whites had to be counteracted to prevent slaves from gaining the upper hand in the domestic economy.[35]

This problem of regulating local commerce is also revealed in conditions in the labor market. In a word, slave labor drove out free labor, tending to perpetuate and increase the dependency not just of the planter class but of the whole white community on slavery. Planters were so eager for trained slaves that they would pay for the apprenticeship of black boys, and artisans seemed unwilling to train white boys, explaining why few of the latter are found in the record.[36] Slaves either arrived with skills from Africa or learned them as apprentices in the New World. Houali probably was a doctor when she arrived in America, whereas teenaged Louis learned surgery in the Charity Hospital.[37] Antoine, a slave of the Church, was instructed by a local master blacksmith. Catherine was a sailor who, when some English pirates killed her master and seized their vessel in the Gulf of Mexico, rowed a boat to New Orleans carrying her mistress and Dame Le Veuf's children to safety. When a planter sought in 1763 to found a sugar mill and rum distillery, he hired a white British West Indian to teach two of his slaves the secrets of the process. As part of a peculiar contract in 1767, a little boy named Jupiter was apprenticed to a wig maker.[38] The planter with a skilled slave not only saved the cost of paying for specialized work by white workmen on contract but also could hire the slave out to work for other masters: self-interest usually outweighed racial interests.

The degree to which slavery structured society and that whites were dependent upon skilled black labor is epitomized by the King's Plantation, first developed by the Company of the Indies. Located across from the town center on the west bank, its slaves were taught special skills essential to the construction of the colony's public infrastructure and to the maintenance of internal navigation.[39] When promoting the foundation of such a work force, the first commissaire ordonnateur pleaded that these slaves "would not only save the wages of [white] workmen, but also their food, that of the slaves being of very little expense."[40] Upon his arrival in the colony, Delachaise immediately advocated the training of a force of black mariners, who were known to have highly developed sailing skills in Africa.[41] The Ministry of Marine repeatedly complained after 1731 that the King's Plantation made no profit and should be liquidated, and the New Orleans authorities refused to comply, detailing the slaves' many savings to the crown. When the king took over the plantation from the company its force numbered 241 people.[42] Despite the efforts of royal ministers to rid the crown of this expense by periodically selling off slaves, 84 still labored for Louis XV at the end of the regime.[43] This not only made the king one of the largest slaveowners but also helped stunt the colony's growth by discouraging white artisanry.[44] Dubreuil also contributed to that problem. As Bienville groaned in 1743, Dubreuil had trained so many slaves in specialized skills that white workmen could not be held in the colony: they "languish[ed] in misery" because they could not compete with slave artisans on the labor market.[45] The same problem was recognized in South Carolina at this time, where local authorities took more vigorous action to discourage black enterprise and encourage white immigration.[46] It was more than ironic: the master class of New Orleans could not attract more slavers because the white population and its buying power remained so small, and it remained small both because so few slaves were available for sale to attract new settlers, and because those who already lived there dominated the local labor market.[47]

The interaction of whites and blacks in the market place is the single most revealing theater of slave relations, but the Catholic Church also shaped the creole generations to some degree. The physical presence of the Church was substantial. Indeed, in terms of the proportion of its personnel in relation to the number of communicants (about 1 to 240 before suppression of the Jesuits in 1763), the New Orleans religious establishment was equal to that of Boston or Montreal. The administrative role of the clergy was as important as its spiritual role: priests maintained vital records and stood guard over the entry into civil society by their control of baptism.[48] Its role in slave society was highly ambiguous from the slave's perspective.

In the French American slave colonies there were three major orders of the Roman Catholic Church represented in various mixes. They existed in various states of good order, depending on how nearby the closest bishop was. Most important in Louisiana were the Jesuits, the most crusading evangelical Catholics, who were famous for living among Indians or with their African slaves in self-contained communities. But they were everywhere thought to be far too attentive to the enlargement of their temporal wealth. Second, the Franciscan suborder of Capuchins was an expanding group, with many thousands of members. Also evangelical, they were nonetheless considered less uncompromising than the Jesuits toward less-than-pious white people and therefore a good choice for colonies. Perhaps most important to the crown, their greatest theologian had been an ardent anti-Jansenist.[49] Finally, the Ursuline Nuns were important in French colonies. Girls were exposed to rudimentary schooling in their convents, and the sisters tended the sick.[50]

At the outset of colonization, Iberville and Bienville were determined to establish the Jesuits in the Mississippi Valley because they knew from experience in Canada that these priests would live among the Indians in the hinterland, learn their languages, and become important go-betweens for the colonists.[51] The crown was ambivalent about encouraging the ultramontane Society of Jesus in the colonies, however, and in 1722 the Capuchin friars were awarded the spiritual domain in New Orleans. But Law's scheme detached Illinois, in which the Jesuits were already well founded, from New France and joined it to Louisiana.[52] So the Jesuits had an excuse to establish a residence in New Orleans in 1726: Illinois priests would now communicate home more conveniently through the lower Mississippi Valley.[53] According to the agreement, only the Jesuits' superior was authorized to live in New Orleans, and he was strictly prohibited from exercising any ecclesiastical function there without the Capuchins' permission. Interpretation of this rule was the source of all future troubles.[54] The contest between the two orders for dominance in New Orleans began immediately, and a battle of nearly forty years was sustained.[55] Priests had absolute jurisdiction over the traditional sacraments, the source of both prestige and income, so the struggle between the clerical orders was for high stakes. It was the policy of both the company and the crown to oppose the establishment of a bishop for New Orleans because the clergy competed with everyone else for labor and land, and a resident bishop would only contribute to the problem.[56] Thus the colony was under the jurisdiction of the distant Bishop of Quebec and that meant unrefereed quarreling between priests of different orders in New Orleans.

The contest between Jesuits and Capuchins provided a vehicle for the expression of contests between planter factions in the Superior Council: the clerical feud was entwined with the struggle between Bienville and Jacques Delachaise and contributed to the latter's success in ousting the former in the 1720s.[57] The upshot of the first round was that the company had the Jesuit Father Beaubois recalled in 1728, who returned to France in the wake of his disgraced protector, Bienville. This nearly cost the colony the Ursulines, who were linked to the Jesuits and threatened to decamp for Saint Domingue.[58] Beaubois returned to New Orleans in triumph with Bienville in 1733, where in three years they established the Jesuits securely in the hinterland and at the capital, where their large estate near the town center became a fine slave plantation producing indigo for export and several products for local consumption.[59] When he was replaced in 1735, Beaubois was on the verge of supervising the construction of a canal between the town center and Bayou St. Jean, a project that had to wait until the 1790s.[60] Even after the Capuchins' feisty Father Raphael died in 1734, however, the quarrel between the two orders simmered on, culminating in the Father Hilaire Génévaux affair in the 1750s and 1760s.[61] Capuchin Génévaux got himself appointed vicar by the pope himself and was repeatedly and forcefully banished from the colony by the planters of the Superior Council, who refused to recognize his credentials.[62] The point of all this is that whatever moral authority the clergy had among the people must have been corroded by this indecorous quarrel over several decades.

The planters' reaction to a papal envoy was not extreme in the context of the times. Everywhere in the eighteenth century the priests suffered from a crisis of confidence as Enlightenment rationalism encouraged open expressions of contempt for the clergy. The great wealth of the Catholic orders tended to reinforce that contempt. The local clergy were virtually all immigrants from France (only one Louisiana-born man became a priest in the colonial period, and few women became nuns), and they arrived with insufficient stipends.[63] The only way they could support their missions and, equally important, gain any respect from other white people, was to become members of the planter class. And so they did: all three orders purchased or were advanced a small number of slaves upon their arrival and they proceeded to build up slaves and land into major estates. The Louisiana clergy not only became slaveowners but also actively promoted the slave trade to the colony in their reports to superiors.[64] Jesuit historians credit their order for the establishment of everything from the Ursuline nuns to the missions among the Indians, from indigo and sugar production to the early boys' school.[65] But they glide over the order's accumulation of wealth. Because their ideological commitment, austerity, and fraternal common property made them the ideal paternal slave masters, the Jesuits' wealth expanded dramatically.[66] When the Jesuits were suppressed in 1763, their plantation must have appeared to contemporaries almost as a town within a town, with one dozen brick buildings and an industrious atmosphere all its own, producing indigo and other products. When the slaves of the three orders are combined, it can be said that the Church was the single largest slaveowner in 1763. The effect of this wealth cut both ways. It made the priests and nuns respectable allies of the secular members of the ruling class, who appreciated the strategic value of a slaveholding alliance with the clergy, but the imposing clerical estates seemed to betray the higher calling, and it caused jealousy.[67]

It is clear that the Catholic Church was an important institutional prop for slavery, and it is not at all clear that, in contrast to Protestant clergy, it had a special role as "the guardian of the moral, religious, and even social life of the untutored Indian and Negro races within its New World domain."[68] No comparative study has demonstrated that this contrast existed, but this is not the place to go into that issue. The questions here are: Was the clergy's attention to the spiritual lives of slaves in any sense methodical, and, if so, was it beneficial to slaves, and was Christianization a major mode of acculturation? To proceed, it is important to avoid the unwarranted, ethnocentric assumption that Christianization of slaves by clergy was a "good" thing, that Christian slaves were "happier," which ignores the fact that their own religions were suppressed as heretical.

Unfortunately, little is known about the religion of New Orleans slaves in the eighteenth century, other than some basics gleaned from the archives of St. Louis Church: most slaves were baptized by the second half of the century, but only a handful were married "before the church." Of 607 slave infants baptized between 1744 and 1750 in St. Louis Church, only 47 (or 7.7 percent) were presented by parents who had been formally married, and more than a third of these belonged to just four slaveholders, including the Capuchin fathers.[69] Moreover, nothing is known about the actual ceremony performed by the priests; there is no proof that it was canonical, and, in any case, it did not alter the slave's civil status. Slaves were no more likely to attend church on Sunday than white people, who were described repeatedly as quite lax, especially the men. As Rhys Isaac notes of early slaveholding Virginia, the male population's ardent devotion to a "display of prowess" militated against religious piety.[70] It seems reasonable that slave men were disinclined to Christian observance for the same reason.

It is useful to turn to descriptions of the situation in the French West Indies, which has been studied by historians in some detail. The slaves' response to religion had some universal characteristics in all French colonies, so that it is safe to make certain arguments about New Orleans by extension from these works on the islands. Gabriel Debien has studied the question of Christianization over the whole colonial period in the French Antilles. He finds that for much of the seventeenth century, when the islands were still colonies with slaves rather than the slave societies they eventually became, the Catholic clergy were zealous in the performance of sacramental rites for slaves.[71] But by the end of the century, slave gang labor and the increasingly important role of the overseer made him hostile to competing authority, especially that of the clergy, and the latter coincidentally became proportionately fewer and far less evangelical toward slaves. This decline was less true in Martinique, it was less true wherever Jesuits were established, and it was less true in the sugar regions than in the later coffee regions, where churches were few. But by the second half of the eighteenth century, even though masters permitted baptism, most were openly hostile toward the catechizing of slaves because they regarded it as subversive.[72]

Debien shares with other historians a tendency to inflate the value of sacraments in evaluating the clergy's capacity or intent to minister to slaves' spiritual needs. This is particularly true in the comparative context, where historians rate Protestant clergy as lax in the performance of sacraments, which ignores the fundamental thrust of Protestantism, which is to replace rituals ("works") with more personal, individualized demonstrations of faith. In particular, Calvinists regard the baptism of infants as an act of little spiritual significance, and the baptism of unregenerate adults or teenagers as sacrilegious. From this perspective, sacraments without religious understanding not only fail to prevent dehumanization, they contribute to it and make it impossible for an individual to achieve Christian freedom.

According to one white observer in Saint Domingue at the end of the colonial period, in the days before religion declined there, "the slave imputed glory to and found consolation in being of the same religion as his master; he enjoyed the hope of sharing one day in another life the same goods and the same advantages."[73] If this is true, hope of reward in the afterlife is hardly an empowering sentiment. Even if, as the same informant concluded, religious commonality inspired masters to moderate their treatment of slaves—which is not substantiated by evidence—it could still be interpreted as functioning merely to perpetuate slavery by reconciling slaves to the system.

Similar testimony is provided by another observer, J. Félix Carteau, a planter driven from Saint Domingue in the 1790s who blamed "negrophiles" for the upheaval there. He defended slavery by arguing that slaves put a high value on the rituals of baptism and marriage, that they believed in "a good God, a bad Devil, in Paradise and Hell."[74] The skeptic would respond that they could have enjoyed virtually the same beliefs in non-Christian Africa, and that these alone amounted to little more than "consolation" in slave society. The writer goes on to another point that is more telling, however, when he notes that the clergy's most important source of income was from the surplice fees "arising from masses purchased by the Blacks" for their souls.[75] Again, this is consolation, which prevented not dehumanization but desperation. Some slaves gave into this sentimental dead-end, lavished their pathetic savings on priests, and hoped that it would buy some respite. The majority, however, were divided into two groups: those who snorted or raged at all gods as cruel jokers and those who "interpreted Christianity to fit the world views inherited from their African past."[76] Only the slaves, not the clergy, could save themselves from losing all spiritual value, either by a fierce secular philosophy, or by adapting the rituals and beliefs of the only sanctioned religion to their own purposes, or by some combination of the two. Carteau may have been right about the importance of baptism, but what it meant to the African Americans is unknown.

Nevertheless, it is true that baptism was administered to the majority of slaves in New Orleans, and all were presented by one or two "sponsors" or godparents. The registers of St. Louis Church indicate that this wove together the lives of whites and blacks in the early period, at least formally, for the great majority of slaves in the first creole generations had white godparents listed. How these sponsors were selected is unknown: most often a godparent was not the slave's master or a member of his family. Equally unclear is the sponsors' role in the slave's life: nowhere is it indicated that they intervened actively in any way to defend the godchild's interests. It does not appear that this ritual was anything more than a formality. That conclusion is sustained by a sample of 1,617 blacks without surnames listed in the sacramental registers, comprising 393 people baptized in the three years 1731 through 1733, 1,036 people baptized in fifty-four months between 1744 and 1750, and 188 people baptized in 1759. In the early period, virtually all were sponsored by white people.[77] By the 1740s, a decline was detectable: 93 percent of slaves had 2 white sponsors, and 12 others had 1 white sponsor who was paired with either a slave or free black. In 1759, however, whites were clearly avoiding participation in this sacrament (see fig. 4). Of 186 slaves listed for that year, only 47 (25 percent) were sponsored by whites, whereas the majority had slave godparents (68 percent) or a mixture of slave and free black godparents (7 percent).[78] The decline continued in later periods. Clearly, most whites had decided that it was socially acceptable to avoid this annoyance, and blacks were permitted to turn to their own community for godparents. As for free blacks, whereas whites had spon-

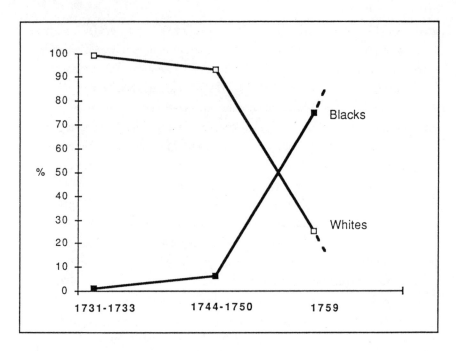

Fig. 4. Racial classification of slaves' baptismal sponsors, St. Louis Cathedral, 1731–33, 1744–50, and 1759.

sored 22 of them in the 1740s, they sponsored none in 1759. By that time the godparentage of all blacks was largely a responsibility of the black community.

To sum up, all slaves in New Orleans were likely to come in contact with members of the clergy and see the inside of St. Louis Church from time to time. Most slaves were baptized at birth, but few slaves were formally married by priests, and nothing is known about the catechizing of slaves belonging to secular masters, who probably resisted it like their counterparts in the rest of North America and in the West Indies.[79] Nothing can be assumed about the clergy's attitude toward slave treatment, but their failure to administer the sacrament of marriage to most slaves is the best indication that they were able to do very little to interpose the Church's authority between masters and slaves for any reason. This is the same conclusion reached by Morris S. Arnold concerning the role of the Catholic clergy in the lives of slaves in early Arkansas.[80]

The attitude of the secular planters toward the Jesuits suggests that they were offended by these priests' special treatment of their own slaves, or at least by their separatism and immunity from the usual "costs" of being members of the planter class, like raising families. Moreover, it was one thing to become special, unmarriageable members of the planter class, it was another to grow so rich that the clergy threatened to diminish the prestige of the secular planters. This was well underway in the islands early in the eighteenth century, and by 1763 the clerical establishment of New Orleans must have appeared to be aiming at the same goal.

Bourbon kings fulminated against the slaveholding of the colonial clergy, but the parlements were even more hostile to clerical wealth.[81] When a West Indian Jesuit obtained an enormous amount of credit against the society's assets and went bankrupt, the Parlement of Paris seized upon the opportunity to force Louis XV to suppress the Jesuit order in all French territory. In 1763, the secular planters joined in the spoliation of the Jesuits' estate, with what one Catholic historian describes as an "almost savage spirit," the moment they received orders from the crown to sequester the Jesuits' property in America to cover the defaulted loan.[82] By this time the Jesuits' enormous amount of property in the New World must have annoyed those many planters who were envious of all priests and especially the Jesuits.[83] Immediately after the expulsion order arrived in New Orleans, the planters rushed to an auction of the Jesuits' plantation, snapped up their goods, divided and sold off their land, and destroyed their chapel.[84] The auction also meant the dispersal of one of the most stable slave subcommunities in town.[85]

This dispersal of the Jesuits' slaves occurred in a period when several large slave communities were broken up, in part because of one particular European cultural element that could have a big effect on the lives of slaves: money. On one hand, the weakness of a currency supply in New Orleans was one important barrier to the elite's economic dynamism. Specie was almost always in short supply because Louisiana's economy could not attract and hold onto it any better than other North American colonies. The commissaire ordonnateur issued treasury notes on the king's credit to pay for the expense of government, designed to pay major contractors who could afford the inherent delay before this kind of paper was actually converted into wealth by whoever was willing and able to accept it at its face value. Sometimes a lot of this paper had to be issued, especially to equip troops in time of war, and the problem of an unleashed, inflationary currency appeared in the early 1740s in the wake of the expensive campaign against the Chickasaws.

Under Commissaire Ordonnateur Rochemore during the Seven Years' War inflation became a nightmare.[86] In so remote a place as New Orleans, when bills came due and so little aid arrived from France during the war, the ordonnateur was forced to issue a lot of bills of exchange drawn on the Treasury of France. Rochemore issued three million livres to locals for their produce to supply the servants of the king. Thus, from the conditions of 1719, when the planters could not buy company slaves for want of cash, the second generation had enormous sums to pay for all labor and goods that came their way, but little came that way. Nearly seven million livres circulated by 1762. Then Louis XV was forced to repudiate vast sums of letters of exchange issued in the colonies that he could not pay, including those issued by Rochemore. This was a heavy blow to colonists in America, yet less devastating in New Orleans than might have been expected.[87]

The bankruptcy of the French crown after 1760 should have been anticipated, but some colonists continued to use or speculate in discounted currency they hoped would be redeemed. It is impossible to separate the gathering currency crisis from a major social change in these years: a major reorganization of property because of the passing of the founders' generation. This happened in a great variety of ways.

The first of these huge capital-displacing events was not in fact an estate liquidation but the largest slave sale in the colony for many years, one-third of the cargo of a captured English slaver in September 1758. About 120 slaves were auctioned for 170,297 livres, at very high prices for "new Negroes," in the early days of the inflation that peaked in 1762.[88] This sale was soon followed by the death of the planter Claude Villars Dubreuil in 1758. His enormous plantation, brickery, and other works soaked up about 436,105 livres more in movables. His adult slaves brought around 3,000 livres each, but those with special skills were bid up over 6,000 livres because planters had such pent-up demands for labor and such large cash reserves.[89] Several other large judicial auctions followed, culminating with that of the Jesuits' plantation, which soaked up another 1 million livres or so.[90]

One dramatic example of how slaves were redistributed in this era is the Carrière family fiasco. Royal ordinances on tutorship, which were reissued in 1741, included Article 7, forbidding minors to alienate slaves from their estates before they were twenty-five years old.[91] Minors were thereby protected from youthful indiscretions, and creditors such as the Company of the Indies were protected too. The Superior Council could ignore the law and the will of the tutor if convinced the minors believed it was in their interest. The most common problem was when one or more heirs of an estate turned twenty-five but others were still too young to be emancipated: theoretically, the estate could not be divided until all were twenty-five. The Superior Council was inclined to set aside the law and let young adults take over their property, but this might not be wise, as in the case of the ten Carrière heirs. When several of the eldest passed their twenty-fifth birthdays and ran into debt, they demanded a division of their deceased parents' large estate into shares. The tutor of the minors was the planter Alexandre Bauré, and he was utterly opposed to the demand. He argued convincingly that the heirs each enjoyed up to twelve hundred livres annually in rent from the estate (enough to buy a young slave) and that the younger heirs would suffer from a probate, when currency was wildly inflated. When the court sided with the heirs, Bauré resigned the tutorship and angrily swore that he would sue to defend the younger children from the folly of their siblings.[92] The estate was promptly thrown on the block on April 16, 1763, and each heir received thirty-one thousand livres, but it was in the form of currency that was soon repudiated by the crown, and it was a complete disaster for the family.[93] The estate's whole value would have been reduced by division at any time, but selling the slaves at this particular time destroyed their market value for the Carrières.

In other words, when the crown repudiated the bills of exchange, a few unlucky individuals were caught holding vast sums of this now worthless paper, which had served as the instrument by which hundreds of slaves had been redistributed, and slaves were the most valued form of capital in town. Thus, most planters managed to dispose of their letters of exchange in the last hour of the inflation so that they devolved prejudicially upon a pathetic minority. Dubreuil's widow fell from one of the richest women in the southern colonies to destitution, and the receivers of the Jesuits' estate sales took home the crown's worthless securities too. The redistribution of primary forms of wealth—slaves, land, and tools—benefited the slaveholders as a group at the expense of a small number of their fellows. Although a few names took many lots in the Jesuit auctions, no one dominated the sales. No sort of privilege counted at the sales but cash. Governor Dabbadie had to pay the highest prices to obtain first choice of four of the Jesuits' eleven yoke of oxen.

Nothing illustrates better than these climactic events the vulnerability of planters to economic and political forces over which they had virtually no influence. Nothing demonstrates better the degree to which everything in slaves' lives was so contingent, so vulnerable to decisions of white people and complex market or imperial forces that neither slaves nor masters could control. Nothing had more effect on the lives of New Orleans than the series of events between 1758 and 1763 that led to the breaking up of these plantations. Years of shrewd investment by a slaveholder could go up in smoke in a moment because of the peculiar nature of his capital. All of the effort that slaves put into making black community a nurturing environment for individuals could also be lost in a moment, with the flourish of a quill in Paris or the stroke of an auctioneer's gavel in New Orleans.

A North American Slave Society: 5

New Orleans in Comparative View

All of this goes to prove the infinite difference between the habitants of the Islands and those of Louisiana.

—Joseph Lassus, c. 1749

New Orleans presents a unique opportunity to study slave society in comparative context because it developed under two of the major metropolitan powers and then became part of the United States. No less than three different legal systems and sets of attitudes need to be considered (French, Spanish, and Anglo-American). The overarching thesis here is that New Orleans was distinctive, like any community, having its own unique history resulting primarily from local social factors, and the prevailing cultural model of comparative analysis is unsound: only a social model works consistently, a model in which culture plays an important but secondary role. In this chapter it will be demonstrated that New Orleans was not recognizably "French" or "Caribbean," although its language, religion, and law were French. Similarly, in later chapters, it will become clear that it did not in any sense become "Spanish" after 1769, even though the official language, clergy, and law were Hispanicized. These three characteristics were of strictly secondary importance, the basic character of the community and its social structure being determined by its classes, demographic profile, export economy, and geographic situation, which made it a North American slave society. After 1803, New Orleans continued to develop according to long-established local factors or imperial policies having little or nothing to do with language, law, or religion. It suddenly became the capital of an American republic, yet that transition was nearly seamless because New Orleans resembled other slave societies of the North American continent from the beginning far more than it did either French or Spanish Caribbean slave societies. The social model of analysis shows that, unlike the Antilles and like the North American slave societies, it had a comparatively high proportion of resident planters and white women, a comparatively low influx of African slaves for much of the eighteenth century, a growing population of nonslaveholding farmers in the hinterland, many Indians in the interior blocking the emergence of maroon societies, and a less spectacularly profitable slave economy than those of the Antilles.

The comparing of slave systems has been dominated since the 1940s by an unusual little book, *Slave and Citizen*, written by a Latin Americanist, Frank Tannenbaum. Most remarkable is its great popularity, one of the few works of modern historical scholarship to remain in print half a century after it first appeared (1947) and to have sold more than one hundred thousand copies. Its thesis, based on a cultural model, is that blacks were less dehumanized by the law in Spanish and Portuguese colonies and by clerical practice in Catholic colonies than they were elsewhere. Specifically, under Spanish and Portuguese law, slavery was "a contractual arrangement between the master and his bondsman," and where Catholic clergy wielded authority, "slave and master were equal in the sight of God."[1] Above all, the condition of free blacks was the key to slave society, and "if the Latin-American environment was favorable to freedom [manumission], the British and American were hostile."[2] French Catholic planters and their culture were supposedly intermediate, between the English at one extreme and the Spanish at the other. Although this argument has been attacked by a wide range of scholars because of its essentially idealist character and the existence of an abundance of contrary evidence, it has retained a strong hold on the popular imagination. It is embedded in much of the recent scholarship concerning Louisiana.[3]

With Tannenbaum's cultural thesis as a heuristic device, we will see the clear superiority of a social model of analysis: a specific slave society can be understood best by studying the social implications of its local slaveholders' expectations, the demographic profile, the relative abundance of labor and natural resources, and the particular institutional array, and, in the second instance, by evaluating mores and cultural traditions.[4] This approach owes much to the work of Sidney W. Mintz. In his analysis of sugar in modern history, for example, he seeks to keep the reader's attention riveted on the social imperatives that formed the cultural meanings of sugar. Discovering "a culture" is not a worthwhile pursuit because "large, complex societies, composed of many overlapping subgroups, usually lack any assemblage of social practices [or common culture] by which life is endowed with meaning; their members differ widely in the way they can live, and in their historically influenced access to the acts, objects, and persons through which they validate their knowledge of life's meaning."[5] Even as late as the eighteenth century, for example, the consumption of refined sugar was largely restricted to the culture of the upper classes. But primary subgroups do incorporate specific cultural elements from one another, like the adoption of sugar consumption by the lower classes, thereby internalizing the meanings attached to them by the other group and adding new meanings of their own. By this model two groups with significantly unequal access to power can profoundly influence one another, even create something in common that mitigates class conflict.[6] Given the interpenetration of the lives of whites and blacks seen in the last chapter, this concept of reciprocal influence is ideal for the study of a slave society.

A cultural model may have more relevance to exceptional, small isolates like the little slave society at Pointe Coupée, several days journey upriver from New Orleans. Gwendolyn Midlo Hall describes an "Afro-Creole" culture there.[7] She is convinced, for example, that this culture was marked by its own language. She also asserts that the slave family was "scrupulously protected" in early Louisiana, a nod to the Tannenbaum thesis.[8] Curiously, she almost ignores the effect of European law codes and religion—the two major cultural institutions. Hall's work on Pointe Coupée is important, but New Orleans was socially and culturally a world apart from Pointe Coupée: one cannot detect a Louisiana-wide culture.

The cultural model resists comparative investigation: the most efficient comparative method is to outline African and European social structures and institutions and measure how these were modified in the New World according to local factors: the analysis cannot be driven by cultural "ways." Rather, essential structural features determine hierarchy and the distribution of power. Social structure is the central historical process, mediated by constantly transforming culture (as defined by Mintz), which is recreated on a day-to-day basis by individuals seeking to cope with, preserve, or alter their status in the social structure. Individuals are shaped by their struggle to transcend or gain the power to modify and redefine a given status into which they are born. In that struggle, some inspired individuals in any group seek to broaden behavioral norms, or "culture," but always driven by power and status. Individuals are not the products of "a culture" but are primarily shaped by their class, color, and gender and form a constantly changing culture. To focus on *a* culture is to try to force the naturally protean to gel, to ascribe to all individuals unshakable beliefs about which many members of a society are deeply ambivalent, and to privilege preservers over changers. Here, the comparative model will feature class, population trends, agriculture, and physical relation to the transatlantic world. In general, to read the evidence of social relations in early New Orleans is to discover that the internal and universal logic of slave society was far more important than any other factor. At the same time, to the degree that slave societies can be classified scientifically, it most closely resembled those in the North American English colonies. Historically, of course, like any human community with its own local events and traditions, it was unique.

To summarize the argument, contrary to the vague, cultural interpretation of "Latin" or "Catholic" attitudes, New Orleans was "Latin" only in that French was spoken there and Catholic only in that this religion was the only one officially recognized. The evidence strongly supports Tannenbaum's caveat that, despite differences between Latin American and Anglo-American slave societies, "similarities were undoubtedly greater." He argues that "slavery proved a pervasive influence that enveloped all of life and patterned it in a way peculiar to itself"—indeed, the very concept of a slave society (as distinct from a society with slaves) appears to have originated in Tannenbaum's work.[9] New Orleans was a slave society like any other because of the essential contradictions built into its social relations. Nevertheless, particularly on account of its demography, economy, and low rate of planter absenteeism, New Orleans fell into a North American class of communities resembling coastal South Carolina far more than French Saint Domingue. Finally, it departed in some ways both from the universal pattern of eighteenth-century slave societies and from the North American norm because of the peculiarities of its external slave supply, its role as the port for a huge hinterland economy that began on the other side of the parish border, and its highly vulnerable position vis-à-vis the Indian population of the Mississippi Valley. Still, it would slip into its place in the American Old South with surprising ease after 1803.

The French first made a successful establishment in the Caribbean on the little island of Saint Christophe in 1627. They settled the much larger islands of Martinique and Guadeloupe in 1635, which rivaled English Barbados in productive capacity by the end of the century. In this same era, the French began settling what was to become the richest colonial establishment, clinging to the edge of another great power's island, Spain's Hispaniola, the western portion of which they renamed Saint Domingue. Colonists gradually overwhelmed the local pirates to farm the richest volcanic tuff soils in the Caribbean. Over the course of the eighteenth century, Saint Domingue surpassed Martinique and Guadeloupe and yielded immense wealth by supplying Europe's growing appetite for sugar and coffee.[10]

In all their seventeenth-century colonies the French first attracted settlers of all classes, but as African slaves began pouring in by the end of the century, common white men no longer had any incentive to indenture themselves there since they were treated almost like black slaves. Moreover, the armies in France's European wars absorbed many young men who might have emigrated to the colonies. By 1789, Saint Domingue had the largest concentration of black slaves of any colony in the New World. Even by 1775, slaves came to outnumber whites by fourteen to one in Saint Domingue, as can be seen in table 9.[11] This extraordinary disproportion, together with the maroon communities in the mountains, epitomized society in the islands.

According to contemporary observers, white people in the islands were given to overindulgence in gambling, food, sex, and opulent display, especially by surrounding themselves with a superfluity of domestic slaves.[12] In all of them plantations were often managed by overseers while owners lived in France.[13] As for the slaves, planters mostly preferred to buy Senegalese Africans because they were presumed to be good farmers, well-built, tireless, sober, and oblig-

TABLE 9

CENSUSES OF SAINT DOMINGUE, 1681–1788

| | Year of Census | | | |
	1681	1754	1775	1788
Whites	4,336	12,859	20,438	27,717
Free blacks	210	4,732	5,897	21,808
Slaves	2,101	164,859	287,806	455,089
Total	6,647	182,450	314,141	504,614

ing, qualities that compensated their own distaste for work. Nonetheless, most masters would buy slaves of any origin, and hence the slave subcommunities on the plantations were ethnically mixed.[14]

Demographic conditions in New Orleans differed sharply from Saint Domingue and resembled those in other North American slave societies because of the comparatively larger number of whites, who were outnumbered by blacks only by two to one by the 1760s. Moreover, unlike New Orleans, central Africans would become numerically dominant in Saint Domingue over the course of the eighteenth century. Contemporaries were well aware of this distinction and others that made New Orleans so different from the islands. One of them, Joseph Lassus, spent many years in both places and in 1749 wrote a good comparative analysis.[15]

Lassus described society in Saint Domingue as terribly warped by a combination of the quick fortunes to be procured from sugar production and the excessive crowding of the land so that it was oversubdivided, which partly explained why it became impossible to retain many white immigrants in the colony. Obsessed with gain, enjoying virtually no strong community ties in a sea of black slaves, forced to send their children to France for schooling, whence they seldom returned, the planters dreamed only of the day they could also return to France and make up for their former misery by rapidly wasting their fortunes. Those who retained title to their plantations when they traveled to France risked leaving them to the care of men who did not know how to manage slaves. "All of this goes to prove," Lassus wrote, "the infinite difference between the *habitants* of the Islands and those of Louisiana."[16] In the latter colony the local planters were committed to permanent residence and enjoyed a pleasant civil society adorned by lovely and intelligent girls and enlivened by a general passion for music. Lassus was at a loss for words to describe the bounty of the soil and the commercial potential of New Orleans. The catastrophe of John Law's system had discouraged the French from settling in the colony, and all that was required was for Louis XV to send enough "Negroes and Whites" and the town of "New Orleans will be the most flourishing in the universe."[17]

The list of contrasts provided by Lassus can be extended. The white populations of the West Indian slave societies included larger numbers of nonslaveholders living in the vicinity of the plantations, who hated the *grands* while not appreciably affecting the gross, colonywide disproportion between white and black.[18] As has been already demonstrated, the proportion of the slaveholders to nonslaveholders in New Orleans was low: less than two-fifths of white families remained outside the slaveholding class by 1766. On the other hand, only one or two very large slaveholders lived there. There was a greater sense of egalitarian sentiment among whites than in Saint Domingue. Indeed, the term *petit blanc* was not current in New Orleans. On the other hand, the *colony* of Louisiana had something Saint Domingue lacked: a huge hinterland of arable beyond the capital peopled by two kinds of natural allies of the planters in New Orleans—first, nonslaveholding white farmers whose numbers grew gradually and who were not neighbors of and thus not envious of the planters and, second, Indian nations such as the Choctaws. Both of these groups depended on the planters of the capital to take off their surplus production in return for trade goods. Both of these groups could be depended upon to support the planters' regime if it were attacked from within. The Native Americans were particularly important; in the eighteenth century the free native populations were extinct in the French West Indies.[19] The number of Indians in the lower Mississippi Valley declined sharply over time, but their places were taken by increasing numbers of immigrant farmers beginning in the 1760s.

For all of these trumps held by New Orleans slaveholders, it is true that the planter class was weakened by a similar division there and in the islands: over time there developed a basic split between those of creole birth and Frenchmen.[20] Throughout the eighteenth century new men from Paris and western French ports arrived in Louisiana and Saint Domingue with connections to someone in the capital by which they secured credit or even office in the colonies.[21] They were reported to look down on creoles with contempt and to treat slaves with more brutality than did the creole planters, which endangered the slaveholding class by undermining its unity.[22] Nonetheless, this division appears to have been comparatively muted in New Orleans, where the core of early founding families remained very strong, able to absorb the trickle of newcomers by intermarrying with them.

The most important factor distinguishing New Orleans from the Antilles is the increasing supply of slaves to the Caribbean islands over the entire course of the eighteenth century. Because of it, two sets of sharply contrasting conditions emerged in regard to slave treatment and slave rebelliousness in the two societies. In Saint Domingue, the attitudes of both masters and slaves were affected by the ability of the planter to stroll down to the slave market and purchase "new" Africans whenever he or she had the cash or credit. This was true even though planters in the islands never stopped complaining that supply did not satisfy their insatiable demand. But the planter in New Orleans had much more to complain about because the slavers stopped sailing there in 1731.[23] The effect of this steady supply to Saint Domingue was that Saint Domingue planters could more easily afford the risk of exploiting slaves physically to the maximum, for which they became justly infamous by 1791, allowing for those individuals whose paternalism did not fit the pattern.[24]

The supply of slaves to Louisiana was almost completely shut off in the years between the small cargo of 1743 and the 1760s, except for an uncertain trickle.[25] When Bienville tried in 1734 to obtain permission for coasting vessels to bring slaves from Saint Domingue, Minister of Marine Maurepas flatly refused because it would violate the Company of the Indies' monopoly.[26] All of Maurepas's efforts to encourage the company to carry Africans to Louisiana yielded small results.[27] By 1735 it was obvious that company slavers avoided the town because New Orleans planters had less cash than the islanders and because slavers regarded the long upriver voyage as prohibitive, a time when slaves' illnesses were likely to worsen, which killed some and lowered the value of others.[28] The slaveholders who could afford to buy more slaves were so desperate for them that two of the richest of them mounted one small joint venture to import a cargo of 190 Africans in 1743 under a license provided by the company, but these were the last to be legally imported into French Louisiana.[29]

Thus, without a slave supply, New Orleans could hardly expect to attract many white people from France. Free white farmers without slaves in an aristocratic slave society were only lowly non-slaveowners who worked with their hands, a status no higher than they enjoyed in France, and perhaps lower. Few whites were attracted to a colony where there was a tendency to cut costs by replacing white free labor whenever possible with black slave labor. The colony's reputation among the common people of France continued to be very bad. As late as 1750, false rumors that little children were being taken up from the streets of Paris by the police and shipped to Louisiana to feed silkworms their mulberry leaves caused terrible riots.[30] In addition to the ill repute of Louisiana, another factor limiting immigration was the fundamental, still somewhat mysterious disinclination of the French to emigrate, even to a nonslave society like New France.[31] The crown's vague plan to people Louisiana with discharged soldiers was fanciful, because the men who became soldiers were usually fit for no regular occupation.[32] Thus the hinterland did not begin to be thickly peopled until much later in the colony's history, and then mostly by farmers from places other than France. The major factor limiting the colony's growth was the failure of the crown to overcome slavers' reluctance to carry Africans to Louisiana.

These two conditions—a limited supply of slaves and a limited number of immigrants—could have had a significant effect on the conditions of slaves. The dearth of new African imports meant those in the colony carried a premium value. The limited supply of colonists minimized the number of strategic marriages that would break up slave families through geographic extension of slave society in Louisiana. Members of both racial groups underwent the process of creolization in close proximity: the predictability of social relations made the whip and the gallows less frequently necessary, and they were less economically sensible because of the lack of a slave market. In other words, if relations between masters and slaves were somewhat moderated in this period, it did not mean any basic change in the regime nor any lessening of planters' willingness to resort to terror if they thought it necessary, as they did in the 1760s under Lafrénière's leadership. It is hard to be more specific than Dumont as to the treatment of slaves in New Orleans: "Some of these slaves can really rejoice at having fallen into good hands; but there are many, too, who suffer."[33] As always, the most important variable was the attitude of a given planter, but on the whole the creole slave generation could exploit comparatively favorable conditions.

So far, little has been said about the effect of crop regimes and their effect, to which we now turn. Only a little sugar cane was grown in New Orleans before 1795, and no coffee or cacao, the three big crops in Saint Domingue. Recent scholarship on production in the islands has been a revelation. College texts cling to the perennial notion that sugar production was a living hell for slaves by comparison to other kinds of production. Nothing would suit the thesis of this chapter better than to affirm the prevailing orthodoxy that sugar cane was a more labor-intensive crop that resulted in higher slave mortality, for that would accentuate the difference between the French Antilles and French New Orleans. But close observation of the evidence shows that this old idea has to be suspended. Neither the sugar regime in Saint Domingue, studied by David Geggus, nor that in Antigua, studied by David Barry Gaspar, can be clearly linked to high mortality rates in the Antilles, although it is easy to show that working sugar cane was hazardous if not in itself fatal. Mortality rates seem to have fluctuated with the condition of the African slaves purchased, the sexual division of labor, the precise position of a plantation, and other factors.[34] In an overview of new research on the issue, Robert Fogel argues emphatically that labor intensity does not account for the differing rates of natural increase of slave populations in sugar and nonsugar societies. Seemingly innocuous factors affected mortality rates, such as the use of manure, which improved yields but spread disease among barefoot workers.[35]

The labor intensity of indigo cultivation In New Orleans appears to have been no less than that of sugar: cultivating and rendering the plants was a backbreaking job and the production of dye was dangerous to health. Since it seems necessary to underpin this argument with care, and since the crop shaped the daily work routine of a majority of New Orleans slaves, it is important to recreate the production routine in detail. As was true of tobacco, "indigo production was troublesome and uncertain of results."[36] Fortunately for their masters, West African slaves arrived with some knowledge of its culture.[37] Planted in the spring from seed obtained originally from the West Indies, the soil had to be carefully prepared and furrowed in advance and then slaves had to tend the fields daily after sowing to keep out weeds, caterpillars, and other pests. A canal had to be maintained next to the field, controlled by a sluice in the levee, from which the plants were watered either by hand or irrigation if possible. By June, a plant resembling broom was about two and a half feet high and ripe for cutting. This had to be done carefully without disturbing the roots because a second crop would sprout from them by August, and, in Louisiana, perhaps a third crop after that. Harvested plants had to be handled with great care to avoid brushing or knocking off the blue plush on the leaves. The harvest was carried to an open-air pavilion covering a series of vats constructed of wood or brick, about ten feet square and three feet deep, arranged in descending order. The plants were piled in the highest vat (the "steeper") and covered with water for about twelve hours to pass through the first stage of fermentation. At a very particular moment—before a second stage of fermentation began—the water had to be drawn off from the steeper into the vat next to it (the "beater"). "The great difficulty is to know this proper point of fermentation, which cannot sometimes be ascertained to any degree of certainty," and slight errors of judgment might destroy months of work.[38] The water in the beater contained the indigo dye in suspension, and slaves now had to churn the water with beaters to separate the grains of dye from the water. All of this took place during the hottest months and attracted swarms of insects. Once it began to drift toward the bottom of the vat, one added a precipitant like limewater to carry all the dye to the bottom. The water was then drawn off into the final vat. The precipitant was scooped into cloth bags and hung up to dry, perhaps dumped into cloth-lined boxes and pressed to speed the drying process, laid out to sweat almost completely dry, and then cut into squares, packed in barrels, and sold to a merchant for the equivalent of about one Spanish dollar per pound.

The cultivation of rice on several plantations was no less exacting. To it the slaves of Louisiana contributed more than mere labor. Long familiar in the Old World with complex hydraulic systems of sluices, floodgates, and ditches that made rice an important crop there, it was a particularly delicate operation in New Orleans because controlled flooding of fields was accomplished by a breach in the levee, and even a small error in judgment could lead to a "crevasse" and catastrophic inundation by one of the most powerful rivers in the Western Hemisphere.[39] It was a nearly year-round process, the fields for the following year's crop being prepared immediately after the harvest. Nevertheless, it complemented the indigo-production cycle nicely on the same plantation because their respective periods of intensive and slack labor were different.[40] Since the rice production regime has been described in such detail and in such elegant prose by several writers, in particular Charles Joyner and Julia Floyd Smith, it would be impossible to improve on their work here.[41] It is sufficient to point out that the arduousness of rice culture was at least as threatening to health in Louisiana as sugar cane was in the Antilles. According to one observer, "the cultivation of it is dreadful: for if a work could be imagined peculiarly unwholesome and even fatal to health, it must be that of standing like the negroes, anckle and even mid-leg deep in water which floats on ouzy mud, and exposed all the while to a burning sun which makes the very air they breathe hotter than the human blood; these poor wretches are then in a furness of stinking putrid effluvia: a more horrible employment can hardly be imagined, not far short of digging in Potosi."[42] On the other hand, however, we must assume that indigo and rice production also made possible the adoption of the task system in New Orleans, as in South Carolina. So far, no direct evidence has come to light, but the New Orleans planters' strong dependence on local self-sufficiency in food (by contrast to West Indian planters, who imported much of their slaves' food to maximize the exploitation of their labor), suggests that a task system gave slaves a few hours of daylight for their own gardens, hunting, and gathering.

Finally, as for the wood industry, few occupations are more dangerous than lumberjacking: in Louisiana falls, cuts, snakebites, and drownings were all associated with the production of lumber. Since sawmills were also powered by making careful breaches in the levee, the same risks were run in that regard as in the cultivation of indigo and rice.[43] Theoretically, labor regimes were equally bad in New Orleans and the islands, yet the slave population of the lower Mississippi Valley grew by about 36 percent between 1731 and 1766, and most of that was by natural increase in that the external slave supply was minimal. New Orleans was a successful slave society. It had a respectable rate of growth for a new slave population by comparison to the islands, where contemporaries and historians alike have argued that the slave force could not have grown without continuous supply by the African slave trade.

To explain this basic difference between New Orleans and Saint Domingue may not be as difficult as it appears. Curiously, one factor is overlooked by Fogel and other historians: the role of the African slave trade itself in the epidemiological situation. Several factors may account for the fact that the plantation regions with the highest mortality and lowest fertility were the lowland sugar plantations in the West Indies, but it may not be necessary to go beyond the simple fact that the great majority of African slaves were imported to precisely those plantations because sugar was so profitable, the cargo of every ship carrying vigorous strains of African diseases that could spread in the slave quarter. In fact, the French recognized the danger posed by slavers to the local colonial population as early as 1685, when authorities in the islands began quarantining ships coming in from Africa.[44] Historians tend to treat the disease climate in Saint Domingue as if it was of purely indigenous origin. Geggus argues that while the slave trade screened out Africans with congenital disorders, it introduced them "into an unfamiliar disease environment," as if they contributed nothing to it.[45] In fact, they may have been the single most important source for mortal disease epidemics in New World slave societies. That is why New Orleans had a quarantine station located on the right bank of the river away from the main concentration of slaves. The experience of New Orleans would seem to bear out the hypothesis that the slave trade was the single most important factor determining mortality rates, for diseases do not seem to have been an important factor in shaping the slave population between the dangerous founding years and the advent of smallpox at the end of the century, which corresponded with the great increase in the slave trade in the last phase of the colonial period.[46]

Throughout the Antilles, working conditions for slaves improved modestly after 1760, when the plough gradually replaced the hoe, mule-powered coffee-bean pulping mills replaced human-powered ones, and mule-powered, double-cylindered cane-crushing mills made sugar production much safer and a bit easier.[47] Another trend over time, however, was to increase slaves' responsibility for feeding themselves, which was paired with a little quasi-free time for truck-farming in a slave's assigned garden, or for hiring out; or one might work for the master for wages. This never replaced the necessity of supplying slaves with basic provisions, however, like those purchased from the New Englanders.[48]

Certain other factors must have affected day-to-day slave treatment in the two colonies. Above all, since so few common white people went to New Orleans, many slaves acquired skills, perhaps proportionately more of them than in the islands, and these would have been empowering in their relations with masters. Deforestation on Saint Domingue meant most slaves lived in houses prefabricated by New Orleans slaves, which meant living quarters were smaller than in New Orleans because Saint Domingue planters had to house as many people under one roof as possible to hold down costs. In general, French historians of the French slave regime regard it as having been harsh.[49] In particular, despite the efforts to provide an adequate diet, poor nourishment was "the constant menace."[50] For all their similarities, of course, each of the French islands was unique. Malnutrition was probably a significant problem on Saint Domingue because masters supplied little food to slaves, in contrast to Martinique, where a number of planters specialized in growing provisions for the other plantations.[51] "New" slaves were branded by planters in Saint Domingue but not in Martinique or Guadeloupe.[52] Racial intermixture was absolutely greater but comparatively less extensive and mulattoes proportionately fewer in Saint Domingue than in the other colonies. Finally, the permanent maroon population of Saint Domingue became especially large.[53]

The immensity of its population, the gross disproportion of whites and blacks, and the relentless drive to make quick, fabulous profits made Saint Domingue the supreme Caribbean slave society. Maroons who escaped the regime lived in mountain strongholds in all the islands from an early date, becoming so powerful that authorities actually signed treaties with them in a desperate attempt to limit their plundering activity. The first of these treaties appeared in Martinique in 1665.[54] But maroon societies became a serious problem on the extremely mountainous Saint Domingue.[55] Conditions were bad enough that society began falling apart after 1750. One runaway was Guinea-born François Macandal, who had lost one hand in a sugar cane mill and "went maroon," as the French put it. From a secret stronghold he organized a vast conspiracy of slaves to poison all whites. He was captured and burned alive on January 20, 1758. He struggled so violently that he toppled his stake and fell off the pyre, inspiring a roar of approval from the slaves forced to witness his execution: "Macandal is saved! He's invincible and incombustible!"[56] Authorities responded by reducing Macandal to ashes and burning other slaves on a regular basis for several months, but the blood of white people ran cold for years after that. By contrast, no such horrendous confrontation occurred in New Orleans after 1731.

One way to illustrate the difference between New Orleans and the islands is to evaluate carefully the interrogation of some slaves who were imported from Martinique into New Orleans in 1765. The reputation of Macandal had become so notorious by 1763 that the Superior Council passed a resolution prohibiting the introduction of any slaves from Saint Domingue, except by licensed African slave traders who had merely refreshed there on the way to Louisiana.[57] This was the origin of a permanent policy designed to distinguish between ignorant and therefore acceptable slaves direct from Africa and slaves who had been corrupted by knowledge of Macandal in the islands. In practice, the ban applied not just to the "domiciled" slaves of Saint Domingue, for it was soon extended to Martinique as well when a vessel brought a small shipment from that island in 1765. Before they were admitted, the Superior Council ordered that they be quizzed in order to weigh their fitness to be sold locally.[58]

Even though Martinique had long ago suffered a declining growth of its black population because of competition with Saint Domingue, it had many more slaves than Louisiana, so conditions were closer to those in Saint Domingue, as planters in New Orleans clearly recognized by carefully screening this group of castoffs. They asked each slave *why* he or she had been brought to Louisiana and examined their bodies for evidence of severe corporal punishment, that is, for signs that a slave was "bad." In fact, only a few had scars on their buttocks from whipping. But most of them knew why they had been deported and their stories reveal that their former masters could and did exercise a more intensely rigorous regime than was possible for New Orleans planters, for Martinique saw at least some slavers arrive from time to time to replace slaves they deported. The record of the interrogation also has the virtue of being a rare peek into the "immigrant" experience of African Americans who were uprooted from familiar surroundings and transported across the sea.

The first slave questioned, Julie, fifty years old, born a Congo but for long a slave in Martinique, did not know why she had been brought to Louisiana. Neither did Marie-Rose (twenty), a creole who was just doing the washing one day when she was suddenly arrested, jailed for five months, and then carried away in the ship, although she claimed never to have done anything wrong. The rest had stories. Jeannette (thirty), a Mina, had raised six children for her mistress, a free Negress, whom she detested and asked to be released to a white slaveowner. (It is not clear if she meant a specific person for a specific reason or just any white owner.) As often happened to dissatisfied slaves in any colony in which masters had the luxury to rid themselves of potential runaways, her owner had her clapped in prison and exiled. Cupidon (thirty-five), an Arada, made the big mistake of sleeping with his master's mulatto lover. Isabelle (twenty-five), an Angolan with a four-year-old son, belonged to a man who had to sell them because he needed cash and could not get the price he wanted in the islands. Angélique (eighteen), a creole, had been a street peddler when the authorities decided to crack down on that activity. The mistress wanted to get rid of her but the master resisted, so the mistress had her imprisoned and shipped off on a pretext. Agnès (thirty), creole, "had to do" with the overseer, and her mistress did not like it and exiled her. Adélaide (thirty), probably a creole, was sent to "Mississippi," as it was still called outside Louisiana, because her mistress was besieged by creditors and hoped to recover the value of her slaves secretly. Finally, no less than five slaves reported that their masters simply wanted to get rid of them because they were too sick to work well. In Martinique, such slaves could easily be replaced with more productive ones.[59]

With the exception of this last group, slaves in New Orleans were unlikely to be sold either for the reasons provided by these slaves nor in the manner they were sold. This is directly related to the low volume of the African slave trade, which was in turn the result of a less dynamic economy in New Orleans. Slaves were simply too few to sell them without very careful consideration, and it would have been difficult to conceal their faults from prospective local buyers in this earliest period because they were all neighbors. And slaves were too hard to come by to sell out of the colony for minor faults: there is not a single case on record of a slaveowner trying to sell a slave out of the colony in order to conceal the act from creditors, the most likely reason for a New Orleans planter to try such a subterfuge. The implication of all this for local slaves is clear: they enjoyed a greater degree of security than the islanders against being plucked out of their families and sold to some distant and unknown master.

Finally, the degree of acculturation of whites and blacks was higher in New Orleans than in the islands because of the small size of the population and its relative stability: familiarity also helped to mitigate the regime in the early decades. The prevalence of the French language is one good sign of the common culture: in the courtroom local slaves were reported to speak either their native African language, at first, or, increasingly, French. As Thad W. Tate remarks of Virginia, despite the popular view, "one of the most misunderstood facts about the Negroes of the eighteenth century is the relative skill with which they spoke English," even within a few years after arrival from Africa.[60] Father Mongin reported the same thing about French in the Antilles.[61] Many slaves from Africa undoubtedly spoke French with a strong accent, and their creole children's French was as distinctive as the African American English of the southern English colonies. This was not, however, a distinct language.

Two thoughtful observers who had been in both Saint Domingue and Louisiana discussed language and stated positively that they heard no patois in New Orleans.[62] One transcription of speech by a slave in the Mobile Bay region comes down to us from this era, spoken in 1762 by one Jupiter, recorded by Jean-Bernard Bossu. The author "translates" this speech into standard French, but the slave's own words are readily understandable, "good" French, and Bossu does not, in fact, translate but provides an exaggeratedly correct version designed to mock the slave's uncertain command of minor subtleties (ça instead of ce), accent (ly instead of lui), and exotic vocabulary of Canadian origin (ferdoches).[63] The more distinctive speech of slaves (and some whites) in nineteenth-century rural Louisiana is a product of the very last phase of the slave trade, when the lower Mississippi Valley was flooded with slaves from every point in the compass. The Haitian refugees probably introduced their dialect early in the nineteenth century, although Louisiana may have produced its own black dialect that closely resembles that of Haiti.[64] This "Creole" is today and always was confined to regions beyond New Orleans Parish.[65]

The evidence points to a modest amelioration of slave treatment in New Orleans by midcentury, as suggested by the tone of the Regulations of Police code of 1751. To put that local code in perspective, it is necessary to look more closely at French slave laws developed by the crown, the Code Noir, which had little to do with the conditions of slaves' lives. In 1685, when the French West Indies were developing into slave societies, Louis XIV decreed a Code Noir for them, the only royal black code (with several subsequent modifications) that was ever implemented in the New World. The king's purpose was complex, but the main purpose was to introduce the king's order into his colonies. The bulk of the code was addressed to *masters*, not slaves, instructing them how to treat slaves as property in courts and the fields.[66] A few protective features give the code a humanitarian gloss, but the king's object in defining the parameters of slave treatment was to set standards to modify the behavior of brutal masters and encourage the indulgent ones to be more strict, all in the interest of order. In 1724 his successor, Louis XV, issued a new code for Louisiana that was quite similar to the old code.

In practice, all protective clauses of the Louisiana Code Noir were interpreted to the masters' advantage. A copy of the Code Noir that is fully annotated by an anonymous critic in a position of authority sometime before 1750 is preserved, hereinafter the "Annotations."[67] The critic states that in practice the major "protective" articles are ignored in Louisiana. This was certainly true in all matters concerning the authority of the clergy. For example, in reference to Article 2, requiring that slaves be converted to Catholicism, the "Annotations" note that "Execution of this article is neglected in the Colony."[68] Even before New Orleans was founded, clergy in the Antilles had learned to be satisfied with administering a single sacrament to slaves—baptism—for which they were required merely to recite the elements of the Trinity and a basic definition of the miracle of the mass.[69] The requirement that slaves be buried in consecrated ground was complied with if, in such a hot climate, the corpse could be interred immediately with no inconvenience to the planter, which was untrue of the corpses of most slaves, who died outside the town center where the consecrated grounds were located.[70] While a few slaves were permitted the rite of Christian marriage, it conferred no civil rights: the law did not protect any slave from rape. Article 8 forbade slaves to marry without permission but also forbade masters to force a slave to marry, but what evidence there is suggests that masters pressured slaves to choose spouses from among those available on the same plantation, and couples received no protection by these informal rites in any case.[71] The provision of Article 10 that the children of a free black woman were free even if her husband was a slave was of no consequence, according to the "Annotations," because this kind of marriage did not exist in Louisiana, meaning it was not permitted.[72]

Much the same was true of articles in the Code Noir requiring basic physical care. In regard to Article 5, which barred labor on Sundays and holidays, all evidence suggests that only the sabbath and a few major Christian holidays were days of rest, as in all slave colonies. However, although Article 19 forbade masters from allowing slaves free time to earn their own food and raiment, the "Annotations" state that a number of Louisiana slaveowners did so anyway, giving their slaves nothing.[73] Since the code sets no penalties for noncompliance with Article 18, ordering the adequate provisioning of slaves, the crown obviously intended to allow planters to establish their own standards, and the "Annotations" declare that no standards were set.[74] Article 20 empowers slaves who are "not at all" fed and clothed to inform officials, who are to prosecute an offending master. A number of runaway slaves who were brought to trial told the judges that they were mistreated, underfed, but no evidence suggests that they had tried to lodge complaints; they did not seem to know they had the right to do so, and this right was reserved only to slaves suffering from total neglect or barbaric treatment in any case. No instance is to be found in which the court interfered with a master's authority over a slave in order to protect the slave.[75] Even if a slave lodged a complaint, Article 24 of the code forbade him or her actually to testify in court against (or for) the master.[76]

Evidence of enforcement of Article 21, which forbids the abandonment of old slaves, is lacking. As for Articles 38 and 39, which forbid the torture or murder of slaves by their owners, authorities did have the right to torture, mutilate, or execute accused criminals. Moreover, Article 39 delegates power to the court to pardon the murderer or mutilator of a slave.[77] The article forbidding the breaking up of young families may have been enforced, but only those few slaves who had been married by a priest were regarded as truly married, and children could be sold away from their parents after they reached puberty in any case.[78] It is impossible to determine whether slaves were separated by sale less often in French Louisiana than they were in other colonies.[79]

Finally, there is no indication that free blacks enjoyed all rights and privileges of free people: more emphasis was placed on Article 53, which required them to show "profound respect" to whites. While it is true that they could sue for recovery in court, in practice this was very rare, allowed only when they were obviously cheated by white people.[80] They could be reenslaved for misconduct: Jeannette was reduced from freedom to slavery by the court in 1747 because she could not pay her debts.[81] A Superior Council decree provided that free blacks who could not pay stiff fines for harboring runaway slaves were to be sold as slaves.[82] Free blacks had the same status as their counterparts in the English colonies.[83]

Nor did free blacks ever become numerous in the French period. Orlando Patterson seeks to avoid the pitfalls of the cultural model by concentrating emphasis upon the socially determined factor of manumission and the number and status of free blacks. Using this measure he obtains six categories of slave societies, but the method suffers from two serious faults.[84] The generalization that planters in the United States were more hostile than other planters to manumission of selected slaves has never been demonstrated. The idea that "there was literally no place for the freedman" in the southern states is contradicted by many success stories of individual free blacks despite strong discrimination against them by whites, including a few with a place in the slaveholding class, albeit a subordinate one, as was true in all slave societies.[85] Patterson also shares a widely held assumption that racially mixed free blacks were a "buffer" between the white masters and slaves where whites were a small minority, that is, throughout the Caribbean.[86] How they could have formed a buffer if they shared the same interests with white planters vis-à-vis slaves (as Patterson argues) is unclear. If Patterson's categories have the virtue of emphasizing social categories, the latter still seem to be derived from the point of view of the slaveowning class, as if it somehow created the free black population to serve specific needs.

In fact, wherever conditions were ideal to limit the free black population—as in New Orleans before 1769, and in Virginia up to the 1780s—the number of free blacks remained few because they were regarded as an inherently disorderly social element whether or not they were born of mixed race. Only a few were freed gratuitously and fewer yet were allowed to purchase their freedom, although they did have the right to possess property (*peculium*) while not owning it outright.[87] The Code Noir of 1724 angrily discouraged if it did not prohibit freedom purchase (Article 50), capping a campaign initiated by Louis XIV against the practice in the Antilles.[88] If one takes into account every single reference to a free black mentioned in all records, and compares this incidence with the free black population at the end of the French period (perhaps two hundred), one would estimate between fifty and one hundred emancipations for the entire period, or one or two per year. When free black populations grew by liberal manumission policies, it was always because of some special external factor (ideology on the part of some planters in Virginia in the last years of the eighteenth century, or the urgent Spanish policy to divide internally a rapidly increasing slave population in Louisiana after 1769), not because they served as buffers. It is possible to construct a more practical set of comparative categories from the point of view of free blacks: their population size and dispersal, economic opportunities, and cultural and social stability. In that scheme, New Orleans blacks would fall into the same category with those of the Virginia Tidewater: they were far fewer in number than in the French Antilles, with limited opportunity, although they enjoyed a small measure of community consciousness by 1769.

It certainly appears that the Code Noir was "a weak barrier to the tyranny of masters."[89] While evidence is lacking that the protective measures of the code had much effect in either New Orleans or Saint Domingue, proof is abundant that the repressive measures were applied: slaves could expect to suffer exemplary punishment in and out of court.[90] Yet it cannot be shown that the punitive provisions were ever applied with consistency by judges. For example, while Article 32 specified the corporal punishments to be administered to runaway slaves, including execution of slaves who repeatedly went maroon, in fact, none of the recidivist runaways was ever executed merely for that crime. The Code Noir is a guide only to certain ideals concocted at Versailles and tells almost nothing about slave treatment in any comparative sense. As seen earlier, local codes are more revealing.

The revised Code Noir of 1724 was completely successful in one respect: the version of 1685 did not include sufficient measures to discourage miscegenation and these were added to the code of 1724. Because of a continuing imbalance of the sexes in the white population of the Antilles, authorities were concerned about mixed-race free people in the New World: if those who were "neither black nor white" became numerous enough, it would challenge the basic logic of the whole racial system and threaten it with eventual dissolution. It has not been established that there *was* a significant growth in the mixed-race population in the French islands early in the eighteenth century. As for racial intermarriage, all the evidence suggests that it was rare because it did great harm to the social status of any white person who entered into such a union. In fact, a priest reported home from Guiana that it was only socially accepted there in a limited sense when a poor white man (with no status to lose) married a free black woman with money. This was the attitude in the islands as well: a white man with "Negro" money was only technically better off than a white man with nothing at all.[91] Such a man, according to one analyst, "falls from the white ranks and becomes equal to freedmen, and even they regard him as their inferior: in effect this man is contemptible."[92] Any white person married to a black, whatever his social position, was officially proscribed.[93] Louis XIV made clear his hostility to racial intermarriage by refusing to register even a minor title of nobility claimed by any man who was married to a nonwhite woman.[94] Gabriel Debien studied the case of one Gaspard-Alexis La Barre, who tried to make respectable his bronze-colored wife by claiming she had some Indian ancestry, causing a big scandal in Saint Domingue.[95] Nonetheless, interracial concubinage seemed to be a growing problem, and the very existence of "mulattoes," as they were labeled by whites, led the crown to decree in 1713 that only top royal officials could authorize manumissions of slaves by masters. That impediment to the conjugal or paternal benevolence of individual white men was regarded as the only way to discourage interracial procreation by concubinage and protect the planter class and the social order as a whole.[96]

The new code of 1724 for Louisiana included a fully explicit policy to minimize both miscegenation and the population of free blacks. Article 6 prohibited interracial marriage, set a heavy fine for those who engendered mixed-race children, and, if a master fathered a child by his own slave in concubinage, both mother and child were to be forfeited to the hospital without possibility of emancipation.[97] While the law did not prohibit interracial sex, the new policy proved effective in Louisiana, facilitated by the fact that white women were comparatively numerous in the colony by 1740. It was not unlike the situation in Georgia, with its unusually strict code that forbade not only a gross disproportion of blacks to whites in households and the training of blacks as artisans, but also interracial sex itself, which was highly unusual. "But in all these things," as reported by John Martin Bolzius, "an unrestricted liberty exists and is exercised in the other colonies," which would become more true of Georgia in time.[98] But mere "carnal" mixture of whites and black slaves did not lead to a high rate of emancipation of mixed-race offspring because social prejudice against it was strong, as in Louisiana. A statistic is in order here. Unfortunately, the census of 1766, while complete, does not provide information on the ancestry of slaves. Conversely, the census taken by Alejandro O'Reilly in 1769, while it indicates numbers of mulattoes, does not include Tchoupitoulas, where the slaves were concentrated, so the count of mulattoes in that census gives a skewed profile of the population. Thus, we can turn to a sample. Of 1,036 baptisms of slaves and free blacks in St. Louis Church listed in the register between February 1744 and July 1750, only 38 are listed as being of mixed African-European birth, about 4 percent, even lower than the standard estimate for the other North American slave societies of about 8 percent (see table 10).[99] Race mixture occurred and for some individuals it might lead to freedom, but neither was particularly true of French New Orleans.

This point requires emphasis: the commitment of the French to keep their supposed "race" pure was carried to great lengths, most successfully in the mother country itself. The crown began trying to keep blacks from the colonies out of France as early as 1698, when Louis XIV threatened to free automatically any slave sent to France from the islands.[100] He clarified his purpose in 1707 by explaining that this rule would discourage masters from bringing blacks to France, except those whom they knew to be so well behaved and loyal that they would not try to claim the privilege of emancipation the king promised to those on French soil.[101] Under the regent, however, the rule was somewhat modified in 1716, when it was decreed that while a master could bring a slave to France, if he did so without permission from local authority, or gave a slave permission to marry in France, he would be punished by the emancipation of the slave in France.[102] In 1738, the crown inexplicably annulled the clause forbidding marriage but strictly limited to three years the sojourn in France of any colonial slave.[103] This was apparently ineffective, for in 1763 colonial administrators were ordered to prohibit any slave from traveling to France, specifically because it was leading to "mixed blood" in France.[104] Free

TABLE 10

BAPTISMS OF BLACKS AND INDIANS IN ST. LOUIS CHURCH, 1744–50, BY RACIAL CLASSIFICATION (N = 1,036)

Classification	N	%
Slave Negroes	969	93.5
Slave mulattoes	29	2.8
Free Negroes	17	1.6
Free mulattoes	9	0.9
Slave Indians and métis	12	1.2
Total	1,036	100.0

mulattoes adopted the names of their fathers and disrupted whites' successions of estate.[105] A good example of the problem is afforded by the retirement
of Ordonnateur Edmé Salmon. When he and his wife sailed to France in 1745,
they took with them five slaves: Negroes Dominique, Marquise, and Marie-
Louise, and Indians Charlotte and Padouka.[106] Thus, the campaign was continued under Louis XVI, and much more decisively. The king's council reviewed
the situation and decided that it was out of hand. Colonists exploited the
privilege of having a favored slave trained in a trade or religiously instructed in
France simply to bring them to the mother country to use as domestic servants. The result was that there were too many of them, especially in Paris, and
that this meant "the inconvenience of the mixture of colors."[107] The resulting
decree by the king in 1777 that no people of color were to enter the kingdom
henceforth was dressed up in the bare-faced rationalization that it was to protect the *colonists* and the *slaves:* for when slaves returned to America from France,
"they carried back [a] spirit of independence and disobedience [*indocilité*] and
became more miserable than useful."[108]

It is clear from the background documentation and subsidiary decrees
that the main object was to keep France white. The advice of the legislative
committee to the king was to expel all colored people who were already in
France because "they corrupt the population [i.e., its color] and manners."[109]
Blacks of any status were forbidden to marry without express authorization, in
order that the realm be "purged of a pernicious germ."[110] When some blacks
sought to confound the decree by marrying whites so they could stay in France,
the crown responded with a thundering decree that any white person who
married a black would be deported to the colonies with the offending Negro.[111] The Louisiana Code Noir provisions that aimed to prevent miscegenation were part of an all-embracing national policy, and any notion that somehow
the French were culturally more predisposed to soften or cross the color line
than, say, the English, is utterly insupportable.

In contrast to the French islands, where the distribution of the sexes
among whites was so unequal that interracial marriage sometimes occurred,
no interracial marriage is recorded in the sacramental records of French New
Orleans. No master was ever called to account before the Superior Council for
interracial concubinage.[112] This is not to argue that race mixture did not occur, for it occurred in all colonies. It is to argue that mixture between white
colonists and blacks was not exceptionally high in New Orleans and that race
relations were not more relaxed than they were elsewhere. Only 443 blacks of

mixed ancestry were counted in the entire province of Louisiana shortly after the Spanish took over, again, only 4 percent of the total population (although blacks were undercounted), and most of these mulattoes were slaves, probably the issue of rapes of black women or of fleeting liaisons of convenience with them by unmarried soldiers, other poor white men, and masters.[113] The oft-repeated assertion that interracial concubinage or marriage was typical or acceptable behavior in early New Orleans is erroneous.[114]

In sum, the Code Noir's main effect was to guide judges in the rules of transferring slaves as chattels. The crown did absolutely nothing to enforce the provisions that might have moderated masters' treatment of slaves. The crown's highest colonial officials also did nothing, except when the interests of two planters conflicted. Thus, French law did not impose any distinctive degree of unity on French slave societies.

As for the clergy, they definitely had more resources (priests and nuns) to Christianize slaves in New Orleans than the clergy in the Antilles, but it is not clear that they did so. In his excellent discussion of African religion in the New World, Albert Raboteau shows that African cultural survival had its greatest success in those areas where the transatlantic slave trade brought the most slaves and where the slave trade persisted deep into the nineteenth century. Thus, voudou played an important role in Haiti by the end of the eighteenth century, santeria in Cuba, candomblé in Brazil.[115] People in the United States have always associated "voodoo" with Louisiana, but this practice was not introduced before the second decade of the nineteenth century, although it may have been introduced in Pointe Coupée by the end of the eighteenth century.[116] As discussed in a later chapter, there is indirect evidence in the police code of 1778 that planters campaigned against the practice of African rites, and the ban on slave imports from the islands was definitely motivated in part by the belief that voudou was practiced there: Macandal was condemned in part for a blasphemous use of blessed Christian objects for magical purposes.[117] But the rest of the record is silent, except that a majority of blacks appearing in the courtroom in New Orleans by about 1750 were baptized Catholics: it appears that most slaves shared with the colonists at least a superficial identification with Catholicism by then. Certainly it is true that all New Orleans slaves were given Christian names (which they sometimes combined with African names), whereas in Saint Domingue fantasy names, those borrowed from pagan antiquity, diminutives, and other non-Christian, degrading names were more common.[118] This indicates that Louisiana clergy may have had more success in stamping out African religion than they did in the islands, but, again, as noted earlier, slaves were the main agents, for their own reasons, in the creation of African-American religion in the quarter. By the end of the colonial period, religion in New Orleans was nominally Catholic, modified to various degrees by both Europeans and Africans.[119] This mark of extreme acculturation is another explanation for the lack of slave rebelliousness in the creole generations of the French regime.

New Orleans appears to have provided a less brutal regime for slaves in the middle of the eighteenth century than that of Saint Domingue. But the laws themselves explain nothing and the evidence of work regimes is not very helpful: if families were more stable and customary liberties more common this was because of the intimate scale of New Orleans, the local commitment and relative security of the planter class, and the lack of a regular and bountiful supply of slaves from Africa. Perhaps it goes too far to argue that the settlers were able to "incorporate the African population within the dominant value structure."[120] Yet there was no Macandal and the decades of dread experienced by whites in Saint Domingue. The two societies shared all the basic characteristics of a slave society, but beyond that they were so different that it is simply impossible to isolate anything about them that was distinctively "French," "Catholic," "Caribbean" or culturally distinctive by any meaningful definition.

The final proof of the striking difference between these two "French" slave societies came in the 1790s. By 1760, the planters of Saint Domingue were frightened of their slaves and could never "sleep on both ears," as the French say. As the population of blacks swelled relentlessly over the next three decades, it became increasingly likely that any demonstration of weakness by metropolitan authorities would put the planters at great risk. And so it happened. When radical abolitionism came to the fore in Paris, Saint Domingue exploded in 1791, and twelve years later the last whites were driven from the colony or killed. Aside from very minor disturbances, the planters of colonial New Orleans never faced a serious threat of major slave revolt after 1731. After Périer's administration, no slave was ever again burned at the stake, like Macandal, in New Orleans.[121] Unlike the planters in the Antilles, those of New Orleans did not yearn to take their profits home to squander them in high style in France, hoping never to return to the New World. Land and opportunity were unlimited in Louisiana, and besides, planters there did not make fabulous profits to take to France in the early days, so they thought of

New Orleans as their home. The low rate of absenteeism, combined with a demographic profile in which the planters were not vastly outnumbered, meant that New Orleans looked quite unfamiliar to visitors from the islands. At the most basic level, social relations were similar in all slave societies, but New Orleans had its own historical web of events and traditions that made it quite distinctive from both the Antilles and other North American slave societies. So it had a unique political history, to which we now turn.

PART II.
THE SPANISH REGIME,
1769–1803

The Cession to Spain, the Insurrection of 1768, the Visitation of Alejandro O'Reilly, and the Reconsolidation of the Planter Class, 1769–1803

6

Its inhabitants enjoy robust health, are generally well built, agile, strong, and of a rare penetration. . . . Industry and agriculture have reached a point little known in America.

—Martín Navarro on Louisiana, c. 1785

[The Louisianians] have attained a state of opulence never before so soon acquired in any new country. And this was effected under all the discouragements of an indolent and rapacious government.

—Gilbert Imlay, 1792

Here indeed the banks of the river have a beautiful appearance, elegant houses encompassed by orange groves, sugar plantations, fine gardens, shady avenues, and the river covered with multitudes of market boats rowing, some up and others down, all tend to enliven the views of the passenger, and form a scene truly delightful.

—Anonymous observer approaching New Orleans
on the Mississippi River, 1799

In the series of bargains that made up the Treaty of Paris in 1763, Louis XV finalized his gift of Louisiana to Charles III of Spain.[1] After the fall of Montreal in 1760, the French crown saw Louisiana as an expensive liability and used it as a pawn to induce the Spanish to join in the war against England in 1762. While Charles III was not at all sure he really wanted the colony, it was clear that Louis would abandon it, and Charles knew he must take it to prevent it from falling into the hands of Britain: it was potentially the gateway to Mexico for the Anglo-American colonists. So Charles III accepted the gift but was unable actually to take it over for several years because of disturbances in his own kingdom and in other colonies. He sent a hapless governor, Antonio Ulloa, who co-ruled with a French army captain, but the colonists were understandably indignant and never gave Ulloa a chance.[2] He did not challenge what were by war's end in 1763 de facto local rules of free trade, adopted by necessity during the long years of war; moreover, he encouraged immigration to the colony, especially by Acadians and Canary Islanders.[3] But Ulloa made several faux pas on the social scene, the soldiers he awaited to shore up his dignity never arrived, and he was always strapped for money.

Then, in 1768, as part of a larger plan to modernize his empire by declaring free trade within it, Charles III decreed a commercial regulation for Louisiana that would impede or terminate its trade with ports outside the Spanish domain. As a result, a powerful faction of planters headed by Attorney General Nicolas de Lafrénière organized a mass demonstration in New Orleans by thousands of colonists from several parishes who frightened Ulloa into taking ship for Spain.[4] It should be emphasized that this revolt occurred not because Ulloa had ruined the colony: it was prosperous, and the regulation appeared to threaten that prosperity.[5] The rebels desperately sought the protection of Louis XV or even England's George III, discreetly pondered the possibility of declaring a republic, and enjoyed about ten months of quasi-independence.[6]

In response to the revolt, Charles III sent General Alejandro O'Reilly with a large flotilla to New Orleans in the late summer of 1769. One of the many Irish gentlemen who soldiered for Spain, O'Reilly was a dedicated imperialist who had recently participated in a royal team charged with the reformation of Cuba. Backed up by over two thousand soldiers, he arrested all the head conspirators, tried them in secret, sequestered their estates, and shot five of them by firing squad.[7] A sixth tried to escape, was bayonetted to death by his guards and buried "with much less ceremony than used for a Negro boy."[8] O'Reilly expelled other rebel leaders and forced everyone else to sign loyalty oaths. The effect of all this was to cut down a portion of Louisiana's upper class, an unusual climax for a colonial insurrection. O'Reilly abolished the Superior Council and established a Spanish bureaucratic superstructure that ran the colony until 1803. The day-to-day affairs of New Orleans Parish were managed by the cabildo, or town council, and the town was policed by a significant portion of the large Fixed Regiment of Louisiana, composed of Hispanophones from Cuba and elsewhere.

While many colonists must have felt sadness and uncertainty in their situation, some townspeople saw the arrival of the Spanish as a personal boon. The auctions of the rebel estates and the subsequent departure from the colony of a number of the rebels' closest relatives gave other people the opportunity to buy their land and slaves. Individual men and women quietly obtained somewhat more respectable positions in New Orleans society than they might have hoped for, positions vacated by the rebels. A majority of men readily accepted places in the new militia O'Reilly organized, and the list of militia officers he appointed shows many new names.[9] Finally, O'Reilly spent a lot of pesos settling Spain's immediate accounts in the colony, which initiated a steady flow of silver into the local economy.[10]

Contributing further to their acceptance, the Spanish increased the overall number of public offices available for locals, which meant somewhat broader civic participation at the expense of real political power. The Spanish did away with the Superior Council because it had policy-making and judicial powers that were unknown in Spanish America, and because it had been the center of the rebellion. In its place, they established an *ayuntamiento* (cabildo) to administer New Orleans; they also set up a separate, decentralized court system. Destruction of the Superior Council meant that the individuals of the ruling class could not join together and concentrate their power in one major body.[11] The responsibilities of local officials in Spanish towns were minimal. The cabildo brought local leaders squarely under the governor's thumb by confining them to the restricted dignity and initiative of mere *regidores* who had no part in colonial policy.[12] On the other hand, O'Reilly somewhat compensated colonists of the ruling class when he increased available military honors in both the militia and the Fixed Regiment of Louisiana, which included loyal locals as adjunct officers.[13] Above all, he signaled his commitment to maintain the slaveowners' regime intact by immediately publishing a decree ("nothing being more essential for good order") to confirm the Code Noir. Except in minor details, where Spanish law or policy overrode this code, it remained the pillar of the social structure throughout the Spanish period.[14]

While the town was superficially Hispanicized by O'Reilly and his successors, society remained composed of Francophones, white and black, who mostly rejected Spanish culture, although a few Spanish and Latin American immigrants came to settle in New Orleans. The government and ruling royal servants of the town were Spanish, and Spanish law was given precedence, but the town's basic social structure remained unchanged and its culture retained its local traditional character. For all the turmoil between 1768 and 1771, considerable continuity marked the town's history in this period.

After their humiliation and despite their lasting resentment, most colonists soon adapted to the new domination. While some reasons have been suggested here, the rapprochement was not finalized until the locals and Spanish commandants joined together against a traditional common foe during the American Revolution: in 1779–80 they attacked and won British West Florida, forcing Britain to cede both Floridas to Spain in 1783. The revolt of 1768 was not a lasting revolution like that of the Anglo-Americans, but the townspeople had succeeded in attracting the full attention of a powerful metropole. Over the following thirty-four years, a combination of authoritarian rule and liberal policies of internal development made New Orleans one of the least democratic but most rapidly growing seaports in North America.

O'Reilly's purge was effective: the town was subjected to Charles III through his local administrators after 1769. The French planter class did regain its social supremacy, however, based on internal reorganization, loyalty to Spanish kings, and alliance with the local Spanish bureaucracy. The Spanish tried in many ways to conciliate the people of New Orleans, especially by successful attempts to stimulate the economy, which greatly benefited the planters. The governors won the allegiance of some people and the acquiescence of the others, introducing Spanish institutions without trying actually to Hispanicize local culture by force. It is true that Spanish law was accorded superior authority and Spanish courts and officials deferred to it when it departed from French law, but the rich were those primarily touched by these minor changes. The male branch of the clergy was now Spanish, although the female branch remained partly French. All official documents were required to be in the Spanish language or in Spanish and translated into any other tongue. Architecture was Hispanicized beautifully on the central plaza, the result of two catastrophic fires in 1788 and 1794 that destroyed the old town center, but Spanish influence was weak beyond the plaza. In the end, New Orleans was never Hispanicized in any basic way. The ceramic plaques with the names of the "calles" in the Vieux Carré today were donated by the Franco regime in the twentieth century and are as misleading as the endless parade of "Marías" and "Santiagos" in the judicial records: the streets were not called "calles" by most townsfolk and they addressed one another as Marie or Jacques, Spanish officials spoke French, and only some educated people learned more than a few words of their rulers' language. The first newspaper, established toward the end of the Spanish period under official sponsorship, was in French. Relatively few Spanish immigrants settled in New Orleans. Thus the light glaze of Spanish culture did not cause unpleasantness after the initial tragedy of 1769. Equally important, Spain had a highly capable body of colonial administrators, and the men who came to rule Louisiana were diplomatic, even ingratiating, adapting to local conditions and needs: they tended to identify with and vigorously defend the colonists' interests. Several Spanish governors and other officials facilitated the adaptive process by marrying local women and knitting the Spanish minority into the majority population.[15] The result demonstrates the great adaptive capacity of a slaveholding class under favorable economic conditions and competent administration, despite adverse historic and ethnic factors.

The planters' institutional means to knit themselves back together into an integrated and stable class after O'Reilly's visitation have been studied in

Fig. 5. Madame John's Legacy, 632 Dumaine Street. Built in 1788 by an American builder, Robert Jones, for a Spanish officer, Manuel Lanzos, it is constructed, nevertheless, in the French style typical of New Orleans houses throughout the city's early history. Photograph taken in the early twentieth century, courtesy of the Historic New Orleans Collection.

some detail. The cabildo acquired an impressive lists of responsibilities that effectively chart the transformation of the town into a city by 1803. Especially because of its control of a wide range of public works and the ever more demanding police of slaves, the New Orleans cabildo had more authority than other local governments in the Spanish borderlands, where the military was gaining control in this period despite efforts of locals and crown to the contrary.[16] C. Richard Arena is willing to attribute even more power to the cabildo. He paints it as the instrument of power of the planter class, in which they had all or partial authority over local public lands, taxes, roads, and the police. They were sufficiently well organized that they were able to prevent the introduction of the royal slave code of 1789 and an intendant's attempt to tinker with the land laws in 1799.[17] If the bare facts of this description are reliable, they are not, however, situated in the imperial context. The cabildo had no authority over land as such, the vast majority of Louisiana's acres, of which the crown would dispose as it saw fit, for the regidores merely regulated spaces owned by the town. The cabildo collected license fees but no property taxes as such, except head taxes on slaves that planters paid into a fund as insurance against an individual planter's loss of a slave to criminal justice. Their regulation of roads was drudgery. The alcaldes sat as members of the cabildo, but the cabildo itself had no judicial capacity, their technical judicial authority being overridden by executive fiat. Their policing of blacks was, in fact, their main duty.[18]

The relationship between cabildo and governor (who could veto any act of the cabildo) did have a political dimension. Arena is right that after 1769 the planters had, in common with planters in every slave society, a royally patented institution where they could at least demonstrate their unity. But it was a major object of Bourbon reformers to shift the fiscal and police power from the cabildo to the intendant, and this was certainly true in New Orleans.[19] The New Orleans Cabildo had much less imposing authority than the old Superior Council, and it was much weaker than local governments in neighboring English colonies, where planters also had legislatures in which to organize, and far weaker by any measure when compared to a true municipal council like those of the United States. Despite these limitations, however, the planters were sufficiently united for basic purposes.

The general did not disrupt local legal tradition with his so-called Code O'Reilly.[20] The rule of thumb was that French private law not explicitly countermanded by this code was allowed to stand. O'Reilly's code was a general distillation of laws perfectly familiar to anyone from Bourbon France or Bourbon Spain. It is true that the planters were ignorant of Spanish procedure, which dragged some of them into ruinous litigation.[21] In general, however, judges did not refer to a single, true unified code of law in the modern sense, which baffles legal historians. As Thomas Jefferson was informed by experts in 1803, "No correct code can possibly be procured; excepting only for a few ordinances promulgated by order of General O'Reilly, respecting principally the laws of inheritance and rights of dower."[22] In actual judicial practice, both Spanish authorities in New Orleans and post commandants in the hinterland were permitted to exercise a large degree of latitude in deciding all but the most serious causes: the Spanish were far less literal-minded about sticking to codes than are some historians.[23]

The Spanish colonial judicial system has been the subject of much speculation and debate since the eighteenth century concerning the "black legend" about Spanish injustice. The legend was inspired among French and English speakers because of the absolutist Bourbon regime in Madrid, the existence of the Spanish Inquisition long into the eighteenth century, and Jenkin's ear of 1739 and the war it caused. Yet it was not merely a legend; there was some foundation to the belief that Spanish justice was typified by courts without juries and jails in which prisoners rotted.[24] And when it came to politics, there was no comparison: the rebels of 1768 were treated far more harshly than the Bostonians who drove Francis Bernard out of town.

The evidence from New Orleans court records during the Spanish regime is mixed. Certainly the Spanish never conducted another secret "bloody assize" in New Orleans.[25] But the records do give the strong impression that justice was expensive. The courts continued local tradition by providing the equivalent of a public defender, and *assessors* attached to the courts were supposed to counsel both sides with impartiality. On the other hand, O'Reilly introduced the Spanish practice of permitting selected independent attorneys to practice and collect fees according to an official tariff, a change from the French period, when the only attorneys allowed were administration officials.[26] The Spanish also introduced a system of judicial appeals to courts in Havana and Madrid that the colonists employed, sometimes to their advantage but always at great expense.[27]

The whole judicial system was decentralized by comparison to the old Superior Council. There were separate judges for town and hinterland beyond New Orleans, and a variety of judges in the town gave colonists a choice, in some cases, of resorting to the courts of the *alcaldes* or that of the governor.[28] As for criminal executions, although the Spanish still employed torture, it was rarely ordered in New Orleans.[29] Conditions in jails are hard to determine. Jailers were poorly paid and probably sought to squeeze as much money from prisoners or prisoners' masters as they could.[30] In summary, the groaning descriptions of Spanish law by American officials who arrived in 1803 were based mostly on conditions that developed in New Orleans at the very end of the period, when government did indeed become rotten with the love of gold.[31] The colonists probably resented the imposition of Spanish law, but not much because of its basic similarity to French law. The same may be said of French and Spanish land tenure systems, which differed in only minor respects.[32]

Hispanicization of the religious establishment was not provocative.[33] The French male clergy were replaced by Castilians, plus a few Irish at the end of the period. Over time, Cuban nuns arrived and gained control of the Ursulines' convent under Mother Superior Antonia de Santa Monica Ramos, but enough recruits were sent out from France to keep the sisters' house bicultural.[34] Several reasons explain why none of this caused serious trouble. First, it was an obvious necessity to replace a group of men (the French priests) who would have a highly privileged access to parishioners, local administrators, and clerical superiors in France, a conduit of information that would not be in the interest of Spanish officials. Second, most planters cared little as to the national origin of priests, so long as they kept to their sphere and did not catechize slaves beyond basic ritual and crude doctrine. Third, secular authorities restrained the efforts of Father Antonio Sedella to introduce the methods of the Inquisition to denounce heretics (Protestants and Jews), scoffing libertines, and French Enlightenment books on the Index that he found in planters' homes.[35] Fourth, the generally jealous and restrictive attitude of Charles III toward the clergy was in accord with that of a majority of the planters. On the other hand, the establishment of a separate diocese in Louisiana, the arrival of a bishop in 1795, and the beautification of the visible edifice of the Church in New Orleans made the town look more important, and that could only enhance the dignity and power of the planters too.[36]

The key to the political success of the Spanish governors was their policy of economic liberalism, which greatly benefited the planters. Contrary to assertions that the Spanish depopulated the colony, at most only a few hundred left as a result of O'Reilly's repression and reorganization.[37] More than compensating for this outflow, the new governors promoted immigration that became gradually free of restrictions by the end of the Spanish regime, so that even Protestant Anglo-Americans were welcome for a time in the 1780s and 1790s. By then, the Spanish had stocked southern Louisiana with many Catholic settlers like Acadians, Canary Islanders ("Isleños"), and a few Málagans, mostly farmers and trappers who were offered generous land terms and government support.[38] These new settlers in the hinterland had their effect upon the seaport of New Orleans because they swelled both local domestic demand for European goods and the total of local production and exports.

As a result of Spanish policies, an economically expansive New Orleans grew rapidly, as indicated by the census of 1785 (see table 11), which listed 14,853 inhabitants, whereas in 1766 the town had only 6,375. This was nearly half the population of the entire colony, stretching from the Gulf to Illinois, which was 32,062.[39] The white population had nearly doubled in nineteen years, despite the outflow caused by O'Reilly's visitation, and the slave population had more than doubled. One-third of the people lived in the town center, nearly one-half in Tchoupitoulas, and the remainder scattered along the river and Bayou St. Jean. This indicates a significant decline of the Lower Coast neighborhood, previously very populous, relative to the Upper Coast neighborhood of Tchoupitoulas, now by far the most populous. The distribution of slaves was extremely uneven: they comprised only one-third of the population of the town center but four-fifths of the population of Tchoupitoulas.[40]

Fortunately, the acquisition of New Orleans coincided with the rise within

TABLE 11

CENSUS OF NEW ORLEANS, 1785

	Whites	Slaves	Free Blacks
Men	721	1,167	149
Young men	1,428	3,892	164
Boys	133	211	60
Women	772	978	158
Young women	1,275	3,080	263
Girls	104	185	113
Total	4,433	9,513	907

the Spanish empire of men who could see that state activism and a carefully limited degree of economic laissez-faire were required to end stagnation in Spanish American colonies. The English seizure of Havana in 1762 had alarmed the Spanish enough to review thoroughly their colonial policy. Charles III was deeply traditional in his guiding political philosophy but he proved daring enough to update the structure of Spain's empire. In the two decades after 1763 his colonial program created a meritocratic bureaucracy, economically feder-ated colonies, and free trade within the empire. His aims should not be mis-taken as "liberal" in the modern sense: it was a new "age of authority."[41]

In 1769, however, neither Spain nor any other imperial power had any experience in managing a large, racially polarized American society with a for-eign culture like Louisiana. The bureaucrats hoped to endear the people to Spain's rule by increasing the trade and economic prosperity of the colony, but the economy of New Orleans also raised its own special problems. In the course of the Great War for Empire, the British had come to dominate trade along the lower Mississippi River. After 1763, the boundary between English and Spanish territory ran down the middle of the Mississippi River, in which English barges could legally anchor: they could not be effectively restrained by the Spanish. Few Spanish or French vessels came to Louisiana, so the English supplied the plantations.[42]

Hoping to end this dependency on the English traders, O'Reilly actively suppressed them, but he tried to mollify the colonists by linking their port to that of nearby Havana, the largest and richest in the Caribbean. O'Reilly or-dered the Cubans to accept Louisiana's lumber, furs, indigo, cotton, corn, rice, tar, and pitch, meat and birds, although not its tobacco, which would compete with Latin American suppliers of the royal monopoly.[43] This policy could have succeeded only if O'Reilly had kept an army on twenty-four hour alert indefinitely in order to police the commerce of New Orleans. Instead, he and many of his soldiers had to leave in March 1770. He had expanded the ranks of permanent regulars stationed in the colony and reorganized the local militia, but only a permanent governor with his rank and energy could have used these forces to keep out illegal traders.

Thus, before he left, O'Reilly drove off the provisioners who had domi-nated the town's external flour trade in the 1760s, but their places were soon taken by Scottish, Welsh, Irish, and American traders with a legal right to sail up the river to the strip of English settlement on the east bank above the West Florida border.[44] O'Reilly himself opened the door to the same elements he so dramatically banished. For example, when an Irish immigrant to Philadelphia named Oliver Pollock offered O'Reilly a bargain on a cargo of Pennsylvania flour for his troops in the winter of 1769, the general rewarded him with the privilege of free trade in New Orleans and the contract for supplying the garrison.[45]

When he departed, the general left enforcement of imperial trade restrictions to an untried governor with too small a force to patrol effectively against smuggling. Anglophone traders and French colonists could meet at innumerable places either on the Gulf Coast or at the planters' very docks along the Mississippi River. Without these suppliers, the townspeople would have experienced severe shortages of merchandise. Ironically, Governor Unzaga was soon complaining that the inhabitants of the town center experienced corn and rice shortages because planters up and down the river traded so heavily with the interlopers at their own docks that they carried fewer provisions to the town market.[46] It is important to keep all of this in perspective: throughout the Western world, "smuggling" flourished in opposition to mercantilist restrictions. Nowhere was this more true than in the mother countries themselves. In Spain itself, where smuggling was "long a major Spanish industry," it "rose to new heights of efficiency" and profitability in this period.[47]

Governor Unzaga had to tolerate smuggling because it was the essential supply of the region. In such a remote place everyone was glad to see vessels flying under any flag.[48] The local Spanish troops were not only no help in suppressing illegal trade but also worked in their off hours as stevedores unloading illegal cargoes.[49] Surrounded as it was on the north and east by English territory and in the Atlantic by English naval might, the town could not get along without an outlet for its produce in the transatlantic trade that the English dominated. Although the town experienced hard times at the beginning of the Spanish domination, within a short time, according to a letter by a colonist of April 6, 1775, the local economy flourished as a result of Unzaga's involuntary leniency toward illegal trade.[50] "Never has the farmer had so much income," the planter exulted, for ships swarmed in the river to take away their produce. Planters went to the foreign vessels in pirogues and traded as they pleased.[51]

This situation at New Orleans was in one sense a reflection of the explosive rise of transatlantic commerce after 1763.[52] By 1776, the colony was importing $700,000 in goods from British traders but countering the debit with only $500,000 worth of exports in return. The planters serviced their debts to traders in Spanish silver.[53] The reason so much silver was available was that just in the years between 1776 and 1785 Spain spent the astounding sum of 48 million reales ($6 million) on the administration of Louisiana.[54]

If unable to keep the Anglophone traders out, Spanish officials tried to attract any traders who were not Anglophones. In 1776, France was granted trade privileges and the right to have commercial representatives in New Orleans with the virtual powers of consuls. For example, by the mid-1780s, France and the West Indies provided 60 percent of all legal ship arrivals via the Gulf Coast.[55] This is by no means an accurate measure of New Orleans' commerce, however, which was dominated by smugglers.[56] In fact, Spanish toleration of illegal trade resulted in a substantial improvement of the merchants' condition. In slave societies, this meant that men devoted to commerce became almost respectable, and it meant that planters who branched out into commerce had nothing to be ashamed of so long as their main pursuit was planting. By 1803, the reign of the profit motive was less restrained than ever before, and one of the most respected men in town was a man like Daniel Clark Jr., who was planter, merchant, trader, slave dealer, land speculator, manufacturer, and urban developer. Nonetheless, this should not be exaggerated. In New Orleans, as elsewhere, "individual merchants, or even merchants as a class, did not suddenly humble a once-dominant landowning elite."[57] In fact, they helped increase its income and glamour.

Thus Spanish economic policy contributed to the rapid rehabilitation of the slaveholding class of New Orleans. They were not impeded by the creoles-versus-*peninsulares* struggle that plagued other Spanish colonies, because suddenly and unmistakably the *peninsulares'* political domination was absolute in 1769. But the colonists' local cultural matrix was never seriously threatened by their rulers, and they had the secret satisfaction of their conviction that French culture was vastly superior to that of the Spanish.[58] It is true that while the fundamental social structure and cultural traditions continued in traditional patterns, certain minor Spanish innovations became more important over time. For example, some blacks took advantage of a Spanish policy to guarantee freedom purchase for slaves of unblemished character. A stream of white newcomers from the West Indies, Europe, and North America did settle in New Orleans with the approval of Spanish governors during these decades, and they helped link the planters to the wider transatlantic world. In general, however, the basic fabric of society was the same in 1803 as it had been in 1769.

Curious Europeans with inquiring minds visited Louisiana and other

North American societies after 1776, and a number of their accounts of New Orleans survive from this period, some of which are misleading.[59] One remarkable critique of slave society by an immigrant to Louisiana must be highlighted. This book, *Voyage to Louisiana, 1803–1805,* was written by an obscure Parisian named Claude-Cézar Robin, an author of tracts on the national currency and natural religion.[60] Robin went to Louisiana as an immigrant, accompanied by a son who soon died in one of the epidemics that began to plague New Orleans in the 1790s. This loss may account for some of the passion with which the Bonapartist Robin advocated the development of Louisiana in his book. The volume ended with perhaps the most advanced methodical analysis of slavery in the early nineteenth century. It was a dual study of a system of social relations and its specific manifestation in New Orleans. Since the value of *Voyage* has not been sufficiently recognized, Robin's insights, now regarded as commonplace among historians of slavery, will be quoted liberally.

Following Robin on his guided tour of the town at the end of the Spanish era, we find that however much the people gravitated to the town center for socializing and marketing, New Orleans remained at the dawn of the nineteenth century a thoroughly agricultural society, but one with a touch of elegance. Robin arrived by the back way on one of the flat-bottomed schooners that took the lakes route from the Gulf Coast. He described the handsome country houses along Bayou St. Jean as being "of the most varied form. Some built of wood, surrounded by galleries in the Chinese fashion, others built of brick are surmounted by a gallery in the Italian manner. Several have colonnades and there are among them some that would do credit to the suburbs of Paris. All of them have a garden in front. Avenues of magnificent orange trees can be seen."[61] When he arrived in the town center during a hellish storm, he found the few town houses of the rich planters and merchants and a mass of half-drowned "miserable hovels."[62] In other words, as Robin could see, the French planters, like their American counterparts in Charleston, basically regarded their great house amid the plantation family to be the natural principal residence, where the lord or lady had plenty of room for self-expression. Robin saw mostly "hovels" of the poor people who dominated the residential part of the town center.

As was true in South Carolina, Robin later discovered that the planters, "whose tables [are] always loaded," were extremely hospitable to visiting foreigners, even those somewhat below them socially. On closer view of the North

American slave societies like New Orleans, however, European gentlemen like Robin invariably were more impressed by the unbridled acquisitiveness of the colonists.[63] Europeans were glad that society was not burdened with either old regime great nobles or beggars, for the extremes of wealth and poverty that set the boundaries of society in the Old World did not exist among whites. Yet they were concerned that the colonists perhaps admired only wealth and not merit. As Robin put it, "The universal desire to acquire wealth insures that no profession is despised as long as it makes money. The baker, the tailor, the shoemaker, are prominent people. They are rich and are the equal of the most important people. But woe to the worthy man who is poor. In Louisiana one needs more courage than elsewhere to brave misfortune, but there also, hard work and good conduct are more likely to lead to success."[64] This was the same thing observers wrote about other North American communities. Compared to the Old World it was more dangerous but far more mobile and free of class restrictions for the individual with capital, and people could afford to be more generous to one another from the bounty of the land.[65] Other immigrants reported that the planters were well-informed, well-bred, and dominated mainly by the "passion . . . to develop their fields" to advance their fortunes.[66]

In this society, a man was measured "by naming the Negroes he has."[67] Those without slaves fell into a nonslaveholding class of whites, composed of small farmers, shopkeepers, and innkeepers, whose status was higher than their counterparts in the Old World. Yet they were inferior by definition as non-slaveholders: a man without Negroes could not be measured at all. To escape that lowly condition and achieve "success" meant to invest capital in slaves.[68] Despite the increase in the volume of the slave trade, impressionistic evidence suggests that the proportionate size of this group grew somewhat in the Spanish period, although a majority of whites continued to belong to the slaveholding class. Nonetheless, as Robin could see, the basic determinant of the character of this society was slavery.

As always, family formation was linked inextricably to economic success, and in the interest of success domestic relations were mostly orderly, still dominated by the moral rectitude of patriarchal authority. Most observers did not, as did the Frenchman Robin, disparage Louisiana women. Father Cyrilo de Barcelona, who was disapproving of the French priests in New Orleans, thought the townswomen were well bred. "They are more honest than in Spain, and live more in accordance with the precepts of the church," he wrote, a remarkable admission by a Spaniard.[69] Governor Unzaga praised local women as exceptionally observing of religious rites. This is hardly surprising from the social point of view, given the fact that the church was the main place where white women by their deportment and clothes reaffirmed their special status.

The great importance of the special relationship between the clergy and women in the eighteenth century is still not very well understood. The secular part of the ruling (male) class was hostile to the privileged status of the clergy if not to the clergy as such. For their part, the clergy were forced to make reasonable concessions because the tide of public opinion against their privileges was so strong, but their main strategy was to pursue the same goals as the secular slaveowners and share their hostility toward fomenters of disorder, for "most of the economic activities of clerics were concentrated in real properties," including many slaves.[70] Nonetheless, the jealousy of secular men in regard to the growth of that property meant that priests had to be shrewd in their spiritual ministrations to women.

In general, white women and children continued to enjoy a racially privileged status and laws that subjugated them to men less than in many other places. Changes did occur. For example, the worst cases of marital discord were handled not by a superior court, but by priests' arbitration in ecclesiastical court: the Spanish liked to keep the civil courts out of suits between spouses if possible. On the other hand, the king was jealous of the church and sought to restrict carefully the role of the clergy in domestic affairs: separations were their business but payment of alimony, for example, was not.[71] One case illustrates how it worked. Marguerite Meilleur had been estranged from her husband, Claude Lacoste, for six years when the hat maker liquidated his property to retire to France. With creditors buzzing nervously around this estate, Marguerite presented her own suit for dowry, community property, and six years alimony. After a long proceeding at high cost, Miró granted her only two-thirds of the eighteen hundred dollars in alimony and flatly denied her appeal for more. It would require a whole chapter to sort out the Lacostes' lives and decide whether she was fairly dealt with by the court. Most important in this case, however, was the role played by new Spanish Capuchin superior Cyrilo. His ecclesiastical court had granted her physical separation, and he must have actively guarded her, because she claimed that Lacoste threatened to spirit her from the colony and reduce her to servitude if Cyrilo was ever absent.[72] Nonetheless, the actual authority of priests in these matters and their frequency of intervention is not clear, for this court's very existence is known only from scattered indirect evidence.[73]

The Lacostes' situation suggests that women's position in marriage improved slightly because Spanish priests seem to have instituted a new vigilance in regard to domestic relations after 1769. Under French rule, the situation was the reverse: civil authorities were paternal and generous to distressed wives, but if French Capuchins offered women any outright protection, the records do not reflect it. The Spanish priests, by contrast with their French brethren, appear to have worked actively to prevent the need for state intervention. Yet this is hard to interpret: an increased clerical role made it harder for some women to escape violent men because of the reluctance of the civil courts to act. Although Marguerite did not claim to be beaten, others did. The convent of the nuns was the last refuge for battered wives, but convents could never "be regarded as genuine oases of female liberty."[74] As usual, the outsider or immigrant factor was at work: many separation cases concerned outsiders, especially Spanish couples.[75]

Other aspects of the law show how women were held in contempt. In regard to rape, O'Reilly's code distinguished between classes of women: a man who ruined a "reputable" female was to be executed, whereas the judge had complete latitude to decide the fate of one who raped an ordinary person.[76] The code set out harsh punishments (the stocks and prison) for any man who permitted the concubinage of his wife with another man, but was shamelessly silent on the subject of married males with mistresses. The masculine image was further fortified by horrendous penalties (death, cremation of the corpse, confiscation of the offender's estate) for male homosexuality, while female homosexuality was ignored.[77]

The most important change in domestic relations resulting from the Spanish takeover was an alteration in the conditions of the marriage market because immigration from France declined after 1769. That decline can neither be described with great accuracy nor explained except by a murky combination of factors, including the French distaste for Spanish rule, the greater attraction of the French West Indies to prospective immigrants, and the war between Spain and France in the 1790s. That immigration decline led to or at least facilitated two changes, the first of which was gradual and long-term, a modernizing trend toward a later age at first marriage for women and an improvement in the consensual quality of marital matches.

Fig. 6. Marie-Anne-Céleste Dragon (1777–1856) of New Orleans, c. 1795–1800. Attributed to José de Salazar. Daughter of Greek-born merchant Miguel Dragon and Marie-Françoise Chauvin Beaulieu de Montplasir, of the numerous Canadian clan of the Tchoupitoulas neighborhood, she married a Greek-born immigrant in 1799 at the age of twenty-two. She bore five children within eight years. Both mother and daughter typify the tendency of New Orleans–born women to marry European-born men. From the collection of the Louisiana State Museum.

As seen in fig. 7, the average age at first marriage for women married in New Orleans in the 1760s had been a distressingly low 15.7 years, but it rose in the 1770s to 19.5 years, and by the end of the colonial period to nearly 21 years.[78] The age at first marriage for New Orleans–born men rose as well, to an overall average of 25.7 years in the last decade of the colonial era and then to an all-time high of 28 years by 1802. Moreover, while husbands were almost always older than wives, extreme discrepancies were unusual. This can only

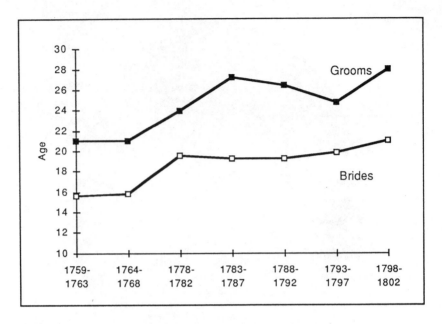

Fig. 7. Age at first marriage of brides and grooms born in New Orleans, married in St. Louis Church, 1759–1768 and 1778–1802.

have improved the basic conditions of marriage, certainly for women, because men were marrying mature adults rather than mere girls who were ill prepared for the responsibilities of wife and mother. Girls in their early teens still married, but a clear social prejudice against early marriage was in place and would become prevalent after 1803. That the marriage market was not bursting at the seams with ambitious men from France facilitated this trend.

In their quest for brides in the earlier creole generations, local men had faced a high degree of competition from men born in France in the 1760s. Competition declined after 1769, as is clear in table 12, showing the birthplaces of husbands of locally born women during the Spanish period.[79] Whereas no less than 53.4 percent of locally born women were marrying men born in France at the end of the French regime, thereafter only 27.1 percent did so. Of course, a new element was introduced in the form of a number of suitors from elsewhere in the Old World, particularly Spain, so that collectively foreign-born men still had proportionately greater appeal to local women. Moreover, Europeans' appeal was still very great for women born in other places in Louisiana and other New World colonies, as seen in table 13.[80] Of these 321 women, 193

(60 percent) married Europeans. Even if the rather anomalous Canary Islanders are removed from this "American"-born group, the proportions would be
similar. The attraction of all creole brides to European-born grooms remained
strong, even if creole men had a somewhat better chance of marrying local
women in this period. Future historians may be able to explain this attraction
more carefully, but the figures suggest that outsiders were presumed to have
more "polish" than local men, possibly better financial resources in some cases,
and were favored disproportionately by either brides, their parents, or both.

Women and children appear to have retained their leverage in the courts
in more routine matters. Widows exercised rights over their estates to a degree
unthinkable in New England, preventing their dissolution and division among
minors and perhaps even rigging evaluations in their own favor vis-à-vis outside creditors.[81] A widow's dowry, at the very least, was always protected from
creditors.[82] Henry P. Dart suggests that under Spanish laws women were
coresponsible for debts contracted by husbands alone, but a close examination
suggests that judges made decisions on an individual basis. Only if a woman

TABLE 12

BIRTHPLACES OF GROOMS OF WHITE BRIDES BORN IN NEW
ORLEANS, MARRIED IN ST. LOUIS CATHEDRAL, 1772–1803

Birthplace	N	%
New Orleans Parish	233	40.0
French North America (other)	37	6.3
Other French colonies	6	1.0
Spanish colonies	33	5.6
English colonies (U.S.)	12	2.0
New World (subtotal)	321	54.9
France	159	27.1
Spain	77	13.2
Europe (other)	28	4.8
Old World (subtotal)	264	45.1
Total	585	100.0

TABLE 13

BIRTHPLACES OF GROOMS OF WHITE BRIDES NOT BORN IN
NEW ORLEANS, MARRIED IN ST. LOUIS CATHEDRAL, 1772–1803

		Grooms						
Brides	New Orleans	French North America	French West Indies	Spanish Colonies	Anglo-America	Subtotal	Europe	Total
French North America	9	18	0	5	2	34	43	77
French West Indies	1	0	0	0	1	2	5	7
Spanish colonies	1	0	0	64	0	65	62	127
Anglo-America	3	3	0	5	2	13	11	24
Europe	4	3	0	5	2	14	72	86
Total	18	24	0	79	7	128 (40%)	193 (60%)	321

appeared to be engaged actively in managing the estate was she held to be liable. It is hard to tell how often this happened.[83] A woman whose husband squandered her dowry could protect herself by appealing to the court to prevent notaries from drawing up any contracts or instruments of indebtedness by him.[84]

Especially when her husband was out of the province on an extended trip to France, Illinois, or the islands, a woman could come into her own. Since letters by Louisiana women are rare, one written to her daughter by Catherine Edme des Rouaudières of Saint Domingue can serve to illustrate this point. She reported that her husband was to make a long business trip home in preparation for selling the plantation, "but it appeared very clearly to me to be impossible for us both to leave," so she ran the place while he was gone for years.[85] Planter absenteeism was less common in New Orleans, however, and women probably had less opportunity for management than they had in Saint Domingue. If white women married to slaveowners ran the household and sometimes acted for their husbands, their economic opportunities for gaining actual personal autonomy remained few. In France in this period, some women began to play a more dynamic role in society, dominating whole sections of the manufacturing sector, especially in the production of luxury goods; but in New Orleans and other colonies the making of clothes or wigs and the coiffing of hair was the work of slaves or free blacks.[86] Insofar as merchant capitalist values permeated the atmosphere of the local planter class, it seems that New Orleans white women were like other women in the colonial world, that is, increasingly "key instruments rather than active agents in the business and social organization of the period."[87] This was true in spite of wives' important role managing the family's household, and there was an added dimension to the subordination of slaveholding women.

Women in the domestic sphere of the household in a slave economy and society were locked into a very specific role. While required to affect for the benefit of other whites the refined femininity appropriate to a southern lady, the mistress had to be tough in command of a large domestic labor force. This central contradiction and the exaggerated concern about her chastity degraded women in a slave regime. A woman was caught in the humiliating situation of having to be at once soft and fine and the mistress of slaves, driven by special urgency because of her softness to command their respect:

> Their slow and soft demeanor, the meticulous tasks which they impose, are given in a manner of apathetic indolence, but if a slave does not obey promptly enough, if he is slow to interpret their gestures or their looks, in an instant they are armed with a formidable whip. No longer is this the arm which can hardly support a parasol, no longer is this the body that appears to be so feeble. Once she has ordered the punishment of one of these unfortunate slaves, she watches with a dry eye as she sees the victim attached to the four stakes.[88]

Luxuriating in conspicuous consumption and the lavish service of domestic slaves, women thereby committed themselves to the profoundly sexist order that coarsened them.

In one way only did the condition of women under the Spanish change. As always, white women were forced to maintain extreme vigilance against the ever-present threat that women of color might be raised to an equal status with white women, which would destroy their only compensation for the subjugation of their sex—their racial superiority. The latter was enforced by the marriage contracts of white couples, who had to prove *pureza de sangre*, meaning that their "blood" was free of that of "Moors, Jews, Mulattoes, and Indians."[89] Prospective white spouses inquired of each other's priests to certify this purity. Always essential to respectable membership in the planter class, this inquiry had been practiced less formally but no less strictly during the French domination. Against the constant threat that husbands would abandon them for more vulnerable and complaisant sex partners among blacks, white women had to maintain despotic vigilance over all social institutions to exclude women of color. The increase in the free black population and the rising incidence of interracial cohabitation and concubinage by white men with black women beginning in the 1770s was of greatest concern to white women. That behavior threatened the individual woman who had to compete with a mistress for her husband's affections, and it threatened all white women with assimilation to a "gender class" of individuals that included members of the degraded race.[90] They would thereby lose the special respect they commanded before the law, lose what customary rights they gained by their privileged color. So white women were perforce more vulnerable and more militant on the racial front in this period, although they exaggerated the real threat. To this subject we will return in later chapters.

The colonists raised their children as might be expected under these conditions. Slaveholding parents "idolized" their children, and fed them a diet rich in red meat, so that they grew up to be undisciplined, willful and domineering, whipping slaves their own age "as a pastime" or to soothe their easily wounded pride.[91] People raised their sons in "total independence," allowing them to travel freely on horseback by age ten and to marry too early by Robin's European standards. It remained true in these years that only those who were sent home to France received more than rudimentary education. In the mid-1790s a Spanish governor greeted with derision a proposal by the Spanish church to establish a seminary in New Orleans, for local boys would not study Latin.[92] The Spanish school that was opened provided an alternative but no higher education than had been offered previously. Many were educated by plantation overseers, and for this office the planter hired "the first Frenchman who comes along." Moreover, the smaller planters particularly needed their sons' assistance on the plantations.[93] Even so, no less than 140 students of all kinds, including some from other colonies, were enrolled in the Spanish school by 1794.[94] Moreover, by 1788, the French established eight private schools in town, which were reportedly attended by 400 students.[95]

Opportunities for children of nonslaveholding families to learn a specialized artisanal skill through apprenticeship remained few. A search for apprenticeship agreements in the judicial and notarial records uncovers only six white boys and one girl who were formally apprenticed during the Spanish period.[96] Even allowing for an indeterminate number of informal apprentice-ships, this is an impressive statistic, illustrating declining artisanal opportuni-ties for nonslaveholders in a slave society.

One modest Spanish legal change in the planters' control over family relations was the suppression of the legal authority of the family meeting, a peculiar French institution called by the court in the interest of a minor with his tutor or godparent presiding. In his first year as governor, Unzaga denied in his court an appeal by the Cazelard minors' tutor, who protested the low winning bid on the lease of the family plantation and demanded a family meeting early in 1771.[97] Unzaga ruled that family meetings had no place in Spanish civil law, and it was his experience that the institution "does not con-tribute to the profit of the minors, it ruins them without leaving them recourse against the relatives." It is likely that Unzaga had in mind some disastrous family meetings in the early 1760s, in which decisions were made that led to the ruin of families like the Carrières or Dubreuils. In the future, the governor ruled, a bonded curator would be appointed and have absolute power, so "the minors will know for a certainty of whom they have to demand restitution."[98] This alteration could have actually increased the personal power of planters as individual tutor/curators at the same time as it decreased the prestige of the family meeting, although the meetings were undoubtedly still held by many families without judicial sanction. It is not clear if this change helped or harmed minors. Shortly after the ruling, sixteen-year-old Pierre Cazelard sued his cu-rator for an accounting and discovered that his $4,066 estate was so encum-bered that its net value was only $235. It resembled most estates in being heavily indebted, and illustrates why it was often unwise for minors to liquidate their deceased parents' property. Yet the fact that these suits by minors against cura-tors were rare suggests that the institution of tutorship continued to operate mostly smoothly and aboveboard even without judicial sanction.

This question of patriarchal authority leads to the question of parental control of boys' and girls' choice of spouses and timing of marriage. As seen in part 1, during the French regime various indicators suggest a degree of free-dom of choice. In New Mexico at this time, Ramón A. Gutiérrez finds that a former degree of freedom was lost in the era of Charles III because of the rising worry that parents had to have substantial power to prevent children from marrying beneath their class, and especially from marrying outside their race on the impulse of "the blind passions of youth."[99] This explains the im-perial decree of 1776, the Royal Pragmatic on Marriage prohibiting the legitimation of unequal unions and insisting on parental consent for all persons below the age of twenty-five. There was nothing new about this in New Orleans except that the Spanish king not only weighed in on the side of parental authority but also for the first time specifically denied the authority of the clergy to meddle in this matter, ending a centuries-old struggle between the clergy and the crown.[100]

The major transitional institution for boys on their way to becoming men was in the local militia or, perhaps, the Fixed Regiment, where a boy's rank reflected his parents' slaveholding status. Those with the wealth to acquire and maintain a cadetship in the Fixed Regiment did so, but Governor Gálvez created the elite Distinguished Company of Carabineers Militia in 1779, which provided a special place for big slaveholders' sons, where they first acquired their military titles.[101]

On militia field days and every other day, the planters were most often preoccupied by their own highly stylized jousting with one another to gain regard as the patriarch with the most dependents. One could cock one's snoot at the town center from the opposite shore, like old Chevalier Pradel in the 1750s, but most planters preferred to live in town at regular intervals. There they appeared in their most effective roles, finely groomed, in pursuit of genteel social pastimes like gossiping over cards, and arranging with their factors about crops and supplies. The demands of running a plantation kept one fixed to that domain much of the time, but the ultimate social moments of the planters' lives occurred in the town center where they collectively asserted the solidarity so necessary to effective control of the subordinate classes. There, in public view, the planters displayed their marks of status by the tables they kept and frequented, the money they lost on bets, but above all by naming the slaves they owned.

Slaveowners could bank on a better supply of slaves after 1769, and this enlarged the horizons and standards of the patriarchs and made entry into the slaveholding class easier for some. The opportunities for those who were unconnected with the rebel leadership of 1768 were broadened because rebel property—especially slaves—was redistributed among them by O'Reilly's auctions. Yet outsiders who arrived after 1769 had the greatest opportunity to move to the top in these years of Spanish rule. All the key government posts were filled by Spanish immigrants, most of them well-bred, unmarried young men chosen for their posts because of special talents, ambition, and inconsiderable property. Most of them used their manners and ability to speak or learn

Fig. 8. Nicolas-Charles-François Favre D'Aunoy, born in New Orleans 1773, and his son, Charles-Manuel-Nicolas, born in New Orleans, 1796. Unidentified artist. The father was at this time (c. 1800) lieutenant colonel in Charles III's royal artillery corps and its commander in New Orleans. He married the seventeen-year-old Manuela-Isabel-Francisca Perez in 1794, the daughter of a Castilian and a native-born woman. The son looks very military for his tender years. From the collection of the Louisiana State Museum.

to speak French to weld themselves to the planter class. They thereby improved their property by marrying well-to-do local women and reconciled the class as a whole to the Spanish regime. A number of Spanish and French civil immigrants also arrived and found entry into the planter class. Several of the first officers permitted to buy seats in the cabildo were relatively recent arrivals, and the wills in the notarial archive show many men who arrived from Europe with no capital and acquired large estates. Andrés Almonester y Roxas arrived from Spain with O'Reilly and labored as a notary while he became one of the richest men in North America.[102] John Pope was informed that Almonester had arrived "hung with Rags that flutter'd in the Air," and had risen to a degree of wealth by the early 1790s such that he could afford anything to finance "Rascalities" or "soothe his Vanity."[103] Within this top stratum of society, then, although political power was monopolized by Spanish *peninsulares,* mobility was not only possible but also characteristic of the slaveholding class as a whole, and ethnic background was no hindrance to mobility.

A particularly good example of how it could work is that of Francisco Bouligny and Marie-Louise Dauberville. Grandson of an Italian merchant who had settled in Alicante in the early eighteenth century, Bouligny came to Louisiana with O'Reilly as a lieutenant in the Cuban forces. Thirty-three years old in 1769, he settled and was quickly promoted to the rank of captain in the fixed regiment that O'Reilly established in the colony. He also wooed and wed Marie-Louise Le Sénéchal d'Auberville (or Dauberville), daughter of a former commissaire ordonnateur of the colony. She was twenty years old and brought to her marriage the very substantial dowry of $10,800. Unfortunately, this was in merely potential form in 1770, an instrument of indebtedness by Joseph Villars Dubreuil, son of the founder who had done so much to shape the development of New Orleans. The younger Villars (as he was known) purchased the Dauberville plantation in 1758 in the grossly inflated livres of that era. Since he had never paid off the purchase price, Bouligny now convinced Governor Unzaga to bring the matter to a head. In fact, one might speculate that the marriage of Francisco and Marie-Louise may well have been founded (if not solely) on the calculated strategy to bring together a highly vulnerable dowry and a Spanish officer with no money but the kind of influence necessary to rescue the dowry.[104]

Mobility meant the possibility of downward movement as well as success, and the rise of the Boulignys meant the fall of the Villars. Besides O'Reilly's seizures of rebel estates, the most dramatic collapse of an estate in this era was that of Villars, who had fallen deeply into debt in the 1760s. In 1768 his creditors secured a writ against him, but he successfully drove the sheriff away from his plantation and somehow secured a moratorium.[105] That ended in 1771, and now when his creditors again initiated judicial seizure of his property with

Unzaga's support he again shut himself up in his house and shouted at bankruptcy commissioners that their writ was not legitimate. Unzaga then had him arrested on criminal charges.[106] Although he was not prosecuted, he was ruined, like his mother a decade earlier.

Once Villars was evicted, his holdings were auctioned off in order to create a net amount to distribute among his creditors, of whom Marie-Louise was only one. The process is not altogether clear, but somehow Francisco and Marie-Louise got the plantation. We know very little about how judicially mandated auctions were conducted. One often suspects that there is sometimes an implicit agreement among the bidders to stand off and permit deserving heirs to purchase an estate at an advantageous bid. Theoretically, the auction was supposed to produce returns according to prevailing market prices. The question is: Did members of the community behave at these auctions in any sense according to moral principle, whether a Christian or a "moral economy" principle that operated to preserve estates whole and in the established line of descent? There is some evidence that the introduction of sugar production in the 1790s made the preservation of estates more imperative than ever. The milling of cane and rendering of sugar required significant capital investment in plant, which could be neither subdivided nor shared without risk of dangerous quarreling at harvest time. So there was a strong disinclination to auction sugar plantations by lots to satisfy heirs or other creditors of estates.[107] At any rate, Francisco and Marie-Louise obtained the plantation and slaves, a lumber enterprise on the right bank. When several Villars heirs sued to recover a portion of it, Bouligny still had Unzaga in his camp, and the governor's court was where such a case was decided because of the rank of the principals. Nonetheless, Bouligny sought to mollify the heirs with a small cash payment and the right to use the canal on the plantation, which was the essential link between the forest and the sawmills by the river.[108]

Francisco and Marie-Louise went on to have many children of Italo-Hispano-Franco-American descent, to join the rank of the largest slaveholders (with eighty by 1778), and to enjoy the spectacular rise of Francisco in the bureaucracy to become lieutenant governor, commander of the Fixed Regiment of Louisiana, and finally military governor for a time following the death of Governor Gayoso in 1799. The future King Louis-Philippe of France (the duke of Orléans) visited New Orleans with his brothers the Duke of Montpensier and the Count of Beaujolais in 1799, all exiles from France on a tour of North America. Far and away the most illustrious visitors the town ever received until Lafayette arrived one quarter century later, they were fêted extravagantly. The Bouligny family was able to orchestrate what may have been the most expensive party of all, costing thousands of dollars. Here was a superb example of extraordinary social mobility and successful ethnic intermarriage.[109] As for downward mobility within the planter class, it was usually not so precipitous as Villars Dubreuil's fall. Class structure and mobility is virtually impossible to illustrate more empirically in this period, for the colonists continued to pay no property taxes, and exact records of slave distribution do not exist for the most populous neighborhoods.[110]

Ethnic jealousy did not threaten the unity of the planter class. Because the immigration from France and Spain tended to increase competition among males for the hands and dowries of local women and to contribute to inflationary pressure on slave prices, individual planters could have regarded newcomers as potentially disruptive intruders as well as potential allies and consumers. Yet the record contains no hint of hostility to outsiders on the part of New Orleanians, although ethnic remarks in private were probably uttered. Even though the population shifted from one composed of a creole majority in 1769 to one with many foreign-born settlers by 1803, ethnic antagonism focused on a few individuals whose ambition seemed inordinate, chief among them the Andalusian Almonester. He underwrote the transformation of St. Louis Church into a Cathedral and rebuilt the presbytery, introduced the first Holy Week procession, and paid for other extraordinary pious works like the hospital, in the most spectacular instance of public mindedness in New Orleans before John McDonogh endowed the public school system in the nineteenth century. By the time of his death in 1798, Almonester dominated the church, the hospital, and the militia of New Orleans, and some people did not like it.[111]

Nonslaveholding whites continued to be comparatively fewer than in the southern United States, where they formed the most numerous portion of society by 1776. Unlike their Anglo-American counterparts, these common people of New Orleans had no institutions in which to organize politically. They enjoyed a special status because of their color, presumably a slightly higher status than the laboring classes of small property in the northern seaports—but their political potential was not feared by the gentry as it was in the North on the eve of the Revolution.[112] The bourgeoisie included merchants, shopkeepers, and artisans in New Orleans, most of whom in time acquired at least a slave or two. Below them was a stratum of white overseers and contract day laborers, mostly off-duty soldiers, plus those second- or third-generation settlers who lived on farms, lacking their own slaves for a variety of reasons.

The record suggests that relations between the white classes was cordial, marked by relatively few suits for payment by artisans or purveyors. Class harmony was not perfect, however, because planters still enjoyed a privileged position that relegated nonslaveholders to second-class status. Planters carried canes, which were not merely the fashion but a necessary tool to discipline both blacks and whites. The gentlemanly use of a cane was supposed to be restricted, but the limits were open to interpretation, as in the case of two young planters named Lacoste and St. Pé. In the mood for having a party in 1768, they began their day by caning a soldier who may have resisted their plans for him, and when a wagoneer admonished them to desist they caned him badly too. When the latter pressed charges, the assailants got off with light fines.[113] Cases like this were rare, however, because planters were usually more favorable to race solidarity and nonslaveholders needed no reminding from planters of their inferior status.

As in the French period, one reason for interclass harmony was the relatively easy movement upward in status if one managed to buy slaves. The way out of the lower class was relatively open in New Orleans, although it was quick only for a man lucky at cards. The same day Lacoste and St. Pé cudgeled their social inferiors an artisan named Henri Roche sued a planter for payment of a six-month loan of twenty-two thousand livres, his savings from a long career as a shoemaker, enough money to propel himself into the ranks of the ruling class, a sum he was ill advised to put in the hands of a planter. Perhaps he had no confidence in his ability to manage slaves himself.[114]

Evidence from the criminal record shows that nonslaveholders' privileged position as whites in a labor-starved slave economy ensured their economic security. Imprisonments of whites for debts or crimes against property were unusual. A rare entry and exit record by the jailer in the late 1790s shows that few white men other than soldiers turned up in jail. In January, 1797, thirty-eight soldiers were jailed plus a male slave, a Choctaw Indian, and a Spanish-surnamed civilian, virtually all for disorderly behavior. For the entire year, only fourteen white civilians were jailed.[115]

The Spanish judicial record includes two hundred cases in the civil courts that originated in, or at least involved residents, of New Orleans, summarized in table 14. As might be expected, even though whites were a racial minority, they dominated the formal criminal record because slaves were seldom prosecuted in courts for major crimes. Defendants were white in two-thirds of the cases, although whites made up less than one-third of the population. Some broad generalizations can be ventured on the basis of the following chart. First, prosecutions for crimes against property represented less than one fourth of the total: most were crimes of violence. Second, although non-French outsiders were a minority of the white population, defendants were outsiders in over half the cases. Third, although it is not indicated in the chart, capital punishment of whites was extremely rare: of five judicial executions for the entire period none involved the local French colonists.[116] Most sentences of imprisonment and hard labor also were meted out to members of groups other than the local French. Only one sentence of whipping of a white civilian is recorded, that of a Mexican former convict from Los Angeles found guilty of

TABLE 14

CRIMINAL PROSECUTIONS IN NEW ORLEANS
UNDER THE SPANISH REGIME, 1769–1803

	Murder	Assault	Theft	Libel	Disorder	Other
Whites						
French	6	14	11	16	5	7
English	0	4	4	6	1	2
Spanish	4	15	7	7	11	1
Other	2	1	4	1	0	2
Subtotal	12	34	26	30	17	12
Blacks						
Slaves	13	2	18	1	0	8
Free blacks	0	10	10	0	0	7
Total	25	46	54	31	17	27

SOURCE: Based on the summary by Derek N. Kerr, "Petty Felony, Slave Defiance and Frontier Villainy: Crime and Criminal Justice in Spanish Louisiana, 1770–1803" (Ph.D. diss., Tulane University, 1983), 317–61.

theft in New Orleans.[117] Even when a free man and a slave were equal partners in crime, whipping was reserved to the slave and some less degrading punishment for the free culprit.[118]

As in the period of the French regime, colonists were almost never charged with theft of goods, and this bears out the thesis that they usually had too good an opportunity to exploit the labor of others or profit from their own labor to risk engaging in petty illegal activity. Most of the cases listed for them under "theft" actually involved some kind of fraud like misrepresenting goods, forgery, or attempting to enslave free blacks. The theft of money and goods was almost the exclusive preserve of the outsiders and slaves.

As in the period of the French regime, slander (usually called "libel") was the most prosecuted crime of white colonists. A few cases involved the professional reputations of artisans. Barrelmakers Louis Delagrouet and Baptiste Jourdain sued one of their patrons, Charles Chabot, for berating them as rogues even after they promised to agree to his demand that they not permit slaves to deliver his barrels because they "would break the braces with sticks" according to Chabot.[119] The defendant was forced to apologize and sign a statement of recantation. Pastrymaker René Chouteau was angry when Bernard Chiloc, previously a carter, went into pastry making too. Chouteau publicly announced that a Negress on the levee had confided to him that Chiloc's pastry was poisoned, which harmed Chiloc's reputation.[120] There was a substantial upsurge in these kinds of cases at the end of the Spanish regime: three fourths of all slander cases derived from the decade after the outbreak of war between France and Spain in 1793. Some of these may have derived from ethnic jealousies, but most appear to have involved the honor of men arising from personality not from ethnicity.[121] A handful of exceptional cases involved the moral reputation of women.[122]

If there was any change in crime rates during the Spanish period, it was caused by the influx of free white propertyless newcomers. This phenomenon is obscure because the largest group of these people, the "Cuban" troops, were disciplined in military courts and little is known of them. Reports by the governor commandants to their captains general in Havana reveal that they sent a few soldiers home on account of serious transgressions, but there were no major incidents in New Orleans social life relating to men or officers of the garrison. There was no Major Membrède to terrorize the citizenry because no Spanish governor would dream of sharing authority with such a man. The soldiers did represent a crucial element in favor of whites in the racial balance of power, and they do not appear to have been substantially intrusive on the patterns of everyday civilian life.

Most impressive is the degree to which Spanish men dominated the criminal record. Fully one-third of all defendants had Spanish surnames, even though they constituted a small part of the town's civilian population. The explanation for this disproportion is that most Spaniards were marginal men, except for the select handful of crown servants, who soon entered the ranks of the slaveholders. Because of their frustrations as economically vulnerable outsiders in a settled slaveholding society and their more personal motives, ordinary Spaniards were most likely to commit crimes of violence, especially upon one another. Next to slaves they were most likely to be sentenced to incarceration. When the petty crimes of soldiers are added in, the New Orleans French resident by 1803 was likely to regard the Spanish as an element comprising a few dedicated Castilian gentlemen, plus a rabble of Catalans and soldiers. But to all appearances, locals neither disliked nor quarreled with Spaniards, appearing to have nothing against Spaniards as such.[123]

Since quarrels of a personal nature were unusual among the planters, trouble between them usually concerned debts, but even in many of these cases one discovers that what commonly troubled their relations was the behavior of their slaves. One judicial case that serves as a general guide to the structure of the slave regime is that of *Charles-Joseph Loppinot v Jean Villeneuve* for recovery of the value of a slave in 1774. Loppinot had a mulatto slave named Mulet, a talented blacksmith, mason, cooper, and roofer about forty-five years old, whom he allowed to hire out to Villeneuve. Mulet constructed a chimney for Villeneuve on his day off, Sunday. When he was finished, Villeneuve allowed him to dine and entertain himself on the plantation until midnight. When Mulet headed home, alone, he drowned in the river. Loppinot charged that it was Villeneuve's responsibility for "guarding imprudently" a slave he employed on the day of rest and treated to brandy. Villeneuve denied making Mulet drunk and was contemptuous of the notion that Mulet should have had a pass to work and should not have worked on Sunday. Slaves were routinely permitted to hire out without passes on any days the courts were closed and employers were not liable for damages to slaves who performed casual labor. Villeneuve had no trouble lining up planters to attest to this customary state of affairs, and Unzaga denied Loppinot's petition. Loppinot exhausted the entire appeals process, which ultimately cost him more than the value of Mulet.[124]

The case of Mulet reveals much. At bottom was the strong competition among planters for the quasi-free labor of slaves in their free time and the strife it could inspire.[125] Whatever may have been Loppinot's policy on hiring out, his capital loss was total, and Mulet would not have drowned if he had not worked for Villeneuve, so it seemed perfectly logical to Loppinot that the latter had been imprudent. If Mulet had been an ox, Villeneuve would have had to pay. Mulet was a man, however, and on his free time was expected to act like a rational, free man, making wages "to clothe himself" and guarding against being drowned. In fact, the ultimate beauty of this logic and the reason that the case was so hotly contested, was that it was really nobody's fault that Mulet drowned. As his peers would have agreed with the judges, Loppinot was just unlucky. These things happened. Negroes could be careless of their lives, especially those who were treated to brandy after a seven-day week.

As this case illustrates, it was the contest among white male gentlemen to control slave laborers that caused the most trouble among them, found in disputed estate successions, in cases concerning the hiring of runaways, in suits for damage to slaves legitimately hired out like Mulet. These records give the impression that it was a constant chore for masters not only to maintain vigilance against willful action by their slaves but also to make sure other planters did not appropriate illicitly or exploit excessively the labor of their slaves. Despite these contests of will, the slaveowners effectively regrouped and maintained the solidarity of their class after the disaster of 1769.

O'Reilly's purge did not set the stage for an amicable development of political life after 1769, but external and internal pressures soon created a climate in which the slaveholding class was closely allied with the small Spanish bureaucracy that governed the colony. The cabildo was primarily a municipal council with little political impact on the colony as a whole and no judicial function, but it gave the slaveholding class an important symbol of its corporate identity nonetheless. The Spanish officials appointed to serve in New Orleans were generally dedicated and competent, at least until 1799, when the administration became incompetent and corrupt. The Spanish promoted immigration to the colony, strengthened its defenses, promoted legitimate trade and tolerated a large degree of illicit trade, and generally contributed significantly to the colony's growth and prosperity.[126] War with Britain between 1779 and 1783 gave the colonists and their governors the opportunity to seize control of the Gulf Coast under the command of Governor Bernardo Gálvez.[127] The war also led to two decades of tension between the Spanish government and the United States about American navigation of the Mississippi River, which convinced the people of New Orleans that in the absence of Spanish protection they would be overrun by half-wild "Kaintucks."[128] The rapprochement between colonists and rulers was a little strained when Spain declared war on the French Republic in the 1790s. A relatively small degree of political sympathy with revolutionary France was briefly expressed by some, especially merchants in hopes of improving their commercial freedom. But the alliance of the colonists and their Spanish rulers held together because slaveowners were deeply impressed that the Haitian Revolution and slave unrest in Louisiana threatened their regime.[129] Above all, a few refugees from Saint Domingue arrived in the town in the early 1790s and frightened the colonists with stories of slaves' bloody revenge in the French colony, convincing slaveholders in Louisiana that a secure regime headed by white Spaniards was better than the possibility of a black regime. As always, the main source of public disorder in New Orleans lay not in ethnic antagonism or quarrels between planters, and not in any clash between the nonslaveholders and the slaveholders the former hoped to emulate: disorder continued to arise mainly from relations between masters and the slaves who resisted their domination.

Blacks, the Slave Trade, and the Advent of Sugar, 1769–1803 7

To the best of their ability they try to do each other as much good as they can.

—Claude-Cézar Robin on the black community, 1803

The advent of Spanish administration meant a strange and disruptive combination of new circumstances for New Orleans blacks. On one hand, it marked the introduction of an unprecedented legal right of a small number of slaves to free themselves. But it also meant the increase of the African slave trade and the disruption of the heavily creolized black community by Africans. In addition, in the last decade of the period the majority of planters switched from the production of indigo to that of sugar, increasing local demand for more slaves to make higher profits than the planters had ever known. These were the two major changes in the "Spanish" period: the increase of the slave supply and the intensification of profit making. Except for a moratorium on the slave trade between 1795 and 1800, many new slaves poured into the province, and the problems of assimilating these Africans into the slave community must have been numerous. Basic conditions of life for most slaves may have declined during the Spanish period because of the slave trade.

Certainly our outside observer, Claude-Cézar Robin, in the final chapters of his *Voyage*, thought slavery was harsh in New Orleans at the end of the Spanish period. He offered an extended critique of the institution based on his observations there. He described how slavery rendered society economically dysfunctional and coarsened the personalities of individuals. The "deep gulf between the two colors," regarded by local whites as an absolute necessity, was "certainly the greatest scourge of the colonies" because it impeded the natural development of commercial capitalism.[1] Slavery accorded the highest social status to the absolute plantation lord with aristocratic values. Since color and class rather than ability determined status, "from the lack of the competitive spirit on all sides proceeds the indolence and the lack of progress in their agriculture." Planters enjoyed an enviable life-style, but "aside from conviviality, they scarcely care for anything but ephemeral luxuries."[2] Slavery degraded the master along with the slave. The constant battle to overcome the slaves' resistance not only dissipated planters' intellectual faculties but also led them to be slaves to their emotions, to "play heavily" by gambling extravagantly or compulsively, to neglect education and religion. All of this was intensified as the New Orleans population swelled with new arrivals from Africa and planters enjoyed rising profits in an expansive economy but faced resistance from more and more slaves. Much of this seems familiar to anyone who has read the work of Kenneth Stampp or other recent historians, but it was an unusually perceptive analysis for Robin's time.

The typical plantation work rhythm reported by Robin accords well with what is known of it in many colonies outside the West Indies. Slaves worked six days a week governed by "a Negro foreman or a white overseer, or most commonly, by the proprietor himself," who strode among them with a whip.[3] Those guilty of special offenses, men or women, were spreadeagled and tied down for up to one hundred consecutive lashes with a coach whip, the master perhaps badgering the whipper to lay it on well. Robin implied that some kind of corporal discipline was unavoidable because of the slaves' low-grade but never-ending and partly effective resistance to the regime.[4] Conditions varied: there were "numerous plantations where the Negroes [were] tolerably well-treated," but at least some planters scoffed at the Code Noir and went so far as to give slaves only unground corn to eat, so their off hours were filled with procuring and preparing food.[5]

Most of the planters would not have agreed with Robin's criticism, and the Spanish official Francisco Bouligny expressed their views well. Offering a comparative framework with Cuba in mind, he praised the local slave regime as more humane. He agreed that most planters gave slaves only one barrel of corn each month but emphasized that they were allowed to keep their own fields and domestic animals to raise money for clothes and food. He believed that they were of robust health by comparison to slaves in Cuba. In the winter they worked only four or five hours in the morning and again in the afternoon, and in the summer the whole of the hot midday hours from eleven to three o'clock were a rest period.[6]

To understand fully how much more sophisticated Robin's critique was, one must keep in mind that when he visited New Orleans the racist reaction to the age of democratic revolution was in full swing. In the first years of the nineteenth century, Bonapartist France was in the throes of that reaction and the hope of reenslaving the French West Indies. The dominant view in France and among French colonists was expressed crudely by a former Louisiana planter, Louis-Narcisse Baudry des Lozières, in a full-blown proslavery argument countering Robin point for point. Slavery in the Americas was better than barbarism in Africa, Baudry argued, and egalitarian ideology led to a bloodbath in the islands. As for the slaves of Louisiana, they were "the most content of their kind."[7] Besides, whites absolutely could not work in that climate, a timeworn "fact" Robin assailed by pointing to the many white non-slaveholders (like the Acadians or Isleños) who did toil in the Louisiana sun.

The control of slaves mainly involved the everyday humiliation of less-than-severe public whipping, use of the pillory and various restraints, and denial of privileges by masters, overseers, drivers, or judges. No historian has been able to measure these things quantitatively with any accuracy for comparative purposes. The sentences handed out by Spanish courts perhaps reflect the standards applied by masters. Julie received two hundred lashes and then had to stand in the pillory for two hours each day for eight days for trying to poison her mistress with powdered glass in 1785. This kind of punishment broke the spirit of almost any human being. Alexandre got three hundred lashes for slandering his master. Jean-Baptiste received two hundred lashes and six months in prison for trying to steal a hat. Demba received a sentence of thirty lashes, labor in chains for five years, and banishment, for breaking and entering.[8]

The treatment of slaves is also revealed in cases in which a slaveowner sued a third party for injuring a slave. They ranged from the trivial, like Basilio Ximenes's demand that François Broutin follow custom and shoot his dog because it bit one of Ximenes's slaves, to much more serious cases. Jacques Porte sent fifteen-year-old slave Charles to claim lumber from a neighbor, François Delery, who owed it to repair fences ruined by Delery's stock. Delery beat up Charles, incurring forty dollars in doctors' bills that Porte wanted covered. Alexandre Bienvenu recovered the value of Baco when another planter's overseer and driver whipped him to death; Bienvenu pressed charges and got them sentenced to hang too, a highly unusual case.[9] Unfortunately, these records tell us less about slaves than about slaveholders, who were always more concerned about the value of the slave than about the slave's suffering.

Slave treatment hardened during the Spanish regime not because of some condition impossible to measure like the number of beatings, but because Spanish imperial policies fed rising profits. The main problem for Spanish colonists at the beginning of the post-1763 era was the feeble development of the mother country's slave trade: Spain had no supply stations in Africa. Moreover, it was a strategic policy of the English and Anglo-Americans to control the slave trade to the Spanish colonists, who bought about half a million new African slaves in the eighteenth century. The trade was valued by interlopers both for the sake of its profits and because it provided cover for the illegal sale of other commodities.[10] To remedy the basic weakness of his empire's economy, Charles III had a complex and ambitious plan to extend slave society throughout his underdeveloped colonies. Thus, he gradually removed virtually all barriers to the importation of African slaves into places like Louisiana and Cuba, both of which became important sugar colonies based on the labor of black slaves. When sugar production collapsed in Saint Domingue in the 1790s, New Orleans planters discovered that they could make the crop not just commercially feasible but fabulously profitable there, and overnight many abandoned indigo, which was threatened by a pest anyway, and switched to sugar. This was facilitated by the increased supply of Africans to the colonies over the previous years: growth of the African slave trade was the central Spanish policy reconciling the slaveholders to their rulers.

Thus in New Orleans, Spanish authorities permitted the settlers to carry local cargoes to any port in the "American islands" to buy slaves after 1777.[11] The Spanish governors usually could not hope to convince large licensed European slaving companies to venture to the distant town of New Orleans, even though the port was exempt from duties on slaves. Companies preferred safe harbors with sure markets like Kingston, Le Cap, or Cartagena. The few slaves brought to New Orleans were insufficient to bring down prices and in fact seemed only to drive them higher. According to one sample of bills of sale, the average price of a seasoned slave in New Orleans rose from $257 in 1771 to $561 by 1787.[12]

Estimating the slave trade to colonial New Orleans is still a numbers game, but it is time to retire Philip Curtin's old guesstimate of 28,300.[13] Employing the adjusted figure of 5,544 for the first phase of the trade (1719 to 1731), an estimated 250 for the period of 1731 to 1763, a total of 5,794 is reached for the period of the French regime down to 1766. Employing the unusually detailed censuses of 1766 and 1785 to obtain base figures, the black population of the parish of New Orleans grew from 3,971 to 10,420 in that period, or 162 percent, a remarkably high rate of growth. There is good reason to attribute a substantial portion of this increase to natural reproduction by the population of 1766. The black population of British North America became self-sustaining quite early and achieved substantial rates of natural increase in the eighteenth century.[14] There is no reason to believe that New Orleans was any different, given that its demographic profile was similar to that of the English slave societies and the community suffered no major epidemiological crises until the end of the Spanish period with only brief bouts with smallpox before that.[15] Thus a normal rate of natural increase for the English colonies has been determined for these decades, and it can be applied to New Orleans to determine the contribution of the slave trade to population growth. The result is an estimate of 3,811 Africans imported between 1763 and 1785.[16]

A remarkably liberal royal decree of 1782 lifted the import duty on slaves and granted permission to export silver to pay for them if they derived from neutral or friendly ports.[17] By the late 1780s, several New Orleans merchants were deeply involved in the reexport trade of Africans from holding stations in the West Indies.[18] These were still mostly small lots, like the cargo of twenty-seven on the *Jason* purchased in Kingston in 1783, of which seven died before they reached Louisiana, a good illustration of investors' high risks.[19]

These slaves were mostly people fresh from Africa who had been landed for refreshment in the islands but not exposed to local slaves. Since 1763, the planter class had tried to prevent the introduction of slaves who had been exposed to the slave system in Saint Domingue. It was conventional wisdom that the slaves of that colony should be avoided because they were "tired of life" and in desperation tried to kill their masters, the legacy of the Macandal conspiracy. Still, the reexport trade from the islands offered opportunities for abuses by individuals against the interest of their class. Thus Govenor Esteban Miró included in his "Decree of Good Government" of 1786 an angry denunciation of those traders who insinuated a few non-"bozal" (African) slaves into their cargoes.[20] It would appear, however, that most slaves were Africans, and the trade flourished.[21] The better-capitalized traders bought up to two hundred at a time and carried them to New Orleans on vessels like Daniel

Clark Sr.'s *New Orleans* or Jérôme Lachapelle's *El Mississippian.* At least twenty-six of these reexport merchants can be identified in the record by the early 1790s, and the town seemed to be plentifully supplied with slaves.[22] The range of origins is impressive: they were coming from all over Africa, routed through Jamaica, Martinique, and Cuba.[23]

This rosy picture for slaveholders came under a shadow in the early 1790s because of the Haitian Revolution, and slave disturbances in Louisiana itself in the first half of the 1790s led planters and royal authorities to restrict the slave trade in 1795 and to shut down the slave trade to the colony entirely in 1796 to keep out subversive elements. This policy was facilitated by the ample supply the colony had received during the previous decade.[24] Ironically, this occurred at the very moment when the transition to sugar production by New Orleans planters would boost demand for slaves higher than ever. By 1800, demand was clamorous, and although the question of reopening the slave trade bitterly divided the cabildo on the question of internal security for a time, the slave trade was reopened, although only Africans direct from Africa were acceptable.[25] According to notarial records, 2,700 slaves of all kinds were imported from 1787 to 1803.[26] Adding this figure and the estimate for the 1763–85 period, plus a guesstimated 600 for the period between the end of the American War of Independence and 1787, when notaries were ordered to record the sale of Africans more routinely, we reach a grand, estimated figure of 12,905 Africans for the entire colonial period. Even with all of its obvious faults, this estimate is more useful than Curtin's extrapolation from the voyages of the 1720s.[27]

Renewal of the African slave trade affected the local slave population in several ways, beginning with its disruptive impact on the slave quarter. Some statistics are available to measure these conditions in the Spanish era as an introduction to a renewed discussion of slavery in a comparative context in the next chapter. Inventories of estate provide rough sketches of the domestic structure of plantation subcommunities. The discussion that follows rests on a collection of thirty slave rolls, including ten large plantations of 54 to 144 slaves, ten medium groups of 22 to 46 slaves, and ten small groups ranging from 10 to 18 slaves, for a total sample of 1,191 slaves. These slave inventories or rolls reveal great variety, which should serve to warn against easy generalizations or comparisons of plantation societies based on selected plantations.

First, let us examine the age and sex distribution of the plantation slave population, as laid out in tables 15, 16, and 17.[28] These tables reveal both startling continuities and variations. The sex distribution within the entire slave population was 5.3 males to 4.2 females according to the census of 1785, but males were comparatively even more numerous in the plantation neighborhoods, a disproportionate number of slave women being stationed in the town center. Yet there was a clear tendency for maldistribution to be less pronounced

TABLE 15

NUMBER, SEX, AND AGE DISTRIBUTION OF SLAVES
ON TEN LARGE PLANTATIONS IN NEW ORLEANS, 1765–1805

Roll	Slaves	Sex M:F	Age Distribution (%)					Average Age
			1–14	15–30	31–45	46–59	60–100	
I	144	55:43	32	37	18	7	6	25
2	78	32:22	31	42	II	II	5	25
3	69	33:36	37	26	22	10	5	26
4	68	31:19	30	28	22	7	13	30
5	63	23:19	33	35	22	6	3	26
6	60	36:14	17	46	12	15	10	30
7	58	27:16	27	19	45	4	5	29
8	58	21:17	36	14	29	7	14	30
9	56	28:22	—	—	—	—	—	—
I0	54	33:11	24	37	24	II	4	29

SOURCES: Roll I is that from the Succession of Jean-Baptiste Destréhan, 26 Feb. 1765, NONA, Garic book I; the other slave rolls, in order, are those from the Succession of Jean-Baptiste Noyon, 22 Oct. 1763, LHC; Succession of Louis Favre, 10 Oct. 1780, LHC, WPA translation only; Succession of Charlotte Dapremont, 5 Oct. 1788, LHC; Succession of Jean Piseros, 28 Aug. 1777, LHC; Succession of Marie Battasar, 14 Feb. 1789, LHC; Succession of Barba Harang, 25 Jan. 1776, NONA, Garic No. 7, 19–26; Succession of Jacques Livaudais, 29 Apr. 1773, NONA, Almonester; Succession of Antoine-Philippe Marigny, NONA, Garic No. 8; Succession of Jean-Baptiste Bienvenu, 11 Sept. 1790, LHC.

NOTE: Sex Distribution refers to adults only (male:female ratio), except in roll 3, in which children are included in the figure.

TABLE 16

NUMBER, SEX, AND AGE DISTRIBUTION OF SLAVES
ON TEN MEDIUM PLANTATIONS IN NEW ORLEANS, 1765–1805

Roll	Slaves	Sex	Age Distribution (%)					Average Age
		M:F	1–14	15–30	31–45	46–59	60–100	
1	46	29:13	9	73	18	0	0	25
2	45	33:12	9	40	16	22	13	37
3	40	14:11	38	35	17	5	5	26
4	39	22:8	25	46	25	2	2	26
5	33	24:9	20	50	27	3	0	26
6	33	19:14	—	—	—	—	—	—
7	31	8:8	45	45	10	0	0	18
8	30	15:7	28	44	28	0	0	22
9	26	13:10	12	54	34	0	0	28
10	22	14:7	4	67	25	4	0	29

SOURCES: Roll 1 is from the Succession of Pierre Marigny, 14 May 1800, LHC; the other slave rolls, in order, are from the Succession of François Reggio, 5 Oct. 1787, LHC; Succession of Marie-Joseph Harang, c. 1769, NONA, Garic No. 1; Succession of Pierre Loriot of Des Allemands, 15 Mar. 1790, NONA, Unmarked Miscellaneous Volume Shelved at U9R-H5; Succession of Louis Boisdoré, 10 Oct. 1788, LHC; Succession of Patrick Macnemara, 19 Jan. 1788, NONA, Rafael Perdomo; Succession of Francisco Bouligny, 25 Nov. 1800, LHC; Succession of Pierre-Joseph Favrot, 15 May 1805, LHC; Succession of Martial Berthelot, 12 Oct. 1776, NONA, Garic No. 7; Succession of Guido Dufossat, 5 Oct. 1794, NONA, Antonio Ximenes.

NOTE: Sex Distribution (male:female ratio) refers to adults only, males to females, except in rolls 2, 5, and 6, where children are included in the figure.

in the largest and smallest plantations (3 men to 2 women) than in the middle-sized plantations (almost 2 to 1). No single factor was more debilitating to the black community than this inability of one-third to one-half the men to marry women either on their own or neighboring plantations, and the inability of many women in the town center to find marriage partners there. The unequal

TABLE 17

NUMBER, SEX, AND AGE DISTRIBUTION OF SLAVES
ON TEN SMALL PLANTATIONS IN NEW ORLEANS, 1765–1805

Roll	Slaves	Sex	Age Distribution (%)					Average Age
		M:F	1–14	15–30	31–45	46–59	60–100	
1	18	8:6	22	39	11	0	28	36
2	18	4:7	39	22	33	0	6	24
3	16	5:4	44	31	25	0	0	20
4	15	11:4	7	46	33	7	7	34
5	15	8:7	33	27	33	7	0	26
6	14	9:5	0	21	15	21	43	50
7	12	10:2	0	83	17	0	0	27
8	10	4:5	13	50	37	0	0	27
9	10	4:2	40	30	30	0	0	22
10	10	5:4	10	70	20	0	0	27

SOURCES: Roll 1 is from the Succession of Alexandre Vielle, 25 Sept. 1764, NONA, Garic No. 1; the other rolls, in order, are from the Succession of Louis De Velle, 14 July 1773, NONA, Garic No. 7; Succession of Antoine Bienvenu, 13 Nov. 1771, NONA, Garic No. 2; Succession of Pierre-François Olivier, 16 Apr. 1776, NONA, Almonester; Succession of Jean-Baptiste Senet, 31 July 1776, ibid.; Succession of Jonathas Darby, 18 Feb. 1767, NONA, Garic and Perdomo 1765–78; Succession of Louis Boisdoré, 27 Feb. 1787, LHC; Succession of Joseph Cassenave, 20 Sept. 1797, LHC; Succession of Marguerite Devin, 12 May 1797, LHC; Succession of Valentin Leblanc, 12 May 1796, LHC.

NOTE: Sex Distribution (male:female ratio) refers to adults only, males to females, except in rolls 4, 5, 6, and 7, where children are included in the figure.

distribution of men and women was maintained by the greater availability of men on the slave market. The imbalance was even more grievous for the African newcomers in the Spanish period in that they were less attractive to creole women as spouses because they were less likely to have personal property or savings and were "saltwater" outsiders who did not know how "to act" in creole society. In fact, the preponderance of males with African names on slave rolls were unmarried young African men.

The origins of slaves were usually recorded because masters believed they could use this information to police slaves more effectively. These lists show that the prevalence of Africans by the end of the Spanish era is remarkable, distinguishing this black community from its successor in the antebellum era.[29] Those with African names were to be found on every plantation, ranging from only one or two names up to 22 percent of the slave roll. The estate of Pierre Marigny was further distinguished in that all of those with African names were from West Africa and none from Central Africa, whereas the African component was usually more mixed. The most African of all these thirty slave rolls was that of a small rental plantation to which Louis Boisdoré assigned a force of young newcomers combined with only a handful of his oldest creole slaves. All plantations in the sample included African-born slaves, meaning those with memories of Africa and enslavement. Especially the oldest slaves in the 1770s, sixty years old and above, would have had particularly important roles in preserving slaves' sense of historical continuity. We know that older slaves allayed the fears of the unknown suffered by new slaves. The role of these older slaves in the politics, consciousness, and other aspects of the slave quarters, however, is not recorded.

Slaves were most naturally distributed among age groups on the largest plantations. In those slave quarters every age group was represented by two or more people on all nine large plantations for which ages were given. On the middle-sized plantations, by contrast, no less than four of nine known age profiles included no people over forty-five years of age, being dominated by young adults in their twenties. In the smallest groups, half had no one listed over forty-five years, three others had only one or two individuals that age, whereas two groups were exceptionally old, like the Darby group (slave roll number 6), where no children were included and two-thirds of the slaves were over forty-five.

Beyond these generalizations lies a forest of particularities. One slave force not included in the sample but belonging to the middle range of that group illustrates particularly well the impossibility of singling out a "typical" plantation or planter. André Jung was a New Orleanian born in Bordeaux of a Canadian father and French mother; he left an estate including forty-one slaves on two plantations in 1784. Late in life he had married Pelagie Loreins, the daughter of Indian trader and planter Jacques Tarascon, an original founder. Jung was survived by three children, Rosette, aged twenty, whose mother was free Negress Goton; Goton, twenty-three, whose mother was the deceased Negress slave Louison; and Jean-Louis, twenty-two, son of free Negress Isabel. "These children since their birth have been fed, educated, and maintained in his home," the will read, "as his own family."[30] Only a handful of men made such open acknowledgments and Jung may have been a unique case of such a large planter making such an open admission at this early date. He left two thousand dollars to support his son in the care of his executor, and he gave Rosette two thousand dollars and Goton one thousand. He left the remainder of his estate to his best friend, François-Marie De Reggio.

Jung's slave force of forty-seven was actually broken into three groups. At his townhouse on the levee he had seven domestic slaves, of whom he freed, without explanation, a mulattress named Vénus, and a young woman with a newborn boy. At his plantation on Bayou St. Jean behind the town center, he had sixteen slaves whose average age was forty-five, nearly half of them fifty years old or older. No children are listed and since the notaries were usually scrupulous about listing all slaves in inventories this plantation was very odd indeed, almost as if Jung allowed among this group of slaves only a few women who were over child-bearing age. The situation was even worse on his tar-making plantation across the lake. Of twenty-five slaves, only the Hibou woman named Marthe and the octogenarian Liva varied the otherwise male slave force: no children were listed and the average age was forty years. The ethnic content of the gang appears to have been deliberately designed as well. Jung carefully crafted a group including eleven African slaves representing nine different nations or tribes, five creole men in their fifties, three younger creoles, three "English" slaves, and three of unknown origins. This combination of creoles and Africans and the various nations of the Africans, all under the rule of the free mulatto overseer Alexandre, appears designed to keep them divided, probably of special importance when black society was as bleak as it was on the opposite shore of Lake Pontchartrain.

For the sake of contrast, the slave inventory of one of Jung's neighbors, Jean-Baptiste Destréhan, drawn up in 1765, can be presented. Known for their Catholic piety and their rigid Christian plantation discipline, the Destréhans had 144 slaves. Theirs was one large community in 1765, thoroughly structured on the basis of the completed family, in striking contrast to Jung's slave force. The Destréhans had 55 adult men and 43 women, with 21 conjugal families including 46 children fourteen years or younger. The average age was twenty-five, and there were 18 people over fifty years of age, including one centenarian. Field slaves could hope for no better situation than this in New Orleans—a large and supportive black subcommunity where families were encouraged and seem to have been protected from separation.[31]

It must have been difficult to form and maintain families under conditions in most of the other slave subcommunities described above. This is particularly true in that the planters were explicitly permitted by law to meddle in the choice of spouses by their slaves and the clergy did nothing to encourage formal weddings by slaves, which, never numerous, virtually ceased by the end of the eighteenth century. Domestic servants who lived in the master's house suffered the most direct meddling. On a visit to New Orleans in 1797, the soon-to-be governor of the province, Manuel Gayoso, carefully selected a body servant for his American wife, Margaret Watts, writing her a detailed description. Bisa had been raised by Madame Maxent, which gave the slave a special cachet even without reference to her personal qualities.[32] As for those qualities, she was trilingual, thoroughly trained in the duties of a housekeeper and lady's maid, and, although forty years old, looked as if she was "a very young wench," which indicates that a female house slave's appearance was at least as important a consideration for a mistress as for a master.[33] As for her morals, "they say that she is a libertine. . . . One defect which almost all of her colour have." By this, Gayoso meant that she would consort with a man without the sacrament of marriage. He planned to deal with this by indulgence, to "allow any husband she may have," but she must not be told of his intention so that he could maximize the advantage of manipulating her through this privilege.[34] Here is the domestic slave's predicament exemplified.

Robin's overall impression of the slaves was that those of the opposite sex were likely to form strong attachments and support one another economically and emotionally. He was not without prejudice and thought they tended to choose lovers or spouses off the plantation in order to add spice to the intrigue of love. This ignored the tragedy that so few blacks were able to form convenient domestic relationships on the same plantation, given the small size of most plantations and the overall sex imbalance. Nonetheless, he admitted to being much impressed by a black community united by a strong network of warm familial ties. Free blacks were so rigidly excluded from white society that many of them of all complexions sought the society of slaves, attending Sunday slave dances, where, according to another observer, "vast numbers of negro slaves, men, women, and children, assembled together on the levee, druming [*sic*], fifing, and dancing, in large rings."³⁵ All seemed "to form a single family united in their abjection. . . . To the best of their ability they try to do each other as much good as they can."³⁶

The introduction of sugar cultivation fed the demand for slaves, compounding the negative effects of the slave trade on slaves' lives. The indigo crop in New Orleans was attacked by a blight that almost completely destroyed production by 1794: it was hardly worth the risk to grow it. Although the Jesuits and a few colonists had cultivated sugarcane, according to a self-serving account of how he singlehandedly revived the crop, Étienne Boré claimed that it

Fig. 9. Jean-Étienne Boré, born 1741, Illinois, died New Orleans 1820. Attributed to Mouchette. Boré was the indigo planter who produced the first large-scale commercial crop of sugarcane, exporting a large quantity of refined sugar in 1796, thereby inaugurating a new crop regime in the parish. Boré was New Orleans' first mayor (appointed), in 1803–4. Courtesy of Howard-Tilton Memorial Library, Special Collections Division, Tulane University, New Orleans.

was not grown at all between the mid-1760s and his experiments in 1794–96. The revolution in Saint Domingue and resulting collapse of sugar production drew attention to the crop in New Orleans once again. After Boré made a huge amount of sugar, seventy sugar mills were set up by his neighbors by 1803, and this became New Orleans' principal staple export until it destroyed the local soil and forests sometime before 1850.[37] This development meant a great extension of slavery in the lower Mississippi Valley.

As seen in an earlier chapter, the prevalent conviction that sugar production as such is linked to high mortality rates for slaves, which has a long tradition, is not supported by the evidence. In the 1820s and 1830s, scientifically minded planters looked at the issue and concluded that the mortality rate exceeded the birth rate on sugar plantations because of the very intense labor required at harvest season.[38] But modern scientific inquiry refutes the theory that sugar production itself meant higher mortality rates.[39] Moreover, the task system was reported to prevail on Louisiana sugar plantations, a labor routine associated with a greater degree of autonomy for slaves than dawn-to-dusk gang labor typical of cotton planters.[40] Many sugar plantations set aside plots for slaves to produce food by independent production, according to the belief that "the more happy and rich the Negroes, the more hard-working they are."[41]

So if contemporaries were right that mortality was high in sugar growing regions, and if the production process itself was not responsible, what might have caused it? James Pitot claimed that Boré sold his first crop, produced by thirty slaves, for one hundred thousand dollars, a princely sum in 1795.[42] That kind of profit fueled demand for slaves, which poured in at an unprecedented rate after 1800. To expand on a theme introduced in chapter 5, intensification of the slave trade brought together people from a great variety of locales together with their local strains of viruses, protozoans, and other microbes to which they had partial immunity, which they spread in the host community into which they were introduced, to whose own diseases they were themselves exposed. Thus, particularly high mortality is directly and related to the *rate and volume of the slave trade* and the degree to which it concentrates slaves in a given region. The more profitable the crop, the higher the rate of influx and geographical concentration of slaves, the higher the mortality. Kenneth F. Kiple and Virginia H. King discussed this issue in some detail in their 1981 work. Kiple and King show that malaria and yellow fever were major killers, the latter particularly where slaves were highly concentrated, like cities, especially New Orleans, which remained closely ringed by its sugar belt for several decades.[43] Even if the African slave trade had completely ceased soon after 1808, the immense influx of slaves from the older states, who had long been isolated from yellow fever in scattered interior farms and plantations, could easily explain elevated mortality rates throughout the antebellum period in lower Louisiana without any reference to the crop regime itself.[44] Pitot came within two fingers of the truth about the connection between the slave trade and disease when he lambasted the Spanish administration for not policing the infrastructure sufficiently (crevasses in the levee, improper disposal of garbage) to prevent the production of noxious air that spread disease, which made slave importation risky.[45]

Finally, it is reasonable to conjecture that the effect of the great influx of African slaves was an increase in both the inclination of the white minority to intimidate blacks into submission and to have less care for their well-being when they could be easily replaced in the marketplace. The combination of a good supply of slaves, and, after 1795, the rising profits of sugar, had the tendency to make masters feel more confident, ambitious, and exploitative, also more defensive. The evidence on this issue is mixed: certain general trends run counter to the hypothesis of a rising degree of exploitation, whereas certain specific incidents, especially the establishment of a militant maroon camp for a time, suggest the opposite. It is possible that the slave society of New Orleans became more disorderly during the Spanish period.

The judicial record of slave crime in the Spanish period is not an ideal source, and evidence of day-to-day police procedure against blacks is almost entirely lacking, so we are forced to rely on the record of important cases, as is true of white crime. The list of the most shocking crimes by slaves and their punishments in the thirty-four years of Spanish rule is short. In the summer of 1771, an abusive master hated by his slaves was shot and killed on his gallery when responding to the midnight fire set by his murderers. The culprits were Temba, or Pierre-Nicolas, a forty-year-old creole who hunted for the plantation, and his accomplice Mirliton. They were tortured into confessing, perhaps on the rack, and sentenced to be dragged to the gibbet and hanged. Their heads and hands were to be nailed up by the side of the road.[46] This was typical procedure in slave societies for such a crime in this period. The incident must have inspired storytellers in the slave camps for many years. Other cases of violent assaults upon whites by blacks were few.[47] One case was important because it involved denying a murderer sacred asylum in the church. The governor enforced the royal decree of March 15, 1787, that denied sacred asylum to felons.[48] The man was imprisoned in Honduras for ten years and then hanged in New Orleans upon his return in 1802.

Judicial cases of slaves' assaults upon one another were exceptionally rare. The only one of note in the record is that concerning a small band of runaways who stole an Englishman's trunk. They quarreled over the loot and one stabbed another to death. The accused was named Jacques, a carpenter, and a native of South Carolina. He ran away from his mistress on the Acadian Coast and gravitated, like most maroons who had lived in the hinterland, to New Orleans. His case is important because it reveals how infrequent such a prosecution was, indicating that slave theft must have been mainly of a petty nature and punished by masters, but for two other reasons. First, the court did not think the murder of a fellow slave warranted capital punishment and Jacques was only sentenced to ten years in El Morro prison in Havana and eternal exile from New Orleans. Second, the court did think the crime was serious enough to insist upon the banishment despite a pathetic plea for mercy from the 64-year-old widow who claimed Jacques was her only property and source of support.[49]

The court tried to punish both the errant slave and the master in cases not involving capital punishment. In the court's view a slave's delict was virtually always the fault of the master for insufficient overseership, and judges tried to punish the master by denying him or her the slave's labor and by forcing the master to punish the slave. When a storekeeper charged one Charles of stealing handkerchiefs, the white man dropped charges once he got his property returned. The court went on to give Charles a stiff sentence anyway because his theft had occurred while he was a runaway: he received two hundred lashes by the public executioner, and his master was ordered to keep him in solitary confinement for two years and working in chains for two more years.[50] The master's compliance in cases like this in unknown. A slave out of work two years and in chains for two more was a big loss. One final point is that Charles was a native of Jamaica, and outsiders continued to be disproportionately represented in the ranks of accused slave criminals. One other case of robbery is important because the culprits were caught wearing some of the clothes they stole, which shows that this kind of crime was unwise in such a small town. Second, this is a rare instance of poor white men in league with a slave in crime, showing that it could happen on rare occasions.[51]

Marronage remained the most common crime by slaves. While in some slave societies Maroons banded together in settled villages at a distance from and openly hostile to slave society, this was virtually unknown in the region of New Orleans, where runaways typically remained on or near a plantation but away from the fields for a while, before returning to work, or for as long as possible until they were captured. The impetus to go *grand maron* could arise from a variety of circumstances. Sale to a different master always carried a risk of marronage. Free Negro Bastian petitioned in 1788 to pay for the freedom of his father Paul, who had run away when he was sold.[52] Slaves who lived hired out to themselves might use their mobility to escape. The free quadroon François Monplaisir sued Guillaume Le Compte in 1785 because he hired Monplaisir's slave Gregoire for a trip to Natchez and the slave ran away from there to Illinois. The defendant, a naive outsider, angrily insisted that Gregoire had represented himself as a free man.[53] Nonetheless, the *grands marons* were few.

Aside from the exceptional case described below, Spanish authorities never mentioned permanent maroon villages in their reports, and the judicial records eloquently testify to the small number of maroons, who faced severe deprivation, constant fear of arrest, and the lack of the organized support they would have received from maroon villages. One roving band of maroons, composed of escapees from New Orleans, was arrested at distant Attakapas in the summer of 1771. They had not formed a maroon village. The commandant sent seven captives back to New Orleans. They confessed to have gathered behind the Ursulines' plantation but eventually removed deep into the interior. These were remarkably successful maroons, including a child and two women, each of whom had enjoyed between one and two years of freedom, but their success was owing to the fact that they kept moving.[54]

Another case is instructive, that of Bobo and Jacob in 1772. Caught napping in the woods, they were hauled to jail and interrogated at length. Bobo had absconded a full sixteen months earlier. While he had spent some time as far away as Barataria on the coast, he had mostly lurked in the forest behind various plantations for a while in company with as many as two other maroons, living on stolen corn, and the fish and game they collected. He admitted to stealing a gun from Jacques Chaperon's son, and to trading with some slaves provisions he stole from Chaperon for their powder and shot. From one of Sieur Chabert's slaves he filched a signed pass, but he denied having killed any cattle, a serious crime. Jacob had run away six months earlier, angry that he had been punished with shackles, and two other maroons chopped them off with an axe. He also hid in the woods. He was asked if some other master had put him to work in the interim, revealing the usual concern that planters were suspected of ruthlessly exploiting the misfortunes of their neighbors. Jacob's response that "he had not given one stroke of the axe for anybody" appears to carry a subtext of bitter pride: whatever the consequences, not working as a slave for so many months was worth it. The rest of his testimony is similar to Bobo's and follows the usual pattern of maroon behavior: theft from planters or from other slaves, an occasional night spent in a helpful slave's cabin, an attempt (in Jacob's case) to shift blame for serious thefts to other maroons, and, despite the great area the two had traveled, not the slightest indication that there existed any maroon community to which they might have sought entry.[55]

Early in the summer of 1781, however, militia Captain Jean-Baptiste Bienvenu exposed a scandal when he mounted a patrol to capture cattle rustlers, probably the largest maroon case to that time in New Orleans. He caught five local runaways and two others from Pointe Coupée, including the three women who had taken and butchered his cow. They turned out to be among the fifteen runaways that one Albert Bonne employed supplying and operating his sawmill deep in the woods on New Orleans' outer boundary. Men like Bonne, who existed in any slave society, confounded the class unity planters needed to control their slaves. By encouraging quasi-free labor status for runaways, whites themselves undermined the system, just as slaves undermined it in their own ways by breaking the rules. Bonne even assigned his illegal workers their own plots for their crops. Over and over, captured maroons confessed to working for wages for planters who eagerly accepted any labor available. The latter were sufficiently numerous to be singled out for special mention in Article 18 of O'Reilly's code of 1770: when the king's lieutenants captured maroons they were ordered to "determine exactly if they were not drawn off and employed by some one of the inhabitants."[56] Bonne proved he was no friend of blacks, however, when he took advantage of free black Barthélémy while he was away fighting with Gálvez. They had made an agreement that the freedman would keep part of the six-arpent plantation he cleared for Bonne, but the white man evicted Barthelemy's family and sold the land while he was gone.[57]

Only once in the entire history of early New Orleans was a maroon camp, or pair of camps, formed in the nearby hinterland for a time. Celebration of Gálvez's victory over the British was marred by a divisive aftershock: the American War of Independence created unusual opportunities for blacks to get free of masters by running away, and in both South Carolina and Louisiana maroon camps formed during the latter part of the war. South Carolina masters lost up to 25 percent of their slaves, some of whom formed small secreted communities, even close to Charleston itself for a time.[58] The disruption of the slave system in New Orleans was minor by comparison, but the episode was highly instructive nonetheless. For a slave to run away was not a political act, but collective resistance to recapture did have a political dimension, as the story of the Gaillard Land maroon camp illustrates. Moreover, when the planters suppressed it, they quarreled and revealed fault lines among themselves.

Early in the Spanish era, planters formalized the system of periodically pursuing maroons. The public advocate proposed that the inhabitants create a general fund to reimburse those masters who lost slaves either to the gallows or to slave hunters who killed them. All of the citizens "of the better class" gathered in one of their rare meetings to approve this plan, and to establish a schedule of bounties: three dollars for a maroon seized in New Orleans. That was about equivalent to the hire of a male slave for a week. A group of eighteen free blacks was then specially commissioned to comb the hinterland for maroons.[59] Within a few weeks, planters put in claims for two men and a woman shot to death by pursuing slave catchers. But the cabildo appeared wholly unconcerned with maroons for several years, and this shows that while *marronage* was endemic it was not a serious problem just before the war.

In 1779 the slaveholders met to deal once again with the "*cimarrones* whose number increases daily."[60] Yet they still were not a serious problem. The masters agreed to make a small, one-time payment of four reales per slave to restore the compensation fund, but there is no other indication that marronage was in fact prevalent or even that this sum was actually collected.[61] Gálvez ordered a general amnesty for runaways who turned themselves in, but the planters mounted no major expedition to reclaim maroons. The meetings and resolves were in fact designed to raise the awareness of whites and intimidate slaves on the eve of the declaration of war upon the English.[62]

Slaves ran away because they were driven to it by abusive masters, but they took special advantage of the disorder of war, when large numbers of local free men marched off and the police of slaves was more lax. By the time of the treaty ending the American war in 1783, a band of maroons had formed at what they called "Gaillard Land" in the wild Chef Menteur district that stretched toward Lake Borgne. A small force of free black slave catchers could not suppress remote and organized groups of maroons.[63] Only a military campaign with a strong show of force could invade such an enclave effectively. In mountainous islands of the West Indies, determined maroons were irrepressible and planters made treaties with them. In flat Louisiana with its many knowledgeable Indian and black guides, a maroon camp was at a decisive disadvantage. Hence, in February 1783, the planters mounted a large expedition against Gaillard Land.

A flotilla of pirogues took the lakes route guided by a former runaway slave in exchange for emancipation. To understand why a slave would risk severe retaliation from other slaves for cooperating like this is to appreciate how much slaves could desire freedom.[64] The detachment surprised one of the maroon villages, seized twenty-three maroons, killing one other. In carrying away the captives, the victors encountered a pirogue bearing the leader of the maroons, St. Malo (named after a major port of departure for many Louisiana immigrants), and some others. In an exchange of gunfire, one died on each side and the remaining maroons capsized. They swam to the pursuers' lead boat and tried to capsize it. One was shot, but three fugitives made shore, where two were captured, but St. Malo escaped.[65]

The examination of the captives back in New Orleans was very revealing. The leaders of the group, Jean-Pierre with his wife Marie and son Jolicoeur, had fled in 1780 when their master had beaten Marie. All the slaves explained that they had run away from the whip. They lived by growing corn, stealing from the plantations, and by the money Jean-Pierre received peddling fish in New Orleans at night, with which he bought powder and shot. He also worked on Madame Mandeville's plantation at times. Another entire family, including two children, had joined the group only two months earlier, so the Gaillard community was twice distinguished by this unusual phenomenon of runaway families who lived by their wits. Asked by the nervous examiner why they were all armed when captured, one Jasmin reassured them that maroons "never go about without arms" because they needed them for hunting and they could be stolen if left unattended.[66] The court, unmoved by their explanations, was severe. The judges had all of the leading offenders hanged. Long-term maroons received three hundred lashes and were forbidden to live in New Orleans. Women were sentenced to two hundred lashes and branding of the latter M on a cheek. Other slaves were condemned to lashes, brands, or terms of shackling to a ball and chain.[67]

These punishments were only the beginning. By the following spring it was evident that outlying plantations suffered from a continuing drain of their resources by marauders from a remaining maroon settlement. One captive maroon yielded much information about the ways in which maroons were involved with slaves, the runaways performing unpleasant forest chores like fuel gathering for slaves, who in return drove beasts into the woods where the maroons could butcher them. The planters passed many ordinances and penalties to make all planters and retailers more accountable for preventing slave disorder. It was strictly prohibited to allow slaves powder, shot, liquor, or separate living conditions, for example.[68]

A reconnoitering expedition was launched against Gaillard Land in 1784. The maroons repulsed a paltry force sent against them and even killed a white man. When St. Malo and his lieutenants bragged openly in May 1784 of killing some American whites who tried to arrest them, Attorney General François De Reggio proclaimed that the planters must imitate the Jamaicans or the infamous Louisiana governor Périer by introducing ferocious measures. A substantial force then utterly destroyed Gaillard Town. No account of the affair remains, but the expedition was so large it cost the hefty sum of $2,261. St. Malo and about fifty other maroons were taken.[69]

At the executions of the Gaillard rebels a dramatic confrontation of the religious and civil authorities occurred. The Spanish Capuchins were zealous in the cause of the Church and jealous of their traditional privileges.[70] For all their religious commitment, the Spanish priests had little moral authority over the slaveowning class to which they belonged. Most white men scorned communion, ritual fasting was unknown, heretical books were read openly, and some men lived with concubines. Yet the priests dared not clash openly with civilians. They enjoyed a degree of residual respect by serving as one pillar of the slaveholders' order.

The trials and executions of the St. Malo rebels rent the peace between the secular and religious slaveholders in the spring of 1784. After the St. Malo captives were hauled back to town in triumph, Father Cyrilo de Barcelona had encouraged the secular authorities in their plan to dispense with the technicalities of a formal trial and conduct summary proceedings.[71] Then it was discovered that one of the Capuchins' own slaves was caught up in the dragnet. The man was condemned by the court to a potentially fatal number of lashes because he was connected to a murder case in the past and refused to cooperate. Moreover, the hypocritical planters charged, he had been hired out by his masters, which was illegal. Father Cyrilo then angrily protested that his Christian sentiments would not allow him to permit the execution of the sentence by a summary court on uncertain evidence. More to the point, the judicial murder of one of their slaves was an intolerable affront to the dignity of the clergy. The Capuchins withdrew support for the proceedings and insisted that a regular court intervene. The planters went ahead anyway, so when it came time for the executions on June 19, the clergy stood on their balcony on the plaza and protested by turning their backs on the hangings of four maroons, discrediting the civil procedure.[72]

To this challenge the planters reacted furiously through spokesman François De Reggio. All slaveowners knew that instant, harsh retribution was required against a concerted slave conspiracy, De Reggio argued, and that long court trials only spoiled "the principal fruits of justice," namely, maximizing the terror for all blacks.[73] The anger of the planters at the clergy's method of embarrassing them is a good measure of how highly they valued the clergy's public approval. Cyrilo threatened to lay everything before the king, so the planters beat him to it before there was time for the bodies of the maroons to rot on the gallows. They sent copies of relevant records and vigorous denunciations of the priests to both the bishop in Havana and the King of Spain. They pleaded pathetically that they were faced with the possibility of a general uprising, that the country was laced with paths known only to the maroons, and that a slaveowner was "entirely at the mercy of the slaves if the judge does not protect him."[74] So the slave regime could not tolerate this show of disunity. The cabildo followed up by requesting that the bishop investigate the rates charged by Capuchins for marriages and burials, which had been set at the beginning of the Spanish regime and subsequently crept up to burdensome levels.[75] In his own report, Governor Miró, who had been absent during the crisis, sought safe ground in a dangerous confrontation by mildly disapproving the way the trials were rushed by his subordinates. Eventually, however, imperial authorities exonerated the officials. Even though the churchmen suffered no repercussions from the planters' complaints, they had lost an important showdown.[76]

This discussion of crime and runaways does not yield to any easy generalization: no clear index of rising exploitation and indiscipline emerges, but the stout resistance of the Gaillard rebels is suggestive. It appears beyond doubt that the growth of the slave trade and, later, sugar cultivation was a tragedy for the great majority of slaves because (a) it permanently committed the planters to the expansion of slave society, (b) it disrupted slave communities with many new arrivals, (c) it nurtured a disease environment that would attain legendary dimensions by 1819, and (d) it *may* have raised the level of brutality suffered by specific work forces because higher profits corroded humane considerations, which incited a growing spirit of slave rebelliousness.

These negative results of economic expansion during the Spanish era are to a minor degree offset by benefits enjoyed by a small number of slaves. One of these, a serious potential threat to the slaveowners' power over individual slaves, was the gradual transformation of the tiny community of New Orleans into a city, which began during the Spanish period as port activity rose and an increasing number of people lived in the town center. Urbanization provided settings and spaces where the barrier between the two "races" might erode or be actively challenged by blacks or held in contempt by nonslaveholding whites. Several cases in the judicial record illustrate how weak the rules of slave society could be. The intermingling of blacks and whites was epitomized in an incident at the height of the Gálvez campaigns during the American War of Independence. The cabildo decreed that carnival had to be modified as a wartime measure: masking and nighttime dancing by blacks were prohibited because of the arrival of so many out-of-town troops, free blacks, and slaves for the festivities.[77] The decree argued that the event gave blacks a chance to steal, but the real motivation was a more generalized fear of the mixture of blacks with large numbers of the lowest class of whites—soldiers—both groups being people who had to work with their hands. Familiarity between the races at the lowest levels had to be discouraged lest the poor discover too much in common and act together across the color line.

Whites and blacks were known to cooperate together in crime on occasion, which confirmed slaveowners' concerns about human tendencies left unchecked. In one case, a Spaniard incited a cabaretier's slave to steal some indigo from his master; the slave was lashed and the Spaniard was lightly fined. A white tavern keeper was punished for fencing stolen goods for a slave. Another Spaniard was tried for selling liquor to slaves, a widespread and apparently irrepressible traffic endlessly decreed against; this was a freak case of prosecution in which the accused was absolved.[78] The other references to interracial criminal cooperation mostly referred to gambling—games of craps, especially—attended by men of all colors and conditions. These were attacked fiercely by Governor Carondelet during the early years of the Haitian Revolution.[79] When the cabildo installed nighttime street lamps for the first time in 1795, it was justified as discouraging disorders caused by slaves and transient whites.[80]

The campaign by the planters in the 1790s against slaves' public venues suggests that blacks tried to establish customary rights and that they had more disposable income. In 1791, the public advocate conducted a crackdown against the cabarets that operated outside the city wall because maroons and other slaves fenced stolen goods in them in return for drink—again, the anonymity of a special urban space undermining the regime.[81] His successor renewed the campaign a few years later but now also against the new dance hall operated by Jacques Coquet for free blacks because it admitted some slaves of both sexes. The latter were encouraged to steal from their masters, it was charged, in order to dress in the appropriate style. Moreover, sailors and other poor whites were admitted, who could only give blacks "bad ideas."[82] Tellingly, masters protested the cabildo's decree against Coquet because the privileged slaves they allowed to attend these balls protested to them. The cabildo backed down and passed another decree in its place merely excluding whites from the hall.[83] All of this conflicting evidence on slave crime can be called upon by proponents on both sides of the debate about its role in affirming slaves' economic rights: from one perspective, slaves' crime undermined their masters' power, from another, it indirectly sustained the regime by degrading the criminal's own self-image.[84]

Above all, growth in the urban market for blacks' manual labor and services increased the threat of eroding racial barriers. The economic expansion was a boon to a select group of blacks because it sustained demand for blacks with specialized skills. The phenomenon of skilled slave labor driving out white labor showed no signs of abating. The phenomenon of the individual slave who by his or her skill commanded a crucial stage in production was carried to a remarkable extreme in the figure of Adam. Of Virginia background, Adam was sixty years old in 1782, when he was the slave of New Orleans planter Jack Mather. In a complex suit over the quality of some tobacco delivered by an upriver planter to another in New Orleans to settle a debt, it was revealed that while the King's Receiver General officially and cursorily examined tobacco before entering it in the royal warehouse, Adam was the only examiner in the colony whose decisions were honored by all planters. The judge ruled in favor of his judgment in this case.[85] The record also reveals many slaves with multiple skills. Especially men in the construction trades like Mulet in the case of *Loppinot v Villeneueve* were described as able to perform not just one but several of the specialized steps in building. One Jérôme was billed in a sale as "an equally good wigmaker and tailor" and "an excellent hunter." In a case illustrating service skills, Widow Alarie protested angrily when Josette tried to buy her own freedom at the price of her official court valuation, since

Josette was worth twice as much because she was a good cook, pastry maker, washer, and ironer.[86] It is impossible to quantify the extent of slave skills, especially because apprenticeship of slaves was often not recorded by a formal contract, perhaps to avoid the expense of the notary's office.[87]

These economic opportunities for blacks able to take advantage of them enabled them to earn the dollars they needed to either buy their freedom or reconstitute families and build estates after they were free. They were now to be found in the notary's office or the courtroom recording the accumulation of property. It was slow going at first. In 1770, free mulattress Marguerite showed how well she understood the value of her property by registering her will, written with respect to God and to "the perils of the sea" she would face on a trip to Havana. She requested to be buried "in the same place as other true Christians . . . as modestly as possible." She willed that her house in Royal Street be sold and the proceeds be used to buy the freedom of Geneviève, her mother, slave of Andry. If her mother died, the estate was to go to Louis, her

Fig. 10. Destréhan Plantation, 1787, remodeled in the 1840s. Constructed by free mulatto Charles, in exchange for a male slave, a cow and her calf, fifty *quarts* each of rice and corn, and one hundred dollars. See Samuel Wilson Jr., *The Architecture of Colonial Louisiana*, 370–73. Courtesy The Historic New Orleans Collection, New Orleans.

brother, slave of Maxent, and in the case of his death to a white woman, Catherine Moreau, wife of Antoine Olivier, Marguerite's executor.[88] A somewhat unusual early will by a free black, this reveals how closely entwined one's life could be with those of whites, even to the point that one might make one an heir. Censuses show that many free blacks lived with white people, mostly as servants, and one's security was buttressed by having a white employer or other light-complexioned people as sponsors.[89] A few whites left small bequests to free blacks.[90]

The extreme to which white protection might be carried by a powerful planter is illustrated by the case of Bernabé Lenes against Negress Marguerite Toutant, whom he believed to be free, for the collection of a note for $106. When Lenes called at her home on the plantation of Jacques Toutant Beauregard to collect, he was curtly informed by the planter that he had a slave named Marguerite, not a free servant, and that as a slave she owned nothing Lenes could seize against the debt. In fact, Beauregard had written up an emancipation of Marguerite in 1779 on the condition that she serve him throughout his life, a common form of conditional emancipation. Even if she was free, her property could not be identified among Beauregard's things without his cooperation, which Lenes could not compel.[91] This indirect protection of the slave may explain why a given slave might accept or even prefer this kind of ambiguous emancipation.

Another indication that humanitarian considerations figured little in the creation of the free black community is that outright manumissions were not protected by alcaldes just because they had been promised. Sometimes masters simply changed their minds and tried to annul emancipations. Fanchon won the promise of emancipation by falling dangerously ill nursing her master in 1773, but then he sold her in Saint Domingue for four thousand livres in 1775.[92] A slave who was granted freedom by testament actually acquired it only if heirs or creditors could not show that he or she was encumbered by the claim of a free creditor.[93] In one tragic case, after Pierre Degout died, his slave Joseph had to sue the estate. A carter and butcher with character references and good witnesses as to Degout's intentions to free him, Joseph had never secured his master's signature on a deed of emancipation. Degout was an ill-tempered drunk, and Joseph had never been able to lead him to the notary's office before he died. The court denied Joseph's petition, and when he tried to open the case again seven years later, he was silenced.[94] Thus guaranteed freedom purchase was a better road to freedom than oral promises of no legal value. The subject of emancipation and free blacks is taken up in greater detail in chapter 9.

Most free blacks remained so poor and subject to such intense white social discrimination that the majority of them continued to form virtually a single subcommunity with slaves, or at least those who lived in the town center. They are found in the sacramental registers very frequently serving as slaves' godparents, for example, and occasionally intermarrying with them. "They never approach each other," Robin observed, "without displaying signs of affection and interest, without asking each other news of their relations, their friends, or their acquaintances."[95] This alliance was an advantage to members of both groups because it presented something of a common front to the white community, it undoubtedly involved mutual trust in joint commercial and financial endeavors, and it enriched social life for members of both groups. Yet there were some signs that forces were pulling the two groups apart, especially because at least some free blacks thought that their status would improve if they did not associate with slaves.

One important suit illustrates the rising economic prospects for some free blacks, the intimidating web of power relations with which they had to contend, and a compelling need to mark their social distance from slaves. In 1776, Marie Pechon and her mulatto son François sued a white planter, the Hiberno-Frenchman Patrick Macnemara, for $250 in damages. One night, en route from New Orleans to their own farm or plantation, they slept over in a slave cabin on the Tixerant place. Macnemara discovered them and accused them of being maroons and tried to arrest them, and when François resisted, Macnemara beat and stabbed him and locked him up. Probably drunk, Macnemara stubbornly ignored his own white subordinate and the black owner of the cabin, who both assured him that the pair were free. In court, Macnemara was contemptuous of the Pechons' claim for doctor's bills and lost work time and insisted on his right to arrest any Negro not bearing freedom papers. To this Marie answered, convincingly, that Macnemara "knew very well" like everyone else that the Pechons were free and that blacks did not carry papers "in hand" because everyone knew who was free and who was not. The Pechons could not win a suit against a prominent white man, but they dared to lodge and try it and thereby defend their right not to be mistreated at will.[96] A suit for fraud by a slave against a free black in 1802—the same François Pechon beaten by Macnemara in 1776—shows that free blacks may have been entrusted with cash earned by slaves. This case illustrates perfectly the twin themes of cooperation between slaves and free blacks and the potential for problems arising from that relationship.[97]

Although the majority of free blacks were poor, their future prospects seemed promising if not unlimited, with the result that most were at least as law-abiding as whites. Of the two hundred major criminal cases during the Spanish period, free blacks were defendants in only twenty-seven cases and only ten of these were crimes against property. In fact, about two-thirds of the defendants were by non-Louisiana free blacks who had been expelled from other colonies, especially from the West Indies. Despite the generally law-abiding character of free blacks, whites profoundly mistrusted them as a group because they were suspected of resentment that could lead to rebellion. The planters in all slave societies regarded the Haitian Revolution as the fulfillment of their worst fears and their concern about free blacks grew accordingly.[98]

Free blacks formed a small and vulnerable but dynamic community that grew to about one seventh of the whole population of New Orleans by the end of the Spanish domination.[99] They became more visible and essential to the local economy. Opportunities were so numerous that a few rich people at the very top of black society went on to become slaveowning planters by the end of the century. One of the earliest of them was Nicolas Bachus of the Tchoupitoulas coast, who in 1785 sued his neighbor for damages. Widow Bienvenu's slaves had hunted rabbits by fire which spread to Bachus's plantation and destroyed his house.[100] According to Robin, the black population was growing faster than that of the whites, and blacks would "one day be the master of the whites; perhaps one day exterminate them entirely."[101] What Robin failed to perceive was that the black community was in the process of becoming more and more deeply divided between free and slave, and, in time, between free mulattoes and blacks (symbolized by the fact that whites formed separate militia units for the two groups), and incapable of that kind of mass political action against an adversary enjoying a monopoly of force. This was being demonstrated dramatically by the Haitian Revolution when Robin arrived, which succeeded only because France was deep in its own revolution and because the black slave masses largely maintained their autonomy, allying with free mulatto planters where and when it was expedient but never trusting them and abandoning the alliance if it stalled the revolution.[102] When a lone free mulatto named Pierre Bailly briefly spoke out for mulatto rights in Louisiana in the Jacobin era, he was not interested in a black revolution.[103]

Blacks could create a fragile local community together, but they could not govern it in any real sense because it completely lacked an institutional superstructure, their politics were criminal by definition, and they were divided. Some demonstrated a kind of political behavior in the St. Malo affair, but they must have been deeply impressed by the relative ease with which the whites rallied, when sufficiently frightened, to destroy the alternative society the runaways tried to establish. It is possible that the violent resistance by these slaves marks the transition from "restorationist" revolts to ideological revolution, a decade before the ideological Haitian Revolution, but so little is known about Gaillard Land that this is mere speculation. The creation of these maroon camps took place during a violent struggle about "freedom," the American War of Independence, and since the planters were exposed to that ideology in imported newspapers, so were the slaves who eavesdropped on masters' conversations or who were able to read. But the single most important factor in their lives was that under white pressure the slave community was deeply divided between creoles and Africans, and the black community was bifurcating into two groups—slave and free—with increasingly distinct interests, under the influence of the new Spanish policy of freedom purchase.

The Slave Society of Spanish New Orleans in Comparative Context 8

> The [planters of New Orleans] do not consider that between them and their slaves they should maintain the eternal relationships of justice and humanity. . . . One should not be astonished to learn that the laws designed to protect the slaves are mostly disregarded by such masters.
>
> —Claude-Cézar Robin, Voyage to Louisiana, 1803–1805

> The Negro slaves have only the name "slave" since in reality they are as happy as the day workers of Europe can be.
>
> —Francisco Bouligny, Louisiana in 1776:
> A Memoir of Francisco Bouligny

The Spanish made some minor alterations in the town's economy, demography, and cultural character, but the social structure of New Orleans was profoundly conservative. Above all, the idea that Spanish institutions or cultural traditions were less dehumanizing for slaves is not supported by evidence from New Orleans. Two very important changes took place after 1769. One resulted from a strictly imperial policy: the great increase in the African slave trade. The other change was not a result of Spanish policy but the work of local planters: the explosive growth of sugar production in the 1790s.

Spanish authorities had unrestricted power to introduce all things Spanish, but they governed within constraints set by the constant battle of wits known as slave society, which was conducted according to existing rules the Spanish did not change. Neither attitudes toward racial mixture and emancipation, nor the clergy's attitude toward slavery, nor the law's effect on master-slave relations changed in any significant way during the era of Spanish rule in New Orleans. Certainly, the evidence does not confirm the assertion by one historian that slaves were more like serfs than slaves in Spanish Louisiana: in 1803, as in 1769, they were slaves in every sense of the word.[1]

Socially, New Orleans was a world apart from Spanish America in 1769, and it remained so in 1803. The Spanish colonies were founded by minuscule groups of men motivated primarily by a quest for gold, who typically inserted themselves at the top of indigenous hierarchies to become the beneficiaries of preexisting tributary obligations paid by sedentary agricultural peoples. In the principal regions of Spanish colonization, the Indian commoner owed labor to a cacique of his own nation, who delegated it to a Spanish *encomendero* in response to force or the threat of force. Even as the native population declined rapidly because of European diseases and Spanish wars of conquest, even as a mestizo population became numerically dominant, the *encomienda* (and its successor, *repartimiento*) remained the enduring system of labor throughout Spanish America, controlled by a tiny Spanish elite whose estates were diversified profit-oriented enterprises.[2]

The sharp contrast between this profile and the situation in New Orleans is obvious. New Orleans was founded by a highly diverse population seeking to establish a colony of settlement, one in which European society was meant to be reproduced, or at least reflected. Neither the mining of precious metals, nor the forced labor of Native Americans (besides a handful of slaves), nor the payment of tribute played a role in the town's development.[3] The social implications of this contrast were great. New Orleans was a slave society based on color, which existed nowhere in Spanish America, although the social structure in Cuba and Peru included many blacks and was gradually developing into slave society.[4] Unlike black slaves, the Indians of the encomienda were seldom bought and sold individually, and, rather than being removed from their nations to live in close association with Europeans, like African slaves, the Indians "stayed on the same lands as always and retained their group organization even when they went in parties to work for the encomendero."[5] Black slaves imported into Spanish America typically were "the Spaniards' auxiliaries in skilled, intensive, or permanent tasks and their intermediaries in dealing with the indigenous population."[6] Outnumbering the Spaniards here and there at times, in no colony were black slaves the majority of the population sustaining the primary mode of production, as was true in New Orleans from the beginning.

These differences in the systems of production and the founders' expectations had further implications. Because the Spaniards were a minority in a sea of non-Europeans, the ethnic development of Spanish colonies was strikingly different from that in New Orleans. Where they were few, blacks tended to cleave to the Spanish and serve as their implements of domination of the Indians, so there was little fear among Europeans (as existed in New Orleans) of a dangerous conjunction between these two groups.[7] Because of a markedly unbalanced sex distribution among both blacks and whites in Spanish America, domestic relations of all sorts between the men of these groups and Indian women created an assemblage of marginal peoples of many different colors. At the highest level of society investigations of *pureza de sangre* supposedly prevented nonwhite "blood" from seeping into the veins of the most respectable people. Even so, because white people were so few, the barrier between their privileged society and a select stratum of mixed-race individuals (even some of those of the first generation) was permeable, and this was decidedly not true in New Orleans. One of Antonio Ulloa's most serious problems was that his Peruvian bride, the Marchioness of Abrado, was scandalously familiar with her dark-skinned servants, provoking the townswomen to deride them all as "mulattoes."[8]

Despite these marked dissimilarities between Spanish colonial societies and New Orleans, the ruling classes in all of them shared a conviction that the Europeans' supremacy depended on their supposed racial purity: Spaniards did not have a liberal attitude toward racial mixture. A rising number of mixed-race people and rising white concern about them occurred throughout the Atlantic world in the last four decades of the eighteenth century. Ramón A. Gutiérrez describes "the concerns voiced by New Mexico's nobility over miscegenation and the necessity of closing ranks to protect their corporate identity" in this period.[9] Concerns were greater where black-white mixture was the main "problem." Concerted efforts were made in the 1770s and 1780s to cap or even reduce the black population of France and Britain, specifically because of the threat of racial mixture.[10] In the United States, worry about a breakdown of the racial barrier was great during the age of democratic revolution.[11]

Where the racial disproportion was marked and white men did not greatly outnumber women, as in the mainland North American slave societies in the eighteenth century, whites particularly oppressed free blacks and held in contempt interracial domestic relations with blacks of any status, which is not the same as arguing that these relations did not occur. The power of the Sally Hemings story to threaten Thomas Jefferson's political career illustrates this attitude.[12] Normally these things were not discussed in Virginia, much less recorded in documents. Only from the surprised report by the exile Louis-Philippe d'Orléans, future king of France, do we know that nearly white slaves were found among George Washington's personal house servants.[13] That is why we know so little about racial mixture in the southern states outside Louisiana, whereas New Orleans, with its busy notaries recording every transaction in conformity with a royal edict, appears on the surface to have been a society where interracial concubinage was prevalent and led to high rates of manumission. As will be seen, that cannot be demonstrated from the evidence.[14] The incidence of interracial domestic relations rose in the Spanish period in New Orleans: a few white men kept house with black women, some had long-term liaisons with blacks but did not live with them under the same roof. But these relationships were not prevalent, did not reflect more tolerant race relations, more humane conditions for slaves, or fundamentally different social rules than those prevailing in the southern United States.

The French Code Noir condemned the offspring of interracial concubinage to perpetual slavery. In general, this harsh measure, aimed at the white master whose children of a black woman might arouse his parental impulses, had been effective: only one interracial couple asked Governor Ulloa's Spanish chaplain to marry them, regarded as intolerably scandalous by local whites. By the time the Spanish arrived, after half a century, the free black population of the parish was very small. When O'Reilly ordered the men of that group to swear an oath of allegiance on September 20, 1769, just thirty were counted. Many had surnames mirroring those of leading white families (Bienville, Vaudreuil, Cazenave, Graveline), but this was not necessarily the key to their social structure: their militia captain, Simon Calfat, was African-born with a French artisan surname (caulker).[15] About the origin of these men and their families we know little except for the original acts of emancipation for a few of them, but it is reasonable to imagine that a majority were those blacks freed during the crisis of 1729–30 to help battle Indians, or their sons. Interracial concubinage had played a distinctly minor role in the creation of this community before 1769.[16] Public opinion continued to condemn interracial marriage and to hold concubinage in disrepute during the Spanish regime.[17] In New Orleans, no white men or virtually none married black women, and the majority of white men did not cohabit with black women.

The best way to study the question of race mixture is through the notarial records and judicial records of emancipations. The following discussion rests on a careful count of all emancipations in New Orleans through 1810. Let us begin with gratuitous emancipations, as distinct from freedom purchases. Between 1770 and 1810 whites freed 1,258 slaves outright, for an average of 31.5 per year, most because they had provided long and faithful service to earn their freedom. The rate was higher than in the past because rates of manumission were rising throughout the Americas in the last quarter of the eighteenth century, the result of ideological and social reasons in an age of liberty, economic expansion, and creolization. For many gratuitous *libertads*, or emancipations, in New Orleans, no reason is given, but those that are noted cover a fairly broad spectrum.

A few are aged slaves whose fidelity is being rewarded at the last minute. Jean-Louis Trudeau explained that he manumitted his Negress, Marguerite (fifty-eight years old), because her service to his mother "merits just reciprocation."[18] Very particular services might be rewarded. Pierre Rousseaux freed mulatto Marie Noel (twenty-four) because she nursed him through an illness.[19] Sometimes this service could win freedom for a slave in a remarkably short time. For some reason, Jacinto Panis freed Negro Miguel (fifty) soon after buying him from the Kerouette estate.[20] William Garland freed his cook, Nero (age not given), only fourteen months after he bought him from Manuel Monsanto in 1794.[21] Governor Miró freed the grif, Tany (Tony?—age not given), who had been captured from the English during the American war only a few years earlier, because he served as interpreter at the Spanish conferences with the Talapoosas.[22] For others it took longer. Several heirs joined together to free one of their mother's slaves, Catin, because she had raised a large family, presumably her own, which could be taken as rare evidence of a pro-natal policy.[23] Liberal ideology seems to have played little part in the increase of manumissions. *Never* did an emancipator say to the notary that he or she was acting in a spirit hostile to slavery itself. Virtually never did an emancipator suggest that he or she was committing a pious act, although the typical will included a brief expression of piety in its preamble.[24]

What must be avoided is the assumption that any man who freed a young woman or mulatto children had an intimate relationship with the woman or a kin relation with the mulattoes.[25] That assumption is often based in turn on the supposition that white women were few and white men had relations with black women because of sexual necessity.[26] Just a few examples should inspire a more conservative approach. The most frequently stated motives for gratuitous emancipations were the good service of the slave or the "love and tenderness" *(amor y cariño)* felt by the emancipator for the manumittee. This particular combination of words does sometimes appear to be code for "my lover" or "my children," but this is not a reliable indicator of sexual intimacy or kinship.

Jacques Carrick's emancipation of Negress Laruba (thirty) and her mulatto children, Antoine (six) and Delmace (four) because of "the service of the mother and [Carrick's] love and tenderness for the children" would certainly appear to be a family situation.[27] We are justified in assuming it. But far more certain is that Andres Armesto was *not* freeing a love child, the *black* boy Joseph (ten), when he explained that he did it for "love" of the boy's mother.[28] We know this because the notaries knew or could easily verify the bloodlines of all the residents of this small community, and they carefully recorded specific racial designations, which were based on parentage, not color as such. (Unfortunately, the names of black fathers were seldom recorded by notaries or priests.) Thus it is certain that free Negro Noel Carrière was not the father of mulatto Marianne (four), the slave he freed he freed in 1791, and so probably was not the lover of the child's mother, Negro Louise (twenty-four), both of whom he freed out of "much love."[29] Charles De Reggio was clearly not the father of fifteen-month-old Negro Celestin when he freed him in 1784.[30] Charles Delachaise would not have been the father of the Negress Catherine's son, grif Elias (five), whose father was necessarily a mulatto.[31] Louise Dutisné Grondel was certainly not the mother of mulatto Marie-Esther (three), whom she freed for the service of Marie's mother mulatto Victoria—and Louise's deceased husband was just as certainly not the father.[32] The only way Francisco Soler could have been related to the griffe Catalina (age not given), whom he freed in 1779, was in the highly unlikely circumstance that he was her grandfather despite the fact that both of her parents were colored.[33]

White women often freed mulattoes. Jeanne Fadet, Widow Piquery, freed François (seventeen) and Marguerite (sixteen), the mulatto children of the Piquerys' Negress, Françoise, out of the widow's "love for their mother." Would she openly admit that she "loved" her husband's mistress?[34] The same question is raised by Anne Recoquillo's liberation of mulatto Charlotte (five) for the love of the child's mother, Negress Marie.[35] Likewise, a white woman was capable of freeing a *Negro man* on account of her "love and tenderness" for him, as did Catherine Hebert when she let go Martin, age forty-two.[36] The ages of the principals are often telling. Presumably, Barthélémy Le Bretton, age twenty-six, was not the lover of the creole Negress, Jeanne, age fifty-five, when he freed her out of "love and tenderness" in 1792.[37] What would justify an assumption that Jacques Terrebonne's liberation of Negro Joseph (three), on account of the good service of his mother Henriette, was payment for her service as a bed mate?[38] By setting aside three hundred pesos in his will, Antonio Ramis freed Negro girl *("negrita")* Poñon, one of the thirty slaves he had on his brickworks just behind the town center's wall, without explanation, but, we must assume, not because she was the concubine of a man who had long been married and had a respectably married white daughter.[39]

Further proof that the words "love and tenderness" are not a reliable guide to intimate ties between master and slave lies in the fact that in many cases one suspects that an emancipator *is* freeing his family but does *not* express love and tenderness. Jean-Baptiste Nicolet appeared to acknowledge indirectly that he was engaged in a very personal act when, without comment, he freed the mulatto Madeleine (thirty) and the quadroon Louis (four) and gave them two thousand dollars, while denying emphatically that he was the father of the children of *another* mulatto woman.[40] Charles Pascal's paternity is suggested by the fact that he freed mulattoes Madeleine and Celestin on condition that they serve free Negress Angélique, the probable mother, whom he had freed sixteen years earlier when she was thirty-three years old.[41] It requires only a little imagination to conclude that Pierre Nitard had an intimate tie of some kind to another man's mulatto slave Rosette, whose freedom his executors were ordered to purchase with proceeds from the sale of his *only* slave, Cézar.[42]

Nevertheless, some unmistakable permanent domestic liaisons appeared in the New Orleans records in this period, arrangements that might be called "common-law marriages" if that had been possible in a Catholic colony. But wills and emancipations revealing these liaisons were almost never explicit about kin relations. Louis Laumonier was an exception when he stated outright that he freed Negress Catherine because she was the mother of their three children, also freed.[43] François-Jacques Lemelle was a creole trader of New Orleans and lived with his longtime mulatto companion, Jacqueline, and three quadroon daughters under the same roof. He was careful to leave them a comfortable and unencumbered estate. His daughters were well educated and ran a business together.[44] A small number of other similar arrangements are found in the record.[45] People like the Lemelles should be distinguished from those cases of temporary liaisons, in which partners did not live under the same roof.[46]

What motivated those men who created families that could not be legalized is unclear, but sexual necessity is not a satisfactory answer. A sample of all wills in the New Orleans Notarial Archive indicates an extremely high rate of male testators who had never married. This situation is even more extraordinary because the sex ratio within the white civilian population dropped nearly to par by 1785 (2,282 males to 2,151 females), although the census probably did not include a number of transient men. One factor, almost certainly, is the rate of foreign immigration. The immigrant stream was overwhelmingly dominated by men. As seen earlier, an important number of locally born young women preferred grooms born in the Old World. At the same time, despite that preference, a number of these men would not find brides in the marriage market. That meant a significant number of all men were without hope of legitimate domestic relations and would be tempted to take up with black women to obtain the comforts of hearth and home, not mere bedmates but women who would be companions, mothers of children, washers of clothes, preparers of food, perhaps business partners. Some with connections to the greater Louisiana marriage market would obtain white wives outside New Orleans, but others would be shut out. Even after we take into account the distribution of the sexes, however, some New Orleans white men, including men with all the socioeconomic means to attract white wives even in a highly competitive marriage market, appear to have been rejecting legitimate marriage.

As seen earlier, eighteenth-century Frenchmen suffered increasing anxiety about the status of women, who had the strongest legal position of any European women, controlling half of a deceased husband's estate. Moreover, in the days when matches were often made according to considerations having nothing to do with affection, wives were often regarded with suspicion by husbands. Charles Casaux made this point in 1781. A Grenadian sugar planter, he defended slavery as a form of extended childhood, and he argued that people who complained that slaves were especially mischievous were wrong. Without regard to color, "you will find a natural and implicit league among all servants to deceive the father, mother, and children [of a household]; among the children and the servants to deceive the father and mother; among the woman, the servants, and the children to deceive the husband."[47] Casaux claimed that men could only manage their dependents by a combination of moderate treatment and absolutely predictable correction by force. Nonetheless, French law gave women a better status than anywhere else. As a result, many French men, led by Jean-Jacques Rousseau, reacted by trying to degrade the status of women in the eighteenth century, some indirectly by choosing to avoid marriage and legitimate reproduction altogether.[48]

A man in a liaison with a black woman in the colonies would have absolute power to dispose of his estate as he saw fit because blacks had no secure legal rights to inheritance, thereby solving the patriarchy problem. Several pieces of good evidence support this theory. The acute observer of New Orleans society Claude-Cézar Robin explained that those men who lived in concubinage with black women did so "rather than to give to a white woman the title of spouse."[49] Amos Stoddard was even more explicit. "The [white] women have more influence over their husbands than is common in most other countries," especially because of their property rights.[50] Their authority over the household was absolute.[51] Thus, according to Perrin du Lac, a number of men preferred liaisons with black women because it gave them "the double advantage of being served with the most scrupulous exactness [since the concubine had no legal rights over the estate], and in case of discontent or unfaithfulness, of changing their housekeeper" at will.[52] To the limited degree that a change is detected at this time, the structural trends that led to a measurable increase in domestic relations across the color line at the end of the eighteenth century had deep roots prior to 1769 and were of a social nature. Moreover, other men, whatever their supposed sexual needs, were content to purchase domestic comforts from innkeepers and go without intimate sexual relations with women.

Intimate relationships with black women were of two different orders, the adulterous (undertaken by married men) and the nonadulterous, the former being more dangerous to white women and their families. One of the best accounts of New Orleans in the 1790s is that by Baudry des Lozières, a refugee army officer with no axe to grind and high praise for Louisiana. His book is a rambling commentary that includes a detailed project to import Angolan slaves to the colony, a formal argument that the lightest mulattoes should be made legally equal to whites, and a lengthy, sad sermon on mulatto temptresses. One had to give them their due, for they did inspire "stronger passion," but they inflamed the jealousy of white women, who campaigned to keep these darker rivals officially degraded by enforcement of the sumptuary law that was designed to keep them out of the best clothing.[53]

The relatively detached commentaries of Perrin du Lac and Baudry des Lozières have always been overshadowed by the inflammatory and outlandish screeds by Paul Alliot and Pierre Berquin-Duvallon. Both men were refugees from Saint Domingue, both were quarrelsome, and both wrote detailed libels aimed at Louisianians out of revenge. Alliot was a quack who claimed to be able to cure everything from syphilis (without mercury) to all sorts of cancer.[54] Moreover, he practiced without a license, and within months of his arrival in New Orleans was jailed and subsequently deported. Unfortunately, Alliot's studied purpose in his subsequent unpublished memoir was to discredit the government of Louisiana, which had refused to permit him to settle there. To Alliot we owe the absurd statement that is the origin of the myth of *plaçage*. He claimed that most free men of color gave their daughters a "special education" and "placed" them with white men at a young age.[55] Berquin-Duvallon also soon ran afoul of both his neighbors and local authorities. His account was published and it is a thoroughly dishonest description of the colony, easily refuted by reference to the many other contemporary accounts. Both men painted the local planters as morally corrupt, to the last man living in concubinage with black women, which was the most effective slander available to writers in this era, and historians have readily accepted these slurs as objective analyses.[56] A more worthy informant is Francis Baily, who, even though he was primed by hatred of slavery and anger at Spanish authorities to find the worst in New Orleans, did not mention interracial concubinage in his detailed description.[57] As shown by the many sorts of evidence laid out here, interracial concubinage was not an "institution" or universal practice by either white men or black women. As for *plaçage*, neither the word nor evidence of its being common is to be found in the archives.

That concubinage played a minor role in emancipation is indicated by more positive evidence, especially when the role of the underground or parallel economy is considered. Isaac Holmes reported that "several female blacks having been permitted to attend the markets, have acquired thereby many hundred dollars. The blacks indeed are the only persons who serve the inhabitants with vegetables, fish, &c. and with the sums they thus acquire many have purchased their freedom."[58] Other evidence supports the view that black women had substantial economic advantages over black men. The slaveowners' domestic servants in town were more likely to be women, and relatively poor slaveowners who possessed only one or two slaves were more likely both to live in the town center near the markets and to possess women because they were easier to discipline, cheaper to buy, and more likely to produce more slaves. In the case of gratuitous emancipations, it is only reasonable to assume that the majority of them were granted to domestic servants (especially, for example, the nurses of white children) because masters were most cognizant of their dedication and labor, and women dominated the domestic force. Holmes went on to lament that "many of the whites constantly cohabit with females of colour," but like every other report of this nature, that "many" is too vague to support glittering generalizations about concubinage, and in fact he specifically referred here not to New Orleans but to "the Southern States."[59] Certainly it can be said, however, that at least some white men in New Orleans evaded the collective moral police exercised by white women and chose illicit domestic arrangements over legitimate marriage, and a small number of these liaisons led to gratuitous emancipations in this period. Moreover, a few white men with children in slavery were also buying their freedom, which was facilitated by a policy introduced by the Spaniards.

The Spanish did introduce a novel element that made a big difference to a small number of blacks, guaranteed freedom purchase. Only a handful of slaves were permitted to buy freedom in the French period because generally it was not in the interest of slaveholders and it was discouraged by the Code Noir. But in 1769 slaves with unblemished reputations suddenly acquired the right to purchase their freedom or that of other slaves, and those with cooperative masters might even pay on an installment basis *(coartación)*. The right to *coartación* has been exaggerated by Tannenbaum and his followers as one that always existed in Spanish law and one that marked a major distinction between slavery in Spanish and Anglo-American colonies or states.[60] In fact, the right of well-behaved slaves to freedom purchase was an interesting policy, but it was introduced late in the eighteenth century, its rationale was never spelled out, and its full effects were felt only gradually and experienced by only a handful of slaves. There was certainly no such thing as an "abstract ideal of His Most Catholic Majesty that at some date all of his people might be free."[61] Tannenbaum simply does not provide any evidence that the right to self-purchase was guaranteed before that time, that it arose from a more humane cultural attitude, or that it affected an important number of slaves.[62]

Above all, O'Reilly's introduction of the *coartación* policy (it was never promulgated as a formal law but had the force of a law) suggests that the Spanish may have regarded the growth of free black classes in their colonies as intrinsic to a broad economic plan.[63] The single most outstanding feature of the Spanish administration is that they increased the slave supply to New Orleans. An expanded slave trade called for a freedom-purchase policy to channel the energies of the most ambitious and privileged slaves, to give them a reason to preserve the social order that kept the rest of the black population in their place. Giving a few blacks a way out of the system would serve to divide and weaken blacks' potential for united hostile action at a time when their number was increasing.[64] It could split the black community because a few would have a stake in the social order by using their free time gardening, hunting, gathering, fashioning, peddling, and otherwise serving for wages or fees and saving up their freedom money.[65] New Orleans suffered two great fires that demolished the core of the town center in 1788 and 1794, in which 856 and 212 buildings were destroyed, respectively. Both disasters brought a substantial infusion of cash to rebuild, which provided some free blacks and slaves with a special opportunity to supply the labor required for construction projects.[66] The system of freedom purchase favored those closest to the town center at the seaport, that is, the economic hub of the colony. It also promoted specialized black workers who provided essential services to the New Orleans economy in selected vocations. This did not subvert the social order because most were restricted to livelihoods that white men generally scorned.[67] Finally, *coartación* was also intended to counteract the outflow of specie resulting from free trade in slaves. Thousands of slaves saving the required *pesos fuertes* (silver dollars) toward their own freedom or that of a relative would tend to keep specie in the town, for slaves held much of the circulating coin in any slave society.[68] In sum, *coartación* was neither emblematic of the slave regime in New Orleans nor indicative of any humanitarian tradition or trend in Spanish slave regimes in general.

Under the influence of the freedom-purchase policy, the black community released a lot of pent-up energy in a few years. The law generated excitement among those few slaves with savings on hand. The sales of the estates of the executed or banished New Orleans rebels of 1768 provided the first opportunity for several slaves to test the new policy. Free mulatto Jean-Baptiste Horry purchased and immediately freed Antoine of Guinea, seventy-five years old, and Antoine's wife, Marianne, fifty, from the estate of Balthazar Masan.[69] From the same sale, one François was purchased by three siblings.[70]

Throughout the period during which the Spanish policy was in effect, 1,330 blacks achieved freedom under *coartación*, in increasing numbers until 1803 (see fig. 11). With this number should be included the 166 slaves freed by free blacks in this period because a majority of these people were undoubtedly family members purchased from whites in order to free them. That makes a total of 1,496 blacks freed by cash payment at the enormous price of at least $511,254, a stunning achievement in a town the size of New Orleans.[71] By the

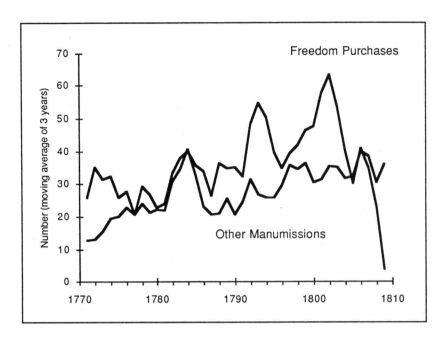

Fig. 11. Freedom purchases and other manumissions, New Orleans, 1770–1810.

end of the period, the rate peaked at one *coartación* every week, and by 1803 free blacks had become an important subclass in the population.

Many planters hated this interference with their absolute power over blacks, angrily insisting on the highest possible prices to permit it, and they usually obtained very high prices. When owners refused to agree to a reasonable *coartación*, blacks had recourse in the courts.[72] They sued masters to secure more fair evaluations, and these court settlements provide important insights into race relations in New Orleans. Slaves did what they could to avoid disputes, especially by waiting for a sale or the death of the master or mistress for a public valuation by an appraiser. A twenty-five-year-old black named Noel beat all of the odds early in the movement. Antonio Ximenes was forced to free Noel four months after buying him because Noel had savings and used Ximenes's recent low purchase price as his judicial price of *coartación*. The court would not permit a challenge to a market valuation that was so fresh.[73] The slave of good character was always fully guaranteed freedom by the court if he or she could pay, and court suits were rare once masters understood that the policy could not be defeated by their resistance.

Still, the road to self-purchase could be heavily obstructed. When a slave like Catherine of the Destréhan estate sued its administrator, Étienne Boré, she was put through a prolonged system of angrily contested evaluations, but Boré was forced to come down on the *coartación* of Catherine and her daughter Félicité.[74] On the other hand, when Marie-Louise Saly petitioned that she had paid her market price to her master and former lover, block maker Mathieu Parin, the court did not believe her and condemned her to silence.[75] When Isidore complained that Madeleine Brasillier Desprès was trying to cheat him on his credit toward freedom, presenting written evidence that seems to support his argument that "the laws divine and human are in my favor," the court silenced him because the mistress argued that he had not been sufficiently dutiful.[76]

Some other slaves were in the humiliating situation of trying to convince the court of their faults or debilities in order to secure a fair price of freedom. Free Negress Hélène petitioned to have her son, Magloir, freed for the six hundred dollars sent by the boy's father, Jason. Two appraisers evaluated him at six hundred and eight hundred dollars, and she asked for a mediator, who said six hundred dollars. The judge then took the unusual step of ordering a second mediator, who said eight hundred dollars. (This has the odor of bribery.) Hélène's attorney denounced the decision by arguing, correctly, that a fourth appraiser was not allowed by law, and then argued that several witnesses had testified that Magloir was a drunk and a thief and should not be so highly valued.[77]

Some slaveowners flatly refused to cooperate, especially when they felt betrayed by a particularly valued slave. Marie-Françoise Girardy, widow Deruisseau, apparently had fifty-year-old Marie-Thérèse locked up for demanding her freedom in 1782. The slave initiated a *coartación* action, and the judge proceeded to an evaluation, even though the widow refused to appear in court. Her plantation was nearby at Bayou St. Jean. Put on twenty-four-hour notice to respond to Marie-Thérèse's suit, Girardy sent in an appeal that the slave was "one of the most perfect servants in this colony" and that it had cost much labor to train her. Moreover, Marie-Thérèse had been a runaway since May 1781, and the widow demanded lost wages. The judge ordered Girardy to appoint her appraiser, who evaluated the slave at nine hundred dollars as opposed to the figure of five hundred offered by Marie-Thérèse's appraiser. The judge appointed a third appraiser who arbitrated a price and restitution to Deruisseau. This case is remarkable in many ways, revealing both a tough female slaveholder's anger that her slave would insult her by leaving and a

determined female slave's ability to set her own terms, working off the plantation to earn her freedom dues.[78]

Another case of a slave unable to get a fair price without a quarrel because of his superior skills was that of Michel, who had to sue Girardy under
the same circumstances one year after Marie-Thérèse.[79] Girardy was the exception because most contested *coartacións* involved male planters. Over time, however, disputed cases became relatively fewer, and customs regarding credit and
hiring out became established.[80] It must be acknowledged, moreover, that some
freedom purchases were quite amicable. The immigrant Scots physician Robert Dow purchased the Philadelphia-born doctor, James Durham, from a British officer after the fall of West Florida and soon allowed him to purchase
himself for five hundred dollars. The trilingual Durham went on to build a
lucrative local practice, keeping in touch with Philadelphia physicians.[81] But
Durham was not typical. Moreover, in 1801 authorities singled him out to limit
his practice to throat ailments, and Durham tried to get out of Louisiana.[82]

That neither slaveowners nor Spanish officials were actuated by any liberal principle is further emphasized by the overall stability of the line on the
chart indicating the incidence of outright emancipations: the rate declined
over time in proportion to the rising slave population. At the beginning of the
Spanish regime, twenty-six slaves per year were freed outright, a rate that rose
to thirty-three slaves at the end of the period, only a 27 percent rise in an era
when the size of the slave population at least doubled. The concurrent rise in
freedom purchase and decline in the rate of gratuitous emancipation by whites
was no coincidence. Slaves' increasing ability to pay must have encouraged
some masters to demand payment rather than emancipate a slave for good
service. Other masters were simply opposed to the growth of an anomalous,
potentially hostile racial "class."[83]

Certain groups were especially favored in the era of *coartación*. Least likely
to be freed were young adults between the ages of fourteen and thirty-four.
Various conditions explain this. It became increasingly likely that freedom
purchasers would buy children out of slavery as soon as they appeared to be
healthy infants. It was possible for a slave mother to buy her infant at a market
price of perhaps as little as $100, whereas for most slaves it must have seemed a
hopeless task to save up one's own price of $350 or more. Young adults at the
peak of their productive ages and market value were discouraged for that reason from banking on the many years it would take to save the price of freedom. Older slaves demanding *coartación* had been saving for years and were also

more likely than younger ones to be freed outright for "good service," which also relieved masters of caring for slaves too old to work.

Women clearly had a greater opportunity to buy freedom than men. Tables 18, 19, 20, and 21, based on the data outlined in fig. 11, reveal several patterns, above all the greater likelihood that females would be emancipated was of exactly the same magnitude (two to one) in both gratuitous emancipations and freedom purchases. This alone cast a shadow over the popular notion that the free black population derived mainly from irregular domestic relations between masters and female slaves. If interracial heterosexual intimacy played a major role in gratuitous emancipations, then women should be measurably or even substantially more favored in these emancipations than in freedom purchases, which were mostly based on the ability to pay; and clearly, the rates were the same. If the role of concubinage was major, the percentage of all female slaves freed gratuitously by white men should have been significantly higher than the percentage freed by white women by contrast to freedom purchases; in fact, white men liberated 73 percent of females freed gratuitously and 76 percent of those freed by purchase, which is not a statistically meaningful difference.

Other evidence presented in the tables supports the same conclusion. In gratuitous emancipations, freed persons unmistakably having two black parents (all Negroes and griffes) comprise 57.4 percent of the total, and in freedom purchases they comprise 60.9 percent: none of these people were freed because they were the children of white men. But, again, what about the relationship between adult black females who were freed and their male masters? Here the age of the manumittee is instructive. The age of women manumittees is known in 839 cases of the total. Of these, one-fourth were over forty years of age, and the likelihood of an emancipation arising from an intimate relationship must have declined sharply at this advanced age. And no less than 43 percent of those whose ages are given were children under the age of fifteen years, with whom masters were unlikely to have intimate relations.

In time, a number of common white men did pay for the *coartación* of their children by other men's slaves, and some could afford to buy the slave woman herself. Of 612 cases in which a third-party payer of a *coartación* was indicated, however, only 200 were white, almost all white men. Most of these were nonslaveholders, most of them unable to attract and marry white women. Cavalry Lieutenant Jean Bordenave paid $950 for Negress Jeanne, who was relatively old at twenty-eight years, at the auction of a rebel estate late in 1769.

TABLE 18

GRATUITOUS EMANCIPATIONS, NEW ORLEANS, 1769–1810:
RACIAL CLASSIFICATION AND SEX OF FREED PERSONS AND
NATIONALITY AND SEX OF EMANCIPATOR

| | Freed Person | | | | | | | | | | Total |
| | Quadroon | | Mulatto | | Griffe | | Black | | Indian | | |
Emancipator	M	F	M	F	M	F	M	F	M	F	
French											
Male	10	19	134	182	4	4	112	285	4	6	760
Female	5	7	42	40	0	3	42	104	0	1	244
Spanish											
Male	5	4	22	17	1	3	14	50	0	2	118
Female	0	0	2	0	0	0	2	3	0	0	7
Anglo-American											
Male	1	1	6	2	0	0	11	14	0	0	35
Female	0	0	0	0	0	0	3	1	0	0	4
Other											
Male	0	0	2	5	0	0	6	15	0	0	28
Female	0	0	0	0	0	0	0	1	0	0	1
Total	21	31	208	246	5	10	190	473	4	9	1,197

The very next day he was beseeched by Ensign Louis Mallet, who expressed "an ardent desire" to buy and free Jeanne. Bordenave agreed. The emancipation of Jeanne by Louis suggests that only a romantic interest could inspire this act.[84] The New Orleans garrison of regular soldiers may have been the single most important factor in racial mixing: most of the Hispanic soldiers were single, and venereal disease was one of the leading causes of their hospitalization.[85] Another early case illustrating payment of *coartación* for a child by a white man is suggestive but not explicit. Pierre Dupart sold to Louis Lanvy five-year-old Eugène, the mulatto son of slave Françoise, for $120, by the express consent of Françoise on condition Lanvy free the boy. Lanvy emancipated Eugène the same day, and it must be assumed that a parental bond was at work.[86] Nonetheless, white *coartación* payers almost never acknowledged pa-

TABLE 19

GRATUITOUS EMANCIPATIONS, NEW ORLEANS, 1769–1810:
RACIAL CLASSIFICATION AND SEX OF FREED PERSONS
AS PERCENTAGE OF TOTAL

Race and Sex of Freed Person	N	%
Black females	473	39.5
Mulatto females	246	20.6
Mulatto males	208	17.4
Black males	190	15.9
Quadroon females	31	2.6
Quadroon males	21	1.8
Griffe females	10	0.8
Indian females	9	0.7
Grif males	5	0.4
Indian males	4	0.3
Total	1,197	100.0

NOTE: All females: 64.2 percent of total freed; all males: 35.8 percent of total freed.

ternity.[87] White public opinion was against a man who appeared to be under the sway of a concubine. Joseph Claret provided a rare piece of evidence in 1790 when he requested a moratorium on his $1,000 in debts. His creditors angrily protested because he openly lavished money on a mulattress named Catherine who went about in high style.[88]

The most important restraint on adulterous concubinage, however, was exercised by white women: a wife was likely to attack a black woman upon the slightest suspicion of a liaison with her husband.[89] The offspring of interracial concubinage faced debilitating prejudice throughout Spanish America: "The disdain of both Spaniards and criollos for mestizos and other 'castas' was as good as boundless."[90] In the end, interracial domestic relations played a distinctly minor part in the growth of the free black population.[91] As in the islands, the great majority of mulattoes died in slavery.[92] In other words, the evidence is overwhelming that most slaves freed themselves by their own

TABLE 20

FREEDOM PURCHASES, NEW ORLEANS, 1769–1810: RACIAL CLASSIFICATION AND SEX OF FREED PERSONS AND NATIONALITY AND SEX OF EMANCIPATOR

| | Freed Person | | | | | | | | | | |
| | Quadroon | | Mulatto | | Griffe | | Black | | Indian | | Total |
Emancipator	M	F	M	F	M	F	M	F	M	F	
French											
Male	0	0	126	138	0	0	145	314	18	36	777
Female	0	0	30	54	0	0	46	108	10	15	263
Spanish											
Male	0	0	18	20	0	0	37	44	1	5	125
Female	0	0	1	1	0	0	1	0	0	0	3
Anglo-American											
Male	0	0	5	4	0	0	4	17	1	2	33
Female	0	0	3	0	0	0	2	2	0	1	8
Other											
Male	0	0	1	3	0	0	6	17	0	0	27
Female	0	0	1	2	0	0	1	2	0	0	6
Mulatto											
Male	0	0	4	4	0	0	5	10	0	0	23
Female	0	0	1	5	0	0	3	12	1	1	23
Black											
Male	0	0	0	0	0	0	7	6	0	0	13
Female	0	0	4	1	0	0	8	12	0	0	25
Indian											
Female	0	0	0	2	0	0	0	2	0	0	4
Total	0	0	194	234	0	0	265	546	31	60	1,330

TABLE 21

FREEDOM PURCHASES, NEW ORLEANS, 1769–1810:
RACIAL CLASSIFICATION AND SEX OF FREED PERSONS
AS PERCENTAGE OF TOTAL

Race and Sex of Freed Person	N	%
Black females	546	41.0
Black males	265	19.9
Mulatto females	234	17.6
Mulatto males	194	14.6
Indian females	60	4.6
Indian males	31	2.3
Total	1,330	100.0

NOTE: All females: 63.2 percent of total freed; all males: 36.8 percent of total freed.

efforts or those of parents or other relatives, not because they were the lovers, children, or heirs of whites.[93] Apart from scattered exceptions, the evidence as a whole does not support casual assertions that free blacks were given their wealth by generous white people.[94] Liaisons between white men and black women were responsible for less than one-fifth of the 2,693 emancipations discussed in this chapter.

If the purpose of introducing guaranteed freedom purchase had been to provide a fair process of self-liberation for all deserving slaves, Spanish authorities would have established routine evaluations more in keeping with the interests of freedom buyers and thereby removing all impediments that forced many slaves into costly court suits. The free black population would have ballooned immediately instead of growing very gradually: from a total of about 200 at the beginning of the Spanish era, over thirty-seven years the free black population grew to 2,312 when counted in 1806.[95] During this same period, the growth in both the absolute number of free blacks and in their proportion of the black population was at least as impressive in the slave states of the United States as in Louisiana.[96] Above all, the Spanish would not have made a great effort to increase the slave population by importations. The restricted and generally promaster character of the freedom-purchase policy in Louisiana bears out the conclusion of numerous historians that the Spanish regarded blacks in general and free blacks in particular with distrust.[97]

The case of Trinidad offers a useful basis of comparison. As in New Orleans, the population, including the free black population, grew rapidly because of Charles III's policies. Nonetheless, all of the laws were distinctly biased against free blacks, and white hostility to them was pronounced.[98] Thus, to speak of free blacks in either New Orleans or Trinidad as "privileged" or living in "affluence" is highly misleading.[99] While freedom purchase was an important boon to those slaves who were able to take advantage of it, they comprised a tiny minority of the whole slave population, as little as 3 and no more than 5 percent. And no evidence suggests the Spanish had a policy to create a free black buffer to oppose the white population.[100] New Orleans was the subject of a major experiment in imperial reorganization, one that was not intended to create a buffer or to make slavery more humane but to augment it and make it more productive and secure.

The causes and frequency of manumisson figure prominently in debates about the Tannenbaum thesis. Clearly, the growth of the free black population in New Orleans was owing to the economic opportunity open to slaves in a bustling port combined with the Spanish freedom purchase guarantee, which was tied to the slave trade policy. Parenthetically, much the same can be said of the policy to include special militia units of free blacks. These units were formed primarily to patrol to recover runaway slaves.[101] The French had created a militia company of free blacks in Bienville's time, so that was nothing new.[102] And the Spanish units were small and certainly did not have the social respectability of white units. By the mid-1790s, New Orleans had one company of mixed-race militia numbering 116 and one of blacks numbering 85, and creation of all-black and all-mixed-race units served to divide the free black community racially.[103] In short, race relations in New Orleans were not "relaxed" and free blacks were not especially protected by "a paternalistic Spanish government" in order to fabricate a buffer caste.[104]

The Spanish did not demonstrate "both public and private commitment to manumission from the beginning to the end of slavery" because of a supposed "legal stratification system with its dual citizenships" and other factors.[105] Typically, historians of the Tannenbaum school insist that large *numbers* of free blacks in Latin American colonies in the nineteenth century are the major evidence of high *rates* of manumission.[106] First, that ignores the fact that most blacks in Spanish colonies did not live in polarized slave societies (those with large disproportions of free and slave): manumissions presented no threat to the regime. Second, more to the point, free black populations originated in Spanish colonies a full century before the French, English, and other colonies were even established, and had been growing primarily by natural increase for two and a half centuries by the time guaranteed freedom purchase was introduced in the 1760s. Manumissions had seeded this growth, but no one has been able to provide a contemporary Spaniard enunciating a cultural or ideological commitment to manumission.[107]

The colonists were basically hostile toward the free black population. One good piece of evidence comes from the papers of Pierre-Joseph Favrot. A Louisiana-born career military man, Favrot served the Spanish faithfully throughout the regime as commandant of several posts. He also assiduously built up an unusual collection of thirty slaves. Of these, ten were of mixed blood, one of which he permitted to purchase his freedom, but it would be inappropriate to assert that any of these people were the children of the family man and leading citizen Pierre-Joseph.[108] In 1795, he wrote up a detailed program to deal with what he regarded as a serious social problem, the increasing number of free blacks in New Orleans, which was "very prejudicial to the Citizens."[109] Presumably written to inspire Carondelet to act in an era of crisis (the Haitian Revolution), it called for the expulsion of free blacks and mulattoes from the entire parish and the settling of them on lands chosen with care to separate them from all criminal elements. This would have several benefits: it would encourage the development of the white artisanal class and increase the white population overall, and it would reduce race mixture (*"le mélange du sang"*). He also advised that they be strictly prohibited from acting as intermediaries in the market by buying provisions at the plantations and reselling them in the town center; to be prohibited from enjoying cabaret life; and to be prohibited from displays of wealth because it threatened the distinction between the races and led them to "impudence toward ladies." Far from showing any favoritism toward free blacks, the planters saw them as a menace to order, and, more fundamentally, to the white "race." Obviously, however, no colonial governor could have considered a forced mass resettlement scheme of the kind suggested by Favrot.

The two secondary elements of Tannenbaum's argument—the cultural distinction of the Spanish clergy and the law—are even less important to the study of slavery in New Orleans than government policies concerning free blacks. While the Spanish kings had earned their honorific "His Most Catholic Majesty" by pious acts, Charles III was a man of his age and decidedly more cool toward the Church (if not toward religion) than his predecessors. He had a systematic if unannounced policy to reduce the property of the Church in the New World, and his suppression of the Spanish Jesuits in 1767 was the first step. The Spanish planned to retire the few remaining French priests in New Orleans and install Spaniards in their places. This also meant the suppression of the Capuchins' slave plantation.[110] None of this appears related to any plan to change the role of the clergy: there is no indication that slaves received more thorough religious instruction than they had in the past.[111] The newborn and the newly arrived from Africa were soon baptized, but there is no indication that this conferred any particular benefit on a slave.

Priests carefully recorded all slave marriages over which they presided in the period between 1777 and 1803, a time for which records are complete, and a grand total of thirty-nine marriages of slaves are recorded in their sacramental books. The majority of these were by slaves belonging to the nuns, who were permitted to keep their plantations. Thus, the secular planters appear to have been under no pressure from the clergy to permit their slaves to be married before the Church. Scholars of Spanish American slavery have not found evidence to sustain the assertion by the Tannenbaum school that for slaves in those colonies, "marriage was a sacred rite and its sanctity protected in law."[112] There is no indication that the Spanish priests who dominated the Church for three decades were "responsible for whatever human rights were conserved for the slave."[113] Not only is there no evidence they encouraged manumissions, but the declining rate of gratuitous emancipations clearly suggests the opposite. Nor did they encourage free blacks to form religious brotherhoods.[114]

The slave law of Louisiana changed hardly at all during the tenure of the Spanish. Nonetheless, the subject of the law is very complex. The variety of slave laws has led historians into great confusion, especially because of a naive willingness to credit those laws having the oldest lineages or an origin in the royal court as having the highest authority. In fact, at the local level, slaveowners had highest authority and determined the operative slave laws. And it may be said that, in general, "Spanish slave law in America developed haphazardly and was mainly concerned with security measures."[115] This is clear in the famous *Recopilación de Leyes de los Reynos de las Indias.*[116] Compiled in Madrid by royal mandate, its laws addressed specific local colonial problems, and it is not a code as such, merely a topical encyclopedia. Those portions concerning blacks and people of mixed race are drawn together in one section of Book VII and show no indication of being designed to govern a slave society according to a consistent plan. There is no indication that judges in New Orleans methodically used the *Recopilación* as a guide to settling issues brought before them concerning slaves. This is even more true of the thirteenth-century code of Spain, *Las Siete Partidas.*[117] The willingness of historians to attach great significance to a few supposedly protective clauses in this code, despite the fact that they were not appealed to by either slaves or judges, is mystifying.[118] Finally, there is the slave code developed by Charles III, also touted by some, the most pathetic product of the Spanish Enlightenment and certainly of no benefit to New Orleans slaves, as discussed further below. From the point of view of actual judicial application, all of these laws together were of no lasting significance compared to the local laws already in place in 1769 and modified by local slaveowners as they saw fit.

Aside from guaranteed freedom purchase, the only other minor change in judicial practice introduced by the Spanish was to tolerate inheritance of property by blacks from whites, although technically it was illegal.[119] Again, far too much can be made of this occasional practice. In one case, the alcalde explicitly overrode the old Article 52 to allow a free woman of color to carry away the movables from a deceased white man's house, as provided in his will.[120] The explanation for this is that the Code Noir was at odds with the Code O'Reilly (Article 3) that estates be liquidated and distributed "with equity," namely in conformity with the Code Noir but with some deference to the principle of fairness. Clearly, the judge believed the black woman in this case had a legitimate claim to the household goods, which she may have actually brought with her to the menage and which were of little value in this highly contested estate anyway. More to the point, this issue almost never arose because white people seldom left property to black people.[121] This isolated case does not prove that the Code Noir was completely annulled, and to blow up the importance of this isolated judicial decree obscures the social reality that the basic laws of slavery were unchanged after 1769.

In the 1770s, the New Orleans planters wrote their own slave code. The Code Noir of 1724, which was reconfirmed by O'Reilly in 1769, was never repealed, but it was implicitly superseded by the Code of 1778. Upon Charles III's authorization in 1777, the composition of this "Code Noir, ou Loi Municipale" was directed by the cabildo.[122] This Loi Municipale is fascinating because of what the planters revealed about themselves by those parts of the Code Noir of 1724 they reaffirmed and those parts they left out. The judicial records suggest that this code accurately reflects the inclinations of Louisiana slaveowners, and, generally speaking, the actual administration of justice.

Of the seventy-two articles in the new slave code, a few are shifted nearly intact from the Code Noir of 1724, beginning with the first six articles concerning religion.[123] Slaveowners must now, on pain of a fine, "entirely forbid assemblies held by Negroes in observance of the deaths of their fellow [slaves]" (Article 4).[124] The language of the old code in regard to labor on holidays is also altered. While the old code strictly forbade labor throughout the twenty-four hours of a Sunday or other holy day, the corresponding part of the new law is a laconic assertion that colonists "will observe" Sundays and holidays. Not only are there no penalties for violaters, but the possibility is left open that slaves may voluntarily work for pay on the indicated days. In fact, attorneys in the case of Mulet, the mulatto slave mason who drowned on his way home from work on a Sunday wage-job, revealed in their pleadings that slaves commonly worked the seventh day to earn the price of their clothing.[125] Moreover, like the old code, this article specifically exempts those masters who send their slaves to supply the Sunday market on the levee, in order to sustain the "public subsistence." This was, in fact, common practice in New Orleans.

The old policy of preventing a breakdown of the morphological distinctions between the "races" is strengthened in the new code. The new Article 6 goes even further than the Code Noir of 1724 by declaring that any white person who marries a black will be "driven from the colony in shame." This reflects the planters' outrage that one of the first Spanish clerics in Louisiana had performed an interracial marriage.[126] Articles 9 and 10 merely reiterate provisions of the old Article 6 punishing white men who live in concubinage with black women.[127]

While Article 7 echoes the Code Noir in forbidding a master to force a slave to marry, two new articles increase masters' power to interfere in this most personal of all relationships. Article 8 represents a departure from the old code by forbidding a master to allow a slave to marry another master's slave because, the code charges, such a practice leads spouses of such unions to absent themselves from their labors to visit one another. The master who permits such a union is obliged to sell his slave to the other master, probably the most effective way to discourage masters from granting permission.

Protective clauses in the old Code Noir do not disappear, but they are much altered in the new code. Masters are enjoined to supply slaves with unspecified provisions "as determined by custom since the founding of the colony."[128] More telling is the language of a new clause requiring a master to provide a pension to any old or sick slave whom he frees because even "the oldest slaves desire freedom so strongly that, without regard for the future, they will do anything to acquire it so as to indulge their fondness for idleness."[129] The callousness of this remark reveals the essence of the slave system. Articles 17 and 18 restate the old rule against separating slaves married before the Church, but they modify the rule about "prepubescent" children: it is no longer prohibited to separate children from their parents by sale, only from mothers. Article 65 forbids the mutilation of slaves, but torture is not prohibited and the murder of slaves by masters is not mentioned. There is no provision for slaves to appeal to authorities if brutalized by their masters. Nor is there evidence for the supposed right of slaves by Spanish law to force a change of masters by marrying another master's slave; as seen above, masters could forbid any marriage.[130] The new code of 1778 repeats all of the old police measures of both the royal code of 1724 and the local code of 1751, but with a more elaborate schedule of penalties for runaways.

The code was far more pointed than the Code Noir of 1724 in its hostility to free blacks and to those slaves who tried to free themselves. Thus, at least twenty of the seventy-two provisions of the code are directly or indirectly concerned with restricting the behavior of free blacks or slaves who hope to purchase freedom. The most important of these is Article 15, which attempts to prohibit the common "abuse" by which certain masters allow certain slaves to work on their own for cash and turn over a fixed portion of it to the master. By Article 70, the slave who does manage to earn the price of freedom is not permitted to purchase it unless four respectable free people attest to his or her good character. This was the slaveholders' crucial limiting amendment of the freedom-purchase policy. No less than seven articles limit free blacks' economic opportunities by restricting the carrying of guns and riding of horses by blacks. Other articles are concerned with what masters defined as problems of public disorder by free blacks. Any emancipated black without a specialized skill must quit the town center, establish a household, and take up "field work," according to Article 71. The new Article 11 lashes out at "the multitude of abuses" resulting from marriage between free blacks and slaves: the article declares these liaisons to be "absolutely forbidden." Finally, free blacks are strictly required by Article 72 to defer to their former masters, as in the old code, but they are now also forbidden "to insult, injure or strike Whites, or to pretend to an equality with them." The last article (number 73) adds the further refinement that free blacks are forbidden to wear the finest clothing available to whites. This was the effective slave law of this society, not royal decrees, and no document from the history of early New Orleans is more revealing of the basic tension in this society.[131] It required a united effort by the slaveholding class and constant vigilance by the white "race" to prevent black slaves from liberating themselves either by peaceful, industrious means, or by flight.

A comment is also required on Tannenbaum's conviction that slaves had recourse to the courts for redress against their masters and could bear witness against white persons only under Spanish law. The Code Noir also accorded the right of recourse, and in reality Spanish law allowed a slave to testify against a slaveowner only in felony cases where the testimony was required to protect the interests of a free (white) person.[132] In practice, there is no indication that the right of judicial recourse was enforced consistently by any court, except in freedom cases.[133] In all slave societies slaves or free blacks were allowed to sue in courts to gain promised freedom or to protect it from illegal encroachment.

In 1789, the royal government of Spain belatedly introduced a slave code for those of its colonies with developing slave societies, written in the last years of Charles III's reign.[134] One historian lauds the Codigo Negro Carolino of 1789 as a sophisticated product "of years of practical experience of Negro slavery in the New World."[135] In fact, this code represents a typically clumsy bureaucratic response to a growing problem in an absolutist empire, the problem of order in societies with some slaves, and this absurd confection was enacted but could not be implemented.[136] Full of unenforceable clauses designed to enlarge the rights of the state to intervene in the master's relations with his chattels, the twin ultimate objects were to diminish the potential for slave rebellion, a serious threat to the crown's interests, while at the same time "promoting natural reproduction of the slave population."[137] Another member of the Tannenbaum school is at least willing to concede that in failing even to mention manumission the code represents "a radical departure" from the supposed Spanish cultural tradition.[138] In fact, it was well within the tradition of Bourbon Spanish slave policy, although it actually clarified by omission the fact that freedom purchase was a privilege based on a policy rather than a legal right. The full weight of evidence from New Orleans, aside from a freedom-purchase policy that benefited a fraction of the slave population, contradicts the argument that "eighteenth-century Spanish slave law was essentially a humanitarian doctrinal adaptation of Roman-law sources."[139]

The planters who represented their class in the cabildo were outraged by the Codigo Negro.[140] They appointed a commission to draw up a detailed appeal to the king not to implement the code, perhaps after learning that their brethren in other Spanish colonies were doing the same.[141] The combined resistance of slaveowners in Spanish colonies made the Codigo Negro a dead letter, and it was quietly suspended in 1794.[142] In 1792, Governor Hector Carondelet issued his personal, short decree on slave treatment to post commanders, but it included none of the more exceptional aspects of the Codigo Negro; his prohibition of more than 30 lashes per day carried no enforcement mechanism and could be ignored with impunity.[143] Thus, the relations between masters and slaves continued to be determined by local customs and conditions.[144] No incident better illustrates the ultimate power of the colonial slaveowning class even where an absolutist king ruled.

One last body of slave law in colonial Louisiana remains to be discussed, the one included in an emergency decree by Carondelet in 1795. It was precipitated by events deep in the Louisiana interior at Pointe Coupée, a small and isolated slave society where slaves grew tobacco and indigo. Some slaves created an incident at the same time that the Spanish worried about the loyalty of the French colonists during the French Revolution. Authorities executed a few people and deported scores of others together with a few free people of both colors.[145] Then Governor Carondelet and the planters cooperated to implement new police regulations for Louisiana that were, in regard to slaves, of a traditional nature, but coincidentally marked an important turning point in New Orleans history.[146]

The Code of June 1, 1795, was a typical Spanish governor's "decree of good government," but it was also something more because it was especially formulated to police the capital and marked the development of the New Orleans town center from a cluster of shops, government buildings, and planters' townhouses into a town in its own right.[147] The decree outlines several police districts for the town, each under the responsibility of a syndic drawn from "the most notable and respectable Inhabitants," who are supposed to supervise appointed rounds by citizen patrols.[148] Carondelet's regulations of slavery were innovative in Louisiana only in the sense that the syndics were supposed to exercise surveillance powers over their fellow slaveowners to make sure that they treated slaves neither too generously nor too harshly. In effect, however, the planters had always exercised a kind of internal police over one another. Otherwise the articles of the code were unexceptional, in no sense in conflict with either the old Code Noir or the Loi Municipale of 1778. One article reveals that "the custom of the colony" is for each slave to receive one barrel of corn or an equivalent each month.[149] Nothing is said of meat, molasses, salt, or other necessities. Slaves are to be given *either* a set amount of clothes *or* a plot of land on which to raise provisions by which to gain the means to buy their own clothes. Slaves who work Sundays are to be paid half a dollar in cash. One close observer described the corn as being in the husk, so that it was only one-third of a barrel shelled, and he reported that slaves were compelled to work Sundays to provide for themselves.[150] Carondelet's code points out that the personal plot system also has the advantages of keeping slaves out of "mischief" (that is, working virtually every day instead) and keeping the public market supplied. Carondelet issued supplementary orders providing for the compensation of masters whose slaves were killed by maroon hunters or judicial decree, prohibiting gatherings of more than six slaves, requiring all slaves from the plantations to quit the town center before sundown, and promising freedom to informers who turned in seditious conspirators.[151]

The courts rarely punished a white man for cruelty, and it was always prompted by a special condition, especially when the interest of another master was harmed, such as when Claude Tremé shot dead another man's slave, or when the victim was a child, such as when Vincent Lesassier brutalized a little girl, or when a planter had a reputation for cruelty, like Guy Dreux, who ran his sword through Agathe's back, killing her instantly, because he suspected her of petty theft.[152] Planters lived in constant fear of a slave uprising beginning in the 1780s, even to the point of cutting off the external supply of slaves from 1795 to 1800 as a security measure.[153]

In the fall of 1800, Louisiana's Governor Casa Calvo took umbrage at the cabildo for debating a reopening of the slave trade and subjected the illustrious members of that body to a furious message. He lectured them that if they Christianized their slaves, supplied them with sufficient food and clothes, and disciplined them prudently, the slave trade would be less problematic. As admirable as the sentiment may be, it was a rare and pointless harangue that was merely tolerated by the planters and illustrated the bankruptcy of Spanish paternalism.[154] The Spanish had not altered the basic fabric of slave society in New Orleans since 1769.

PART III.
THE REPUBLICAN PERIOD, 1803–1819

Napoleon's Louisianicide and the New Republican Order: 9

The Planter Class Supreme

There is not in the United States a more hospitable people than the Louisianians, nor do the inhabitants of any part of America live in the midst of greater abundance or in greater style and elegance.

—James Brown to Henry Clay, 1804

On the whole, the state of society is similar to that of every city rapidly rising into wealth. . . . Their business is to make money. They are in an eternal bustle.

—Benjamin Henry Latrobe, *Impressions Respecting New Orleans*, 1819

A dozen years, and the French of Louisiana are cementing themselves with their new fellow citizens and rearing up their children, more or less, in the language of the nation.

—Frances Wright, *Views of Society and Manners in America*, 1820

The Spanish could congratulate themselves that their political and economic government of Louisiana was a success. Most colonists were soon reconciled to Spanish rule and showed little inclination to overthrow it: the slaveholding class's compelling need for solidarity against menacing Anglo-American pioneers and Caribbean slave rebellion had overridden all other considerations. Nonetheless, the same combination of American expansion and Haitian Revolution that wed the colonists to the hidalgos' government spelled the ultimate demise of Spanish rule in Louisiana. For the Americans, the British, and the French all eyed Louisiana and its seaport capital with a growing appetite for the rich natural resources the province contained. Several years of extraordinarily intense and complex intrigue resulted in the brief attempt of France to rule Louisiana again. Napoleon Bonaparte hoped to make the colony into a vast breadbasket to feed the slave societies he hoped to reestablish in the Antilles. In 1800 he persuaded Charles IV to exchange the province for a handsome Italian principality. Although the Spanish retained control until 1803, in that year Napoleon sent a colonial prefect, Pierre-Clément de Laussat, to New Orleans to prepare the town for the arrival of a French army. When another of his armies was defeated by that of the black Haitian rebels in 1803–4, however, ending his dream of reestablishing a French empire in the Antilles, Bonaparte committed what he called, with rueful sarcasm, "Louisianicide": he sold Louisiana to the United States, hoping at least to exasperate the British and appease the young American Republic.[1]

The people of Louisiana had the good fortune to come under the republican flag of the United States at an ideal time, facilitating their transition. The Louisiana Purchase gave President Thomas Jefferson a great public relations coup, and the weakness of his new administration gave him a strong motive to make the acquisition as popular as possible. He also had good reason to expedite the full political independence of the colonists because loyal citizens would ward off the intriguing foreigners who eyed the region jealously. At first he planned to reform the colonists, but Jefferson tempered his zeal with genuinely liberal restraint when he saw that Louisianians could be Americanized in his perfect image only by force. That he refused to employ. He appointed a complaisant Tennessee planter as territorial governor, William C. C. Claiborne, who was sufficiently popular by 1812 to be elected the state's first governor in his own right.[2]

In the territorial phase, Louisiana had a territorial legislature and New Orleans had a municipal council, both dominated by local Francophones.[3] New Orleans was the site of some minor political and cultural clashes, for residual distrust between Francophones and Anglophones did not dissipate overnight. Ethnic heterogeneity actually smoothed the development of democratic apparatus rather than impeding it, however, by introducing a fault line into the opposition party that quickly formed against Claiborne, one composed mostly of Francophones but led by dissident Anglophones. Moreover, Francophones were divided politically between the locally born and the "foreign" or recent French immigrants.[4] Democratic politics also gave white planters the means to unite and override cultural variety to keep free blacks out of political life and, above all, to fight a particular federal policy, the ban on the local slave trade in 1804. Congress made an ill-advised effort to arrest the African slave trade to Louisiana four years before it would be banned on a national basis, but angry protests from New Orleans slaveholders led to a virtual lifting of the ban in 1805.[5] The Aaron Burr affair of 1806, when the former vice president was arrested on his way to New Orleans, on Jefferson's charge that he planned to lead the West into a rebellion against the federal government, was fundamentally a product of politics outside Louisiana: the people of New Orleans were at no time on the verge of rebelling against the United States.[6] Moreover, General Andrew Jackson briefly threatened to alienate New Orleanians by imposing a harsh regime of martial law on the town late in 1814 when the British threatened to invade it. Francophone and Anglophone political leaders united to resist his bullying.[7] As always, above all, slavery united whites and made them willing republicans.

The slaveowning classes of the other southern states readily adopted their natural allies in New Orleans, who realized the importance of joining with the others to promote their mutual interests. The result was a remarkably smooth transition to statehood in nine years.[8] Thus, on January 6, 1815, the Francophone Anne-Louis de Tousard could announce to a relative: "Nationalities no longer count; we are all Americans."[9] Two days later, slaveholders' affection for their republic and the strength of their class unity were both dramatically confirmed in the Battle of New Orleans. They created their own political culture, especially their elaborate January 8 festivities, when Francophones and Anglophones stood shoulder to shoulder to applaud orators "indulging in severe observations with reference to the defeated enemy."[10] The gallery of the principal hub of wealthy Francophone society, the Exchange Coffee House in Chartres Street, was dominated by paintings of George Washington, Napoleon Bonaparte, and the Declaration of Independence.[11]

The remarkable speed of political adaptation was a reflection of a similar degree of rapid social adaptation: in 1803, New Orleans society was already so much like that of Charleston that it required no wrenching changes to become "Americanized." By 1819, it was one of the most fascinating, ethnically diverse cities in the United States, one of its major ports, and this had occurred with little friction among the various sections of white society despite the suddenness of its transformation into a large city. Locals experienced some mixed emotions at first, and during the early years they endured meddling by President Thomas Jefferson (who tried to introduce the common law), Congress (which tried to ban the slave trade), General James Wilkinson (who bullied the townspeople during the Aaron Burr affair), and General Andrew Jackson (whose cruel martial law left bitter memories after the Battle of New Orleans), but it was never enough to inspire hatred or rebellion. The local planters understood well enough that the differences between them and other North American slaveholders were cultural and secondary: they shared the same social structure, status system, and conservative views. As Joseph G. Tregle Jr. has put it, they "labored under no illusion as to their true self-interest, clearly aware of the certain promise of improved fortune implicit in their new status as citizens of the great republic."[12] They took readily to free institutions. As a class, the slaveholders were divided by ethnicity as the number of non-Francophones grew, but not bitterly divided. Together, the planters devised and put into place a slightly variant American legal regime. Louisiana was quickly and easily assimilated into the American South because the combina-

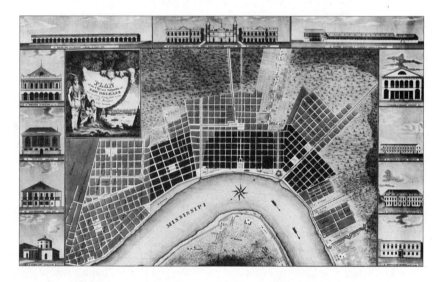

Map 3. Plan of New Orleans, 1815, by Jacques Tanesse. Surrounding vignettes (*left to right*) are: fire pump house (1813), government house (1761), customs house (1809), Théâtre d'Orléans (1813), meat market (1813), cabildo or "hôtel de ville" (1796), St. Louis Cathedral (1795), Presbytère (completed 1813), military hospital and barracks (1758), Théâtre St. Philippe (1810), Collège d'Orléans (1812), Ursuline Convent (1750), Charity Hospital (1786). Courtesy the Historic New Orleans Collection, Acc. No. 1971.4.

tion of republican institutions and the political clout that came with membership in a huge regional slaveholding class was irresistible.

Benjamin Latrobe will pull aside the curtain on this chapter. It would be hard to find a more American icon for this role because of his mixed background. He was English born and bred, of French and German descent, the son of a second-generation American mother who happened to be in England at the time and left him to be raised there. He emigrated on his own to Virginia as a young man in 1796. His architectural and engineering skills soon took him to the North, where he gave Philadelphia its first waterworks in 1799. In 1803, Jefferson appointed him as national surveyor of public buildings and charged him with completing the capitol.

In subsequent work, Latrobe became an important agent of the Americanization of New Orleans architecture. He designed the federal customs house for the port, thereby introducing the neoclassic style of the Republic into the town in 1809 from his workroom on the Chesapeake Bay. In 1811, he won a contract to establish a waterworks in the town. His son died in New Orleans securing this contract and designing houses for locals. The elder Latrobe then visited New Orleans for the first time, arriving early in 1819. Over the next nine months he designed not only the waterworks but also the Louisiana State Bank Building, the clock tower on the cathedral, and improved designs for sugar processing plants. Then, at the height of the dangerous season in the fall of 1820, yellow fever killed Latrobe.[13]

In keeping with the transient character of life for many in New Orleans in the nineteenth century, Latrobe thought the town would change rapidly. Its physical face, which had "at first sight a very imposing and handsome appearance, beyond any other city in the United States," would be almost completely remodeled or replaced within a century.[14] That highlights the story of New Orleans' rapid growth in its early national period. By 1819, the population of the parish had experienced strong growth. A house-by-house census of the town center in 1805 indicates a total of 8,164 people (3,543 whites, 3,056 slaves, and 1,565 free blacks), but over half the total population of 17,001 reported in 1806 remained in the plantation neighborhoods of the parish, as seen in table 22. Of the whole population for the territory (52,998) the town had nearly one-fourth of its white population, just over one-third of its slave population, and over two-thirds of its free black population.[15]

The town's population was only about 14 percent larger than it was in 1785 (14,853) because of the murderous mortality rate: in 1787 smallpox began attacking the townspeople periodically with gale force until it was brought under control in about 1803. Thereafter, the population grew because of immigration and natural growth (see table 23), so that the town expanded impressively by about 146 percent in the fourteen years between 1806 and 1819![16] According to one observer, the actual population by the 1820s was up to 50,000 in the winter, when the population was highest after the end of the sickly season.[17] By comparing the two censuses, one also sees the beginning of the demographic trend that will mark the city's development until the Civil War: the slave proportion of the population slid from one-half to one-third by 1820 and would continue to slide toward the vanishing point by 1861.

The legal definition and the social character of New Orleans changed after 1803. The territorial legislative council created twelve counties in 1805, that of Orleans being defined the same way New Orleans Parish has been

TABLE 22
CENSUS OF NEW ORLEANS, 1806

	Whites	Slaves	Free Blacks
Males	3,530	—	—
Females	2,781	—	—
Total	6,311 (37%)	8,378 (49%)	2,312 (14%)

TABLE 23
FEDERAL CENSUS OF NEW ORLEANS, 1820

	Whites	Slaves	Free Blacks	Total
Males	12,168	7,331	2,835	22,334
Females	7,569	7,615	4,326	19,510
Total	19,737 (48%)	14,946 (34%)	7,161 (18%)	41,844 (100%)

defined in the present work, namely all "country lying on both sides of the Mississippi from the Balize to the beginning of the Parish of St. Charles [German Coast]."[18] The First General Assembly under territorial government then created nineteen parishes in 1807, modeled on the old ecclesiastical parishes but now endowed with most of the police and judicial responsibilities granted to the counties two years earlier, yet the counties themselves were maintained for electoral and taxation purposes, causing endless confusion for historians.[19] Moreover, the *parish* of New Orleans was substantially smaller in area than the *county* of Orleans because the eastern and southern boundaries of the former were now reduced by the erection of new parishes on the lower coasts. This does not, however, seriously change the definition of the *community* under study in the present work because those new parishes were by this point lightly populated areas. After the erection of St. Bernard Parish in 1807 on the left bank below town and Plaquemines Parish below St. Bernard, the geographic area in which the community or town of New Orleans was concentrated was the one delimited by today's parish boundary lines plus the eastern portions of today's Jefferson Parish, right and left banks. The cultivated part of New Orleans was some tens of thousands of acres, but the residential portions were substantially larger than that by 1819.[20] By then, suburbs stretched toward Tchoupitoulas (St. Mary and Annunciation), toward Bayou St. John (St. Claude and St. Johnsburgh), and toward the Gulf of Mexico (Marigny, Daunois, Declouet). In other words, the area of the town under study here, the main settled part of the parish, was much the same area in 1803 as it was in 1731, but between 1803 and 1819 its agricultural portion gave way with remarkable rapidity because of population growth and the subdivision and settlement of the old plantation regions adjoining the town center.[21] This population growth benefited the planter class above all: it meant growing domestic demand and that meant profits for plantations and commercial investments alike. Every shipmaster who dropped anchor before the levee was a potential customer for Daniel Clark's ropewalk or a possible carrier for Étienne Boré's sugar. Every immigrant or voyager depended on provisions carried to the town center by slaves from their masters' plantations. Planters who speculated in land saw values rise with the population.

The character of this new immigration was closer to the original founding population, containing far more poor than gentry. Outside Faubourg St. Mary, where many fine brick homes were built by 1819, most new homes in other areas were modest, single-story, cypress wood houses, and most streets remained unpaved, turning to knee-deep mud after a downpour.[22] It was a city of great contrasts: the regular design of a Philadelphia cheek by jowl with an unhealthy swamp; some public theaters and other buildings as large as anything found in the northern cities overlooked a mass of cheaply made cottages as plain as those of Norfolk. As seen earlier, planters preferred to embellish their plantation homes, coming to the town center often but not to stay for long periods. Thus as the city of New Orleans gradually made itself more distinct from the old plantation region by becoming a more urban space with suburbs, the white residential part of the urban area became primarily the domain of ever more numerous nonslaveholders.

The emergence of the increasingly populous and anonymous city brings up once again the question of whether or not this community suffered great moral disorder: Was the slaveowning class able to discipline society in conformity with its own image of respectability? New Orleans had a ready-made image problem in 1803 because of Anglo-American prejudice against French and Spanish Catholic Europeans, especially in regard to their supposed lax attitude toward vices. According to the more objective William Darby in 1817, "much distortion of opinion has existed, and is not yet eradicated in the other parts of the United States, respecting public morals and manners in New-Orleans."[23] A well-traveled man like Darby, however, would "find little to condemn in New-Orleans more than in other commercial cities," and will find a commensurate "urbanity of manners."[24] The same view was expressed by Massachusetts-born, Yale-educated Reverend Theodore Clapp, who was much irritated that when he traveled outside Louisiana he was forced to listen to ignorant people condemn the town as a wicked fleshpot. In his view, despite the low state of Christian observance, there was as much Christian spirit among the people as in Massachusetts.[25]

It must be acknowledged that the disorders for which New Orleans became justly infamous over the course of the nineteenth century—crime, disease, and vice—began to develop in this period. Timothy Flint was a keen observer who spent over seven months in New Orleans, and he wrote in his careful description that the town was "exposed to greater varieties of human misery, vice, disease, and want, than any other American town."[26] Still, Flint argued forcefully that "the police of the city is at once mild and energetic. And notwithstanding the multifarious character of the inhabitants, collected from every country and climate, notwithstanding the multitudes of boatmen and sailors, notwithstanding the mass of people that rushes along the streets is of the most incongruous materials, I have seen fewer broils and quarrels here than in any city where I have resided so long."[27] Parson Clapp singled out that "floating population" of the maritime community as being responsible for the town's crime.[28] Some of the pirates in the Gulf of Mexico were closely associated with New Orleans, but the U.S. Navy suppressed the worst of these in 1819, trying and hanging the notorious John Desfarges and his lieutenant Robert Johnston in New Orleans despite threats by their friends to rescue them. By 1819, local sentiment was almost uniformly on the side of the federal government on this issue.[29] Flint concluded unequivocally that New Orleans was "about on a footing with the other cities of the Union in point of morals."[30] That was because slaveowners roused themselves, although spasmodically, to address the most serious problems.

The town council tried to establish a reliable white constabulary or gendarmerie, for example, supported by a tax on slaves, and this entailed the same problems that police departments present everywhere: their staff is frequently just as "outlaw" as the people they are designed to restrain.[31] Policemen provoked several violent incidents in which citizens were wounded.[32] It is not possible to evaluate the rates of crime in New Orleans in this period carefully because records of the criminal courts were destroyed. There is no reason to suppose that rates were higher than in American cities of the same size. Certain disorderly practices may have been comparatively more prevalent than in northern cities. At one end of the spectrum was the rather minor crime of graffiti: in 1810 the city set fines for those guilty of scrawling the "indecent inscriptions and figures with which most houses walls and fences of this town are covered."[33] More serious was gambling, a traditional southern diversion that seems to have reached the level of a mania in New Orleans by the 1820s.[34] In 1823, there would be an attempt to suppress it by statute.[35] Some forms of gambling were not amenable to any kind of policing, however, such as the old tradition of gambling on slaves by various means. For example, the British carried away many captured slaves after the battle of 1815, and as late as 1827 James Johnston was willing to pay $13,920 cash for the claim of Jacques Villeré against the British government for $18,560 for thirty-two slaves, the former betting the British would pay the full claim and the latter betting they would not.[36] Blood-sport spectacles were staged in New Orleans, like cock fighting and even bull baiting, but these were still to be found in other states or Europe.[37] Finally, at the extreme end of the spectrum, there is evidence that dueling by gentlemen was common. While we have certain knowledge only of scattered incidents, such as the duel between Governor Claiborne and Daniel Clark, one observer claimed that it was frequent as late as 1838.[38] With the possible exception of graffiti, these were all typical southern problems not peculiar to New Orleans.

One problem affected all classes but especially those without the means to avoid its worst effects: the inadequate and dangerous infrastructure. Public health deteriorated badly, partly because so little was done to improve it, and partly because pathogens flourished throughout the Americas in this period. Some reform was attempted by 1819. Over the years the town council tried to move hogs, dogs and noxious workshops off the streets, to clean up the scandalously filthy jail, to wall in the cemeteries to keep out horses and cattle, to require speedy unloading of barges carrying perishables, to have incoming vessels examined by doctors, to require butchers to dispose of their refuse more often, to clean city streets, and to restrict the disposal of fecal sewage in the river.[39] Drainage remained a serious problem, alleviated somewhat by Carondelet Canal, which carried runoff water and much of the city's sewage into Bayou St. Jean.[40] Benjamin Latrobe got the city's first running water pumping through pipes of bored cypress trunks in 1819.[41] It must be acknowledged that public spirit remained weak, dominated by the notion that "government" was responsible for such matters. Francophone newspaper editors groaned about this, especially when crowds just gaped instead of making the slightest effort to extinguish dangerous house fires.[42] Nonetheless, the well-traveled and highly critical Anne Royall, who visited the city a decade after Latrobe's death, went so far as to report that "there is not a more orderly city or town, perhaps, in the world than New Orleans."[43]

Despite improvements, the rate of mortality from epidemic diseases seemed to rise inexorably because of immigration. Unfortunately, it is not possible to be very specific about the role of yellow fever. Historians have found references to it before 1817, but Father Sedella stated very clearly in his marriage register for June 1817 that the city was experiencing its first epidemic of that disease, describing it carefully as "the black vomit."[44] Several observers reported that in 1817–18 up to six thousand people died of yellow fever.[45] If true, New Orleans' growth rate would have been even more spectacular if not for this malady. According to the astute analysis of Amos Stoddard, yellow fever and the other less terrifying killers favored the outsiders as hosts. He noted that "the constitutions of those born and educated in that country, are adapted to the climate; and the creoles can hardly conceive of a portion of the

Fig. 12. Father Francisco-Antonio-Ildefonso Sedella ("Père Antoine"), c. 1800 (born in Granada, 1748; died New Orleans, 1829). Attributed to José de Salazar. Sedella arrived in New Orleans in 1781, was appointed commissary of the holy office in 1786, appointed pastor of St. Louis Church in 1787, deported to Spain by Governor Miró in 1790 on the advice of the bishop of Santiago Cyrillo de Barcelona, reinstated by the crown and returned to New Orleans in 1795, elected pastor of St. Louis Cathedral by acclamation in 1804, and repeatedly refused to bow to authority of papal representatives and refused an offer of the episcopate. On loan to the Louisiana State Museum by the Archdiocese of New Orleans.

globe more healthful than their own."[46] He also credited the large proportion of vegetables in their diet and their avoidance of ardent spirits in preference to red wine.[47] Only in 1818 was a Board of Health established, although New Orleans had long been famous for its hospitals and doctors.[48] Meanwhile, the class factor was not without its effect on the mortality rate. Bad public health conditions disproportionately affected the crowded, exposed city dwellers, whereas many slaveowners could afford to travel to avoid them. Accounts of winnowing visits by yellow fever and cholera would reach truly epic proportions beginning, in the 1830s, with the ghoulish description by John B. Wyeth. And according to him blacks were more likely than whites to die of these diseases, even though whites were more likely to get them: "A negro gets very sick ... refuses all remedies ... believes that he shall go into a pleasant country where there are no white men or women."[49] Still, it is hard to refute one contemporary writer (thought to be Daniel Clark), who argued vigorously that New Orleans was not more unhealthy than Philadelphia or New York City.[50]

Historians' preoccupation with moral disorder and ethnic conflict in New Orleans have obscured more important social issues. Class distinctions among white people had never been disruptive, because the slaveholding class was not a tiny minority forming a closed and all-powerful elite. As seen earlier, about two-thirds of households were slaveholding in the 1760s. After 1803 that would change somewhat: the slaveholding proportion of the free population declined in the direction of the norm for the South (between one-fourth and one-third), and its domination of social and political institutions became, in the absence of metropolitan authorities, more complete and more obvious. That was a recipe for class disharmony, and the planters did not help matters by erecting a political system in which the mass of common people had no direct voice outside their local communities.

Despite the possibility of mobility, wealth was distributed very unequally and more so over time. The historian who studied this subject systematically would undoubtedly find that New Orleans resembled Charleston, where inequality grew to the point that by 1860 the top 10 percent of wealthholders owned over three-fourths of all personal wealth.[51] Like other conservative southern states, not only did property requirements limit major offices to members of the wealthy elite, but the suffrage was limited to property owners. To vote for governor and members of the state legislature, one had to be a free white male, twenty-one years old, resident in a given county one year (except those who purchased their land from the United States government), and a taxpayer. Since taxes were levied on a select few—mainly slaveowners and members of the commercial and professional classes—somewhat less than half the state's free white males were qualified to vote in 1812, similar to Virginia.[52] City elections were more democratic, but not at first. The first suffrage law required the elector either to own five hundred dollars, to pay one hundred dollars in rent, or to own an equivalent amount of property. The rent requirement was lowered in 1812 to fifty dollars, so all a nonslaveholding white man had to do to distinguish himself from the poor whites and the blacks was to pay a modest rent.[53] City officers were men of very little power, however, so democracy at this level merely served to mask the real extent of domination by the slaveholding class.

Despite their growing numbers, white laboring people could not form a class and challenge the supremacy of the slaveholding class because of their ethnic diversity, the weak development of the industrial sector, and the ability of some to join the slaveholding class. Any man not too proud to work with his hands could make two and a half dollars per day, according to Isaac Holmes. Living expenses were high (boarding, five to six dollars a week; clothes washing, one dollar per dozen) but it was also true that someone with a two-mule cart could clear eight to ten dollars per day—so much that a person could buy a slave within a year.[54] Because of this potential for mobility, rather than becoming a class with the potential for concerted hostility to slavery, the incoming stream of nonslaveholding white men (mostly men) benefited the slaveholding class because they strengthened the collective force of white people, augmented the labor supply, and improved domestic consumer demand. The potential for true working-class formation was constantly enervated by slavery and race.

The real challenge to the supremacy of the slaveowning class was posed not by nonslaveholders but by the potential for ethnic antagonism: contemporaries had legitimate concerns about the cultural cleavage. In the end, however, their fears were exaggerated. Latrobe imagined that he detected profound incompatibility separating Francophones and Anglophones. He thought that "national hatred and jealousy seems to be implanted in the very essence of the human mind," seemingly unaware that nationalism had been artificially inflated by the struggle generated by the French Revolution.[55] In fact, Latrobe's other observations suggest that white ethnic hatred in New Orleans did not exist and that even mere prejudice might soon disappear. Ethnic friction was a weak, gaseous melange of the natural resentment of bumptious newcomers, French chauvinism, newsprint rhetoric, and, above all, the pressing need of the Francophone community to use anti-Anglophone dudgeon to paper over their own deep internal divisions.

Latrobe did not have time before he died to discover how much real variety existed within each of the two main language groups. The heterogeneity of the white population was amazing by 1819, and many factors contributed to this mixture. The American/non-Francophone group became steadily more numerous, augmented by some unusual arrivals. With the end of Spanish rule, Jews began arriving again, expanding what would become the largest group of Jewry of any state in the South by 1860.[56] Among contributors to a growing white working population were Irish and German redemptioners, the first groups of indentured adults to arrive in a long time.[57]

The Francophone group was extraordinarily variable. As a result, it was fragmented by major blocs that moderated hostility to non-Francophones. Far and away the largest wave of immigration was that of the Saint Domingan refugees, many thousands of whom were welcomed into the territory by Claiborne between 1803 and 1810. Haiti spun off virtually all of its white population between 1791 and 1805, with waves of exiles departing according to their geographic position in the former colony of Saint Domingue. Small groups of them reached New Orleans in 1791, again in 1798, when the British evacuated after failing to subdue the colony, and in 1803–4, when the colonial regime finally fell and the Republic of Haiti was declared. Other exiles went to other colonies, especially Cuba, where the local governor gave the masters lands to work with their slaves while waiting to return to their estates when Haiti was pacified, for whites assumed that was inevitable.

The last great exile of French planters from the Caribbean began in 1809 after Napoleon invaded Spain. The Spanish people believed he would oust the hated first minister, Manuel Godoy, who actually ruled the country, so that Charles IV could reign again. But Napoleon removed both Godoy and the royal family to principalities and crowned his own brother, Joseph Bonaparte, as king of Spain, sparking a revolt that began in Madrid on May 2, 1808. Nationalistic reaction against all French residents led to violent clashes in the Spanish colonies, and in 1809–10 the French exiles were almost completely expelled from Spanish colonies in the Caribbean.[58]

Many French refugees from Cuba went to New Orleans, and so little is known of them that even the size of the group is uncertain.[59] According to a report in the *Moniteur de Louisiane* early in 1810, the local French-speaking population had been enlarged by the entry of 2,731 whites, 3,102 free blacks, and 3,226 slaves, or a total of 9,059—although the origins of these people was not given, perhaps including people who were not refugees.[60] Remarkably, a handful, both white and black, were Louisiana–born immigrants who had settled in Saint Domingue or Cuba.[61] The governor praised the generosity of New

Orleanians to the refugees, many of whom arrived in desperate condition, having escaped mobs with nothing more than their lives and a few slaves.[62] Nonetheless, evidence of the reception of the refugees by locals is mixed. Planters' fears of the tainted ideas of anyone from Saint Domingue remained strong. Moreover, a number of Saint Domingans had been greater planters than anyone in New Orleans, in some cases being the former owners of hundreds of slaves. Proud men and women of these ranks must have embarrassed leading locals, upsetting standards and lines of deference and alliance.[63]

Much evidence shows that white refugees did not fit into local society easily and were convinced that their sojourn in New Orleans would be brief. In his will, Thomas Bignerier wrote of the time "when the French regain their property in St. Domingue," where he had left 50 slaves.[64] André Duconge dutifully distributed among his heirs the 330 slaves he believed would one day be recovered on the island.[65] In fact, by 1820, only 1,700 of the white refugees remained in New Orleans, as estimated by Paul F. Lachance.[66] If a majority of the approximately 1,300 refugees arriving before the big group of 1809 were white, and if at least some of the approximately 1,000 people who arrived in a last wave in 1810 were white, then the total of white refugees would have been perhaps 4,000, for a remarkably low persistence rate of 43 percent. That the white refugees did not fit in is also confirmed by Lachance's painstaking determination of indices of homogamy: the refugees showed a pronounced tendency to intermarry with one another, which declined only as their willingness to marry the "foreign" (new immigrant) French rose, which is to say that they showed a strong disinclination to marry locals.[67]

The new immigrants from France after 1815 would become remarkably numerous by 1861, and their capacity for snobbery vis-à-vis the Louisianians was great and their predilection for marrying "les grands" of Saint Domingue marked.[68] One thing tended to unite all white Francophones and bind them to the Republic: an undertone of resentment of their mother country, which had abandoned them to their fate. This was true despite lingering Bonapartism here and there. For example, an unkind book written in French about the New Orleanians was answered in the French-language paper, Ami des Lois, by the sarcastic comment that the people of Louisiana were merely "better spouses, better fathers, [and] better farmers than the grammarians or scribblers of France."[69] The influx of these refugees and immigrants served to sustain a stronger French character of the town for several decades, but this should not be exaggerated: the lazily broad vowels of Louisiana French provoked snide contempt from European-born Francophones, as do Louisiana and Canadian French vowels to this day.[70] Still, the French language was temporarily reinforced by other new arrivals; in the two decades following 1819, no less than 8,264 people arrived from France.[71] Lachance also makes the important discovery that to the degree Anglophones married Francophones the former were absorbed into the latter group in this early period.[72] But the language declined in the later antebellum period despite this infusion, and after 1862 French cultural elements rapidly approached the vanishing point, not because they were actively suppressed by Anglophones but because the rapprochement and acculturation of the two groups began immediately in 1803.[73] As Joseph G. Tregle Jr. has shown, the locals suffered from a sense of inferiority to and envy of all the newcomers. If the new immigration by the better-educated "foreign" French from France seemed for a time to act as a buffer group between the Louisiana Francophones and other North Americans, in the final accounting locally born French speakers would sense that they had more in common with Anglophone North Americans than with people from Europe.[74]

One way to get a closer look at the white population is to sketch a profile of it from the record of those who died in New Orleans in these years. The St. Louis Cathedral register of the funerals of whites in the three years 1810 to 1812 contains 838 entries; both age and place of nativity are given for 797 of these. Their distribution according to origin and average age at death is shown in table 24.[75] This data confirms several key facts about the town's population. First, the dominant position of Francophones is undeniable; those from Louisiana, Saint Domingue, France, and Quebec constitute about 88 percent of the whole. The profile of the Saint Domingans is important because it suggests that a great many white refugees were advanced in age, no less than one-third of them being fifty years old or older at death. If this is typical of the refugee group, it helps explain low persistence rates: many died of old age shortly after arriving.

Finally, the locally born who died in these years are the most revealing. First, children five years old or younger account for the extraordinary proportion of 59 percent of all deaths recorded for locals. When this figure is combined with the fact that only a small number of the locally born lived beyond the age of sixty (6 percent of the total), claims as to the robust health of the locals seem exaggerated. Of great importance about the locally born is the fact that when children are removed from the totals, men are significantly outnumbered by women: men fifteen years or older constitute only 40 percent of

TABLE 24

AVERAGE AGE AT DEATH OF WHITE PEOPLE IN NEW ORLEANS BY BIRTHPLACE, 1810–12

| Birthplace | Males | | Females | | Children |
	N	Average Age	N	Average Age	%
New Orleans	161	11.9	146	18.6	59.0
Louisiana (other)	13	44.9	8	32.0	—
Canada	12	40.5	2	36.5	—
Saint Domingue	106	35.6	87	30.6	28.5
Spanish colonies	9	46.2	7	37.6	6.2
English colonies (U.S.)	8	14.8	3	33.3	36.3
New World (subtotal)	309		253		
France	155	36.0	14	55.0	—
Spain	27	51.6	1	35.0	—
Southern Europe	22	40.1	0	—	—
Central Europe	7	39.8	2	72.0	—
Great Britain	5	35.2	2	42.0	—
Total	525		272		

adults, women 60 percent. This cannot be a fluke in so large a sample and must indicate a substantial degree of outmigration by men born in New Orleans but squeezed out of the marriage market by immigrants. Although this stream of men heading for Opelousas and other upcountry districts had existed for decades, competitiveness in the local marriage market may have been worse than ever. The great disproportion between the overall number of males (66 percent of the whole) and females (34 percent of the whole) in the funeral register, which is even greater if children are eliminated from the totals, is striking.

The English speakers had been confident that they would quickly outnumber Francophones until the refugee wave of 1809–10. After that, however, the glum territorial secretary reported to the secretary of state that he disapproved admitting Louisiana as a state, which was advocated only by "dissatisfied" European and West Indian immigrants. He complained that "the principles and habits which prevail in this country instead of approximating towards those of the U States [sic] are becoming every day more and more dissimilar."[76] From the perspective of some Anglophones, the fractures in the Francophone population described above were less obvious and of little comfort. Yet Claiborne scotched his secretary's analysis by garnering votes from French speakers to become the first elected governor in 1812.[77]

A large degree of good will was expressed by local planters for Americans. As reported by outsider James Weir just before the Louisiana Purchase, the local French and Spanish gentlemen had treated him with "the greatest civility & friendship."[78] If some observers were impressed by the degree of conflict between Anglophones and Francophones, when their evidence is examined closely, it is found to derive from the fact that some politicians tried to profit by exploiting cultural differences between the two groups. William Sparks described what he called political "race" (white ethnic) rhetoric in detail, but especially in the decade after 1819, when it played a greater role as the rate of immigration by Americans increased. But Sparks acknowledges several key, contradictory facts. Above all, ethnic competition was characteristic of the city and not "in the country parishes [where] these prejudices of race had never been so strong as in the city, and were fast giving way."[79] In other words, it was *not* universal, not "racial," but a feature of life in the capital. It was inflamed above all by issues concerning development of the city's infrastructure. For example, while no strict housing barrier existed between the Anglophones and Francophones, there was a tendency for the former, the newcomers, to settle in the new Faubourg St. Mary (above Canal Street), while the locals remained in the neighborhoods where they were in 1803 or moved into Francophone suburbs. Inevitably, this caused hard feelings when it came to funding local improvements. St. Mary lay on the river too, the old population reasoned, and if its streets were improved, the town's focal point of commerce might shift a bit further up the crescent, out of the hands of the old population at the levee in front of the Place d'Armes.[80] This was a typical urban phenomenon, not a sign of bitter ethnic relations. As the historian Tregle concludes, even after the extreme ethnic political jockeying of the 1830s is taken into account, "as individuals, [Francophones and Anglophones] had gotten along remarkably well."[81]

Another major cultural phenomenon might have exacerbated trouble between the two major language groups but did not: religion. The introduction of religious toleration in New Orleans was an important change wrought by republican government, and it presented slaveholders with another potential threat to their unity. If there was no sudden enthusiasm to introduce non-Catholic sects, the door was now open to them. The small group of Protestants immediately came together to select a denomination, and, as well-to-do southerners, the natural choice was the Anglican church. They explained the move, however, in the ecumenical spirit that "it was a less remove from the Popish service to which all were familiar here."[82] It was actually several years before there was any settled Protestant church.[83] Doctrinal heterodoxy seems to have caused no social unpleasantness. The only real division was not between Catholics and non-Catholics but within the Catholic community, another factor that diminished the potential for Francophone-Anglophone tensions.

The Roman Catholic Church experienced great internal tension in the age of democratic revolution. A dramatic incident shows that at least some of the common people in New Orleans regarded the Church as an institution in which they had a stake. In 1803, the Church was maintained primarily by the Spanish crown at substantial annual cost, an income the clergy now lost. Moreover, the inauguration of republican government initiated a crisis about the cathedral. The pope had appointed an Irish vicar general for the region, Father Patrick Walsh, who was behaving as if he was bishop when the Americans arrived because no one had replaced the first bishop, Peñalver, who had departed in 1801. Father Sedella was pastor of St. Louis Cathedral but suddenly resigned in 1805, partly because of a long-simmering feud with the subordinate clergy (Jean-Pierre Koune and François-Pierre L'Espinasse), and partly because he was inclined to leave New Orleans with other Spanish nationals anyway.[84] Just as suddenly, he changed his mind, but Walsh had already appointed himself pastor of the cathedral in Sedella's place and now refused to annul the resignation.[85] This split the Catholic community, and in defense of local authority against that of Rome, Sedella refused to turn over the keys of the cathedral to Walsh. Antoine was a very popular figure and the confrontation produced an explosion. On March 14, *Moniteur de La Louisiane* published a call to the people to *elect* a pastor and assistants for the cathedral, and that very day a tumultuous crowd declared Sedella and his assistants elected by popular acclamation. The mayor himself urged the priest to accept the decision when it was presented by the new independent board of church wardens; the city council had turned over administration of the cathedral to the congregation.[86]

Walsh sued and protested hopelessly to the supreme court and the governor, but the subordinate clergy disclaimed any association with him.[87] The wardens then launched a campaign to have Sedella appointed bishop, but Rome instead appointed a series of luckless outsiders to represent the Church in New Orleans.[88]

From his office in Maryland, Bishop John Carroll sent a new vicar general to replace Walsh, but he was greeted by rough music in New Orleans. According to Claiborne, the "mob" that refused admittance to the cathedral of this papal representative was composed of "low Spaniards, free Mulattos, and negroes," but it also represented the sentiments of the anticlerical planters.[89] Sedella's very broad personal popularity resulted in part from his Franciscan selflessness. He dressed in a coarse habit and did not attempt to make individuals feel uncomfortable about their vices. These qualities endeared him to the poor, but to the planters he also represented their own home rule by snapping his fingers in the face of the foreign Church hierarchy.[90]

In 1813, the Church appointed as Bishop of Louisiana Louis DuBourg, the enterprising founder of St. Mary's College of Baltimore. As he probably knew when he took the post, his authority was unlikely to be established despite his birth in the former colony of Saint Domingue. He immediately refused to lodge in the presbytery because Sedella's assistants lived there with mixed-race families that DuBourg took to be their own, the same objection raised by the Spanish priests about the French Capuchins when they arrived in New Orleans in the 1760s! He at first stayed with the Ursulines and began trying to ease out the Sedella crowd, which caused an uproar, infuriating Sedella, who accused DuBourg of being a royalist, a remarkable charge from a priest but unquestionably a popular move in New Orleans. The bishop's situation became impossible—he feared for his life and fled New Orleans. The Church remained firmly in the hands of the people.[91]

Despite all this excitement about control of the cathedral, piety remained at a low ebb. Latrobe was disappointed by the drab services on Sunday. Regular congregations were four-fifths female, he observed, of which at least one-half were black. As another observer put it, "Few gentlemen except officers attend."[92] Holy Week processions that had formerly wound through the streets since the 1790s were now confined to the cathedral once again.[93] As Amos Stoddard put it gently, the planters' "health and prosperity in some measure divert their attention from [religion]."[94] Representatives of the Protestant Missionary Society of Connecticut were flabbergasted when, in 1813, Father

Sedella embraced them as allies, warmly encouraging them to distribute their supply of Bibles, of which, they were told, there were "not ten" in the whole state.[95] When the missionaries subsequently imported a load of French-language Bibles, they were besieged by "a large crowd of hundreds of people of all colours and ranks."[96]

It is clear that ethnic friction was a very minor problem in the first stage of the Americanization of New Orleans because the towns' leaders welcomed allies among any and all white newcomers. Sedella's embrace of Bible men from New England is an epitome of the way white society coalesced. Of supreme importance was the fundamental need of the slaveholding class for unity. The closer one looks at such a class in any slave society, the more hairline cracks one discerns: between big planters and small, or between ethnic groups.[97] But their unity of purpose and the racially unified front they welded to restrain black ambitions always countered any tendency to severe dislocation.

Above all, despite the emergence of ethnic neighborhoods, people mixed at every social stratum in every social activity.[98] Men and women could and did intermarry according to considerations other than their languages. If pre-existing kinship networks determined the marriages of many people within their language groups, it was not because they would be ostracized for marrying outside that group, only outside their class. The marriage registers of St. Louis Cathedral and St. Marie Church show numerous marriages across the language line. Just to name a few, Claiborne married the Attakapas belle Marie-Clarisse Duralde, and when she died soon thereafter, he married Suzanne Bosques, daughter of a Mallorcan immigrant and a local Francophone. Edward Livingston married Marie-Louise Davezac. Marylander Thomas Guy married Euphrozine Sauvagin. Georgian Thomas Simson married Maria-Rosa Montes de Oca. New Yorker Benjamin Levy married Emelie Prieur. Bostonian Joshua Prentice married the Saint Domingue refugee Renette Rey.[99] Members of all white ethnic groups mixed in the public ballrooms, dancing being the principal pastime, as it was throughout the South.[100] It is striking that there was only one serious incident during the years of the national embargo, a riot between the ethnic groups of common people, many of whom must have been out of work and irritable, during several days in the summer of 1808.[101]

If the French and American legal systems were as different as some experts have suggested, the law would have been a major stumbling block to smooth and rapid acculturation of the major ethnic groups; in fact, it was not. Lawyers like Jefferson and historians attentive to fine legal distinctions have built up a mountain of work on the peculiarities of law in Louisiana, but the legal transition after 1803 shows clearly that the basic law in New Orleans continued to be what it had always been: what the planters said it was, and planters everywhere had similar laws. The attempt by the Jefferson administration to introduce the common law was a political mistake, not because it was so different from existing law, however, but because it was so *similar* to what the planters already had that they regarded Jefferson's project as merely an attempt to demonstrate American power. The locals did embrace the English tradition of jury trials in criminal cases, and Francophones and Anglophones served together as jurymen.[102] Even in the domain where the greatest variation existed, family law, women and children were in about the same condition as their counterparts in Jefferson's Virginia.

In the two decades after 1783, Anglo-American white women were, despite their legal inferiority, somewhat better off than those of Louisiana: the American Revolution had made them republicans.[103] Nonetheless, they also became increasingly restricted to a domestic sphere in their roles as "republican mothers."[104] Conditions were different for southern white slaveholding women, who, because of the peculiar nature of their duties, did not develop networks or clubs northern women had that both sustained and transformed the cult of domesticity.[105] Southern women had strong kin networks, but these are not the kind of associations that led to abolitionism and suffragism as female associations did in the North. The domestic sphere over which the plantation mistress reigned was marked less by republican ideology than by crucial class interests. Rather than the smooth contours of the bourgeois paradigm of true woman and mother, southern women of the planter class lived in a fractured and ragged-edged world in which they had to be at once fragile and ruthless, vulnerable but cunning: feminine but first and foremost slaveowners. This basic contradiction of playing incompatible roles—one role shaped by gender and the other by slavery—shaped the lives of these women. The power denied one by the law of men was partly compensated by the privileges one enjoyed in administering a large white and black "family." But under these conditions, she "could envision no alternative to the system."[106] Slavery set strict limits to the potential for progressive liberalization of the patriarchal regime. The fundamental racial imperative meant that male household heads could never yield significant ground to the principle of the individual's right to self-ownership, which came to prevail in bourgeois capitalist society.[107]

The basic premise upon which family law was erected in Louisiana, as in all states, was declared unequivocally in Book 1, Title 1, Chapter 1 of the Louisiana Code of 1808: "Whilst men are capable of all kinds of engagements and functions . . . women are, by their sex alone, rendered incapable of various civil engagements and functions; thus, for example, women cannot exercise the offices of magistrate or representative, nor have they the right to elect or to be elected representatives of the people."[108]

Women merchants could keep their property legally separate from their husbands', but they were incapable of any legal action on their own, denied even the right to witness a will or commit any legal act without specific, written authorization from a husband or father. Husbands were prohibited from giving wives any general legal authority.[109] A man could demand separation from his wife for her adultery, but his own infidelity was not a cause unless he kept a concubine *in the house*. Finally, only the woman was forbidden to remarry until ten months after the dissolution of a marriage.[110] It should not be imagined that all women were incapable of influence, despite their legal degradation. As will be seen, they exercised considerable pressure to maintain racial boundaries. Moreover, some women evaded the bars to sexual equality so far as to be successful planters. One in West Feliciana Parish named Rachel Swayze O'Connor has been studied. An immigrant to Louisiana in 1778, she died there after building up a slave force of eighty-one worth $27,875, and her biographer concludes: "Few men had done as well."[111] Even politically women were not necessarily inert: Étienne Boré's talents were "below mediocrity" but he was highly motivated because his wife was "a great politician."[112]

The one, relatively minor exception to this generalization about the legal degradation of women was the French institution of community property established at marriage and widows' inheritance rights: fathers' power over inheritances was restricted.[113] Although the men now had an opportunity to change this to conform to American law, in which women were more strictly subsumed in the persons of their husbands and entitled only to one-third of the estate for life, they did not. Perhaps a combination of the force of tradition and vigilant wives employing domestic politics prevented any changes.[114]

New Orleans women may have enjoyed slightly more respect than other southern women because of the special contribution of the nuns. And a few locals now saw membership in one of the Catholic orders as a real alternative, even though most women submitted to the great pressure to marry and take up the "sacred calling" of motherhood.[115] Nonetheless, evidence about the Ursulines in this period is mixed. The prestige of the convent declined after

1803, partly because of the political change in 1803, but more because of the sisters' own money-making activities. Sixteen of the twenty-seven nuns decamped for Havana in terror when Prefect Laussat arrived, believing that the French republicans would suppress the clergy or worse, although Napoleon in fact intended to preserve the Church intact. The Americans showed them no ill will either.[116] This was, in fact, the coincidental resolution of an ethnic schism bubbling in the convent since the 1780s: those who left were the Cuban nuns, while the eleven who stayed comprised nine locally born, two from France, plus two coadjutrix, one local-born and the other Acadian.[117] But this decline in the sisters' total forces also weakened them, to the point that the treatment of their orphans was subjected to a rude official inquiry in the 1820s, which may well have been related to their now considerable wealth, for they profited from numerous land sales as they subdivided into residential lots their large Tchoupitoulas plantation.[118] The Ursulines' moral authority appeared to be declining. Moreover, regardless of the preponderance of women at mass, the Church remained a male preserve at the top just like any other major institution.[119] Women's status was indicated by the rule in the Church's catechism "that wives must respect and show deference to their husbands in all regards."[120] The planter class was by definition male.

Continuity with tradition was strong: even rich women were subject to public humiliation in ancient ways if they violated the code of female behavior. In the spring of 1804, Claiborne reported to Secretary of State James Madison that a full-scale *charivari* had been held at the expense of a rich widow who married a much younger man. A large crowd besieged the newlyweds with heartless taunts and a demand that the couple finance separate fêtes for the rich and the poor of the city. By this means the couple was expected to compensate society for the embarrassment caused by their folly or sin.[121] Thus, if community property continued to give Louisiana women a somewhat stronger position in the family than in the rest of the nation, its effect on her overall subordination should not be exaggerated.[122]

One provision of family law was new in Louisiana: with the disestablishment of the Catholic Church, marriage was a civil contract and divorce possible after 1803, of undoubted benefit to some women. A special act of the legislature was now required for a divorce, however, a public scandal that must have acted to dissuade the timid, but people with surnames of every description soon applied for such acts.[123] The territorial legislature also assisted women separated from their husbands with a law empowering county courts to make seizures to provide alimony payments.[124] Discussion of severe matrimonial discord and irregularity should be offset by a clear statement that the great majority of marriages were free of it. Of 738 marriages of whites recorded in St. Louis Cathedral registers in the decade between 1810 and 1819, only a few ended up in courts.[125] Contrary to some extravagant statements by other historians, only 11 of these marriages were by couples who had been living in concubinage prior to marriage: a formal church wedding by a couple who had not yet produced children was the norm for whites. The evidence bears out Jane Turner Censer's findings for the South as a whole: a modest liberalization of attitudes toward divorce in this period favored women but directly affected only a few.[126]

Few suits for separation on account of incompatibility reached the Supreme Court, in part because there was great effort to settle such matters at lower levels, in part because legal separation short of divorce became easier to settle once divorce was acceptable, but also because the court appears to have disliked hearing appeals from these women.[127] One recorded case is particularly revealing. Louis-Marie Durand, native of Martinique, age unknown, married Lucie Bardon, local born, age twenty-two years, in 1785.[128] They started with nothing but twenty-seven years later had a house, three young children, three slaves, and numerous debts owed to them. Now because he abused her she wanted to separate, keep the children, half the property, and receive alimony. Father Sedella had tried and failed to arbitrate a reconciliation. She had been refused by a parish court because there had been "reciprocal excesses and outrages," as the law put it, so she had lost the right to be protected by the court. It was true that witnesses had seen him beating her with a stick, but some claimed her shrewish tongue required it. She was likely to use such coarse epithets as "brigands of St. Domingue!" It is interesting that witnesses made it a special point to describe her cruelty to the slaves, as if this substantiated their evaluation of her character. She beat them "so hard as to fall down herself with rage and fatigue."[129] She warned the Supreme Court that her appeal had infuriated Louis even more: he told her twenty men had a pact to whip her publicly to silence her tongue. The court was unimpressed by the appeal and upheld the parish judge. It shows that a woman in a bad marriage could not expect to be granted automatic release from her spouse's authority.

Suits arising from marital separations are most revealing when they involve significant quantities of property, as close attention to several key cases will demonstrate. The courts were by no means chivalrous when it came to property. Judges protected women who naively cosigned notes with their husbands for loans against their community property, but women who tried to use their marriage contractual rights to plunder an estate verging on bankruptcy were treated as frauds. Courts retained great flexibility by splitting some very fine hairs where women and property were involved.[130] In the case of *Brognier v Forstall*, for example, when loans for which both Celeste Delavillebeuvre (widow Forstall) and her husband signed had ruined them, she separated from her husband in property and tried to claim three slaves as part of her dowry.[131] She claimed she did not know her liability when she signed the obligation *in solido* with her husband. The parish judge found in her favor. But when the chief creditor of the estate appealed, the supreme court ruled against her, acknowledging the law that her obligation was technically void because she was a mere woman and wife, but arguing, astoundingly, "yet it is admitted in practice . . . she may, nevertheless, bind herself," obviously convinced Celeste knew exactly what she was doing.[132] Thus judges reserved a great degree of latitude on this point; it was common practice to obtain a wife's consent to debts against the community, but judges carefully evaluated her personal role. This curious judicial ambiguity would have helped some women, hurt others.[133]

Another very distinctive and historic case is that of Marie-Julie Carrière. Daughter of immigrant merchants from France, "Zulime" was born in New Orleans in 1777. In 1794, she married a French-born immigrant, Desgranges, who was subsequently suspected of bigamy. Meanwhile, Zulime and Daniel Clark Jr. fell in love, and when they thought they found evidence (but not decisive proof) of Desgranges's prior marriage in Philadelphia, they married there and then settled in New Orleans. But Clark forced her to live in seclusion, to bear their child, Myra, in secrecy, and then sent the child to be raised by friends in Delaware. He meant to protect his family from scandal until Desgranges's marriage to Zulime could be definitely annulled by proof of his prior marriage. But to this humiliation and deprivation, Clark added to Zulime's unhappiness by abandoning her domestic comforts for those of another woman. To top off the first act in this sordid drama, Clark tried to bestow his fortune on Myra, but his business associates and sisters united after his death in 1813 to exclude both Myra and Zulime from the inheritance. Myra's struggle to rectify this injustice in the United States court system until her death in 1885 would become the most notorious legal case in the country. It demonstrates that even an adult woman from a prosperous family like Zulime was not immune to a minor misadventure that could totally destroy her peace of mind and leave her with only arduous and unreliable legal recourse.[134]

The sad case of Alexandrine Dusuau is instructive as to just how vulnerable to abusive men women and girls could be, little protected by courts. A penniless man with debts named Zénon Nouchet wooed the thirteen-year-old girl in New Orleans and carried her off to Natchez, Mississippi, to marry her against the will of her widowed mother. According to the Supreme Court file, he was obviously after the girl's marriage portion, which was over ten thousand dollars, and when Alexandrine soon died, he insisted that it was all his according to Mississippi law, although he protested his innocence, never having imagined while she was alive that he might inherit anything. In fact, the district court in Louisiana allowed him the standard 25 percent in intestate cases, and the Supreme Court upheld it when the widow appealed to protest that anything was too much.[135] This "theft" of Alexandrine (akin to slave stealing) was not typical behavior in New Orleans, it was a scandalous affair, but it reveals how vulnerable planters' girls were, a dowry's price tag attached to them for the marriage market, sometimes mere children in grown men's hands.

In fact, however, far fewer children of Alexandrine's age were married in the republican era. A clear pattern emerges over the first two decades of the nineteenth century: the proportion of locally born girls marrying under the age of 16 dropped from 25 percent of the whole in the middle of the Spanish period (1786–90) to only 11.7 percent at the beginning of the antebellum era (1813–17). This steady elimination of young adolescents from the local marriage market helped sustain the rise in the average age of first marriage for women born in New Orleans to an all-time high of 20.23 years. Moreover, as can be seen in fig. 13, which summarizes the age-at-marriage data for six decades, the average age at first marriage for the spouses of these women dropped slightly to 23.53 years by 1817.[136] It can only be regarded as salutary for domestic relations, and particularly for the mental health of brides that they were more often young adults and that the degree of age equality between spouses increased. These trends are congruent with those in the rest of the United States, although Americans in all regions were able to marry earlier than their counterparts in Europe.[137]

This brings up the question of the conditions of the marriage market, which remained remarkably stable, aside from a slight decline of the competition European men offered locals in the pursuit of brides. As seen in table 25,

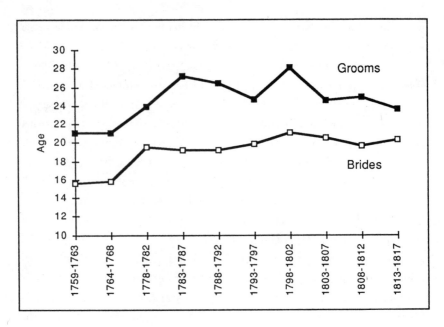

Fig. 13. Age at first marriage of women born in New Orleans and their spouses, married in St. Louis Church, 1759–1768 and 1778–1817.

however, that competition continued to shut nearly four of every ten New Orleans–born men out of the local marriage market. Presumably, many sought brides in the small Francophone communities sprinkled throughout the interior of North America. What we know of young women from the hinterland, however, suggests that they were just as likely as New Orleans women to seek out European-born spouses, as seen in table 26. Thus of 1,062 couples of all origins for whom the nativity of both husband and wife are known in the American period, fully 506 women (47.6 percent) chose husbands born in Europe. Again, as in the discussion of this phenomenon in the earlier history of New Orleans, speculation is the only recourse. Given that their age of marriage was higher than ever in the past, brides were young adults who must have been exercising some degree of choice in partner selection: marrying a man from the "cultivated" Old World must have served to improve a bride's social status in New Orleans.

While it is scarcely necessary to mention that only heterosexual intimacy and marriage were sanctioned, a remarkable commentary on homosexuality was published by Edward Livingston that suggests a hardening of attitudes at this time, which forms a natural bridge between the discussions of marriage and children. Livingston was commissioned to rewrite the state's criminal code, and in his treatise in defense of the final product he explained why he had eliminated homosexual acts from the list of crimes. Of his four reasons, the first is that "in our country . . . the repugnance, disgust, and even horror, which the very idea inspires, will be a sufficient security" against such acts.[138] Then, appearing to contradict himself without skipping a beat, he argues that including it as a traditional capital offense in a code that would be studied by republican youth would be dangerous, for "the familiarity their minds must acquire with the most disgusting images, would, it is firmly believed, be most injurious in its effects"—in other words, the very idea of it could corrupt morals.[139] Third and fourth, it was an offense "difficult of proof," and a charge from which "the innocent might suffer."[140] While these latter explanations may be congruent with the modern spirit of criminal reform, the first two reasons are suggestive of something more profound at work here. They are consistent with David F. Greenberg's thesis that this was a period of rising anxiety about masculinity. With the growth of capitalist market economies

TABLE 25

BIRTHPLACES OF GROOMS OF WHITE BRIDES BORN IN
NEW ORLEANS, MARRIED IN ST. LOUIS CATHEDRAL, 1804–19

Birthplaces	N	%
New Orleans Parish	234	38.2
French North America (other)	40	6.5
Other French colonies	34	5.6
Spanish colonies	13	2.1
English colonies (U.S.)	44	7.2
New World (subtotal)	365	59.6
France	161	26.3
Spain	33	5.4
Europe (other)	53	8.7
Old World (subtotal)	247	40.4
Total	612	100.0

TABLE 26

BIRTHPLACES OF GROOMS OF WHITE BRIDES NOT BORN IN
NEW ORLEANS, MARRIED IN ST. LOUIS CATHEDRAL, 1804–19

Brides	New Orleans	Grooms						Europe	Total
		French North America	French West Indies	Spanish Colonies	Anglo-America	Subtotal			
French North America	18	41	3	3	3	68	56	124	
French West Indies	16	4	46	0	6	72	101	173	
Spanish colonies	2	0	0	6	1	9	10	19	
Anglo-America	7	2	8	0	6	23	14	37	
Europe	8	2	4	0	5	19	78	97	
Total	51	49	61	9	21	191 (42%)	259 (58%)	450	

and the gradual disengagement of men from child-rearing responsibilities, men experienced increasing disquiet about maternal domination, the demasculinization of boys, and their supposed resulting sexual orientation, as revealed in Livingston's muddy discourse.[141]

Those who study women and the family and posit a dramatic change in the status of white children in the era after 1800 will welcome evidence from New Orleans. Changes in the laws concerning children were few, and one suspects that this accurately reflects unchanging conditions: boys and girls of the planter class continued to have markedly different experiences, but at least they were coming to be regarded as children whose childhood was something to be shielded from adult realities.

The greatest difference between the condition of children in Louisiana and the other states (and particularly the free states) was taxpayers' reluctance to establish public schools. A shift in this regard had developed over the course of the eighteenth century in British America, particularly among middle-class families. For the first time, large numbers of bourgeois people came not only to see children as individuals in their own right but also to regard childhood as a period to be cherished and extended. Of a piece with the emergence of the "cult of true womanhood," that development was also marked by a decrease in the importance of fathers in child rearing, as mentioned above, and a gradual decline in the employment of corporal punishment of children. Underpinning all of this was the basic Lockean ideological premise that infants were born innocent of innate characteristics or sin, that early childhood experiences were crucial, so that formal education of children was important. But signs of this modern attitude were weak in Francophone New Orleans in 1819.[142]

Americans were in universal agreement that the people of Louisiana were deeply anti-intellectual, indifferent to the liberal arts. One girl, Mary Ann Hunter, wrote sadly to her correspondent in Philadelphia in 1815 that "reading is not fashionable in New Orleans, we feel the want of books very much."[143] Numerous private tutors continued to function for the benefit of planters' children, but despite Claiborne's campaign to promote public schools nothing happened for years. The planters were not interested in taxing themselves to support schools for nonslaveholders' children, and the Catholic clergy feared that universal public education would threaten its influence.[144] Claiborne's initiative to establish a local university also met with formal approval by the planters in 1805 but did not come to fruition until many years later, and then it was little more than an academy.[145] Rather than schools, the foremost institution of socialization for children of the slaveowning class, which a child entered at age four, was their own series of public balls. One was described by an amazed New Englander in the early 1830s, who had "never beheld a more pleasing sight."[146] Troubled that Francophone and Anglophone children danced in separate regions of the ballroom, he was reassured by his guide that it was merely owing to the inconvenience of language, and that "a universal unanimity of feeling" existed between the two groups.[147]

Children of the working poor had no balls in which to promenade, were more vulnerable to distressed circumstances, and had to work at an early age. Yellow fever created so many homeless orphans that even the Protestants organized orphanages for both girls (1817) and boys (1824), a project initiated by Phoebe Hunter.[148] Records of indentures show that more white boys were put under these contracts than in the past as the town became flooded with immigrants, a reflection of the growth in the hitherto tiny stratum of laboring whites. Of ninety-six indentured children recorded between 1811 and 1817, the birthplace of the child is stated in seventy-five of the apprenticeship contracts, and only a third were born in New Orleans.[149] In yet another indication of the fact that there was only one true class in town, that of the slaveowners, the indentured were racially variable: 55 percent of the children were white, 41 percent were of mixed race, and 4 percent were listed as free Negroes.[150] This was like a mirror of the free skilled working population, and such a mixture could not form an urban working class like those developing in northern cities, where blacks were few. It is uncertain whether the figures indicate a trend, but in 1811 the average age of the children was 14.2 years, whereas it sank to 12.7 years by 1817, including many children under 12 years of age. Consistent with that trend is that half of the contracts in 1811 made the master responsible for providing a minimum of instruction in reading and writing, and in 1817 two-thirds of them provided for it because so many children were very young.

Conditions for apprentices were still unpleasant and potentially cruel, as illustrated by one revealing case from the records of the supreme court. In a shop containing several apprentices of both colors, one of the white boys quarreled with one of the black boys "about coming nearer the light," and the former stabbed the latter with scissors, causing a superficial wound. The enraged artisan hauled the white boy into the back room and gave him thirty lashes on his bare back. The boy's father sued to annul the contract with a cruel master and the parish court obliged him. The shop owner appealed, however, and upon submission of depositions from other artisans who swore that "a master cannot do without a cowskin," and a deposition by the boy's fellow workers that they were generally treated well and were whipped only when they deserved it, the court reversed the lower court's decision, agreeing with the attending physician that it was a bad, bloody beating, but not bad enough to annul a contract. The plaintiff's deponents were judged to be overwrought because it involved "a helpless white boy severely whipped for a struggle with a slave."[151] In other words, protecting the slaveowner's interest was paramount, as usual. The beating of this lad was not an isolated incident. In 1817, J. G. Flügel and a friend tried to restrain a silversmith who was sadistically beating a young apprentice, his hands tied, for stealing a dollar.[152] As in the rest of the country, it would be another century before reformers would better protect children from such inhumanity. Meanwhile, only the children and slaves of the planters were protected from abusive exploitation by others.

In summary, neither ethnic consciousness, nor religion, nor attitudes and laws regarding domestic relations caused serious trouble in New Orleans after 1803, for basic institutions remained the same. Nothing stirred more than a passing ripple on the glassy surface of the planter class, and the development of other groups was shaped primarily by social not cultural factors. It was not a question of becoming Americans, but of finally becoming members of the group for which eight decades of North American colonial status had naturally prepared them. Even if that had not been true, the need to maintain slavery and the planter class overrode all other considerations. Frances Wright's remark that Louisianians quickly adapted "the language of the nation," meaning its democratic-republican language of public virtue, indicates that chauvinism was quickly dispelled by the prospect of joining fellow slaveowners in other states and sharing their collective power. The planters were assimilated with ease into the class structure of the South via republican institutions, a structure in which there was no power on earth above the planters. They now made the rules more explicitly than ever in racial terms that would ensure their domination, but the structure and methods of their class had not changed since 1718, a class marked by fundamental conservatism or lack of dynamism. Above all, at a time when there appeared in the cities of the North wage relations between an entrepreneurial class and working classes, this occurred but feebly in New Orleans. The only change in the planters' condition was that their traditional domination was now improved to the point of absolute supremacy.

The transition after 1803 was facilitated by the sea of money being generated by sugar production. A newspaper laid out the accounting for a sixty-slave, eight-hundred-acre New Orleans sugar plantation in 1806. On an initial investment of $84,000, one would produce 250,000 pounds of sugar worth $20,000, plus 160 hogsheads of molasses worth $2,400. Expenses would be only about $3,000, including a mere $1,280 to feed, clothe, and medicate the slaves, or just under 6 cents per slave per day if their children were left out of the calculation. The rest was profit, depending on debt service. This citizen would pay the grand sum of $60 in taxes.[153] Even more impressive are actual production figures for eleven of the largest sugar plantations in 1806: a total of 494 working hands turned out $2,158,117 worth of sugar and molasses, an astounding average return of $439 per hand.[154] The economic surge was also nourished by local "manufacturing establishments," no less than 590 of them by the beginning of the 1820s. On close inspection, however, this is just a list of artisanal shops and the 31 sugar mills of the parish. A remarkably varied list, it nevertheless includes nothing more sophisticated than distilleries, no factories as such.[155] Yet it reflects a sharp rise in local demand for services and goods to sustain the sugar boom. Rapid social mobility was possible in these prosperous times.

John James Audubon arrived in New Orleans in 1819 or 1820 "destitute of all things" (except for "two of My Slaves"), terribly depressed, and soon became well-to-do, painting portraits of monied locals.[156]

A list of the port's principal exports in 1802, set out in table 27, reveals the extraordinary fertility of the Mississippi Valley and the main reason for the town's expansion.[157] Although the cotton, Campeachy wood, deerskins, and several other commodities on the list were not produced at New Orleans, the town provided the services that were essential to get these products to market.

In basic ways the planters were like capitalists everywhere in that they put a high value on their public reputations for the sake of their credit, so that they could borrow investment capital to increase their profits. The planters would never develop into bourgeois industrial capitalists, however, for that would mean creating a large free industrial class that would threaten their ideology and interests. Instead, without ever seriously questioning the moral and economic soundness of slavery itself, they perpetuated a remarkably simple capitalist (or "precapitalist") ethic according to which neither manual labor nor mere commercial endeavor without investing the profits in order to become a slaveholder was honorable.[158] Moreover, they faced a rather different set of risks than those encountered by bourgeois capitalists in the more closely calculated marketplace. Acts of God could be cataclysmic for an entire community that was based on the cultivation of crops for export. A hurricane in August 1812 destroyed crops and killed people, and in the middle of the night on May 6, 1816, the river made a crevasse in the levee in front of the Macarty plantation, causing a flood that nearly overwhelmed the core of the old town.[159] In the free-for-all atmosphere of the first decades following 1803, the prospective buyer of plantations had to be wary of ingeniously unscrupulous real estate speculators like John McDonogh, who artificially inflated the market value of his properties by documentary chicanery.[160] The greatest challenge, however, as always, was that of exacting labor from slaves. The planters exalted their special talent to command slaves as a veritable art that only select, tough men could master. Planters were keenly conscious of the difference between wage relations in the marketplace and slave relations on the plantation, which required distinct ways of thinking and acting, as illustrated in the following case argued before the supreme court.[161]

Joseph Fouque was a successful storekeeper in 1812, when he decided that he was ready to fulfill the dream of any ambitious man and liquidate his for-

TABLE 27
PRINCIPAL STAPLES ON WHICH DUTIES
WERE PAID AT NEW ORLEANS, 1802

Cotton in bales, pounds	375,137
Cotton thread, pounds	400
Sugar, pounds	1,333,330
Indigo, pounds	80,572
Tobacco (Louisiana), pounds	80,380
Tobacco (Kentucky), pounds	44,294
Campeachy wood, pounds	353,200
Deerskins, pounds	181,562
Beaver and other furs, pounds	1,072
Fox and other furs, pounds	702
Bearskins	834
Cowhides, pounds	2,429
Tabasco pepper, pounds (?)	5,050
Iron in plates, pounds	78,432
Sugar cases	23,065
Tar, barrels	5,977
Pitch, barrels	1,442
Planks (10- to 12-foot)	850
Salt pork, barrels	344
Salt beef, barrels	204

NOTE: Totals do not include exports from the American deposit.

tune in order to buy the Harang slave plantation. Apparently, Alexandre Harang wished to retire to the town center: part of the transaction included the sale by Fouque of his house in Royal Street to Harang.[162] Fouque joined the top rank of slaveholders. Like most merchants of any standing, he had owned some slaves—domestic servants—but his commercial success had not depended primarily on his ability to manage them. Unfortunately, the bad hurricane of August 1812 wrecked his first crops. More drastically, however, the planter class jeered at the idea that a former retailer could run a plantation. From the moment he was observed to switch, one deponent explained, "his credit declined." Another was more specific: "The great price he gave for [the plantation], the high levee, and his reputed inability to conduct the negroes of the plantation" ruined his credit.[163] Early in 1813, one year after the purchase, he appealed to the parish court for respite from his creditors: although he was able to show that on paper his assets exceeded his debts, others did not agree that the plantation was still worth the two hundred thousand dollars he had paid.[164]

The planters' conviction that there was something very special and even mysterious about the ability to manage slaves meant that the prediction of Fouque's ruination was a self-fulfilling prophecy. This was technically capitalist behavior by all parties involved, but remarkably unsophisticated behavior. Fouque put himself in a far too risky position by acquiring slaves he could not feed after one crop failure. His peers judged him partly on his lack of acumen with capital, but the main reason they ruined him by refusing him credit was that the labor relations he knew from his store made it unlikely, they supposed, that he could learn how to "conduct" slaves. That judgment was based not on a balanced appraisal of the man's demonstrated abilities or disabilities but upon a highly stylized preconception of the arduous and dangerous business of managing slaves who had nothing to lose. This kind of judgment, based as it was on intangible considerations, was arbitrary and unreliable. For the records are full of other gentlemen to whom their peers did lend huge sums before their inability to pay was recognized. A big bankruptcy could cause a domino effect all over town.[165]

At the same time, certain peculiarities of the Harang work force might have given creditors good reason to doubt his prospects, although they were never mentioned. The plantation's slave inventory reveals marked imbalances. Out of sixty-five slaves purchased from Harang by Fouque that were subsequently auctioned, thirty-eight were mature Africans in their thirties and forties, purchased in the heyday of the Spanish-era slave trade.[166] They hailed from no less than twenty-one different nations in Africa from the Congo to Senegal. Moreover, most of the adults who were listed as creoles were born somewhere other than Louisiana. In other words, these were all people who were regarded as more difficult to manage than locally born creoles who belonged to rooted kin networks in the community. Exacerbating these ethnic conditions was the extremely unequal sex distribution—forty-five men and twelve women—and the small number of eight children. This was a bizarre subcommunity with a built-in potential for instability. Only a savvy planter could maintain control of this group, and a former shopkeeper seemed an unlikely candidate.[167] Still, others had made the transition successfully, and Fouque appears to be the victim of what might be called mob psychology.

The crudity of the planters' capitalist behavior was somewhat alleviated by their relatively modern attitudes toward credit and banking.[168] Thus, in 1819, Governor Villeré called passionately for an end to the jailing of debtors as the "last remains of the barbarous establishment of despotism."[169] Several banks were established in the town for the first time, allowing planters to mobilize capital more effectively than in the past.[170] The most important of these symbolically was a branch of the Bank of the United States. President Jefferson resisted this, regarding the BUS as a tentacular "powerful enemy" that could, if allowed to penetrate everywhere, "in a critical moment, upset the government," and meanwhile it was creating a legal structure "shaped on the model of England."[171] Secretary of the Treasury Albert Gallatin and the merchant-financiers bore down on the president, however, and Louisiana was drawn into the national banking system.[172] The need for currency and credit was obvious. Before the banks appeared, the town was cash-short, particularly since the Spanish subsidies had ceased. Vincent Nolte, a German trader raised in Italy and Hamburg, arrived in New Orleans in 1806 and began his extraordinary career. Discovering that "there was not a single [commercial] house there possessed of any capital worth mentioning," he flabbergasted the town when he soon had three ships deliver to him half a million silver dollars.[173] Men like Nolte needed banks to hold their money, and the planters were eager to borrow it from the bankers.[174]

The year 1819 marks a watershed in the town's socioeconomic development in several ways. Above all, the local community of planters was on the point of disintegration at the very moment it had reached the apogee of its development. Sugarcane was rapidly exhausting the parish soils and wood supply, and the residential portion of the town was expanding: plantations were becoming fewer and planters would either seek new lands outside the parish (nearby St. Charles Parish was the current favorite destination of migrants) or remain and become members of the small rentier class. All of this was "natural," aside from the wholesale harm to the natural environment. That is, it was not the result of unfair competition or the failure of government to protect the planters. The federal government faithfully maintained a protective tariff of three cents per pound on foreign sugar and five cents per pound on foreign molasses, an indirect tax on consumers that drew the fire of both northerner and southerner.[175] Although this was a boon to sugar planters in other parishes, within only ten years after 1819, New Orleans would sink to tenth place in the list of eighteen sugar-producing parishes, producing a mere 2,787 hogsheads in 1828, and virtually no sugar by midcentury.[176] It also meant that New Orleans was becoming increasingly white.

The feverish pace of economic growth in New Orleans after 1815 was suddenly interrupted by a crisis in the market for another Louisiana crop. In November 1818, news of collapsing cotton prices in London reached New Orleans. While little or no cotton was grown for export in the parish, it was one pillar of the port's export economy.[177] The nation was plunging into a major economic crisis brought on in part by the huge migration to the Old Southwest and the explosive rise in cotton production.[178] Moreover, the manufacturing sector that had expanded in many states during the war was not sufficiently protected by the Tariff of 1816. The Bank of the United States did not have sober investment policies. The expansion of banking had flooded

Fig. 14. The Port of New Orleans, view from the roof of a house on the levee, 1819, by Benjamin H. Latrobe. The economic life of the town can be measured by the sea of masts huddled in the crescent, even in a period of commercial crisis. The white man on the roof is being served by a person of color, probably a mulatto slave. From Latrobe, *Impressions Respecting New Orleans.*

the country with paper of little value. The result was a panic and a sharp recession.[179]

By December 1818, northern banks began suspending specie payments, interest rates soared beyond the legal rate of 12.5 percent in Louisiana, and by early 1819 commerce in New Orleans suffered "terrible embarrassment."[180] By April, commerce was described as being "in a critical situation" because "money does not circulate."[181] Planters could not sell their sugar, and one of them was so overwhelmed by three hundred thousand dollars in debts that he drowned himself, setting off a chain of other bankruptcies. The discovery of the body of the cashier of the Planter's Bank floating in the Mississippi River caused a riotous run on that bank.[182] Thus, the story of the planter class closes as it began one century earlier, in a general capitalist crisis of confidence, one seemingly touched off in a distant European capital: the cotton market in London.

Unlike the John Law crisis, this time the planters knew they were saved from the worst consequences because they were members of a dynamic republic and had the only seaport used by thousands of inland farmers in several states. Thus, the local economy had great vitality despite the crash. According to Edward Dana, in the year prior to October 1, 1819, no less than fifteen hundred flatboats and five hundred barges from those upcountry farms unloaded in New Orleans, and five hundred steamboats plied the river out of the port.[183] Momentarily frightened like the rest of the country's capitalists, Louisiana's slaveholding class quickly rebounded in 1820 and went on to four more decades of breakneck growth and fabulous wealth. The aristocratic quality of their lifestyle was exemplified by their public and private ballrooms, which the well-traveled Henry B. Fearon claimed he had "never seen exceeded in splendour."[184] Flint believed that "the influence of slavery" made the locals "more reckless of the value of money than any people that I have seen."[185] Truly impressive is how confidently the slaveholding class maintained its supremacy in spite of the closure of the African slave trade in 1808, in spite of the disruptions of the War of 1812 and the crash of 1819, and in spite of the sudden growth and increasing ethnic complexity of both the masters' class and the slave community.

An Old Regime Made Anew: 10

Slaves and Free Blacks in the Postcolonial Era

I congratulate you, fellow-citizens, on the approach of the period at which you may interpose your authority constitutionally to withdraw the citizens of the United States from all further participation in those violations of human rights which have been so long continued on the unoffending inhabitants of Africa, and which the morality, the reputation, and the best interests of our country have long been eager to proscribe.

—Thomas Jefferson, 1806

The time may not be far distant when we shall be called to the field against a more formidable foe than the banditti lately quelled.

—Manuel Andry, after the Deslondes Revolt, 1811

Lay not up for yourselves treasures upon earth, where moth and rust doth corrupt, and where thieves break through and steal.

—Matthew 6:19

Since the slaveholders' regime was perfected by their political liberty, American government was no boon to blacks. The former colonists now had unrestricted rights to shape their society under a powerful republican government committed to the preservation of slavery. Deep and wrenching changes occurred in the black social structure, which was vastly altered because of trends with roots in the colonial period and because of certain technical changes the planters made in the laws after 1803. Slavery became a much *bigger* enterprise involving many more slaves because of the continuing sugar boom and the inauguration of free trade for Louisiana producers. Not only the size but also the variation of the slave population increased dramatically. At the same time, the continuing process of urbanization that had begun during the Spanish period meant that urban and rural slaves in the parish became more distinct as groups, with their own social patterns. The black community was also divided because free blacks' separate identity became more distinct. All of these changes centered on the central long-term trend that reached a crescendo in the years following 1803: the last phase of the African slave trade. Nonetheless, at a time when the black population of the parish was growing dramatically, 1815 marks the beginning of a new influx of white immigrants that would in future decades progressively diminish the black proportion of the city's population and its collective strength of community. The planters were able to contain tensions produced by the town's dramatic transformation because they now had undivided authority and because the black community was undergoing divisive internal changes.

Benjamin Latrobe's observations, written one and a half decades after the beginning of self-rule by Louisianians, provide an introduction to the routine context of life at the center of this urbanized slave society. Latrobe pictures slaves at work, play, funerals, and under the regime of the whip. Seeking to demonstrate how little the sabbath was kept in New Orleans, the Protestant Latrobe walks the reader through town one Sunday morning in 1819. He buys a breakfast of oranges from a black woman and watches the mooring of a crowded local market boat gaily flying Napoleon Bonaparte's pendant, from which four old slaves unload farm produce and game under the lash of their master's tongue. He watches sailors being helped into new "slops" by a black woman storekeeper. After eavesdropping on a group of well-dressed free blacks discussing their Methodist preacher, and attending church himself, he strolls up Bourbon Street and finds the stretch dominated by black artisans to be open for business.[1] In one of them, a mulatto is arguing a play at draughts with a well-dressed young white man, but most men are black and "hard at work at their trade."[2] At the corner of St. Louis Street, a fifteen-year-old black boy hawks his catch of birds. Later, Latrobe sketches a cabriolet in which a white man and light-skinned colored woman ride, driven by "a ragged black boy."[3] In other words, he finds the city's economy dominated by the labor of blacks, even on Sunday. On any day but Sunday he also would have seen the supreme mark of black degradation, the all-black city chain gang of men and women offenders, cleaning streets and levees, providing muscle for artisans on city projects, driving piles, spreading oyster shell on the levee, burying dead animals, and other lowly tasks as part of their public humiliation.[4]

Socializing was permitted after mass, and when he sees blacks at play, Latrobe gives full reign to his cultural and racial prejudice. His description of the Sunday afternoon slave dances in Congo Square includes important details, however, especially the remark that he saw musical instruments of African derivation and heard songs in a tongue he could not identify. Since the only languages spoken in New Orleans that Latrobe would be unable to identify would be those of Africans or Indians, this comment reveals the synthetic cultural mixture to which New Orleans blacks were making their personal contributions. It also indicates, however, that the speed and completeness of the citification of Orleans Parish should not be exaggerated, for this was obviously a mixed urban-rural crowd. Nonetheless, the increasing distinction between urban and rural space as plantations became relatively fewer in the parish meant an increasingly marked distinction between urban and rural people. At first an imperceptibly gradual trend, it was quickened by the last influx of

Fig. 15. *Market Folks*, 1819, by Benjamin H. B. Latrobe. From Latrobe, *Impressions Respecting New Orleans.*

African slaves, such that the creole, French-speaking, city-born slaves and free blacks felt some degree of separation from "saltwater Negroes" with African accents or "hick" creole slaves and free blacks who lived in the culturally distant, proportionately declining plantation region. Equally revealing, Latrobe notices that the crowd is entirely black. If Robin was right in 1802 that blacks and mulattoes danced together in the square, and Latrobe was right that they did not in 1819, it suggests a new social distance between these two groups.[5]

A funeral procession passing through the town center to the cemetery was the occasion for another observation by Latrobe about this matter of skin color. He watched a funeral for a one-hundred-year-old African slave woman attended by two hundred relatives. He described how the shallow, water-filled grave in the crowded cemetery was carved out of a muck of decomposing human remains in which little boys made sport with the skulls, and he described how one overwrought granddaughter threw herself upon the coffin. Once again, he pointed out that all participants were black, that is, neither the slave's family nor connections included any mulattoes, suggesting that these groups had been pulled apart by the planters' policy of discouraging emancipation and according a distinct status to mixed-race people.[6] This should not be exaggerated, for the slave population was mostly black anyway. The baptismal register of St. Marie Church at the town center offers a statistic that illustrates both the extent of race mixture and the danger of overestimating it. Of the baptisms of eighty-three slaves between 1804 and 1819, fully sixty-nine of them (83 percent) were either African or creole Negroes, but that does leave eight mulattoes and six quadroons.[7] However, the distinction between blacks and mulattoes was now legally embodied: the onus was on blacks to prove their freedom in case of a dispute, whereas those of mixed blood were presumed to be free unless someone could prove otherwise.[8]

Unfortunately, Latrobe did not combine his observations on blacks and mulattoes with any questions about the recent history of the slave trade, which was the most important factor affecting conditions in the slave community. As indicated earlier, although the question of the slave trade was the most serious problem arising from the Louisiana Purchase, it proved temporary and the trade remained open between 1804 and 1808. While it is impossible to count the number of slaves imported in those years with precision, demand for slaves was always strong, partly because of local demand for labor but also because the town was the central slave market for the entire region.[9] For Orleans Territory, including slaves brought in from other parts of the United States, *it is likely that a total equal to all slaves imported into the region before December 20 1803 was imported between 1803 and 1810.*[10] Slave prices are a good indication of the strength of demand, and prices rose to breathtaking heights in New Orleans. The joint commission established after the War of 1812 to compensate masters who lost slaves to the British army had to establish average values. Forced sale, the means of transferring title that yielded the *lowest* prices, showed an average value of slaves in New Orleans of $474, far higher than in South Carolina ($317) or Georgia ($268).[11] Slaves sold by more typical means averaged far higher, and higher in New Orleans than elsewhere. Even an illegal cargo of slaves from Africa seized and sold in 1818 brought an average of $768. The average value of the slaves actually carried away from New Orleans by the British was $1,068.[12]

The African and domestic slave trades made the town a seething cauldron of new, unfamiliar black faces coming and going over the auction blocks in the early American period. The illegal African trade after 1807 was sustained in some volume by the pirates in the Gulf of Mexico until about 1820: it was, in fact, the principal reason they collected and organized at Barataria and other hideouts.[13] Officials in New Orleans reported that the Baratarians who were temporarily dispersed in 1814 by the United States government simply regrouped after the Treaty of Ghent, shamelessly affecting the role of Latin American revolutionaries and setting up "republics" (first at Galveston) for the transfer of slaves and other stolen property into Louisiana.[14] Precise evidence is rare. The thoroughly respectable Jacques Pitot is found in 1810 selling eighteen slaves born in an amazing variety of places, one-third denoted as "brut," or African-born.[15] The Lafitte brothers sometimes noted where they had purchased their Africans, sometimes not, like Sujuire, a Congo who was twenty-two years old, whom Pierre Lafitte sold to the Ursuline nuns in 1810.[16] James E. Alexander was informed by a planter in 1830 that a regular slave-smuggling operation existed that was linked to Cuba.[17]

Evidence that the illegal trade in Louisiana was all but completely suppressed by 1820, however, is to be found in the records of the United States District Court for the Eastern District of Louisiana, a court particularly concerned with admiralty cases. The great majority of the indictments in this court fall into three groups, first, the approximately sixty ships that carried the refugees from Cuba between June and December 1809, which were formally charged in accord with federal law but then released because the refugees were allowed to enter on humanitarian grounds. A second group comprised ships that were seized because the vessel master or a passenger had among his or her possessions one or more African slaves presumably intended to serve as personal domestics, often coming from the islands. These cases were also usually dismissed. A small third group concerned true cases of slave smuggling, ships that carried between one and two hundred slaves either directly from Africa or through a port like Havana. In several of these cases, pirates seized Spanish vessels en route to Spanish American ports, intending to smuggle the slaves into the United States. This was true of the *Alerta* in 1810, or the famous case of the *Josefa Segunda* in 1818, which was plundered by René Beluche.[18] Indictments for slave smuggling were rare after 1820, although the trade undoubtedly never completely disappeared, so part of the local population was African throughout the antebellum era.[19]

The Africans brought in during the last years of the legal slave trade had the greatest potential to divide the local black community. Quasi-class divisions existed within the slave community, but in these first two decades of the nineteenth century they were overshadowed by ethnic divisions because of the immeasurable influx of an astounding variety of slaves.[20] Slaves gathered by the thousands in Congo Square, but they were clannish: "The Minahs would not dance near the Congos, nor the Mandringos [*sic*] near the Gangas."[21] Fragments of African class structure arrived in the slavers and were evident in Congo Square. One day in 1817, three former kings of the Congo region could be discerned there, of "genteel address [and] richly ornamented," whose dancing was spectacular.[22] Kings from the Old World could not slip into the existing structure of the black community without friction.

The profile of just one modestly large Tchoupitoulas slave force indicates how great this variety could be, that for Louis Avart's plantation of fifty slaves: twenty-nine creoles and twenty-one Africans. That was the fundamental divide, even though one finds considerable variety within each group. Of the creoles, no less than ten were of mixed blood, but these were mostly children. As for the Africans, they represented no less than eight different nations. The overall sex distribution was wildly unbalanced at twenty-three men and twelve women (sixteen years or older). Even more telling, although eight out of sixteen creole adults were men (50 percent), fifteen out of twenty African-born adults were men (75 percent). While it is impossible to say anything certain about competition for marriage partners, since neither the paternal nor marital status of men was recorded, it is easy to speculate that there was stress in the slave quarter in this regard. The master's favoritism in regard to the division of labor was clear: the great majority of the locally born were either domestic servants or artisans, whereas the great majority of the Africans were field slaves working under the command of a driver named Hyacinth, a Poular. Social status in the slave force is clearly revealed in the evaluations assigned by the appraisers: $300 to $400 for field hands, $400 to $750 for artisans and peddlers, and up to $1,050 for house servants.[23]

Given that two-thirds of the "Cuban" refugees in 1809 were black, moreover, they must have presented the slave community of New Orleans with a major challenge. Of the total, 3,102 were free blacks and 3,226 were slaves. Most refugees were penniless upon arrival, and the blacks among them would have competed with locals in those economic activities reserved to blacks. At least some of the refugees, in particular the free blacks, would have shared the wounded pride of the white newcomers in being Saint Domingans rather than hick Louisianians. Some of them introduced voudou to New Orleans at this time, which must have had a disruptive effect on the community because of the special powers claimed by its practitioners.[24] The refugees also brought diseases with them from the islands that were held responsible for the extra high mortality rate in New Orleans in 1809. Only 985 baptisms were recorded as opposed to 1,238 mortalities. Disease always fell heavily on the poorest, above all slaves. In the following year, once again, more people died than were born.[25]

Another, particularly anomalous element in the town's slave population was the odd collection of Indian slaves that had been developing over one century in lower Louisiana. Latrobe was the grandson of Pennsylvania Moravians killed by Indians, and he was prejudiced against them. Those he saw in New Orleans streets (presumably free visitors from the hinterland) roused him to condemn those who were trying to "improve . . . *our Red brethren*"—he looked forward to the day when the Indians would be extirpated.[26] In the context of building black community, they formed another, uncertain piece in the mosaic that made its internal structure unstable.

The efforts of masters to keep slaves divided by deliberate policy can never be underestimated. Equally important to avoid, however, is the notion that the whites were strong enough or clever enough to create a hierarchy among blacks based on color or ethnic background, with mulattoes at the apogee. The slave community was divided by color: a majority of mulattoes were slaves, and sometimes these were privileged over others either because of their complexion or because of a kin relation to the master's family. But this hardly means that all mulatto slaves were privileged and all blacks ranked lower in the

Fig. 16. Slaves from the upper South being conducted to the lower South, c. 1839. From James S. Buckingham, *The Slave States of America*, 2 vols. (London: Fisher and Son, 1842).

estimation of either their masters or fellow slaves. When Peter Blancq took his family on a voyage to Bordeaux in 1818, he revealed that his children's nurse was a twenty-three-year-old African named Charlotte, "having several of her country marks on both temples."[27] Many free blacks in 1803 were African-born people who owed their success to something other than a light complexion.

If the direct-from-Africa supply of slaves was cut off in 1808, no corresponding solicitude prevented the forced march of masses of unoffending black Americans from the older states into the lower Mississippi Valley.[28] The ethnic cornucopia of new slaves that were moved into Louisiana from the United States must have contributed to the disruption of the local black community, a constant challenge to its integrity. Whether on foot from the Atlantic states or on groaning flatboats from Kentucky, slaves arrived in Louisiana by the thousands by 1819.[29] While the majority of these particular new arrivals were taken to parishes outside New Orleans Parish, especially to "the Florida parishes" on the other side of Lake Pontchartrain, for example, more than a few were sold to local planters. Even before 1803, the New Orleans market had been used by planters in the United States to sell slaves they did not want, such as the eight leaders of Gabriel's Rebellion who were exiled there in 1801.[30] Such an exile rid Virginians of a problem and it helped keep their slaves in line to demonize Louisiana as a horrible destination for outcasts. Whether or not the Virginia rebels actually arrived in New Orleans, it does lead to the question of whether there is evidence of "Gabriels" among the town's own slaves: Was the rebelliousness of this rapidly growing and divided slave population on the rise?

Scholars of the American Revolution have shown how strongly blacks reacted to and contributed to the ideology of liberation, and, given the establishment of the Haitian Republic at the beginning of New Orleans' territorial period, it is reasonable to wonder about the extent of ideology among slaves in New Orleans. There is scattered evidence that free blacks were as ardently republican as any group in 1803, but we know next to nothing about the slaves for want of sources.

A peculiar incident in 1805 tends to underline the limited potential for rebellion among New Orleans slaves. A mulatto slave named Celestin reported to authorities that a white refugee from Saint Domingue for whom he worked (Grandjean) was trying to draw him into a plot for a slave uprising. The response of city fathers was to set up Grandjean by soliciting a few "Mullattoes of note and integrity" to enter into the man's confidence to find out all they could. The upshot was that Grandjean was the sole plotter, having labored for several months in vain to draw slaves into his scheme. He was promptly arrested, and the sole beneficiary of the incident was Celestin, whose freedom a grateful town council resolved to purchase.[31] It is true that whites were jittery throughout the period and undoubtedly had reason to be. In retrospect, however, the slaves' ability to inspire fear is much more impressive than their ability to mount serious, organized challenges to the system. Nonetheless, one event does suggest that Louisiana slaves were explicitly ideological, which lies in the records of the insurrections of 1811–12.

Any lingering spirit of Haiti in Louisiana appeared to have abated by the beginning of 1811. At the start of Mardi Gras that year, Claiborne had to call out the city guard and the troops of the garrison to put down a free-for-all between white boatmen and sailors that took place on January 5. This is one of the few riots mentioned in these years, and, in Claiborne's estimation, the public peace was still most threatened by the "Burrites," supposed adherents of Aaron Burr, accused of planning to revolutionize New Orleans in 1806.[32] In the days following the mariners' riot, however, some slaves at German Coast began one of the largest slave uprisings in the history of North America.

As always in Louisiana history, aside from the broken conspiracy of 1731, this rebellion took place in a region outside the boundaries of New Orleans Parish. On January 9, a group of slaves at German Coast rose up under the leadership of a mulatto slave born in Saint Domingue named Charles Deslondes. What is most intriguing is that it began with little or no advance planning the day after reports were published in New Orleans that Henri Christophe had defeated Alexandre Pétion in a bloody battle and seized control of Port-au-Prince.[33] This was a contest between the former black slaves, under Christophe, political heir of Toussaint Louverture and Jean-Jacques Dessalines, and the quadroon, Pétion, who had at one time fought against slave insurrection and was still thought to be "inclined to the French."[34] Christophe's victory was that of black slaves over free mulattoes, a story that had been followed in the local press, and it is hard to resist speculating that Charles Deslondes's rebels were emboldened by the fall of Port-au-Prince to the former slaves.[35]

The German Coast rebels wounded their master and killed his son and then rushed from plantation to plantation to gather adherents until they had up to five hundred people, many of them armed and prepared to carry out what whites believed to be "a mature plan" by Deslondes.[36] Meanwhile, the local whites, some of them warned in advance by loyal slaves, packed up their valuables and fled to New Orleans in terror before the rebels, who marched defiantly, "colors displayed and full of arrogance."[37] The rebels prepared for a pitched battle, but the militia and federal troops under General Wade Hampton attacked and routed them.[38] The final tally was two whites killed, three houses burned, several pillaged, on one side, and sixty-six slaves killed in battle, seventeen missing and assumed to be dead of wounds, and many others captured. Thirty suspected leaders (twenty-eight blacks and two mulattoes) were interrogated for two days by an impromptu jury of six planters, and twenty-one of these were condemned and executed on the fifteenth. One more was tried and executed February 20. These leaders were executed by firing squads, their heads being then cut off and mounted on poles to provide masks of terror to other slaves.[39]

The reaction of whites to these "brigands" and "assassins" reflected the basic assumptions and varieties of thought about the policing of slaves. Claiborne seized upon the opportunity to blame the planters themselves for introducing too many slaves into the territory, including many banished from other states and colonies because of their bad character. His supporters immediately introduced a bill in the legislature that would have restricted the entry of slaves into the territory by the domestic slave trade.[40] The answer of the planters was an angry demand that Claiborne abandon his "doctrine of passive obedience and non-resistance" and establish a full regiment of federal troops at New Orleans on a permanent basis.[41] They also responded to the emergency with the usual publication of police rules to limit the freedom of movement of slaves in the city.[42]

Nothing illustrates more vividly the planters' conviction that they could never be sure that they controlled their slaves. Claiborne assured superiors that it had not been a major conspiracy, suggested that it was mainly caused by "indiscriminate importation of Slaves from the Southern States," but it had given whites an opportunity to make "an impression upon the Blacks that will not (I suspect) for a length of time be effaced."[43] General Hampton, one of the richest of all slaveowners, was convinced, on the other hand, that "the plan is unquestionably of Spanish origin, & has had an extensive combination."[44] From three different perspectives the blame was differently cast but upon white men in each case: Claiborne blamed slaveholders' insatiable demand for slaves, slaveholders blamed Claiborne, and Hampton blamed foreign agitators. Carefully avoided was the idea that slaves would rebel against slavery of their own accord because they wanted to be free or were inspired by Christophe.[45] In the end, no substantive action was taken besides the executions.[46] Importers were soon advertising cargoes of slaves from as far away as Baltimore ("guaranteed good subjects"), and the periodic complaints of unsupervised slaves (going to fish in the lake, enjoying "sports and dances") continued to appear.[47]

Nonetheless, the effect of the Deslondes Uprising on New Orleans was profound. Slave rebellion had always occurred so far away from the town in the raw interior that the townspeople had minimal cause for concern. This time they believed that a savage horde was descending upon them from a position less than two hours distant. According to Hampton, "the confusion was great beyond description."[48] This direct challenge to slavery must have momentarily unnerved planters because their orthodoxy that blacks were reconciled to the regime came undone. They rallied quickly, however, and taught blacks, as they put it, "an important lesson—their weakness."[49] Even so, New Orleans planters shared with Thomas Jefferson and other southern planters a horror of politicized black rebellion that was now based on a fresh and vivid memory.[50]

The horror was soon reinforced by other incidents. Planters shuddered in fear through the Christmas eve of 1811 because a rumor arose that the German Coast rebels were preparing another surprise assault in concert with slaves in New Orleans. The militia marched through the night and nothing happened.[51] Eight months later, however, the thing whites feared most nearly came to pass in New Orleans, the possibility that "in case there should arise a Man of desperate courage amongst us, exasperated by a desperate fortune, he might with more advantage than Cataline kindle a Servile War."[52] After a slave betrayed them, two presumably white leaders were convicted of "endeavouring to excite a revolt among the blacks."[53] The incident was so well covered up by authorities at the time that almost nothing is known of it. Joseph Wood was executed September 11, the entire militia marching through the night again. The fate of the second man, Paul Macarty, is unknown. This was an old family name in New Orleans by 1812, but a parallel mulatto family of Macartys had existed for some time, and it is interesting that he expressed "inimity against the whites" and hoped that the Spanish would regain Louisiana.[54] If he was a mulatto, this would help explain General Andrew Jackson's determination a few years later to recruit freedmen for the Battle of New Orleans (January 8, 1815): men like Macarty would be in the field of battle under his surveillance rather than back in the bosom of the black community of New Orleans while the British were attacking. As for Wood, the attempt by white Americans to incite slave rebellion was hardly peculiar to Louisiana, for the same thing occurred in Virginia at this time.[55]

During the war years (1812–15), concern about the "loyalty" of slaves mounted as the British army approached. Ultimately, however, no slave plot troubled the glorious moment of the Battle of New Orleans. Claiborne had been right about the German Coast incident: it was a spontaneous uprising that did not threaten to obtain the dimensions of a "Saint Domingue." In fact, although planters could never rest easy after 1812, the era of slave insurrection in Louisiana was over. The slave community of the state and its New Orleans subcommunity were both too divided to rebel successfully on the basis of African culture, and too carefully restricted by white surveillance to do so on the basis of revolutionary ideology—and most slaves knew it. Plots were uncovered at German Coast in 1829, and New Orleans in 1830, when handbills were posted calling on slaves to kill all whites on the principle of divinely ordained equality and in the military tradition of Hannibal. But it does not appear that the regime was ever seriously threatened.[56] Perhaps because it followed so closely on the heels of those handbills in 1830, Nat Turner's uprising in Virginia inspired a severe reaction among New Orleans whites, but that revealed more about them than about the real potential of their slaves to overthrow them.[57] Slaves sometimes demonstrated by violent means their ardent desire for freedom in other states, and it can be said that eventually slaves destroyed slavery and "consciously sought to rebuild society on a new property base."[58] By 1862, Louisiana slaves were just as ideologically prepared to do that as slaves throughout the South. But from the perspective of 1819, that new golden era must have seemed almost impossible for an ethnically divided slave community in the face of a planter class more powerful than it had ever been in the colonial period.

The Deslondes Uprising and the growing urban anonymity of New Orleans made authorities increasingly anxious and vigilant in regard to slaves. It should be stressed that the everyday problem of urban control, rather than the threat of rebellion, was the most important spur to white "reforms" in the town council and legislature. Nonetheless, in the wake of the German Coast incident the New Orleans Town Council published thumping new ordinances to intimidate all blacks. Not unlike the code of 1751, these restrictions reveal the heavy dependency of consumers on certain slaves to supply the local markets, which led to all manner of subversive activity. Thus, the council led off with a stern warning to slaves to live with their masters rather than in rented dwellings of their own. A variety of masters from the indigent to the wealthy allowed favored slaves freedom of movement in return for a regular weekly or monthly cash payment or other recompense. As always, this was good for free people because it kept their larders full, and it was good for masters because it brought in a steady cash income. But collectively these people posed a special problem. If a self-hired slave was from a plantation in the outer limits of the parish, naturally she or he would want to live at the town center where economic opportunities were greatest, that is, where the market for specialized labor was the strongest. A slave hired to herself basically lived free of all the normal restraints and yet was not thereby cured of the natural, dangerously resentful attitude all slaves were assumed to harbor toward the system. This parallel economy where slaves might enjoy semi-autonomy was becoming a particularly acute problem (from the point of view of masters) because of the size of the city and its booming economy.[59]

The other ordinances of 1811 were also predictable. Absolutely no assemblies of slaves were to be allowed except for preapproved funerals, or dances and sports on Sundays before sunset at designated places. Only blind or handicapped slaves were permitted to carry "a cane or baton"; others would get twenty-five lashes. As usual, negligent masters were specially targeted: anyone who allowed an assembly of slaves or resisted police when they broke it up was subject to a fine up to one hundred dollars. Nonetheless, some masters found it useful for preserving good order on their own domains to allow slaves such recreation, and these masters undermined the security of their class.[60]

An example of such a master is provided by a rare criminal record surviving from this period. Jacques-Philippe Guinault, member of an "old" and prominent local family, gave a dinner for some friends early in 1812 at his Bayou Road home, and he invited them to stay to watch the ball held by his slaves. The slaves were not only permitted to start the festivities in the kitchen of his house, when the kitchen proved too small for the twenty-five women and fifteen men who showed up (belonging to a variety of masters), they were permitted to use Guinault's own dining room. According to depositions by white guests, the party was perfectly decent. Suddenly, however, the police burst into the house, which "occasioned a great uproar and tumult among the negroes." When one of the white gentlemen demanded an explanation, the leader of the intruders snarled at him that they had "an order for which they did not have to account." The police broke furniture, took some money from one slave woman, made threats, and then left. When order was restored and the party recommenced, the police returned at midnight and struck terror again.[61] The head of the patrol later explained coolly that he had been ordered by the chief of police to break up the party, where, he snorted, "the women appeared elegantly dressed," and he had been much abused by the white people, one of them having the gall to yell at him that it was outrageous "that a proprietor has not the right to have his slaves diverted."[62]

If masters thought they could pacify slaves by controlling their movements, on one hand, and on the other hand by granting them the privilege of having parties, the records are full, nevertheless, of many indications that slaves resisted the regime in a variety of ways short of rebellion. Given the bountiful supply of slaves in this era, for example, masters had the luxury of trading slaves to rid themselves of problematic individuals, which led to many "redhibitory" suits in the courts. According to the customary rule followed by judges, leprosy, epilepsy, malignant fevers that exhibited themselves within three days of a sale, and mental defects were unquestionably redhibitory faults guaranteeing annulment of a sale.[63] The most common cause pleaded in these cases was, as always, redhibitory vices, regarded as mental defects, especially when a slave was "addicted" to running away, which forced the court into a variety of contortionate positions, revealing both the assertiveness of slaves and the profound contradictions of slavery for masters.[64]

Sometimes the seller had obviously tried to shift the burden of an afflicted or unruly slave onto the buyer. This must have happened far more often than the number of redhibitory suits would suggest. The slave Charles, who was finally shot in flight by slaves authorized by their master in St. Charles Parish, was tried and executed on October 13, 1808, convicted of many burglaries and attempted rapes of white women. A "compulsive runaway," Charles had belonged to a great variety of masters from Natchitoches to New Orleans, all of whom had passed the incorrigible slave off to another unwary buyer rather than suing in court.[65] One also suspects, in some cases, that the buyer was trying to exploit the right of redhibition to salvage a loss that was not the fault of the seller. In general, the court leaned against the seller in redhibitory suits, especially when the fault was marronage, even when the seller acknowledged the addiction to running away in the bill of sale. Otherwise it is hard to generalize, but these cases reveal much of interest about slaves.

The fault of marronage caused the most problems in the transfer of slaves between masters. In a contract of sale for nine slave men for $10,500 it had been stipulated by seller Prosper Foy to buyer Manuel Andry that six of the nine openly threatened to run away rather than go to Andry's, which was far from their home. This is a fine example of how slaves tried to exert pressure to prevent their dispersal. The six slaves did run away from Andry's and the court found against Foy despite his open admission of the problem at the time of sale and the fact that he was selling the slaves only because he was liquidating the estate to retire to France. The court was impressed by Andry's evidence that, on one hand, Foy knew the slaves "were notoriously bad characters, addicted to every sort of vice or defect," and, on the other, that Andry had treated them "with gentleness [douceur]" because he "only punishes negroes when they deserve it."[66] The sale of any slave was bristling with tension and risk: the slave could cause both buyer and seller a good deal of trouble and money. Marigny sold Delabarre a slave for $800 in 1797 who ran away as soon as he was delivered to the buyer. Somehow he managed to get to Havana, where he lived four years before being recaptured and jailed. All that time, Marigny refrained from demanding payment, the neighborly thing to do until the slave actually started working for Delabarre. But then the latter died, causing an angry court suit in the American period between two families about the value of the runaway.[67]

The court could not adhere to an unvarying guideline in redhibitory suits and was capable of contrary decisions. In the case of *Duncan v Cevallos' Executors* in 1817, Duncan was angry that a slave he had bought on the guarantee that he was a good domestic, coachman and bricklayer, was also a runaway, a drunk, and a thievish one. The seller produced witnesses that the slave did not have that character when he was sold. Remarkably, the court accepted this and found for the seller with a comment on this slave and the disorderly ambiguity of the system itself, especially when a slave was forced to change masters: "[The slave] might conceal his skill from his dislike of a new master; a great indulgence might render him idle, and free access to liquors might induce him to drink to excess, and he consequently would appear idle, drunk, and worthless [but not necessarily *not* a good coachman at the time of the sale]."[68] The bad faith with which the system was riddled is epitomized in this case.

The old problem of marronage took no new forms after 1803, but the character of the runaway population changed slightly in this period in two ways. First, while maroons were able to establish a temporary refuge in the 1780s, that option was now permanently closed off because the region was sufficiently populous that maroons could not hide in groups for long. In 1813, the town's police jury met "in consideration of the fires to which the city has just been exposed, by which it is threatened" and organized a general maroon hunt for July 1.[69] There was no mention of maroon villages, which had never existed on a permanent basis in a region where mountainous retreats were unavailable. A whole family might hide out in the canebrake to avoid being separated by sale, like the one John James Audubon came across and assisted, but maroon villages just were not possible.[70] A slave from the outlying plantation areas might hide out in or near the slave quarters (called "camps" in Louisiana). As one Bayou Sara planter explained, in the night runaways took pumpkins and corn from the fields or hogs belonging to slaves, but they kept moving from camp to camp.[71] On the other hand, because of the growing population of the town caused by an influx of many strangers, maroons were now likely to seek refuge in the anonymity of a mixed population in the residential neighborhoods of the town. Messieurs Clark and Turner notified the public that two slaves were missing from their Point Houmas plantation, blacksmith Levin, formerly of Baltimore, who "carries his head high," and Betsy, late of New Orleans, both of them having probably fled to her former home in New Orleans in the skiff they stole.[72]

A second change in marronage patterns was that a growing number of Louisiana slaves learned of and ran to other states or Spanish colonies in an effort to pretend their way into free status, and slaves from other states fled to Louisiana for the same reason. The mulatto slave named Horace, fifteen years old, included in the Prosper Foy group above, had been a maroon for seven months, during which time he had traveled to New York, Liverpool, and Charleston, where he was arrested and returned to Louisiana.[73] A slave woman of Maryland escaped to Louisiana, where a man she lived with eventually sold her to another, whom the Supreme Court ruled liable when the original master located and reclaimed her.[74] Slaves were sometimes in the company of white people on these long flights. Jack Morgan was believed to be traveling with two common white men and would probably "attempt to go to the Spanish country."[75] When Pierre Lafitte broke jail in 1814 he took Sam, Caesar, and Hamilcar with him, and they undoubtedly headed for Barataria, where the blacks could join the pirate population that lived under no flag.[76] A quite different kind of case concerned a man named either Jeffrey Nash or Charles Jefferys ("Jeffers"). Born in Detroit in 1787, the firm of Henry and Forsyth purchased Nash there in 1803 and took him to New Orleans. He ran away, and, when captured, adamantly insisted that he been emancipated by his master in 1802 and sued his jailor to free him. Yet when he was brought before the mayor he admitted that his master had only promised him his freedom; he could not prove that he had been freed. He obtained an attorney, however, who tacked hard to the left, raising the large principle that according to the Northwest Ordinance of 1787 slavery was prohibited in Detroit. The parish court scoffed at this, but Nash started a family and plotted his appeal, and when he was finally heard before the state Supreme Court in 1816, he won on the basis of that very argument.[77]

No new patterns of marronage emerge from the evidence. For example, search of a complete run of the newspaper *Moniteur de la Louisiane* from September 4, 1802, to February 18, 1804 (seventeen and a half months), yielded ads for twenty-four different maroons, and no generalizations are possible. In the fall of 1802, Alexandre Harang advertised an interesting group escape one morning by Pierre-Marc, Senegalese, thirty years old, who spoke Spanish, French, English, and the old generalized Indian language called Mobilier, who ran off with three other adult Africans including a woman. In the fall of 1803, a mulatto named Honoré ran away with Negress Isabel; they belonged to two different masters. In one case, two young girls ran away together, an unusual couple because Finette was a creole and her companion was a *"brute,"* African-born slave; their master could describe them and their clothes in remarkable detail. Two young Congo men advertised by Harang early in 1804 were so newly arrived from Africa that they would not know their master's name when asked.[78]

The only constant in this sample is that outsiders were overrepresented. This accords well with the pattern seen earlier: outsiders were usually overrepresented in the criminal record. They were likely to have been sold away by masters dissatisfied with their unruliness, and they faced the same problem of all immigrants in learning "how to act" to be accepted in the host community. Madame De Cruise of Esplanade Street advertised the flight of Jamaica-born Louis-Calixte, age fifteen, blue eyes and brown hair, who would have found himself set apart in the Francophone slave community on account of his foreign birth and accent (he spoke French, but undoubtedly with an accent), his complexion, even his height, which at four feet four inches was short for a fifteen year old, even for a slave in an age when median stature was low.[79] The outsider's acceptance in the slave community was never automatic. The slave who was not trusted by either fellow slaves or the master was more than likely to flee such an intolerable situation.

The court heard one case that shows how masters could not agree on the correct way to pursue maroons. Guillot and Dossat entered into an interesting arrangement by which Dossat purchased a 5 percent share in slave Dimanche and worked him. When Dimanche ran away, Guillot angrily charged Dossat for taking neither of the measures that "most men" did: "some advertize them in the gazettes; others think that this step puts the slave on his guard" and instead tell a constable that they will pay a reward.[80] According to the law, in fact, runaways were supposed to be advertised. In practice, the newspapers are not a reliable guide to the full extent of marronage.

The curious willingness of planters to gamble on the purchase of maroons at a discount has been noted earlier, another illustration of the strong market demand for slave labor. For example, a man posted a notice that he had purchased runaway Jean-Louis, baker, and that he would be pardoned if he returned immediately.[81] Evidently, the buyer bet on the slave's willingness to gamble on the humanity of a new master by returning. Some maroons would rather die than return to a cruel master. Valère managed to escape his Bayou

St. Jean master, Evariste Blanc, and make his way to Cuba. When a neighbor of Blanc's on a trip to Cuba had him arrested and conducted back to New Orleans, "he threw himself in the river the day we anchored before the town and perished."[82] Edouard de Montulé claimed that suicide was mainly intended to spite the master rather than to escape misery, but this appears to be an overly refined distinction.[83]

When maroons were caught, the master had already sustained a loss of the slave's labor, and severe punishment might incapacitate the slave for several more days, provoke another attempt at flight, or, as just seen, lead to suicide. The application of weights was a popular technique because it permitted the slave to work, causing extreme drudgery rather than pain, a kind of slow torture that was less likely than the whip to drive the slave to run away again. Nevertheless, the African Jean-Louis (a Canga) was advertised as having absconded, with eighteen-pound rings on each foot linked by a chain, which may explain why he went maroon, although it was unlikely that he literally "ran" away, given that he also had a hernia.[84] Free woman of color Justine Seguin used a similar method with Marthonne, fastening an iron collar around her neck. Either Seguin did not trust the slave or she tried to run away again because Seguin sold her and her infant to Louis Feriet, who promptly appeared in court to annul the sale when Marthonne disappeared. He was armed with depositions from Seguin's neighbors who claimed that she "often went maroon" and had worn the iron collar.[85]

The planters' explicit image of themselves was marked above all by the belief that they were not cruel. In fact, the Supreme Court adhered to the principle that "cruelty and inhumanity ought not to be presumed against any person," especially a slaveowner.[86] The image can be evaluated by looking carefully at several instances in which masters cast blame on other white men for their own slaves' costly misbehavior. As usual, these cases involved both the master's pecuniary interest and personal honor. Marronage led to some interesting examples that illustrate the dangerous complexity of relations between planters. Bayon's mixed-race slave escaped to New Orleans and was jailed there, and as a courtesy his neighbor, Prévôt, reclaimed the slave to take him back up the country, but the slave escaped on the way. Bayon could not risk being made a fool by a neighbor and sued for the slave's value, arguing that Prévôt should not have allowed his charge to walk on the shore en route up the river. Prévôt's rejoinder convinced the court: the slave had dysentery from his stay in prison, and if he had kept him in the boat, it would have "fix[ed] on his [Prévôt's] character the stain of brutality."[87] This shows an informal code of slave treatment at work, although we will never be certain how consistently it worked to restrain excessive brutality.

Masters were reluctant to charge their own slaves with crimes, but not out of humanity toward their slaves: formal criminal charges often meant a loss to the master, a loss of face and the slave's services. After the mulatto slave Charles stabbed a Catalan shopkeeper to death in the Faubourg Marigny, his master, Cadet Monlon, still had "the effrontery to say that he [Charles] was a good lot" and would try to save him from the gallows (as reported by one indignant citizen), presumably because he believed that the Catalan must have provoked the stabbing. When Charles could not be found, the public suspected that Monlon was concealing him, and there was a violent scene when he would not let the sheriff search his home.[88]

A continuing legal problem that remained unresolved was the assignment of blame when a slave misbehaved after imbibing illicit intoxicating liquors, one of the most common (and least effective?) demonstrations of slave defiance. Delery sued Mornet for the loss of his slave. The latter had sold liquor to a pirogue full of slaves who became drunk and quarrelsome. A white man came upon them and threatened to have them flogged if they did not calm down. Two of them were so unnerved by this threat that they jumped in the river, probably to escape, although the man believed they were trying to drown themselves, and Delery's slave did drown. Mornet's claim that he did not know the men were slaves was treated by the court with laconic contempt: it was the prevailing rule that all blacks were assumed to be slaves in any circumstances unless they could prove they were free. The court upheld the parish court's finding that Mornet had caused the slave's death, without even mentioning the responsibility of the man who had actually incited the drowning.[89] It was widely accepted that it was natural for slaves to desire liquor and that they should not be denied modest quantities—but woe to the man who gave or sold liquor to *other* men's slaves. All of these slaveowners—Bayon, Monlon, and Delery—were motivated to protect both the value of their property and their reputations as men who would not be blamable for harm to their servants.

An important arena of resistance was the slave family, and it is here that cruelty is more accurately measured. In an overview of recent scholarship on the general history of the black family in slavery, Barbara Bush indicates both how much has changed during the most recent period of scholarship and how much remains to be done.[90] Above all, the older view (first developed by proslavery thinkers as a rationale) that the slave family was unstable and typically matrifocal has been debunked, most notably by the work of Herbert Gutman.[91] Historians' acceptance of the stereotype arose primarily from ignorance of conditions in West Africa and also from a failure to distinguish between differing conditions before and after 1865. That is, African women had significant authority over child rearing and certain economic activities, which, retained in slavery in America, gave the false impression of matriarchal rule. The misimpression was reinforced by historians' failure to recognize nonnuclear families. In fact, black women may have enjoyed more leverage in regard to black men in American slavery, even though African patriarchy was strong and was preserved to some measurable extent in America. Deborah Gray White takes the argument another step to argue that "slave families were unusually egalitarian" because African patriarchy was eroded if not destroyed by the degradation of male slaves.[92]

African women were slaves in America, however, and masters could interfere in the most intimate family matters. We know that families were formed in New Orleans in this period because of the steady supply of black babies presented at the baptismal font, although their parents' names were not consistently recorded and were seldom noted as married before the Church. Beyond that, unfortunately, the kind of judicial records that survive from these years tell much less about the condition of the slave family than in the colonial period. One rare series of letters shows that some masters were merely interested in keeping slaves pregnant by any means necessary, not a policy conducive to wholesome family life. The case of Amazilie, belonging to the absentee planter Henri de Ste-Gême, is instructive. The plantation manager Jean Boze reported early in 1819 that Amazilie had "aborted herself" rather than bring another slave into the world.[93] The overseer punished her severely. He also followed certain unspecified instructions by Madame de Ste-Gême, who took an active interest in every detail concerning the slaves even while in France. The slave immediately got pregnant again but gave birth after only seven months, so the child "could not survive."[94] Regardless of her behavior in the past, the naive overseer did not suspect that Amazilie may have induced premature labor. Soon he reported that she was trying dutifully to get pregnant again.[95] The slave's marital status or sex partner were of no interest to her mistress, just her ability to reproduce.

The major comfort a slave enjoyed was the community of family and friends: losing that was demoralizing, and dramatic changes could occur at any time that a master's circumstances or attitude changed. Here again, probably the single most important factor determining whether or not a person was able to live in a completed family under one roof was New Orleans' transformation into a city. In 1819, the plantation regions still began just at the outer boundaries of the faubourgs, and the extreme extent of urbanization the city would attain by 1860 was just beginning. On the plantations, as Ann Patton Malone has discovered, a remarkably high degree of family formation was possible even in the volatile decade of 1810–19, when three-fourths of all slaves lived in simple families. Half of all slaves lived in fully formed nuclear households, composed of a married couple and children.[96] Since Louisiana had both important sugar and cotton parishes, Malone is able to compare families in the two. Contributing to the debunking of the myth that sugar was a slave killer, she finds that plantation slaves in sugar parishes like New Orleans enjoyed higher rates of family formation and stability than the cotton parishes.[97] Nonetheless, the situation was different in the town center and residential suburbs, where an increasing proportion of masters and slaves lived as the rural portion of the parish was morselized by faubourgs.

Slaves who lived in the city faced challenges to domestic stability that must have forced many into the habitual subterfuge of "petit marronage." Since so many of these slaves were live-in house servants, many were isolated black individuals in white households, as shown in the census of 1805. This count of the residential quarters shows that of 653 slaveholding households headed by a white person fully 284 of them (about 44 percent) had only one adult slave of either sex or only children under sixteen years.[98] This is one crude guide to the limited opportunities for slaves to create households under the same roof in the urban environment. If we include those households in which two or more adult slaves lived who could not have formed a family based on a heterosexual pair, the statistic is even more impressive. Moreover, unlike the situation in the plantation neighborhoods, even when families under the same roof were possible, the city slaves were highly dispersed. Of 1,451 households, over half (765) included one or more slaves, and they were found in every street, in every micro-neighborhood of the town center. They do not appear to have been concentrated anywhere: there was no residential center of the slave community. Slaveowning households were most numerous in the homes and shops in the commercial district radiating from the port, least numerous at the rear of the town center, where those slaveowning households headed by blacks tended to concentrate. All of this suggests that weak family formation marked the lives of city-dwelling slaves, and that the typical person who tried to maintain a family was constantly tempted to steal five minutes from her master here, an evening there, forever looking over her shoulder and dreaming up excuses to visit loved ones. Granting family privileges gave masters a vital tool in slave control. At the same time, the impediments to free association exaggerated the importance of kin and quasi-kin relations, which served to inhibit the growth of class consciousness among slaves.[99]

Some masters believed that a policy of paternalistic solicitude would more efficaciously guarantee slaves' gratitude and obedience. A particularly detailed description of this behavior is described by Edward Derby on one of the largest sugar plantations in the parish, the Michel Labranche plantation of 120 slaves, at harvest's end.[100] Derby noted that it had one of the first sugar mills to be operated by steam. Formerly, the crushing cylinders were rotated by a pair of horses harnessed to the gears, driven by a slave boy perched on a board dragging behind the team, a dangerous and boring occupation. As for

Fig. 17. Sugar production in Louisiana. Even though this engraving dates from the post–Civil War period, showing both the full development of steamboat transportation and the electrification of a part of the process, little else had changed since the introduction of commercial sugar production nearly one century earlier. From *Harper's Weekly*, 21 July 1883, reprinted in Leonard V. Huber, *New Orleans: A Pictorial History* (Gretna, La.: Pelican, 1991).

the other working slaves, the harvest took two months, was "a time of severe work," but it was "commonly remarked" (defensively?) that the slaves' health was "better at this time than at any other" because they were well fed.[101] Arriving on the last day of harvest, Derby witnessed the beginning of "a negro fête" slated to last several days, the last load of cane arriving escorted to the mill in a gaily beribboned oxcart surrounded by "singing, dancing and laughing" slaves, who were serenaded by a band composed of homemade barrel drum, horse-jaw-with-teeth played washboard style, split cane struck percussively, a gourd rattle and possibly a gourd stringed instrument. This hailed the beginning of "a Congo dance . . . chiefly a sort of shuffle, and a violent agitation of all the muscles of the body," and marked by "mock flirtation."[102] Then the party shifted to the front lawn of the big house, where the slaves erected a pole "with a popinjay figure of a bird on the top," then

> an old merry looking negro, a native Guinea man, came out with a crooked stick which he carried in imitation of a gun, to perform a series of pantomime. Keeping all the while the most perfect time, he shouldered his gun, presented it at the bird . . . [repeatedly, until finally he] fired, and was knocked backwards by the recoil—a dénouement which seemed to afford infinite amusement. He then returned, and made a speech, in what language I know not, in a sort of recitative, several others occasionally joining in a chorus.[103]

We can only speculate about the deeper meaning of this ritual, with its wistful air of a free-ranging hunter's frustration. Its communal expression and African roots are what counted. Throughout the festivities, however, individual slaves approached the master and guests "for small supplies of silver."[104] This supplement to the income slaves had from plots of waste ground was the highest expression of planter paternalism: the African cultural idiom was strictly limited to that context of fatherly generosity and surveillance.[105] The next morning, some Labranche slaves rowed Derby's party through the swamp to Lake Pontchartrain to fish and fowl, pulling their oars "merrily," and singing. Some songs praised the master ("Mon bon ami, c'est Monsieur Labranche"), others praised themselves "as the best and most industrious negroes—That their fields were better worked, and their sugar got in quicker than any other gang could do it."[106] Derby described this seemingly idyllic situation in the interest of fairness, to balance off his description of the regime of physical force that lay at the foundation of the system. The greatest tragedy of the system was that masters were taken in by these supposed demonstrations of contentment and gratitude, discovering their "catastrophic misunderstanding" only four decades later, when freedmen would gladly take their leave of the plantation.[107]

Ultimately, as Derby noted, all masters relied on the threat of the infliction of pain. Methods described in New Orleans were those common throughout the South, as discussed briefly above. At the lowest level of intensity was the public chain gang. Edward Derby was disgusted when he first saw it and noticed women chained side by side with men, lugging spades and pickaxes, punished for some minor "domestic offense," the masters compounding their shamelessness by accepting compensation from the city for their slaves' labor.[108] More severe was the whipping that was routinized on plantations and in the jail in the town center. The slaveowner might send an offender to the public jailor with a note specifying a given number of lashes and whether or not the victim was to be spreadeagled and bound, and "in passing the prison in the morning, the cries of the poor creatures are dreadful."[109] The ultimate penalty, hanging, was now staged on the site of slaves' one sanctioned venue for socialization, Congo Square.[110]

Fig. 18. *Street in the Faubourg Sainte-Marie,* c. 1821, by Félix-Achille Saint-Aulaire. Note the public chain gang of slaves cleaning the streets. From a photograph of the original in the Bibliothèque Nationale, Paris.

Free blacks were affected less by the urbanization of New Orleans than by the legal changes imposed on them. At the beginning of the territorial period, they were numerous, industrious, and prosperous, with their numbers growing daily. Their ebullience was checked between 1807 and 1819 by a consensus among local planters to adopt policies to reduce dramatically the free black community's growth rate. That growth was owing to the great wealth of the port and its special labor needs, which promoted manumission indirectly, and to the little escape hatch the Spanish had opened in the form of freedom-purchase rights. In the next chapter, this legal campaign against free blacks is taken up in detail. Here, the social structure, living conditions, and resistance of free blacks living in residential parts of the city is described.

In one sense, because of the increasing anonymity of big city life, free blacks enjoyed marginally more freedom from direct surveillance. Paradoxically, that anonymity also meant they also suffered greater risk of being re-enslaved by fraudulent means. For there was a rising local incidence of the kidnapping of free blacks by whites to sell them into slavery in other states. The experience of free black woman Betsy Sives illustrates the kidnapping phenomenon and the amazing twists of fate possible in a black person's life. Born free in New Jersey, she had to move to Nova Scotia with her godmother, probably a Tory, during the American Revolution. She then hired as a servant to a lady who took her to Saint Domingue; from there she fled during *its* revolution with a free woman of color to Cuba. In 1809 she fled again, arriving in New Orleans with the other refugees. Her last employer, the mulatto Marianne Delogny, now "wickedly and fraudulently" tried to sell her as a slave to a white man and held her daughter. The court ordered both Betsy and her daughter seized by the sheriff and hired out until their status could be determined. Delogny had her story ready, and since Sives had no proof of her freedom the court probably would have accepted her version. Incredibly, however, Sives produced a white man named William Francis, who had hired her as a servant in New Orleans, knowing well that she was free because his father-in-law, who was also in town, knew Sives's mother in New Jersey and remembered the little girl! Sives and daughter were freed, and the white man who had intended to buy them was fined and charged with court costs, evidently because the judges knew that he was the real culprit.[111]

William Francis's role in the Sives case was not a fluke: other white people knew slaves individually and intimately enough to remember them years later, and their willingness to testify in their defense shows that white solidarity was spiderwebbed with hairline cracks. Lest Cuba be imagined to have been a haven for blacks because slaves occasionally fled there and passed themselves off for a time as freed persons, the case of Marie-Louise is revealing. Born free in Louisville, she was kidnapped there and taken to New Orleans where she was sold to François Bernoudy, who violently kept her in slavery despite "her repeated solicitations to be set at liberty."[112] Being too poor to get a lawyer on her case at first, she became more highly motivated when she had a son, Jim, and Bernoudy made plans to sell them both to a planter in Cuba, where her free birth would be almost impossible to prove. In the nick of time, Joseph Lynd and Betsy Currie deposed that they had known her: Lynd remembered her as a little girl in Indiana Territory and Kentucky. After a delay of three and a half years the Orleans Parish Court freed Marie-Louise and Jim.

Free blacks might fall victim to a variety of other stratagems. The pirates of Barataria, headed by the Lafittes, were willing to steal and traffic in anything, especially slaves, and they seemed to regard all blacks as fair game. They either kidnapped Marie-Zabeth or at least captained the ship that became her prison in 1805. We know of her case only because she was lucky enough to come before Claiborne and prove her freedom.[113] Nine years later, the Supreme Court heard another case of a Marie-Zabeth, mulatto, although it could well be the last act in the drama the Lafittes' prisoner had begun in 1805. Constable Jean-François Meunier sued Jean Duperron because the latter had fraudulently ordered him to arrest Marie-Zabeth, claiming that she was a maroon living with another man. When all of this occurred is not stated, as is often true in these appeals. At any rate, the constable "shipped her off" (to the Lafittes because the constable could not determine if she had an owner and was afraid of being sued?), but she got free, got a judgment of punitive damages in the parish court against both Duperron and Meunier (since this was a denial-of-freedom case), and the attorney general also stepped in to punish Meunier with jail time and a fine, which he insisted Duperron should pay. The court regarded this as a criminal appeal and refused to rule. Clearly this was a case of jealousy and vengeance. It shows both how vulnerable free blacks could be because of their weak legal status and how they might fight back when white people took advantage of that status.

The legislature expressed indignation about the crime of kidnapping free blacks into slavery and tried to make it less attractive. In 1819, it set the stiff penalty of a prison sentence of up to fourteen years and a fine of one thousand dollars or twenty years for the second offense.[114] To keep this in perspective and avoid giving the impression that whites took any special care to protect free blacks, it is notable that it was twenty years hard labor for the *first* offense of *slave* stealing. Concealing slave maroons was subject to such astronomical fines that the guilty party who was unable to pay might go to jail for what amounted to a lifetime.[115] The law against kidnapping free blacks was primarily designed to protect unwary masters who might buy the victims and all the trouble the victims could cause. Moreover, it was not clear that the law of 1819 would have protected undocumented free blacks born outside the United States like Jacob, who was shanghaied in Jamaica, carried to New Orleans and sold to Antoine Demarchy, who promptly sold him in turn to Louis Milhet. The latter forced Demarchy to take him back as soon as Jacob filed his suit, but it is not clear that Jacob was believed by the court and freed.[116]

A more subtle way of "kidnapping" free blacks was by legal technicalities. The suit of Augustine and three other freed persons against Caillau Lafontaine in 1814 shows how absolutely essential it was for free blacks to have their documentation in order and how even then it might be to no avail. Saint Domingan refugees, the four had been freed by Widow Marie-Françoise Letourneur during their exile in Cuba early in 1809 "in recognition," she wrote in the particular case of the Guinea-born Zilia, "of the good and loyal services that she has unfailingly rendered to me."[117] But Lafontaine was one of the deceased Letourneur's creditors and had the blacks jailed because without them the estate could not settle his account. The blacks' argument that they had been Marie-Françoise's separate property and that she had renounced her community property with her husband upon arrival in New Orleans was a typical ploy to bypass laws limiting the capacity of debtors to liberate slaves. Judges did not like it, and besides, Lafontaine had the most powerful attorney in the Old Southwest, Edward Livingston, and he easily prevailed over the unlucky slaves, which the court now ruled was their status.

Another case, *Delphine v Doctor Raimond Devèze*, shows that even when freed persons were successful at escaping the clutches of someone holding them illegally, it could take many years. Delphine was born free near Cap Français, Saint Domingue, to freedwoman Caroline, who died when she was still little. She was committed to the care of an aunt, who was the concubine of an apothecary, Belzons, and the whole family fled in the last wave of whites and free blacks to be driven from the country in 1803. In Cuba briefly, they went on to New Orleans in 1804. Probably broke and desperate, Belzons sold Delphine as a slave to Widow Gauteraud even though she claimed to be free. Gauteraud sold her to Guterat, and he in turn sold her to Devèze. This amazing succession of masters was not unusual for a slave who claimed to be free. Under Devèze's regime, Delphine "suffered unjust corporal punishment" and her eldest son (eight years old) was also "beaten and cruelly treated," Devèze having broken open his head with a metal pot and crockery. In other words, Delphine was in slavery for two decades after arriving in New Orleans until she could get her case heard and finally settled by the Supreme Court in her favor in 1824. She was freed but received none of the wages she claimed (thirty cents per day) since her enslavement.[118]

A case linked to that of the slave Nash of Detroit, discussed above, is *Lunsford v Coquillon,* which also turned on the Northwest Ordinance. Rebecca Lunsford was definitely born a slave in Kentucky. Then her master, James Riddle, moved to the other side of the Ohio River, where she served him several years. They then spent some years in New Orleans, where, if the confused testimony is read with some imagination, it appears that Riddle in fact sold her for a time to another man (circa 1816), who soon forced Riddle to take her back, and in 1817 they were back in Kentucky. She had either gotten wind of the prohibition of taking slaves to live in Ohio—had she heard of Nash's case, which was in court at this time?—or she had found out in Ohio and only now worked up her courage, but she threatened to initiate a suit for freedom. This shows that masters took this kind of threat very seriously. Her legal inclinations scared Riddle and he sold her down river in New Orleans to the (presumably) unsuspecting Michel Fortier, who promptly sold her to Marie Girard, who in turn unloaded her on Louis Coquillon, all sellers being, we suppose, threatened with lawsuits. She sued Coquillon and the Supreme Court freed her in 1824.[119]

The most effective mode of resistance by free blacks was their striving to become economically independent and socially respectable by relying on their own initiative. That story is heavily obscured by the fact that they typically were not entered in the city directory as merchants or artisans, in part because they were seldom successful enough to have their own stores or shops, peddling their wares or their skills from door to door on the strength of their reputations.[120] Little by little, however, they were leaving their slave origins and the slave community behind in an effort to prove that they were equally entitled to the benefits of republican liberty. It was primarily by these efforts, the most effective means of resistance available to them, not the personal protection of white benefactors, that the group avoided the degree of degradation the legal regime would have imposed on them. It explains why free blacks were sufficiently wealthy to be the heads of 1,831 households in New Orleans in 1830, many of them property owners, many of them artisans, painters, writers, inventors, Catholic nuns, and Protestant ministers.[121] It explains why at the end of the antebellum era an impressive list of the two hundred leading free men of color, in association with so many free black women who are harder to trace, had built a community of impressive dimensions. The list included men who had participated in the Battle of New Orleans in 1815 and were still living, men like Paulin C. Bonseigneur, shoe store owner, or Bazile Brion, shoemaker, or François Escoffié, teacher.[122] Orleans Parish free blacks owned real estate worth a total of $2,628,200 in 1860.[123]

Some of these free blacks were slaveholders, although their reasons for owning slaves is open to debate because many of them were either assisting individuals on their way to freedom or keeping relatives in slavery for their protection according to their rights as slaveowners.[124] Free mulatto Perrine Daupaine, for example, is frequently found in the archives liberating Negroes such as Angélique, aged fifty, never with an explanation.[125] Marie-Joseph Piron described the ten slaves she would take with her in applying for a passport to travel to Cuba on business in 1816.[126] A few free blacks were slaveowners who regarded themselves as full, profit-oriented members of that class. They are difficult to identify in the record except when they had large estates. Of the 112 slaveholding households headed by a black householder in the residential portion of New Orleans Parish at the beginning of the American period (7.7 percent of all households), it is virtually impossible to pinpoint that minority who were holding slaves for profit rather them to protect them with their master's legal rights.[127] Moreover, holding slaves for profit was not hypocritical: most free blacks did not regard themselves as members of a "race" and merely sought the most logical road to respectability. More to the point, the great majority of free blacks in the residential portion of the parish were common people: 62 percent of free blacks' 296 households in the town center at the beginning of the American period were nonslaveholding, and few ever attained a rank higher than an artisan or shopkeeper. In 1861, the majority of free blacks would still be laborers of modest means, either because they had chosen not to be members of the slaveholding class or because they were excluded from the means to acquire slaves.[128] Finally, the arrival of a large number of refugee free blacks from Saint Domingue and a few Protestant Anglophone free blacks from the states split the free black community, enfeebling its collective power. Free black spouses had a strong tendency to search out one another within their respective subcommunities based on place of birth.[129]

It is a wonder that either slaves or free blacks found the strength to resist dehumanization and create subcommunities to the extent that they did. Both were under great pressure both from long-term trends (the slave trade) and new tendencies, like the planters' rising concern about slave rebellion in the age of Deslondes and Christophe. That concern was disproportionate to the real threat because both slaves and free blacks were so legally degraded, racially outnumbered in the region, and socially atomized by ethnicity that neither group could form a conscious class with revolutionary potential. That is not the same thing as arguing that masters did not believe slaves to be capable of class formation and revolution. John Ashworth is undoubtedly right that slaves gave masters good reasons to believe that, but he goes too far in insisting that slaves formed a (non-"conscious") class and engaged in "class conflict" with slaveholders.[130] On the other hand, the high level of both active and passive slave resistance, perfectly typical of slave societies throughout the South, is persuasive evidence that no "Latin" cultural tendencies of the planters mitigated the regime in New Orleans. But it is now time to delve more deeply into the character of slave society in New Orleans: Was it essentially different from those elsewhere in the slave South before 1803, and did it change in any fundamental way after 1803 because Americans imposed an "alien" culture on the local population?

Black Manon
in the Capital City of the Slave South 11

In no part of the world are slaves better treated than in the Mississippi
Territory. . . . When we pass into Louisiana, we behold a different and more
disgusting picture. The French and Spanish planters, in particular, treat their
slaves with great rigor.

 —Amos Stoddard, *Sketches, Historical and Descriptive, of Louisiana,* 1812

The condition of the slaves here, the treatment, which they receive, and the
character of their masters have been much misrepresented in the non-slaveholding states. . . . At present, we are persuaded, there are but few of those
brutal and cruel masters, which the greater portion of the planters were
formerly supposed to be.

 —Timothy Flint, *A Condensed Geography and History*
 of the Western States or the Mississippi Valley, 1828

"Do you mean she was prettier than any of the pure white Creoles of her day?

 "Definitely so! Let me tell you something that you probably don't know.
That particular mixture and the ones that followed at 93.75, 96.875, 98.4375 and
99.21875 per cent white were the most beautiful women in the world."

 —Pierre Paul Ebeyer, *Paramours of the Creoles,* 1944

The slave society of early national New Orleans was unique because, unlike
the rest of the slave South, which remained mostly rural, this singular parish
became a populous residential and commercial urban space by 1819, its major
plantation neighborhoods beginning to give way to suburban development.

Many historians have embraced the view that New Orleans was "far removed from the patterns developed in early Massachusetts or Virginia" and, after 1803, "long remained a strange province in the American South" because of its supposedly distinct race relations.[1] The argument throughout this book has been that the social patterns in early New Orleans were, indeed, unlike those in Massachusetts but remarkably similar to those in the slave society of the Virginia Tidewater. Early national New Orleans was "strange" mainly because it was a fast-growing city in a region where slavery usually worked against the development of large cities: the town grew large because of its geographic position and its role as an entrepot for local planters, fur-trading Indians, and the farmers and planters of the vast interior who sent staples down the rivers to New Orleans. Any changes in its race relations after 1803 resulted from urban conditions.

The three leading comparative views of New Orleans are, first, that French and Spanish cultural traits restrained the planters so as to limit the dehumanization of slaves; second, that New Orleans was the primary site of a fundamental re-Africanization of the slave South in the first decade of the nineteenth century, which reduced the ability of the planter class to dominate the slave population; and third, that the social structure of Louisiana was fundamentally different from that of upper South states because its free blacks formed a special protected caste.[2] All three of these "cultural" views are supported by thoughtful historians and have inspired useful debates. The cultural model has been consistently refuted here, but not because culture is of no importance: Tannenbaum raised important issues, and the question of comparative dehumanization deserves to be addressed. It is true that the huge influx of new slaves at the end of the colonial period and during the territorial period enriched the southern black population with one last major infusion of African influences, the effect of which should be explored. By 1860, the free black population of New Orleans did look different from those in upper South towns, for which there is a social, obscure explanation. This chapter will show that most of what was truly distinctive about New Orleans resulted from its urbanization, and that cultural influences were much less important than any cultural model would suggest.

New Orleans blended easily into the social landscape of the South in 1803 and became the region's economic capital city. Other southerners and an important minority of northerners crowded into the parish because, as William Darby put it, "there are few places where human life can be enjoyed with more pleasure, or employed to more pecuniary profit."[3] Masters brought in their slaves from other states because they found nothing about Louisiana to be repellently strange: they knew that neither law, nor religion, nor other cultural impediments would restrain their ambition in unfamiliar ways. On the contrary, as indicated in this chapter's first two epigraphs, some Anglo-Americans thought the exact opposite was true, that the locals treated slaves more cruelly. Moreover, African cultures were quickly swamped, if not destroyed, by the extraordinary heterogeneity of the slave population. As for free blacks, as seen below, they were degraded as in the rest of the South. Part of New Orleans' uniqueness is that it provides one of the best examples of the extraordinary resilience of the slaveholders' class solidarity, a unity that held firm despite its own members' cultural diversity, the potential for an "African" revolt against their power, the unsettling ambitions of free blacks, and the challenge of large-scale urbanization. The town's urban condition became the single most important determinant of its character. More important than any cultural factors were the decline of the proportion of the population living on plantations, the extraordinary demand for a flexible labor supply to meet the port's seasonal marketing demands, the increasing anonymity possible for individuals in the large population, and the existence of a huge number of transients and settlers from outside New Orleans. The implications of these trends for the slaveowning class were several.

While the political power of the planters was unleashed after 1803, the importance of their alliance with both non-planting slaveholders and non-slaveholding white property owners, especially commercial capitalists, increased. As the number of both slaves and non-property-owning white people grew in proportion to property owners, the social distance between the slaveholding elite and their natural allies was reduced, all the more true because of the introduction of democracy. Moreover, if planters expressed doubts about the ability of a shopkeeper like Joseph Fouque to join their ranks, one also sees little contempt expressed for those like him who succeeded or for their bourgeois values. Nor are the planters found heaping contempt on common white people. Meanwhile, the planters' traditional appetite for entertainment at the town center was unabated. All of this contributed to what might be called the bourgeoisification of the slaveowning class of New Orleans, which was well under way by 1819, in part on account of taste but more because urbanization and the rising number of blacks in the region required a strong union of all white people. Urban problems required greater vigilance to preserve the racial order, with an urgency rising in direct relation to the size of the population, which nearly tripled in the first two decades of the nineteenth century.

A brief stroll through the town's newspapers and town council records will explain this need for white solidarity. Every day the slaves and rootless whites seemed harder to control. Runaway slaves were harder to find because they no longer had to hide out in forests but could blend into a large, increasingly anonymous population. In 1815, for example, one Rodriguez of Faubourg Marigny offered a reward for his milk vendor, Neri, "a black woman of the Heboo nation," recognizable for her inveterate pipe-smoking, cancerous leg, and ability to speak English and French. She had been on her own for two months simply by crossing over into Faubourg St. Mary and pretending to have a different master, with permission to hire out.[4] In the face-to-face conditions of the town center of colonial days, Neri would not have been able to elude capture so long in the residential portion of the parish: ads of this kind were new. The old problem of slaves and free blacks gaining too much control over the direct marketing of consumer goods and casual labor was as bad as ever.[5] The problem of policing poor whites grew in importance, epitomized in the struggle to create an effective gendarmerie, which was aimed at all the lower orders, as is clear from the General Police Ordinances of 1817.[6] With these preliminary remarks, it is now time to apply the social model more systematically and demonstrate its superiority to one dominated by cultural considerations.

The weight of evidence suggests that slaves' day-to-day living conditions, conditions of life, and opportunity to be manumitted were much the same as in the other southern states. These three categories, as originally suggested by Eugene D. Genovese, will serve to structure the discussion here.[7] To begin with day-to-day living conditions, Louisiana in general and New Orleans in particular came to have a terrible reputation for cruelty by 1861, which proponents of the Tannenbaum thesis accept, attributing that supposed harshness to Anglo-Americanization after 1803. In fact, many sojourners left accounts of slavery there in the three decades after 1803, which, taken as a whole rather than in isolation from one another, reveal that this argument is just not convincing: the Anglo-Americans could not and did not change much. Louisiana's slaves were at least as dehumanized by masters before 1803 as after, and not measurably more so after 1803 than in the rest of the slave South. For the colonial period, in previous chapters it has been shown that both the law and judicial practice indicate that slaves were "protected" only as property, not as individuals with rights.[8] Thus, as Judith Kelleher Schafer has shown, advertisements placed by masters of all ethnic groups concerning slaves in antebellum New Orleans newspapers "reflect almost every conceivable abuse of the slave and few mitigating circumstances."[9] As David C. Rankin puts it, "Louisiana's Latin heritage failed to soften slavery, encourage manumission, and foster egalitarian race relations" after 1803.[10] A closer look at the whole body of contemporary published accounts supports these views, showing that race relations in New Orleans were much the same as in other North American slave societies.

Benjamin Latrobe arrived in New Orleans with an impression received from other sources that the locals treated their slaves harshly. He probably read books about Louisiana on his long trip there, perhaps the one by the

Fig. 19. *Maid of the Douglas Family, New Orleans,* c. 1840, attributed to Julien Hudson. From the collection of the Louisiana State Museum.

disgruntled Pierre-Louis Berquin-Duvallon, who charged that slaves were especially deprived in Louisiana.[11] Latrobe described in detail a variety of blacks working on Sunday, and he did not approve, believing that blacks should be guaranteed one day for worship and recreation. In all fairness, he explained, "the slaves are by no means obliged to work anywhere in this state on Sunday, as has been stated & is believed in the Eastern states by many, excepting in the sugar boiling season, & when the river rises, on the levee to prevent danger from inundation."[12]

In fact, many did work on the Sabbath, for the law guaranteed them a wage of fifty cents, although it was often paid in kind. Many carried provisions they raised to the central market on Sunday, and this, Latrobe believed, they regarded as a "frolic" rather than work, without which the "city would starve."[13] This market activity must have been a very important source of pride and opportunity for black socializing. Another visitor stated that the Sunday market was managed "entirely by negro slaves, who spread out the different articles in petty quantities . . . charging . . . about 100 per cent for the trouble."[14] On those sugar plantations that remained in the parish in 1819, independent production by slaves and their participation in the market remained important.[15] Other slaves, who lived in the town center, peddled dry goods purchased wholesale by their masters.[16] A "parallel" local domestic economy existed in any slave society, and it has been the subject of close attention recently.[17] But in such a large and growing city, this economy was especially important. Latrobe was fascinated that either poor or rich masters might subsist directly on their slaves' commerce. "I have heard," he wrote, "of mistresses who beat their slaves cruelly if they do not bring them a sufficient sum of money to enable them to keep the house, or fuel to warm them."[18] Louisiana's first historian, Judge François-Xavier Martin of the Supreme Court, hired out some of his slaves to themselves on the condition that they keep his larder full.[19]

Beyond the issue of Sunday labor, in the end, Latrobe regarded the locals as hard task masters by comparison to Anglo-Americans. He gave a few specific examples. The wife of the president of the Bank of Louisiana was known to have whipped two slave women to death with impunity.[20] Latrobe's sweeping judgment of the planters was seconded by Amos Stoddard, who wrote that "the scenes of misery and distress constantly witnessed along the coast of the Delta . . . torture the feelings of the passing stranger and wring blood from his heart."[21] Those who believed that "the slaves in the United States were always worse treated than those in Louisiana" (i.e., the future Tannenbaum thesis) were mistaken.[22] New Orleans' reputation would reach a new level of luridness in the work of Harriet Martineau in the 1830s. An English intellectual who hated slavery, she thought New Orleans was not a place "where one who prizes his humanity would wish to live."[23] She described in detail the awful story of Madame Lalurie, the local-born Marie-Delphine Macarty. First married at the tender age of thirteen to a prominent local Spaniard who was much older, she may have been deranged by it.[24] Married to a third husband in 1833 and living in a comfortable Royal Street mansion, she acquired a reputation for cruelty. One day an exasperated slave started the house on fire, and it was discovered that Marie-Delphine had chained down, whipped, and let starve some of her slaves, beating her own daughters when they protested. Martineau acknowledged that the French-speaking white community was outraged and a lynch-mob drove the woman out of the country into exile, but it was the image of a hothouse of human cruelty that was seared into the reader's memory.[25]

Countering this tradition in outsiders' accounts of New Orleans, however, is its equally convincing polar opposite, the tradition of defending local slaveowners from charges of harsh treatment, as in Timothy Flint's statement in one of this chapter's epigraphs. How can this issue be settled? The subject of day-to-day treatment has been aired in a number of important works, and New Orleans has been a special object of econometric research.[26] What has emerged from the confusing debate is a new and more healthy wariness in regard to statistical data about diet or the frequency of whipping, which can easily become reductive and mask larger realities, like, for example, the demoralizing fear of being whipped, felt even by those who were never whipped. In the absence of other kinds of records for this period, such as criminal records, the laws formulated by the planters are, faute de mieux, our most promising source on day-to-day treatment.

The laws written by the local planter class in New Orleans in the territorial period reflect the sudden transfer of Louisiana and the concurrent black triumph in Haiti, both of which made it imperative that slaveowners avoid the appearance of a conquered class before their slaves. So they moved on a broad front, immediately writing a new slave code in their territorial legislature in 1806, which would lengthen to thirty pages of fine print by 1827.[27] Latrobe studied and admired the code, some clauses of which were written in more humane language than could be found in the codes in other states, "but no law of this kind can be fully inforced [*sic*]; the slave cannot possibly be acquainted with all its provisions in his favor."[28]

The Black Code is a synthesis of those in force over the preceding century. It is divided into three parts. The first section merely repeats old injunctions concerning the treatment of slaves: they must be fed regularly, rested according to a schedule (two hours at midday in the six hot months, one and one-half hours from November to May), provided either with clothes *or* a plot, and guaranteed care when ill or disabled. As Latrobe pointed out, what this all meant in practice is simply not clear. When the occasional plantation management records worked their way into the judicial or notarial archives and were preserved, we have evidence that the expense "for the supplying of Negroes with meat," for example, was comparatively minuscule.[29] At this time, as the city expanded and the forest receded, slaves must have had greater difficulty supplementing their diet by local hunting.

The second part of the code is composed of thirty sections reiterating the police measures enacted in the local codes of 1751, 1778, and 1795.[30] Much of this part of the code is, as usual, directed at masters. Two articles, however, numbers 16 and 39, were new. The former prohibits slaves from witnessing against white people in court, but slaves had virtually never testified against whites under the more liberal Spanish law anyway, except, as always and in all slave societies, in freedom cases. Section 39 provides that anyone (presumably whites) could lodge a complaint with authorities against a master who violated the code. No evidence suggests that this section had any significant effect.

The third section was a new format in that its twenty-two sections represented an attempt to create a separate criminal code for slaves. The only thing new here is the provision for special juries to handle offenses by blacks, including free blacks accused of capital crimes: justice was now completely in the hands of slaveowners themselves. A county judge and three to five freeholders not related to the master were to decide capital cases within three days of the crime, but only three freeholders were required to judge noncapital crimes. Enforcement of the code was now so planter-controlled that the Louisiana Supreme Court did not even entertain criminal appeals of any description because "our mode of trial gives every chance for innocence to vindicate itself."[31]

Finally, certain remnant Spanish laws lingered because they were not explicitly repealed and were not directly contrary to common law, published in two hefty volumes in 1820.[32] Although most are unrelated to slavery, included are some of those slave laws that have attracted so much attention, unjustifiably so in that they were without effect. Above all is Law 6 of Title XXI of Partida Fourth of Las Siete Partidas, forbidding a master to kill or wound a slave without a judge's leave, and allowing a judge to sell to another master a slave treated so cruelly "that they cannot bear it."[33] First, it is important to point out the profound weakness of the latter law. It was up to the slave to complain and hope that a judge would sympathize. Even if the judge were to agree, all the slave got for his trouble was a new master who *might* be less cruel, and the only loss to the original master was immaterial: the court was to turn over proceeds of the sale to him. Neither judicial records nor contemporary observations suggest that New Orleans slaves even knew of this law or ever benefited from it. As for other Spanish laws, like the one guaranteeing freedom to a runaway slave who successfully eluded recapture for thirty years, the chance that they may have had some effect in a handful of cases is remote. Efforts to attach significance to peculiarities in French and Spanish laws in regard to the treatment of slaves are misdirected.[34] The laws before and after 1803 grew naturally out of the basic condition of slave society, which was over eighty years old in New Orleans in 1803. Not only had pre-1803 judicial practice shown no particular solicitude for slave criminals, Judith Kelleher Schafer goes so far as to argue that "the English common-law tradition furnished the greater protection" to slaves accused of crimes, if for no other reason than that masters had greater power to shield their chattels under the elaborate property rules of common law.[35]

Given that the vast majority of slaveowners in New Orleans were Francophones, the instances of cruelty that observers saw, which they were bound to see in any slave society, were almost inevitably committed by Francophones, so generalizations by contemporaries must be treated with care. Moreover, like most such reports, Edward Derby's account of his visit in 1824–25 mixes some uniquely interesting detail with equal amounts of hearsay. Of the latter type is his remark that the immigrant minority of American planters were "universally acknowledged to have caused a great improvement in the state of the slaves. . . . [They] taught the Creoles, that it is their interest, more especially since the importation of slaves is next to impossible, to treat their stock more humanely, and to feed and clothe them better."[36] One might respond that closure of the African slave trade had a like effect on all slaveowners. One might also be tempted to accuse Derby of ethnic bias. On the other hand, his principal informants appear to have been Francophones, including the planters whose domains he describes in admiring detail. In fact, not a single published account of New Orleans in this period by a writer of any background suggested that Anglo-Americans were more cruel than local slaveowners or introduced cruel policies.

Following Genovese's schema, a second category of "slave treatment" concerns the conditions of life, defined as "family security, opportunities for an independent social and religious life, and . . . cultural developments."[37] These things are determined mainly by individual planters, and, once again, they are very hard to measure accurately for comparative purposes. The slaveholder's personal circumstances and attitudes determined whether he or she would break up a family, allow a degree of autonomy, or permit a slave cultural pursuits. The recent work of Norrece T. Jones Jr. and Brenda Stevenson has reinforced our understanding of how vulnerable the slave family could be to the external forces that could destroy it.[38] The threat of selling a slave or a family member was a major instrument of social control, and Louisiana's legal prohibition against selling a child under the age of ten years away from its mother was neither expressed in humanitarian terms nor an effective restriction on family disruption by sale. The relevant clause in the new slave code was, in fact, a change for the worse, for under earlier law children were not separable from the mother's hearth before the age of puberty. This meant a minor increase in the liquidity of slaveowners' property and less supportive and wholesome family life for some black children. But the courts were not discerning when it came to the ages of slaves, and planters evinced no particular scruples about selling children. In 1811, Jean-Baptiste Bacqué sold Sanitté and her five children to Joseph Gournier, on the account of Jamaica slaveholder Teresa Morgan. Two and a half years later, Gournier sold the children (aged eighteen months to thirteen years) to Antoine Prudhomme, without their mother.[39] Jean-Baptiste Bergé bid $310 at auction for a nine-year-old girl who swooned on the way to his house. The auctioneer sneered at his demand to annul the sale, saying Bergé must pay even if she was "dead on a slab," which she was three days later.[40] Clearly, the law did not restrain slaveholders on the account of age. One study of the disruption of slave marriages by interstate sales in New Orleans concludes that dissolution was infrequent, but persuasive critics show that the authors base their study on a small sample and are guided by several insupportable assumptions.[41] Moreover, the breakup of marriages is hardly an accurate measure of the overall extent of family disruption:

most of the unmarried adult slaves imported from the other states and sold in New Orleans had been removed from the comfort of their families of birth. The most comprehensive study of the domestic slave trade in New Orleans reveals that four out of ten children under the age of thirteen years sold there were separated from their parents.[42]

As for independent religious life, there is no indication that the clergy either promoted or protected it or ameliorated slavery in any way.[43] By the beginning of the nineteenth century, the priests had separate schedules of surplice fees for funerals for whites, free blacks, and slaves, but only one schedule for marriages (seven pesos, six reales just for the sacrament), and the vast majority of slaves obviously were not likely to pay for this luxury, for they all but disappear from the marriage registers by this time.[44] Latrobe saw some blacks going to churches, but all blacks were excluded from the Catholic priesthood, whereas the Protestant evangelical sects introduced a true alternative. According to one historian, "only the Methodist and Baptist organizations allowed the city's Negroes the freedom of expression and the luxury of a semiautonomous black clergy."[45] Little is known of the development of independent religious life in the slave quarter.

As for the slaves' opportunity for independent cultural development in other respects, this has been discussed at some length in the preceding chapter. The immediate effects of the "re-Africanization" of the slave population meant that ethnic diversity undermined the potential for cultural coherence or pride.

Fig. 20. A slave auction in New Orleans, c. 1839. From Buckingham, *Slave States of America.*

Of much greater concern than culture to most slaves at this time, however, were the social factors that set new boundaries to their ambitions and their ability to form a community that protected and nurtured individuals. Above all, the slaveowning class made it much more difficult for anyone to get out of slavery than in the past.

The third category of slave treatment is access to freedom and citizenship, associated with attitudes toward miscegenation, and many scholars consider it the most useful factor in comparative analysis, certainly the most prominent feature of Frank Tannenbaum's argument. For the racial views implied in the comparative willingness to emancipate individual slaves must reflect basic cultural influences if rates of manumission vary with masters' national origins.[46] Central to the comparative analysis, therefore, is the problem of measuring manumission rates. In all slave societies, many people in bondage exerted pressure on masters to provide them with some escape hatch from their condition, and many of them negotiated a deal—this was as true in the United States as anywhere else. So the main issue is how often it was permitted, *not* how many free blacks existed, which was determined by a combination of the age of a given society, the number of blacks, and local economic conditions. This was especially true in New Orleans, to which thousands of free blacks, including many mulattoes, immigrated between 1803 and 1810. No one has been able to demonstrate that actual rates of manumission were higher in any slave society outside North America, nor that any planter class had a predisposition to favor manumission.[47] In New Orleans, both the absolute number of free blacks and their proportion of the population had grown in the Spanish period, and the effort of the planters to stop this trend during those years and after 1803 is the key: it shows that they shared a basic ideology with American slaveowners. In fact, free blacks were in an increasingly vulnerable position not because of policies introduced by the Americans but because the slaveowners of 1803 finally were able to "normalize" the growth and status of this special group by law by tightly restricting the exits out of slavery into the growing free black subclass.[48]

Hostility to free blacks was the natural and most obvious result of planters' anxiety about race. While free blacks were not, collectively, disposed to rebellion, the behavior of free blacks as individuals seemed to represent an insidious threat to the whole system in several ways.[49] Whites saw free blacks gain considerable economic power in New Orleans by 1803. A handful of black planters challenged the whites' monopoly of the slave supply in the market place. When the free mulatto Louis Dusuau died in 1814, he was a member of that tiny free black elite. Besides his home in Conti Street he had a sugar plantation with thirty-seven slaves at Bonnet Carré, a small farm in Metairie with three slaves, another city lot, and a big piece of land out in Attakapas he may have been preparing to become a plantation.[50] The economic success of free blacks could destroy the racial rationale for slavery: blacks were obviously not inherently inferior to whites.

Beyond mere economic insolence, certain individual free blacks seemed devoid of the personal respect they owed white people. Attorney Étienne Mazureau filed a complaint in 1813, claiming that when he and his wife strolled opposite Maspero's Exchange one afternoon, free woman of color Félicité Fouché, coming up the sidewalk in the opposite direction, not only refused to step aside but also gave madame a shove. When admonished, Félicité snarled, "I don't give way to anybody, the road is for everybody—you could have passed by shifting a bit." When Mazureau threatened to have her punished, she mocked him, said he would not dare, and went off showering the Mazureaus with "abusive expressions."[51] This sort of thing had to be stopped. Incidents like this fed whites' fear that the nonslaveholding majority of free blacks had a racial motive to stir slaves to revolt. In fact, one outside observer pointed out that by restricting full citizenship to whites the planters exposed the state to precisely that danger.[52] Legislators saw it the other way around, and now tried to arrest the growth of the free black population and to restrict their economic opportunities.

The planters' most pressing goal was to reduce dramatically the number of emancipations. The territorial legislature and the city fathers of the Town Council of New Orleans went into action immediately in 1804 in an attempt to stiffen the racial regime, capped in 1807 by a law passed in the legislature that abolished the *coartación* system in its entirety. In eight terse sections, the lawmakers eliminated the privilege of guaranteed self-purchase. Section one prohibited the compelling of any man to free a slave except by a special act of the legislature. This meant that a slave might acquire his or her value several times over and act with perfect sobriety, but the master could and probably would refuse to emancipate the slave. This section was in effect immediately, whereas slaves on the verge of purchasing freedom had a grace period until September 1, 1807, to complete their payments.[53]

The other sections of the anti-*coartación* law made it extremely difficult for masters to liberate slaves for any reason. Perhaps the most important deterrent of all was that a slave could not be freed if under the age of thirty years. No slave could be freed whose behavior had not been exemplary for at least four years. The master had to file an intention to emancipate forty days prior, during which time creditors were invited to produce evidence that the slave was collateral on a debt and could not be freed. Even if this waiting period was passed and the slave was freed, if a mistake was made the creditors of an estate could convince a court to reenslave him or her years later to recover their capital. The emancipator was required to maintain the emancipee if necessary, to prevent any inconvenience to the public. Unauthorized emancipations were subject to stiff fines. The law eliminating the right to purchase freedom was thereafter sustained by the Louisiana Supreme Court.[54] Only a handful of slaves were able to buy their freedom in the decades thereafter: the spigot was closed on the outlet of slaves into the free black subclass.[55] The final logical step was taken in 1830 when the legislature ruled that an emancipator had to post a bond of one thousand dollars to guarantee that the manumittee would leave Louisiana within one month.[56]

It was also of great importance to limit the influx of free blacks into Louisiana from other states and colonies. Their entry was forbidden by the legislature in 1807, on pain of a fine, incarceration, and sale into temporary slavery if an illegal entrant could not pay the fine. The refugee free blacks of 1809 were allowed to enter, but over time the law was effective.[57] In 1830, it was reinforced with harsher penalties, and free blacks who left the territory of the United States for any reason were debarred from reentering Louisiana.[58] The next legislature decided that was unfair to those property owners "who have always conducted themselves in an orderly and respectful manner," and these were permitted to travel anywhere except the West Indies, the most important destination of Louisiana free black travelers since the eighteenth century.[59]

In direct conjunction with the policy to limit emancipations was the policy to reinforce the developing breach in the free black community between those who were born light-colored and those who were darker. One way was to limit their marriage partners: the new civil code recapitulated the law of 1778 outlawing marriages between free people of any color and slaves, to emphasize the complete degradation of the (largely black) slave population.[60] Another measure was more subtle but more effective. It was noted in the last chapter that according to a judicial decision of 1810 someone of mixed race was presumed to be free unless it was discovered the person was a slave.[61] Obviously, mulattoes who were dressed as slaves or found working with slaves were not presumed to be free. But the customary distinction was part of the strategy to widen the gulf between slaves and freedmen, not to "privilege" mulattoes, aside from the dubious privilege of not being treated as a slave runaway when found unsupervised by a white person. And the distinction was not unusual: runaway advertisements in all states note the link between "yellow" complexion and the presumption of freedom. Court rulings from Louisiana in the Deep South to North Carolina in the upper South indicate that a mulatto who dressed and behaved as a free person was presumed to be free of suspicion of slave status.[62] The planters drove a wedge between the very lightest skinned "mulattoes" and everybody who was darker to divide and weaken the free black community, on the one hand, and by so doing to divide and weaken the black community as a whole.

At the same time, the possibility that mixed-race people might "pass" as white was drastically reduced by a seemingly minor technical adjustment. The legislature passed an innocuous-sounding law that went into effect in 1808 requiring notaries and other people acting in an official capacity to designate any and all free blacks in their records as either "free man of color" (FMC) or "free woman of color" (FWC).[63] At one stroke this eliminated the method by which free blacks could document their lineages, especially their transition through the traditional three generations to white legal status. Throughout the colonial world, either law or custom stipulated, as did the law of Virginia in 1705, that "the child, grand child, or great grand child, of a negro shall be deemed, accounted, held and taken to be a mulatto."[64] This was an exclusionary rule implying that a great-great-grandchild of a Negro having only white ancestry for three generations was regarded by the law as a white person. In practice, this meant that a few people "passed" legally from "the Negro race" into "the white race" in all slave societies. By the beginning of the nineteenth century, the rule was somewhat liberalized in Jeffersonian Virginia, where a person with only one eighth or less "Negro blood" was allowed to pass legally. Moreover, that person could escape whatever residual social prejudice attached to remote black ancestry by removing from the locale.[65] In New Orleans, until 1808 a person could verify the first two steps toward social passing because notaries and priests faithfully recorded either "Negro, mulatto, or quadroon" after a black person's name. If a quadroon, the grandchild of a Negro, had a daughter by a white man, the children of that daughter by a white man would be white, according to custom. On the other hand, there had been an extralegal custom in New Orleans even during the Spanish period *not* to facilitate passing by recording any degree of admixture beyond the second degree. That is, the term "octoroon" is not encountered in the records: anyone lighter than a mulatto was a "quadroon." It is precisely because of this strict avoidance of any term indicating a third consecutive generation of racial mixture that proves the "third-degree" customary rule of passing was acknowledged, but never documented by authorities, in New Orleans.

In other words, the so-called one-drop rule, by which a person with any black ancestry, no matter how remote, *was already effectively adhered to in New Orleans before 1803.* While technical, morphological passing occurred, real, social passing (general acceptance of a person as "really" white) was next to impossible in a town where status and ancestry were so well recorded. One might be morphologically white, say she was white, and yet everyone would whisper "the truth" behind her back. Real passing might have happened occasionally because of lax surveillance at the lowest level of the social spectrum, as it could in all states, but not at the other end of the spectrum. One does find some hints in the sacramental records of slippage across the color line when children of quadroons were entered in the white registers.[66] But the "correction" of one such entry in 1817 as belonging in the "colored" register reveals official vigilance to prevent passing.[67] To insist on positive evidence for all this is to miss the point because it was a system of lies of omission: the passing of light-skinned free blacks was limited more effectively by public opinion than by explicit laws or rules. There was no law that priests could not use the term "octoroon," for example, but they never did, for reasons deduced only from the results— the limited ability of free blacks to pass. As Lewis Clarke of Kentucky put it so well in 1842, "There never was anything beat slavery for lying."[68]

After 1803, it was the intention of the planter class to make the one-drop rule the de facto law of the land. However many people had broken the customary technical (if not the social) third-degree barrier by 1808, it was clear that many aspired to do so in the future, even though by no means all mixed-race people yearned to pass. This was a grave threat in a community where the gemeinschaft-type of face-to-face organization and policing of social relations was no longer possible. The passing of the third degree of admixture by many people, who had acquired the surnames of virtually every leading white family in town, could lead to insufferable confusion of property rights. This was true even though only some free blacks bore the surnames of white people to whom they were directly related.[69] Creation of the labels "free man of color" and "free woman of color" eliminated all pretension to any presumptive right to

Fig. 21. *Head of a Black Wearing a Turban*, c. 1818, by Eugène Delacroix. The artist carried out an intensive study of this young man in a series of paintings. From a photograph by the author.

pass because no individual's specific admixture was legally recorded: it created an undifferentiated degraded free black subclass of people who could be surveiled to make sure they did not intermarry with whites. Isaac Holmes could see how it worked: "Although the term quatroon [*sic*] would infer a person of three-fourths white extraction, yet all between the colour of a mulatto and a white acquire in New Orleans this appellation. Some, indeed, are to all appearance perfectly white; yet as it can be traced that they are of black descent, were they to intrude into the company of a white female, or even into the boxes appropriated to the whites at the theatre, they would be expelled with every mark of disrespect."[70] It was by this disrespect that social passing was prevented. This was the beginning of the modern era "of instituting legal constraints to racial self-determination."[71] It was inaugurated not by the tiny minority of Anglo-Americans but by the local white Francophones.

A revealing pair of incidents shows the strength of race prejudice against even that one damning drop in New Orleans. Saint Domingue refugees had to battle rumors about their ancestry because it was undocumented in Louisiana, as seen in the case of André-Martin Lamotte. He took out a lengthy ad in a newspaper in 1811 to complain that he had just learned that rumors had been afloat for years "raising humiliating doubts about our [my family's] origin." So he had somehow managed to buy and file with a local attorney copies of the entries in the parish books of Les Cayes documenting his entire ancestry. "Talk of this nature," he concluded sadly, "and perhaps just as unfounded, is bruited about here by half the refugees of St. Domingue against one another."[72] Another refugee suffered from rumor-mongering many years later. John Cauchoix was on the verge of marrying Mademoiselle Smith, "a young lady of very respectable connections," when a rival started a rumor about the color of Cauchoix's aunt, whom witnesses had seen among the refugees in Cuba, a rumor that spread through town like wild fire. Naturally, the match fell through. He sued for a large sum and a jury did award him a token amount. He had produced documentation of his lineage going back over one century and depositions from other refugees proudly attesting that extreme color prejudice in Saint Domingue had kept its white race "pure."[73]

When the color policy in regard to free blacks was combined with the restrictions on manumission and the peculiar French culture of New Orleans, an odd circumstance arose that did not arise in other southern states. The so-called quadroons or free people of color formed a distinct subset of the free black population that avoided association with free blacks of a darker hue, and with slaves of any color, as was true in all states in which color was degraded by law. But they came to form the great majority of the town's free black population because the laws of 1807 all but ended the entry of dark-skinned blacks into the free population. The free people of color married only among themselves, becoming lighter as a group because of their language, their distinctive cultural marker, which tended to confine them to New Orleans or satellite Francophone communities.

This was the key: in slave society, if "one drop" of black "blood" meant that a person might be subject to white social prejudice, by removing to a place where people did not know about the "drop," one might escape prejudice altogether. In Louisiana, however, the one-drop rule was more tyrannical. Not only was it impossible to expunge black "blood," but, by contrast with the other states of the union, it was next to impossible for Francophone free blacks to get away from that blood by distancing themselves geographically from their community of origin. In the other states, once one could "pass" morphologically, one might also pass socially by moving to another state, especially a free state, or to the southern frontier, where one's labor or purchasing power was so eagerly welcomed by pioneer communities that origins might not be carefully looked into. Thus, the free black populations of the states where emigration was possible (especially those of the upper South geographically closest to the free states accessible to migrants) remained comparatively smaller and darker than that of New Orleans because the light-skinned tended to migrate out of slave society. The lightest-skinned free blacks of New Orleans enjoyed a certain degree of social superiority over all other local blacks and in some cases had substantial estates, which would disincline them to head for the frontier. Most spoke French, however, and that was a decisive barrier to passing quietly outside the region, where anybody with a French accent was assumed to be from Louisiana, their ancestry drawing close attention precisely because of Louisiana's exaggerated reputation for race mixture. The risks such a person took by trying to pass outside of Louisiana have been immortalized in the most popular musical melodrama of the twentieth century, "Showboat." If such a person's "black blood" was discovered, it was a violation of laws prohibiting the entry of free blacks in most states.

Thus, free blacks stayed in Louisiana, where the ancestry of the quadroons was carefully recorded, each generation in succession, an endless litany of FMCs and FWCs, marrying one another, virtually sealed off genetically from the black population. The result was that by the 1860s New Orleans had a remarkably white population of free "blacks" that surprised all outsiders. Whitelaw Reid described them:

> There were elegantly dressed ladies, beautiful with a beauty beside which that of the North is wax-work; with great, swimming, lustrous eyes, half-veiled behind long, pendant lashes, and arched with coal-black eyebrows; complexions no darker than those of the Spanish senoritas one admires in Havana, but transparent as that of the most beautiful Northern blonde, with the rich blood coming and going, under the olive skin, with every varying emotion; luxuriant flowing stresses, graceful figures, accomplished manners—perfect Georgian or Circassian beauties. Yet every one of these was "only a nigger."[74]

This passage is also marked by the erotic undertones with which white men typically spoke of the "quadroons." Reid was describing the new Manon, bizarrely epitomized in the twentieth-century, racially obsessive popular history by Pierre Paul Ebeyer quoted at the head of this chapter.

Up to this point, people of mixed race and racial passing have been discussed without very specific reference to the social dynamics of genetic intermixture, a remarkably confused subject that requires very careful exploration. Let us begin with a startling anecdote, one illustrating the fact that some free blacks of mixed race were beginning to embarrass private property in the generational successions of white families. This was the most immediate threat to the security of the slaveholding class. From one perspective, an interracial liaison is cooptation of the vulnerable black woman. From another perspective, however, it can also appear to be cooptation of the master and subversion of the regime by the creation of customary rights usually denied to black women.[75] Marie Darby's dramatic confrontation with her relatives illustrates both the continuous growth of the problem of racial mixture over time (all of the circumstances of the case developed during the Spanish period but it was fought out in American courts), and a major change in the period after 1803: larger and richer estates meant higher stakes and the greater vulnerability of white heirs to challenges from their black siblings or other relatives. The reader should not be confused by the name Darby: all principals were Francophones.

In 1805, Marie Corbin Baschemin Darby, widow of an important member of the founding generation, Jonathas Darby, found herself in a very difficult position. They had had several children, of whom only three were still living. Daughter Jeanne cared for her dutifully, but the two sons profoundly disturbed the peace of her last years. Her youngest son, Louis, had become violently insane. Marie struggled to prevent her daughter-in-law, Joanna Dessalles, from seizing control of Louis's large estate, charging that Joanna was not qualified and that guardians should be appointed by the court to protect the property.[76] This contest between two white women helps to put in perspective Marie's other court battle at this same time.

Two years earlier, a more serious threat to Marie's family and respectability was presented by a quite different set of grandchildren, her oldest son Pierre's three boys and three girls by his concubine Nanette (or Jeannette), a Negress. Pierre had died in 1803, leaving a will that donated everything he owned to these children (apparently Nanette was deceased), and Marie fought it tooth and nail. She got a ruling from Pierre Derbigny in the new Court of Common Pleas in June 1804, annulling the will. That foiled the suit by Nanette's children, headed by eldest brother François Darby, to carry out the succession. Marie stormed that they had no proof of being free nor even that they were Nanette's children, and, above all, such an inheritance would be "an action also contrary to the manners of this country."[77] That much was true: while some men freed slaves in the Spanish period and a few made donations to them, major transfers of property like this were rare. According to Marie, the rule had always been that when a man died without legal offspring he could donate up to one-third of the estate to illegal children, but only if they were born to a marriageable free woman, which Nanette clearly was not. In fact, as seen earlier, that rule could be evaded and black heirs could inherit if no white heirs protested, but Marie wanted the estate to go to the ascendant forced heir, namely to her. The scandal of being shoved aside by these dusky reminders of her son's lifelong misbehavior would have been intolerable, and the judge agreed.

The black Darbys took the case into Superior Court, however, and in 1806 they finally vanquished Marie. Crying helplessly that according to "laws as ancient as that of the establishment of this colony the marriage of Whites with Blacks was and is prohibited," Marie charged grandson François with trying "to assimelate [sic] the blacks with white persons."[78] It should be pointed out that the decision in no sense changed the laws banning intermarriage because that was not the issue anyway: Pierre and Nanette were not married. And given the nature of the civil law and the ambiguity of the status of the common law in 1806, this case created no precedent for other blacks to exploit. Nevertheless, this case undoubtedly helped spark the ensuing campaign by the planters to make this kind of saucy challenge by free blacks more difficult in the future.

To maintain racial slavery, henceforth the assumed biological line between whites and blacks had to be patrolled more strictly or the logic of race would collapse. "Society" as defined by whites could only benefit by limiting the number of free blacks and their opportunity to adulterate the whites' blood and trouble their estates. One could not police by law sexual relations between white men and black women (the ultimate cause of a mixed-race population, if not the proximate cause of the birth of a majority of its members)—in no slave society were laws designed to prevent these sexual relations as such.[79] But the legitimacy of mixed offspring must be prevented, which foreclosed inheritance rights, for such inheritance would disgrace a white family. White women had the most to lose by this disgrace: people like Marie Darby were on the front line of battle against free blacks.

It is necessary to state as emphatically as possible before going forward that illicit sexual relations between white men and black women were not primarily responsible for the growth of the free black population after 1803.[80] The free black population of New Orleans had grown because of a combination of factors more important than interracial sexual liaisons. The arithmetic is simple: the record of marriages in the St. Louis Cathedral Archives register for blacks shows that of 127 marriages by free people of color recorded between 1777 and 1807, 57 were by blacks and 70 were by people of mixed race.[81] While it is true that a number of free mulattoes themselves resulted from race mixture in New Orleans, in creating their *own* families they were producing a majority of mulattoes and quadroons *before* 1803. The other major factor was immigration; the number of free mulatto refugees arriving from the Antilles may have equaled or actually exceeded the number of free mulattoes already living in New Orleans. In other words, the number and proportion of mixed-race people became pronounced in New Orleans in the first two decades of the nineteenth century because of social or historical factors, not cultural dispositions to racial intermixture.

The actual racial mixture that did occur between whites and blacks was not proportionately greater where whites were of French or Spanish origin as opposed to Anglo-Americans. Even Tannenbaum felt compelled to refute the notion that there was a difference: "Every traveler in the [Anglo-American] South before the Civil War comments on the widespread miscegenation. . . . [It was] as characteristic in southern slave states as in other slave societies in this hemisphere."[82] Interracial concubinage may have been marginally more common in a big city like New Orleans than it was in rural Kentucky, and it was less effectively veiled by the code of silence, but racial mixture was not comparatively greater or fundamentally more acceptable in New Orleans because of cultural conditions than it was in Kentucky. As was stated frankly in one court case from that state's records, interracial concubinage was "but too common, as we all know, from the numbers of our mullatto [*sic*] population."[83] A key difference between Kentucky and New Orleans is that in the latter notaries and clerics recorded methodically vital statistics, emancipations, and property transfers, and the racial classifications of the principals involved. Gary Mills found in his study of Alabama that the proportion of mulattoes in the antebellum free black populations of Anglo-American counties and "Latin" counties was comparable.[84] The key was that everywhere in the South, those of mixed race seemed to be concentrated in and gravitate to the towns. When Anne Royall arrived in Alexandria, Virginia, in 1825, she described a population of "every shade of colour, from the fairest white, down to the deepest black," which filled her with "horror and disgust."[85] Thus one is not surprised to find the most noticeable and best-documented mixed-race population in the South's largest city, New Orleans. Moreover, by 1819, blacks of mixed race probably constituted a majority of free persons of color—for blacks of any shade were mostly prevented from freeing themselves after 1807.

Frances Trollope explained how quadroons were kept in their place: slaveowning white women played a very special role. Describing their elegant entertainments, she notes that "every portly dame of the set is as exclusive in her principles as a lady patroness" because she had to compete with parallel social gatherings, those where white men might mix with black women, who were, according to an astonished Carl David Arfwedson in 1833, "as white, if not whiter, than the Creoles."[86] Thus, white women exercised "the most violent, and the most inveterate" prejudice against free mulatto women: if some white men formed liaisons with women of color, these liaisons were condemned by respectable female society as disgraceful.[87]

Pierre Darby and Nanette were among a tiny minority of couples who engaged in lifetime concubinage, but Trollope was describing a second category of more casual liaisons in which a somewhat larger number of unmarried white men indulged. Readers have been too willing to ignore Trollope's qualifier: she wrote that "such of the gentlemen" who slipped away from the company of white women formed these illicit liaisons, not all white men. Historians have typically grouped all interracial sexual unions under the heading of *plaçage* and exaggerated their incidence and social acceptability, based on the practice of—at most—a handful of young white men and free black women.[88] In chapter 8 it was revealed that a slanderous generalization by the disgruntled writer Paul Alliot was the unique origin of the historians' myth of *plaçage* (i.e., the "placing" of a free black girl by her parent in a menage with a white man).[89] By contrast, voluntary liaisons entered into by adults like Pierre and Nanette certainly occurred. But the myth that these mixed couplings were universal was popularized in print by Thomas Ashe. Like Alliot, Ashe was a scapegrace, an Anglo-Irish novelist who catered to a scandal-loving reading public. His description of New Orleans mulatto concubines reads like a soft-pornographic

Thousand and One Nights: they strolled the town center heavily laden one and all with gold, pearls, diamonds and other jewels dripping from their hair and clothes, a description seconded by no other observer. It is symptomatic of the wealth of his imagination and the worthlessness of his book, one written by a man who probably never saw New Orleans and went on to a shameless career of smut and blackmail that eventually led to prison.[90] One of the most thoughtful of all visitors to antebellum New Orleans, a dour Scot named James Stuart who hated slavery and had every reason to paint race relations in the most lurid colors, stated flatly that accounts of widespread interracial mixing were "merely travellers stories."[91]

Short-term interracial liaisons might be arranged beginning in 1805 in the so-called quadroon balls in the St. Philip Street Ballroom, where some of the light-skinned free women of color danced with white men, gatherings at which black men of any hue or status were prohibited.[92] These dance halls have provided the most sturdy lore of old New Orleans down to this day. Careless reading of carelessly written sources has inspired exaggeration. An observer who was equally as informative and as misleading as Trollope, Karl Bernhard, Duke of Saxe-Weimar, spent the 1826 carnival season in New Orleans, and gave a good deal of attention to the various types of balls given between Epiphany and Lent. He agreed with Trollope that at the most respectable balls "most of the gentlemen . . . [were] far behind the ladies in elegance" and soon slipped away to the quadroon ball, where they could be "more at their ease."[93] But he never provided exact numbers of these gentlemen, clearly implied that they went to the quadroon ball not to seek sexual liaisons but to relax in the company of people who would not express disapproval of their inelegance (coarse language and drunkenness), and he never knew that the tiny St. Philip Street Ballroom could not have held more than a fraction of the town's free black women and an even smaller proportion of its white men. In fact, his descriptions suggest that the quadroon balls were substantially more about male posturing than flirtation with the women.[94] He skittered out as soon as possible "that I might not utterly destroy my standing in New Orleans, but returned to the [white] masked ball and took great care not to disclose to the white ladies where I had been."[95] He also referred to "the greatest contempt, and even . . . animosity" with which white women spoke of free blacks, and of the whites' privilege to have any free black whipped "upon an accusation, proved by two witnesses."[96] In his detailed description of New Orleans, Paul Wilhelm, Duke of Württemberg specifically reported that quadroon balls were only "occasionally attended by white gentlemen, but white women may under no circumstances appear there, and the native Creoles also avoid these gatherings, at least publicly, so as not to get into a quarrel with the ladies of New Orleans, who are most intolerant in these matters."[97] According to Paul Wilhelm, only "foreigners or unmarried young men" engaged in interracial liaisons, and he did not suggest that it was universal even among those groups.[98] At least as impressive as the contemporary published accounts that mention interracial concubinage are those that do not, even when the purpose is to catalogue the town's sins.[99] The New England missionary Timothy Flint argued repeatedly and with some heat that he knew "of no people among whom . . . [an immoral] man would sink into more certain contempt."[100]

Even stable interracial liaisons were certainly not socially acceptable, not something that would be discussed openly, and to cross the boundary of concubinage and marry was infamy. Any man who married a black woman was automatically "reduced to a level" with her in public opinion, and they "must then live en retraite in New Orleans, or quit the country for another part."[101] And only a white man of means would dare brave that ordeal with a light-skinned quadroon woman who might be exposed even then. This is not to argue that interracial marriages never happened, for they happened in all states; it is to argue that they were neither more common nor acceptable in New Orleans than elsewhere in the South.

While *plaçage* is a myth, New Orleans certainly did have street-walking prostitutes of all colors. What was different about New Orleans was that it was more open than in the rest of the South, becoming a serious *urban* problem in the booming queen city.[102] But many (probably most) prostitutes were white women, especially Irish and German immigrants. By midcentury, the trade was attacked by Know Nothing reform politics mounted by a coalition of Whig businessmen and householders.[103] These women primarily served the city's floating population, the kind of illicit sex that occurs wherever it is not suppressed systematically.

Racial mixture is a difficult subject that defies easy summary. What is clearly implied in the sacramental records of St. Louis Cathedral is that most free women of color did not dance at quadroon balls and did not live in concubinage with white men: they married free men of color and led as respectable lives as they were permitted to do under the circumstances.[104] New Orleans was different from Richmond, Virginia, only in that illegal (adulterous) or merely disgraceful (nonadulterous) liaisons with blacks were less veiled and more numerous in the larger urban population. And the evidence that white people in New Orleans had the same attitudes as prevailed in other southern slave societies is clear in the notarial archives. Those white men who married, for example, typically did not mention concubines or children of color in their wills.[105]

Occasionally, emancipations clearly indicate an intimate relationship with the slave, but usually when the principals were from Saint Domingue. It was unlikely that a white woman born in conservative New Orleans would have written, as did Widow Marie Perou, formerly of Saint Domingue, that she freed mulatto Marie-Françoise, twenty-three years old, because she was the "natural daughter of my husband."[106] Local men who never married were more likely to mention illegitimate families in their wills. Jean-Baptiste Picou, born in New Orleans in 1758, never married but fathered ten mixed-race children by free woman of color Victoire Deslonde, and he left half of his estate to them, the other half to his brother.[107] Joseph Roux, born in St. Tropez, never married and left his estate to free mulatto Marie-Elizabeth, obviously his life companion because she was required to split the estate with her quadroon son Jean-Baptiste when he reached his majority.[108] Jean-Baptiste Macarty openly acknowledged his natural son, quadroon Théopile, about six years old, born of free mulatto Rosette Beaulieu, and instructed his executor to establish a trust fund of six thousand dollars. The interest would pay for Théo's education, the sum to be managed by Rosette unless "she would not make good use of it." He left two thousand dollars more to Rosette, which she was instructed to leave to Théo when she died. The boy should be trained as a refined artisan, a goldsmith or gunsmith. Macarty included an unembarrassed caveat for the benefit of his three white children: if they thought Théo's bequest was too large they had permission to reduce it to four thousand dollars.[109] In a similar instance, Jacques Moquin, native of Montreal, made his white daughter his universal heir, yet only love seems to explain why he left free mulatto Jeanneton Dubois four thousand dollars plus the twelve-year-old Bambara slave Azore, a fortune on which any free black could live at ease for the rest of her life.[110] These are examples of that minority of men whose wills nourished the greatly exaggerated accounts of quadroon concubines.

The motive of a single man to emancipate a slave, however, could be totally obscure. A good example is the will of Thomas Hassett, an Irish priest in the "foreign" clergy group engaged in a desperate struggle with Père Antoine for control of St. Louis Cathedral. In a will written on April 19, 1804, he freed

Fig. 22. Julien Hudson (active New Orleans 1830s to 1840s), believed to be a self-portrait. A portrait painter and free person of color of New Orleans. From the collection of the Louisiana State Museum.

Negress Brigid and her two children and left her a bequest of one hundred dollars. The next day he annulled that will and ruled that only her son, Thomas ("Thomas Hassett, Jr."?), would be freed and collect the one hundred dollars, whereas Brigid and the other son were to be sold. The estate went to his sister in Ireland. As in so many cases, no definite conclusion is possible about the relationships between these four people.[111]

   In fact, moreover, most of the mothers of white men's illegitimate children were *not* quadroons. Roux was more typical in his choice of a mulatto, but long-term liaisons with unmixed blacks were by no means rare. Jean Dubreuil, never married, fifty-nine years old when he wrote his will in 1811, left the bulk of his estate to his mulatto daughter Manette by free Negro Marie-Jeanne Dubourg.[112] The slaveowning free mulatto Valentin Bauré's will in 1810 declared that he was the natural son of Sieur Bauré and free Negress Louise Bauré (and Valentin, in turn, although a mulatto, chose a Negress to be the mother of his own daughter).[113] As for Frederic Bancroft's old story that light-colored female mulatto slaves commanded premium prices in the domestic slave trade because of their sexual allure, Laurence J. Kotlikoff has decisively refuted this notion in a fine quantitative study.[114]

Side by side with these exceptional cases are scattered throughout the notarial archives many other wills written by men who did not leave mixed-race heirs. François Chauvin Delery Desillet's testament breathes the air of a man whose wife and seven children could have absolute confidence in his moral rectitude and have no fear that he left a parallel black family.[115] At the other end of the social scale, Sebastien Ferrer, a Catalan cabinetmaker who never married, declared that he had no children of any status, and there is no reason to believe that his emancipation of Catiche for her "good service" meant that she was his lover.[116] Two of the city's richest citizens, John McDonogh and Judah Touro, are excellent examples. Both were outsiders (one a Maryland Protestant and the other a Rhode Island Jew) who settled in New Orleans during the Spanish regime. Both had their hearts broken by beautiful young white women in their early years and remained bachelors thereafter, pining for their true loves. Both became exceptionally liberal philanthropists, despite the fact that they could never become full-fledged accepted gentlemen at the pinnacle of society because of their eccentricity (McDonogh, a miser and apparent misanthrope until his will was unsealed) or origins (Touro, a non-Christian). Neither would have risked much damage to his reputation among men by enjoying the comfort of a liaison with a woman of color, and yet evidence suggests that neither ever did. In shunning interracial commitments they were typical of the majority of white men.[117]

In all of the attention devoted to interracial sex, historians have ignored two important social phenomena, first, the power and motivation of white women to police these matters collectively and defend the respectability of their sex, a peculiar kind of southern "feminism," and second, the inclination of most free people of color to seek respectability through legitimate domestic relations with one another.[118] That neglect has been combined with the erroneous assumption that the sheer number of all individuals of mixed race is some kind of mathematical guide to the degree of sexual interaction between blacks and whites. To repeat for emphasis, by 1819, the majority of mulattoes seen in New Orleans streets were the children of couples composed of two married mulattoes, not the children of white men.

What was most distinctive about interracial sex in New Orleans was its large-scale urban character and the disproportionate contribution to it by male outsiders. The faithful representatives of the slaveholding class, the courts, led by the jurist of French background, Martin, struggled to restrain renegade planters from donating property to concubines and offspring of color. This same battle was fought out in every southern courtroom, as evident in the cases cited by Helen Tunicliff Catterall in her digest of legal decisions concerning slavery, a campaign against "Jezebel," as Deborah Gray White has called the menacingly seductive black women of popular southern mythology who drew white men into a life of shame as if by magic.[119] For us, she was the black Manon, the laughing, carefree, irresistible icon who obscures the pervasive pain and humiliation of slavery.

Anxiety about free blacks and the patrolling of blood lines was not at all incompatible with the tendency of some white men, including some rich ones, to extend their special protection over and economic support to their parallel mixed-race families. This played some part in the logic behind the presumption that black equals slave, mulatto equals free: it incidentally helped protect white-allied free mulattoes from police and other white people who might otherwise harass these "blacks." But these relationships were of little consequence in the overall scheme of things. The great majority of free blacks did not form a common social network with white relatives and depend on them for protection from hostile Americans.[120] Mulattoes tended to enjoy higher socioeconomic status than darker free blacks because their white blood supposedly made them superior: general belief in this pseudo-biology made it socially true, *not* the specific white parentage of those mulattoes who had white parents.[121]

In fact, the result of the campaign to limit the growth of the free black population was remarkably successful in Louisiana. Their number mounted from 10,476 in 1820 to only 18,647 in 1860, representing a remarkable decline in their proportion of the black population to only 5.3 percent, exactly one-half the proportion of free blacks (10.6 percent) in Virginia, far smaller than the one that would have been created if the freedom purchase policy had not been annulled.[122]

Thus, although a broad distinction between upper South and lower South has been posited in regard to the status and role of free blacks, the difference between New Orleans and the upper South shrinks to the vanishing point in light of these statistics.[123] Lower South whites did not feel more comfortable about the free mulatto population and create a "three-caste" system.[124] As seen above, legislators in Louisiana were clearly as concerned about the free black population as in the upper South. Michael P. Johnson and James L. Roark show that throughout the antebellum period many bills were introduced in the other key state of the lower South—South Carolina—to degrade free blacks, some of them were passed, and South Carolina slaveowners joined in the general crackdown against free blacks in the 1850s.[125] Moreover, the most sustained rationale provided by a South Carolina slaveholder for not utterly suppressing free blacks was that their degraded, disfranchised status was "a check upon the insolence and profligacy" of nonslaveholding whites, who threatened slaveholders' supremacy: free blacks' economic competition with white workers was a healthy antidote to Jacksonian mechanics' power.[126] The anti–free black movement that swept the South in the wake of Nat Turner's Rebellion and intensified in the 1840s and 1850s was harsh in New Orleans and other lower South slave societies, and the most obnoxious "scientific" racism, directed at all blacks, was concocted by men of the lower South.[127]

The whole concept of a three-caste system in either the West Indies or the lower South has been subjected to withering fire by Stephen Small: the notion of a "privileged" free black caste or a three-tier system in any slave society is insupportable.[128] One might agree with Paul Lachance's schema of a "tri-level" society in New Orleans in the very limited sense that any mature slave society defined three "races" (whites, blacks, and mixed, plus Indians), as was true in Petersburg, Virginia. But unlike castes, individuals might move into and out of these groups in various ways, by the lightening of blacks and by the darkening of white people's children or by the fall from grace that occurred on those occasions when a white person married a black person and became presumptively a member of a degraded race. Nor were the races strictly divided according to status: most mulattoes were slaves and some blacks were free. Castes are fixed social entities into which one is born and in which one dies, entities that are regarded as natural and religiously ordained. None of this was true of the free black population in any state.[129] The proportion of that population declined over the course of the antebellum era, its color became increasingly lighter overall, and hostile attitudes toward it became more explicitly codified precisely because it was not a caste.

Extra emphasis is required: the free black community of New Orleans was largely self-created and evinced an extraordinary degree of industriousness in its ambition to achieve respectability and earn equality. In this regard, although he wrote no account of his own parish, the white New Orleans engineer Nicolas De Finiels did make a remarkable comment in his official report on Illinois in 1803. The free blacks were "more active and vigorous than the whites; they endure hard labor more courageously, and they could become as good warriors as they are hunters."[130] Most of them worked to obtain moral respectability too, not to sell their daughters into whoredom. Free blacks were the focal point of racial policy because they threatened to subvert all the traditional arguments about black inferiority and white superiority by their determination to succeed against heavy odds. Whether as smooth-palmed planters and artists, or calloused farmers and artisans, male and female, the thoroughly American values and diligence of the majority of free blacks was the supreme embarrassment to the slaveholding class. The dogged insistence by some historians that a free black caste was created, privileged, and protected by doting white fathers in New Orleans utterly obscures not only the real lives of individual free blacks but the fundamental nature of antebellum society.

Besides limiting the future growth of the free black community, local slaveholders launched an unceasing campaign of discrimination against free blacks of all complexions, beginning immediately at the end of 1803. Legislators rigidly excluded them from all the new democratic institutions, barring them from voting and holding positions of responsibility in government itself. The free blacks protested this exclusion in the first election of the House of Representatives in 1812, but they were ignored.[131] The planters tried mightily to abolish the free black militia, but they were stymied by Governor Claiborne until his death. They were immediately successful, by contrast, in declaring juries to be the preserve of whites.[132] There was a crackdown on taverns run by free blacks.[133] Midwives, many of whom were black, were limited and subordinated to white doctors.[134] As seen earlier, new market regulations aimed at restricting all blacks.

The planter class also attacked on the cultural front. Measures were taken to keep slaves out of free blacks' public ballrooms. A white fencing master named Regnier was restrained because his clientele was black. When some free people of color tried to provide instruction to their peers in this gentleman's art, the city council moved against them.[135] The first Protestant church founded in Louisiana in 1805 excluded people of color.[136] The resistance maintained by planters against establishing a public school system was motivated in part by the expected demand by free blacks to participate.

Legislators erected a bristling battery of new laws to restrain the personal freedom of movement of all free blacks. By Section 21 of the Black Code of 1806, free blacks were required to carry freedom papers if armed, which would have applied to all blacks in the militia, and in effect to most free black men, given the popularity of hunting.[137] Free blacks were required to have their freedom officially documented, as is clear from the law requiring free black refugees from the West Indies to register proof of their freedom with city officials.[138] At critical moments, as in December 1814, all free blacks were required to carry passes issued by the city.[139] While the penalty for rape committed by a white man on a white woman was life in prison, for a free black it was death. In 1818, even attempted rape of a white woman would become a capital crime for a free black.[140] Until 1816, judges could hear the testimony of slaves against free blacks but not against whites; although after 1816 slaves' testimony was barred except against other slaves.[141] Free blacks were permitted to testify in any kind of criminal case, but in practice this was rare, except in criminal denial of freedom cases; obstructionist lawyers were likely to challenge successfully any would-be black witnesses.[142] As always, free blacks were strictly ordered to show deference to any and all whites.[143] They were subject to special fines and prison terms for striking a white person, whatsoever the provocation.[144] A lone newspaper advertisement for the opening of a private school for free blacks in 1813 stated that no such school had existed, and the fate of the little academy is doubtful.[145] By a law passed in 1830, free blacks were made subject to harsher penalties than whites for inciting slaves or free blacks to be disorderly.[146] By another law of that same year, a free black was required like a white person to post bond when opening a tavern, but he or she also had to have special permission from the local police jury.[147] Free blacks were the target of a vicious campaign of slander. They were denounced as "the heaviest scourge of New Orleans," wallowing in debauchery and crime, despite the clear evidence to the contrary.[148]

The result of this regime was that not only did the free black population abruptly ceased to grow at the rate it was growing in 1807, but its collective economic and social power was severely limited. By 1850, even though New

Orleans free blacks were more likely to own real estate (6.56 percent of all free blacks) than in any other city in the South, it was the result of the town's peculiar economy and opportunities. What they owned, as is true of free blacks throughout the South, "must be considered a monument to [their] energy, enterprise, and frugality."[149] The vast majority of the town's free blacks were unskilled laborers, and they were under constant competitive pressure from poor white immigrants (especially the Irish) who wanted their jobs. Tiny groups provided artisanal and professional services, but by 1850 all were subject to increasingly restrictive laws and some individual free blacks were beginning to abandon Louisiana for Haiti in desperation.[150] It was possible for judges of the Supreme Court to announce with perfectly straight faces that free blacks were just as distinct from slaves as white men, "with the exception of political rights, social privileges, and the obligations of jury and militia service."[151]

The attack by slaveowners on the growth and status of the free black population was not a sideshow but the focal point of southern racial policy in this era. The movement to fence off free blacks by special laws in New Orleans was in accord with trends in the other southern states, in an era of growing enthusiasm for the dynamic future of black slavery. By the 1790s, most planters were obsessed with cotton, sugar, and Haiti and lashed out at free blacks to secure the racial regime.[152] Certainly, there were individual exceptions. Both Julien Poydras and John McDonogh emancipated their slaves in their wills.[153] A progressive newspaper (Libéral) appeared briefly sometime in the 1820s and was targeted for censorship by the legislature when it "occasionally inserted articles favourable to the black population."[154] But in all the southern states, the slaveowning class as a whole moved to exert the full force of the law to erect absolute barriers to free blacks' liberty and racial equality. In all major towns in the South, free blacks had been increasing in number, making economic gains, and creating a parallel system of cultural institutions, especially their own churches and schools. "Ironically," Ira Berlin writes, "the more the free Negro became like them, the more enraged whites became."[155] The white backlash was incited by a combination of personal resentment of the flow of ambitious free black individuals up the social scale and the compelling need of the planter class to stop the flow of black blood across the color line. That could dissolve the white and black races, replace them with a brown race, and wreck the rationale for the whole system.[156]

Everywhere in the New World, "the hard core of slavery was much the same" and free blacks constituted an annoying contradiction.[157] They could not behave as a true class, conscious and assertive, because they were distributed along a socioeconomic gradient, carefully sorted into racial subclasses, everywhere feared and oppressed as former slaves. Without this degradation, the natural affections that arose between people regardless of color would have led to intermarriage and an obliteration of the racial distinctions upon which slavery was based. The color barrier was always artificial, and slaveowners' behavior proves that they knew it was liable to collapse the moment they relaxed their vigilance, in an era of rising black revolutionary consciousness, decline of the African slave trade, and intensification of production.

The slaveholding classes of Louisiana and the other southern states methodically used their new republican institutions to legislate the social structure in the most striking example of government intervention in the nation's history before the Civil War. By concerting all of the powers of the state, local, and federal governments against free blacks to degrade them, the planters dramatized and sharpened the distinction of color that guaranteed their own supremacy over blacks and nonslaveholding whites. Because of the success of that campaign, the financial crash and the Missouri crisis of 1819 proved to be only minor, temporary setbacks to the empire of American slavery, of which New Orleans had become the tragic capital.

Epilogue:

Madame Plantou's Mardi Gras Mask for New Orleans, 1819

On March 18, 1819, Benjamin Latrobe strolled to the Girod home opposite Maspero's Coffee House to view a twelve-by-seven-foot oil painting. He was with Anthony Plantou, who advertised himself as "surgeon, occultist, dentist . . . [and] reader to the Paris Athaneum."[1] The man's wife, Julia, had painted the canvas: *The Treaty of Ghent.* One could view the work for one dollar (children fifty cents) and buy an engraved copy for ten dollars. Little is known of Julia except that she continued her career as an artist in Washington and Philadelphia. Where she learned her craft is uncertain. Advertisements for the exhibition claimed she was a student of Jacques-Louis David, and her work shows his influence, but today's authorities suggest she was a student of John Francis Renault, a Frenchman who had been working in the United States since the early 1780s.[2]

The New Orleans Town Council was so taken with Madame Plantou's work that it appropriated fifty dollars to purchase a coy of the engraving, signed by the plenipotentiaries who signed the treaty. The council displayed this art in its session hall. It was a work so full of dislocated abstractions that it reflected faithfully the profoundly contradictory society that passed beneath it.

Latrobe cast his skeptical artist's eye over the painting and wrote a mixed review. Technically, parts of it were admirable. Of the thematic structure, however, he disapproved on two counts. First, "its inherent sin, especially in America, is its being an allegorical picture," because the classical deities depicted there "are known by character only to those few who have had classical educations."[3] In other words, it mocked the extreme class disparity between the planters, who could afford the best education (even if not all of them sought it out), and everybody else. Second, he was embarrassed by the "caricature" of depicting a people in "riotous & unreasonable triumph," whereas the actual negotiation of a treaty "has nothing picturesque about it."[4] He missed the real caricature: the celebration of a "triumph" in a contest historians regard as having been entered into for dubious reasons in 1812, by which nothing substantive was gained in 1814, in which the country had suffered considerable humiliation that was forgotten after the battle of January 8, 1815, which was an accidental engagement after the treaty was signed.

To go deeper yet, Plantou's painting is a grotesque Mardi Gras mask for the town in several respects. First, the theme: it was a very old set piece popular throughout the Ancien Régime, and as such indicates the cultural conservatism of revolutionary republicans despite their political subversiveness. A symbolic female riding a chariot of triumph drawn through a jubilant throng is precisely the same arrangement seen a century earlier, for example, in Picard's *La Fortune conduite par la Folie*, satirizing the Mississippi bubble in 1720.[5] New Orleans too was profoundly conservative, remodeled by republican freedom but retaining the old form of the social structure unchanged. Second, the work

Fig. 23. The Treaty of Ghent, 1817, by Julia Plantou. From Latrobe, *Impressions Respecting New Orleans.*

is an imperfect marriage of American and French republican symbolism that captures the deep fault line between the two revolutions and the two countries, which had been lightly papered over by the Louisiana Purchase and then deeply embittered again in the era of Napoleon's Continental System. We see the capitol in Washington City in the background, we see an indisputably American eagle sweeping over the crowd, but just beneath the bird we also see a French *bonnet rouge*, with its drooping peak derived from the Phrygian cap, rather than an American one derived from the helmet-shaped Roman *pileus*, probably an unconscious error by Plantou. Both were symbols of liberty based on caps given to emancipated slaves in antiquity.[6]

Third, the figure of America as a young Native American woman (the antithesis of Manon) completes the final stage in the development of a symbol over the preceding half-century that begins with Robert Rogers's *Female American* (1767), "offering a white-Indian woman as a prototypical American hero."[7] Her emergence was possible only because the Indians east of the Mississippi River were confined to reservations and destined to be "removed," and in the area of the former Province of Louisiana they were convinced of the superior might of the United States and declined rapidly because of epidemic diseases. By 1819, the stoic maid in Plantou's painting serves to veil that grim reality. Fourth, Plantou chose to humble Britannia before three classical figures who inadvertently symbolize New Orleans' transformation into a commercial giant. We see Hercules (à la Jackson) being unshackled, with Mercury at his right delivering the treaty while Minerva stands guard to keep the peace. What neither Plantou nor Latrobe realized was that all three were associated with commerce. Hercules was the special guardian of Roman merchants because of his long journeys and ability to avert all kinds of evils; Mercury was associated with shopkeepers and grain-traders; and Minerva was the Italian goddess of handicrafts.[8] Plantou intended to project the indomitable strength of republicans (Hercules the hero of the twelve labors dressed in the skin of the Nemean lion), watched over by a combination of Christian angels and pagan gods. But we see Mammon embodied variously in these central figures, the god of a burgeoning, tempestuous, and periodically riotous and destructive capitalism in what was suddenly becoming a major seaport city.

What makes the Plantou engraving most disturbing, however, is the near-perfection with which is obscures the racial chasm that made New Orleans such a horrendously difficult, unpeaceful place for a majority of its population. At first glance, everyone in the painting is white, including "America," who is merely dressed as an Indian. In the crowd directly behind her, however, is one figure, arm upraised, dressed in coarse garb, also seemingly white but with pronounced African physiognomy, apparently meant to be a slave. Black Manon is not present, of course, because her very existence must be denied absolutely in order to maintain the structure of civilization. But one representative of the subordinate race is permitted to follow discreetly in the train of the nation's chariot, making his gesture not in defiance but in admiration of his superiors. We have seen over and again that nothing could be further from the truth: like blacks throughout the South, those of New Orleans had made special contributions to the forging of American values—ambition, diligence, creative expertise, moral austerity—and had pursued the American dream of personal and economic independence with the same enthusiasm as their white fellows. Only in 1862, however, when New Orleans fell to the Union Army, could they even begin to make their greatest and most painful contribution: teaching their white fellow citizens how to transform equality from an assertion in the Declaration of Independence into an effective universal principle.

Notes

ABBREVIATIONS

AGI, PPC   Archivo General de Indias, Papeles Procedentes de Cuba

AGI, SD   Archivo General de Indias, Sección V, Gobierno, Audiencia de Santo Domingo, the Historic New Orleans Collection

AHR   *American Historical Review*

AN, AC   Archives Nationales, Archives des Colonies, Paris

Brown Papers   James Brown Papers, 1765–1867, Manuscript Division, Library of Congress

Claiborne   W. C. C. Claiborne, *Official Letter Books of W. C. C. Claiborne, 1801–1816*

CDV   Conseil de Ville: Proceedings of Council Meetings

CFHC   Charles F. Heartman Collection of Manuscripts Relating to the Negro and Slavery, Special Collections, Xavier Univ. Library

DSG   Despatches of the Spanish Governors: Translations from Archivo General de Indias, Audiencia Santo Domingo and Papeles Procedentes de Cuba by the Works Progress Administration of Louisiana, Howard-Tilton Memorial Library, Special Collections Division, Manuscripts Section, Tulane Univ.

DSG/HBC   Despatches of the Spanish Governors: Translations from Archivo General de Indias, Audiencia Santo Domingo and Papeles Procedentes de Cuba by the Works Progress Administration of Louisiana, Howard-Tilton Memorial Library, Special Collections Division, Manuscripts Section, Hector Baron de Carondelet Series, Tulane Univ.

HAHR   *Hispanic American Historical Review*

JNH   *Journal of Negro History*

Laussat Papers   Laussat Papers, Historic New Orleans Collection

LH   *Louisiana History*

LHC   Louisiana Historical Collection, Louisiana Historical Center, Louisiana State Museum, New Orleans

LHQ   *Louisiana Historical Quarterly*

MVHR   Mississippi Valley Historical Review

NONA	New Orleans Notarial Archive, Civil District Courts Building, New Orleans
PLHS	*Publications of the Louisiana Historical Society*
RHAF	*Revue d'Histoire d'Amérique Française*
RSTC	Records of the Superior [Territorial] Court, 1804–13, Louisiana Division, New Orleans Public Library
SCLA	Supreme Court of Louisiana, Collection of Legal Archives, Earl K. Long Library, University of New Orleans
Sedella Collection	Antonio Sedella Collection, 1787–1815, Manuscripts Section, Special Collections Division, Howard-Tilton Memorial Library, Tulane Univ.
SMV	Lawrence Kinnaird, ed., *Spain in the Mississippi Valley, 1765–1794*
Ste-Gême Papers	Ste-Gême Family Papers, the Historic New Orleans Collection
TPO	Clarence E. Carter, ed. and comp., *The Territorial Papers of the United States*, vol. 9, *The Territory of Orleans, 1803–1812* (Washington, D.C.: GPO, 1940)

INTRODUCTION

1. Gary B. Nash, "Social Development," in *Colonial British America: Essays in the New History of the Early Modern Era*, ed. Jack P. Greene and J. R. Pole (Baltimore: Johns Hopkins Univ. Press, 1984), 234.

2. Peter H. Wood, *Black Majority: Negroes in Colonial South Carolina from 1670 Through the Stono Rebellion* (1974; reprint, New York: Alfred A. Knopf, 1975).

3. Allan Kulikoff, *Tobacco and Slaves: The Development of Southern Cultures in the Chesapeake, 1680–1800* (Chapel Hill: Univ. of North Carolina Press, 1986), 205.

4. Robert W. Fogel, *Without Consent or Contract: The Rise and Fall of American Slavery* (New York: W. W. Norton, 1989), 187.

5. For the concept of the planters as a class, see, in particular, Eugene D. Genovese, *The World the Slaveholders Made: Two Essays in Interpretation* (New York: Vintage Books, 1971).

6. Deborah Gray White, *Ar'n't I a Woman? Female Slaves in the Plantation South* (1985; reprint, New York: W. W. Norton, 1987), 43.

7. Herbert Asbury, *The French Quarter: An Informal History of the New Orleans Underworld* (1936; reprint, St. Simons Island, Ga.: Mockingbird Books, 1984), 25.

8. Frank Tannenbaum, *Slave and Citizen*, intro. Franklin W. Knight (1947; reprint, Boston: Beacon Press, 1992).

9. I am particularly indebted to Gary B. Nash, *The Urban Crucible: Social Change, Political Consciousness, and the Origins of the American Revolution* (Cambridge: Harvard Univ. Press, 1979).

10. On the confusion concerning this word, see Joseph G. Tregle Jr., "On That Word 'Creole' Again: A Note," *Louisiana History* (hereafter cited as *LH*) 23 (1982): 193–98; and JoAnn Carrigan, "Introduction," in *A History of Louisiana*, by Alcée Fortier, 2d ed., 5 vols. (Baton Rouge: Claitor's Book Store, 1966), 1:xxix–xxxii.

CHAPTER 1. FATAL GOLDEN DREAMS

1. John R. Swanton, ed., *Final Report of the United States De Soto Expedition Commission* (1939; reprint, Washington, D.C.: Smithsonian Institution Press, 1985).

2. Patricia K. Galloway, ed., *La Salle and His Legacy: Frenchmen and Indians in the Lower Missis-

sippi Valley (Jackson: Univ. Press of Mississippi, 1982); Robert S. Weddle, ed., *La Salle, the Mississippi, and the Gulf* (College Station: Texas A&M Univ. Press, 1987); Robert S. Weddle, *The French Thorn: Rival Explorers in the Spanish Sea, 1682–1762* (College Station: Texas A&M Univ. Press, 1991).

3. On the Indians' resentful memory of the Spanish, see François Le Maire, "M. Le Maire on Louisiana," in *A Jean Delanglez, S.J., Anthology: Selections Useful for Mississippi Valley and Trans-Mississippi American Indian Studies,* ed. Mildred Mott Wedel (New York: Garland, 1985), 143; and Captain Charles-Philippe Aubry to Duke of Choiseul, 5 Feb. 1765, in Carl A. Brasseaux, ed. and trans., *A Comparative View of French Louisiana, 1699 and 1762: The Journals of Pierre Le Moyne d'Iberville and Jean-Jacques-Blaise d'Abbadie,* 2d ed. (Lafayette: Center for Louisiana Studies, Univ. of Southwestern Louisiana Press, 1981), 140.

4. Verner W. Crane, *The Southern Frontier, 1670–1732* (1928; reprint, New York: W. W. Norton, 1981), 47–72; Mathé Allain, *"Not Worth a Straw": French Colonial Policy in the Early Years of Louisiana* (Lafayette: Center for Louisiana Studies, Univ. of Southwestern Louisiana Press, 1988).

5. Marcel Giraud, *A History of French Louisiana,* vol. 1, *The Reign of Louis XIV, 1698–1715,* trans. Joseph C. Lambert (Baton Rouge: Louisiana State Univ. Press, 1974), 80–101.

6. Guy F. Frégault, *Iberville le conquérant* (Montréal: Société des Éditions Pascal, 1944).

7. Pierre Goubert, *Louis XIV and Twenty Million Frenchmen,* trans. Anne Carter (New York: Vintage Books, 1972), 314.

8. Marcel Giraud, "France and Louisiana in the Early Eighteenth Century," *Mississippi Valley Historical Review* (hereafter cited as *MVHR*) 36 (1950): 657–74.

9. For a different view, according to which Louisiana before 1718 was a "failure," see James T. McGowan, "Planters Without Slaves: Origins of a New World Labor System," *Southern Studies* 16 (1977): 5–26. The "planters" of the title—actually a tiny handful of army officers—had no illusions that they might create a plantation society based on the labor of indentured Frenchmen or Canadian bush rangers.

10. "Lettres patentes de 24 Septembre, 1712," *Publications of the Louisiana Historical Society* (hereafter cited as *PLHS*) 4 (1908): 13–20; Albert G. Sanders, trans., "Documents Concerning the Crozat Regime in Louisiana, 1712–1717," *Louisiana Historical Quarterly* (hereafter cited as *LHQ*) 15 (1932): 589–609; *LHQ* 16 (1933): 293–308; and *LHQ* 17 (1934): 268–93, 452–73. On Crozat's governor, Antoine de La Mothe Cadillac, see Charles E. O'Neill, *Church and State in French Colonial Louisiana: Policy and Politics to 1732* (New Haven: Yale Univ. Press, 1966), 75–81.

11. Hubert to the Council, 26 Oct. 1717, Archives Nationales, Archives des Colonies, Paris (hereafter cited as AN, AC), ser. C13A, 5:49v–51.

12. Giraud, *History of French Louisiana,* vol. 1; see also Marcel Giraud, *Histoire de la Louisiane française,* vol. 2, *Années de transition, 1715–1717* (Paris: Presses Universitaires de France, 1958).

13. Marc De Villiers du Terrage, "The History of the Foundation of New Orleans, 1717–22," *LHQ* 3 (1920): 163–64, 171–74.

14. For the choice of the site, see also Pierre Margry, ed., *Découvertes et établissements des Français dans l'ouest et dans le sud de l'Amérique septentrionale, 1614–1754: mémoires et documents originaux,* 6 vols. (Paris: D. Jouaust, 1886), 5:599–608; Nancy M. Surrey, *The Commerce*

of Louisiana During the French Regime, 1699–1763 (1916; reprint, New York: AMS Press, 1968), 32–54; and Sally Dart, "French Incertitude in 1718 as to a Site for New Orleans," *LHQ* 15 (1932): 37–43, 417–27.

15. Pierre de Charlevoix, *Journal of a Voyage to North America*, 2 vols. (1744; reprint, Ann Arbor: University Microfilms, 1966), 2:290.

16. Ibid., 301.

17. For the key clause in the royal patent guaranteeing that nobles would not suffer derogation by participating, a momentous change in French policy, see Letters Patent, Aug. 1717, AN, AC, A, 22:25v. This document, which was published, runs between folios 25 and 33. The best general introduction to Law's project is Émile Levasseur, *Recherches historiques sur le système de Law* (1854; reprint, New York: Burt Franklin, 1970). See also Herbert Lüthy, *La banque protestante en France: de la révocation de l'édit de Nantes à la Révolution*, 2 vols. (Paris: S. E. V. P. E. N., 1959), 1:275–327, esp. 288–90 for ridicule of Law's "magical formula"; Jacob M. Price, *France and the Chesapeake: A History of the French Tobacco Monopoly, 1674–1791, and Its Relationship to the British and American Tobacco Trades* (Ann Arbor: Univ. of Michigan Press, 1973), 196–220; and Fernand Braudel, *Civilization and Capitalism, 15th–18th Century*, vol. 3, *The Perspective of the World* (1979; reprint, New York: Harper and Row, 1984), 326–35. For a derivative English-language account of the whole episode, see H. Montgomery Hyde, *John Law: The History of an Honest Adventurer* (London: W. H. Allen, 1969).

18. Levasseur, *Recherches historiques*, 62–65; Pierre Heinrich, *La Louisiane sous la Compagnie des Indes, 1717–1731* (Paris: E. Guilmoto, 1907), 4–6.

19. Levasseur, *Recherches historiques*, 156–89.

20. On the bubble, see J. H. Shennan, *Philippe, Duke of Orleans: Regent of France, 1715–1723* (London: Thames and Hudson, 1979), 97–125; Jean Egret, *Louis XV et l'opposition parlementaire, 1715–1774* (Paris: Librairie Armand Colin, 1970), 34–39.

21. Daniel Roche, *The People of Paris: An Essay in Popular Culture in the 18th Century*, trans. Marie Evans and Gwynne Lewis (Leamington Spa, U.K.: Berg, 1987), 266–68.

22. On the fascination with the discovery of mines in Louisiana, see [Jonathas Darby], "A Chapter of Colonial History: Louisiana 1717 to 1751," trans. Gustave Devron, *LHQ* 6 (1923): 565.

23. Edmond Barbier, *Chronique de la régence et du règne de Louis XV, 1718–1763*, 8 vols. (Paris: G. Charpentier et Cie., 1885), 1:32–106. See also Saint-Simon, *Historical Memoirs of the Duc de Saint-Simon*, trans. and abr. Lucy Norton, 3 vols. (New York: McGraw-Hill, 1972), 3:144–46, 269–71.

24. Franklin C. Ford, *Robe and Sword: The Regrouping of the French Aristocracy after Louis XIV* (Cambridge: Harvard Univ. Press, 1953), 84, 87, 98–99; Ralph Davis, *The Rise of the Atlantic Economies* (Ithaca: Cornell Univ. Press, 1973), 209–11, 225–30. For defenses of Law's scheme, see Emmanuel Le Roy Ladurie, *The Peasants of Languedoc*, trans. John Day (Chicago: Univ. of Illinois Press, 1976), 260–61. The English also had a bubble in 1720, but it was soon patched up deep in the bowels of a constitutional government by a smooth fixer, Robert Walpole.

25. Timothy Flint, *Recollections of the Last Ten Years in the Valley of the Mississippi*, ed. George R. Brooks (1826; reprint, Carbondale: Southern Illinois Univ. Press, 1968), 253.

26. These figures are based on the data in Jean Mettas, *Répertoire des expéditions négrières*

françaises au XVIIIe siècle, vol. 2, *Ports autres que Nantes*, ed. Serge and Michèle Daget (Paris: Société Française d'Histoire d'Outre-Mer, 1984).

27. "Journal du Voyage que le Sr. Roussel natif de Versailles a fait," in France, Colonies, 1702–1750, 4 vols., 3:512–42, Edward E. Ayer Collection of Americana and American Indians, Manuscript Division, Newberry Library, Chicago; [Charles Le Gac], *Immigration and War: Louisiana, 1718–1721*, ed. and trans. Glenn R. Conrad (Lafayette: Center for Louisiana Studies, Univ. of Southwestern Louisiana Press, 1970), 12–49; Anonymous Narrative, 6 Aug. to 2 Sept. 1719, AN, AC, C13A, 5:303–14; Bienville to the Council, 20 Oct. 1719, AN, AC, C13A, 5:274–80v; Minutes of the Council of Marine, Nov. 1722, AN, AC, C13A, 6:280–83.

28. Dumont de Montigny, "History of Louisiana," in *Historical Memoirs of Louisiana, from the First Settlement of the Colony to the Departure of Governor O'Reilly in 1770*, ed. Benjamin F. French, 5 vols. (1853; reprint, New York: AMS Press, 1976), 5:19–21.

29. Ibid. For the difficulties involved in making the transfer from Biloxi to New Orleans, see Lieutenant-General Le Blond de La Tour to the Company, 30 Aug. 1722, AN, AC, C13A, 6:321–34v. Reports of the number of deaths varied widely. Jonathas Darby reported in "Chapter of Colonial History," 546, that "a very great number" of people of all races died, but especially Germans. For the estimate that five hundred people died of starvation, see Antoine-Simon Le Page Du Pratz, *The History of Louisiana, Or of the Western Parts of Virginia and Carolina*, ed. Joseph G. Tregle Jr. (1774; reprint, Baton Rouge: Louisiana State Univ. Press, 1975), 32. See also Jean-Baptiste Bénard La Harpe, *Historical Journal of the Settlement of the French in Louisiana*, trans. Virginia Koenig and Joan Cain, ed. Glenn R. Conrad (1724; reprint, Lafayette: Center for Louisiana Studies, Univ. of Southwest Louisiana, 1971), 167, 190; "Journal of Diron d'Artaguiette," in *Travels in the American Colonies*, ed. Newton Mereness (New York: Macmillan, 1916), 19–21, 38–39. On the continuing poor supply of provisions, see Superior Council to the Company, 27 Feb. 1725, AN, AC, C13A, 9:51–52v, 56v–59. See also James D. Hardy Jr., "The Transportation of Convicts to Colonial Louisiana," *LH* 7 (1966): 207–20.

30. See Glenn R. Conrad, trans. and comp., *The First Families of Louisiana*, 2 vols. (Baton Rouge: Claitor's Publishing, 1970), 2:76–123, recording the deaths of 487 whites in New Orleans between 1724 and 1729 alone, virtually none of them the result of advanced age. These records are incomplete. See also Marcel Giraud, *Histoire de la Louisiane française*, vol. 3, *L'époque de John Law, 1717–1720* (Paris: Presses Universitaires de France, 1966), 323–35.

31. Most of twelve thousand people sent to Guiana between 1763 and 1766 were French, and nine thousand of them died before the end of 1766. See Jacques Michel, *La Guyane sous l'Ancien Régime: le désastre de Kourou et ses scandaleuses suites judiciaires* (Paris: Éditions L'Harmattan, 1989), 89–91. For the opposing argument that the planters' "indenture and wage systems rapidly broke down because of lower class white and Indian desertion," see James T. McGowan, "Creation of a Slave Society: Louisiana Plantations in the Eighteenth Century" (Ph.D. diss., Univ. of Rochester, 1976), 45. McGowan consistently emphasizes the number and power of free workers and underestimates the decisive reduction of their population and collective force by diseases and redistribution to the posts.

32. The best sustained attack upon the Company of the Indies is by Giraud, *Histoire de la Louisiane française*, 3:316–60, and vol. 4, *La Louisiane après le système de Law, 1721–1723* (Paris: Presses Universitaires de France, 1974), 384–89.

33. Barbier, *Chronique de la régence*, 1:131, 137–40. See also discussions by Giraud, *Histoire de la Louisiane française*, 3:274–76; Carl A. Brasseaux, "The Image of Louisiana and the Failure of Voluntary French Emigration, 1683–1731," in *Proceedings of the Fourth Annual Meeting of the French Colonial Historical Society, April 6–8 1979*, ed. Alf A. Heggory and James J. Cooke (Washington, D.C.: Univ. Press of America, 1979); Glenn Conrad, "*Émigration forcée*: A French Attempt to Populate Louisiana, 1716–1720," in *Proceedings of the Fourth Annual Meeting of the French Colonial Historical Society*, ed. Heggory and Cooke, 57–69. For merciless satires aimed at Law's Louisiana by writers and medalists of bourgeois Holland and England, see Benjamin Betts, *A Descriptive List of the Medals Relating to John Law and the Mississippi System* (Privately printed, 1907).

34. The governor of New Orleans persecutes Des Grieux and his lover, driving them into "the sterile countryside," where Manon dies. See De Villiers du Terrage, "History of the Foundation of New Orleans," 201–12, on the supposed derivation of Prévost's characters from real settlers in New Orleans. For Buffon's theory of the degenerate New World, see Clarence J. Glacken, *Traces on the Rhodian Shore: Nature and Culture in Western Thought from Ancient Times to the End of the Eighteenth Century* (Berkeley and Los Angeles: Univ. of California Press, 1967), 679–85. For the wealth of cultural manifestations of Manon since 1731, see the catalogue, *Manon Lescaut: À travers deux siècles* (Paris: Bibliothèque Nationale, 1963).

35. Mother Superior Theresa Wolfe, *The Ursulines in New Orleans and Our Lady of Prompt Succor: A Record of Two Centuries, 1727–1925* (New York: P. J. Kenedy and Sons, 1925), 196.

36. The table is based upon the report of Le Gac in *Immigration and War*, 51–52; see also Albert L. Dart, in "Ship Lists of Passengers Leaving France for Louisiana, 1718–1724," *LHQ* 14 (1931): 516–20; *LHQ* 15 (1932): 68–77, 453–67; and *LHQ* 21 (1938): 965–78.

37. "Jonchère Concession, October 26, 1719," *LHQ* 11 (1928): 553–56, provides a glimpse of one of these contracts for a huge tract.

38. On mercantilism, see Charles-André Julien, *Les Français en Amérique de 1713 à 1784* (Paris: Centre de Documentation Universitaire et Société d'Édition d'Enseignement Supérieur, 1977), 23–62. For a defense of mercantilism, see Charles Secondat Baron de Montesquieu, *The Spirit of the Laws*, trans. Thomas Nugent (New York: Hafner Press, 1949), 364–69.

39. Some concessions lay as far away as Arkansas. See Dumont de Montigny, "History of Louisiana," 22; and Dumont de Montigny, "Census of Louisiana, 1721," *PLHS* 5 (1911): 95–98.

40. For an example, see Jay Higginbotham, "The Chaumont Concession: A French Plantation on the Pascagoula," *Journal of Mississippi History* 36 (1974): 353–62.

41. Giraud, *Histoire de la Louisiane française*, 3:167–220; Henri Gravier, *La colonisation de la Louisiane a l'époque de Law, octobre, 1717–janvier, 1721* (Paris: Masson, 1904), 70–76.

42. Dart, "Ship Lists of Passengers," *LHQ* 21 (1938): 970–74.

43. See Archives de la Bastille, series 10600 and *passim* for the case histories of deportees, especially those whose families requested their deportation.

44. Ibid.

45. Ibid., series 10644.

46. Ibid., series 10672.

47. Ibid.

48. The mass transportation of criminals to all colonies was abruptly terminated during the regency. See Decree of the Council of State, 9 May 1720, AN, AC, A, 23:29v–30. In fact, transportation of criminals to most French colonies virtually ceased. See Royal Declaration, 5 July 1722, in Médéric Moreau de Saint-Méry, *Loix et constitutions des colonies françaises de l'Amérique sous le vent*, 6 vols. (Paris: Author, 1784–90), 3:14–15. But officials sometimes specifically requested that a few be sent. See, for example, Bienville and Salmon to Maurepas, 1 June 1737, AN, AC, C13A, 22:40v–41, complaining that none had arrived as promised. Bienville and Salmon to Maurepas, 10 Aug. 1739, AN, AC, C13A, 24:10v–11, specified either black slaves or French salt smugglers. See also Gabriel Debien, "Les engagés des Antilles au travail (XVIIe siècle)," *Bulletin de la Société d'Histoire de la Guadeloupe* 55 (1983): 3–14.

49. For examples of reports that have been singled out to support these arguments, see Capuchin Father Raphael to Company Spiritual Director Abbé Raguet, 15 May 1725, AN, AC, C13A, 8:399v–404; and Governor Jean Jacques Blaise D'Abbadie to Choiseul, 7 June 1764, AN, AC, C13A, 44:58–62.

50. The same conclusion is reached by Mathé Allain, "L'Immigration Française en Louisiane, 1718–1721," *Revue d'Histoire d'Amérique Française* (hereafter cited as *RHAF*) 28 (1975): 561–64.

51. Reinhart Kondert, "German Immigration to French Colonial Louisiana: A Reevaluation," in *Proceedings of the Fourth Annual Meeting of the French Colonial Historical Society, April 6–8 1979*, ed. Heggory and Cooke, 70–81. Kondert's work supersedes J. Hanno Deiler, *The Settlement of the German Coast of Louisiana and the Creoles of German Descent* (1909; reprint, Baltimore: Genealogical Publishing, 1970), 14–17; but see 37–38 for Deiler's estimation that ten thousand Germans actually left their homes in Germany with the intention of settling in Louisiana. See also Marcel Giraud, "German Immigration," ed. and trans. Glenn R. Conrad, *Revue de Louisiane* 10 (1981): 143–57. On a later addition to the German Coast population, see Glenn Conrad, "L'immigration alsacienne en Louisiane, 1753–1759," *RHAF* 28 (1975): 565–77.

52. For an overview, see René Le Conte, "The Germans in Louisiana in the Eighteenth Century," ed. and trans. Glenn R. Conrad, *LH* 8 (1967): 67–84. The author believes that estimates of the number of Germans recruited have been exaggerated.

53. This is figured from Military Budget for Louisiana, 30 Jan. 1731, AN, AC, C13A, 13:268. Theoretically the common soldier received a monthly allowance, plus forty-five pounds of bread, twelve pounds of meat, and some clothing; see Council to the Company, 5 June 1723, AN, AC, C13A, 7:123v.

54. On soldiers' circumstances, see Beauchamp to Maurepas, 5 Nov. 1731, AN, AC, C13A, 13:200v–201v, complaining that they were likely to sell their clothes just to get their corn ground. According to Bienville and Salmon to Maurepas, 12 May 1733, AN, AC, C13A, 16:63–64v, many lived in wretched huts before the barracks were built.

55. Commissaire Ordonnateur Hubert to the Council, 26 Oct. 1717, AN, AC, C13A, 5:51–52

56. Diron d'Artaguiette reported on 29 September 1722 that soldiers were restless because civilian workmen got meat. See "Journal of Diron d'Artaguiette," 27–28. See Minutes of the Counseil de la Regie, 28 May 1723, AN, AC, C13A, 7:119–21v, for the threatened insurrection of that year; and Delachaise to the Company, 6, 10 Sept. 1723, AN, AC, C13A, 7:22v–25v, reporting that soldiers and their officers claimed they could not subsist on their wages.

57. Bienville to Maurepas, 4 Feb. 1743, AN, AC, C13A, 28:37–38; Vaudreuil to Maurepas, 28 Oct. 1744, AN, AC, C13A, 28:234v–35; and Vaudreuil to Maurepas, 28 Oct. 1745, AN, AC, C13A, 29:53–54.

58. On desertion, see Superior Council to the Company, 22 Feb. 1725, AN, AC, C13A, 9:64v; "Journal of Diron d'Artaguiette," 18, 25; Noyan to Maurepas, 8 Nov. 1734, AN, AC, C13A, 19:145–46v; Vaudreuil to Maurepas, 24 Nov. 1746, AN, AC, C13A, 30:100–100v; Vaudreuil and Michel to Rouillé, 20 May 1751, AN, AC, C13A, 35:16v, that even if supplied, they were naturally debauched types "who breathe here nothing but desertion and revolt." See also Vaudreuil to Maurepas, 23 May 1748, AN, AC, C13A, 32:57–58, on the king's general amnesty for deserters; Vaudreuil to Rouillé, 20 July 1751, AN, AC, C13A, 35:158–60v, on desertion of new troops; and Michel to Rouillé, 18 May 1751, AN, AC, C13A, 35:205v–6, on the unusual punishment of some deserters by beheading.

59. The Swiss troops were more harshly treated than the French and were probably more obedient and easier to exploit, but only by their own officers; see LeBlond to the Company, 9 Dec. 1721, AN, AC, C13A, 6:133v; and Delachaise to the Company, 6 Sept. 1723, AN, AC, C13A, 7:18–18v; Vaudreuil to Maurepas, 22 May 1748, AN, AC, C13A, 32:54–56. On the policy of ethnic division, see Vaudreuil and Michel to Rouillé, 22 May 1751, AN, AC, C13A, 35:33v–34; see also David Hardcastle, "Swiss Mercenary Soldiers in the Service of France in Louisiana," in *Proceedings of the Fourth Annual Meeting of the French Colonial Historical Society, April 6–8 1979*, ed. Heggory and Cooke, 82–91, for an excellent discussion. He points out that very few Swiss ever actually settled over the years.

60. The table is based on recruiters' ledgers found in AN, AC, D2A5, Troupes, Recrues: Louisiane, 9 Sept. 1726 to 8 Apr. 1730, 5–93; and AN, AC, D2A6, Compagnie des Indes, Troupes, Recrues, 30 Apr. 1730 to 10 Sept. 1733, 1–9v. Only those recruits specifically recorded as arriving alive in Louisiana are included.

61. Cadillac to the Naval Council, 7 Feb. 1716, AN, AC, C13A, 4:203.

62. Bienville to Maurepas, 18 May 1733, AN, AC, C13A, 16:226–26v.

63. Conrad, *First Families of Louisiana*, 1:205–6.

64. Even those soldiers who served the longest terms in the colony still returned to France. See Vaudreuil to Maurepas, 17 Nov. 1748, AN, AC, C13A, 32:145–46.

65. Remonstrance against Outlaws by Deputy Attorney General Raguet, 2 Sept. 1724, Louisiana Historical Collection, Louisiana Historical Center, Louisiana State Museum, New Orleans (hereafter cited as LHC, all citations being to the Records of the Superior Council).

66. Bienville and Salmon to Maurepas, 9 May 1733, AN, AC, C13A, 16:33–39v, on the departure of dozens of all classes; Bienville and Salmon to Maurepas, 5 Aug. 1733,

AN, AC, C13A, 16:141–42v, on more; Bienville and Salmon to Maurepas, 11 Aug. 1733, AN, AC, C13A, 16:147–49.

67. Bienville and Salmon to Maurepas, 9 Aug. 1734, AN, AC, C13A, 18:96–97; Salmon to Maurepas, 18 May 1733, AN, AC, C13A, 16:258; see Surrey, *Commerce of Louisiana,* 273–77.

68. In 1723 the Superior Council forbade billiards on Sundays and holidays and late at night; it forbade gambling at home and nullified all gambling notes over one hundred livres. It is difficult to determine how scrupulously these decrees were enforced. Public houses were subject to an early curfew, although nighttime sports like shining deer were very popular, and celebrations of feast days disregarded the curfew. See Decrees of Superior Council, 29 Apr., 13 May 1723, AN, AC, C13A, 7:99v–100; Minutes of the Council, 20 July 1721, AN, AC, C13A, 6:148v, on informing.

69. This is based on tabulations of Glenn Conrad's translations of AN, AC, G, 1:464 ff., in *First Families of Louisiana,* 1:57–64. The community of New Orleans includes all people living below Cannes Bruslées. All the other settlements in the lower Mississippi Valley are lumped together. The number of soldiers given is according to the garrison established in 1732, consisting of four hundred soldiers posted in the town and four hundred at the other posts throughout the colony, although the active garrison was usually far below quota. The whites and slaves not accounted for in the table were those of Illinois and other distant posts. For slightly different totals, see Charles R. Maduell Jr., *The Census Tables for the French Colony of Louisiana From 1699 Through 1732* (Baltimore: Genealogical Publishing, 1972), 113, 123.

70. Memoir on the Condition of Louisiana, 1746, AN, AC, C13A, 30:256. The figures for whites are extrapolated, based on a total of 1,500 women and children for the whole colony: I attribute the same proportion of these to New Orleans as the fraction of the colony's men specified as living in the town (800). For the whole colony the figures are 3,200 whites and 4,730 blacks. These figures are provided in an extremely detailed, anonymous report.

71. Joseph Zitomersky, "Urbanization in French Colonial Louisiana, 1706–1766," in *Annales de Démographie Historique,* ed. L. Henry (Paris: Mouton, 1974), 273–74. Zitomersky focuses on the town center, but his finding holds true for the parish as a whole.

72. Iberville carefully estimated the population of the entire Mississippi Valley in 1701 at 36,100 armed men with their families in twenty-four nations; see Margry, *Découvertes et etablissements,* 4:601–2. See also Bienville's Memoir on Louisiana in 1726, AN, AC, C13C, 1:362–74; Commissaire Ordonnateur Edmé Salmon to Minister of Marine Jean-Frédéric Maurepas, 8 Feb. 1733, AN, AC, C13A, 17:39–41; John R. Swanton, *Indian Tribes of the Lower Mississippi Valley and Adjacent Coast of the Gulf of Mexico* (Washington, D.C.: GPO for the Smithsonian Institution, 1911), 39–45; John R. Swanton, *The Indians of the Southeastern United States* (Washington, D.C.: GPO for the Smithsonian Institution, 1946), 11–14; Patricia D. Woods, *French-Indian Relations on the Southern Frontier, 1699–1762* (Ann Arbor: UMI Research Press, 1979), 2, 14; Charles Gayarré, *History of Louisiana,* 5th ed., 4 vols. (1854–66; reprint, Gretna, La.: Pelican, 1965), 1:349–52; Giraud, *History of French Louisiana,* 1:76; Marc De Villiers du Terrage, ed., and

George C. H. Kernion, trans., "Documents Concerning the History of the Indians of the Eastern Region of Louisiana," *LHQ* 8 (1925): 28–40.

73. For a discussion of the Indians in the vicinity of New Orleans, see Marco J. Giardino, "Documentary Evidence for the Location of Historic Indian Villages in the Mississippi Delta," in *Perspectives on Gulf Coast Prehistory*, ed. Dave B. Davis (Gainesville: Univ. Presses of Florida, 1984), 232–57, especially 238 for the map.

74. La Harpe, *Historical Journal*, 18–19, 32–33, 40. On the supply of meat, see Bienville's Memoir on Louisiana, in 1726, AN, AC, C13C, 1:369v.

75. Minutes of the Superior Council, 18 Sept. 1724, AN, AC, C13A, 8:127v.

76. Daniel H. Usner Jr., *Indians, Settlers, and Slaves in a Frontier Exchange Economy: The Lower Mississippi Valley before 1803* (Chapel Hill: Univ. of North Carolina Press, 1992). See also William A. Read, "Louisiana Place Names of Indian Origin," *Louisiana State University Bulletin* 19 (Feb. 1927); and "More Indian Place-Names in Louisiana," *LHQ* 11 (1928): 445–62.

77. André Pénicaut, *Fleur de Lys and Calumet: Being the Pénicaut Narrative of French Adventure in Louisiana*, ed. and trans. Gaillard Richebourg (Baton Rouge: Louisiana State Univ. Press, 1953), 105, 115–16, 133, 220; D'Artaguiette to Pontchartrain, 12 May 1712, AN, AC, C13A, 2:803.

78. Bienville's approach was so expert that the company's investigators charged him, absurdly, with favoring the Indians' interests over those of the French; see Delachaise to the Company, 6 Sept. 1723, AN, AC, C13A, 7:26v–27. See Crane, *Southern Frontier*, 83–84, 97–98, for praise of Bienville as a gifted diplomat.

79. The legendary injustice of the conquistador was strong enough that the Indians were completely relied upon to repulse the Spanish if they attacked from Pensacola; see d'Artaguiette to Pontchartrain, 12 Feb. 1720, AN, AC, C13A, 2:535–36.

80. William Beer, "The Visit of Illinois Indians to France in 1725," *LHQ* 6 (1923): 189–93.

81. Even the Chickasaws were impatient to obtain fourteen-year-old St. Michel. See Pénicaut, *Fleur de Lys and Calumet*, 25, 30, 67–68, 73–79. The English colonists had a similar policy. See also Patricia K. Galloway, "Talking with Indians: Interpreters and Diplomacy in French Louisiana," in *Race and Family in the Colonial South*, ed. Winthrop D. Jordan and Sheila L. Skemp (Jackson: Univ. of Mississippi Press, 1987); and J. Frederick Fausz, "Middlemen in Peace and War: Virginia's Earliest Indian Interpreters, 1608–1632," *Virginia Magazine of History and Biography* 95 (1987): 41–64.

82. Bienville to Pontchartrain, 25 Feb. 1708, AN, AC, C13A, 2:100–102; Bienville to Maurepas, 20 Dec. 1737, AN, AC, C13A, 22:115v–16; Bienville to Maurepas, 15 June 1740, AN, AC, C13A, 25:105–6; Noyan to Maurepas, 4 Jan. 1739, AN, AC, C13A, 24:234–35; Bizoton to Maurepas, 9 May 1739, AN, AC, C13A, 24:246–46v, for the Barthelemys. See also Patricia K. Galloway, "The Barthelemy Murders: Bienville's Establishment of the *Lex Talionis* as a Principle of Indian Diplomacy," in *Proceedings of the Eighth Annual Meeting of the French Colonial Historical Society, 1982*, ed. E. P. Fitzgerald (Lanham, Md.: Univ. Press of America, 1985), 91–103.

83. On the failed policy, see George F. G. Stanley, "The Policy of Francisation as Applied to the Indians during the Ancien Regime," *RHAF* 3 (1949): 333–48. Most of the French were disinclined to marry Indians for their own local, social reasons, and

both intermarriage and concubinage were unusual in New Orleans. Moreover, the number of Indians who actually lived in New Orleans—almost all slaves—was always very small. On the period before the foundation of New Orleans, see Minutes of the Council of Marine, 1 Sept. 1716, AN, AC, C13A, 4:255–57; and Duclos to Pontchartrain, 25 Dec. 1715, AN, AC, C13A, 3:819–24, who concluded that neither the women or the men involved really wanted to marry, and it would only produce a "Spanish" type of colony of mixed bloods. See also O'Neill, *Church and State in French Colonial Louisiana*, 71–72, 84–87, 106–8, 248–54; Gary B. Nash, *Red, White, and Black: The Peoples of Early America*, 2d ed. (Englewood Cliffs, N.J.: Prentice-Hall, 1982), 104–10; Jean Delanglez, S.J., *The French Jesuits in Lower Louisiana, 1700–1763* (Washington, D.C.: Catholic Univ. of America, 1935), 394–403; Cornelius J. Jaenen, *Friend and Foe: Aspects of French-Amerindian Cultural Contact in the Sixteenth and Seventeenth Centuries* (Canada: McClelland and Stewart, 1976), 153–85. On New Orleans, see Périer and Delachaise to the Company, 25 Mar. 1729, AN, AC, C13A, 11:332, reporting the successful prevention of Indian-white domestic alliances, and after that concubinage disappeared from reports on New Orleans. The problem could not be completely contained, however, in lonely Illinois; see Father Tartarin's Statement of 1738, AC, C13A, 23:241–43v.

84. See Woods, *French-Indian Relations*, 33–34, 46.

85. Pénicaut, *Fleur de Lys and Calumet*, 255. For a different view, see John J. TePaske, "French, Spanish, and English Indian Policy on the Coast, 1513–1763," in *Spain and Her Rivals on the Gulf Coast*, ed. Ernest F. Dibble and Earle W. Newton (Pensacola, Fla.: Historic Pensacola Preservation Board, 1971), 34–36.

86. Bienville to Pontchartrain, 28 July 1706, AN, AC, C13A, 1:525, on the scalp policy, derived from the practice in New France. On the rate of exchange, see La Harpe, *Historical Journal*, 66; and Bienville to Maurepas, 26 Aug. 1734, AN, AC, C13A, 18: 185–86.

87. For a typical early plea for better supply, see Bienville to Pontchartrain, 27 Oct. 1711, AN, AC, C13A, 2:570–74. See also Lawrence H. Gipson, *The British Empire before the American Revolution: Provincial Characteristics and Sectional Tendencies in the Era Preceding the American Crisis*, vol. 2, *The Southern Plantations* (Caldwell, Idaho: Caxton Printers, 1936), pt. 4; and Norman W. Caldwell, *The French in the Mississippi Valley, 1740–1750* (Urbana: Univ. of Illinois Press, 1941), 101.

88. Minutes of the Superior Council of Louisiana, 18 Sept. 1723, AN, AC, C13A, 7:143v–47v; Representation by Bienville, 1 Dec. 1724, AN, AC, C13A, 8:155–57v. See Woods, *French-Indian Relations*, 1–44, for the origins and development of the basic alliance system of French/Choctaws versus English/Chickasaws.

89. On the Natchez and related tribe of the Taensas, see Du Pratz, *History of Louisiana*, 279–85, 306–57; Pierre F. X. Charlevoix, *History and General Description of New France*, vol. 6, trans. John G. Shea (1870; reprint, Chicago: Loyola Univ. Press, n.d.), 232–56; and Pénicaut, *Fleur de Lys and Calumet*, 84–96. For the other nations, see Fred B. Kniffen, Hiram F. Gregory, and George A. Stokes, *The Historic Indian Tribes of Louisiana from 1542 to the Present* (Baton Rouge: Louisiana State Univ. Press, 1987), 44–82; and Grayson Noley, "The Early 1700s: Education, Economics, and Politics," in *The Choctaw Before Removal*, ed. Carolyn Keller Reeves (Gainesville: Univ. Presses of Florida, 1985).

90. Major Jadart Beauchamp to Maurepas, 5 Nov. 1731, AN, AC, C13A, 13:199v–200. The governor actually allowed Carolinians to come and go, as reported by Périer and Delachaise to the Company, 25 Mar. 1729, AN, AC, C13A, 11:334.

91. For the general confusion of French policy under Périer, with army officers jostling for control of the various nations, see Diron d'Artaguiette to Maurepas, 17 Oct. 1729, AN, AC, C13A, 12:148–59; Regis du Roullet to Maurepas, 11 Nov. 1729, AN, AC, C13A, 12:92–98.

92. To penetrate the governor's series of reports at various crucial moments, see Périer to Maurepas, 5 Dec. 1729, AN, AC, C13A, 12:33–35; Périer to Maurepas, 1 Apr. 1730, AN, AC, C13A, 12:352–55; *idem* to Controller General Orry, 1 Aug. 1730, AN, AC, C13A, 12:328–37. For other key reports, see Broutin to the Company, 7 Aug. 1730, AN, AC, C13A, 12:405–10; Diron d'Artaguiette to Maurepas of 9 Feb. 1730, AN, AC, C13A, 12:362–66; *idem* to *idem*, 10 Jan. 1731, AC, C13B, 1:110v–13v; Charlevoix, *History and General Description of New France,* 6:80–116; Du Pratz, *History of Louisiana,* 73–87; Dumont de Montigny, "History of Louisiana," 61–66; Darby, "Chapter of Colonial History," 550–54; Jean-Charles Pradel, *Le Chevalier de Pradel: vie d'un colon français en Louisiane au XVIIIe siècle d'après sa correspondence et celle de sa famille,* ed. A. Baillardel and A. Prioult (Paris: Librairie Orientale et Américaine, 1928), 63–66, 70–72. See Patricia K. Galloway, "The French and the Natchez Indians in Louisiana: 1700–1731," *LH* 19 (1978): 413–35, for a different view, suggesting that the massacre was the result of inevitable imperial rapaciousness. A discussion of the large secondary literature on the Natchez War is in Woods, *French-Indian Relations,* 95–109. See also Marcel Giraud, *A History of French Louisiana,* vol. 5, *The Company of the Indies, 1723–1731,* trans. Brian Pearce (Baton Rouge: Louisiana State Univ. Press, 1991), 388–439. The harshest evaluation of Périer is by Jean Delanglez, in "The Natchez Massacre and Governor Périer," *LHQ* 17 (1934): 631–41.

93. Périer to Maurepas, 18 Mar. 1730, AN, AC, C13A, 12:38.

94. See McGowan, "Creation of a Slave Society," 82–86, for the argument that "the French dreams of a tobacco empire" were destroyed by this "war for liberation fought by an alliance of Indians and Africans." This interpretation overemphasizes the strength of the two latter groups, their unity, and their success in setting limits to white behavior, and it ignores the many factors that limited the development of Louisiana before 1729. On the other hand, the subsequent victory of the whites can be overemphasized; see Daniel Usner Jr., "From African Captivity to American Slavery: The Introduction of Black Laborers to Colonial Louisiana," *LH* 20 (1979): 25–48.

95. The best overall account is Périer to Maurepas, 18 Mar. 1730, AN, AC, C13A, 12:37–45. See also La Harpe, *Historical Journal,* 73–87.

96. Father Le Petit to Father Avaugour, 12 July 1730, in *The Jesuit Relations and Allied Documents,* ed. Reuben G. Thwaites (Cleveland: Burrows Brothers, 1900), 68:223, wrote that "although they have nothing to fear at New Orleans, either from the smaller neighboring Tribes, whom our Negroes alone could finish in a single morning, or even from the Tchactas [Choctaws], who would not dare to expose themselves on the Lake in any great numbers, yet a panic terror has spread itself over almost every spirit, particularly with the women."

97. Périer to Maurepas, 18 Mar. 1730, AN, AC, C13A, 12:39v–40. According to Dumont de Montigny, "History of Louisiana," 99–102, Périer assembled all local slaves, accused them of harboring treacherous thoughts, and demanded that volunteers step forward to prove their loyalty. The number of these blacks can only be estimated at about fifteen, for the first four names on the list are the only legible ones (Caesar, Crispin . . . (?), Legro, and Trudy); see Attorney General's Proposal to Free Negroes for Military Merit, 13 May 1730, LHC. Périer reported to Maurepas that fifteen blacks accompanied the French troops in the expedition against the Natchez in his report of 18 Mar. 1730, AN, AC, C13A, 12:45v.

98. Charlevoix, *History and General Description of New France*, 6:96. See also John A. Green, "Governor Perier's Expedition Against the Natchez Indians, December 1730–January 1731," *LHQ* 19 (1936): 546–77.

99. Femme Brulée au Poteau, 1730, AN, AC, F3, 24:187–87v.

100. Carl F. Klinck and James J. Talman, eds., *The Journal of John Norton, 1816* (1816; reprint, Toronto: Champlain Society, 1970), 46–47.

101. La Harpe, *Historical Journal*, 87–96, on the Natchez' conjunction with the Chickasaws. See Orry to Périer, 1 Nov. 1730, AN, AC, C13A, 12:338–51, for the company's denunciation of Périer. Périer was completely confused by the end of 1731, when he interpreted the natural ploy of the Chickasaws to exploit the ambitions of blacks for freedom as proof that the Chickasaws were under black domination. See Périer to Maurepas, 10 Dec. 1731, AN, AC, C13A, 13:63–64; and Périer's last words were to warn Maurepas that Bienville would make peace with the Chickasaws, as if that was not absolutely essential until a suitable army could be mobilized; see his letter of 6 Mar. 1733, AN, AC, C13A, 16:204v.

102. Bienville to Maurepas, 15 May 1733, AN, AC, C13A, 16:206–17v; Bienville to Maurepas, 18 May 1733, AN, AC, C13A, 16:227–28v.

103. Bienville to Maurepas, 26 Aug. 1734, AN, AC, C13A, 18:183v–84.

104. Bienville to Maurepas, 15 Feb. 1737, AN, AC, C13A, 22:70–73; and d'Artaguiette to Maurepas, 8 May 1737, AN, AC, C13A, 22:223–32v; Bienville to Maurepas, 28 Apr. 1738, AN, AC, C13A, 23:58–68. Bienville and d'Artaguiette agreed, despite their rivalry, that the main reason for the failure of the first expedition was the reluctance of their troops to engage the enemy. On the second campaign, see Louis XV to Bienville, 1738, in AN, AC, C13A, 23:54–57v; Salmon to Maurepas, 2 Jan. 1740, AN, AC, C13A, 25:138–38v; Minutes of the Council of War, 15 Feb. 1740, AN, AC, C13A, 25:82–85v; Bienville to Maurepas, 6 May 1740, AN, AC, C13A, 25:42–68v. See also Woods, *French-Indian Relations*, 144–45; and Michael J. Foret, "War or Peace? Louisiana, the Choctaws and the Chickasaws, 1733–1735," *LH* 31 (1990): 273–92. The argument that the campaign against the Chickasaws was a success despite the inglorious outcome of the major engagements is ably developed by Charles J. Balesi, *The Time of the French in the Heart of North America, 1673–1818* (Chicago: Alliance Française, 1992), 174–87.

105. Surrey, *Commerce of Louisiana*, 335–66, 388–89.

106. Ibid., 379–80; John G. Clark, *New Orleans, 1718–1812: An Economic History* (Baton Rouge: Louisiana State Univ. Press, 1970), 57–58; John H. Moore, "The Cypress Lumber Industry of the Lower Mississippi Valley during the Colonial Period," *LH* 24 (1983): 25–47.

107. See Périer and Delachaise to Maurepas, 30 Mar. 1728, AN, AC, C13A, 11:71–74, for specific emulation of "Virginia and Carolina."

108. French West Indian planters had tried and abandoned the production of tobacco. In 1674, Louis XIV established a royal monopoly on the sale of tobacco to obtain revenue. At the end of the century the monopoly yielded him only about one-fourth of the two hundred thousand pounds the English king collected. Price, *France and the Chesapeake*, 4–11, 21–30, 53, 75–76.

109. Louisiana only exported between 100,000 pounds and 400,000 pounds annually until the 1780s. Virginians remained the main suppliers to France, shipping 6 million pounds annually by the end of the 1720s. See ibid., 247–67, 302–28; see also Lewis C. Gray, *History of Agriculture in the Southern United States to 1860*, 2 vols. (1932; reprint, Gloucester, Mass.: Peter Smith, 1958), 1:69–73; Surrey, *Commerce of Louisiana*, 164–65, 177–78, 197–98; Lauren C. Post, "The Domestic Animals and Plants of French Louisiana . . . ," *LHQ* 16 (1933): 571–73. See Périer and Delachaise to Company, 22 Apr. 1727, AN, AC, C13A, 10:171–71v, on Périer's importation of three "English" tobacco specialists, at least one of them from South Carolina; and Périer to Maurepas, 30 Apr. 1727, AN, AC, C13A, 10:217v–218. The fate of the original French tobacco workers sent out in 1718 is unclear; see Conrad, *First Families of Louisiana*, 1:23–24. See also Memoir on Tobacco in Louisiana, c. 1727, AN, AC, C13A, 10:135–36, on the necessity to acquire Virginia seed because the French market demands Virginia tobacco. The Memoir on the Present State of the Inhabitants of Louisiana in 1750, AN, AC, C13A, 34:393–94, reported that the Natchez uprising ruined tobacco there and production was confined to Pointe Coupée; see also Clark, *New Orleans, 1718–1812*, 79–80.

110. Jack D. L. Holmes, "Indigo in Colonial Louisiana and the Floridas," *LH* 8 (1967): 329–49. See also Price, *France and the Chesapeake*, 312–13, 346–51; Clark, *New Orleans, 1718–1812*, 56; and Gray, *History of Agriculture*, 1:73ff.

111. Wood, *Black Majority*, 35–37; Henry P. Dart, "The First Cargo of African Slaves for Louisiana," *LHQ* 14 (1931): 173, 176. Elizabeth Donnan, ed., *Documents Illustrative of the History of the Slave Trade to America*, vol. 4, *The Border Colonies and the Southern Colonies* (Washington, D.C.: W. F. Roberts for Carnegie Institution, 1935), 636.

112. Hemp grew well, but the crown prohibited it to protect growers in France. Périer and Delachaise to the Company, 2 Nov. 1727, AN, AC, C13A, 10:194v–95.

113. Du Pratz, *History of Louisiana*, 203.

114. Council of Louisiana to Company, 1725, AN, AC, C13A, 9:240v–41, claimed that during the space of four to five months slaves could only harvest wood; see also Darby, "Chapter of Colonial History," 564. On single-crop planters, see T. H. Breen, "The Culture of Agriculture: The Symbolic World of the Tidewater Planter, 1760–1790," in *Saints and Revolutionaries: Essays on Early American History*, ed. David D. Hall, John M. Murrin, and Thad W. Tate (New York: W. W. Norton, 1984), 247–84; on South Carolina, see John J. McCusker and Russell R. Menard, *The Economy of British America, 1607–1789* (Chapel Hill: Univ. of North Carolina Press, 1985), 169–81.

115. Du Pratz, *History of Louisiana*, 204–5. See also Clark, *New Orleans, 1718–1812*, 85–87, 139–48.

116. Maurepas to Rostan, 2 Sept. 1738, AN, AC, B, 67:126–26v. The Crown hoped that

New Orleans might provide a port from which French traders could breach the Spanish crown's carefully guarded markets in nearby port towns, but trade by either the wet route to Vera Cruz or the dry, overland route to Santa Fe never came up to extravagant expectations. See Memoir by Bienville, 1725, AN, AC, C13C, 1:401v–2v; Jean-Marie Loncol, "La Louisiane et les colonies espagnols d'Amérique, 1731–1748," *RHAF* 18 (1964): 196–201; Herbert E. Bolton, *Texas in the Middle Eighteenth Century: Studies in Spanish Colonial History and Administration* (Berkeley and Los Angeles: Univ. of California Press, 1915), 66–69.

117. Clark, *New Orleans, 1718–1812,* 61–87. Clark gives more credit to metropolitan authorities than the results seem to suggest, but any reader must sympathize with his honest effort to evaluate the extent of commerce using very incomplete records.

118. Its formal name was Le Cap Français, or "Guarico" as it was known by the Spanish. See Médéric Moreau de Saint-Méry, *Description topographique, physique, civile, politique, et historique de la partie française de l'isle Saint-Domingue,* ed. Blanche Maurel and Étienne Taillemite, 3 vols. (1797; reprint, Paris: Société de l'Histoire des Colonies Françaises et Librairie Larose, 1958), 2:297.

119. Bienville et al. to Company, 14 Jan. 1724, AN, AC, C13A, 8:6–7v; Samuel Wilson Jr., "Early Aids to Navigation at the Mouth of the Mississippi River," *Proceedings, United States Naval Institute* 70 (1944): 278–87.

120. Manuel de Las Heras, "Summary of a Representation, 1778," in *Documents Relating to the Commercial Policy of Spain in the Floridas with Incidental Reference to Louisiana,* ed. and trans. Arthur P. Whitaker (Deland: Florida State Historical Society, 1931), 5; Thomas Hutchins, *An Historical Narrative and Topographical Description of Louisiana and West Florida* (1784; reprint, Gainesville: University Presses of Florida, 1968), 32–36.

121. Bienville to Maurepas, 28 Jan. 1733, AN, AC, C13A, 16:223, described his voyage of fifty-two days from France to Saint Domingue as "fortunate." In 1729, a ship spent forty-seven days ascending the river from its mouth to New Orleans; see Périer and Delachaise to the Company, 26 Aug. 1729, AN, AC, C13A, 11:361.

122. This was true despite the crown's modest attempt in the 1730s to interest traders of Bordeaux and La Rochelle to sail beyond the islands to the distant colony; see Surrey, *Commerce of Louisiana,* 36–38, 67–69, 83, 76–77, 218–24.

123. Ibid., 367–87.

124. Giraud, *History of French Louisiana,* 5:144–59.

125. Louis XV to Kerlérec and Rochemore, 25 Mar. 1758, AN, AC, C13A, 40:6, on sugar; Bienville and Salmon to Maurepas, 12 May 1733, AN, AC, C13A, 16:76v–77, on the vulnerability of sugarcane to frost; Delanglez, *French Jesuits in Lower Louisiana,* 389–92, traces sugar production by the Jesuits (1740s), by Dubreuil (1750s), and by Balthasar Masan (1760s); d'Abbadie reported on the problems with Masan's mill but characterized the sugar made in New Orleans as of "very good quality"; see Brasseaux, *Comparative View of French Louisiana,* 133.

126. Périer and Delachaise to Maurepas, 30 Mar. 1728, AN, AC, C13A, 11:71–74; Périer and Salmon to Maurepas, 10 Dec. 1731, AN, AC, C13A, 14:169–69v; Bienville and Salmon to Maurepas, 10 June 1736, AN, AC, C13A, 21:26v–27v. By 1737, the roughly one dozen indigo planters produced fifteen thousand pounds; see Bienville and Salmon to Maurepas, 13 Dec. 1737, AN, AC, C13A, 22:51–51v. For the best discus-

sion of this foolhardy and costly incident, see Giraud, *History of French Louisiana*,
5:130–40.

127. "Captain Harry Gordon's Journal of 1766," in *Travels in the American Colonies*, ed.
Mereness, 483.

128. John C. Rule, "Jérome Phélypeaux, Comte de Pontchartrain, and the Establishment
of Louisiana, 1696–1715," in *Frenchmen and French Ways in the Mississippi Valley*, ed. John F.
McDermott (Urbana: Univ. of Illinois Press, 1969), 179–97; John C. Rule, "Jean-
Frédéric Phélypeaux, Comte de Pontchartrain et Maurepas: Reflections on His Life
and His Papers," *LH* 6 (1965): 365–77. For an example of direct intervention to
encourage trade, see Maurepas to Rasteau, 30 July 1733, AN, AC, B, 58:169–72.

129. Davis, *Rise of the Atlantic Economies*, 313.

130. John Reps, *Town Planning in Frontier America* (1965; reprint, Columbia: Univ. of Missouri Press, 1980), 3–10, 58–72.

131. Samuel Wilson Jr., "Colonial Fortifications and Military Architecture in the Mississippi Valley," in *The French in the Mississippi Valley*, ed. John F. McDermott (Urbana:
Univ. of Illinois Press, 1965), 116–17.

132. For a similar definition of a community, as opposed to defining the small urbanized
portion of it as a "town," see Louis Lavallée, *La Prairie en Nouvelle-France, 1647–1760:
étude d'histoire sociale* (Montreal: McGill-Queen's Univ. Press, 1993), 12 and *passim*. For
a different view, see Clark, *New Orleans, 1718–1812*, 156–57.

133. On the human costs (to slaves) of building and maintaining the levee, see "Relation
de la Louisianne," Edward E. Ayer Collection of Americana and American Indians,
Manuscript Division, Newberry Library, Chicago, no. 530, 29–31. On the marine
integration of the region and the levee, see Claude-Cézar Robin, *Voyage to Louisiana,
1803–1805*, trans. and abr. Stuart O. Landry Jr. (1807; reprint, New Orleans: Pelican,
1966), 33–35, 40. See also Giraud, *History of French Louisiana*, 5:194–95.

134. Marion Tinling, ed., *The Correspondence of the Three William Byrds of Westover, Virginia,
1684–1776* (Charlottesville, Va., 1977), entry for 8 Nov. 1710. On the neighborhood
of Bayou St. Jean, see Edna B. Freiberg, *Bayou St. Jean in Colonial Louisiana, 1699–1803*
(New Orleans: Harvey Press, 1980); on that of the lower coast, see Carl A. Brasseaux,
"The French Presence Along the Mississippi River Below New Orleans, 1699–1731,"
Southern Studies 22 (1983): 417–26.

135. The descriptive aspects of this section are based primarily upon the work of Samuel
Wilson Jr. See especially the following works: "Gulf Coast Architecture," in *Spain and
Her Rivals on the Gulf Coast*, ed. Dibble and Newton, 78–126; "Ignace François Broutin,"
in *Frenchmen and French Ways*, ed. McDermott, 231–94; "An Architectural History of the
Royal Hospital, and the Ursuline Convent of New Orleans," *LHQ* 29 (1946): 559–659;
"Colonial Fortifications and Military Architecture"; "Architecture in Eighteenth-
Century West Florida," in *Eighteenth-Century Florida and Its Borderlands*, ed. Samuel Proctor
(Gainesville: Univ. Presses of Florida, 1975), 102–39; "Almonester: Philanthropist and
Builder in New Orleans," in *The Spanish in the Mississippi Valley, 1762–1804*, ed. John F.
McDermott (Urbana: Univ. of Illinois Press, 1974), 183–271; *The Architecture of Colonial
Louisiana: Collected Essays of Samuel Wilson, Jr., F. A. I. A.*, ed. and comp. Jean M. Farnsworth
and Ann M. Masson (Lafayette: Center for Louisiana Studies, Univ. of Southwestern
Louisiana, 1987); and, with Leonard Huber, *The Cabildo on Jackson Square* (Gretna, La.:

Pelican, 1970). See also James M. Fitch, "Creole Architecture 1718–1860: The Rise and Fall of a Great Tradition," in *The Past as Prelude: New Orleans, 1718–1968* ed. Hodding Carter et al. (New Orleans: Pelican, 1968), 71–87; and Jonathan Fricker, "The Origins of the Creole Raised Plantation House," *LH* 25 (1984): 137–53. A contemporary description can be found in Philip Pittman, *The Present State of the European Settlements on the Mississippi,* ed. Frank H. Hodder (1770; reprint, Cleveland: Arthur H. Clark, 1906). In the beginning, the isles, measuring 300 feet square, were divided into twelve lots with 60 feet on the front, five that were 120 feet deep on the streets parallel to the river, and two on each of the perpendicular streets 150 feet deep.

136. Rudolph Matas, *History of Medicine in Louisiana from the Earliest Period,* ed. John Duffy (Baton Rouge: Louisiana State Univ. Press, 1958), 1:17, argues that medical care in New Orleans was superior by comparison with English colonies. For a good overview of epidemic diseases, showing that after the founding era they became a serious problem only at the end of the eighteenth century, see John Duffy, "Pestilence in New Orleans," in *The Past as Prelude,* ed. Carter et al., 88–115.

137. See Surrey, *Commerce of Louisiana,* 253–72, for the general abundance of food but high prices in town.

138. Wilson, *Architecture of Colonial Louisiana,* 117, 53, 149, 154, 242, for several maps, which should be compared.

139. Ibid., 115–30, especially 121 on Vauban.

140. The town was carefully planned by a colorful group of royal engineers; see especially Wilson, *Architecture of Colonial Louisiana,* 1–23, and "Ignace François Broutin."

141. Wilson, *Architecture of Colonial Louisiana,* 263–64, for a general physical description.

CHAPTER 2. FORMATION OF THE PLANTER CLASS AND A STABLE ORDER

1. The phrase is from a blurb on the cover of Asbury's *French Quarter,* which has been reprinted many times, a book based on original scholarship that pictures colonial New Orleans as dominated by criminal elements; see 25–27.

2. Joe G. Taylor, *Louisiana: A History* (1976; reprint, New York, W. W. Norton, 1984), 15.

3. Carl A. Brasseaux, "The Moral Climate of French Colonial Louisiana, 1699–1763," *LH* 27 (1986): 40.

4. Gwendolyn Midlo Hall, in *Africans in Colonial Louisiana: The Development of Afro-Creole Culture in The Eighteenth Century* (Baton Rouge: Louisiana State Univ. Press, 1992), 9, 276.

5. Giraud, *History of French Louisiana,* 5:269.

6. Gayarré, *History of Louisiana,* 2:105. His view has filtered down through most works on the subject. See Émile Lauvrière, *Histoire de la Louisiane française, 1673–1939* (Baton Rouge: Louisiana State Univ. Press, 1940), 164–66, 203–10; Harold Sinclair, *The Port of New Orleans* (Garden City, N.Y.: Doubleday, Doran, 1942), 55; Edwin A. Davis, *Louisiana: A Narrative History,* 3d. ed. (Baton Rouge, La.: Claitor's, 1971), 57, 83–87; and Maurice Denuzière, *Je te nomme Louisiane: découverte, colonisation, et vente de la Louisiane* (Paris: Éditions Denoêl, 1990), 279–81. The sole contemporary document from the post-1731 period making a sustained charge of hedonism is the anonymous *The Present State of the Country and Inhabitants. . . of Louisiana. . .* (London, 1744). Full of demonstrable errors, designed to persuade the English public to seize the potential eco-

nomic bonanza of lower Louisiana, it was probably written by one of a group of Virginia interlopers who had seen New Orleans briefly from the inside of its jail. See also Howard H. Peckham, ed., *Narratives of Colonial America, 1704–1765* (Chicago: R. R. Donnelly, 1971), 53–70; Fairfax Harrison, "The Virginians on the Ohio and Mississippi in 1742," *LHQ* 5 (1922): 316–32; and *Christopher Gist's Journals*, ed. William M. Darlington (Pittsburgh: J. R. Weldin, 1893), 253–60. The same argument in regard to the outlying posts ("the general weakness of bourgeois legal and moral values"), where it is more accurate, is made by Morris S. Arnold, in *Unequal Laws unto a Savage Race: European Legal Traditions in Arkansas, 1686–1836* (Fayetteville: Univ. of Arkansas Press, 1985), 203–8. See also his *Colonial Arkansas, 1686–1804: A Social and Cultural History* (Fayetteville: Univ. of Arkansas Press, 1991). For a similar debate about New France, see Jean Blain, "La moralité en Nouvelle France: les phases de la thèse et de l'antithèse," *RHAF* 27 (1973): 408–16; and Robert-Lionel Séguin, "La Canadienne aux XVIIe et XVIIIe siècles," *RHAF* 13 (1960): 492–508.

7. Carrigan, "Introduction," 1:xxix.

8. Bienville made large grants of land to himself above, below, and across from the town center and then parceled them out to settlers, who agreed to pay dues or quitrents to Bienville. The directors of the Company of the Indies protested when they found that he had appropriated the best lands, so the crown annulled grants over a certain size and assumed all seigneurial obligations owed by settlers, but it is not clear that the colonists ever paid these to anybody. This struggle between Bienville and the company about land policy was bitter and was partly responsible for his recall in 1725. Many of the basic documents concerning Bienville's lands have been translated and published by Henry P. Dart, editor of the *Louisiana Historical Quarterly.* *LHQ* 10 (1927): 6–24, 161–75, 364–80, 538–61; and *LHQ* 11 (1928): 87–110, 209–32, 463–65. See also "Royal Edict of August 10, 1728," *PLHS* 4 (1908): 107–13; and Henry P. Dart, "Bienville's Claims Against the Company of the Indies for Back Salary, 1737," *LHQ* 9 (1926): 210–20. The quarrel was unresolved at the end of Bienville's administration. See Maurepas to Vaudreuil and Salmon, 22 Oct. 1742, AN, AC, B, 74:649–50.

9. On the arpent, see Jack D. L. Holmes, "The Value of the Arpent in Spanish Louisiana and West Florida," *LH* 24 (1983): 314–20. According to the measurement used at the beginning of the nineteenth century in the Pintado Collection of Land Surveys, deposited in the Louisiana State Univ. Library, Baton Rouge, the standard measure was the square arpent, which was ten square *perches* of eighteen French feet, slightly longer than English feet.

10. Of the twenty-two, seven were from Paris or the Isle de France; four from the Argonne; two from Beauce; and one each from Picardy, Brittany, Orleanais, Saintonge, Artois, Poitou, Franche Comté, Lyonnais, and La Rochelle; Dart, "Ship Lists of Passengers," *LHQ* 15 (1932): 68–69.

11. For example, people who lived above the "Maggiolo line" running between St. Malo and Geneva were significantly better educated than those who lived below it. See R. R. Palmer, *The Improvement of Humanity: Education and the French Revolution* (Princeton: Princeton Univ. Press, 1985), 10–11. Nuclear households and partible inheritance were dominant in the north; the *famille-souche* type (in which only the eldest son

could marry and inherit) was dominant in Brittany and Alsace, and the *famille-communitaire* type (in which all children were permitted to marry and live under the authority of the eldest male) was dominant in the south. See Fernand Braudel, *L'identité de la France: espace et histoire,* 2 vols. (Paris: Arthaud-Flammarion, 1986), 1:88–94. The country was a welter of local microeconomies and dialects, with a standard French-speaking majority only in the Isle de France and northwestern central region. See Braudel, ibid., 55–56, 72–88.

12. Gary B. Mills, "The Chauvin Brothers: Early Colonists of Louisiana," *LH* 15 (1974): 117–31.

13. Goubert, *Louis XIV,* 162. The proscription of Protestant emigration to the colonies was enforced by Louis XV as well; see Rouillé to Keeper of the Seals, 28 Jan. 1753, AN, AC, B, 98:65.

14. The Capuchin Father Raphael worried about Protestants in powerful positions like the commandants of German Coast (Darensbourg), Mobile (Louboey), and Natchez (Merveilleux). Moreover, they lived in "concubinage" with white women, according to Father Raphael, who also suspected that Councillor Gerard Pery was an atheist. See Raphael to Abbé Raguet, 15 May 1725, AN, AC, C13A, 8:405v–6. In 1725, the company complained of one Lieutenant Reboul, "Lutheran," in command at *La Balize,* the lighthouse and little fort at the mouth of the river, because he allowed an English ship to go upriver to trade. See Superior Council to the Company, 8 Mar. 1725, AN, AC, C13A, 9:76v. Most Protestants in the Swiss regiment refused to convert even after many years of effort by the priests. See Memoir by Rochemore, c. 1749, AN, AC, C13A, 33:150v.

15. O'Neill, *Church and State in French Colonial Louisiana,* 256–82.

16. Bertram W. Korn, *The Early Jews of New Orleans* (Waltham, Mass.: American Jewish Historical Society, 1969), 6–28; and see Gérard Lafleur, "Les Juifs aux iles françaises du vent, XVIIe–XVIIIe siècles," *Bulletin de la Société d'Histoire de la Guadeloupe* 65–66 (1985): 77–131, for the story of Jews in the major French West Indian colonies.

17. Marriage of 17 Feb. 1727, St. Louis Cathedral Marriages, 1720–1730, 122.

18. Henry P. Dart, "The Career of Dubreuil in French Louisiana," *LHQ* 18 (1935): 267–331.

19. Henry P. Dart, "The Legal Institutions of Louisiana," *LHQ* 2 (1919): 72–103; Henry P. Dart, *Courts and Law in Colonial Louisiana* (New Orleans: Montgomery-Andree, 1921); Henry P. Dart, "A Criminal Trial Before the Superior Council of Louisiana, May 1747," *LHQ* 13 (1930): 367–76; Jerah Johnson, "La Coutume de Paris: Louisiana's First Law," *LH* 30 (1989): 145–55; James D. Hardy Jr., "The Superior Council in Colonial Louisiana," in *Frenchmen and French Ways,* ed. McDermott, 87–101; Jerry A. Micelle, "From Law Court to Local Government: Metamorphosis of the Superior Council of French Louisiana," *LH* 9 (1968): 85–107, emphasizes the ambiguous status of the Council; and Donald J. Lemieux, "The Office of "Commissaire Ordonnateur" in French Louisiana, 1731–1763: A Study in French Colonial Administration" (Ph.D. diss., Louisiana State Univ., 1972), 185–200, argues that justice in the hands of the French *commissaire ordonnateur* was well-administered. See also Jean-Claude Dubé in *Les intendants de la Nouvelle France* (Montréal: Fides, 1984).

20. Joseph Zitomersky, "Espace et société en Amérique coloniale française dans le

contexte comparatif du Nouveau Monde," in *Les Français des États-Unis d'hier à aujourd'hui,* ed. Ronald Creagh and John P. Clark (Montpellier: Éditions Espaces 34, 1994), 43–74.

21. Roland Mousnier, *The Institutions of France under the Absolute Monarchy, 1598–1789,* vol. 1, *Society and the State,* trans. Brian Pearce (Chicago: Univ. of Chicago Press, 1979), 428–638, for a description of the lower levels of France as a society of corporations.

22. According to Henry P. Dart, "The method of trial seems to have been wholly practical, informal, and simple." See "The Law in Louisiana," *Loyola Law Journal* 2 (1921): 10. For typical injunctions to keep attorneys out of the colony, see Louis XV's Instructions to Bienville, 2 Sept. 1732, AN, AC, B, 57:797; Louis XV to Rochemore, 25 Mar. 1758, AN, AC, C13A, 40:5v, where *les gens de pratique et de palais* are denounced for harming commerce by their expense, wherever they are tolerated.

23. Giraud, *History of French Louisiana,* 5:15–53.

24. Grace King, *Jean-Baptiste Le Moyne Sieur de Bienville* (New York: Dodd, Mead, 1893); Michael J. Forêt, "The Failure of Administration: The Chickasaw Campaign of 1739–1740," *Revue de Louisiane* 11 (1982): 49–60.

25. For a different view, see Guy Frégault, *Le grand marquis: Pierre de Rigaud de Vaudreuil et la Louisiane* (Montréal: Fides, 1952).

26. The essential documents are brought together by Abraham P. Nasatir and James R. Mills in *Commerce and Contraband in New Orleans During the French and Indian War: A Documentary Study of the Texel and Three Brothers Affairs* (Cincinnati: Hebrew Union College-Jewish Institute of Religion, 1968). See also Marc De Villiers du Terrage, *The Last Years of French Louisiana,* ed. Carl A. Brasseaux and Glenn R. Conrad and trans. Hosea Phillips (Lafayette: Center for Louisiana Studies, Univ. of Southwestern Louisiana, 1982), 102–16.

27. For an important combined list of planters, traders, and army officers who signed a condemnation of Rochemore, see Copy of a Declaration by Fifty-seven Citizens, 25 Apr. 1760, AN, AC, C13A, 46:114–14v.

28. De Villiers Du Terrage, *Last Years of French Louisiana,* 378–406.

29. Bienville to Maurepas, 25 July 1733, AN, AC, C13, 16:269v–70v.

30. Minutes of the Council of Commerce, 5–13 Sept. 1719, AN, AC, C13A, 5:333–34, on the Company's terms for slaves; Superior Council to The Company of the Indies, 17 Mar. 1726, AN, AC, C13A, 9:245v–246, for a demand for negroes for *les petits habitants* to relieve their *misère.* See also Adrien Pauger to the Company, 6 Apr. 1726, AN, AC, C13A, 9:378–378v; Delachaise to the Company, 18 Oct. 1723, AN, AC, C13A, 7:59 bis v–60 bis v. Governor Périer reported toward the end of his administration that the distribution of slaves was still prejudicial to the small planter, in Périer to Maurepas, 1732, AN, AC, C13A, 14:171. Salmon to Maurepas, 14 Dec. 1731, AN, AC, C13A, 15:186v, stated flatly that the big planters monopolized slaves.

31. Périer and Delachaise to Company, 25 Mar. 1729, AN, AC, C13A, 11:322–36.

32. Census by Governors Ulloa and Aubry, May 1766, Archivo General de Indias, Sección V, Gobierno, Audiencia de Santo Domingo, microfilm copy in the Historic New Orleans Collection (hereafter cited as AGI, SD, followed by legajo:folio), 2585:1–26v.

33. Edith Day Price, "La Dame de Ste. Hermine," *LHQ* 21 (1938): 671–73.

34. George C. H. Kernion, "The Chevalier de Pradel," *LHQ* 12 (1929): 238–54.

35. Giraud, *Histoire de la Louisiane française*, 3:201–4. On titles, see Stanley C. Arthur and George C. H. Kernion, *Old Families of Louisiana* (1931; reprint, Baton Rouge, La.: Claitor's Publishing, 1971).

36. Sigmund Diamond, "An Experiment in 'Feudalism': French Canada in the Seventeenth Century," *William and Mary Quarterly*, 3rd. ser., 18 (1961): 3–34; see also James T. Lemon, "Spatial Order: Households, Local Communities, and Regions," in *Colonial British America*, ed. Greene and Pole, 88, for a capsule discussion of the need for alternative marks of status in a New World without the familiar code of aristocratic society.

37. Roche, *People of Paris*, 36–63.

38. Rev. Mgr. Earl C. Woods and Charles E. Nolan, eds., *Sacramental Records of the Roman Catholic Church of the Archdiocese of New Orleans*, 10 vols. (New Orleans: Archdiocese of New Orleans, 1987–1995), vols. 1 and 2. This is a continuing publication project.

39. Henry P. Dart, "Imprisonment for Debt *(Contraint de Corps)* in French Louisiana, 1743," *LHQ* 8 (1925): 549–56.

40. Authorities were enjoined to report all duels, so the following record of duels should be complete. See "Journal of Diron d'Artaguiette," 16 Nov. 1722; Delachaise to the Company, 18 Oct. 1723, AN, AC, C13A, 7:73v–74; Périer and Delachaise to the Company, 26 Aug. 1729, AN, AC, C13A, 11:361v–62; Fleuriau to Maurepas, 17 Nov. 1729, AN, AC, C13A, 12:182–83; Louboey to Maurepas, 4 Jan. 1740, AN, AC, C13A, 25:208–11.

41. Delachaise to the Company, 18 Oct. 1723, AN, AC, C13A, 7:79–81, on the first scramble for pews; *D'Ausseville v Baron*, Records of the Superior Council, 28 May 1729, Louisiana Historical Collection, Records of the Superior Council, Louisiana Historical Center, Louisiana State Museum, New Orleans (hereafter cited as LHC, all citations being to the Records of the Superior Council); Bienville to Maurepas, 28 Apr. 1734, AC, C13A, 18:171–74; and Salmon to Maurepas, 29 Apr. 1734, AC, C13A, 19:53–53 bis; *Paul Dalcour v Lafrénière*, 6 Oct. 1736, LHC.

42. Jean-Louis Flandrin, *Families in Former Times: Kinship, Household and Sexuality*, trans. Richard Southern (Cambridge: Cambridge Univ. Press 1979), 63, 119–21. See also Vaughan Baker, Amos Simpson, and Mathé Allain, "*Le Mari est Seigneur:* Marital Laws Governing Women in French Louisiana," in *Louisiana's Legal Heritage*, ed. Edward F. Haas and Robert R. McDonald (Pensacola, Fla.: Perdido Bay Press, 1983).

43. Paul Lachance, "L'effet du déséquilibre des sexes sur la comportement matrimonial: comparaison entre la Nouvelle France, Saint-Domingue, et la Nouvelle Orléans," *RHAF* 39 (1985): 211–15, shows that the initial 2-to-1 distribution in New France fell to near parity in 1715 (or 110 to 100); the 4-to-1 distribution in Saint Domingue grew to 5 to 1 after 1770, whereas it nearly reached parity in New Orleans by the 1760s and then rose again.

44. Flandrin, *Families in Former Times*, 125–26; see also Léon Abensour, *La femme et le féminisme avant la Révolution* (Paris: Éditions Ernest Leroux, 1923), 13–22; and Le Roy Ladurie, *Peasants of Languedoc*, 110–13, on the disproportionate decline of women's wages in the sixteenth century. Flandrin is echoed in part by James F. Traer, *Marriage and the Family*

in *Eighteenth-Century France* (Ithaca: Cornell Univ. Press, 1980), 15–18, who labors less convincingly to show that the "modern family" was a product of the age of reason.

45. Flandrin, *Families in Former Times*, 126–29, 182.

46. Carolyn Lougee, *"Le paradis des femmes": Women, Salons, and Social Stratification in Seventeenth-Century France* (Princeton: Princeton Univ. Press, 1976), 5, 21–26, 59–110. The writer employs the word "feminist" with suitable reservations.

47. Many philosophes were no more enlightened on this than they were on other modern social issues. Condorcet was the main exception when he advocated civil equality for men and women in 1791. See Jean H. Bloch, "Women and the Reform of the Nation," in *Woman and Society in Eighteenth-Century France: Essays in Honour of John Stephenson Spink*, ed. Eva Jacobs et al. (London: Athlone Press, 1979), 3–18. For a sarcastic, misogynist work published in London in 1770 by the Chevalier de Champigny, who spent time in Louisiana in the 1760s, see *Reflexions sur le gouvernement des femmes* (London: Author, 1770).

48. Louis-Sebastien Mercier, *The Waiting City: Paris, 1782–88*, ed. and trans. Helen Simpson (1781–88; reprint, London: George G. Harrap, 1933), 49–51; see also John Lough, "Women in Mercier's Tableau de Paris," in *Woman and Society in Eighteenth-Century France*, ed. Jacobs et al., 110–22.

49. Dart, "Ship Lists of Passengers," *LHQ* 21 (1938): 969–70.

50. Unfortunately, marriage registers for the three decades following 1733 have not survived.

51. Based on the number of adult men (574) and women (424) between Tchoupitoulas and the Lower Coast, computed from the census of 1766.

52. Henry P. Dart, "Marriage Contracts of French Colonial Louisiana," *LHQ* 17 (1934): 229–45; Hans W. Baade, introduction to *Louisiana Marriage Contracts: A Compilation of Abstracts from Records of the Superior Council of Louisiana during the French Regime, 1725–1758*, ed. Alice Daly Forsyth and Ghislaine Pleasanton (New Orleans: Polyanthos, 1980).

53. Périer and Delachaise to the Company, 25 Mar. 1729, AN, AC, C13A, 11:325v.

54. Laurence Fontaine, "Droits et stratégies: la reproduction des systèmes familiaux dans le Haut-Dauphiné (XVIIe–XVIIIe siècle)," *Annales ESC* (1992): 1259–77.

55. *Piquery v Boisclair*, 25 Feb. 1752, LHC, showing that she had so little time to attend to her Tchoupitoulas Plantation her neighbor filched from it.

56. *Pierre Charpentier v Madame Goudeau*, 29 Aug. 1763, LHC.

57. Proxy by Jean-Baptiste Bunel to Sheriff Lenormand, 1 Nov. 1763, LHC, to sell slaves and land to settle gambling debts so he could leave jail, in which it was indicated that his wife had left him; *Elizabeth Bunel v Beauregard*, 1–5 Nov. 1763, LHC, to make good a note he gave her for six thousand livres that he had from Malteste, who refused to honor it because he signed it when drunk and was cheated at cards by Beauregard; also Registry of Purchase of Slaves, 17 Feb. 1767, LHC, by Bunel shows her continuing prosperity.

58. The somewhat murky presentation of this case is owing to a record that is incomplete; see *Azemard v Laseigne and Flottmanville*, 13 Apr. *passim* to 3 Sept. 1763, LHC.

59. Bertram Wyatt-Brown, *Southern Honor: Ethics and Behavior in the Old South* (Oxford: Oxford Univ. Press, 1982), 254–71.

60. St. Louis Cathedral Baptisms, 1731–1733, Archdiocese of New Orleans, Archives, New Orleans. A conservative principle was employed, so as to exclude any entry

that was partly illegible, any of the entries listing only one sponsor, any entries including sponsors without surnames, and any entries marred by other ambiguities. For a comparative basis, substantially lower figures have been established for New France on the basis of signatures on marriage contracts. See Michel Verrette, "L'alphabétisation de la population de la ville de Quebec de 1750 à 1849," *RHAF* 39 (1985): 68. Bride and groom signed most of the 233 marriage contracts cited in *Louisiana Marriage Contracts,* ed. Forsyth and Pleasanton.

61. This was a modestly substantial fortune.

62. *Jean-Baptiste Gauvin v Louis Cheval and Marie-Louise Soulande,* 16 May, 22 Sept. 1740, LHC.

63. For an angry denunciation of "the hypocrisy, the sacrilegious thrills of . . . playacting" by women in romance, see Edmond and Jules de Goncourt, *The Woman of the Eighteenth Century . . .* , trans. Jacques Le Clercq and Ralph Roeder (1928; reprint, Westport, Conn.: Hyperion Press, 1981), 119.

64. On the high rate of domestic violence in France at this time, see Nicole Castan, "La criminalité familiale dans le ressort du parlement de Toulouse, 1690–1730," in *Crimes et criminalité en France sous l'Ancien Régime, 17e–18e siècles,* ed. André Abbiateci et al. (Paris: Librairie Armand Colin, 1971), 91–107.

65. Flandrin, *Families in Former Times,* 122–4.

66. *Louise Jousset v Pierre Manadé,* 15 Feb. 1728, LHC, and his response of 20 Mar. Her renunciation of the community of 8 July would appear to be part of the bargain for the pension; she was probably not renouncing very much besides debts. Translations of crumbling depositions in the LHC for 8 July 1728 by Works Progress Administration workers show that the couple's friends believed that his gambling losses made him envious of his wife's property. In some cases these reliable translations have been admitted into evidence in lieu of the original documents.

67. *Marie-Louise Marganne v Michel Rossard,* 18 Aug. 1736 and 7 Dec. 1737, LHC. Women were not generally privileged before the Court in nondomestic matters. For example, when Marie Coupart assaulted Françoise Goublaye under the mistaken belief that this merchant had shortchanged her for some sugar, Marie was thrown into prison, fined forty livres, and warned of exemplary punishment if she misbehaved again. *Antoine Goublaye and Françoise Martin v Marie Coupart,* 5 Aug. *passim* to 14 Aug. 1728, LHC.

68. *Angelique Prévost v Jean Guillot,* 5 Feb. 1738, LHC.

69. *Marné v Hardy,* 30 Aug. *passim* to 9 Sept. 1743, LHC.

70. *Marné v Hardy,* 4 July *passim* to 1 Aug. 1744, LHC; *Hardy v Marné and Barbaut,* 24 June, 7 July 1746, LHC; *Hardy v Barbaut,* 7, 14 Aug. 1747 and 24 May 1748, LHC. Documents of 16 Dec. 1758, ff. mention Hardy de Boisblanc as Administrator of Vacant Estates. For all separation suits of the 1760s, see *Marie-Rose Larche v Tisoneau,* 5 Sept. 1766, LHC, for separation because he had detained her in a convent in France, but only a WPA abstract of the documents remains; *Ursule Trepagnie v Dubuisson,* 26 May 1768, LHC, for separation of property to preserve against creditors the cash and slaves she had brought to the community; *Marie-Françoise Eloy v Pierre Lambremont,* 10 Feb. 1769, LHC, to renounce the community to protect her children because she was "tired of his dissipation and bad conduct"; *Marie Erou v Jean Brunet,* 13 Feb. 1769, LHC, was a lurid case for which the documentation has disappeared, concerning

the husband's open affair with another woman; and *Marie-Thérèse Leveillé v Philippe Flotté*, 12 June 1769, LHC, for full separation, because he bought a remote plantation with her money and submitted her to seventeen years of cruelty. She was awarded full separation and maintenance in New Orleans, along with his bond to alienate nothing from the community. In *Philippe Flotté v Marie-Thérèse Leveillé*, 25 May 1773, LHC, he began a fierce court campaign to prevent her from alienating community property (selling slaves) to pay her debts; see also *Jacquet v Leveillé and Flotté*, 18 Jan. 1774, LHC, demanding payment of her room and board.

71. *Françoise Ruellan v Jean-Baptiste Membrède*, 6 Feb., 25 and *passim* 1745, LHC; *Françoise Ruellan v Jean-Baptiste Membrède*, 30 Aug., 1 Sept. (filed 2 Sept.), 2 Oct. 1745, LHC. For another interesting separation case, see *Jeanne Kerouette v Louis Populus*, 7 Oct. 1761, LHC; *Jeanne Kerouette v Louis Populus*, 16 Mar., 4 June 1763, LHC. See also *Jeanne Kerouette v Louis Populus*, 7 May 1770, LHC.

72. The evidence does not support the view that "common law and bigamous marriages were widespread, even among the social elite." See Brasseaux, "Moral Climate of French Colonial Louisiana," 35.

73. This is based on the unions recorded in St. Louis Cathedral Baptisms and Marriages, 1759–1762, St. Louis Cathedral Baptisms and Marriages, 1763–1766, and St. Louis Cathedral Marriages, 1764–1774, and on the baptisms recorded in the appropriate registers, Archdiocese of New Orleans, Archives, New Orleans. Here and throughout this book, the names of registers will be given as assigned in Woods and Nolan, *Sacramental Records.* In the text, St. Louis Cathedral will be referred to as a "Church" for events prior to its consecration as a cathedral. In all cases, I have worked with the original registers, which were assigned a variety of titles by priests. Many marriage records for the French regime were destroyed in the fire of 1788, so this is a sample that was preserved by chance. This finding agrees with A. J. B. Johnston's for Louisbourg in this period. See his *Religion in Life at Louisbourg, 1713–1758* (Kingston: McGill-Queen's Univ. Press, 1984), 134–38.

74. *Laurent Blanc v Réné Manne*, 5 Feb. 1738, LHC; Salmon to Maurepas, 22 Oct. 1734, AN, AC, C13A, 19:90–91. See *Louisiana Marriage Contracts*, ed. Forsyth and Pleasanton, 13, 54, for the marriage contract with Françoise-Laurence LeBlanc and its annulment. See also Maurepas to Champigny, 16 Aug. 1735, AN, AC, B, 64:292–92v; Bienville and Salmon to Maurepas, 15 Apr. 1736, AN, AC, C13A, 21:7–8; Salmon to Maurepas, 19 June 1736, AN, AC, C13A, 21:284–84v, reporting the return of the woman's slaves; see Salmon to Maurepas, 14 May 1737, AN, AC, C13A, 22:28–28v, for the report that Manne was on his way to Carolina *"chercher fortune."*

75. Périer and Delachaise to the Company, 2 Nov. 1727, AN, AC, C13A, 10:198v–99. See also Delachaise et al. to the Company, 26 Apr. 1725, AN, AC, C13A, 9:135v; Superior Council to the Company, 17 Mar. 1726, AN, AC, C13A, 9:249.

76. Father Raphael to Abbé Raguet, 28 Dec. 1726, AN, AC, C13A, 10:50–50v.

77. Wolfe, *Ursulines in New Orleans*, 196.

78. Father Raphael to Abbé Raguet, 18 May 1728, AN, AC, C13A, 10:46v. See Usner, *Indians, Settlers, and Slaves*, 50, 235.

79. Périer and Salmon to Maurepas, 29 Mar. 1732, AN, AC, C13A, 14:8–9.

80. Flandrin, *Families in Former Times*, 216–17, 240–42; Castan, "Criminalité familiale dans le ressort du parlement de Toulouse," 96–97, challenges this view.

81. Flandrin, *Families in Former Times*, 216.

82. Ibid., 130–40, 153–54. See also David Hunt, *Parents and Children in History: The Psychology of Family Life in Early Modern France* (New York: Basic Books, 1970), 26, 113–79.

83. Delachaise to the Company, 18 Oct. 1723, AN, AC, C13A, 7:68. See Carl J. Ekberg, *Colonial Ste. Genevieve: An Adventure on the Mississippi Frontier* (Gerald, Mo.: Patrice Press, 1985), 269–83, on children in upper Louisiana.

84. Périer and Delachaise to the Company, 3 Nov. 1728, AN, AC, C13A, 11:145; but see Father Le Petit to Father Avaugour, 12 July 1730, in Thwaites, *Jesuit Relations and Allied Documents*, 68:199–201. According to Conrad, *First Families of Louisiana*, 2:154, after the Natchez killings, orphans at the Ursulines included thirty girls (aged three to twelve years) and three infant boys, for which the crown would pay a 150-livre pension per orphan; see also Kerlérec and Rochemore to Berryer 18 Oct. 1759, AN, AC, C13A, 41:10–11, for a summary of the history of orphans in the colony, indicating that they were never numerous.

85. Raphael to Raguet, 18 May 1726, AN, AC, C13A, 10:46.

86. *Raphael v Company of the Indies*, 4 Apr. and 25 July 1731, LHC, on the schoolhouse, but see *LHQ* 5 (1927): 116 and 243–44, for a translation of this crumbling document. See also Raphael to Raguet, 12 Mar. 1726, AN, AC, C13A, 10:42V; Bienville and Salmon to Maurepas, Sept. 1742, AN, AC, C13A, 27:27–28; Gerard Pery's Petition of 21–24 Sept. 1740, LHC; Delanglez, *French Jesuits in Lower Louisiana*, 287–91; Samuel Wilson Jr., *The Capuchin School in New Orleans, 1725* (New Orleans: Archdiocesan School Board, 1961).

87. Salmon to Maurepas, 16 Feb. 1733, AN, AC, C13A, 17:57–59; Roger Baudier, *The Catholic Church in Louisiana* (New Orleans: N.p, 1939), 101–2; John P. Dyer, "Education in New Orleans," in *The Past As Prelude*, ed. Carter et al., 117–19.

88. In the absence of a boys' school, freelance teachers must have found work. One is known because he sued his indignant employer in 1729, a woman who had borrowed from him and refused to repay. In a receipt from the year 1740 to a parent there is a clear indication that one J. Sautien accepted boys "at his school" in New Orleans, but nothing more is known of this instructor; see *Réné Galbée v Madame Rivard*, 16 Aug. 1729, LHC; Sautien's Receipt to Carrière, 28 Mar. 1740, LHC.

89. Marion Ware, ed., "An Adventurous Voyage to French Colonial Louisiana: The Narrative of Mother Tranchepain, 1727," *LH* 1 (1960): 227. See also Giraud, *History of French Louisiana*, 1:122–23.

90. R. Cabon, "Une maison d'education à Saint-Domingue: les religieuses du Cap," ed. Gabriel Debien, *RHAF* 3 (1949–50): 3, 79; Joan Marie Aycock, "The Ursuline School in New Orleans, 1727–1771," in *Cross, Crucible and Crozier: A Volume Celebrating the Bicentennial of a Catholic Diocese in Louisiana*, ed. Glenn R. Conrad (Lafayette: Archdiocese of New Orleans and Center for Louisiana Studies, 1993), 203–18.

91. Pradel, *Chevalier de Pradel*, 145–73. On girls' schools in France, characterized by conservative curricula and other limitations, see Martine Sonnet, *L'éducation des filles au temps des Lumières* (Paris: Éditions du Cerf, 1987), 285–87.

92. For a typical straightforward example, following a family meeting, see *Pierre Daniel v Daniel Estate*, 27 Feb. 1740, LHC.

93. John F. McDermott, "Auguste Chouteau: First Citizen of Upper Louisiana," in *Frenchmen and French Ways*, ed. McDermott, 1–13; William E. Foley and C. David Rice, *The First Chouteaus: River Barons of Early St. Louis* (Urbana: Univ. of Illinois Press, 1983).

94. "Royal Edict of Dec. 15, 1721," *PLHS* 4 (1910): 67–71; and *LHQ* 10 (1927): 533–37; Royal Ordinance on Tutors, 1 Oct. 1741, LHC.

95. Agnès Fine, *Parrains, marraines: la parenté spirituelle en Europe* (Paris: Fayard, 1994), 41–65.

96. One dramatic example illustrates the power of tutors. In the summer of 1743, Joseph Chaperon sued the Ursuline nuns for encroaching on the land of his ward Françoise Larche; the Sisters' plantation was next to the girl's, and they allegedly moved the surveyor's posts to their own advantage. The disposition of this case is unknown because the court-ordered surveyor's investigation was not recorded; but it shows how tutors would sue even the most venerable of parties who tried to take advantage of a minor. See *Joseph Chaperon v Ursulines*, 3 July, 3 Aug. 1743, LHC.

97. Petition of Tixerant and Arlut, 13 July, 3 Aug. 1743, LHC.

98. Carrière Estate, 4 Nov. passim to 13 Dec. 1743, LHC; *François Jahan v André Carriere*, 2, 26, 29 Nov. 1743, LHC. The outsider's angry suit for damages against André was quashed by the governor himself. Unfortunately, the marriage register for this period is lost, and the story of André and St. Martin sinks from view. For a discussion of the issues in which a somewhat different view is expressed by Micheline Dumont, in *Quebec Women: A History*, trans. Roger Gannon and Rosalind Gill (Toronto: Women's Press, 1987), 66–68.

99. See, for example, Orest Ranum, *Paris in the Age of Absolutism* (Bloomington: Indiana Univ. Press, 1968), 172–74.

100. Succession of Fazende, 17 Mar. 1760, LHC; *Piquery v Boisclair*, 26 Feb., 4 Mar. 1752, LHC; *Bobé v Hery Duplanty and Company*, 9, 12 Jan. 1763, LHC.

101. Prearranged marriages remained common in this era in France, and pressure to knit family alliances may have meant unhappy matches for some girls; see René Pillorget, *La tige et le rameau: familles anglaise et française XVe–XVIIIe siècle* (France: Calmann-Lévy, 1979), 144–50.

102. St. Louis Cathedral Baptisms and Marriages, 1759–1762; St. Louis Cathedral Baptisms and Marriages, 1763–1766; St. Louis Cathedral Marriages, 1764–1774, Archdiocese of New Orleans, Archives, New Orleans.

103. Pradel, *Chevalier de Pradel*, 199–200.

104. Ibid., 380–90.

105. Ibid., 410–24.

106. Ibid., 424–30.

107. Contract of Tixerant and Aufrère, 29 Dec. 1738, LHC, for the large project involving the commitment of twenty-two male and fifteen female African slaves.

108. Contract of Pradel and Foucault, 6 Oct. 1763, LHC; Contract of Pradel and Martin, 26 Jan. 1766, LHC. An unknown number of contracts were either not recorded or have been lost. Moreover, in such a small community informal agreements to accomplish a variety of minor enterprises must have been common. In general, however, contracts were rare in this period.

109. Perhaps the most notable suit for a broken contract was that by Petit and Durand in 1767 against Evan Jones, who was at the start of a long career in New Orleans, for failure to deliver a cargo of slaves as agreed, another piece of evidence on the slight slave trade to New Orleans. See Contract of Petit and Durand with Jones, 20 Dec. 1765, LHC; *Petit and Durand v Jones*, 10 May 1767, LHC; Arbitrators' Report, 18 May 1768, LHC. Other broken contracts ran the gamut from the trivial *Chaperon v Blanpain*, 31 May 1748, LHC, about an ass that would not cover mares; to the more serious *Jacques Nicolas v Louis Langlois*, 9 May 1749, LHC (now found in WPA abstracts only), because apprentice Augustin Langlois had run away from the master gunmaker; finally, see *Julien Bidaux v Philippe Adam*, 21 June, 6 July 1748, LHC; and *Jean-Baptiste Darieux v Gaillard*, 30 May *passim* to 29 June 1768, LHC, for apprenticeship contracts broken by runaway boys.

110. Second May 1747, LHC; he was soon engaged, for example, in a suit for payment against the Tixerant-Arlut couple.

111. On the succession, see Inventory and Sale of Rasteau Estate, 6 June, 1 July 1747, LHC; *Broutin v Rasteau Succession*, 3 and 7 Sept. 1747, LHC; Rasteau père to Curator, 23 Jan. 1749, LHC; Rasteau Succession, 27 Sept. 1763, *LHQ* 25 (1942): 1170–73. The evidence is a muddle, but Rasteau *père* wrote an anguished letter from France insisting that huge sums were unaccounted for. For a similar case of plunder, involving a large cache of money belonging to some Spanish traders, see *J. F. Delatorre v Gerard Pery*, 23 Mar., 5 Apr. 1741, LHC.

112. *Piquery v Boisclair*, 26 Feb., 4 Mar. 1752, LHC; *Bobé v Hery Duplanty and Company*, 9, 1 2 Jan. 1763, LHC, in the name of his father who had returned to France when the Spanish arrived.

113. D'Ausseville Succession, 6 Feb. 1745 *passim* to *Procureur André Aufrère v Attorney for Vacant Estates Godefroy Barbin*, 13 Mar. 1747, LHC, for a rare instigation of appeal to superior judicial authority in France; and D'Ausseville Succession, 20 Apr. 1765, LHC.

114. Other possibly fraudulent cases include Jacques Judice Succession, 16 Feb. 1747 and *passim*, LHC; *Françoise Petit v Lasource*, 5–6 July 1748, LHC. *Jean-Pierre Vilemont v Councillor Lesassier*, 7 May (filed 9 May), 14 Sept. and 15 Oct. 1767, LHC, provided the opening shot in the dénouement of the Dauberville Succession, to which the Dubreuils were deeply indebted, in the nastiest of these suits in the French period.

115. Eugene Genovese, *Roll, Jordan, Roll: The World the Slaves Made* (New York : Random House, 1974), 27.

116. Evidence of the costs of free labor is rare because most labor contracts concern slaves. See Heloise H. Cruzat, trans., "Agreement between Louis-Cézar Le Breton, and Jean-Baptiste Goudeau as Overseer on his Plantation, 1744," *LHQ* 9 (1926): 590–92, for an overseer's contract; the Canadian was to receive on an annual basis his lodging, twelve barrels of rice, one pound of beef or one-half pound of bacon daily, twelve pounds of tobacco, one pair of shoes, one bed, eight hundred livres, six linen shirts, and the services of one slave.

117. Minutes of the Conseil de Regie, 28 May 1723, AN, AC, C13A, 7:119–24.

118. Giraud, *History of French Louisiana*, 5:257–61.

119. John A. Dickinson, *Justice et justiciables: la procédure civile à la prévôté de Québec, 1667–1759*

(Québec: Les Presses de l'Université Laval, 1982), 77–98, 170–76. See also Peter N. Moogk, "'Thieving Buggers' and 'Stupid Sluts': Insults and Popular Culture in New France," *William and Mary Quarterly*, 3d ser., 36 (1979): 533, for the remark that "social inferiors were accorded greater respect in Canada than in France."

120. Council Decisions, 5 Nov. 1725, LHC, resolves a case beginning on 22 August.

121. *Bouet v Goublayes*, 16 July 1727, LHC, and a second document of the same date in oversize section. See also *Antoine Milon v Marchand*, 12 Mar. 1730, LHC; *Jacques Mousset v Lafrénière*, 17 Mar. 1725, LHC.

122. Raphael to Raguet, 18 Apr. 1727, AN, AC, C13A, 10:326.

123. Contract of Longueville and Doyon, 4 Oct. 1747, LHC.

124. Darrett B. Rutman and Anita H. Rutman, *A Place in Time: Middlesex County, Virginia, 1650–1750* (New York: W. W. Norton, 1984), 239.

125. James Perry, *The Formation of Society on Virginia's Eastern Shore, 1615–1655* (Chapel Hill: Univ. of North Carolina Press, 1990), 134–39.

126. Third Feb. 1739, *LHQ* 8 (1925): 382–88.

127. Succession of Jean Tessinard, 15 Sept. 1764, LHC; the slave may not have been paid for, however, because he was not mentioned in the estate auction.

128. Will of Jean Louis, 16 Nov. 1735, LHC; Contract by King's Contractor Joseph Dubreuil, 10 June 1736, LHC; Report by Bienville and Salmon, 20 May 1737, LHC. See Charity Hospital Board of Directors Meetings of 20 Aug. and 1 Oct. 1764, LHC, on the inmates.

129. *Chaumont v LeGros*, 30 Jan. 1745, LHC.

130. On criminal procedure, see André Lachance, in *La justice criminelle du roi au Canada au XVIIIe siècle: tribunaux et officiers* (Québec: Les Presses de l'Université Laval, 1978), 61–103.

131. *State v Baude*, 6 Nov. *passim* to 12 Nov. 1767, LHC. See also Lachance, *Justice criminelle*, 105–33 on the variety of punishments for felonies.

132. Autopsy and Witnesses Depositions, 5, 7 Nov. 1740, LHC.

133. For the most colorful case, see *Lenormant v Taillefer*, 24 Mar. 1747, LHC; Vaudreuil to Maurepas, 25 Apr. 1747, AN, AC, C13A, 31:56–58v. The judicial records for a few years in this period are completely missing. The imperial reports for those years do not indicate unusual crime rates for those years.

134. On the prevalence of arson in France, committed by types of poor people unknown in Louisiana, such as tenants who were refused hunting rights, beggars who "tricked" those who refused to "treat," and the indigent insane, see André Abbiateci, "Les Incendiaires devant le Parlement de Paris: Essai de Typologie Criminelle (XVIIIe Siècle)," in *Crimes et criminalité en France*, ed. Abbiateci et al., 13–32.

135. *Delisle v André et al.*, 8 Jan. (filed 31 Jan.), 8, 10 Mar. 1753, LHC. Delisle and others routinely kept large tracts of land patrolled by slaves. Another important case concerning rustlers was *State v Degout (Fleury) et al.*, 7 Mar. *passim* to 25 Apr. 1764, LHC, which included special features like the partnership of whites and one free black in crime and the torture of the white ringleader because he refused to confess. For a quantitative review of crime in Quebec in this period, see André Lachance, "La Criminalité à Québec sous le Régime Français," *RHAF* 20 (1966): 409–14.

136. Brasseaux, *Comparative View of French Louisiana*, 104–5.

137. Michel to Rouillé, 23 Sept. 1752, AN, AC, C13A, 36:272–73.

138. Rutman and Rutman, *Place in Time*, 143.

CHAPTER 3. BLACK MAJORITY

1. All of the West Indian, North American, and South American colonies had prolonged founding eras in which colonists attempted to establish export economies
based on the labor of either the local Native Americans (Latin America) or indentured servants or peasants from the Old World (Anglo- and Franco-America). Certain technical exceptions might be raised. Tidewater North Carolina may have had
a black majority before that colony was formally set off from the Virginia colony,
from which most of its white settlers hailed.

2. The only slave shipment to New Orleans for which relations among those on a
slaver are known is that of the captive English vessel of 1758, which shows that 15 of
121 had conjugal relations that were honored in the sale; see Sale of Captured Slaves,
27 Sept. 1758, AN, AC, C13A, 40:189–98.

3. Mettas, *Répertoire des expéditions négrières françaises*, vol. 2, voyage number 2911.

4. Statistics are based upon seventeen voyages with known voyage times, in ibid.

5. Périer and Delachaise to Maurepas, 9 Apr. 1728, AN, AC, C13A, 11:28–29; Périer and
Delachaise to the Company, 30 Jan. 1729, AN, AC, C13A, 11:315–15v, on *La Galathée*;
Périer and Delachaise to the Company, 31 July 1728, AN, AC, C13A, 11:51–52; Périer
and Delachaise to the Company, 26 Aug. 1729, AN, AC, C13A, 11:351–51v; Périer and
Delachaise to the Company, 25 Mar. 1729, AN, AC, C13A, 11:333, told the directors
that high mortality resulted from keeping blacks in prisons at Gorée trading station
too long on bad food and water; and Mettas, *Répertoire des expéditions négrières françaises*,
vol. 2, voyage numbers 2901 *(Duc De Noailles)*, 2903 *(Vénus)*, and 2909 *(Vénus)*. On
scurvy and the revelation of an efficient cure by an African doctor, see Matas, *History
of Medicine in Louisiana*, 1:127–34.

6. Governor Feuquières and Intendant Bénard to Pontchartrain, 28 Jan. 1721, AN, AC,
C8A, 28:12.

7. Donnan, *Documents Illustrative*, 4:638–39, showing that the company measured one
pièce as a man over seventeen years of age or a woman over fifteen without flaws; three
children of eight to ten years made two *pièces*.

8. Suzanne Miers and Igor Kopytoff, "African 'Slavery' as an Institution of Marginal-
ity," in *Slavery in Africa: Historical and Anthropological Perspectives*, ed. Suzanne Miers and
Igor Kopytoff (Madison: Univ. of Wisconsin Press, 1977), 1–84.

9. Paul E. Lovejoy, *Transformations in Slavery: A History of Slavery in Africa* (Cambridge:
Cambridge Univ. Press, 1983), 18–20; see also Basil Davidson, *Black Mother: Africa, The
Years of Trial* (London: Victor Gollancz, 1968), 38–40.

10. Du Pratz, *History of Louisiana*, 382–83. See also Lucien Peytraud, *L'esclavage aux Antilles
françaises avant 1789 d'après des documents inédits des archives coloniales* (Paris: Librairie Hachette,
1897), 85–89.

11. For the best discussions, see Daniel C. Littlefield, *Rice and Slaves: Ethnicity and the Slave
Trade in Colonial South Carolina* (1981; reprint, Urbana: Univ. of Illinois Press, 1991), 8–
32; Darold D. Wax, "Preferences for Slaves in Colonial America," *Journal of Negro
History* (hereafter cited as *JNH*) 58 (1973): 371–401.

12. C. R. Boxer, *The Golden Age of Brazil, 1695–1750* (Berkeley and Los Angeles: Univ. of California Press, 1962), 313.

13. Soi-Daniel Brown, ed. and trans., "From the Tongues of Africa: A Partial Translation of Oldendorp's Interviews," *Plantation Society in the Americas* 2 (1983): 52–53.

14. Only a few hundred were shipped to the islands over the decades because the crown disapproved and because it risked ruining Bienville's reputation among the Indians as a just man; see Bienville to Pontchartrain, 28 July 1706, AN, AC, C13A, 1:522–23; Bienville to Pontchartrain, 12 Oct. 1708, AN, AC, C13A, 2:177–78; Robert to Pontchartrain, 26 Nov. 1708, AN, AC, C13A, 2:359–62; Pontchartrain to Bienville, 10 May 1710, AN, AC, B, 32:36–41; Bienville to Maurepas, 28 Jan. 1733, AN, AC, C13A, 16:223v. See also Daniel H. Usner Jr., "American Indians in Colonial New Orleans," in *Powhatan's Mantle: Indians in the Colonial Southeast*, ed. Peter H. Wood, Gregory A. Waselkov, and M. Thomas Hatley (Lincoln: Univ. of Nebraska Press, 1989), 104–27.

15. P. E. H. Hair, Adam Jones, and Robin Law, eds. *Barbot on Guinea: The Writings of Jean Barbot on West Africa, 1678–1712*, 2 vols. (1732; reprint, London, 1992), 1:133–34.

16. For a good example of a combination of poisoning and witchcraft perpetrated by a slave against the slave driver (also a slave) of a plantation, see Petition by Bonnaud, 21 Oct. 1729, and Indictment by Attorney General Fleuriau, 25 Oct. 1729, LHC.

17. Du Pratz, *History of Louisiana*, 377.

18. Philip D. Curtin, ed., *Africa Remembered: Narratives by West Africans from the Era of the Slave Trade* (Madison: Univ. of Wisconsin Press, 1967), 42–43. The first Muslim of whom we have certain knowledge is Abd al-Rahman Ibrahima, who arrived in New Orleans in 1788 in transit to Natchez. There his faith also set him apart as a privileged slave. See Terry Alford, *Prince Among Slaves: The True Story of an African Prince Sold Into Slavery in the American South* (1977; reprint, New York: Oxford Univ. Press, 1986) 48–49, 56–57, 73–75.

19. Hair, Jones, and Law, *Barbot on Guinea*, 1:106–7.

20. Ibid., 1:185.

21. Prosecution of Charlot Kacaracou, 3 Jan. 1748, testimony of 10 Jan., LHC. On the rise of the Bambara states, see Basil Davidson, *A History of West Africa to the Nineteenth Century* (1965; reprint, Garden City, N.Y.: Doubleday, 1966), 266–69. See also Peter Caron, "'Of a nation which others do not understand': Bambara Slaves and African Ethnicity in Colonial Louisiana, 1718–60," *Slavery and Abolition* 18 (1997): 98–221.

22. As for the assertion that "whites were publicly punished by blacks," by Hall in *Africans in Colonial Louisiana*, 131, it is based on one anomalous case in the earliest days before authorities knew that the great majority of people would be black slaves. This particularly heinous crime of robbery by a soldier against one of the colony's highest ranking gentlemen was punished in several ways, including a flogging by a "negro," but this was never repeated. See Court Martial of Jean-Baptiste Porcher, 23 Feb. 1720, LHC.

23. Minutes of the Council, 21 Nov. 1725, AN, AC, C13A, 9:267v.

24. Deliberations of the Superior Council, 21 Nov. 1725, AN, AC, C13A, 9:267v; Appeal by Attorney General Fleuriau to the Superior Council, 17 Aug. 1726, LHC. These slaves undoubtedly were members of the small maroon camp of Natanpallé that

existed somewhere in the vicinity of New Orleans at this time, the only such maroon community that existed in the early period; see Interrogation of Sansouci, 31 Mar. 1727, LHC, but refer to WPA summaries because this document has disintegrated.

25. Petition by Louis Congo, 24 Jan. 1737, LHC. He claimed that one of the men was the runaway slave of Augustin Langlois, named Guy; see Declaration by Louis Giscard Benoit, 8 Jan. 1737, LHC.

26. Martin Klein and Paul E. Lovejoy, "Slavery in West Africa," in *The Uncommon Market: Essays in the Economic History of the Atlantic Slave Trade,* ed. Henry A. Gemery and Jan S. Hogendorn (New York: Academic Press, 1979), 181–212; Patrick Manning, *Slavery and African Life: Occidental, Oriental, and African Slave Trades* (Cambridge: Cambridge Univ. Press, 1990), 110–25; Davidson, *History of West Africa to the Nineteenth Century,* 214–18.

27. Brown, "From the Tongues of Africa," 56–58. On a related theme, according to Oldendorp, some nations did not regard ritual cannibalism as a crime, but most nations did not practice it; see ibid., 58–59.

28. Sidney W. Mintz, *Caribbean Transformations* (1974; reprint, Baltimore: Johns Hopkins Univ. Press, 1984), 12.

29. Hair, Jones, and Law, *Barbot on Guinea,* 1:123; 2:547, 549.

30. Brown, "From the Tongues of Africa," 54.

31. Ibid., 55.

32. Hair, Jones, and Law, *Barbot on Guinea,* 1:85–87, 128–29; 2:502–4.

33. Manning, *Slavery and African Life,* 130.

34. For the thesis that Louisiana slaves created an unusually distinctive "Afro-Creole culture," in the absence of a "cohesive white elite" (160), see Hall, *Africans in Colonial Louisiana,* 159–61.

35. Mettas, *Répertoire des expéditions négrières,* vol. 2, voyage number 2859. For further detail, see Hall, *Africans in Colonial Louisiana,* 69–70.

36. Mettas, *Répertoire des expéditions négrières,* voyage number 2908; see also Hall, *Africans in Colonial Louisiana,* 88–92, for a vivid description.

37. La Harpe, *Historical Journal,* 213.

38. Minutes of the Council of War, 7 Jan. 1724, AN, AC, C13A, 7:174v. The threat of a conjunction was real. Even before the founding of New Orleans, in 1712, seven hundred miles up the Red River a mounted maroon band of twenty-five to thirty black slaves harassed their former Spanish masters in Mexico, living with their Indian allies. See D'artaguiette to Pontchartrain, 12 May 1712, AN, AC, C13A, 2: 807–8.

39. Périer and Delachaise to the Company, 30 Mar. 1728, AN, AC, C13A, 11:99.

40. Périer to Maurepas, 18 Mar. 1730, AN, AC, C13A, 12:40.

41. Périer to the Company, 18 Mar. 1730, AN, AC, C13A, 12:295–95v.

42. Charlevoix, *History and General Description of New France,* 6:100.

43. Lusser or Régis Du Roullet to Maurepas, c. Feb. 1730, AN, AC, C13A, 12:120v–30; Régis Du Roullet to Périer, 16 Mar. 1731, AN, AC, C13A, 13:187–93.

44. Father Le Petit to Father Avaugour, 12 July 1730, in Twaites, *Jesuit Relations and Allied Documents,* 68:197–99.

45. Memoir of D'Ausseville, 20 Jan. 1732, AN, AC, C13A, 14:273–74v.

46. Hall, *Africans in Colonial Louisiana*, 106.

47. David C. Conrad, "Slavery in Bambara Society: Segu, 1712–1861," *Slavery and Abolition* 2 (1981): 69–80.

48. Périer to Maurepas, 21, 28 July 1731, AN, AC, C13A, 13:87–87v; Beauchamp to Maurepas, 5 Nov. 1731, AN, AC, C13A, 13:200–200v; Du Pratz, *History of Louisiana*, 77–79. Périer said he executed six men, Du Pratz reported eight people, Beauchamp claimed it was ten to twelve!

49. Périer to Maurepas, 21, 28 July 1731, AN, AC, C13A, 13:87.

50. D'Ausseville to Maurepas, 20 Jan. 1732, AN, AC, C13A, 14:274v.

51. Ibid.; Salmon to Maurepas, 18 Jan. 1732, AN, AC, C13A, 15:25v.

52. Commissaire Ordonnateur Salmon to Maurepas, 18 July 1733, AN, AC, C13A, 17:152–53, argued that although these thieves deserved to be hanged they were not, for "the Council reflected that if all the Negro thieves were hanged not one would be saved from the scaffold."

53. Périer to Maurepas, 21, 28 July 1731, AN, AC, C13A, 13:87v.

54. Vaudreuil to Maurepas 16 Nov. 1748, AN, AC, C13A, 32:139–39v. See Richard Price, "Introduction: Maroons and Their Communities," in *Maroon Societies: Rebel Slave Communities in the Americas,* ed. Richard Price, 2d. ed. (1973; reprint, Baltimore: Johns Hopkins Univ. Press, 1979), 9–16, for a general discussion of how the race barrier raised by whites between Indians and Africans was the real obstacle to more widespread and successful marronage.

55. Roland McConnell, "Louisiana's Black Military History, 1729–1865," in *Louisiana's Black Heritage,* ed. Robert R. Macdonald, John R. Kemp, and Edward F. Haas (New Orleans: Louisiana State Museum, 1979), 33–34.

56. Albert J. Pickett, *History of Alabama and Incidentally of Georgia and Mississippi from the Earliest Period* (Sheffield, Al.: Robert C. Randolph, 1896), 292–93.

57. Dart, "Ship Lists of Passengers," *LHQ* 14 (1931): 519, and *LHQ* 21 (1938): 965. Also see Conrad, *First Families of Louisiana,* 1:71, for Isaac Matapan (1721), and 117, for cook Perrine (1720.)

58. *Bernard v Cadot,* 9–10 May 1724, LHC; *Bernard v Dumanoir,* 26 July, 20 Sept. 1724, LHC. In 1725, one Jean-Baptiste Raphael, free Negro of Martinique, is listed in the sacramental register as marrying. The coincidence of the unusual name "Raphael" suggests it may be the same person. See St. Louis Cathedral Marriages, 1720–1730, Archdiocese of New Orleans, Archives, entry 201. A "Raphael," free Negro, is also registered as marrying a slave in 1730. See Louis Cathedral Marriages, 1720–1730, entry 357. This one may be named after Father Raphael.

59. Baptism of Marie, daughter of Pinette, 9 Sept. 1731, St. Louis Cathedral Baptisms, 1731–1733; and Marriage of Vanon and Marie Anne (also of Senegal), 19 Mar. 1731, ibid., "Marriages," entry 7.

60. Contract of Darby and Mingo, 28 Nov. 1727, LHC; and Contract of Chavannes and Mingo, 21 Oct. 1729, LHC; *Mingo v Darby,* 21, 25 Nov. 1730, LHC.

61. Marie's Petition for Freedom Papers, 4 June 1735, LHC; Bienville's Emancipation of Zacarie, 16 July 1743, LHC.

62. Pradel, *Chevalier de Pradel,* 304–5, 381.

63. Joseph Meunier's Emancipation of Marie, 28 Mar. 1736, LHC.

64. St. Julien's Manumissions of Marie-Charlotte and Louise, 9 Oct. 1735, LHC; Attorney General's Petition for Emancipation of Marie-Charlotte and Louise, 29 Nov. 1743, LHC; and *Marie Charlotte v Antoine Aufrère, Procurator for D'Ausseville*, 6 Feb. 1745, LHC. For a related case, see *D'Ausseville v St. Julien Estate*, 1 July passim to 7 Dec. 1737, LHC, concerning the ownership of Jeannot and Calais. The significance of this case was that the slaves' testimony was believed and was decisive.

65. Petition of Trudeau, 11 July 1737, LHC.

66. *Fabry v Jean-Baptiste*, 19–14 Aug., Sept. 1743, LHC.

67. By 1691, Virginia planters strongly discouraged manumissions by law because free blacks supposedly threatened order "by their entertaining [runaway] Negroes from masters' service, or receiving stolen goods, or being grown old bringing a charge upon the country." Quoted in A. Leon Higginbotham Jr., *In the Matter of Color: Race and the American Legal Process, The Colonial Period* (New York: Oxford Univ. Press, 1978), 48.

68. On the labor of freedmen see Contract of Chavannes and Mingo, 21 Oct. 1729, hiring him as an overseer, as previously discussed; Contract of François Trudeau and Scipion, 21 Aug. 1736, LHC, for the year, for 200 livres; this could be the same Scipion in the Contract with Réné Petit to command his *voiture* (a large pirogue or barge in Louisiana, often mistranslated as *coach*, rowed mainly by slaves to Illinois). For an example of the skills, risk of social disease, and independence of freedmen, see Contract of King's Physician Prat and Pierre Almanzor, 2 Mar. 1737, LHC, to treat the man's venereal disease, for which Pierre promised to serve as cook or in any capacity "except wielding an axe or working the ground," for five years; mortgage by Jacques Duvergès to Piemont, 7 July 1739, LHC, for clothing, rugs, fabrics, wine, and brandy, which this free black carried to Illinois as a *voyageur*, and promised to repay the following June, mortgaging same by the property of Negress Marie; Receipt by Claude Reynaud to Isabelle, 6 Aug. 1739, LHC, for 750 livres to purchase a herd of mature horned cattle, illustrating that black women too engaged in formal entrepreneurship; and mortgage by Claude Reynaud to Isabelle, 29 July 1740, LHC, probably a copy, apparently indicating that Isabelle was suing either Reynaud or the Pascagoula *métis* from whom he had purchased them, Jean-Baptiste Baudreau, since wolves had devoured some of her calves. Examples of conflicts between freedmen and slaves include *State v André*, 21 Apr. 1730, LHC, for prosecution of a free black André, employed by Bellair, a slave catcher who shot a maroon; *Cézar Blanc v Bellair*, whose free black employee Thomare (Thomas?) shot one of Blanc's slaves; and *Bernard Bouilland v Simon*, 12 Apr. 1738, LHC, concerning a free black's act of multiple assaults inflicted on slaves.

69. Throughout the judicial and administrative records of the French regime, only about sixty free blacks are mentioned, the great majority denoted as being black rather than of mixed race.

70. Arlette Gautier, *Les soeurs de solitude: la condition féminine dans l'esclavage aux Antilles du XVIIe au XIXe siècle* (Paris: Éditions Caribéennes, 1985), 36–54; see also Miers and Kopytoff, "Introduction" in *Slavery in Africa: Historical and Anthropological Perspectives*, ed. Miers and Kopytoff, 7–11.

71. Gautier, *Soeurs de solitude,* 62–124.

72. Based on four voyages of 1721 for which distributions are known from Mettas, *Répertoire des expéditions négrières,* vol. 2. Three later cargoes are known, however, those of 1723, 1728, and 1731, and among these people the sex distribution was extremely unbalanced.

73. Conrad, *First Families of Louisiana,* 2:124–27, 144–47.

74. See Willie Lee Rose, "Childhood in Bondage," in William W. Freehling, ed., *Slavery and Freedom* (New York: Oxford Univ. Press, 1982), 37–48; and John W. Blassingame, *The Slave Community: Plantation Life in the Antebellum South,* 2d ed. (New York: Oxford Univ. Press, 1979), 180–91.

75. Henry P. Dart, ed., "Documents Concerning Sale of Chaouachas Plantation," *LHQ* 8 (1925): 602–15.

76. Bienvenu Succession, 6 Apr. 1753, LHC; Dart, "Career of Dubreuil," 292–330.

77. Philip D. Morgan, "Three Planters and Their Slaves: Perspectives on Slavery in Virginia, South Carolina, and Jamaica, 1750–1790," in *Race and Family in the Colonial South,* ed. Jordan and Skemp, 37–79.

78. Du Pratz, *History of Louisiana,* 380–87.

79. Allan Gallay, ed., *Voices of the Old South: Eyewitness Accounts, 1528–1861* (Athens: Univ. of Georgia Press, 1994), 146–47.

80. Manadé to D'Ausseville, 6 Apr. 1730, LHC.

81. D'Ausseville to Le Roy, 29 Apr. 1730, LHC.

82. *D'Ausseville v Le Roy,* 7 Aug. 1730, LHC.

83. The possibility of suicide was real. While no case of suicide by a white person is discovered in the archives during the colonial period, some slaves took their own lives. A Bellisle slave hanged himself in one of Dubreuil's slave cabins, where his corpse was discovered already decomposing in June. See Official Report by a Committee of the Superior Council, 26 June 1747, LHC.

84. Declaration by Chaperon, 8 Sept. 1737, LHC.

85. *State v François Baraca,* 9 Feb. 1748, LHC.

86. Chauvin Succession, 5 Apr. 1747, LHC.

87. *Seller v Jassemin,* 14 Sept. 1736, LHC; *Bellisle v Louise Bertiche,* 20 Nov. 1737, LHC; *Joseph Larche v Angelique,* 19 July 1739, LHC; *Coustilhas Estate v Hypolite,* 21 Jan. 1741, LHC.

88. *Gueydon v Roujot,* 30 Aug. 1748, LHC.

89. Du Pratz, *History of Louisiana,* 386.

90. *State v Babette,* 9 Oct. 1765, LHC.

91. *Ferrand v Judice,* 17 May 1746, LHC.

92. Philip J. Schwarz, *Twice Condemned: Slaves and the Criminal Law of Virginia, 1705–1865* (Baton Rouge: Louisiana State Univ. Press, 1988), 15, 39.

93. For an introduction to the subject, see Price, ed., *Maroon Societies.*.

94. *State v Sansouci,* 31 Mar. 1727, LHC, a slave who reported that he had lived at Natanpallé, where fifteen men and one Indian woman had sworn to defend themselves to the last person with their eleven guns.

95. Declaration by François Livet, 30 Aug. 1736, LHC; Declaration by Jacques Roquigny, 2 Sept. 1736, LHC; Declaration by Overseer Lange, 2 Sept. 1736, LHC; *State v Guela,*

4–12 Jan. 1737, LHC. Evidence that there was an ordinance to report marronage is in Declaration of Benac, 15 Dec. 1746, LHC, which was made "in accord with the ordinance."

96. *State v Lafleur*, 11 Apr. 1738, LHC.

97. Petition of Livet, 26 May 1738, LHC, to apprehend maroon; Report of Coustilhas' Executor Gerard Pery, 12 Dec. 1738, LHC.

98. *Louis Congo v Maroons*, 17 Aug. 1726, LHC; *State v Maroons*, 10 Jan. 1741, LHC; *Fleuriau v Maroons*, 19 Mar. 1737, LHC.

99. Declaration of Anne Coudra, 7 Feb. 1745, LHC, on the barn; Letter of Jacques Fazende, 17 Feb. 1745, LHC; Deposition on Raguet Fire, 25 Feb. 1745, LHC.

100. *Nicolas Barbin v Pradel*, 26 July to 5 Aug. 1752, LHC, demanding restitution for the canoe.

101. Procuration of Andrés to Jean Gonzalle, 7 June 1739, LHC; Petition of Jean Gonzalle, 15, 20 June 1739, LHC.

102. Deposition by Chaperon, 7 Nov. 1739, LHC, containing no explanation of why it was made months after the fact.

103. Chaperon's Procuration to Destréhan, 1 Sept. 1744, LHC, to seize slaves.

104. Declaration of Dupart, 10 Mar. 1747, LHC.

105. Declarations of Manuel and John, 22 Mar. 1748, LHC.

106. Petition by Lafrénière to Arrest Vagrants, 3 Sept. 1763, LHC. *State v François*, 14 Nov. 1764, LHC, a case of false arrest by an overseer, a very rare mention of a pass in the record. When the Jesuits' slaves asked for a pass in Membrède's henhouse picket case, described in a later chapter, Piquery led them personally rather than writing them a pass.

107. Vere T. Daly, *A Short History of the Guyanese People* (London: Macmillan Education, 1975), 143–52.

108. *State v Sainbas et al.*, 25 Jan. to 4 Feb. 1764, LHC.

109. *State v Nicolas*, 10–14 Feb. 1764, LHC.

110. *State v François*, 17 Feb., 3 Mar. 1764, LHC.

111. *State v Jeannot*, 12–14 Apr. 1764, LHC.

112. Thus, the argument by Gerald W. Mullin that "acculturated slaves . . . were the most successful rebels" and runaways in eighteenth-century Virginia is not borne out by the evidence in Louisiana. See *Flight and Rebellion: Slave Resistance in Eighteenth-Century Virginia* (Oxford: Oxford Univ. Press, 1972), 89. Several problems mar Mullin's book. For example, the "acculturated" are deemed "most successful" because they formed 60 percent of those advertised in newspapers, but this percentage would seem merely to equal their approximate percentage of the population, even if we accept without debate Mullin's questionable measurement of acculturation, a term he uses interchangeably with "assimilation," another problem. See 89–112 for his entire discussion of marronage.

113. *State v Louis*, 3 Sept. *passim* to 10 Sept. 1764, LHC.

114. *State v Cézar*, 20 June *passim* to 24 July 1764, LHC.

115. Pierre Vaissière, *Saint-Domingue: la société et la vie créoles sous l'Ancien Régime, 1629–1789* (Paris: Librairie Académique, 1909), 235–49.

116. Since it is frequently asserted by historians that New Orleanians did not know that the colony had been transferred to Spain until 1765 or even later, it is necessary to point out that while officially the colonists were not informed of the transfer until 1765, it was an accomplished fact—at least on paper—and publicly known in France before Lafrénière sailed for New Orleans in 1763.

117. For a different interpretation, see Hall, *Africans in Colonial Louisiana*, 202–3.

118. Ibid., 203.

119. Philip D. Morgan, "Colonial South Carolina Runaways: Their Significance for Slave Culture," *Slavery and Abolition* 6 (1985): 57–78.

CHAPTER 4. TWO COMMUNITIES, ONE CREOLE SOCIETY

1. Lois Green Carr, Russell R. Menard, and Lorena Walsh, *Robert Cole's World: Agriculture and Society in Early Maryland* (Chapel Hill: Univ. of North Carolina Press, 1991), 158.

2. The judicial records indicate that all slaves spoke French within a few years of their arrival. See also Joseph L. Tisch, *French in Louisiana: A Study of the Historical Development of the French Language in Louisiana* (New Orleans: A. F. Laborde and Sons, 1959), 44–45. A patois was probably introduced to some regions by Haitian refugees in the late eighteenth or early nineteenth century. Kniffen et al., *Historic Indian Tribes of Louisiana*, 97, 124–26, comments on the Mobilian language derived from an Indian dialect and spoken by many individuals of all colors in the region.

3. Declaration of Antoine Bruslé, 7 Mar. 1733, LHC.

4. McGowan has suggested that masters ruled by "raw violence" before 1731, but "the slave system after the Natchez revolt bore the imprint of a humane consciousness" because of specific reforms introduced during the final phase of Bienville's service. See "Creation of A Slave Society," 118. His main evidence is the book by Antoine-Simon Le Page Du Pratz, but that writer did not present his work as advocacy of humane reform and his advice was aimed primarily at manipulating slaves into obedience.

5. Census by Governors Ulloa and Aubry, May 1766, AGI, SD, 2585:1–26v. A microfilm copy in the Historic New Orleans Collection was consulted. Unfortunately, slaves were enumerated only by status, not by sex or age.

6. Inquest of 23 Nov. 1765, LHC. See the misdated judgment of 9 November. He was condemned for murdering himself, and his corpse was hanged in the plaza upside down for twenty-four hours, and then thrown in a sewer.

7. For a particularly entangled situation, see *St. Martin v Duguay Executors*, 25 Oct. 1735; *Bruslé v Duguay Executors*, 26 Oct. 1735, LHC; Succession of Bruslé, 8 Oct. 1738, LHC; *Dumanoir v Bruslé Estate*, 5 Jan. 1740, LHC; Judgment of 6 Feb. 1740, LHC; Receipt by Dumanoir, 26 Feb. 1740, LHC. Petition by Marguerite Piemon, 8 Oct. 1738, LHC.

8. Remonstrance of Widow Bunel, 27 Jan. 1738, LHC. This is in response to Petition of Gaspard and Marie-Françoise Joumard, 3 Jan. 1738, LHC, date of sale given as "1725" in error.

9. Remonstrance of Widow Bunel, 27 Jan. 1738, LHC.

10. Petition of Jean-Baptiste Dumanoir, 1 Feb. 1738, LHC.

11. See, for example, Judicial Lease of Renaud Succession Slaves, 31 Oct. 1763, LHC.

12. *Delisle Dupart v Jung*, 31 July, 5 Aug. 1752, LHC.

13. *Pierre De Lorme v (Jacques or Jean-Baptiste?) Chenier*, 22 Apr. 1740, LHC.

14. *Vielle v Pery*, 5 Oct. (calendered 6 Oct.), 1741, LHC.

15. Antoine and Jacques Fazende to Chantalou, 19 Aug. 1752, LHC; Protest of Layssard, 3 Nov. 1753, *LHQ* 22 (1939): 1198–99, original not found in LHC; *Fazende Heirs v Layssard*, 22 Mar. 1760, LHC, and Receipt to Layssard, 3 Sept. 1760, LHC, may be related.

16. *Delapommeraye v Dubois*, 31 Jan. 1763, LHC.

17. Petition of De Morant, 3 June 1737, LHC. The document is too decayed to determine the outcome.

18. *La Croix v [Mathurin and Nicolas?] Dupré (Terrebonne)*, 24 May 1763, LHC.

19. *Chaperon v Pery[?]* [document is disintegrated], 15 Mar. 1745, LHC.

20. See Report of Runaway Jean-Pierre by Michel Brosset, 24 June 1746; Reports of Runaway Manuel by Michel Brosset and Jacques Judice, 3, 17 Aug. 1746, LHC.

21. *Brosset v Chaperon*, 23 Aug. 1746, LHC.

22. *Father Dagobert v Luquet*, 11 June 1764, Sheriff's Execution, 17 Sept. 1764, *LHQ* 5 (1922): 58–62.

23. *State v Jupiter Louis Gamelle*, 20 Feb. *passim* to 21 Mar. 1744, LHC; also Prevost's Declaration, 2 Feb. 1744, LHC.

24. Mark Tushnet, *The American Law of Slavery, 1810–1860: Considerations of Humanity and Interest* (Princeton: Princeton Univ. Press, 1981), 44.

25. Ibid., 33.

26. *Bauré v Fossier [Faussier, Faucier]*, 10, 13, 19 Jan. and 10 Mar. 1753, LHC.

27. Remonstrance of 2 Sept. 1724, LHC.

28. *State v Degoute (Fleury), Periche, Jacques, and Jacob*, 7 Mar. to 25 Apr. 1764, LHC.

29. Gayarré, *History of Louisiana*, 2:361–67, Article 19.

30. Ibid., Articles 17 and 20.

31. Ibid., 2:366. The word "police" in this context meant general public vigilance, especially by military pickets.

32. Ibid., 2:365.

33. Ibid., 2:365–66. Two other articles override the king's code. Article 22 drastically raises the penalties set in the Code Noir for masters who permit Negroes to assemble on their plantations, including condemnation to the galleys for life on the second offense. Article 10 abolishes the provisions of the Code Noir's Article 34 for free blacks to pay fines for harboring slave runaways: they shall now automatically become slaves of the king.

34. Ibid. Articles 16 and 17 unceremoniously scrap Article 15 of the king's code governing the market transactions of blacks, setting more enforceable penalties. On the guns, see "Ordinance Regulating the Bearing of Arms, 1744," trans. Tamara D. McGinnis, *LH* 29 (1988): 228.

35. Gayarré, *History of Louisiana*, 2:362, Article 3. For discussion of a similar code in a neighboring English colony from this same period, see Wood, *Black Majority*, 323–26.

36. Shoemaker Dupard would not even take on an orphan until a planter compensated the artisan with the labor of a slave for one year, an act of charity for the orphan's

benefit. See Contract of Apprenticeship, 9 Oct. 1737, LHC. For examples of payment to artisans for training slaves and white boys, see *Darieux v Gaillard*, 30 May 1768, LHC; and Deposition by Villars, 14 Apr. 1768, LHC.

37. Noyon Succession, 22 Oct. 1763, LHC; *Marette v Louis and Jean*, 9 June 1748, LHC; interrogation of 10 June.

38. Contract of Apprenticeship between Father Dagobert and Jean Roy, 29 Aug. 1763, LHC; Affidavit of Dame Le Veuf, 12 Oct. 1765, LHC; Contract of Alexandre Boré and William Burdon ("Baudon"), 26 Sept. 1763; Contract of Macnemara and Dortolle, 13 Mar. 1767, LHC. French colonists evidently continued to wear wigs on special occasions until the French Revolution. See also *Villemont v Villars Dubreuil*, 28 May 1766, LHC, in which Dubreuil's apprenticed mulatto cooper Baptiste was the court's first seizure in this big bankruptcy; or *Marette v Louis and Jean*, 9 June 1748, LHC, included testimony of 10 June by eighteen-year-old Louis apprenticed to the hospital by Dubreuil to become a surgeon.

39. Henry P. Dart, "The Slave Depot of the Company of the Indies at New Orleans," *LHQ* 9 (1926): 286–87. For a description of the property as it changed over time, see Samuel Wilson Jr., "The Plantation of the Company of the Indies," *LH* 31 (1990): 161–91.

40. Hubert to the Council, 26 Oct. 1717, AN, AC, C13A, 5:53.

41. Delachaise to the Company, 6, 10 Sept. 1723, AN, AC, C13A, 7:42–42v; Delachaise and Périer to the Company, 25 Mar. 1729, AN, AC, C13A, 11:330v.

42. Salmon to Maurepas, 16 Jan. 1732, AN, AC, C13A, 15:13–14, reported that the Company owned 148 men, 68 women, and 18 children, plus several infants, the number of which I have estimated at 7. Salmon argued that the slaves were essential for working on forts, rowing, building barracks, "and the little boys could be apprenticed as blacksmiths, locksmiths, carpenters, masons." Salmon later informed Maurepas, 3 Sept. 1739, AN, AC, C13A, 24:160 bis verso, that maroons and slaves of poor quality had been sold for 63,070 livres, leaving 79 men and an unspecified number of women and children. See folios 160v–160 bis verso for the whole report.

43. Condition of the King's Negroes, 1 Jan. 1760, AN, AC, C13A, 42:66.

44. Company Report of 25 July 1725, AN, AC, B, 43:535–37, complained of the poor treatment of company slaves and established new regulations for their use. Périer and Salmon to Maurepas, 5 Dec. 1731, AN, AC, C13A, 14:30–32v, complained that the company wished to eliminate one-third of its Negroes, but these were trained in essential métiers, and could not be replaced by whites, who could not work during the hot temperatures of half the year. See Du Pratz, *History of Louisiana*, 186–87, on savings to the crown of fifty thousand livres against the ten thousand it cost to maintain. In response to the report quoted at the head of this chapter, Rouillé to Kerlérec and Dauberville, 27 Nov. 1753, AN, AC, B, 97:350v, ruled against any budget for the king's Negroes and barred excuses to disobey the order to sell them; but Dauberville to Rouillé, 4 July 1754, AN, AC, C13A, 38:147–49, reported on the upkeep of the Negroes, their valuable services, and the necessity to postpone the order to sell them. Dubreuil's Bill for Improvements of the King's Plantation, 2 Feb. 1759, AN, AC, C13A, 41:415–18v, included the building of three cabins, one 30 X 19 and

two 24 X 18, "all enclosed with stakes." Kerlérec to Berryer, 15 Aug. 1760, AN, AC, C13A, 42:64–65v, advocated sale of the remaining slaves.

45. Bienville to Maurepas, 4 Feb. 1743, AN, AC, C13A, 28:38v–39. Louboey to Maurepas, 2 Apr. 1746, AN, AC, C 13A, 30:176–78v, which reported that the best workmen were driven off by Lenormant's stringent financial policy; Michel to Rouillé, 18 Jan. 1752, AN, AC, C13A, 36:251–51v, complained that ship captains seduced away labor of "soldiers, habitants, [and] negroes"; Governor Kerlérec to Rouillé, 19 June 1752, AN, AC, C13A, 36:149v–50, tried to find some skilled whites to take with him to Louisiana. James Oglethorpe's intention to exclude slaves from Georgia in the 1730s was meant to avoid these conditions and create a colony based upon free white labor. See Phinizy Spalding, "James Edward Oglethorpe's Quest for an American Zion," in *Forty Years of Diversity: Essays on Colonial Georgia*, ed. Harvey H. Jackson and Phinizy Spalding (Athens: Univ. of Georgia Press, 1984), 69.

46. Wood, *Black Majority*, 195–233.

47. The virtually direct connection between Maurepas's failure to reestablish the African slave supply to Louisiana and Salmon's request for involuntary white peasants, the next best thing, was quite explicit and summed up the whole situation perfectly. See Salmon to Maurepas, and Bienville and Salmon to Maurepas, 28, 29 June 1740, AN, AC, C13A, 25:185, 29. It should also be pointed out that Maurepas was trying to induce soldiers to stay permanently in Louisiana; see Maurepas to Karrer, 8 Aug. 1734, AN, AC, B, 60:226; and Bienville and Salmon to Maurepas, 8 Apr. 1735, AN, AC, C13A, 20:12, on the effect of land offers; and Bienville and Salmon to Maurepas, 15 Apr. 1736, AN, AC, C13A, 21:51.

48. Based on an estimate of the clergy derived from Abbé de Lisle-Dieu to Rouillé, c.1752, AN, AC, C13A, 36:337v–38, reporting that eleven Capuchins served the colony. See Wolfe, *Ursulines in New Orleans*, 10, 19–21, 39, reporting arrivals but not deaths, from which it may be deduced that about twelve nuns were alive near the end of the French regime; and Delanglez, *French Jesuits in Lower Louisiana*, 75–79, who found eight Jesuits in the 1720s but does not give a precise figure for the later period, so I have guessed arbitrarily that they still had the same number at the end of the period. Subtracting about five priests who would have posted outside New Orleans, that leaves an estimated twenty-six people. On the social role of the clergy see Jean Quéniart, *Les hommes, l'église, et Dieu dans la France du XVIIIe siècle* (Paris: Hachette, 1978).

49. Capuchins have been the targets of some exaggerated contempt by historians. See E. Preclin and E. Jarry, *Histoire de l'Eglise depuis les origines jusqu'a nos jours*, vol. 19, pt. 2, *Les luttes politiques et doctrinales aux XVII et XVIII siècles* (Saint Dizier: Bloud and Gay, 1956), 616.

50. Ibid., 492–93, 514–16, 611–23, 680–702. Marie-Françoise Boisrenaud, chaperone of the small shipment of girls sent by the king in 1704, was the first to provide education to the young Indian slave girls kept by unmarried men; see Giraud, *History of French Louisiana*, 1:178–79.

51. Bienville to Pontchartrain, 25 Feb. 1708, AN, AC, C13A, 2:109–11. Good discussions are found in Delanglez, *French Jesuits in Lower Louisiana*, 109–11; and Baudier, *Catholic Church in Louisiana*, 63–68. On the success of the Jesuits in creating the image of the

"bon sauvage" in Louisiana, see John R. Carpenter, *Histoire de la littérature française sur la Louisiane de 1673 jusqu'a 1766* (Paris: A. G. Nizet, 1966), 341–44.

52. Anonymous Statement on the Church in Louisiana, c. 1725, AN, AC, C13A, 11:217–19. See O'Neill, *Church and State in French Colonial Louisiana*, 118–26, 164–74; Claude L. Vogel, *The Capuchins in French Louisiana, 1722–1766* (Washington, D.C.: Catholic Univ. of America, 1928), 29.

53. "Royal Brevet of August 17, 1726," *PLHS* 4 (1908): 100–101.

54. Treaty with the Jesuits, 20 Feb. 1726, AN, AC, A, 22:155–63. See Article 24.

55. Raphael to Raguet, 28 Dec. 1726, AN, AC, C13A, 10:47–48v; Périer and Delachaise to Company, 22 Apr. 1727, AN, AC, C13A, 10:172v–73, warned of jealousy since the Jesuits would be paid eight hundred livres compared to Capuchins' six hundred; Council of Louisiana to the Company, 23 Apr. 1725, AN, AC, C13A, 9:125v–26, on the Dominican.

56. Royal Memoir, 1722, AN, AC, C13A, 6:410–14v. See also O'Neill, *Church and State in French Colonial Louisiana*, 110–13, 142, 182, 233–34.

57. O'Neill, *Church and State in French Colonial Louisiana*, 283–87; Baudier, *Catholic Church in Louisiana*, 90–99.

58. Périer and Delachaise to the Company, 2 Nov. 1727, AN, AC, C13A, 10:191v; Mother Tranchepain to Raguet, 5 Jan. 1728, AN, AC, C13A, 11:273; Bienville and Salmon to Maurepas, 15 May 1733, AN, AC, C13A, 16:14v–16.

59. For a description of their land, see Treaty with the Jesuits, AN, AC, A, 22:160v–61v.

60. Delanglez, *French Jesuits in Lower Louisiana*, 296–99.

61. Bienville and Salmon to Maurepas, 20 Apr. 1734, AN, AC, C13B, 1:171, reporting that Raphael's death "rendu les pouvoirs aux Jésuites."

62. For an interesting contrast, see John J. TePaske, *The Governorship of Spanish Florida, 1700–1763* (Durham, N.C.: Duke Univ. Press, 1964), 159–92, showing a contest between well-established creole clerics and invading peninsulares.

63. Wolfe, *Ursulines in New Orleans*, 5–43, for the foundation, and the discouragement of converting local girls; the first two local nuns were orphans in 1759 and 1768. Delanglez, *French Jesuits in Lower Louisiana*, 286, shows that girls were not encouraged to become nuns, congruent with colonial policy, for female colonists were too rare to be permitted to escape creole-producing responsibilities. The only male born in colonial Louisiana to become a priest was raised and educated in France and served there until returning to Louisiana decades later. See Charles E. O'Neill, S.J., *Viel: Louisiana's First-Born Author, with "Evandre," the First Literary Creation of a Native of the Mississippi Valley* (Lafayette: Center for Louisiana Studies, Univ. of Southwestern Louisiana, 1991), 8–27. For a different view, see also Mary V. Miceli, "The Christianization of French Colonial Louisiana: A General View of Church and State in the Context of Eighteenth-Century French Colonization and a Theory of Mission," *Southern Studies* 21 (1982): 384–97.

64. The Ursulines were the most acquisitive. They bought a second plantation in 1751, and their big estate on the left bank between the town center and Tchoupitoulas would be subdivided and sold off to form its own faubourg ("Les Religieuses") early in the nineteenth century. See Vaudreuil and Michel to Rouillé, 17 May 1751, AN, AC, C13A, 35:5–6. The promotion of slavery began very early. See Father Gravier

to Pontchartrain?, c. 1706, AN, AC, C13A, 1:570v; Father Raphael to Abbé Raguet, 15 Sept. 1725, AN, AC, C13A, 8:412. The clergy's influence is clear from a similar plea sent to Raguet by the governor; see Périer to Raguet, 25 Apr. 1727, AN, AC, C13A, 10:211–12v.

65. Delanglez, *French Jesuits in Lower Louisiana*, 131, on the Ursulines; 287–99, on school and indigo; 375–490 on Indians.

66. See Herman W. Konrad, *A Jesuit Hacienda in Colonial Mexico: Santa Lucia, 1576–1767* (Stanford, Calif.: Stanford Univ. Press, 1980), 114–25, for a description of this phenomenon, which was poorly recorded in New Orleans because notarial records for the early period have not survived.

67. The earliest known defense of the slave trade published in French put much emphasis on Biblical justifications and the supposed Christianization of slaves in America, and the writer's winning trump was the fact that the clergy had a long and distinguished tradition of slaveholding. See [Bellon de Saint-Quentin], *Dissertation sur la Traite et le Commerce des Négres* (Paris: n.p, 1764), 44–52.

68. Herbert S. Klein, *Slavery in the Americas: A Comparative Study of Virginia and Cuba* (1967; reprint, Chicago: Ivan R. Dee, 1989), 88. Klein focuses on the Spanish Catholic clergy but this comment is intended to refer to the Catholic Church in general.

69. St. Louis Cathedral Baptisms, 1744–1753, Archdiocese of New Orleans, Archives, New Orleans.

70. Rhys Isaac, *The Transformation of Virginia, 1740–1790* (Chapel Hill: Univ. of North Carolina Press, 1982), 120.

71. Gabriel Debien, "La christianisation des esclaves des Antilles françaises aux XVIIe et XVIIIe siècles," *RHAF* 20 (1967): 531–41.

72. Ibid., 548–55; and Gabriel Debien, "La christianisation des esclaves des Antilles françaises aux XVIIe et XVIIIe siècles," pt. 2, *RHAF* 21 (1968): 99–101.

73. An Alsation officer, Golberry, quoted in Debien, "Christianisation des esclaves," 547–48.

74. [J. Félix Carteau], *Soirées bermudiennes ou entretiens sur les événements qui ont opéré la ruine de la partie française de l'isle Saint-Domingue* (Bordeaux: Pellier-Lawalle, 1802), 81.

75. Ibid.

76. Albert J. Raboteau, *Slave Religion: The "Invisible Institution" in the Antebellum South* (New York: Oxford Univ. Press, 1978), 127.

77. Free blacks sponsored the certain exceptions. In several cases, no surname is given for one of two sponsors, probably indicating a slave.

78. For example, whites can be certainly identified as sponsoring only three (or 4.8 percent) of sixty-three blacks baptized between 1 July and 1 October 1790. Unfortunately, later priests were less careful about recording the racial classification of sponsors. Presumably, all those not designated white were black, but some instances in this register are ambiguous. None of these can be identified in other sacramental registers, which strongly suggests that they were free blacks, like so many other sponsors in this era.

79. For a different view, see Sister Mary Veronica Miceli, "The Influence of the Roman Catholic Church on Slavery in Colonial Louisiana under French Domination, 1718–1763" (Ph.D. diss., Tulane Univ., 1979), 57–63.

80. Arnold, *Unequal Laws unto a Savage Race*, 121–25.

81. Déclaration du Roy Concernant les Ordres Religieux et gens de Mainmorte etablis aux Colonies françoises de L'amerique, 25 Nov. 1743, Historic New Orleans Collection, Manuscript Division, Mss. 352.

82. Baudier, *Catholic Church in Louisiana*, 163.

83. A good description of the jealousy they could arouse is found in Konrad, *Jesuit Hacienda in Colonial Mexico*, 1–11.

84. Petition by the Attorney General, 9 July 1763, LHC, to expel the Jesuits for encroaching upon rights of the Capuchins by baptizing and marrying their own slaves, overpowering other missionaries, disturbing the peace, and in general violating restrictions on their letters patent of 1727. It is notable that all recent sales of Negroes by them were declared null, presumably because authorities believed that the fathers would try to anticipate the ruling and sell off slaves. See also Albert H. Biever, S.J., *The Jesuits in New Orleans and the Mississippi Valley* (New Orleans: Archbishopric, 1924), 60–63; Charles T. Soniat, "The Title to the Jesuits' Plantation," *PLHS* 5 (1911): 19–26, on the auction of the plantation in six lots.

85. Sale of the Jesuits' Effects, 18 July and *passim*, 1763, AN, AC, C13A, 43:331–52.

86. Clark, *New Orleans, 1718–1812*, 107–25.

87. This follows Surrey, *Commerce of Louisiana*, 97–151, although she exaggerates the amount of currency circulating at ten million. See Minutes of the Council 5 Sept. 1719, AN, AC, C13A, 5:333–34, on the first terms of slave purchase. Key documents concerning currency in Louisiana include Delachaise to the Company, 6 Sept. 1723, AN, AC, C13A, 7:15v–16v, for his assault on card money upon his arrival; Périer and Delachaise to the Company, 2 Nov. 1727, AN, AC, C13A, 10:193–93v, on the failure of copper coins; Périer and Delachaise to the Company, 31 July 1728, AN, AC, C13A, 11:54–55, reporting torture and condemnation to the galleys of a clerk, Duval, for counterfeiting one-thousand-livre notes, a rare example. See Report to the King, 1 Apr. 1744, AN, AC, C13A, 28:333–40, on Salmon's downfall for issuing too many bills of exchange that circulated as currency; Vaudreuil to Maurepas, 6 Jan. 1745, AN, AC, C13A, 29:27v–30, approving devaluation as strong medicine; but in Vaudreuil to Maurepas, 30 Oct. 1745, AN, AC, C13A, 29:64–65, he pleaded that it caused suffering; Plea of Négociants of New Orleans, 17 Feb. 1753, AN, AC, C13A, 38:233–34, to fix the currency; and the Anonymous Englishman to Maurepas on Louisiana Currency in 1754, AN, AC, C13A, 38:225–32v; Commissaire Ordonnateur Foucault to Choiseul, 12 June 1762, AN, AC, C13A, 43:5–6, reported 6,783,476 livres in circulation and advocated retirement; Summary Table of Abuses . . . by Thiton de Silègues, 12 Dec. 1761, AN, AC, C13A, 42:254–56v, blamed the ordonnateurs; Foucault to Choiseul, 29 Sept. 1766, AN, AC, C13A, 45:213v, on suspensions of letters of exchange: there is no faith in the king's word.

88. Sale of Captured Slaves, 27 Sept. 1758, AN, AC, C13A, 40:189–98; Marine Clerk Brochard to Ministers Massiac and Normand de Mézy, 9 Oct. 1758, AN, AC, C13A, 40:277–82v.

89. Succession Sale of the Estate of Dubreuil, 23 Oct. 1758, in Dart, "Career of Dubreuil," 291–331.

90. See for example, Sale of Delapommeray Slaves, 2 June 1758, LHC, in which sixty-

five slaves sold for 152,834 livres. On the Jesuits, see Delanglez, *French Jesuits in Lower Louisiana*, 515–16.

91. Ordinances, 1 Oct. 1741, LHC.

92. *Bauré v Joseph Carrière*, 4 Dec. 1762, LHC; Carriere Family Meeting, 7 Dec. 1762, LHC; Appeal by Joseph Carriere et. al., 5 Feb. 1763, LHC; *Carrière v Bauré*, 5 Mar. 1763, LHC; Carrière Estate Partition, 26 Apr. 1763, LHC.

93. Petition by Carrière Minors, 4 June 1763, LHC; *Broutin v Carrière Minors*, 1 Oct. 1763, LHC. The case also shows why the office of tutorship was increasingly unpopular. For attempted refusals of tutorships see Petition of Jacques Livet, 5 Oct. 1748, LHC; Rivard Succession, 2 Sept. and 11 Nov. 1752, LHC; *François Briant v Adam Succession*, 14, 22 Mar. 1764, LHC, to be relieved of minors who have cost him four thousand livres; *Fusilier Delaclaire v Pontalba Succession*, 1 June 1765, LHC, to quit a duty that earned only ingratitude, and he was "about to abandon New Orleans forever" anyway; Bunel Succession, 11 Dec. 1764 (filed 17 Oct.) and 1 Feb. 1765, LHC; and Langlois Succession, 9 Dec. 1747 *passim* to 11 Nov. 1752, LHC, in which two tutors in a row refused to serve on account of illiteracy, but the family forced the second to do his duty, which included apprenticing out the youngest boys.

CHAPTER 5. A NORTH AMERICAN SLAVE SOCIETY

1. Tannenbaum, *Slave and Citizen*, 55, 63.

2. Ibid., 65.

3. For the most succinct general critique, see Mintz, *Caribbean Transformations*, 68–75. For more specialized refutations, see Robert B. Toplin, ed., *Slavery and Race Relations in Latin America* (Wesport, Conn.: Greenwood Press, 1974); and, especially, Marvin Harris, *Patterns of Race in the Americas* (1964; reprint, New York: W. W. Norton, 1974). For the very best case possible for Tannenbaum's thesis, or rather for his own qualified interpretation of it, see Eugene D. Genovese, "Materialism and Idealism in the History of Negro Slavery in the Americas," in *In Red and Black: Marxian Explorations in Southern and Afro-American History*, by Genovese (Knoxville: Univ. of Tennessee Press, 1984). For the most recent work epitomizing both the strengths and still greater dangers of the cultural model, see David Hackett Fischer, *Albion's Seed: Four British Folkways in America* (New York: Oxford Univ. Press, 1989).

4. This echoes Harris, *Patterns of Race in the Americas*, 81.

5. Sidney W. Mintz, *Sweetness and Power: The Place of Sugar in Modern History* (New York: Viking, 1985), 154.

6. Ibid., 180.

7. Hall, *Africans in Colonial Louisiana*, 156–200.

8. Ibid., 168. Further research may well reveal that families in early New Orleans were less likely to be disrupted than in Saint Domingue, but simply because slaveowning families took pains to keep their work force as intact as possible in their own interest.

9. *Slave and Citizen*, 118.

10. Peytraud, *L'esclavage aux Antilles françaises*, 7–11.

11. Vaissière, *Saint-Domingue*, 21, 116, 153.

12. Moreau de Saint-Méry, *Description topographique*, 1:33–34. Moreau de Saint-Méry is echoed by Vaissière, *Saint-Domingue*, 55–92, 255–75.

13. Gabriel Debien, *Les esclaves aux Antilles françaises, XVIIe–XVIIIe siècles* (Basse-Terre: Sociétés d'Histoire de la Guadeloupe et de la Martinique, 1974), 106–17.

14. Moreau de Saint-Méry, *Description topographique*, 1:47–55. Congos became very numerous by 1791 despite their generally bad reputation, light color, and supposed disinclination to marry and reproduce. For the African ethnic mixture of a large sample of slaves in Guadeloupe, see Nicole Vanony-Frisch, "Les esclaves de la Guadeloupe a là fin de l'Ancien Régime d'après les sources notariales, 1770–1789," reprint, *Bulletin de la Société d'Histoire de la Guadeloupe* 63–64 (1985): 32–36.

15. Mémoire concernant la Louisiane et Saint Domingue, c. 1749, AN, AC, C13A, 33: 163–73.

16. Ibid., 170v.

17. Ibid., 169.

18. Vaissière, *Saint-Domingue*, 128–52.

19. Peytraud, *L'esclavage aux Antilles françaises*, 28–29.

20. C. H. Haring, *The Spanish Empire in America* (1947; reprint, New York: Harcourt, Brace, and World, 1963), 194–99.

21. A random sample of 258 testators in the New Orleans Notarial Archives between 1771 and 1805 revealed the place of birth for 233 of them, and half were born in France and only 12 percent were born in New Orleans. All wills were canvassed in randomly selected legajos from the New Orleans Notarial Archive, those of Jean-Baptiste Garic, 1771–75; Andres Almonester, 1771–75; Rafael Perdomo, 1785–86; Carlos Ximenes, 1791–93; François Broutin, 1792–94; and Narcisse Broutin, 1800–1802, 1804–5.

22. [Michel-René Hilliard d'Auberteuil], *Considérations sur l'état présent de la colonie française de Saint-Domingue: ouvrage politique et législatif*, 2 vols. (Paris: Grangé, 1776–77), 2:35–36.

23. Pierre Pluchon, *La route des esclaves: négriers et bois d'ébène au XVIIIe siècle* (Paris: Hachette, 1980), 230–33.

24. For the highest expression of this paternalism, see [Poyen Ste.-Marie], *De l'exploitation des sucreries, ou conseils d'un vieux planteur aux jeunes agriculteurs des colonies*, 3d ed. (Point-à-Pitre, Guadeloupe: L'Imprimerie de la République, 1802).

25. Mettas, in *Répertoire des expéditions négrières françaises*, vol. 2, indicates no voyages in this period and none are mentioned in imperial reports, which accords with Jonathas Darby's flat statement that there were none, in "Chapter of Colonial History," 567.

26. Maurepas to Bienville and Salmon, 24 Aug. 1734, AN, AC, B, 61:649v–50, on the proposal by free Negro Larue to import mixed cargoes from Saint Domingue, including slaves. See Gaston Martin, *Nantes au XVIIIe siècle: l'ère des négriers, 1714–1774, d'après des documents inédits* (Paris: Librairie Félix Alcan, 1931),176–83, on the debilitating struggle between the company and the independent armateurs of Nantes. This book contains the best description of the trade. For a rare general commercial account of a slaver's voyage in 1743, see Robert Forster, *Merchants, Landlords, Magistrates: The Depont Family in Eighteenth-Century France* (Baltimore: Johns Hopkins Univ. Press, 1980), 6–7.

27. This extensive correspondence begins with Maurepas to Fayet, 8 Aug. 1734, AN, AC, B, 61:466; Maurepas to Bienville and Salmon, 24 Aug. 1734, AN, AC, B, 61:649 *passim* to 679. Maurepas solicited bids from slavers but rejected them as too costly to

both king and inhabitants; see Maurepas to Rasteau, 15 Mar. 1735, AN, AC, B, 62:148v–49; Maurepas to Bourgine, 29 Mar. 1735, AN, AC, B, 62:153v; Maurepas to Orry, 10 Sept. 1737, AN, AC, B, 65:90v–91; Maurepas to Bienville and Salmon, 24 Mar. 1738, AN, AC, B, 66:318–18v. His successors had no better luck; see Rouillé to Keeper of the Seals, 19 Apr. 1754, AN, AC, B, 100:84–84v; and Machault to Premord, 30 Sept. 1756, AN, AC, B, 104:381–81v.

28. Maurepas to Orry, 27 Sept. 1735, AN, AC, B, 62:84v–85v.

29. Mettas, *Répertoire des expéditions négrières françaises*, vol. 2, voyage number 2170; and the very extensive correspondence that went into promoting this voyage, which begins in AN, AC with Louisiana Planters to Bienville and Salmon, and New Orleans Merchants' Proposal to Form Slave Trade Company, 18, 20 Feb. 1738, AN, AC, F3, 242:n.p.; continuing throughout until at least Maurepas to Governor Vaudreuil and Commissaire Ordonnateur Lenormant, 30 Apr. 1746, AN, AC, B83:312. The company opposed the voyage until it secured a large cash advance against purchases by the armateurs in Africa; see Maurepas to Bienville and Salmon, AN, AC, B72:472–72v; and Maurepas to Dalcourt, 2 Oct. 1741, AN, AC, B73:162v. Gaston Martin, *Histoire de l'esclavage dans les colonies françaises* (Paris: Presses Universitaires de France, 1948), 25, writes that supply was always inferior to demand in the French colonies. But the prolonged hiatus in the slave supply to New Orleans was unique. Given the degree of attention lavished upon the voyage of 1743 in imperial reports it is unlikely that other cargoes would have gone unreported. A unique case of the capture and sale of thirty-three contraband slaves was cause for a special report to France by the governor and intendant. See Vaudreuil and Dauberville to Maurepas, 10 Nov. 1748, AN, AC, C13A, 32:20–22. Demand was so strong that they fetched an average of nineteen hundred livres at the auction. None of the many proposals for slave shipments in the 1750s and 1760s found in this section of AN, AC, C13A were undertaken.

30. Barbier, *Chronique de la régence*, 4:401–3, 414–15, 422–42, 453–54.

31. On the factors that should have impelled more peasants to emigrate and resettle in the colonies, see Le Roy Ladurie, *Peasants of Languedoc*, 243–50, 255–58, 298–99.

32. Maurepas to Vaudreuil, 11 Nov. 1748, AN, AC, B, 87:273–73v; and Vaudreuil and Michel to Rouillé, 20 May 1751, AN, AC, C13A, 35:13v–16v, on the likelihood that soldiers would take advantage of the settlement program to retire from the army early only to flee Louisiana.

33. Dumont De Montigny, "History of Louisiana," 5:119.

34. Geggus, "Sugar and Coffee Cultivation in Saint Domingue and the Shaping of the Slave Labor Force," in *Cultivation and Culture: Labor and the Shaping of Slave Life in the Americas*, ed. Ira Berlin and Philip D. Morgan (Charlottesville: Univ. Press of Virginia, 1993), 88–90; and Gaspar, "Sugar Cultivation and Slave Life in Antigua before 1800," in *Cultivation and Culture*, 110–16.

35. Fogel, *Without Consent or Contract*, 114–53.

36. Ulrich B. Phillips, *American Negro Slavery: A Survey of the Supply, Employment and Control of Negro Labor as Determined by the Plantation Regime.* (1918; reprint, Baton Rouge: Louisiana State Univ. Press, 1966), 93.

37. Hall, *Africans in Colonial Louisiana*, 124.

38. Bernard Romans, quoted in Holmes, "Indigo in Colonial Louisiana," 344. Some indigo was also cultivated in the islands. See Élie Monnereau, *Le parfait indigotier* (Marseilles: Jean Mossy, 1765), 15–84.

39. Judith A. Carney, "From Hands to Tutors: African Expertise in the South Carolina Rice Economy," *Agricultural History* 67 (1993): 1–30; Littlefield, *Rice and Slaves*, 80–98.

40. David L. Coon, "Eliza Lucas Pinckney and the Reintroduction of Indigo Culture in South Carolina," *Journal of Southern History* 42 (1976): 64.

41. Charles Joyner, *Down By the Riverside: A South Carolina Slave Community* (Urbana and Chicago: Univ. of Illinois Press, 1984), 41–89; Julia Floyd Smith, *Slavery and Rice Culture in Low Country Georgia, 1750–1860* (Knoxville: Univ. of Tennessee Press, 1985), 45–63. See also Mildred K. Ginn, "A History of Rice Production in Louisiana to 1896," *LHQ* 23 (1940): 544–88.

42. "American Husbandry" (1775), quoted in Aubrey C. Land, ed., *Bases of the Plantation Society* (New York: Harper and Row, 1969), 86.

43. Moore, "Cypress Lumber Industry," 33.

44. Ordinance of the General Administrators of the Islands, 18 Jan. 1685, in Moreau de Saint-Méry, *Loix et constitutions*, 1:406–7.

45. Geggus, "Sugar and Coffee Cultivation in Saint Domingue," 89.

46. For the onset of the epidemics for which the region became notorious, see Matas, *History of Medicine in Louisiana*, 1:198.

47. Debien, *Esclaves aux Antilles françaises*, 163–69.

48. Ibid., 171–84.

49. McGowan, "Creation of a Slave Society," 219–34; Debien, *Esclaves aux Antilles françaises*, 184–248; Peytraud, *L'esclavage aux Antilles françaises*, 288, summarizing an argument beginning on 228; Martin, *Histoire de l'esclavage dans les colonies françaises*, 124–25; Vaissière, *Saint-Domingue*, 165–205; Jacques Cauna, *Au temps des isles à sucre: histoire d'une plantation de Saint-Domingue au XVIIIe siècle* (Paris: Éditions Karthala et A. C. C. T., 1987), 111–30.

50. Debien, "La question des vivres pour les esclaves des Antilles françaises aux XVIIe et XVIIIe siècles," *Anuario des Instituto de Antropología e Historia* 7–8 (1970–71): 170.

51. Debien, *Esclaves aux Antilles françaises*, 214–18.

52. Ibid., 69–71.

53. Ibid., 60–61; Peytraud, *L'esclavage aux Antilles françaises*, 207–8, claims, however, that morals were more relaxed in Saint Domingue than in the other islands, and that conditions there directly inspired the proscription of racial intermarriage in Louisiana in the Black Code of 1724.

54. Decree of the Council of Martinique, 2 Mar. 1665, in Moreau de Saint-Méry, *Loix et constitutions*, 1:136.

55. Debien, *Esclaves aux Antilles françaises*, 411–30; Vanony-Frisch, "Esclaves de la Guadeloupe," 131–38; Cauna, *Au temps des isles à sucre*, 130–35, discusses marronage and the disinclination of masters to free slaves.

56. The words of the slaves are a pastiche of reports by two eighteenth-century historians. See Moreau de Saint-Méry, *Description topographique*, 3:629–31. See also [Anon.], *Relation d'une conspiration tramée par les negres dans l'isle de S. Domingue; défense que fait le Jésuite confesseur, aux negres qu'on suplicie, de révéler leurs fauteurs & complices* (n.p., n.d., copy in Bibliothèque Nationale), 3–4.

57. Decree of Superior Council, 9 July 1763, LHC.

58. Examination of the Cargo of *La Roue de Fortune*, 12 Nov. 1765, LHC.

59. Ibid.

60. Thad W. Tate, *The Negro in Eighteenth-Century Williamsburg* (1965; reprint, Charlottesville: Univ. Press of Virginia, 1987), 56. Hall's suggestion that slaves imported into the mainland English colonies were English-speaking creoles from the West Indies is incorrect: the vast majority were direct from Africa. See Philip D. Curtin, *The Atlantic Slave Trade: A Census* (Madison: Univ. of Wisconsin Press, 1969), 142–46.

61. Marcel Chatillon, ed., "Lettres du R-P. Jean Mongin: l'èvangélisation des esclaves au XVIIe siècle," *Bulletin de la Société d'Histoire de la Guadeloupe*, 61–62 (1984): 134–35.

62. [Captain Vaugine de Nuisement], "Vie en Louisiane de 1752 à 1756," 57; Jean-Bernard Bossu, *Travels Through that Part of North America Formerly Called Louisiana*, trans. John Reinhold Forster, 2 vols. (London: T. Davies, 1771), 1:24.

63. Jean-Bernard Bossu, *Nouveaux voyages dans l'Amérique septentrionale* ("Amsterdam" [Paris?]: Chez Changuion, 1777), 83–84. A career military man from France who spent most of his Louisiana assignment in Illinois, his book is written for popular consumption, tinged with Rousseauan romanticism, and deficient in reliable historical information. He intends the Jupiter story to be a "Sambo" anecdote, but it would appear that the slave is cunningly avoiding being made the butt of a joke by his master for Bossu's entertainment. Hall discusses some quotations in Du Pratz that she labels "Louisiana Creole," in Hall, *Africans in Colonial Louisiana*, 191–92. The man quoted, however, was an African whose speech was shaped by complex influences, speech that was not typical of the French spoken by Louisiana-born slaves.

64. John Smith-Thibodeaux, *Les francophones de Louisiane* (Paris: Éditions Entente, 1977), 46–51.

65. Ingrid Neumann, *Le créole de Breaux Bridge, Louisiane: étude morphosyntaxique—textes—vocabulaire* (Hamburg: Helmut Buske Verlag, 1985), 488. See also John F. McDermott, *A Glossary of Mississippi Valley French, 1673–1850* (St. Louis: Washington Univ. Press, 1941); and William A. Read, *Louisiana French* (Baton Rouge: Louisiana State Univ. Press, 1931).

66. Thomas N. Ingersoll, "Slave Codes and Judicial Practice in New Orleans, 1718–1807," *Law and History Review* 13 (1995): 23–62.

67. Code Noir of 1724 with Annotations, AN, AC, A23:50–57.

68. Ibid., 50v. Raphael to Raguet, 15 May 1725, AN, AC, C13A, 8:403–3v. Everywhere priests reported that masters refused to send slaves for instruction; on Guiana, for example, see Father Panier to Maurepas, 30 Oct. 1736, AN, AC, C14, 16:264; Justin Girod-Chantrans, *Voyage d'un Suisse dans différentes colonies d'Amérique pendant la dernière guerre* (Neuchatel: La Société Typographique, 1785), 195–201. See also Debien, *Esclaves aux Antilles françaises*, 249–60, 268; Peytraud, *L'esclavage aux Antilles françaises*, 190–94; Gautier, *Soeurs de solitude*, 138–42; Vaissière, *Saint-Domingue*, 205–12.

69. Chatillon, "Lettres du R-P. Jean Mongin," 18–23, 87–88.

70. Code Noir of 1724 with Annotations, 51v.

71. On the plantation of the Jesuits, for example, which was centrally located in New Orleans so that slaves would have exercised some degree of choice of spouses if they could have, all women on the plantation were married to men of the plantation, so

they must have been required to do so; see AN, AC, C13A, 43:331–52. The real value of Code Noir provisions to slaves seem negligible. Christian baptism and monogamous family structures could even be regarded as cultural impositions that hurt more than helped slaves. Few slave marriages actually appear in the church records, indicating resistance to or exclusion from Christian marriage. See Peytraud, *L'esclavage aux Antilles françaises,* 120–32.

72. Code Noir of 1724 with Annotations, 51.

73. Ibid., 52v.

74. Ibid., 52. On this issue in the Antilles, see Debien, "Question des vivres pour les esclaves des Antilles françaises," 131–73.

75. For representative examples, see *Lange v Geula,* 4, 10 Jan. 1737, LHC. In every case in which the court interfered in the master-slave relation, it was to protect the property rights of the master or another white person, not to protect the slave. For a similar conclusion based on evidence from the French Antilles, see Peytraud, *L'esclavage aux Antilles françaises,* 239. As one historian of the subject puts it, the slave's right to complain was "illusory," a mere "legal disposition" rendered worthless by the common interest of magistrate and master. Martin, *Histoire de l'esclavage dans les colonies françaises,* 29.

76. The corresponding article in the code of 1685 is number 30, which states that the testimony of a slave is to serve only as a *"mémoire"* for judges. In a clarification of 1686, the crown changed the rule to read that slaves could be witnesses, except for or against their masters; see Emilien Petit, *Traité sur le gouvernement des esclaves,* 2 vols. (Paris: Knapen, 1777), 1:31–32. The practice in both the Antilles and Louisiana was that when no white witnesses were available judges accepted the testimony of slaves in noncapital cases. The issue almost never arose in Louisiana. For an equally negative assessment of the Code Noir, see Giraud, *History of French Louisiana,* 5:322–23.

77. For an exceptionally rare example of an overseer torturing a slave, see *Merveilleux v Gaullas,* 18 June 1727, LHC. Carl A. Brasseaux presents this case as an instance of enforcement of the Code Noir in "The Administration of Slave Regulations in French Louisiana, 1724–1766," *LH* 21 (1980): 149–50, but the judges sought merely to protect the interests of the slaveowner from harm and did not punish Gaullas for inhumanity to the slave. For examples of judicial mutilation, see *State v Pierre and Jean,* 31 July 1764, sentence of 31 Aug., LHC; for torture, see Laura Porteous, trans., *Lebreton v Temba,* 1 June 1771, *LHQ* 8 (1925): 5–22, sentence of 9 June.

78. On marriage, see Gautier, *Soeurs de Solitude,* 142–45; Herbert G. Gutman, *The Black Family in Slavery and Freedom, 1750–1925* (New York: Random House, 1976), 347–51; Kulikoff, *Tobacco and Slaves,* 352–80; and White, *Ar'n't I A Woman?* 97–110, 142–60.

79. Petition of Joseph Maison, 6 Dec. 1765, LHC; Declaration by Charles-Marie Delalande, 16 Dec. 1765, LHC; Declaration by Joseph LePage, 11 Dec. 1769, LHC. In all three cases the master took the unusual step of citing the Code Noir as the reason for his action.

80. For the travails of a literate free black immigrant from France; see *Raphael Bernard v Cadot,* 9 May 1724, LHC; and *Raphael Bernard v Dumanoir,* 26 July, 20 Sept. 1724, LHC.

81. *State v Jeannette [Connard?],* 8 Apr. 1747, LHC; the indictment included a vague charge of theft. For a unique and neglected comparative legal study of free blacks, see

Auguste Lebeau, *De la condition des gens de couleur libres sous l'ancien régime d'après des documents des archives coloniales* (Paris: Guillaumin et Cie., 1903).

82. Decree of 31 Jan. 1726, AN, AC, A23:67v–68.

83. For a different view, see Ira Berlin, *Slaves Without Masters: The Free Negro in the Antebellum South* (New York: Oxford Univ. Press, 1974), 110.

84. Orlando Patterson, *Slavery and Social Death: A Comparative Study* (Cambridge: Harvard Univ. Press, 1982), 247–61.

85. Ibid., 259. On the ability of some free blacks to succeed despite discrimination, see Leonard P. Curry, *The Free Black in Urban America, 1800–1850: The Shadow of the Dream* (Chicago: Univ. of Chicago Press, 1981), 37–48; and Berlin, *Slaves Without Masters*, 274–77.

86. Patterson, *Slavery and Social Death*, 257.

87. See Thomas N. Ingersoll, "Free Blacks in a Slave Society: New Orleans, 1718–1812," *William and Mary Quarterly*, 3d ser., 48 (1991): 176–79; Tannenbaum, *Slave and Citizen*, 55–56, 74–79. In Article 23 of the Code Noir it is explicitly stated that a master might permit a slave to hold a *"peculium"* and even specifies how creditors may make claims against it. There is clear evidence for de facto customary slave *peculium* in the English colonies and the United States as well.

88. Ordinance of the General Administrators of the Islands, 5 Aug. 1711, in Moreau de Saint-Méry, *Loix et constitutions*, 2:272–73.

89. A. J. T. Bonnemain in 1792, quoted in Louis Sala-Molins, *Le code noir ou le Calvaire de Canaan* (Paris: Presses Universitaires de France, 1987), 207. For additional discussions of physical treatment of slaves in other French colonies not already cited, see Girod-Chantrans, *Voyage*, 130–36; Antoine Gisler, *L'esclavage aux Antilles françaises, XVIIe–XIXe siècle*, 2d ed. (Paris: Éditions Karthala, 1981), 77–127; Sidney Daney, *Histoire de la Martinique depuis la colonisation jusqu'en 1815*, 3 vols. (1846; reprint, Fort-Royal, Mart.: Société d'Histoire de la Martinique, 1963), 2:90–93.

90. For a different view, see Brasseaux, "Administration of Slave Regulations in French Louisiana," 153.

91. Just before the promulgation of the Code Noir of 1685, a census of the principal French colonies in the islands indicated that mulattoes numbered only 245, or less than 1 percent of the population of 12,652 whites and 19,696 black slaves, in spite of the fact that white males outnumbered white females by nearly two to one; see census of 12 Apr. 1683, AN, AC, C8B, 17, no. 9. See also Gautier, *Soeurs de solitude*, 72–73.

92. Hilliard d'Auberteuil, *Considérations sur l'état présent*, 2:78–79. See also [Paul-Ulrich Dubuisson], *Nouvelles considérations sur Saint-Domingue, en réponse à celles de M. HD* (Paris: Cellot and Jombert, 1780), 24–25; and Shelby T. McCloy, *The Negro in the French West Indies* (Lexington: Univ. Press of Kentucky, 1966), 262–65.

93. Letter of the General to the Governor of Le Cap, 7 Dec. 1733, Moreau de Saint-Méry, *Loix et constitutions*, 3:382.

94. Pontchartrain to the Governor General of the Islands, 26 Dec. 1703, Moreau de Saint-Méry, *Loix et constitutions*, 1:716.

95. Gabriel Debien, *Un colon sur sa plantation* (Dakar: Univ. of Dakar, 1959), 7–9.

96. Peytraud, *L'esclavage aux Antilles françaises*, 196–208; Gabriel Debien, "Les affran-

chissements aux Antilles françaises aux XVIIe et XVIIIe siècles," *Anuario de Estudios Americanos* 24 (1967): 1177–81; Gautier, *Soeurs de solitude,* 151–81.

97. Only entry 201 for 4 August 1725 in St. Louis Cathedral Marriages, 1720–1730, Archdiocese of New Orleans, Archives, leaves open some question on this head. Father Raphael joined a Martinique-born mulatto to one Marie Gaspard, her color not given. It is highly unlikely that a priest would have ignored the law and she was probably also a mulatto, one who happened to have been born in Flanders. Alan Watson's assertion that Article 9 of the old code rested unchanged in the code of 1724 is incorrect; see *Slave Laws in the Americas* (Athens: Univ. of Georgia Press, 1989), 88. The exceptional clause of 1685 permitting a "man" to marry a slave concubine if he was not married to someone else during his concubinage with her is changed to specify that only "the *black* man, manumittee or free[born]" (emphasis added), is permitted to marry his slave concubine. In practice, the marriage of white men and black women in the French Antilles was rare, regarded as socially acceptable only in the unusual case where a free black woman became rich and wed a poor white man; see Father Panier to Minister of Marine Maurepas, 25 Sept. 1741, AN, AC, C14, 18:187–87v.

98. Gallay, *Voices of the Old South,* 87. On early Virginia, see Warren Billings, ed., *The Old Dominion in the Seventeenth Century: A Documentary History of Virginia, 1606–1689* (Chapel Hill: Univ. of North Carolina Press, 1975), 151–52, 165–69.

99. St. Louis Cathedral Baptisms and Marriages, 1759–1762, Archdiocese of New Orleans, Archives, New Orleans. For the census of 1763, I used the transcription, corrected as necessary by comparison to the original, in Jacqueline K. Voorhies, trans. and comp., *Some Late Eighteenth-Century Louisianians: Census Records of the Colony, 1758–1796* (Lafayette: Univ. of Southwestern Louisiana, 1973). See Edward B. Reuter, *The Mulatto in the United States* (1918; reprint, New York: New American Library, 1969), 112.

100. Extract of a Letter from the Minister of Marine to M. Ducasse, 5 Feb. 1698, in Moreau de Saint-Méry, *Loix et constitutions,* 2:579.

101. Minister of Marine to Superior Council of Saint Domingue, 10 June 1707, in ibid., 2:99.

102. Royal Edict, Oct. 1716, in *Recueils de réglemens, édits, déclarations et arrêts, concernant le commerce, l'administration de la justice, & la police des colonies françaises de l'Amérique, & les engagés. Avec le code noir et l'addition audit code,* 2d ed., 2 vols. in 1 (Paris: Les Libraires Associés, 1765), 2:89–96.

103. Royal Declaration, 15 Dec. 1738, ibid., 2:128–34.

104. Letter of the Minister, 30 June 1763, in Moreau de Saint-Méry, *Loix et constitutions,* 3:602–3. The crown relented in 1769 by allowing a colonist to bring in one slave upon deposit of a huge surety of forty-five hundred livres and guaranteeing the slave's return to America within eight months. See Intendant's Regulation, 29 Aug. 1769, in ibid., 267–68.

105. Regulation of Administrators, 24 June, 16 July 1773, in Moreau de Saint-Méry, *Loix et constitutions,* 3:448–50.

106. Ship List of *L'Éléphant,* 13 Jan. 1745, AN, AC, C13A, 29:111–11v.

107. Report by Bureau of Colonies, n.d., AN, AC, F1B, 1:35.

108. Royal Declaration, 9 Aug. 1777, AN, AC, F1B, 1:2 (printed).

109. Advice of the Legislative Committee for the Colonies, n.d., AN, AC, F1B, 1:72.

110. Decree of the Council of State, AN, AC, F1B, 1:86v–87. See also the accompanying Memoire, n.d., AN, AC, F1B, 1:95v.

111. Decree of Council of State, 5 Apr. 1778, AN, AC, F1B, 1:10–10v. For a different view of France in this regard, see Mathé Allain, "Slave Policies in French Louisiana," *LH* 21 (1980): 134–35.

112. For other French colonies see Girod-Chantrans, *Voyage*, 180–86; Lebeau, *De la condition des gens de couleur libres*, 90–95; Moreau de Saint-Méry, *Description topographique*, 1:83–85, 103–11; Peytraud, *L'esclavage aux Antilles françaises*, 406–20; Vaissière, *Saint-Domingue*, 63–65, 75–77; E. Hayot, "Les gens de couleur libres du Fort-Royal, 1679–1823," *Revue Française d'Histoire d'Outre-Mer*, 56 (1969): 77–81; Gautier, *Soeurs de solitude*, 157, David P. Geggus, *Slavery, War, and Revolution: The British Occupation of Saint Domingue, 1793–1798* (Oxford: Clarendon Press, 1982), 19–22.

113. Lawrence Kinnaird, ed., *Spain in the Mississippi Valley, 1765–1794* (hereafter cited as *SMV*), pt. 1, *The Revolutionary Period, 1765–1781*; pt. 2, *Post-War Decade, 1782–1791*; pt. 3, *Problems of Frontier Defense, 1792–1794*; Annual Report of the American Historical Association for the Year 1945, vols. 2–4 (Washington, D.C.: GPO, 1946), pt. 1, 196. The census of 1769, sometimes cited by scholars, is worthless because it excludes the Tchoupitoulas neighborhood of New Orleans, the largest single concentration of blacks in the colony. Of 157 free people of color in New Orleans in 1771, 90 were of mixed race, meaning the children of either interracial liaisons or liaisons between people of mixed race. Given the fact that the admixture of any white "blood" at all served to define a "black" person as a mulatto, the demographic logic is inescapable that a mixed-race population would be soon dominated by the offspring of liaisons in which both parents were of mixed race. Moreover, the slave population of 1771 included 280 additional people of mixed race, further discrediting the notion of a strong link between miscegenation and manumission. The argument that a significant number of mixed-blood people were passing into the "white race" before 1769, thereby artificially masking the extent of miscegenation, is not convincing; see Hall, *Africans in Colonial Louisiana*, 239.

114. For a different view, see Hall, *Africans in Colonial Louisiana*, 239–42; Laura Foner, "The Free People of Color in Louisiana and St. Domingue: A Comparative Portrait of Two Three-Caste Slave Societies," *Journal of Social History* 3 (1970): 410–11, 414; and Berlin, *Slaves Without Masters*, 108–10. As Debien shows, concubinage became an important factor in the manumission of slaves in the French West Indies only at the end of the eighteenth century; see Debien, "Affranchissements aux Antilles françaises," 1185–86. Foner's article is most often cited by scholars who argue that interracial concubinage was always widespread in New Orleans. Her evidence consists of assertions by two outsiders from the early nineteenth century who were either hostile to the locals (Berquin-Duvallon) or totally unfamiliar with slave society (Laussat).

115. Raboteau, *Slave Religion*, 4–42.

116. Hall, *Africans in Colonial Louisiana*, 301–2.

117. Council Decree, 20 Jan. 1758, in Moreau de Saint-Méry, *Loix et constitutions*, 3:217–18. See also Raboteau, *Slave Religion*, 76. Raboteau's discussion is marred by his misinterpretation of the New Orleans planters' policy on the islands: they had first banned

slaves from the islands long before 1782, but he is right that it was because the poisoning conspiracy was related to the cult. For a description of voudou, see Moreau de Saint-Méry, *Description topographique*, 1:64–69.

118. Jean Fouchard, *The Haitian Maroons: Liberty or Death*, trans. A. Faulkner Watts (New York: Edward W. Blyden Press, 1981), 181–85.

119. Raboteau, *Slave Religion*, 76–82.

120. McGowan, "Creation of a Slave Society," 120. See also Brasseaux, "Administration of Slave Regulations in French Louisiana," 139–58, for a good review of some of the evidence and a similar argument that slaveholders "tempered their treatment of slaves with paternalism" (142).

121. Debien, *Esclaves aux Antilles françaises*, 430–69; Peytraud, *L'esclavage aux Antilles françaises*, 342–71.

CHAPTER 6. THE CESSION TO SPAIN

1. A. Morel-Fatio and H. Léonardon, eds., *Recueil des instructions données aux ambassadeurs et ministres de France*, sec. 12 bis, *Espagne*, 3 vols. (Paris: Felix Alcan, 1899), 3:337–49. See also De Villiers du Terrage, *Last Years of French Louisiana*, 173–78; Wilson E. Lyon, *Louisiana in French Diplomacy, 1759–1804* (Norman: Univ. of Oklahoma Press, 1934), 16–33; Arthur S. Aiton, "The Diplomacy of the Louisiana Cession," *American Historical Review* (hereafter cited as *AHR*) 36 (1932): 269–80; and Francis P. Renaut, *Le pacte de famille et l'Amérique: la politique coloniale franco-espagnole de 1760 à 1792* (Paris: Éditions Leroux, 1922), 160–66.

2. Arthur P. Whitaker, "Antonio de Ulloa," *Hispanic American Historical Review* (hereafter cited as *HAHR*) 15 (1935): 155–94; R. E. Chandler, "Aubry: Villain or Hero?" *LH* 26 (1985): 241–70; and De Villiers du Terrage, *Last Years of French Louisiana*, 234–375.

3. John P. Moore, "Antonio de Ulloa: A Profile of the First Spanish Governor of Louisiana," *LH* 8 (1967): 189 bis–218; Carl A. Brasseaux, *The Founding of New Acadia: The Beginnings of Acadian Life in Louisiana, 1765–1803* (Baton Rouge: Louisiana State Univ. Press, 1987). Chevalier Champigny, "Memoir on the Present State of Louisiana," *Historical Memoirs of Louisiana, From the First Settlement of the Colony to the Departure of Governor O'Reilly in 1770*, ed. Benjamin Franklin French, 5 vols. (1853; reprint, New York: AMS Press, 1976), 5:127–233.

4. Wilbur E. Meneray, ed., *The Rebellion of 1768: Documents from the Favrot Family Papers and the Rosamonde E. and Emile Kuntz Collection*, trans. Philippe Seiler (New Orleans: Howard-Tilton Memorial Library, Tulane Univ., 1995); R. E. Chandler, trans., "Ulloa's Account of the 1768 Revolt," *LH* 27 (1986): 407–37; "An Exact Collection of the Facts Relating to the Cession of Louisiana to the Spaniards," c. 1770, Historical Society of Pennsylvania, Philadelphia; Decree of the Superior Council in the Name of King Louis XV, October 29, 1768, in Gayarré, *History of Louisiana*, 2:367–68; Statement of the Inhabitants and Traders of Louisiana on the Event of October 29, 1768, n.d. (printed), AN, AC, C13A, 48:245–66. John P. Moore, *Revolt in Louisiana: The Spanish Occupation, 1766–1770* (Baton Rouge: Louisiana State Univ. Press, 1976).

5. Several historians have pictured the colony as being on the brink of mass starvation at this time because it was cash-poor. For the deprivation theory of the revolt of

1768, see Carl A. Brasseaux, *Denis-Nicolas Foucault and the New Orleans Rebellion of 1768* (Ruston: Louisiana Tech Univ. Press, 1987), 11, 45, 91–96; Carl A. Brasseaux, "Confusion, Conflict, and Currency: An Introduction to the Rebellion of 1768?" *LH* 18 (1977): 161–69; Moore, *Revolt in Louisiana*, 124–42. For the assertion that French Louisiana was always "plagued" by "the problem of subsistence," and that "there was a great shortage of food" in the 1760s, see Clark, *New Orleans, 1718—1812*, 28, 160. This interpretation owes something to Charles Gayarré, who harped stubbornly on the absurd notion "that Louisiana had been, since its foundation, that is for sixty-six years, in a starving condition" (*History of Louisiana*, 2:163). For an abundance of direct evidence to the contrary, see Surrey, *Commerce of Louisiana*. The colonists were not dependent on France for their food supply and did not face starvation in the 1760s: they experienced shortages of luxury comestibles like wheat flour and wine. The economic dynamism of New Orleans in this period is proved by comments by several reporters. The planter Pradel reported in 1755 that the colony had become "opulent"; see *Chevalier de Pradel*, 265. See Governor Dabbadie's comments in Brasseaux, *Comparative View of French Louisiana*, 101–2, indicating that in September 1763 the markets were "more than reasonably supplied," especially by the English. Dabbadie does not mention a food shortage. Pittman, in his *Present State of the European Settlements*, 10–12, 23, did not believe there was a subsistence crisis. Hutchins, in *Historical Narrative and Topographical Description*, 29, claimed, on the basis of observations made in the 1760s, that Louisiana colonists had "attained a state of opulence never before so soon acquired in any new country" on their supremely rich soils. He is echoed by another visitor who saw the colony not long after the insurrection. See Pierre-Marie De Pagès, *Travels Round the World in the Years 1767. . . 1771*, 2d ed., 3 vols. (London: J. Murray, 1793), 1:19–20, 26–27. A reliable local observer reported that in the late 1750s Louisiana's exports included beans, corn, peas, and rice. See De Villiers du Terrage, *Last Years of French Louisiana*, 147–49.

6. Charles E. O'Neill, S.J., "The Louisiana Manifesto of 1768," *Political Science Reviewer* 19 (1990): 247–89. Manuel Serrano y Sanz, ed., *Documentos históricos de la Florida y la Luisiana, siglos XVI al XVIII* (Madrid: Librería General de Victoriano Suárez, 1912), 274–95; Pierre H. Boulle, "French Reactions to the Louisiana Revolution of 1768," in *The French in the Mississippi Valley*, ed. John F. McDermott (Urbana: Univ. of Illinois Press, 1965), 143–57.

7. R. E. Chandler, "Eyewitness History: O'Reilly's Arrival in Louisiana," *LH* 20 (1979): 317–20. David K. Bjork, ed., "Alexander O'Reilly and the Spanish Occupation of Louisiana, 1769–1770," in *New Spain and the Anglo-American West: Historical Contributions Presented to Herbert Eugene Bolton*, 2 vols. (1932; reprint, New York: Kraus Reprints, 1969), 1:165–82; David K. Bjork, "Documents Relating to Alexandro O'Reilly and an Expedition Sent Out by Him from New Orleans to Natchitoches, 1769–1770," *LHQ* 7 (1924): 20–39. A collection of transcriptions of documents from the trials is provided in Vicente Rodriguez-Casado, *Primeros años de dominacion española en la Luisiana* (Madrid: Diana, 1942), 443–82. See also Brian E. Coutts, "Martín Navarro: Treasurer, Contador, Intendant, 1766–1788: Politics and Trade in Spanish Louisiana" (Ph.D. diss., Louisiana State Univ., 1981), 70–80; David K. Texada, *Alejandro O'Reilly*

and the New Orleans Rebels (Lafayette: Univ. of Southwestern Louisiana Press, 1970); Bibiano Torres Ramirez, *Alejandro O'Reilly en las Indias* (Seville: Universidad Publicaciónes, 1969).

8. "Exact Collection of the Facts," 56.

9. List of Militia Officers Appointed by O'Reilly, 12 Feb. 1770, *SMV,* pt. 1, 158–59.

10. Coutts, "Martín Navarro," 88–90, 263–69.

11. Decree by O'Reilly, 25 Nov. 1769, *SMV,* pt. 1, 108–9. See Torres Ramirez, *Alejandro O'Reilly en las Indias,* 187–202. The New Orleans Cabildo was even less powerful than those of older Spanish American colonies; see Haring, *Spanish Empire in America,* 147–65.

12. Decree by O'Reilly, 25 Nov. 1769, *SMV,* pt. 1, 109–14; First Meeting of the Cabildo, 2 Dec. 1769, Copia Fiel de las Actas del Cabildo de Nueva Orléans, 4 vols., transcriptions by the Works Progress Administration of Louisiana, Louisiana Division, New Orleans Public Library (hereafter cited as *ADC*), 1:6–7; Gayarré, *History of Louisiana,* 3:1–41, on O'Reilly's procedure in general. See Herbert I. Priestley, "Spanish Colonial Municipalities," *LHQ* 5 (1922): 125–43, on the subject.

13. Torres Ramirez, *Alejandro O'Reilly en las Indias,* 129–41; on the policy concerning the introduction of disciplined militia in Spanish colonies at this time, see Allan J. Kuethe, *Cuba, 1753–1815: Crown, Military and Society* (Knoxville: Univ. of Tennessee Press, 1986), x and ff.

14. Ordinance of 27 Aug. 1769, AN, AC, C13A, 49:69.

15. Four daughters of Gilbert-Antoine St. Maxent, for example, married Governors Luis Unzaga and Bernardo Gálvez and two other Spaniards; see Gayarré, *History of Louisiana,* 3:310–11; John W. Caughey, *Bernardo de Gálvez in Louisiana, 1776–1783* (1934; reprint, Gretna, La.: Pelican, 1972), 84; Jack D. L. Holmes, *Gayoso: The Life of a Spanish Governor in the Mississippi Valley, 1789–1799* (Baton Rouge: Louisiana State Univ. Press, 1965), 124; Coutts, "Martín Navarro," 211. For a useful study of this phenomenon in the Spanish colonies, see Gary M. Miller, "Bourbon Social Engineering: Women and Conditions of Marriage in Eighteenth-Century Venezuela," *Americas* 46 (1990): 261–90.

16. Gilbert C. Din and John E. Harkins, *The New Orleans Cabildo: Colonial Louisiana's First City Government, 1769–1803* (Baton Rouge: Louisiana State Univ. Press, 1996), 53ff. See also Gilbert C. Din, "The Offices and Functions of the New Orleans Cabildo," *LH* 37 (1996): 5–30; and Ronald R. Morazán, "Letters, Petitions, and Decrees of the *Cabildo* of New Orleans, 1800–1803, Edited and Translated" (Ph.D. diss., Louisiana State Univ., 1972).

17. C. Richard Arena, "Landholding and Political Power in Spanish Louisiana," *LHQ* 38 (1955): 23–39.

18. Din and Harkins, *New Orleans Cabildo,* 81, are in agreement with me that the cabildo's overall authority was limited, although they are rather argumentative about its judicial authority (105). See 206–90 on the cabildo's responsibility for public health, public works, and public ceremonies.

19. Louisa Schell Hoberman and Susan Migden Socolow, Introduction to *Cities and Society in Colonial Latin America,* ed. Louisa Schell Hoberman and Susan Migden Socolow (Albuquerque: Univ. of New Mexico Press, 1986), 6–7.

20. See "Digest of the Laws of Louisiana, Nov. 29, 1803," *American State Papers: Documents, Legislative and Executive, of the Congress of the United States, Class X, Miscellaneous,* vol. 1, ed. Walter Lowrie and Walter S. Franklin (Washington, D.C.: Gales and Seaton, 1834), 362–77.

21. Din and Harkins, *New Orleans Cabildo,* 122, stress continuity.

22. "Condition of Louisiana in 1803, When the American Government Took Possession," in Joseph M. White, ed. *A New Collection of Laws, Charters, and Local Ordinances of the Governments of Great Britain, France, and Spain,* 2 vols. (Philadelphia: T. and J. W. Johnson, 1839), 2, 693.

23. Morris S. Arnold stresses procedural informality and a loose interpretation of O'Reilly's code by authorities in his *Colonial Arkansas,* 141–54.

24. For an example of the arbitrary power of a Spanish commandant and indefinite imprisonment without trial, see William Rogers to Oliver Pollock, 1782, *SMV,* pt. 2, 7.

25. Dart, *Courts and Law in Colonial Louisiana,* 26–28.

26. Appointment of *Procuradores,* 23 Dec. 1769, *ADC,* 1:10–13. At the end of the Spanish period, however, legal expertise was weakly established in the town; see Declaration on Attornies, 19 Feb. 1802, *ADC,* vol. 4. no. 4, 168–70.

27. Din and Harkins, *New Orleans Cabildo,* 116–19. See Resolution to Petition the King, 11 July, 29 Aug. 1800, *ADC,* vol. 4, no. 3, 198, 228–29, for a complaint about the slow pace of criminal appeals in Havana; followed by a request to establish an appeals tribunal in New Orleans.

28. Din and Harkins, *New Orleans Cabildo,* 105, 107; Gayarré, *History of Louisiana,* 3:8–19.

29. For a rare instance of torture in criminal procedure, see *Jean-Baptiste Lebreton v Temba,* 1 June 1771, Louisiana Historical Collection, Spanish Judicial Records, Louisiana Historical Center, Louisiana State Museum, New Orleans (hereafter cited as LHC, all citations being to the Spanish Judicial Records), for murder of a master by a slave.

30. On the public *calabozo* and its operation in this period, see Petition by Warden Joseph de la Peña, 29 Nov. 1793, *ADC,* vol. 3, no. 3, 100; Petition by Sheriff François Pascalis, 29 Jan. 1796, City Council: Petitions, Decrees, and Letters of the Cabildo, 1789–1803, New Orleans Public Library; Report by the Governor, 10 Nov. 1797, *ADC,* vol. 4, no. 2, 74–75. Concerning the public executioner, see Appointment of Antonio Zosa, 12 Sept. 1788, *ADC,* vol. 3, no. 2, 34; Order to Hangman, 4 Dec. 1795, *ADC,* vol. 4, no. 1, 78, to move off the plaza; Appointment of Jean-Baptiste, 13 Apr. and 20 July 1798, *ADC,* vol. 4, no. 2, 111, 159, a slave convict.

31. Claiborne to Jefferson, 24 Aug. 1803, in Clarence E. Carter, ed. and comp., *The Territorial Papers of the United States,* vol. 9, *The Territory of Orleans, 1803–1812* (Washington, D.C.: GPO, 1940) (hereafter cited as *TPO*), 19–21; Daniel Clark to James Madison, 3 Sept. 1803, *TPO,* 36–37, for two examples. See also John E. Harkins, "The Neglected Phase of Louisiana's Colonial History: The New Orleans Cabildo, 1769–1803" (Ph.D. diss., Memphis State Univ., 1976), 132–36; Holmes, *Gayoso,* 56; and Caroline M. Burson, *The Stewardship of Don Esteban Miró, 1782–1792* (New Orleans: American Printing, 1940), 188–209.

32. C. Richard Arena, "Land Settlement Policies and Practices in Spanish Louisiana," in *The Spanish in the Mississippi Valley, 1762–1804,* ed. John F. McDermott (Urbana: Univ. of Illinois Press, 1974), 53–55.

33. For an overview, see Alfred E. Lemmon, "Spanish Louisiana: In the Service of God and His Most Catholic Majesty," in *Cross, Crucible and Crozier*, ed. Conrad, 16–29.

34. Sister Jane Frances Heaney, *A Century of Pioneering: A History of the Ursuline Nuns in New Orleans, 1727–1827*, ed. Mary Ethel Booker Siefken (Chelsea, Mich.: Bookcrafters, 1993), 166–73.

35. For a somewhat different view, see Richard Greenleaf, "The Inquisition in Spanish Louisiana, 1762–1800," *New Mexico Historical Review* 50 (1975): 45–72.

36. Charles E. O'Neill, S.J., "A Bishop for Louisiana," in *Cross, Crucible and Crozier*, Conrad, 96–107. For a disapproving description of the local clergy and public religious rites, see John Pope, *A Tour through the Southern and Western Territories of the United States of North-America*, intro. J. Barton Starr (1792; reprint, Gainesville: Univ. Presses of Florida, 1979), 38–41.

37. Dispatch, 1773, AN, AC, C13A, 50:102–3v; Bernardo Gálvez to José Gálvez, 11 Mar. 1778, AGI, SD, 2547:469–73v, reported the building of thirty-two new houses in the town center alone in recent years.

38. Burson, *Stewardship of Don Esteban Miró*, 124–43; Laura L. Porteous, trans., "O'Reilly's Ordinance of 1770," *LHQ* 11 (1928): 237–40; Miró to Campo, 11 Aug. 1792, in Jack D. L. Holmes, ed., *Documentos inéditos para la historia de la Luisiana, 1792–1810* (Madrid: Ediciones José Porrua Turanzas, 1963), 26–41. For an overview, see Francis P. Burns, "The Spanish Land Laws of Louisiana," *LHQ* 11 (1928): 557–81. On the immigrants, see Brasseaux, *Founding of New Acadia*, 73–89, 101–7; Gilbert C. Din, *The Canary Islanders of Louisiana* (Baton Rouge: Louisiana State Univ. Press, 1988), 1–104; Gilbert C. Din, "Early Spanish Colonization Efforts in Louisiana," *Louisiana Studies* 11 (1972): 31–49; Gilbert C. Din, "Proposals for the Colonization of Spanish Louisiana," *LH* 11 (1970): 197–214; V. M. Scramuzza, "Galveztown: A Spanish Settlement of Colonial Louisiana," *LHQ* 13 (1930): 553–609; Francisco Morales Padrón, "Colonos Canarios en Indias," *Anuario de Estudios Americanos* 8 (1951): 399–441.

39. Computed from the Summary of the Census of 1785, Parsons Collection, Humanities Research Center, Library of the Univ. of Texas at Austin. An important contrast is provided in Census of New Orleans, June 1778, *SMV*, pt. 1, 290, which canvassed only the 66 isles of the town center. Officials occasionally took a census of this kind to police the seat of government; it was not intended to define a community as an autonomous social unit.

40. Census of Louisiana in the year 1785, *American State Papers, Miscellaneous*, 381. The totals are the same as in the schedule in the Parsons Collection but the neighborhood distribution is summarized in this source.

41. Mark A. Burkholder and D. S. Chandler, *From Impotence to Authority: The Spanish Crown and the American Audiencias, 1687–1808* (Columbia: Univ. of Missouri Press, 1977), 83–135. See also Guillermo Céspedes del Castillo, *América hispánica, 1492–1898* (Barcelona: Editorial Labor, 1983), 313–18; Jacques A. Barbier, "The Culmination of the Bourbon Reforms, 1787–1792," *HAHR* 57 (1977): 51–68. The King's policies in Spain itself appear far less successful by comparison. See Perry Anderson, *Lineages of the Absolute State* (1974; reprint, London: Verso 1979), 82–84.

42. Gayarré, *History of Louisiana*, 3:44–46; Unzaga to Delatorre, 18 Oct. 1773, Despatches of the Spanish Governors: Translations from Archivo General de Indias, Audiencia

Santo Domingo and Papeles Procedentes de Cuba by the Works Progress Administration of Louisiana, Howard-Tilton Memorial Library, Special Collections Division, Manuscripts Section, Tulane Univ., New Orleans, 25 vols. (hereafter cited as DSG or DSG/HBC for the Hector Baron de Carondelet Series), 5:38, *passim*, for wharf reports, which should be studied with a critical eye for underreporting.

43. O'Reilly to Unzaga, 3 Apr. 1770, *SMV*, pt. 1, 165–67; Arriaga to Unzaga, 20 June 1771, *SMV*, pt. 1, 194–95. Numerous appeals by locals finally got the tobacco restriction lifted; see, for example, Navarro to José Gálvez, 8 Mar. 1782, AGI, SD, 2609:228–30.

44. Jack D. L. Holmes, "Some Economic Problems of the Spanish Governors in Louisiana," *HAHR* 42 (1962): 521–43. On Spanish Louisiana's complex frontiers, see Abraham P. Nasatir, *Borderland in Retreat: From Spanish Louisiana to the Far Southwest* (Albuquerque: Univ. of New Mexico Press, 1976), 2.

45. James Wilkinson, *Memoirs of My Own Times*, 3 vols. (Philadelphia: Abraham Small, 1816), vol. 2, app. 1, Deposition of Oliver Pollock, n.p.

46. Carl Brasseaux, ed. and trans., "Official Correspondence of Spanish Louisiana, 1770–1803," *Revue de Louisiane* 9 (1980): 184. On the official actions against smuggling in Louisiana, see Seventy-Seven Reports 1773–1807, AGI, SD, 2651:1–188. For a review of Spanish trade policy, see Arthur P. Whitaker, "The Commerce of Louisiana and the Floridas at the End of the Eighteenth Century," *HAHR* 8 (1928): 190–203.

47. Max Beloff, *The Age of Absolutism, 1660–1815* (1954; reprint, New York: Harper and Bros., 1962), 93.

48. Caughey, *Bernardo de Gálvez in Louisiana*, 70–71; Clark, *New Orleans, 1718–1812*, 166–67, 178–79.

49. Coutts, "Martín Navarro," 102.

50. Because of the uncertainty surrounding the status of New Orleans and the denial of Louisiana tobacco to the royal monopoly, the town did have hard times in the early 1770s; see Appeal by the Cabildo to the Governor, 16, 23 Aug. 1771, *ADC*, 1:55, 58–59, which refers to *"la grande devastacion"* of the colony because merchants flee the country.

51. De Villiers du Terrage, *Last Years of French Louisiana*, 411, for a letter by one "Lafrénière." See also De Las Heras, "Summary of a Representation," 5.

52. Coutts, "Martín Navarro," 83–106, argues that although the New Orleans economy enjoyed expansion in the 1760s it slumped in the 1770s, but his evidence shows only that the Spanish customs collections were unimpressive. He argues that revenues in New Orleans by the 1780s offset less than 5 percent of royal expenses (123–25). Rather than a sign of economic weakness, however, this is a measure of the cost of maintaining Louisiana as an imperial barrier, not of costs incurred by the colonists themselves or their system of production.

53. Robin F. A. Fabel, "Anglo-Spanish Commerce in New Orleans during the American Revolutionary Era," in *Anglo-Spanish Confrontation on the Gulf Coast during the American Revolution*, ed. William S. Coker and Robert R. Rea (Pensacola, Fla.: Gulf Coast History and Humanities Conference, 1982), 32–35; James A. James, *Oliver Pollock: The Life and Times of an Unknown Patriot* (New York: D. Appleton-Century, 1937), 52–54. See 54 for different figures from a different report.

54. Statement of Expenses of the Province of Louisiana, 31 May 1787, *SMV*, pt. 2, 209.

55. See Clark, *New Orleans, 1718–1812*, 221–31.

56. The shrewd intendant Martín Navarro, who served many years in the colony, begged his superiors in 1785 to do the one thing the English dreaded: declare New Orleans a free port. This would attract many shipmasters, especially the Americans, who would overwhelm the English. The Spanish government continued, however, to fear reducing its mercantilist system to a nullity in New Orleans, the outpost that guarded the route to Mexico. See Martín Navarro, "Political Reflections on the Present Condition of the Province of Louisiana," in *Louisiana Under the Rule of Spain, France, and the United States, 1785–1807*, ed. James A. Robertson, 2 vols. (Cleveland: Arthur H. Clark, 1911), 244–61. See also Clark, *New Orleans, 1718–1812*, 231–37. See Coutts, "Martín Navarro," 154–58, 318–24; and Commercial Privileges Granted to Louisiana and West Florida, 22 Jan. 1782, *SMV*, pt. 2, 1–5; Reduction of Tariff, 5 Aug. 1784, *SMV*, pt. 2, 107–8; Kinnaird, "Introduction," *SMV*, pt. 2, xiii–xiv.

57. Catherine Lugar, "Merchants," in *Cities and Society in Colonial Latin America*, ed. Hoberman and Socolow, 71.

58. Mark A. Burkholder, "Bureaucrats," in *Cities and Society in Colonial Latin America*, ed. Hoberman and Socolow, 91–93.

59. Several outside observers carried such fierce grudges against the townspeople that their work can be used only with careful qualification, particularly true of the well-known accounts by Pierre-Louis Berquin-Duvallon and Paul Alliot, two West Indians who were not welcomed in Louisiana. See Gabriel Debien and Réné Le Gardeur, "Les Colons de Saint-Domingue Réfugiés à la Louisiane," pt. 2, *Revue de Louisiane* 10 (1981): 15–21. Caution should also be exercised in the use of some accounts of New Orleans by Frenchmen. See Georges-Henri-Victor Collot, *Voyage dans l'Amérique septentrionale, ou description des pays arrosés par le Mississippi, l'Ohio, le Missouri et autres rivières affluentes*, 2 vols. (Paris: Chez Arthus Bertrand, 1826), 1, 318–19; François-Marie Perrin Du Lac, *Travels Through the Two Louisianas, and Among the Savage Nations of the Missouri . . . in 1801, 1802, & 1803* (London: Richard Phillips, 1807), 59, 83.

60. Robin, *Voyage*.

61. Ibid., 30.

62. Ibid., 32.

63. For typical comments see Charles-Maurice de Talleyrand-Périgord, *Mémoires du Prince de Talleyrand*, ed. Le Duc de Broglie (Paris: Calmann Lévy, 1891), 1:238–40; John S. Hull, *Remarks on the United States of America, Drawn Up from His Own Observations, And from the Observations of Other Travellers* (Dublin: William M'Kenzie, 1801), 19, 27, 32, 47.

64. Robin, *Voyage*, 36.

65. Ibid., 54–55.

66. Francisco Bouligny, *Louisiana in 1776: A Memoria of Francisco Bouligny*, ed. Gilbert C. Din (New Orleans: Jack D. L. Holmes, 1977), 56.

67. Ibid.

68. The Capuchins proposed to establish a poorhouse in 1759, but the need for one was apparently doubtful and it was never built; see Margulliers to Berryer, 18 Dec. 1759, AN, AC, C13A, 41:372–73v. The rebels of 1768 referred vaguely to poor relief. In the last years of the Spanish regime there were fewer than twelve orphans living on state support at any one time; see Laussat to Salcedo and Casa Calvo, 31 Dec. 1803, Laussat Papers, Historic New Orleans Collection (hereafter cited as Laussat Papers).

69. Gayarré, *History of Louisiana*, 3:57.

70. Paul Ganster, "Churchmen," in *Cities and Society in Colonial Latin America*, ed. Hoberman and Socolow, 159.

71. Sedella to Miró, 16 Aug. 1787, folder 6, Antonio Sedella Collection, 1787–1815, Manuscripts Section, Special Collections Division, Howard-Tilton Memorial Library, Tulane Univ., New Orleans (hereafter cited as Sedella Collection).

72. *Marguerite Lacoste v Claude Lacoste*, 10 Feb. 1783, LHC.

73. The issue of protection from spousal abuse is little discussed here because the judicial records do not yield much information about it. One of the closest students of domestic matters in this era discusses the conflicting evidence on the ecclesiastic tribunal. See Hans W. Baade, "The Form of Marriage in Spanish North America," *Cornell Law Review* 61 (1975): 45.

74. Asunción Lavrin, "Female Religious," in *Cities and Society in Colonial Latin America*, ed. Hoberman and Socolow, 191.

75. See *Maria Antonio Rodriguez v Joseph Molina*, 20 Apr. 1782, New Orleans Notarial Archive, Civil District Courts Building, New Orleans (hereafter cited as NONA, followed by the name of the notary whose bundle for the year of the citation contains the document, unless it is otherwise indicated), Estevan Quinones No. 1 (1778–1783), which apparently represents along with succeeding volumes the records of the ecclesiastical court; note the use of the word *"divorcio"* in this and similar pleas. See also *Augustina Concha v Juan Riquero*, 14 Sept. 1786, LHC, for a case in which the court was unable to protect a woman from a sneak public beating by her husband. Sternly warned by the court, however, he complied quickly when she sued for a settlement in *Augustina Concha v Juan Riquero*, 17 Sept. 1787 and 14 May 1789, LHC.

76. "Digest of the Laws of Louisiana, Nov. 29, 1803," 373.

77. Ibid.

78. Based on links between the marriages of 62 brides and 4 grooms for the period 1759–1768, and of 317 brides and 91 grooms for the period 1778–1802, and their dates of birth given in the baptismal registers of St. Louis Church, found in Woods and Nolan, *Sacramental Records*, vols. 1–7. A conservative principle of selection was applied that eliminated any bride or groom whose date of birth could not be established beyond the shadow of a doubt.

79. Ibid.

80. Ibid.

81. Succession of Louis Ducret, 30 Aug. 1779, LHC; *Madeleine Brazillier v Henri Després*, 9 June 1788, LHC.

82. See, for example, *Isabel Duverge v Pierre Lavergne Succession*, 14 Mar. 1795, LHC.

83. Estate of Bobé Descloseaux, 15 Jan. 1773, *LHQ* 9 (1926): 150–56, entry for 24 Sept. 1777. Another case, however, shows that a native female creditor of an estate might be protected at the expense of a new immigrant widow; see Succession of William Quays, 12 Nov. 1791, LHC.

84. *Marie-Louise Lemaire v Jean Mackies*, 9 Sept. 1785, LHC. It is possible that courts permitted some special protection of vulnerable widows by the official under-valuation of estates to permit the widow to purchase the estate and hold it together or to discourage creditors from demanding liquidation of the estate. For cases in which

inventories are specifically described as customarily assigning low values to movables, see *Valentin v Estate of Jung*, 23 Sept. 1784, LHC; and *Josette v Marie Louise Alarie*, 6 Mar. 1789, LHC.

85. Gabriel Debien, *Lettres de colons* (Laval, France: Université de Dakar, 1964), 140. For a rare instance of women engaged in the highest order of economic activity in a slave society, see Lease of a Plantation by Madeleine Brazillier to Françoise Girardy and Annulment, 12 Apr., 2 May 1771, NONA, Jean-Baptiste Garic, 2, 131–31v, 153v–54v.

86. Léon Abensour, *La femme et le féminisme avant la Révolution* (Paris: Éditions Ernest Leroux, 1923), 181–83.

87. Lugar, "Merchants," 66.

88. Robin, *Voyage*, 239–40.

89. See, for example, Certification of Purity of Blood of Marguerite Wiltz, 7 Feb. 1776, LHC; see also L. N. McAlister, "Social Structure and Social Change in New Spain," *HAHR* 43 (1963): 353–56.

90. See Marriage Contract of Jean Paillet and Catherine Villeré, 16 Nov. 1769, LHC, of a white man with a quadroon at English Turn, an unusual exception to the rule against intermarriage. This may be the couple married by Ulloa's chaplain; see Robin, *Voyage*, 57.

91. Robin, *Voyage*, 240–41. On children, see p. 37.

92. Carondelet to Las Casas, 5 July 1794, DSG/HBC, 4:377–80.

93. Carondelet to the Bishop of Louisiana, 9 June 1796, DSG/HBC, 11:489–91.

94. David K. Bjork, ed. and trans., "Documents Relating to the Establishment of Schools in Louisiana, 1771," *MVHR* 11 (1924–25): 561–69; Navarro to José Gálvez, 12 Feb. 1787, AGI, SD, 2611:41–44.

95. There was a lag for many years before schools were entirely reestablished after the fires of 1788 and 1794; see Miró to Porlier, 7 Apr. 1788, AGI, SD, 2553:253–58v; Wilson, "Almonester," 207–10. On the first library society in 1805, see Roger P. McCutcheon, "Libraries in New Orleans, 1771–1833," *LHQ* 20 (1937): 152–58.

96. Apprenticeship of Étienne Broiart Jr. to Shoemaker Abraham Guidroz, 21 Oct. 1769, LHC; Apprenticeship of Jean Bouquoi to Shoemaker Jean Durant, 7 Nov. 1769, LHC; Apprenticeship of Louis Manière to Sailmaker Antoine Limier, 6 Apr. 1770, LHC; Apprenticeship of Bely Estirguill to Master Tailor John Mackey, 8 Mar. 1785, NONA, Rodriguez No. 4, 209–10v; Apprenticeship of François Robin to "Galatase" Antoine Saubert [*galandage* was the favorite method of construction in New Orleans, called brick-between-posts], 18 Mar. 1785, NONA, Rodriguez No. 4, 236–37; Apprenticeship of Mathieu Hotard to Silversmith William Gross, 27 July 1785, NONA, Rodriguez No. 5, 453v–54v; Apprenticeship of Nancy Lafond to Marie Hognon [apparently in housewifery, reading and writing], 10 Aug. 1786, NONA, Rodriguez No. 9, 971v–72v.

97. Petition of Thomas Porée, 1 Feb. 1771, LHC; and see *LHQ* 12 (1929): 288–99, for the editors' comments.

98. Ibid., 293.

99. Ramón A. Gutiérrez, *When Jesus Came, the Corn Mothers Went Away: Marriage, Sexuality, and Power in New Mexico, 1500–1846* (Stanford: Stanford Univ. Press, 1991), 315.

100. Ibid., 315–18. See also the very useful discussion of the economic issues involved in

this contest in Jack Goody, *The Development of the Family and Marriage in Europe* (Cambridge: Cambridge Univ. Press, 1983).

101. Jack D. L. Holmes, *Honor and Fidelity: The Louisiana Infantry Regiment and the Louisiana Militia Companies, 1766–1821* (Birmingham, Al.: Privately Printed, 1965), 18–25; see also R. E. Chandler, "O'Reilly and the Louisiana Militia," *Revue de Louisiane* 6 (1977): 63–68.

102. Wilson, "Almonester," 185–87.

103. Pope, *Tour through the Southern and Western Territories*, 39–40.

104. Gilbert C. Din, *Francisco Bouligny: A Bourbon Soldier in Spanish Louisiana* (Baton Rouge: Louisiana State Univ. Press, 1993), 42–49.

105. Sheriff's Seizure of 28 May 1766, LHC; Petition by Widow Felicité Dubreuil, 11 Aug. 1766, LHC, to spend the principal of her inheritance; Villars Dubreuil turned his hatred upon the tutor of his biggest creditor, as seen in *Jean-Pierre-Robert-Gérard Vilemont v Dubreuil*, 14 Feb. 1768, LHC; and Debt Arbitration, 6 June 1768, LHC.

106. Unzaga's Order for a Meeting of Dubreuil's Creditors, 11 Apr. 1770, LHC; *State v Dubreuil*, 30 Sept. 1771, LHC.

107. [Hilliard d'Auberteuil], *Considérations sur l'état présent*, 1:112–29.

108. Din, *Francisco Bouligny*, 49–51.

109. Ibid., 211–13.

110. The records of a doomed attempt to collect a chimney tax in the 1790s are worthless, for the number of chimneys is a very uncertain measure of property, and the attempt was soon abandoned because many or even most people refused to pay. See Din and Harkins, *New Orleans Cabildo*, 146. No census of Tchoupitoulas has turned up for this period, except for the summary of 1785.

111. Wilson, "Almonester," 183–235.

112. Nash, *Urban Crucible*, 261–63.

113. *Phoenard v Lacoste*, St. Pé, and Milhet, 13 May to 3 June 1768, LHC.

114. *Roche v Joseph-Marie Armant*, 13 May 1768, LHC.

115. AGI, Papeles Procedentes de Cuba, Legajo 545 f, g, and l.

116. Two were Americans from Natchez executed for counterfeiting; three others were murderers.

117. *State v Josef Silva*, 17 Oct. 1786, LHC.

118. *Antonio Fernandez v Josef Leon, Josef Pivoto, and Yaca*, 16 Feb. 1781, LHC; *Marianne Perthuit v Jacques and Cupidon*, 28 Feb. 1785, LHC.

119. *Delagrouet and Jourdain v Chabot*, 3 Feb. 1785, LHC.

120. *Chiloc v Chouteau*, 20 Apr. 1771, LHC; defendant paid costs and was warned.

121. For some good examples of exceptions, see *Juan Castanedo v Étienne Pellegrue*, 1 June 1799, and Jean-Baptiste Frette, 10 Mar. 1800, LHC, for a pair of unusual cases involving the paternity and race of a girl; and *Arthur Morgan v Joseph Leblanc*, 25 Feb. 1800, and *Leblanc v Morgan and Edouard Forstall*, 22 Aug. 1800, LHC.

122. Most notably *Marie-Jeanne Lerable v Nicolas and Charles Daunoy and François Montreuil*, 10 Jan. 1798, LHC; *Marie-Jeanne Lerable v Marie-Josef Cenas and Jeanne Regnet*, 31 May 1799, LHC.

123. For rare references to ethnic conflict, see Bernardo Gálvez to José Gálvez, 8 Apr. 1782, AGI, SD, 2549:93–93v, reporting on dissension between French and Spanish

troops he gathered in Saint Domingue; and Carondelet to the Bishop of Louisiana, 9 June 1796, DSG/HBC, 11:489–90, requesting Spanish and French priests for posts where the population was mixed and Irish priests for the English speakers at Natchez and Baton Rouge.

124. Denial of a suit in the governor's court could technically be appealed to the cabildo, but this was rarely done, and the Spanish discouraged the cabildo members from exercising this function. After the early years, appeals were remanded directly to judges of the royal Audience of Santo Domingo in Havana. See *Loppinot v Villeneuve*, 15 Apr. 1774, LHC; *LHQ* 10 (1927): 438; *LHQ* 11 (1928): 33–120.

125. For other cases, see *Jacques Beauregared v Étienne Plauché*, 12 Oct. 1774, LHC; *Jacques Chaperon v Julie Larche*, 4 Feb. 1775, LHC, and *François Larche v Julie's Curator*, 11 Dec. 1776; *François Blache v Jacques Tarascon*, 19 Oct. 1778, LHC; *Marie Vizente v Angelique and Pierre*, 27 Feb. 1781, LHC; *Roman Lozada v Pedro Guerrero*, 1 Nov. 1794, LHC.

126. Gilbert C. Din, "Protecting the '*Barrera*': Spain's Defenses in Louisiana, 1763–1779," *LH* 19 (1978): 183–211; Gilbert C. Din, "Spain's Immigration Policy in Louisiana and the American Penetration, 1792–1803," *Southwestern Historical Quarterly* 76 (1973): 255–76; Abraham P. Nasatir, *Spanish War Vessels on the Mississippi, 1792–1796* (New Haven: Yale Univ. Press, 1968); Holmes, *Honor and Fidelity*; C. Richard Arena, "Philadelphia–Spanish New Orleans Trade, 1789–1803" (Ph.D. diss., Univ. of Pennsylvania, 1959); Thomas M. Fiehrer, "The Baron de Carondelet as Agent of Bourbon Reform: A Study of Spanish Colonial Administration in the Years of the French Revolution," 2 vols. (Ph.D. diss., Tulane Univ., 1977), 356–65, 452–65.

127. Coker and Rea, eds., *Anglo-Spanish Confrontation*; J. Barton Starr, *Tories, Dons and Rebels: The American Revolution in British West Florida* (Gainesville: Univ. Presses of Florida, 1976); Robert V. Haynes, *The Natchez District and the American Revolution* (Jackson: Univ. Press of Mississippi, 1976); Light T. Cummins, *Spanish Observers and the American Revolution, 1775–1783* (Baton Rouge: Louisiana State Univ. Press, 1991); Manuel Conrotte, *La intervención de España en la independencia de los Estados Unidos de la América del norte* (Madrid: Librería General de Victoriano Suárez, 1920); James, *Oliver Pollock*; Buchanan P. Thomson, *Spain: Forgotten Ally of the American Revolution* (North Quincy, Mass.: Christopher Publishing House, 1976); Jack D. L. Holmes, "The Historiography of the American Revolution in Louisiana," *LH* 19 (1978): 309–26.

128. Richard B. Morris, *The Peacemakers: The Great Powers and American Independence* (1965; reprint, New York: Harper and Row, 1970), 218–47, 386–410; José A. Armillas Vicente, *El Mississippi, frontera de España: España y los Estados Unidos ante el tratado de San Lorenzo* (Zaragoza: Talleres Editoriales Cometa, 1977); Arthur P. Whitaker, *The Mississippi Question, 1795–1803: A Study in Trade, Politics, and Diplomacy* (1934; reprint, Gloucester, Mass.: Peter Smith, 1962); Eli Merritt, "Sectional Conflict and Secret Compromise: The Mississippi River Question and the United States Constitution," *American Journal of Legal History* 35 (1991): 117–71.

129. Frederick J. Turner, "The Origin of Genêt's Projected Attack on Louisiana and the Floridas," *AHR* 3 (1897–98): 650–71; Frederick J. Turner, "Documents on the Relations of France to Louisiana, 1792–1795," ibid., 490–516; Ernest R. Liljegren, "Jacobinism in Spanish Louisiana, 1792–1797," *LHQ* 22 (1939): 47–97; Gilbert L.

Lycan, *Alexander Hamilton and American Foreign Policy: A Design for Greatness* (Norman: Univ. of Oklahoma Press, 1970).

CHAPTER 7. BLACKS, THE SLAVE TRADE, AND THE ADVENT OF SUGAR

1. Robin, *Voyage*, 252.
2. Ibid.
3. Ibid., 237.
4. Ibid., 241.
5. Ibid., 248, 238–39.
6. Bouligny, *Louisiana in 1776*, 57; Robin, *Voyage*, 240.
7. Louis-Narcisse Baudry des Lozières, *Voyage à la Louisiane et sur le continent de l'Amérique septentrionale, fait dans les années 1794 à 1798* (Paris: Dentu, 1802), 199–200; see also 103–10, on the *"travail lucratif"* of Louisiana slaves. See also his *Les égaremens du nigrophilisme* (Paris: Chez Migneret, 1802), 74–85. For the countertrend toward a more enlightened view, see Isabelle and Jean-Louis Vissière, *La traite des noirs au siècle des lumières* (Paris: Éditions A. M. Métailié, 1982), 28–31.
8. *Jean-Louis Dapremont v Julie*, 28 Oct. 1785, LHC; *Joseph Durreau v Alexandre*, 29 Mar. 1799, LHC; *Sebastien Bury v Jean-Baptiste*, 10 Feb. 1786, LHC; *Livaudais v Demba*, 4 Dec. 1800, LHC.
9. *Ximenes v Broutin*, 3 June 1786, LHC; *Porte v Delery*, 17 June 1786; *Bienvenu v Spiritu Liotaud*, 19 Apr. 1792, LHC. It is not clear that this sentence was carried out.
10. Curtin, *Atlantic Slave Trade*, 150, 200, 212, 268. Charles III experimented with a Spanish monopoly granted to one Miguel Uriarte for a few years, but he went bankrupt, so foreigners dominated the slave supply once again. See James F. King, "Evolution of the Free Slave Trade Principle in Spanish Colonial Administration," *HAHR* 22 (1942): 41; see also Roland Mellafe, *Negro Slavery in Latin America*, trans. J. W. S. Judge (Berkeley and Los Angeles: Univ. of California Press, 1975), 38–84.
11. Bernardo Galvez to José Galvez, 21 Mar. 1777, AGI, SD, 2547:183–85v; and Bernardo Galvez to José Galvez, 18 Aug. 1777, AGI, SD, 2547:339–39v, requesting permission to trade local produce for slaves; Royal Proclamation, 21 Nov. 1777, *SMV*, pt. 1, 242–43.
12. Based on a sample of slave auctions randomly selected from NONA, Notary Jean-Baptiste Garic's bundle of 1771; Notary Andres Almonester's bundle of 1778; Notary Fernando Rodriguez's bundle of 1787; Notary Antonio Ximenes' bundle of 1799–1800; and Notary Marc Lafitte's bundle of 1812.
13. Curtin, *Atlantic Slave Trade*, 83.
14. Ibid., 73.
15. Matas, *History of Medicine in Louisiana*, 1:198–219.
16. Thomas N. Ingersoll, "The Slave Trade and the Ethnic Diversity of Louisiana's Slave Community," *LH* 37 (1996): 151–52.
17. Royal Decree Conceding New Favors to Promote the Trade of Louisiana, 22 Jan. 1782, Manuscritos, Biblioteca Nacional, Madrid, leg. 19247, Article 4; Coutts, "Martín Navarro," 441–44. On the progress of the trade, see Navarro to José Gálvez, 16 June 1786, AGI, SD, 2610:514v–15. In a series of steps beginning in 1789, Spain declared

freedom of trade in slaves for its colonies. See King, "Evolution of the Free Slave Trade Principle," 47–54; Curtin, *Atlantic Slave Trade*, 150; Robert L. Stein, *The French Slave Trade in the Eighteenth Century: An Old Regime Business* (Madison: Univ. of Wisconsin Press, 1979), 211; James A. Rawley, *The Transatlantic Slave Trade: A History* (New York: W. W. Norton, 1981), 130. The shifting sands of Spanish policy are studied by Paul F. Lachance, in "The Politics of Fear: French Louisianians and the Slave Trade, 1786–1809," *Plantation Society in the Americas* 1 (1979): 162–97. The interpretations presented here differ from Lachance's in some details.

18. See Navarro to Gálvez, 28 Apr. 1785, AGI, SD, 2610:140–40v; and Printed Schedule of Imposts, 22 Jan. 1782, AN, AC, C13B, 1:450–57, on the lifting of the royal 6 percent impost on slaves. See also Decision of Council of the Indies, 15 Dec. 1785, AGI, SD, 2530:126–41, reiterating the necessity to restrict the slave trade by the English to minimize opportunity for illegal trade with colonists for other commodities. The only specific report of a large shipment of slaves to New Orleans in these years is in Navarro to José Gálvez, 16 June 1786, AGI, SD, 2610:514v–15, where he writes, "The commerce in Negroes, despite the want of silver, continues but slowly, although there are presently 300 in the River and some more are expected." See also Miró to José Gálvez, 1 May 1787, AGI, SD, 2552:285–92v; Navarro to José Gálvez, 7 June and 19 Dec. 1787, AGI, SD, 2611:211–15, 897–906. The supply of Jamaican slaves to Natchez by Daniel Clark and others beginning in 1787 can be traced in May W. McBee, comp., *The Natchez Court Records, 1767–1805: Abstracts of Early Records* (Ann Arbor: Edwards Brothers, 1953), 44–83.

19. *Pousset v Marmillon*, 3 Mar. 1784 (filed under 5 Mar.), LHC. For another example of the variety of risks to a slaver and its cargo, see Petition of André Duget, 16 Aug. 1784, LHC, about a vessel from Saint Domingue grounded on the bar at the mouth of the Mississippi River, which occasioned the loss of several slaves' lives.

20. Decree by Miró, 2 June 1786, *ADC*, vol. 3, no. 1, 90–96. See also Miró to José Gálvez, 1 May 1787, AGI, SD, 2552:285–87v; and Miró to Lerena, 22 July 1791, AGI, SD, 2557:18–19v. The problem of the introduction of seasoned, suspect slaves was still a problem at the end of the colonial period; see Pierre-Clément Laussat to Decrès, 5 June 1803, and Appeal by Municipal Council to Laussat, 2 Dec. 1803, Laussat Papers.

21. Account of the Negroes that were Introduced into this Port in the Year 1787, Archivo General de Indias, Papeles Procedentes de Cuba, microfilm copy in The Historic New Orleans Collection (hereafter cited as AGI, PPC), 678b:15 bis–15 bis verso.

22. In alphabetical order, Narciso Alva, Alexandre Baudin, Jean-Baptiste Beauregard, William Butler, Daniel Clark, Michel Fortier, Claude Girod, Thomas Irwin, Jaime Jorda, Jean-Baptiste Labattut, Jérome Lachapelle, Jean Ladnier, Lavergne and Siben Cie., Henry Ludlow, Pierre Marigny, François Mayronne, Juan Medina, Jean Merieult, Étienne Pedesclaux, Oliver Pollock, George Proffit, Alexandre Reaud, David Ross, Juan Santa Cruz, Pierre Sauvé, Joseph Trevino.

23. For two outstanding examples, see Bills of Sale by William Butler, 25 Jan. *passim* to 27 May 1794, NONA, Pierre Pedesclaux No. 20, 72 to 538. Bills of Sale by Merieult, 10 May *passim* to 27 July 1803, NONA, Pierre Pedesclaux No. 44, 397 to 630; Bills of Sale by Merieult, 28 July to 29 Nov. 1803, NONA, Pierre Pedesclaux No. 45, 645 to 920. After the outbreak of the Haitian Revolution, Charles IV flatly prohibited the

importation of slaves from Saint Domingue, which led traders to other ports in the Antilles. See Miró to Las Casas, 21 Aug. 1790, DSG, 21:50. On violations of the ban, see Declaration by Jean-Baptiste Poeyfarre, 16 July 1792, ADC, vol. 3, no. 3, 9–10; Governor Hector, Baron Carondelet to Diego Gardoqui, 25 July 1792, AGI, SD, 2665:468–69.

24. See Petition to Carondelet, 20 June 1795, ADC, vol. 4, no. 1, 40–41, at the behest of *"infinitos habitantes"* to keep out all slaves who were not *"enteramente bosales"*; Decree by the Cabildo, 19 Feb. 1796, ibid., 95–97, proscribing all slaves "of whatever class."

25. Declaration by Vidal, 8 Aug. 1800, ADC, vol. 4, no. 3, 206–7; Debate in Cabildo, 16 Aug. 1800, ibid., 207–22; Report on the Slave Trade, 1796–1800, AGI, SD, 2588:321–44, 349v–54; see also Casa Calvo to the Cabildo, 24 Oct. 1800, ADC, vol. 4, no. 4, 13–22. For a different interpretation of these events, see Lachance, "Politics of Fear," 171–76. On the reopening, see Decree by Ramon de Lopez y Angulo, 29 Nov. 1800, AGI, PPC, 550:327–27v. Nonetheless, the policy was not clear. Even at the end of the Spanish regime, royal officers were not sure who was to be allowed to bring slaves into New Orleans; see Pierre-Joseph Favrot to Governor Nemesio Salcedo, 9 Sept. 1803, Favrot Family Papers, Manuscripts Section, Special Collections Division, Howard-Tilton Memorial Library, Tulane Univ., New Orleans, on a Spanish shipload full of slaves from Kingston via Cuba. See also Pierre Clément de Laussat, *Memoirs of My Life, to my Son during the Years 1803 and After . . .* , ed. Robert D. Bush, trans. Agnes-Josephine Pastwa (Baton Rouge: Louisiana State Univ. Press for the Historic New Orleans Collection, 1978), 29–32.

26. This is intended to be a preliminary count based solely on the records in NONA. At least some of these slaves were being sold to planters beyond New Orleans after 1787. See bills of sale by several of the traders listed above in McBee, *Natchez Court Records*, 44–45, 53, 57–58, 69–72, 80, 83. On the other hand, other slaves may have been entered but not registered in bills of sale in NONA. It was not until 28 Feb. 1789, that the Spanish king declared not only free trade in slaves, untaxed, but provided a small bounty for them as well. See King, "Evolution of the Free Slave Trade Principle," 49–52; Stein, *French Slave Trade in the Eighteenth Century*, 211. Governor Miró tried unsuccessfully to convince Madrid to allow him to charge a local tax of one peso per imported slave for the reimbursement fund for those planters whose slaves were killed in the attack on Gaillard land in 1784; see Miró to José Gálvez, 24 Mar. 1787, AGI, SD, 2552:145–50v; and Consultation on the Slave Trade, 1791, AGI, SD, 2531:203–13.

27. Curtin's figure is also based on a census analysis that includes the mistaken assumption that New Orleans was as mortally unhealthful in the eighteenth century as it became in the nineteenth; *Atlantic Slave Trade*, 83. In fact, no major mortalities from epidemic diseases are recorded between the founding years and the last decades of the eighteenth century. Paul Lachance extrapolates backward from census tables as well, and this is a risky procedure, especially given the ambiguity in the census of 1797, for example, although the census material he employs for the period prior to that is reliable. See Lachance, "Politics of Fear," 196–97.

28. The data for Table 14 are based on the following slave rolls, numbered 1 through 10: Succession of Jean-Baptiste Destréhan, 26 Feb. 1765, NONA, Garic Book No. 1;

Succession of Jean-Baptiste Noyon, 22 Oct. 1763, LHC; Succession of Louis Favre, 10 Oct. 1780, LHC, WPA translation only; Succession of Charlotte Dapremont, 5 Oct. 1788, LHC; Succession of Jean Piseros, 28 Aug. 1777, LHC; Succession of Marie Battasar, 14 Feb. 1789, LHC; Succession of Barba Harang, 25 Jan. 1776, NONA, Garic No. 7, 19–26; Succession of Jacques Livaudais, 29 Apr. 1773, NONA, Almonester; Succession of Antoine-Philippe Marigny, NONA, Garic No. 8; Succession of Jean-Baptiste Bienvenu, 11 Sept. 1790, LHC. The data for Table 15 are based on the following slave rolls, numbered 1 through 10: Succession of Pierre Marigny, 14 May 1800, LHC; Succession of François De Reggio, 5 Oct. 1787, LHC; Succession of Marie-Joseph Harang, c. 1769, NONA, Garic No. 1; Succession of Pierre Loriot of Des Allemands, 15 Mar. 1790, NONA, Misc., shelved at U9R-H5; Succession of Patrick Macnemara, 19 Jan. 1788, NONA, Rafael Perdomo; Sale of Half Interest in a Plantation by Nicolas Daunoy to Charles Favre Daunoy, Apr. 1779, NONA, Garic No. 11; Succession of Francisco Bouligny, 25 Nov. 1800, LHC; Succession of Pierre-Joseph Favrot, 15 May 1805, LHC; Succession of Martial Berthelot, 12 Oct. 1776, NONA, Garic No. 7; Succession of Guido Dufossat, 5 Oct. 1794, NONA, Antonio Ximenes. The data for Table 16 are based on the following slave rolls, numbered 1 through 10: Succession of Alexandre Vielle, 25 Sept. 1764, NONA, Garic No. 1; Succession of Louis De Velle, 14 July 1773, NONA, Garic No. 7; Succession of Antoine Bienvenu, 13 Nov. 1771, NONA, Garic No. 2; Succession of Pierre-François Olivier, 16 Apr. 1776, NONA, Almonester; Succession of Jean-Baptiste Senet, 31 July 1776, ibid.; Succession of Jonathas Darby, 18 Feb. 1767, NONA, Garic and Perdomo 1765–78; Mortgage by Louis Boisdoré to Salomon Mallines, 27 Feb. 1787, LHC; Succession of Joseph Casenave, 20 Sept. 1797, LHC; Succession of Marguerite Devin, 12 May 1797, LHC; Succession of Valentin Leblanc, 12 May 1796, LHC.

29. The "nation" was listed after a slave's name and before occupation, age, and market value.

30. André Destréhan Jung Succession, 14 Sept. 1784 *LHC.*

31. Destréhan Succession, 26 Feb. 1765, NONA, Garic, book 1, no. 28.

32. Gayoso to Watts, 1 Sept. 1797, "Family Letters of Don Manuel Gayoso de Lemos, Governor of Louisiana, 1797 to 1799," in *Louisiana Daughters of the American Revolution, Genealogical Records* (N.p.: N.p., 1938), 16. Copy in the Louisiana State Museum Library, New Orleans.

33. Ibid., 18.

34. Ibid.

35. In Fortescue Cuming, *Early Western Travels, 1748–1846,* vol. 4, *Cuming's Tour to the Western Country, 1807–1809,* ed. Reuben G. Thwaites (Cleveland: Arthur H. Clark, 1904), 4:363.

36. Robin, *Voyage,* 248.

37. Boré to Laussat, 27 June 1803, Laussat Papers; James Pitot, *Observations on the Colony of Louisiana from 1796 to 1802,* trans. Henry C. Pitot (Baton Rouge: Louisiana State Univ. Press for the Historic New Orleans Collection, 1979), 73–79.

38. John S. Kendall, "New Orleans' 'Peculiar Institution,'" *LHQ* 23 (1940): 874–75.

39. See also V. Alton Moody, "Slavery on Louisiana Sugar Plantations," *LHQ* 7 (1924): 232–48; John A. Heitmann, *The Modernization of the Louisiana Sugar Industry, 1830–1910* (Baton Rouge: Louisiana State Univ. Press, 1987), 8–14.

40. Victor Tixier, *Travels on the Osage Prairies*, ed. John F. McDermott and trans. Albert J. Salvan (Norman: Univ. of Oklahoma Press, 1940), 47. As discussed in an earlier chapter, the task system may have always been typical in New Orleans. For perhaps the best early description of sugar production, see [Hilliard d'Auberteuil], *Considérations sur l'état présent*, 1:169–228.

41. [Hilliard d'Auberteuil], *Considérations sur l'état présent*, 1:134.

42. Pitot, *Observations on the Colony of Louisiana*, 115.

43. Kenneth F. Kiple and Virginia H. King, *Another Dimension to the Black Diaspora: Diet, Disease, and Racism* (New York.: Cambridge Univ. Press, 1981), 5–61.

44. Ibid., 44.

45. Pitot, *Observations on the Colony of Louisiana*, 30, 79.

46. *Jean-Baptiste Cezaire Lebreton v Temba et al.*, 1 June 1771, LHC; see *LHQ* 8 (1925): 5–22. Three other slaves were whipped, tarred, and feathered for suspicious connections to the murder.

47. The most lurid case occurred at Baton Rouge; see *State v Marie Glass*, 7 Feb. 1780 and 19 Jan. 1781, LHC, and *LHQ* 7 (1924): 589–654, concerning a mixed-race native of North Carolina who virtually tortured a girl to death. See also *Jacques Vilbelmont v Chalinette*, 28 Sept. 1786, LHC; *Renato Beluche v Joseph*, 4 May 1787, LHC; *Josef Delacruz v Unknown Negro*, 15 May 1788, LHC; *Antonio Martinez v Jean-Baptiste*, 13 May 1790, LHC, a serious murder case.

48. *State v François-Joseph*, 9 Jan. 1802, LHC. It is curious that a slave tried to win asylum, since there is no evidence it was ever allowed in New Orleans.

49. *State v Jacques*, 17, 24 Apr. 1790, LHC. Another spectacular case arose in Des Allemands that is full of revealing details; see *State v Clément and Jacob*, 30 Oct. 1777, LHC, concerning the murder of a black slave overseer by his own brother who feared punishment for stealing something in New Orleans, as he had done before. The only fratricide on record, Clément desperately accused others before he finally confessed. For the fratricide he was whipped, hanged, and his corpse was sewn up in a sack with varmints and thrown in the river.

50. *State v Charles*, 28 Feb. 1786, LHC. The master was charged with the costs of court as well, which was routine in these criminal cases.

51. *State v Pierre et al.*, 26 May 1790, LHC.

52. *Bastian v Laurent Caliche*, 10 Jan. 1788, LHC.

53. *Monplaisir v Le Compte*, 2 Mar. 1785, LHC.

54. *State v Marianne et al.*, 29 July 1771, LHC.

55. *State v Bobo and Jacob*, 6 Mar. 1772.

56. Instructions, 12 Feb. 1770, AGI, SD, 2594:67v–68.

57. Report of Bienvenu, 26 May 1781, LHC.

58. Richard S. Dunn, "Black Society in the Chesapeake, 1776–1810"; and Philip D. Morgan, "Black Society in the Lowcountry, 1760–1810," in *Slavery and Freedom in the Age of the American Revolution*, ed. Ira Berlin and Ronald Hoffman (Urbana: Univ. of

Illinois Press, 1983), 138–41. See Jean-Pierre Tardieu, *Le destin des noirs aux Indes de Castille, XVe–XVIIIe siècles* (Paris: Éditions L'Harmattan, 1984), 266–95, on marronage in Spanish colonies.

59. Petitions by the Attorney General, 6, 27 Aug., 8, 15 Oct. 1783, *ADC*, 1:109–11, 113–14, 116, 139–40; Gilbert C. Din, "*Cimarrones* and the San Malo Band in Spanish Louisiana," *LH* 21 (1980): 239–42; Roland C. McConnell, *Negro Troops of Antebellum Louisiana: A History of the Battalion of Free Men of Color* (Baton Rouge: Louisiana State Univ. Press, 1968), 22–23. Din suggests a total figure of 103 maroons captured in all sweeps at this time.

60. Order of Assessment, 12, 19 Nov. 1773, *ADC*, 1:141–42.

61. Petitions by the Attorney General, 19, 26, Feb., 1 Mar., 9 Apr. 1779, *ADC*, 1:266–69, 273–74. Over the decade, only ten claims were lodged against the fund for maroons killed by pursuers. See Claim by Antoine Tomassin for Bombares, 14 Jan. 1774, *ADC*, 1:146–47; Claim by Zacharias Faustin for Charles, 11 Feb. 1774, *ADC*, 1:149–50; Claim by Mademoiselle de Calogne for Martine and Claim by Jacques Beauregard for Charles, 25 Feb. 1774, *ADC*, 1:151–52; Claim by François Pascalis de la Barre for Lozio, *ADC*, 1:184–85, 16 May 1775; Claim by Georges Trugle for a Slave, 10 May 1776, *ADC*, 1:206–7; Claim by François Villière for Indian Slave Pierrot, 31 Oct. 1777, *ADC*, 1:233–34, at Natchitoches; Claim by Pierre Cabaret de Trepis for Clémente, 6 Mar. 1778, *ADC*, 1:244–45; Claim by Georges Steigre for a Slave, 22 May 1778, *ADC*, 1:248–49; Claim by Pierre Lavigne for Pierre, 27 July 1781, *ADC*, 2:64.

62. See Hans W. Baade, "The Law of Slavery in Spanish *Luisiana*, 1769–1803," in *Louisiana's Legal Heritage*, ed. Haas and McDonald, 61–64, for other particulars of Gálvez's racist campaign against blacks to achieve white solidarity in the years of the war emergency.

63. Richard Price has described how difficult it could be to approach their refuges, which were artfully disguised and well-secured by booby traps. See Price, "Introduction," 6.

64. Claim for Compensation by Madame Duparc, 1 Aug. 1783, *ADC*, 2:163–64.

65. Trial of Maroons, 1 Mar. 1783, LHC. These documents must be used in conjunction with the translation by Laura Porteous, in *LHQ* 20 (1937): 841–65. Apparently unrelated cases concerning Gaillard Land maroons of 1784 have been appended to this document. See also Hall, *Africans in Colonial Louisiana*, 202–36.

66. Trial of Maroons, 1 Mar. 1783, LHC.

67. Ibid.

68. Proceedings, 23, 30 Apr. 1784, *ADC*, 2:206–9.

69. Petitions of 28 May, 4 June, 11, 30 July 1784, *ADC*, 2:212–19, and 3, 6–7. See also Burson, *Stewardship of Don Esteban Miró*, 110–19; McGowan, "Creation of a Slave Society," 228–44; Derek N. Kerr, "Petty Felony, Slave Defiance and Frontier Villainy: Crime and Criminal Justice in Spanish Louisiana, 1770–1803" (Ph.D. diss., Tulane Univ., 1983), 178–83.

70. The priests had, with the support of their king, ousted the French Capuchins because of their supposed lax morality and other faults. See Cyrilo to the Bishop of Havana, 6 Aug. 1772, in Gayarré, *History of Louisiana*, 3:57–66; Unzaga to Delatorre, 10 July 1773, DSG 5, 9–14. On the special and fascinating case of Father Hilaire de

Genévaux, see Testimonial against Hilaire Genévaux, 17 Nov. 1781, AGI, SD, 2587:575–90; and Dispatch on Hilaire, 17 Aug. 1784, AGI, SD, 2587:557–74. See also Dispatches on Louisiana Capuchins, 1783, AGI, SD, 2583:162–279; and 21 July 1783–3 Apr. 1786, AGI, SD, 2587:723–60; also Miró to Gálvez, 1 Aug. 1784, AGI, SD, 2549: 461–61v.

71. Authorities may have falsified a confession by St. Malo to justify their actions. The contradiction between St. Malo's apparently contrite confession and his lasting reputation among slaves as a stalwart who "said not a word" to accuse his compatriots is addressed by Din, in "Cimarrones and the San Malo Band," 256–57. The tone of Bouligny's report to Miró, the only report of the summary "trial," is suspect. The supposed quotations from a speech by St. Malo are most improbable and sound deliberately contrived. Din describes Miró's anger at Bouligny about the way the affair was handled (258, 260–61).

72. Ibid., 257; Burson, Stewardship of Don Esteban Miró, 214–15.

73. Petition by Reggio, 25 June 1784, ADC, 2:220–25.

74. Petition to the King, 2 July 1784, ADC, vol. 3, no. 1, 1–4.

75. Petition to the Bishop, 9 July 1784, ADC, vol. 3, no. 1, 4–5.

76. Din, "Cimarrones and the San Malo Band," 261.

77. Cabildo Deliberations, 19 Jan. 1781, ADC, 2:46–47.

78. Guillermo Parbaus v Juan Espinosa, 18 Feb. 1785, LHC; Juan Zerrada v Pierre, 26 May 1790, LHC; State v Antonio Ximenes, 2 June 1794, LHC.

79. State v Juan Freyre, 16 Aug. 1791, LHC; see also commentary by Henry P. Dart on "Juanico the Gallician's Billiard Hall," LHQ 6 (1923): 42–45; State v Pierre Baby, 31 Jan. 1794, LHC; State v Coffigny et al., 6 Feb. 1794, LHC; State v Pedro Diaz et al., 5 May 1794, LHC. One case concerned an interracial assault by a Spaniard and a slave upon an American; see John Jackson v Josef Gonzalez and Pierre, 15 Oct. 1800, LHC. The prominence of Spaniards in these incidents suggests that the outsider effect in criminal behavior is at work as usual.

80. The movement for street lighting actually began in 1792, when the cabildo decreed the necessity of it to eliminate lurking places for maroons and bad characters; the remaining surrounding forests were also to be pushed back for the same reason; see Decree of 5 Oct. 1792, ADC, vol. 3, no. 3, 24–26. For a report, see Carondelet to Llagano, 30 Mar. 1796, AGI, SD, 2565:593–97v, explaining the purpose and requesting that since a chimney tax passed for the support of the lamps has failed they wish to lease out waste commons surrounding the town to the "many poor . . . who could not subsist except by cultivating vegetables [for market]," referring to free blacks, and to use the proceeds to keep the lamps fueled. On the prolonged experimentation in search of a method of taxation to support the lamps, see Deliberations of 20 Apr. 1798, ADC, vol. 4, no. 2, 114–22.

81. Petition by Francisco Riano, 27 May 1791, ADC, vol. 3, no. 2, 134–35.

82. Petition by Gabriel Fonvergne, 22 Jan. 1796, ADC, vol. 4, no. 1, 88–89.

83. Decree of 29 Jan. 1796, ADC, vol. 4, no. 1, 90–91. The attorney general included Coquet's hall in his list of vice palaces in a new campaign a few years later; see Petition by Attorney General, 7–8 Feb. 1800, ADC, vol. 4, no. 3, 133–39.

84. Alex Lichtenstein, "'That Disposition to Theft, with which They Have Been Branded':

Moral Economy, Slave Management, and the Law," *Journal of Social History* 21 (1988): 413–40.

85. *William Strother v Jean-Baptiste Macarty*, 2 May 1782, LHC.

86. Sale of Jerome, 18 Nov. 1784, LHC; Petition by Josette, 6 Mar. 1789, LHC.

87. A suit about two slaves belonging to Jérome Lachiapelle who were hired or apprenticed to bricklayer Joseph Duguet revealed, for example, an informal contract only because the parties fell out over the terms in 1790. See *Lachiapelle v Duguet*, 27 July 1790, LHC; the plaintiff was a recent immigrant to the town, a prominent importer of slaves, who sued for the rent of the slaves, which Duguet claimed were apprenticed to him. The court found for Lachiapelle. Most contracts of apprenticeship in the record (10) are with shoemakers and carpenters.

88. Will of Marguerite, 1 Mar. 1770, LHC.

89. More of the relationship of Marguerite and the Oliviers is not known, so this is typical of interracial relations for its ambiguity. In so many instances, important implicit understandings between participants in interracial civil or criminal matters were not stated in the record or are hard to prove.

90. *Joseph Becat v Marianne*, 12 Sept., 29 Oct. 1767 (filed 14 Sept. and 8, 31 Oct.), LHC; Donation by Jean-Baptiste Maroteau to Samagis, 21 June 1779, NONA, Garic No. 12, 364–65; Will of François Demazillière, 29 Mar. 1783, NONA, Mazange, 282–87; Will of Francisco Soler, 7 Oct. 1783, NONA, Rodriguez, 893v–95; Will of Daniel Clark, 5 Jan. 1780, NONA, Mazange, 34–37 and ditto, 18 Aug. 1787, NONA, Perdomo, 428–32v; Will of Arnault Dubertrand, 16 Sept. 1785, NONA, Rodriguez, 801–3v; Will of Joseph and Louise Barba, 21 Feb. 1786, NONA, Rodriguez, 218–23v; Will of Madeleine Brazillier, 19 Oct. 1793, NONA, Ximenes, 603–7v.

91. *Bernabe Lenes v Marguerite Toutant*, 23 June 1789, LHC; Emancipation of Marguerite, 3 May 1779, NONA, Almonester, 253v–54v.

92. Emancipation of Fanchon, 30 Dec. 1773, NONA, Garic, 366–66v; *Pierre Fauché v François Demazillière*, 5 Feb. 1783, LHC; see also *Marie v Methode*, 6 Nov. 1780, LHC; *Claude Guillory v Michel and Marguerite Barre*, 20 Jan. 1781; *Linda v John Haily*, 19 Apr. 1785, LHC.

93. *Gaspard v André Neau Succession*, 14 Feb. 1771 (filed 15 Feb.), LHC, on a slave baptized as free in France but now pressed back into slavery in New Orleans by an executor for absent heirs; see also *Alexandre Boré v Nanette*, 29 Oct. 1773 (filed 19 Oct.), LHC; Succession of *Jeanne Kerouette v Françoise*, 8 Nov. 1774; Raynoldo Chouteau Succession, 21 Apr. 1776, LHC, which includes an appeal to Havana by slaves demanding freedom; *Alexis et al. v Pelagie Loreins' Executor*, 7 Sept. 1781, LHC; *Cecile v André Dumont's Executor*, 2 Aug. 1786, LHC; *Augustin v Agathe Lacroix Succession*, 3 Sept. 1786; *Baptiste Corce v Françoise*, 6 Oct. 1786, LHC; *Madeleine v Jean-Antoine Soulie's Executor*, 21 Nov. 1787, LHC; *François Carcasses v Baptiste*, 20 May 1788, LHC; *Marie-Jeanne v Chantalou's Heirs*, 18 Oct. 1799, LHC; *Michel v Rillieux's Heirs*, 5 Apr. 1800, LHC.

94. *Joseph v Degout's Executor*, 8 Aug. 1783, LHC; *Joseph v Degout Succession*, 3 Apr. 1790, lodged when the estate's executor died and the heirs were temporarily not represented, showing how a slave could be alert to and take advantage of shifting circumstances in the lives of whites.

95. Robin, *Voyage*, 248.

96. *Pechons v Macnemara*, 19 Dec. 1776, LHC. See Douglas Deal, "A Constricted World:

Free Blacks on Virginia's Eastern Shore, 1680–1750," in *Colonial Chesapeake Society*, ed. Lois Green Carr, Philip D. Morgan, and Jean B. Russo (Chapel Hill: Univ. of North Carolina Press, 1988), 304–5, for attempts by free blacks to stand up for their rights in court.

97. *François v Pechon*, 20 Mar. 1802, LHC.

98. Alfred N. Hunt, *Haiti's Influence on Antebellum America: Slumbering Volcano in the Caribbean* (Baton Rouge: Louisiana State Univ. Press, 1988), 107–46.

99. Census of 31 Dec. 1806, *TPQ* 923–24.

100. *Nicholas Bachus v Marianne Bienvenu*, 20 Jan. 1785, LHC. The widow absolutely denied the claim and the court did not proceed with the trial for reasons left unexplained.

101. Robin, *Voyage*, 250.

102. Carolyn E. Fick, *The Making of Haiti: The Saint Domingue Revolution from Below* (Knoxville: Univ. of Tennessee Press, 1990), 183–203, 245–50.

103. Kimberly Hanger, "Conflicting Loyalties: The French Revolution and Free People of Color in Spanish New Orleans," *LH* 34 (1993): 30.

CHAPTER 8. THE SLAVE SOCIETY OF SPANISH NEW ORLEANS

1. Thomas M. Fiehrer, "The African Presence in Colonial Louisiana: An Essay on the Continuity of Caribbean Culture," in *Louisiana's Black Heritage*, ed. McDonald, Kemp, and Haas, 18–19, 29–30.

2. James Lockhart and Stuart B. Schwartz, *Early Latin America: A History of Colonial Spanish America and Brazil* (New York: Cambridge Univ. Press, 1983), 61–102.

3. General O'Reilly had decreed that Indian slavery was abolished in Louisiana in conformity with Spanish law. In reality, those already enslaved died in that status despite the efforts of a few to sue for freedom, but O'Reilly's decree does seem to have discouraged further purchases of Indian slaves. See Stephen Webre, "The Problem of Indian Slavery in Spanish Louisiana, 1769–1803," *LH* 25 (1984): 117–35.

4. Genovese, *World the Slaveholders Made*, 64–65.

5. Lockhart and Schwartz, *Early Latin America*, 72.

6. Ibid., 91.

7. Frederick P. Bowser, *The African Slave in Colonial Peru, 1524–1650* (Stanford: Stanford Univ. Press, 1974), 7, 100–109.

8. Gayarré, *History of Louisiana*, 2:184; Lockhart and Schwartz, *Early Latin America*, 129–32. On the complexities and historical confusion surrounding this term, see Jack D. Forbes, *Africans and Native Americans: The Language of Race and the Evolution of Red-Black Peoples*, 2d ed. (Urbana: Univ. of Illinois Press, 1993). The word "mulatto" in New Orleans meant a person with some black ancestry, usually one-half.

9. Gutiérrez, *When Jesus Came*, 335.

10. The policy of the government of Louis XVI in the 1770s can be followed in AN, AC, série F1B, discussed earlier in chapter 5. On Britain, see Folarin Shyllon, *Black People in Britain, 1555–1833* (London: Oxford Univ. Press, 1977), 99–105, 249–51.

11. Racial prejudice became much more explicit because of it, and the election of 1802 was affected by wildly inflammatory charges of miscegenation against an important doctrinaire of the new prejudice, Thomas Jefferson. See Winthrop D. Jordan, *White over Black: American Attitudes Toward the Negro, 1550–1812* (1968; reprint, Baltimore: Pen-

guin Books, 1969), 461–81, 542–69; and Fawn M. Brodie, *Thomas Jefferson: An Intimate History* (1974; reprint, New York: Bantam Books, 1975), 450–502.

12. See especially Brodie, *Thomas Jefferson.*

13. Louis Philippe d'Orléans, *Journal de mon voyage d'Amérique,* ed. Suzanne Huart (Paris: Flammarion, 1976), 55.

14. See Jordan, *White over Black,* 138–40; Higginbotham, *In the Matter of Color,* 44–47, on Virginia, which was representative of views in the southern colonies on intermarriage. On the British West Indies, see Mavis C. Campbell, *The Dynamics of Change in a Slave Society: A Sociopolitical History of the Free Blacks of Jamaica, 1800–1865* (Cranbury, N.J.: Associated Univ. Presses, 1976), 50–56.

15. On the interracial marriage, see Statement of the of the Inhabitants and Traders of Louisiana on the Event of October 29, 1768, n.d. [printed], AN, AC, C13A, 48: 253. On the free blacks, see Oath of 20 Sept. 1769, The "Black Books," Document 1-A, LHC. The original has disappeared from the collection.

16. One well-traveled observer stated very clearly at the end of the French regime, for example, that only four racial groups were found in Louisiana: European-born whites, creole whites, Africans, and those with mixed European and Indian parentage. That is, while the métis were distinctive enough to rate a separate category, the number of mulattoes was small and regarded as forming part of the "African," slave population. See Bossu, *Travels Through that Part of North America,* 1:23. The emancipation of mulattoes is virtually never mentioned in the judicial records of that era.

17. For a different view, see Foner, "Free People of Color in Louisiana and St. Domingue," 409–10; James E. Winston, "The Free Negro in New Orleans, 1803–1860," *LHQ* 21 (1938): 1075–85; and Jack D. L. Holmes, "Do It! Don't Do It!: Spanish Laws on Sex and Marriage," in *Louisiana's Legal Heritage,* ed. Haas and McDonald, 20–22. Popular writers have accorded interracial domestic relations and mixed race people a central position in their works; see Alfred Mercier, *L'habitation Saint-Ybars: ou, maîtres et esclaves en Louisiane,* ed. Regimald Hamel (1881; reprint, Montreal: Éditions Pierre-Clément-de-Laussat, 1982), for an example. Suits between whites concerning interracial sex relations are rarely found in the courts; for one example, see *Juan Castenedo v E. F. Pellegrue,* 1 June 1799, LHC, for slander concerning a pregnant slave. Some historians posit a different attitude toward race among Spaniards arising from the multiracial society in some regions in Spain. See Harmannus Hoetink, *The Two Variants in Caribbean Race Relations: A Contribution to the Sociology of Segmented Societies,* trans. Eva M. Hooykas (1962; reprint, New York: Oxford Univ. Press, 1967), 164–68. See Jorge Juan and Antonio Ulloa, *Noticias secretas de America* (1826; reprint, Bogotá: Biblioteca Banco Popular, 1983), 490–91, on the prevalence of concubinage in the Spanish colonies.

18. Emancipation of 13 Aug. 1772, NONA, Jean-Baptiste Garic 3, 222v–23v.

19. Emancipation of 18 Oct. 1782, NONA, Leonard Mazange No. 6, 873v–75.

20. Emancipation of 30 May 1776, NONA, Garic No. 7, 171–72.

21. Emancipation of 22 Sept. 1795, NONA, Carlos Ximenes No. 9, 421v–22v.

22. Emancipation of 24 May 1786, NONA, Fernando Rodriguez No. 8, 671v–73.

23. Emancipation of Catin, 20 July 1773. Probably the same as Emancipation of Catherine by Charles J. B. Fleuriau, 9 May 1775, NONA, Garic No. 6, 141v–42v.

24. Jean Perret's will begins with the usual commitment of his soul to God; he then donates all his personal estate to his former slave, Angélique, now free, but the reader gains no sense that the bequest arises from a religious impulse. See Will of 7 Feb. 1774, NONA, Garic No. 5, 28–29.

25. See, for example, Gwendolyn Midlo Hall, "Raza y libertad: la manumision de los esclavos rurales de la Luisiana bajo la jurisdiccion del capitan general de Cuba," *Anuario de Estudios Americanos* 43 (1986): 365–76.

26. Assertions that "white women were scarce and died young" and that the typical New Orleans couple "did not marry before the church" are insupportable. See Kimberly S. Hanger, *Bounded Lives, Bounded Places: Free Black Society in Colonial New Orleans, 1769–1803* (Durham, N.C.: Duke Univ. Press, 1997), 97.

27. Emancipation of 1 Feb. 1799, NONA, Pierre Pedesclaux No. 33, 65–66.

28. Emancipation of 11 Sept. 1786, NONA, Rodriguez 1786, No. 9, 1159–59v.

29. Emancipation of 9 Apr. 1791, NONA, Pedesclaux 12, 245–46.

30. Emancipation of 8 Oct. 1784, NONA, Rodriguez No. 3, 715–15v.

31. Emancipation of 19 Oct. 1801, NONA, Pedesclaux No. 39, 566v–67v.

32. Emancipation of 28 Dec. 1775, NONA, Garic No. 6, 324–25.

33. Will of 16 Sept. 1779, NONA, Andres Almonester 1779, 489v–93. This is all the more unlikely in that, as a Spaniard, Soler had almost definitely not been in Louisiana long enough at this time to be anybody's grandfather.

34. Emancipation of 3 Dec. 1771, NONA, Garic No. 2, 342–43.

35. Emancipation of 20 Dec. 1771, NONA, Garic No. 2, 359–59v.

36. Emancipation of 7 Feb. 1795, NONA, François Broutin No. 31, 30–31v.

37. Emancipation of 22 Dec. 1792, NONA, François Broutin No. 15, 381v–82.

38. Emancipation of 28 Apr. 1803, NONA, Pedesclaux No. 44, 371–71v.

39. Will of 24 Aug. 1798, NONA, Ximenes No. 15, 553v–57v; see also Emancipation of Josephe and Marie, 1 Sept. 1784, NONA, Rafael Perdomo No. 4, 369–70.

40. Will of 22 June 1795, NONA, F. Broutin No. 31, 142–47v.

41. Will of 1 July 1799, NONA, Ximenes No. 16, 124–28v; Emancipation of 3 May 1783, NONA, Mazange/Rodriguez No. 7, 416v–18.

42. Will of 22 May 1783, NONA, Mazange/Rodriguez No. 7, 479v–82v.

43. Will of 8 Nov. 1798, NONA, F. Broutin No. 47, 243v–47v.

44. Will of Jacques Lemelle, 22 Apr. 1783, NONA, Mazange, 362–65v. See also Lemelle Succession, 21 Mar. 1784, LHC; Emancipations of Agathe (25), Jeanne-Françoise (16), and Marie-Adelaide (14), 29 July 1785, LHC; Petition of Lemelle Sisters, 27 Sept. 1985, LHC. Lemelle was a bachelor. The road to this apparently happy ending had not been smooth. In 1765, Lemelle had received permission to free his slave Jacqueline, and then he went on a business trip to Europe, leaving his affairs in her care. Upon his return, he was so angry at her alleged mishandling of his property and disrespect to her mother ("La Dame Lemelle") that he tried to annul her emancipation. This may be connected with the fact that he apparently returned to find her pregnant with a son Lemelle sold at birth to the infant's probable father, Gaspard Gardelle, for the huge, obviously compensatory sum of eight hundred dollars, on condition that the child be freed when of age. See Petition of Jacques Lemelle, 10 Jan. 1767

(misdated "Nov. 1765"), James Brown Papers, 1765–1867, 5 vols., 1:1–1v, Manuscript Division, Library of Congress (hereafter cited as Brown Papers); and Sale of 10 July 1767, LHC.

45. For a rare outright interracial marriage, see Marriage Contract of Jean Paillet and Catherine Villeré[ay], 16 Nov. 1769, LHC. For the major instances of lifelong matches, sometimes open to interpretation, see Will of Henry Bourky, 16 Apr. 1773, NONA, Garic, 140–40 bis verso; Will of Guillaume Boisseau, 28 Dec. 1781, NONA, Mazange, 1002–7v; Will of Francisco Munoz, 21 Aug. 1784, NONA, Rafael Perdomo, 355–61; but see another version, 23 Aug. 1784, LHC, in which he reneges on donation of a house to the woman; Will of Jean Billaud, 1784, NONA, Rodriguez, 187–88v; Will of André Jung, 14 Sept. 1784, LHC; Will of François Demazillière, 6 Dec. 1787, NONA, Rodriguez, 1143v–51v; Will of Michel Perrault, 5, 9 May 1790, NONA, Pedesclaux, 368v–69v, 394–97; Will of Louis Forneret, 19 Apr. 1791, NONA, François Broutin, 203v–6; Will of Bartholomé Toutant Beauregard, 27 Feb. 1792, NONA, François Broutin, 39v–40v; Will of Baptiste Trenier, 3 Aug. 1792, NONA, F. Broutin, 251v; Will of Pierre Cazelard, 17 June 1797, NONA, F. Broutin, 118v–22; Will of Carlos Guardiola, 11 Sept. 1801, NONA, Pedesclaux, 518–19v; Will of Joseph Dauphin, 2 Nov. 1809, NONA, Pedesclaux, 499v–501. For important cases concerning long-lasting liaisons that went bad, see *Madeleine Canella v Louis Beaurepos*, 20 Jan. 1777, LHC; and *Jeanneton Ducoder v St. Marc Darby*, 21 Dec. 1778, LHC; Will of Jean-Baptiste Macarty, 21 Nov. 1808, NONA, Narcisse Broutin, 491v–92. For a discussion, see Holmes, "Do It! Don't Do It!," 23–26

46. Again, the following list contains cases open to debate. See *Madeleine v Jean Soulie Succession*, 21 Nov. 1787 and 20 July 1791, a fascinating case in which Madame Chauvin's slave sued an estate to execute the donations of five hundred dollars to herself and of slave Guim to Madeleine's quadroon daughter; see also Will of Jean Perret, 7 Feb. 1774, NONA, Garic, 28–29, and *Angelique v Perret's Executor*, 25 May 1774, LHC; Donation by Raimond Gaillard, 7 Oct. 1775, NONA, Garic, 240–42; Will of Joseph Meunier, 15 Sept. 1777, NONA, Garic, 338v–40; Will of Charles Renard, 1 Oct. 1777, NONA, Garic, 366–68; Will of Antoine Demouy, 24 Apr. 1778, NONA, Garic No. 9, 247–49; Donation by François Raguet, 18 Mar. 1782, NONA, Mazange, 285v–87v; Will of Jean Arlut, 29 Oct. 1782, NONA, Mazange, 890–94; ditto, 7 Dec. 1788, NONA, Perdomo, 530–34v; *Marie Coffigny v Widow Coffigny*, 23 June 1795, LHC; Will of Jacques Moquin, 31 Aug. 1807, NONA, Benjamin van Pradelles, 114v–16v; Will of Bernard Cassoud, 18 Mar. 1810, NONA, John Lynd, 269v–71v. For the best-known example in Louisiana of long-term concubinage followed by the man's legitimate marriage, which did not occur in New Orleans, see Gary B. Mills, *The Forgotten People: Cane River's Creoles of Color* (Baton Rouge: Louisiana State Univ. Press, 1977), 12–28.

47. [Charles de Casaux or Caseaux], *Essai sur l'art de cultiver la canne et d'en extraire le sucre* (Paris: Clousier, 1781), 279.

48. Elizabeth Fox-Genovese and Eugene D. Genovese, *Fruits of Merchant Capital: Slavery and Bourgeois Property in the Rise and Expansion of Capitalism* (New York: Oxford Univ. Press, 1983), 299–336.

49. Robin, *Voyage*, 250. Unfortunately, Robin was also given to extravagant expressions concerning interracial concubinage, writing in this same passage that "everyone" engaged in it. On this point his imagination was overstimulated by the fear that the "colored people" would become so numerous as to rise up and "exterminate" the whites. Like so many people then and now, he made the elemental error of deducing the incidence of interracial sex in New Orleans from the number of people of mixed race he saw. He did not investigate the subject methodically and was capable of the contradictory statements on the same page (249) that the population of free people of color grew faster than that of whites because of "their own reproduction," and, further on, because of "the co-habitation of whites with free women of color."

50. Amos Stoddard, *Sketches, Historical and Descriptive, of Louisiana* (Philadelphia: Mathew Carey, 1812), 323.

51. Ibid., 328.

52. Quoted in Robertson, *Louisiana Under the Rule of Spain, France, and the United States*, 1:205.

53. Louis-Narcisse Baudry des Lozières, *Second voyage à la Louisiane, faisant suite au premier de l'auteur de 1794 a 1798*, 2 vols. (Paris: Charles, 1803), 1:281–99.

54. Paul Alliot, "Historical and Political Reflections on Louisiana," in *Louisiana Under the Rule of Spain, France, and the United States, 1785–1807*, ed. Robertson, 1:146–47.

55. Ibid., 85.

56. Pierre-Louis Berquin-Duvallon, *Vue de la colonie espagnole du Mississipi ou des provinces de Louisiane et Floride occidentale, en l'année 1802, par un observateur résidant sur les lieux* (Paris: L'Imprimerie Expéditive, 1802), 243–47.

57. Francis Baily, *Journal of a Tour in Unsettled Parts of North America in 1796 & 1797* (London: Baily Bros., 1856), 300–17.

58. Isaac Holmes, *An Account of the United States of America, Derived from Actual Observation, During a Residence of Four Years in that Republic* (London: Caxton Press, 1823), 327. See also Kimberly S. Hanger, "Protecting Property, Family, and Self: The *Mujeres Libres* of Colonial New Orleans," *Revista/Review Interamericana* 22 (1992): 130–35.

59. Holmes, *Account of the United States of America*, 327.

60. Tannenbaum, *Slave and Citizen*, 90–104; Stanley M. Elkins, *Slavery: A Problem in American Institutional and Intellectual Life*, 2d. ed. (1959; reprint, Chicago: Univ. of Chicago Press, 1968) 72–80; Klein, *Slavery in the Americas*, 74–78, 194–224; Genovese, *World the Slaveholders Made*, 103–13.

61. McGowan, "Creation of a Slave Society," 178.

62. On *coartación*, in addition to the citations above, see Fernando Ortiz, *Los negros esclavos* (1916; reprint, Havana: Editorial de Ciencias Sociales, 1975), 283–90; Elsa V. Goveia, "The West Indian Slave Laws of the Eighteenth Century," *Revista de Ciencias Sociales* 4 (1960): 76–79; Leslie B. Rout, *The African Experience in Spanish America: 1501 to the Present Day* (New York: Cambridge Univ. Press, 1976), 87–93; Frederick P. Bowser, "Colonial Spanish America," in *Neither Slave Nor Free: The Freedmen of African Descent in the Slave Societies of the New World*, ed. David W. Cohen and Jack P. Greene (Baltimore: Johns Hopkins Univ. Press, 1972), 25–26, 31–32; Sumner E. Matison, "Manumission by Purchase," *JNH* 33 (1948): 146–67; T. H. Breen and Stephen Innes, *"Myne Owne Ground": Race and Freedom on Virginia's Eastern Shore, 1640–1676* (New York: Oxford

Univ. Press, 1980), 72–77. The ultimate source of many errors published on this subject is Hubert H. S. Aimes, "Coartación: A Spanish Institution for the Advancement of Slaves into Freedom," *Yale Review* 17 (1908–9): 12–31.

63. For a precedent O'Reilly used to establish the policy, see the Royal Decrees of 21 June 1768 and 27 Sept. 1769, in Richard Konetzke, ed. *Colección de documentos para la historia de la formación social de hispanoamérica, 1493–1810*, 3 vols. (Madrid: Consejo Superior de Investigaciones Cientificos, Artes Gráficas Ibarra, 1953–1962), 3, 337–40, 360–61. Bernardo Gálvez briefly attempted to negate the policy after he arrived in New Orleans. See the exceptionally long, complex case of *Marie Jeanne v Jean Suriray*, 28 Feb. 1776, LHC. Or see the translation of the case in Laura Porteus, trans., "Index to Spanish Judicial Records in Louisiana," *LHQ* 11 (1928): 350 for his ruling on the Cuban law.

64. Parts of this discussion appear in a somewhat different form in Ingersoll, "Free Blacks in a Slave Society," 173–200.

65. For a cross-section of evidence concerning the labor of free blacks, see Contract of Apprenticeship between Raymond Gaillard and Jack Fletcher, 23 May 1787, NONA, Rodriguez, 537v–38, to train mulatto Basile as a silversmith, illustrating the phenomenon of mulatto advantage in the skilled trades; see also *Marie-Anne v Salomon Prevost*, 25 June 1789, LHC, which shows a family of conditionally free blacks virtually running a widow's plantation; or see Bill to Charity Hospital, 3 June 1803, LHC, by Basile Demazillière for installing 129 beds. For a rare piece of evidence that black slaves were polarized into creole and African groups, see Gerard L. St. Martin, trans., and Mathé Allain, ed., "A Slave Trial in Colonial Natchitoches," *LH* 28 (1987): 57–58.

66. Report by Miró, 31 Mar. 1788, PPC, leg. 5, 437; Report by Carondelet, 10 Dec. 1794, Biblioteca Nacional, Manuscritos, leg. 19509, Florida y Luisiana, 218–20v; Lauro A. de Rojas, "The Great Fire of 1788 in New Orleans," *LHQ*, 20 (1937): 578–89; Jack D. L. Holmes, "The 1794 New Orleans Fire: A Case Study of Spanish Noblesse Oblige," *Louisiana Studies* 15 (1976): 32; and Gayarré, *History of Louisiana*, 3:335–36.

67. On economic and vocational discrimination against free blacks in slave societies, see Léo Elisabeth, "The French Antilles," in *Neither Slave Nor Free*, ed. Cohen and Greene, 159–65; and for other colonies see, in the same volume, Bowser, "Colonial Spanish America," 42–53; Franklin W. Knight, "Cuba," 290–300; Jerome S. Handler and Arnold A. Sio, "Barbados," 247–57; and A. J. R. Russell-Wood, "Brazil," 109–22; see Elsa V. Goveia, *Slave Society in the British Leeward Islands at the End of the Eighteenth Century* (1965; reprint, Westport, Conn.: Greenwood Press, 1980), 181–84, 214–29; and Bowser, *African Slave in Colonial Peru*, 302–23.

68. Michael Craton, "Jamaican Slavery," in *Race and Slavery in the Western Hemisphere: Quantitative Studies*, ed. Stanley L. Engerman and Eugene D. Genovese (Princeton: Princeton Univ. Press, 1975), 266.

69. Manumission of Antoine and Marianne, 22 May 1770, NONA, Joseph Fernandez and Andres Almonester (1768–70), 121v–23.

70. Manumission of François, 28 July 1770, ibid., 169v–72. See also Manumission of Victoire and Madeleine, 15 Feb. 1786, LHC.

71. This is a total of recorded cash payments only; the actual total could have been up to 15 percent higher depending on what was paid for the 166 slaves liberated outright by black slaveholders. While most of the emancipations in the rest of the colony of Louisiana have been ignored here, about 8 percent of the total manumissions (freedom purchase and gratuitous combined) discussed here are of slaves who were registered in New Orleans but cannot be shown definitely to have settled there. The population figures are computed from the Summary of the Census of 1785, Parsons Collection, Special Collections, Library of the Univ. of Texas, Austin. See also Glenn R. Conrad, trans. and comp., *Saint-Jean-Baptiste des Allemands: Abstracts of Civil Records of St. John the Baptist Parish with Geneology and Index, 1753–1803* (Lafayette: Univ. of Southwestern Louisiana, 1972); *St. Charles: Abstracts of the Civil Records of St. Charles Parish, 1770–1803* (Lafayette: Univ. of Southwestern Louisiana, 1974); and *The German Coast: Abstracts of the Civil Records of St. Charles and St. John the Baptist Parishes, 1804–1812* (Lafayette: Univ. of Southwestern Louisiana, 1981), from which I have computed 189 total manumissions for the German Coast(s) for the years indicated in Conrad's titles, including 123 outright emancipations and 66 freedom purchases for $22,227 total dues paid.

72. Contrast with Baade's argument on this subject in "Law of Slavery in Spanish *Luisiana*," 67–70.

73. Emancipation of Noel, 30 Dec. 1771, NONA, Almonester, 255–56.

74. Petition of Catherine, 25 June 1773, LHC.

75. Petition of Marie-Louise Saly, 23 Jan. 1781, LHC.

76. Petition of Isidore, 15 Mar. 1788, LHC.

77. *Hélène v Després*, 12 Aug. 1780, LHC. Magloir does not appear to have been emancipated, but in this and its other exceptional aspects this case proves the rule of judicial routine in *coartación* actions.

78. *Marie-Thérèse v Françoise Girardy*, 4 Sept. 1782, LHC; compensation was figured as sixteen months of lost wages at $7 per month.

79. *Michel v Françoise Girardy*, 9 Oct. 1783, LHC.

80. *Loppinot v Villeneuve*, 15 Apr. 1774, LHC, illustrates these routines.

81. Emancipation of Durham, 2 Apr. 1783, NONA, Mazange, 303v–5. See also Betty L. Plummer, "Letters of James Durham to Benjamin Rush," *JNH* 65 (1980): 261–69.

82. Charles E. Wynes, "Dr. James Durham, Mysterious Eighteenth-Century Black Physician: Man or Myth?" *Pennsylvania Magazine of History and Biography* 103 (1979): 325–33.

83. Over these same decades, the planters of the American Revolution also freed an unusual number of slaves and then suddenly not only stopped doing so but subscribed en masse to an absolute racial regime against all blacks. See Berlin and Hoffman, *Slavery and Freedom in the Age of the American Revolution*; Berlin, *Slaves Without Masters*, pt. 1; Luther P. Jackson, "Manumission in Certain Virginia Cities," *JNH* 15 (1930): 279–314.

84. Contract of Borchenave and Mallet, 23 Dec. 1769, LHC.

85. Holmes, *Honor and Fidelity*, 75–76.

86. Emancipation of Eugene, 8 Apr. 1771, NONA, Almonester, 59–60, 64v–65v.

87. See *Antoine Guichard v Daniel Dupain*, 18 Dec. 1782, LHC, disputing the coartación

price of a slave for a rare instance in which the father referred openly to "my son."

88. Petition by Claret, 25 June 1790, and 2 May 1793, LHC. Governor Carondelet granted a two-year delay but refused another appeal when that time ran out.

89. *Rosette v Joseph Bonneville*, 27 July 1791, LHC, for a petition by a slave to auction publicly her niece because Bonneville's wife beats the girl on such a suspicion. See Whitaker, *Mississippi Question*, 43–47. For a typical attack on morals in New Orleans at this time, by a person, as usual, who did not succeed in New Orleans and left the colony under duress, see Andrew Oehler, *The Life, Adventures, and Unparalleled Sufferings of Andrew Oehler* (Trenton: Author, 1811), 185–87.

90. Magnus Mörner, *Race Mixture in the History of Latin America* (Boston: Little, Brown, 1967), 57. See also Rout, *African Experience in Spanish America*, 140–45, 156–59; Edgar F. Love, "Marriage Patterns of Persons of African Descent in a Colonial Mexico City Parish," *HAHR* 51 (1971): 79–91; Robert McCaa, "Modeling Social Interaction: Marital Miscegenation in Colonial Spanish America," *Historical Methods* 15 (1982): 45–66. Spanish judges offered no comfort to white paramours who tried to renege on favors to freed blacks after the affair was ended, and might hold even a respectable planter up to public ridicule; see *Madeleine Canelle v Louis Beaurepos*, 20 Jan. 1777, filed 18 Jan., LHC.

91. Debien, "Affranchissements aux Antilles françaises," 1185–86, stresses the same point for the islands.

92. Dubuisson, *Nouvelles considérations sur Saint-Domingue*, 59–72.

93. Donald E. Everett, "Free Persons of Color in Colonial Louisiana," *LH* 7 (1966): 33–50, argues that concubinage has been overemphasized. Compare with Holmes, "Do It! Don't Do It!" 20–22; Joe G. Taylor, *Negro Slavery in Louisiana* (1963; reprint, New York: Negro Universities Press, 1969), 162.

94. See, for example, Hanger, "Protecting Property, Family, and Self: The *Mujeres Libres* of Colonial New Orleans," 136–38.

95. This is based on a modest extrapolation from the census of 1769, which counted sixty-seven free blacks and ninety free mulattoes in Orleans Parish but did not include Tchoupitoulas. See Census of Louisiana, 2 Sept. 1771, *SMV*, pt. 1, 196. On the 1806 figures, see James Monroe to James Madison, 4 Feb. 1811, "A General Return of the Census of the Territory of Orleans Taken for the Year 1806," *TPO*, 923. Speculation that the free black population of 1769 was much larger is based on treating as a single list a series of militia eligibility lists that form a file covering a long time span. See Hanger, *Bounded Lives, Bounded Places*, 113–14.

96. Berlin, *Slaves Without Masters*, 46–47.

97. Bowser is particularly concise on anti-black attitudes and the insecure position of free blacks in Spanish America in *African Slave in Colonial Peru*, 110, 278–82, 301–25. Magnus Mörner is also skeptical that Spanish or Brazilian manumission policy owed anything to humanitarian motives. See his *Race Mixture in the History of Latin America*, 114–18. Donald Ramos emphasizes the primary ulterior motive of controlling the slave population by extending privileges to a few. See his "Community, Control, and Acculturation: A Case Study in Eighteenth-Century Brazil," *Americas* 42 (1986): 432–33.

98. Unlike New Orleans, by 1789 the whites (2,151) were outnumbered eight to one by black slaves (10,100), free blacks (4,467), and Indians (2,200). A majority of the free blacks were voluntary immigrants who took advantage of Spain's generous policy to grant acreage to settlers, although blacks without slaves received half the size of the whites' grants, and nothing about this policy can be construed as favoring free blacks in order to counter whites. This is clear from the very anti–free black headright system: the intent was to encourage (white) slaveholders to settle. And "white patriots continued to see, or said they saw, the spectre of slave revolt behind every attempt of the free coloured to extend the area of his freedom." See James Millette, *Society and Politics in Colonial Trinidad* (1970; reprint, Trinidad, Colo.: Omega and Zed Books, 1985), 34. See also 33, 106–14.

99. For an example, see H. E. Sterkx, *The Free Negro in Ante-Bellum Louisiana* (Rutherford: Fairleigh Dickinson Univ. Press, 1972), 51.

100. This notion was fixed in the literature of the subject by Laura Foner, who relies on undocumented assertions by previous historians on this subject in "Free People of Color in Louisiana and St. Domingue," 415–16.

101. See Free Negro Militia to Bernardo De Gálvez, c.1778, AGI, PPC leg. 188A, showing their pride in their fidelity as slave catchers and protesting the governor's choice of their officers: he included none from Tchoupitoulas.

102. McConnell, *Negro Troops of Antebellum Louisiana*, 3–14.

103. Company of Militiamen of Color of New Orleans, 6 Sept. 1793, AGI, PPC leg. 191, 47–48; List of Black Militiamen, 17 Jan. 1797, AGI, PPC leg. 213, 5–6. For further information on the colony's black forces in uniform, see Holmes, *Honor and Fidelity*, 54–57.

104. Hanger, *Bounded Lives, Bounded Places*, 162, 168.

105. Herbert Klein, *African Slavery in Latin America and the Caribbean* (New York: Oxford Univ. Press, 1986), 226.

106. Ibid., 217 ff.

107. Ibid., 230–31. See also Klein's *Slavery in the Americas,* a book that shows no regard for chronological context and lacks even an implicit definition of slave society. For critiques of the Tannenbaum thesis, see David B. Davis, *The Problem of Slavery in Western Culture* (Ithaca: Cornell Univ. Press, 1966), 227–88; and C. Duncan Rice, *The Rise and Fall of Black Slavery* (Baton Rouge: Louisiana State Univ. Press, 1975), 265–304.

108. Bill of Sale, 20 Dec. 1781, Favrot Family Papers, Howard-Tilton Memorial Library, Special Collections Division, Manuscripts Section, Tulane Univ., New Orleans; Emancipation of Joseph, 16 Aug. 1783, NONA, Rodriguez, 756–56v.

109. "Abus à réformer," c. June 1795, unsigned but in Favrot's hand, Doc. 550 in the Favrot Family Papers.

110. Proceedings Against Capuchins, 1783–86, AGI, SD, 2587:723–60; Yield of Sale of Capuchins' Property, 18 Aug. 1784, AGI, SD, 2609:708–10.

111. Bowser, *African Slave in Colonial Peru*, 230–53.

112. Elkins, *Slavery*, 73.

113. Ibid., 71. For a typical Tannenbaum-derived argument on this head, see Vincent B. Thompson, *The Making of the African Diaspora in the Americas, 1441–1900* (Harlow, U.K.: Longman, 1987), 218–39.

114. Klein, *African Slavery in Latin America and the Caribbean*, 233–35.

115. Gwendolyn Midlo Hall, *Social Control in Slave Plantation Societies: A Comparison of St. Domingue and Cuba* (Baltimore: Johns Hopkins Univ. Press, 1971), 89.

116. *Recopilacion de Leyes de los Reynos de las Indias*, 3 vols. (Madrid: Real y Supremo Consejo de las Indias, 1791), 2:360–70.

117. *Las Siete Partidas*, trans. Samuel P. Scott (Chicago: Commerce Clearing House for the American Bar Association, 1931).

118. The strongest defense of *Las Siete Partidas* as being protective of slaves is a very weak one. See Watson, *Slave Laws in the Americas*, 42–46.

119. This had been prohibited by the Code Noir in Article 52. According to the Code O'Reilly, Article 24, a man without legitimate heirs could leave his estate to the children of a free woman if "no legal impediment existed" to the marriage of the testator and the mother. Since the planters' code of 1778 (Loi Municipale) prohibited interracial marriage and priests did not perform them in New Orleans, it would appear that any such donation would have been illegal. See "Digest of the Laws of Louisiana, Nov. 29, 1803," 374–75.

120. Baade, "Law of Slavery in Spanish *Luisiana*," 61.

121. In the economic history of the free blacks, inheritance was far less important than the wealth they created themselves. For what appears to be a quite different view, see Hanger, *Bounded Lives, Bounded Places*, 79–87. Hanger's discussion is fascinating but the emphasis is misplaced.

122. *Code noir ou loi municipale: entreprit par délibération du cabildo en vertu des ordres du roi, que Dieu garde, consignés dans sa lettre faite à Aranjuez le 14 de mai, 1777* (New Orleans: L'Imprimerie d'Antoine Boudousquie, 1778); Debates of 19, 26 Feb. and 1 Mar. 1779, *ADC*, 1:266–69. The king's authorization is noted in the preamble to the code. The Spanish transcriptions of the cabildo records have two systems of pagination, numbers in the top left corner of the page that refer to the original ledgers, and, in the right corner, page numbers for the transcription books. Since New Orleans Public Library forbids access to the originals, citations here refer to the pages of the transcription books. My characterization of this in a previous publication as a "royal" code has been criticized. By this I meant merely that its composition was authorized by royal authority and the final product was signed by all major royal officers, but I regret using this misleading adjective. See Din and Harkins, *New Orleans Cabildo*, 160. I cannot agree with Hans Baade's description of this code in "Law of Slavery in Spanish *Luisiana*." For example, rather than a significant change, the article ordering free blacks to respect white people is a recapitulation of Article 53 in the Code Noir of 1724.

123. The articles are numbered from 1 to 73, but there is no Article 33.

124. *Code noir ou loi municipale*, 2. There is a remarkable new tone to these six articles, however, in that they aim to suppress not Protestants or Jews but practitioners of "superstitious or foreign" (African?) religious rites.

125. *Charles-Joseph Loppinot v Jean Villeneuve*, 15 Apr. 1774, LHC.

126. This couple is probably the one recorded in the Marriage Contract of Jean Paillet and Catherine Villeray, 16 Nov. 1769, LHC. Catherine was a quadroon. It is possible that a tiny handful of mulattoes who were married in New Orleans had black mothers and white fathers who were legitimately married, although their matrimony was

not recorded in New Orleans. See, for example, the marriage of Charrayse and Barco, 20 Jan. 1777, Libro Primero de Matrimonios de Negros y Mulatos de la Parroquia de Sn Luis de esta Ciudad de la Nueva-Orleans, 20 Jan. 1777 to 29 July 1830, Archives, Archdiocese of New Orleans, New Orleans, iv.

127. These fines are equivalent to those in the code of 1724.

128. *Code noir ou loi municipale,* 3.

129. Ibid., 4.

130. Tannenbaum, *Slave and Citizen,* 49; Klein, *Slavery in the Americas,* 62. Only two rare appeals can be found in New Orleans, both dating from the early tenure of a Spanish governor who had acquired an unwarranted reputation for favoring the supposed rights of slaves. See Petition of Charlotte, 27 Feb. 1793, LHC; and Petition of Philippe, 7 June 1793, LHC. The plea by free negress Madeleine Hardy to have her son emancipated "for the unrelenting bad treatment" he received from his master is in reality a freedom-purchase case in which she is trying to bargain down the price. See *Hardy v Forneret,* 26 Aug. 1790, NONA, François Broutin, Court Proceedings No. 1, Doc. No. 3.

131. Some ambiguous remarks by the attorney general in the trial of maroons in 1784 has raised questions about the technical status of the code. The essential passage in the cabildo records is found in the Deliberations of 11 June 1784, *ADC,* 2:217–19. See Ingersoll, "Slave Codes and Judicial Practice in New Orleans," 52–54; and Baade, "Law of Slavery in Spanish *Luisiana,*" 64–67.

132. Tannenbaum, *Slave and Citizen,* 49–52, 73.

133. For a rare exception, see *Manuel de Lanzos v Pierre Santilly,* 11 Dec. 1779, LHC.

134. AGI, SD, 2588:1189–97v. On the background, including the influence of the French Code Noir, and the trial version of the code written for Santo Domingo in 1784, see Javier Malagón Barceló, *Codigo negro carolino, 1784* (Santo Domingo, Dom. Rep.: Ediciones de Taller, 1974); and Louis Sala-Molins, *L'Afrique aux Amériques: le code noir espagnol* (Paris, Presses Universitaires de France,1992), which includes a French translation of the code of 1784. See also Hans-Joachim König, "The *Código Negrero* of 1789: Its Background and its Reverberations," in *Slavery in the Americas,* ed. Wolfgang Binder (Wurzburg, Konigshausen & Neumann, 1993), 141–50.

135. Klein, *Slavery in the Americas,* 79.

136. Of interest here are the protective clauses of the Codigo Negro sent to the governor of Louisiana. The key articles prohibit the forced labor of children under seventeen years of age and adults over sixty years, prohibit the most laborious field labor for women, require the strict separation of unmarried men and women, limit disciplinary actions to twenty-five lashes that do not draw blood, and require courts to apply the same judicial sanctions to the serious crimes of both slave and free people. See Ortiz, *Los negros esclavos,* 329–35, 408–15.

137. Hall, *Social Control in Slave Plantation Societies,* 99. It is true that the 1780s were a period of reform in the slave laws of many regions of the Atlantic world, but emphasis on supposed humanitarianism obscures the profound commitment to perpetuate slavery. See Debien, *Esclaves aux Antilles françaises,* 471–95; Jordan, *White over Black,* 346–48, 365–72; Michael Craton, James Walvin, and David Wright, eds., *Slavery, Abolition and Emancipation: Black Slaves and the British Empire, A Thematic Documentary* (London: Longman,

1976), 181, 186–90. On the trade, see Ortiz, *Los negros esclavos*, 329–30; Rout, *African Experience in Spanish America*, 84; and Haring, *Spanish Empire in America*, 203–5. The first act in a series that would establish free trade in African slaves was declared on 28 February 1789, and the Codigo Negro followed on 31 May.

138. McGowan, "Creation of a Slave Society," 278.

139. Baade, "Law of Slavery in Spanish *Luisiana*," 58.

140. Cabildo Minutes, 26 Feb. 1790, *ADC*, vol. 3, no. 2, 90–91.

141. Appeal by the Cabildo, 23 July 1790, Manuscritos, Biblioteca Nacional, Madrid, legajo 19248, "Luisiana," 167–74v; Endorsement by the Governor, 23 July 1790, AGI, SD, 2554:116–16v.

142. Mellafe, *Negro Slavery in Latin America*, 106–9; Franklin W. Knight, *Slave Society in Cuba during the Nineteenth Century* (Madison: Univ. of Wisconsin Press, 1970), 11, 125–26; Klein, *Slavery in the Americas*, 84–85.

143. "Having received the most exact orders from the Court," 11 July 1792, AGI, PPC, leg. 18, 892–93v. This directive comprised a mere six articles. See also McGowan, "Creation of a Slave Society," 296–311, for a different view.

144. Rout, *African Experience in Spanish America*, 81–87.

145. Miró to Las Casas, 15 July 1791, DSG 24, 44–45; Miró to Las Casas, 28 Aug., 23 Sept. 1791, DSG 25, 5, 22; Carondelet to Las Casas, 16 Sept. and 19 Oct. 1792, DSG/HBC, 2:103–6; Cabildo Minutes, 25 Apr. 1795 and *passim*, *ADC*, vol. 4, no. 1, 2–42; Carondelet to the Cabildo, 2 May 1795, *ADC*, vol. 4, no. 1, 13–24; Carondelet to Las Casas, 18 June 1795, DSG/HBC, 5:247–53 and *passim*; Carondelet to Las Casas, 20 July 1795, DSG/HBC, 2:214–18; Intendant Francisco Rendón to Gardoqui, 15 June 1795, AGI, SD, 2612:498–503v. Transcriptions of the trials from Papeles Procedentes de Cuba, Legajo 168j, are in the Roscoe Hill Collection of the Papeles Procedentes de Cuba, Library of Congress, microfilm copy in the Historic New Orleans Collection. See also Jack D. L. Holmes, "The Abortive Slave Revolt at Pointe Coupée, Louisiana, 1795," *LH* 11 (1970): 341–51.

146. For the view that the disturbance at Pointe Coupée and the Code of 1795 represented a kind of watershed in race relations, see Hall, *Africans in Colonial Louisiana*, 343–74; McGowan, "Creation of a Slave Society," 347–85; and Juan José Andreu Ocariz, *Movimientos rebeldes de los esclavaos negros durante el domino español en Luisiana* (Zaragoza: Dto. de Historia Moderna, 1977), 75–87, 117–38. For a convincing refutation of the view that the code represents a new level of repression, see Gilbert C. Din, "Carondelet, the Cabildo, and Slaves: Louisiana in 1795," *LH* 38 (1997): 5–28.

147. Regulation of the general police, 1 June 1795, Manuscritos, Biblioteca Nacional, Madrid, legajo 19509, "Colección de varios documentos para la historia de la Florida y tierras adyacentes, II," 1–17; for a reliable English translation, see James A. Padgett, ed. and trans., "'A Decree for Louisiana,' 1 June 1795," *LHQ* 30 (1937): 590–605; see also Andreu Ocariz, *Movimientos Rebeldes*, 179–220. For Carondelet's further instructions for "neighborhood commissioners" of 1 Jan. 1796, see AGI, PPC, leg. 212b, 129–33v. The preamble justifies the code as arising from the recent disturbances, which threatened "to expose the Province to all the Horrors that have ruined the French colonies," referring to the Haitian Revolution and related slave rebellions in

other West Indian colonies. Carondelet reported home that his real purpose, however, was simply to seize the occasion of an emergency to modernize the administration of New Orleans. See Carondelet to Eugenio de Llaguno y Amirola, 31 May 1796, Manuscritos, Biblioteca Nacional, Madrid, legajo 19508, "Colección de varios documentos para la historia de la Florida y tierras adyacentes," 1, 414–19v.

148. Padgett, "Decree for Louisiana," 593. The word "police" is used here in the same general sense in which it was used at the time. Only in the nineteenth century did New Orleans begin trying to establish a regular white gendarmerie.

149. Ibid., 601.

150. François-Marie Perrin Du Lac, c. 1800, quoted in [Carter G. Woodson?], ed., "Observations on the Negroes of Louisiana," *JNH* 2 (1917): 165.

151. Regulation of 15 June 1795, AGI, PPC, leg. 618:1414–18; Decree of 15 Sept. 1795, AGI, PPC, leg. 22:1179.

152. *State v Claude Tremé,* 21 Dec. 1787, LHC; *State v Vincent Lesassier,* 27 Sept. 1793, LHC; *State v Guy Dreux,* 2 Nov. 1796, LHC. On Dreux's reputation, see Joseph-Xavier Pontalba to Jeanne-Louise Pontalba, 4 Nov. 1796, Pontalba Family Papers, Howard-Tilton Memorial Library, Special Collections Division, Tulane Univ., New Orleans.

153. The debate on the slave trade issue spanned the years between 1795 and 1800; it hinged on the problem of public order and included charges by Spanish officials that disorder was provoked by the brutality of slaveowners; see Cabildo Minutes, various dates, *ADC,* vol. 4, no. 1, 40–41, 95–98, 128, 135–38; vol. 4, no. 3, 206–22; and vol. 4, no. 4, 13–28.

154. Casa Calvo to the Cabildo, 24 Oct. 1800, *ADC,* vol. 4, no. 4, 13–22.

CHAPTER 9. NAPOLEON'S LOUISIANICIDE AND THE NEW REPUBLICAN ORDER

1. Two essential primary sources are Éléonore-François-Élie Moustier, "Memoire sur une Question Interressante; Souvent Agité en Amerique et Quelquefois en Europe: 'S'Il Convient à la France de Desirer la Retrocession de la Louisiane,'" ed. E. Wilson Lyon, *MVHR* 22 (1935–36): 251–66; and "Despatches from the United States Consulate in New Orleans, 1801–1803," *AHR* 32 (1928): 801–24; and 33 (1929): 331–59. The best overview is Alexander DeConde, *This Affair of Louisiana* (New York: Charles Scribner's Sons, 1976). See also Frederick J. Turner, "The Policy of France toward the Mississippi Valley in the Period of Washington and Adams," *AHR* 10 (1904–5): 249–79; Thomas M. Green, *The Spanish Conspiracy: A Review of Early Spanish Movements in the Southwest* (Cincinnati: Robert Clarke, 1891); Albert H. Bowman, *The Struggle for Neutrality: Franco-American Diplomacy During the Federalist Era* (Knoxville: Univ. of Tennessee Press, 1974); Jerald A. Combs, *The Jay Treaty: Political Battleground of the Founding Fathers* (Berkeley and Los Angeles: Univ. of California Press, 1970); Samuel F. Bemis, *Pinckney's Treaty: A Study of America's Advantage from Europe's Distress, 1783–1800* (Baltimore: Johns Hopkins Univ. Press, 1926); Lyon, *Louisiana in French Diplomacy;* François Barbé-Marbois, *The History of Louisiana, Particularly of the Cession of that Colony to the United States of America,* ed. E. Wilson Lyon (1829; reprint, Baton Rouge: Louisiana State Univ. Press, 1976); De Villiers du Terrage, *Last Years of French Louisiana;* Clément de Laussat, *Memoirs of My Life;* Pitot, *Observations on the Colony of Louisiana.*

2. The essential primary source is W. C. C. Claiborne, *Official Letter Books of W. C. C. Claiborne, 1801–1816,* ed. Dunbar Rowland, 6 vols. (Jackson, Miss.: State Dept. of Archives and History, 1917) (hereafter cited as *Claiborne*); *TPO.* See also Stoddard, *Sketches;* Joseph T. Hatfield, *William Claiborne: Jeffersonian Centurion in the American Southwest* (Layfayette: Univ. of Southwestern Louisiana Press, 1976); John D. Winters, "William C. C. Claiborne: Profile of a Democrat," *LH* 10 (1969): 189–209; Gerard J. Toups, "The Provincial, Territorial, and State Administrations of William C. C. Claiborne, Governor of Louisiana, 1803–1816" (Ph.D. diss., Univ. of Southwest Louisiana, 1979).

3. Conseil de Ville: Proceedings of Council Meetings, vols. 1–3, translations by Works Progress Administration of Louisiana, Louisiana Division, New Orleans Public Library (hereafter cited as CDV). See also Marietta M. LeBreton, "A History of the Territory of Orleans, 1803–1812" (Ph.D. diss., Louisiana State Univ., 1969).

4. William B. Hatcher, *Edward Livingston: Jeffersonian Republican and Jacksonian Democrat* (Baton Rouge: Louisiana State Univ. Press, 1940), 2–123. Michael Wohl, "A Man in Shadow: The Life of Daniel Clark" (Ph.D. diss., Tulane Univ., 1984). For a different view, see Richard P. McCormick, *The Second American Party System: Party Formation in the Jacksonian Era* (1966; reprint, New York: W. W. Norton, 1973), 310–20.

5. Everett S. Brown, ed., "The Senate Debate on the Breckinridge Bill for the Government of Louisiana, 1804," *AHR* 22 (1917): 340–64; Claiborne to Madison, 5, 26 July 1804, *Claiborne,* 2:236–38, 271–72. See also Lachance, "Politics of Fear," 180.

6. Two leading accounts by historians are highly prejudiced against Burr. See Thomas P. Abernethy in *The Burr Conspiracy* (New York: Oxford Univ. Press, 1954); and Henry Adams, *History of the United States of America during the Administrations of Thomas Jefferson* (1889–91; reprint, New York: Library of America, 1986), 754–928. A more balanced, now much-neglected account is Walter F. McCaleb, *The Aaron Burr Conspiracy, and A New Light On Aaron Burr,* 2d ed., intro. Charles A. Beard (1903; reprint, New York: Argosy-Antiquarian, 1966). See also [Edward Livingston or James Workman?] "Faithful Picture of the Political Situation of New Orleans at the Close of the Last and Beginning of the Present Year 1807," *LHQ* 11 (1928): 359–433.

7. Henry P. Dart, ed., "Andrew Jackson and Judge D. A. Hall," *LHQ* 5 (1922): 509–70; James A. Padgett, "The Difficulties of Andrew Jackson in New Orleans, including His Later Dispute with Fulwar Skipworth, As Shown by the Documents," *LHQ* 21 (1938): 367–419; Adams, *History of the United States,* 1126–84.

8. Cecil Morgan, ed., *The First Constitution of the State of Louisiana* (Baton Rouge: Louisiana State Univ. Press for the Historic New Orleans Collection, 1975); Lewis W. Newton, *The Americanization of French Louisiana: A Study of the Process of Adjustment Between the French and the Anglo-American Populations of Louisiana, 1803–1860* (1929; reprint, New York: Arno Press, 1980). For the conventional view that "the American domination" was an imposition and led to considerable conflict, see Gayarré, *History of Louisiana,* vol. 4. See also Joseph G. Tregle Jr., "Louisiana in the Age of Jackson: A Study in Ego-Politics" (Ph.D. diss., Univ. of Pennsylvania, 1954).

9. Tousard to John C. Stocker, 6 Jan. 1815, in Norman B. Wilkinson, ed., "The Assaults on New Orleans, 1814–1815," *LH* 3 (1962): 46.

10. Carl David Arfwedson, *The United States and Canada in 1832, 1833, and 1834*, ed. Marvin Fisher, 2 vols. (1834; reprint, New York: Johnson Reprint, 1969), 2:69.

11. Samuel Wilson Jr., "Maspero's Exchange: Its Predecessors and Successors," *LH* 30 (1989): 212.

12. Joseph G. Tregle Jr., "Creoles and Americans," in *Creole New Orleans: Race and Americanization*, ed. Arnold R. Hirsch and Joseph Logsdon (Baton Rouge: Louisiana State Univ. Press, 1992), 145.

13. Samuel Wilson Jr., Introduction to *Impressions Respecting New Orleans: Diary and Sketches, 1818–1829*, by Benjamin Henry Latrobe (New York: Columbia Univ. Press, 1951) xi–xxiv.

14. Latrobe, *Impressions Respecting New Orleans*, 18, 35, 40.

15. Computed from James Monroe to James Madison, 4 Feb. 1811, "A General Return of the Census of the Territory of Orleans Taken for the year 1806," *TPO*, 923; and *New Orleans in 1805: A Directory and a Census*, ed. Charles L. Thompson (New Orleans: Pelican Gallery, 1936). Daniel Clark Jr. suggested in 1803 that the population of Louisiana "considerably exceeds 50,000 souls." See Clark to Madison, 8 Sept. 1803, *TPO*, 32. President Jefferson seized upon one exaggerated estimate and informed Congress that the Isle of Orleans (the several parishes lying below Bayou Manchac) contained no less than 50,150 whites and 39,820 blacks. See his *An Account of Louisiana Laid before Congress by Direction of the President of the United States, November 4, 1803* (Providence: Heaton and Williams, 1804), 28. On the Parish of Orleans, see also Robin, *Voyage*, 97. Those who insist on abstracting the town center out of the larger community of which it was a part when enumerating the people of "New Orleans" create unnecessary confusion. To single out one example of the result, found in an important book: Leonard P. Curry has the free black proportion of the city population jumping by a factor of three between 1800 and 1810, to nearly 29 percent, and then declining by a like degree over the next forty years, oblivious to the fact that his authorities are defining the community of New Orleans quite differently at various points in time. See *Free Black in Urban America*, 251.

16. Matas, *History of Medicine in Louisiana*, 1:345–49.

17. Flint, *Recollections of the Last Ten Years*, 218.

18. Robert D. Calhoun, "The Origin and Early Development of County-Parish Government in Louisiana, 1805–1845," *LHQ* 18 (1935): 75.

19. Ibid., 88–89.

20. As late as 1830, "the island of New Orleans," referring to the general region below Bayou Manchac, could be described as one-third cultivated, two-thirds swamp. See James Stuart, *Three Years in North America*, 3d ed., 2 vols. (Edinburgh: Robert Cadell, 1833), 2:200.

21. For a guide to the complex morselization of the parish, see Meloncy C. Soniat, "The Faubourgs Forming the Upper Section of the City of New Orleans," *LHQ* 20 (1937): 192–211.

22. William Darby, *A Geographical Description of the State of Louisiana, the Southern Part of the State of Mississippi, and Territory of Alabama*, 2d. ed. (New York: James Olmstead, 1817), 75.

23. Darby, *Geographical Description*, 76.

24. Ibid.

25. Theodore Clapp, *Autobiographical Sketches and Recollections during a Thirty-Five Years' Residence in New Orleans*, 3d ed. (Boston: Phillips, Sampson, 1858), 244–54.

26. Flint, *Recollections of the Last Ten Years*, 220.

27. Ibid.

28. Clapp, *Autobiographical Sketches and Recollections*, 253–54.

29. *Courier de la Louisiane*, 22, 24 Nov., 1 Dec. 1819; 14 Jan., 21 Feb., 26 May 1820.

30. Flint, *Recollections of the Last Ten Years*, 224. See also Stuart, *Three Years in North America*, 2:203. This is also the conclusion of Liliane Crété, *Daily Life in Louisiana, 1815–30*, trans. Patrick Gregory (Baton Rouge: Louisiana State Univ. Press, 1981), 54–56.

31. Mayor's report, 17 Mar. 1804, CDV, vol. 1, no. 1, 61–62; Resolution to establish a "purely civil" Police Guard, 15 Feb. 1806, CDV, vol. 1, no. 3, 1–9, and throughout to Resolution to Reduce Police Guard, 23 Jan. 1813, CDV, vol. 2, no. 4, 31, since it now cost twenty-nine thousand dollars annually because of high labor costs; and Resolution to Increase Police Guard, 3 Aug. 1816, CDV, vol. 2, no. 6, 37–38; see Dennis C. Rousey, "The New Orleans Police, 1805–1889: A Social History" (Ph.D. diss., Cornell Univ. Press, 1978), 27–37, 42–45, for a good summary and demonstration that Saint-Domingan refugees were numerous among the police.

32. Protest of 7 May 1806 and *passim*, CDV, vol. 1, no. 3, 56, 58–59, 63. See also the description of a wild police melee in Deposition by Charles Patton, 11 Sept. 1810, and Deposition by Richard Zehender, 25 Sept. 1810, Charles F. Heartman Collection, Xavier Univ. Library, Special Collections, New Orleans. See also Dennis C. Rousey, "Cops and Guns: Police Use of Deadly Force in Nineteenth-Century New Orleans," *American Journal of Legal History* 28 (1984): 41–66.

33. Ordinance of the Conseil de Ville, 6 July 1810, box 5, John Minor Wisdom Collection, General Manuscripts, Howard-Tilton Memorial Library, Special Collections Division, Manuscripts Section, Tulane Univ., New Orleans.

34. See for example, Isaac, *Transformation of Virginia*, 94–104. For one of many shocked descriptions, see J. C. Beltrami's of 1823, in *A Pilgrimage in America Leading to the Discovery of the Sources of the Mississippi . . . and Bloody River* (1824; reprint, Chicago: Quadrangle Books, 1962), 523–25.

35. The legislature's debates on the bill were reported by an amused Philadelphia Quaker who was convinced that none of the gentlemen was the least bit serious about it. See Alice E. Smith, ed., *The Journals of Welcome Arnold Greene: Journeys in the South, 1822–1824* (Madison: State Historical Society of Wisconsin, 1957), 118–19. For earlier attacks by officials on gambling, see Order of Mayor Girod to Restrain Guillot and Fauchier, 3 Aug. 1813, box 6, John Minor Wisdom Collection, General Manuscripts, Manuscripts Section, Special Collections Division, Howard-Tilton Memorial Library, Tulane Univ., New Orleans; Address by James Villeré, 6 Jan. 1818, *Journal of the Senate during the Second Session of the Third Legislature of the State of Louisiana* (New Orleans: J. C. de St. Rome, 1818), 6. The aristocratic origin and social role of gambling might be compared to that of dueling. See Steven M. Stowe, *Intimacy and Power in the Old South: Ritual in the Lives of the Planters* (Baltimore: Johns Hopkins Univ. Press, 1987), 5–49.

36. Agreement of Johnston and Jacques and Gabriel Villeré, 19 June 1827, James Stoddard Johnston Papers, 1821–1839, Historical Society of Pennsylvania, Philadelphia.

37. Henry B. Fearon, *Sketches of America: A Narrative of a Journey of Five Thousand Miles through the Eastern and Western States*, 2d ed. (1818; reprint, New York: Benjamin Blom, 1969), 274.

38. It was a daily affair according to Charles Daubeny, who described it in some detail in his *Journal of a Tour Through the United States and in Canada, Made during the years 1837–38* (Oxford: T. Combe, 1843), 147–48. The opinion of one New Orleanian, writing from his duty post in Paris in 1826, was that "duelling is generally less fashionable, and of course less necessary, than it was some years ago," but this appears not to have been true in New Orleans. See James Brown to James Stoddard Johnston, 13 May 1826, James Stoddard Johnston Papers, 1821–1839, Historical Society of Pennsylvania, Philadelphia.

39. Police Regulations of 17 Mar. 1804, CDV, vol. 1 no. 1, 56–61; of 18 Apr. 1804, ibid., 79–80; of 12 May 1804, ibid., 90–91; of 6 June 1804, ibid., 110; of 9 June 1804, ibid., 111–12; of 20 June 1804, ibid., 121–23; of 25 July 1804, ibid., 143–44; of 26 June 1805, CDV, vol. 1, no. 2, 61; of 9 Apr. 1806, CDV, vol. 1, no. 3, 43; of 25 June 1806, ibid., 81; of 17 July 1811, CDV, vol. 2, no. 3, 66–67.

40. For the beginning of a long, complex, and informative court case on the function of the canal, see *The Orleans Navigation Company v Mayor of New Orleans*, [François Xavier Martin], *Martin's Reports of Cases Argued and Determined in the Superior Court of the Territory of Orleans, 1809–12, and in the Supreme Court of the State of Louisiana, 1813–30*, 12 vols., n.s. (New Orleans: Samuel M. Stewart, 1846–1853), 1:269–80. The private company that took over the canal sought to restrain the city from using it as a sewer. The city's argument was that its public chain gang of criminal slaves and the slaves donated by public-minded citizens had dug the canal and thereby established the city's permanent right to use it. The case dragged on for years.

41. Gary A. Donaldson, "Bringing Water to the Crescent City: Benjamin Latrobe and the New Orleans Waterworks System," *LH* 28 (1987): 381–96.

42. "On the morning of the 6th instant . . . ," *Courier de la Louisiane*, 7 Apr. 1820.

43. Anne Royall, *Mrs. Royall's Southern Tour, Or Second Series of the Black Book*, 3 vols. (Washington: N.p., 1830–31), 3:17. She blamed the city's bad reputation on evangelical fundraisers in the other states, who spread lurid tales to raise money to convert the Louisiana Catholics to Protestantism. See 68.

44. St. Louis Cathedral Marriages, 1806–21, Archives, Archdiocese of New Orleans, 194.

45. Thomas Nuttall, *A Journal of Travels in the Arkansas Territory*, ed. Savoie Lottinville (1821; reprint, Norman: Univ. of Oklahoma Press, 1980), 266.

46. Stoddard, *Sketches*, 170.

47. Ibid., 170–73, 324–25.

48. *Acts Passed at the Second Session of the Third Legislature of the State of Louisiana* (New Orleans: J. C. de St. Romes, 1818), 124–52. See, for example, John Salvaggio, *New Orleans Charity Hospital: A Story of Physicians, Politics, and Poverty* (Baton Rouge: Louisiana State Univ. Press, 1992).

49. John B. Wyeth, *Oregon* (1833; reprint, Ann Arbor: Univ. Microfilms, 1966), 73. See 72–77.

50. "Remarks on Louisiana," in *Travels in the Old South, Selected from Periodicals of the Times*, ed. Eugene L. Schwaab, 2 vols. (Lexington: Univ. Press of Kentucky, 1973), 2:108–11.

51. Peter J. Coclanis, *The Shadow of a Dream: Economic Life and Death in the South Carolina Low Country, 1670–1920* (New York: Oxford Univ. Press), 151–52.

52. Article II, Section 8 of the Louisiana Constitution of 1812, *Constitutions of the State of Louisiana and Selected Federal Laws,* ed. Benjamin W. Dart (Indianapolis: Bobbs-Merrill, 1932), 500; McCormick, *Second American Party System,* 179, 312.

53. *Acts Passed at the Second Session of the Legislative Council of the Territory of Orleans* (New Orleans: James Bradford, 1805), 58–60; *Acts Passed at the First Session of the First General Assembly of the State of Louisiana* (New Orleans: Thierry, 1812), 26, for the reduction to fifty from one hundred dollars.

54. Holmes, *Account of the United States of America,* 282–83.

55. Latrobe, *Impressions Respecting New Orleans,* 110.

56. Korn, *Early Jews of New Orleans,* 222–29; Elliott Ashkenazi, *The Business of Jews in Louisiana, 1840–1875* (Tuscaloosa: Univ. of Alabama Press, 1988), 9.

57. Earl F. Niehaus, *The Irish in New Orleans, 1800–1860* (1965; reprint, New York: Arno Press, 1976); J. Hanno Deiler, "The System of Redemption in the State of Louisiana," *LHQ* 12 (1929): 426–60.

58. For a concise description of the situation in Spain, see Felix Markham, *Napoleon* (New York: Mentor Books, 1963), 164–72, which unfortunately ignores the entire colonial issue; see also Douglas Hilt, *The Troubled Trinity: Godoy and the Spanish Monarchs* (Tuscaloosa: Univ. of Alabama Press, 1987), 167–68, 211–26; Robert S. Holtman, *The Napoleonic Revolution* (Baton Rouge: Louisiana State Univ. Press, 1967), 185–86. The best description of the expulsion from Cuba is Gabriel Debien's, in "Réfugiés de Saint-Domingue expulsés de la Havane en 1809," *Anuario de Estudios Americanos* 35 (1978): 555–610.

59. An opportunity for research lies in the records of the New Orleans French Consul General concerning these people, in the Centre des Archives Diplomatiques, Nantes, France.

60. Gabriel Debien and Réné Le Gardeur, "Colons de Saint-Domingue Réfugiés à la Louisiane," pt. 1, *Revue de Louisiane* 9 (1981): 132; Paul F. Lachance, "The 1809 Immigration of Saint-Domingue Refugees to New Orleans: Reception, Integration, and Impact," *LH* 29 (1988): 109–41; Charles B. Rousséve, *The Negro in Louisiana: Aspects of His History and His Literature* (New Orleans: Xavier Univ. Press, 1937), 25–27; and Thomas Fiehrer, "Saint-Domingue/Haiti: Louisiana's Caribbean Connection," *LH* 30 (1989): 431–37. For a different view, see Hunt, *Haiti's Influence on Antebellum America,* 47. Agreement among Anglophones that the West Indians should be granted asylum was general, without regard to political boundaries. See Claiborne to Poydras, 4 June 1809, *TPO,* 843; Livingston to Giles, 13 June 1809, *Moniteur de Louisiane,* 2 Aug. 1809.

61. Debien, "Réfugiés de Saint-Domingue," 584–606.

62. Claiborne to Julien Poydras, 4 June 1809, *TPO,* 843; see also Claiborne to Gallatin, 21 June 1809, *TPO,* 847–48; Smith to Claiborne, 12 Sept. 1809, *TPO,* 850; Smith to Territorial Legislature, 14 Apr. 1810, *TPO,* 881–82.

63. Debien and Le Gardeur, "Colons de Saint-Domingue Réfugiés," pt. 2, pp. 21, 33–35.

64. Will of Bignerier, 12 Sept. 1810, NONA, Narcisse Broutin, 290v–91v.

65. Will of Ducongé, 30 Mar. 1810, ibid., 247–48v; for another example, see Will of Pierre Conte, 10 July 1809, NONA, Pierre Pedesclaux, 311–12v.

66. Lachance, "1809 Immigration of Saint-Domingue Refugees to New Orleans," 127.

67. Ibid., 135–36. At the highest level of integration between the refugees and the locals, only 15 percent of the former chose partners among the latter. Lachance chooses to emphasize the fact that in time they became much less exclusive than the new French immigrants.

68. For the observation that local-born Francophones were still, three decades later, "yet more distrustful of the new-comers from France [than of Anglo-Americans], often men of superior acquirements," see Francis and Theresa Pulszky, *White Red Black: Sketches of Society in the United States during the Visit of Their Guest,* 2 vols. (1853; reprint, New York: Negro Universities Press, 1968), 2:260.

69. "Mes Etrenes à Berquin," *L'Ami des Lois,* 4 Jan. 1810.

70. Joseph H. Ingraham, *The South-West, By a Yankee,* 2 vols. (1835; reprint, Ann Arbor: University Microfilms, 1966), 1:101.

71. Moreover, in contrast to the general character of immigrants to the United States, the single largest group among these from France were from the more prosperous mercantile class. See Carl A. Brasseaux, *The "Foreign French": Nineteenth-Century French Immigration into Louisiana,* 3 vols. (Lafayette: Center for Louisiana Studies, Univ. of Southwestern Louisiana, 1990–93), 1:xxix.

72. Paul F. Lachance, "Intermarriage and French Cultural Persistence in Late Spanish and Early American New Orleans," *Histoire Sociale—Social History* 15 (1982): 59.

73. Henry Blumenthal, *American and French Culture, 1800–1900: Interchange in Art, Science, Literature, and Society* (Baton Rouge: Louisiana State Univ. Press, 1975), 10–15.

74. Joseph G. Tregle Jr., "Early New Orleans Society: A Reappraisal," *Journal of Southern History* 18 (1952): 29–30.

75. St. Louis Cathedral Funerals, 1803–1815, Archdiocese of New Orleans, Archives, funerals for 1 Jan. 1810 to 31 Dec. 1812. All infants under the age of two years were assigned the age of one year. The category of "Southern Europe" groups those born in Italy and Portugal. The category of "East and Central Europe" groups those born in Germany, Poland, and Hungary.

76. Robertson to Smith, 24 May 1809, *TPO,* 841.

77. *Journal of the House of Representatives during the First Session of the First Legislature of the State of Louisiana* (New Orleans: P. K. Wagner 1812), 27 July 1812, 4. Claiborne received 2,757 votes out of 3,874; five French-surnamed candidates divided the remainder.

78. Quoted in Otto A. Rothert, *A History of Muhlenberg County* (Louisville, Ky.: John P. Morton, 1913), 445.

79. William H. Sparks, *The Memories of Fifty Years* (Philadelphia: Claxton, Remsen and Haffelfinger, 1872), 442.

80. Ibid., 442–45.

81. Tregle, "Creoles and Americans," 162.

82. John Watson's Journal, quoted in Georgia F. Taylor, "The Early History of the Episcopal Church in New Orleans, 1805–1840," *LHQ* 22 (1939): 433.

83. The first minister left after a few years, apparently disgruntled because parishioners

did not pay as agreed. See Philander Chase, *Bishop Chase's Reminiscences: An Autobiography*, 2d ed., 2 vols. (Boston: James B. Dow, 1848), 1:54–62, 2:474–75. On the white Methodists, who finally established a regular church in 1825, see Robert H. Harper, *Louisiana Methodism* (Washington, D.C.: Kaufman Press, 1949), 6–7, 37; and Ray Holder, "Methodist Beginnings in New Orleans, 1813–1814," *LH* 18 (1977): 171–87. The Jews were last to organize because they were so few and often married non-Jews. The first synagogue opened only in 1827, even though a prominent Jew named Judah Touro had lent money to establish both the local Episcopal and Presbyterian churches. See Korn, *Early Jews of New Orleans*, 153–56, 165–66; see also 192–208.

84. Sedella to Walsh, 5, 6, 7 Mar. 1805, folder 6, Sedella Collection.

85. Sedella to Walsh, 11 Mar. 1805, folder 6, Sedella Collection.

86. They did this, they explained, in imitation of Napoleon's concordat with the Church and by authority of Almonester's widow, patroness of the cathedral. Many of the relevant documents are found in Stanley Faye, ed., "The Schism of 1805 in New Orleans," *LHQ* 22 (1939): 98–141. See also Charles E. O'Neill, S.J., "'A Quarter Marked by Sundry Peculiarities': New Orleans, Lay Trustees, and Père Antoine," *Catholic Historical Review* 76 (1990): 237–43; and Baudier, *Catholic Church in Louisiana*, 255–59.

87. Deposition by Koune and Father Charles Lusson, 12 Feb. 1806, Brown Papers, 2: 349–50v.

88. Claiborne summoned Sedella into his office, quizzed him, but merely forced him to take an oath of allegiance to the republic for safety's sake. See O'Neill, "Quarter Marked by Sundry Peculiarities," 243–77; Baudier, *Catholic Church in Louisiana*, 261–72. See also *Father Walsh et al. v Antoine Sedella et al.*, 3 June 1805, box 438-572, Records of the Superior [Territorial] Court, 1804–13, Louisiana Division, New Orleans Public Library (hereafter cited as RSC); Claiborne to Madison, 18, 26 Mar. 1805, *TPO*, 420–21, 425–26; Mayor's Report, 16 July 1806, CDV, vol. 1, no. 3, 88–90.

89. Claiborne to Jefferson, 17 June 1807, *TPO*, 744. For an even more colorful description of the vicar general's attempt to get the keys to the cathedral, see Complaint by Rev. John Olivier, 15 June 1807, NONA, B. Von Pradelles, 92–94.

90. Baudier, *Catholic Church in Louisiana*, 273–80.

91. Andrew Jackson asked DuBourg to officiate at the religious ceremony celebrating the Battle of New Orleans, but then he took off again and did not establish his residence in the city until 1823. See Annabelle M. Melville, *Louis William DuBourg, Bishop of Louisiana and the Floridas, Bishop of Montauban, and Archbishop of Besançon, 1766–1833*, 2 vols. (Chicago: Loyola Univ. Press, 1986), 1:281–82, 286–91, 304–6, 317–19, and 2:731–34. See Randall M. Miller, "A Church in Cultural Captivity: Some Speculations on Catholic Identity in the Old South," in *Catholics in the Old South: Essays on Church and Culture*, ed. Randall M. Miller and Jon L. Wakelyn (Macon, Ga.: Mercer Univ. Press, 1983), 20–38, 34–36, for the argument that lay-trusteeism, or American "congregationalism," was a serious problem for authorities in Rome. Irish clergy took over the New Orleans diocese by the 1850s.

92. [John Sibley] "Dr. John Sibley of Natchitoches, 1757–1837," ed. G. P. Whittington, *LHQ* 10 (1927): 478. See also Edward G. G. S. Derby, Earl of Stanley, *Journal of a Tour in America, 1824–1825* (London: N.p., 1930), 248.

93. Latrobe, *Impressions Respecting New Orleans*, 114, 62.

94. Stoddard, *Sketches*, 330.

95. Samuel J. Mills to the Trustees of the Missionary Society of Connecticut, 1813, *The Connecticut Evangelical Magazine*, 6, no. 7 (1813): 272–73; see also W. O. Hart, "The Bible in Louisiana a Century Ago," *PLHS* 9 (1916): 56–74.

96. *Louisiana Gazette*, 27 Apr. 1815; see also 25 Apr.

97. For a discussion of the issues, see Peter J. Parish, *Slavery: History and Historians* (New York: Harper and Row, 1989), 124–45.

98. Several historians have stressed the great social similarity of the people in the two language groups. Lawrence E. Estaville, for example, has demonstrated the extraordinary similarity of the basic institution: the family. For both Franco- and Anglo-Americans the typical family in Louisiana in 1820 was agriculturally based on a plot of less than one hundred acres, with a forty-year-old male head of household, and three children or less. See "The Louisiana French Culture Region: Geographic Morphologies in the Nineteenth Century" (Ph.D. diss., Univ. of Oklahoma, 1984), 445–50.

99. Selected at random from marriage registers of St. Louis Cathedral and St. Marie Church.

100. R. Randall Couch, "The Public Masked Balls of Antebellum New Orleans: A Custom of Masque Outside the Mardi Gras Tradition," *LH* 35 (1994): 412–16.

101. Claiborne to Thomas B. Robertson, 18 Aug. 1808, *Claiborne*, 4:191–92; Claiborne to Madison, 31 Aug. 1808, *Claiborne*, 4:199–201.

102. Fearon, *Sketches of America*, 275–76.

103. On their greater personal control over the choice of their spouses, somewhat more egalitarian marriages, and rising literacy, see Mary Beth Norton, *Liberty's Daughters: The Revolutionary Experience of American Women, 1750–1800* (Boston: Little, Brown, 1980), 228–99.

104. Ibid., 298–99; Nancy F. Cott, *The Bonds of Womanhood: "Woman's Sphere" in New England, 1780–1835* (New Haven: Yale Univ. Press, 1977), 192–96; Carl N. Degler, *At Odds: Women and the Family in America from the Revolution to the Present* (New York: Oxford Univ. Press, 1980), 26–65. The French Revolution meant a greater submission of some French women too, although it improved rights for minors; see Pillorget, *Tige et le rameau*, 290–94.

105. One exception should be noted: Catholic women communicants were socially active to the point of forming the Female Orphan Society in 1817. See *Acts Passed at the Second Session of the Third Legislature of the State of Louisiana*, 192–98; Resolution, 1 Mar. 1817, CDV, vol. 2, no. 6, 130. See also Dolores Egger Labbé, "Women and Religion in Early Louisiana," *Revue de Louisiane* 5 (1976): 101–14. See also Suzanne Lebsock, *The Free Women of Petersburg: Status and Culture in a Southern Town, 1784–1860* (New York: W. W. Norton, 1984), 202–6, 215–26.

106. Elizabeth Fox-Genovese, *Within the Plantation Household: Black and White Women of the Old South* (Chapel Hill: Univ. of North Carolina Press, 1988), 364; see also 81–85, 109. See also Catherine Clinton, *The Plantation Mistress: Woman's World in the Old South* (New York: Pantheon Books, 1982).

107. Peter W. Bardaglio, *Reconstructing the Household: Families, Sex, and the Law in the Nineteenth-Century South* (Chapel Hill: Univ. of North Carolina Press, 1995), 35–36.

108. Louis Moreau-Lislet, ed., *A Digest of the Civil Laws Now in Force in the Territory of New Orleans* (New Orleans: Bradford and Anderson, 1808), 8.

109. Ibid., 28, 230, 246.

110. Ibid., 28, 30.

111. Avery O. Craven, *Rachel of Old Louisiana* (1975; reprint, Baton Rouge: Louisiana State Univ. Press, 1995), 106. The statistic on slaves is computed from the inventory on 115–22.

112. Claiborne to Jefferson, 27 Oct. 1804, *TPO,* 315.

113. Patricia Seed, "American Law, Hispanic Traces: Some Contemporary Entanglements of Community Property," *William and Mary Quarterly,* 3d ser., 52 (1995): 157–62.

114. George Dargo, *Jefferson's Louisiana: Politics and the Clash of Legal Traditions* (Cambridge: Harvard Univ. Press, 1975), 11–12.

115. Dolores Egger Labbé, "Mothers and Children in Antebellum Louisiana," *LH* 34 (1993): 161–62.

116. Decrès to Laussat, 31 Dec. 1802, AN, AC, C13A, 51:164–64v; Morales to Soler, 31 May 1803, AGI, SD, 2620:68 bis 69; Laussat to Decrès, 5 May 1803, Laussat Papers; Laussat to Decrès, 7 June 1803, Laussat Papers.

117. Heaney, *Century of Pioneering,* 202–14.

118. Ibid., 282–85. In just one notary's book for 1818, for example, Narcisse Broutin's No. 37, there are ten bills of sale for properties ranging from small lots to an entire "islet," or block, plus scattered houses in the old town center. See folios 42v–43, 77v–78v, 98v–99v, 103–4, 109v–10v, 112v–13v, 121–23, 123–24v, 153v–55, 425–26v.

119. On at least one occasion, the nuns were the butt of rude jokes by men in the local theaters. See Claiborne to James Pitot, 8 June 1805, *Claiborne,* 3:84–85.

120. Labbé, "Mothers and Children in Antebellum Louisiana," 167.

121. Claiborne to Madison, 16 Mar. 1804, *Claiborne,* 2:47–48; see also Petition to Governor, 15 Feb. 1805, CDV, vol. 1, no. 1, 240–41, bitterly protesting that the federal soldiers stationed on the plaza tried to prevent the *charivari* festivities there, the incident that probably led to the removal of the federals from town soon thereafter. See Yves-Marie Bercé, *Fête et révolte: des mentalités populaires du XVIe au XVIIIe siècle* (Paris: Hachette, 1976), 56–74, 118–25, on fêtes like carnival or *charivari* that were increasingly feared or managed by both monarchical and republican governments of France.

122. Carole Shammas, Marylynn Salmon, Michel Dahlin, *Inheritance in America from Colonial Times to the Present* (New Brunswick: Rutgers Univ. Press, 1987), 63–79, on the limited changes as a result of the Revolution. The trend in the American colonies had been to exclude wives from the office of executrix over a husband's will. My impression of wills as a whole in New Orleans is that wives frequently served as executrixes there; see ibid., 58–62.

123. Ibid., 24, 30–34. For a description of a debate in the legislature concerning a divorce petition by a man who discovered that his spouse was illiterate, see Derby, *Journal of a Tour in America,* 260–61.

124. *Acts Passed at the Second Session of the Legislative Council of the Territory of Orleans,* 54–58.

125. St. Louis Cathedral Marriages, 1806–1821, 61–236v.

126. Jane Turner Censer, "'Smiling through Her Tears': Ante-Bellum Southern Women and Divorce," *American Journal of legal History* 25 (1981): 24–47.

127. A case illustrating the court's rules of thumb include *Bermudez v Bermudez*, 1812, Martin, *Martin's Reports*, 1:283–84.

128. Durand Marriage, 11 Dec. 1785, Libro de matrimonios celebrados en esta Iglesia parroq.l de San Luis de Nueva Orleans, 1784–1806, Archives, Archdiocese of New Orleans, 43.

129. *Durand v Durand*, No. 130, 4 *Mart.* (o.s.) 174 (New Orleans, 1816), Supreme Court of Louisiana, Collection of Legal Archives (hereafter cited as SCLA, with principals and docket number, if any, followed by the standard legal reference to *Martin's Reports* [*Mart.*], old series [o.s.] or new series [n.s.], according to which the original case file is stored in the archives, followed by the venue and date of decision in parentheses, all cases cited before 1812 being for the territorial Superior Court, all cases thereafter for the Supreme Court, all of the latter having Eastern District docket numbers), Archives, Manuscripts, and Special Collections, Earl K. Long Library, Univ. of New Orleans.

130. See, for example, *Durnford v Gross*, No. 422, 7 *Mart.* (o.s.) 465 (New Orleans, 1820), SCLA.

131. *Louis Brognier Declouet v Celeste Forstall*, 1813, Orleans Parish Court Records, Louisiana Division, New Orleans Public Library, reel 1, case 303.

132. *Brognier v Forstall*, 1815, Martin, *Martin's Reports*, 1:667–69.

133. On the other hand, the court carefully preserved a wife's full status as a privileged creditor of the estate if she initiated a separation suit that had not been decided before the husband died. See *Hannie [Haynie] v Browder*, Nos. 250–51, 6 *Mart.* (o.s.) 14 (New Orleans, 1819), SCLA. For another very interesting case, concerning a white couple living in concubinage who tried to protect their property by a note of indebtedness made out by the man to the woman, see *Delany v. Trouve*, 1815, No. 79, 3 *Mart.* (o.s.) 610 (New Orleans, 1815), SCLA.

134. Nolan B. Harmon Jr., *The Famous Case of Myra Clark Gaines* (Baton Rouge: Louisiana State Univ. Press, 1946), 21–32, 36–38, 63–65, 102–11, 121–53. His hint on page 21 that Zulime may have had Gypsy ancestry is unwarranted, and he is mistaken about her parents' places of birth: Jean was a Gascon and Marie Chaufert was from Bordeaux. See Saint Louis Church Marriages, 1784–1806, 99.

135. *Lebreton v Nouchet*, No. 10, 3 *Mart.* (o.s.) 60 (New Orleans, 1813), SCLA.

136. The data include 265 brides and 54 grooms in the period 1803–1817, listed in the Libro de matrimonios celebrados en esta Iglesia parroq.l de San Luis de Nueva Orleans, 1784 to 1806, and St. Louis Cathedral Marriages, 1806–1821, whose baptisms can be discerned in baptismal registers. Subjects were chosen according to a highly conservative principle: anyone whose identification in baptismal registers was clouded by the slightest ambiguity was eliminated.

137. Michael R. Haines, "Long-Term Marriage Patterns in the United States from Colonial Times to the Present," *History of the Family* 1 (1996): 15–39. Haines employs a formula based on an index of proportions married that has not been used here.

138. Edward Livingston, *Report Made to the General Assembly of the State of Louisiana, On the Plan of a Penal Code* (New Orleans: Benjamin Levy, 1822), 37.

139. Ibid.

140. Ibid., 37, 38.

141. David F. Greenberg, *The Construction of Homosexuality* (Chicago: Univ. of Chicago Press, 1988), chap. 8.

142. Philippe Ariès, *Centuries of Childhood: A Social History of Family Life*, trans. Robert Baldick (1960; reprint, New York: Random House, 1962), 411–15. See also Degler, *At Odds*, 66–110; Cott, *Bonds of Womanhood*, 84–101, Norton, *Liberty's Daughters*, 235–38, 247–50.

143. Hunter to Mrs. C. Y. McAllister, 30 July 1815, "The Western Journals of Dr. George Hunter, 1796–1805," ed. John F. McDermott, *Transactions of the American Philosophical Society*, n.s., 53, pt. 4 (1963): 17.

144. Raleigh A. Suarez, "Chronicle of a Failure: Public Education in Antebellum Louisiana," *LH* 12 (1971): 109–22.

145. Clark's Report, 8 Sept. 1803, *TPO*, 38; Claiborne to Jefferson, 29 Sept. 1803, *TPO*, 60; Claiborne to Jefferson, 16 Jan. 1804, *TPO*, 162, reporting that dancing was the chief accomplishment of local children; Claiborne to Poydras and Ursulines, 6, 8 Apr. 1804, *Claiborne*, 2:82–83, 85–97; John Watkins to Claiborne, 2 Aug. 1805, *TPO*, 487–88. Act to Establish Public Free School, *Acts Passed at the First Session of the First Legislature of the Territory of Orleans* (New Orleans: Bradford & Anderson, 1806), 8–10; *Acts of 1808*, 20–22; *Acts Passed at the First Session of the Second Legislature of the Territory of Orleans* (New Orleans: Bradford & Anderson), 46–48; Claiborne to the Legislature, 29 Jan. 1811, *Claiborne*, 5:126. See Stuart G. Noble, "Governor Claiborne and the Public School System of the Territorial Government of Louisiana," *LHQ* 11 (1928): 535–52; and "Schools of New Orleans during the First Quarter of the Nineteenth Century," *LHQ* 14 (1931): 65–78, for the argument that ethnic factors contributed to a lack of cooperation on the issue. See also Martin L. Riley, "The Development of Education in Louisiana Prior to Statehood," *LHQ* 19 (1936): 595–634. On the university, see Act of 19 Apr. 1805, *Acts Passed at the First Session of the Legislative Council of the Territory of Orleans*, 304–20; Memorial to Congress, 20 Apr. 1812, *TPO*, 1014.

146. Ingraham, *South-West, By a Yankee*, 1:120.

147. Ibid., 121.

148. Priscilla Ferguson Clement, "Children and Charity: Orphanages in New Orleans, 1817–1914," *LH* 27 (1986): 337–40.

149. New Orleans Parish Indentures [*Engagements*], 1809–1818, 2 vols., Louisiana Division, New Orleans Public Library.

150. Assuming that masters still had some slaves trained as artisans, their agreements were not consistently registered with the city and cannot be quantified.

151. *Mitchell v Armitage*, No. 573, 10 *Mart.* (o.s.) 38 (New Orleans, Apr. 1821), SCLA.

152. "Papers from a Journal of a Voyage down the Mississippi to New Orleans in 1817," *LHQ* 7 (1924): 431–32.

153. *Louisiana Gazette*, 19 Sept. 1806.

154. "Description of Louisiana," *Charleston Courier*, 3 Nov. 1807.

155. Walter Lowrie and Walter S. Franklin, eds., *American State Papers: Documents of the Congress of the United States in Relation to Finance*, vol. 4 (Washington, D.C.: Gales and Seaton, 1858), 163.

156. Howard Corning, ed., *Journal of John James Audubon: Made During His Trip to New Orleans in 1820–1821* (Boston: Club of Odd Volumes, 1929), 30, 111–55.

157. *Moniteur de la Louisiane*, 12 Mar. 1803.

158. The rare examples of Louisiana slaveholders who questioned slavery and freed their own slaves include Julien Poydras and John McDonogh. See Crété, *Daily Life in Louisiana*, 272–73; and William Allan, *Life and Work of John McDonogh* (1886; reprint, Metairie, La.: Jefferson Parish Historical Commission, 1983), chap. 4.

159. St. Louis Cathedral Marriages, 1806–1821, 115v, 172v. The best description of the difficulty of maintaining the levees is in Henry Marie Brackenridge, *Views of Louisiana* (Pittsburgh: N.p., 1814), 176–81.

160. Arthur G. Nuhrah, "John McDonogh: Man of Many Facets," *LHQ* 33 (1950): 41–56.

161. For a recent work in which this distinction is accorded the utmost significance, see John Ashworth, *Slavery, Capitalism, and Politics in the Antebellum Republic*, vol. 1., *Commerce and Compromise, 1820–1850* (New York: Cambridge Univ. Press, 1995), pts. 1 and 2.

162. Bill of Sale, 7 Jan. 1812, NONA, Pedesclaux, 13–14.

163. *Fouque's Syndics v Vigneaud*, No. 322, 6 *Mart.* (o.s.) 423 (New Orleans, Mar. 1819), SCLA. The reference to a high levee probably means that it was insecure and could easily break if not watched with an expert eye.

164. *Fouque v Creditors*, 2 Jan. 1813, NONA, Pedesclaux No. 67, 518–21.

165. For a good example, see Tableau of Debts of Eugène Fléchier, 28 Oct. 1815, box 100-209, RSTC, for an extraordinary list of debts totaling seventy thousand dollars.

166. The discrepancy between the one hundred slaves he was asserted to own in the court case involving his son-in-law's claim to some of the slaves, and the sixty-five slaves actually inventoried in the auction of his estate, is not altogether clear.

167. Auction of Fouque Estate, 31 Mar. 1813, NONA, Pedesclaux, 110v–13. Bills of Sale of Additional Slaves are found at ibid., 117–18, and *passim.* Harang bought back the plantation. See Bill of Sale by Michel Fortier to Alexandre Harang, 23 July 1813, NONA, Pedesclaux, 295–96.

168. Peter J. Coleman, *Debtors and Creditors in America: Insolvency, Imprisonment for Debt, and Bankruptcy, 1607–1900* (Madison: State Historical Society of Wisconsin, 1974), 3–30, 87, 179–90, 249–68.

169. Sidney L. Villeré, *Jacques Philippe Villeré, First Native-Born Governor of Louisiana, 1816–1820* (New Orleans: Historic New Orleans Collection, 1981), 95. See also *Acts of 1805*, 60–67; supplemented by *Acts of 1808*, 50–78, establishing rules about bail bonds; the court also enforced a top market rate of interest of 10 percent to prevent usury. For another important case, see *Chiapella v Lanusse's Syndics*, No. 614, 10 *Mart.* (o.s.) 448 (New Orleans, Dec. 1821), SCLA.

170. See the lead article in *Louisiana Gazette*, 28 Dec. 1804, for the argument that the Bank of the United States was "owned chiefly by Europeans," whereas a New Orleans bank would be locally owned. See George D. Green, *Finance and Economic Development in the Old South: Louisiana Banking, 1804–1861* (Stanford, Calif.: Stanford Univ. Press, 1972), 1–22.

171. Bray Hammond, *Banks and Politics in America from the Revolution to the Civil War* (Princeton: Princeton Univ. Press, 1957), 206.

172. Ironically, the panic and recession of 1818–1819 was sparked in part when the Treasury called for $2 million in specie to pay obligations signed for the Louisiana Purchase: the BUS had only a little more than that altogether, which was less than 10 percent of its liabilities, half as much as required by law. Jefferson could take com-

fort in this further proof of his enemy's perfidy. See Hammond, *Banks and Politics in America*, 258.

173. Vincent Nolte, *The Memoirs of Vincent Nolte: Reminiscences in the Period of Anthony Adverse, or Fifty Years in Both Hemispheres*, trans. Burton Rascoe (1854; reprint, New York: G. Howard Watt, 1934), 90.

174. Robert E. Roeder, "Merchants of Antebellum New Orleans," *Explorations in Entrepreneurial History* 10 (1958): 119.

175. Joseph G. Tregle Jr., "Louisiana and the Tariff, 1816–1846," *LHQ* 25 (1942): 32–33, 56–61.

176. Ibid., 52.

177. *Louisiana Gazette*, 25 Nov. 1818.

178. George Dangerfield, *The Era of Good Feelings* (1952; reprint, New York: Harcourt, Brace and World, 1963), 199–245.

179. *Louisiana Gazette*, 25–27, Nov., 7, 16 Dec. 1818. It is likely that research in the future will unearth better evidence of the depression in New Orleans. It may well have been more severely felt than newspapers indicate.

180. [Plantation manager] Jean Boze to Henri de Ste-Gême, 2 Dec. 1818; see Boze to Henri de Ste-Gême, 21 Dec. 1818, 20 Jan. 1819, Ste-Gême Family Papers, the Historic New Orleans Collection (hereafter cited as Ste-Gême Papers).

181. Boze to Henri de Ste-Gême, 17 Apr. 1819, Ste-Gême Papers.

182. *Courier de la Louisiane*, 17, 22 Oct. 1819.

183. Edward Dana, *Geographical Sketches on the Western Country: Designed for Emigrants and Settlers* (Cincinnati: Looker, Reynolds, 1819), 207.

184. Fearon, *Sketches of America*, 274.

185. Flint, *Recollections of the Last Ten Years*, 241.

CHAPTER 10. AN OLD REGIME MADE ANEW

1. Latrobe does not identify the sect, but it was probably the same black Methodist congregation Anne Royall described a few years later. See Royall, *Mrs. Royall's Southern Tour*, 3:21.

2. Latrobe, *Impressions Respecting New Orleans*, 130.

3. Ibid.

4. Report of the Mayor by Surveyor Joseph Pilier, 24 Dec. 1831, Slavery in Louisiana Collection, 1785–1860, folder 9, the Historic New Orleans Collection.

5. Latrobe, *Impressions Respecting New Orleans*, 49–51. On the social life of Congo Square at the rear of the town center, see Jerah Johnson, "New Orleans's Congo Square: An Urban Setting for Early Afro-American Culture Formation," *LH* 32 (1991): 140–45. On the rural-urban, African-creole distinction, see also Philip D. Morgan, "Black Life in Eighteenth-Century Charleston," *Perspectives in American History*, n.s., 1 (1984): 224–26.

6. Latrobe, *Impressions Respecting New Orleans*, 138–9.

7. Baptêmes des personnes de couleur libres et des esclaves, 1805–1844, St. Marie Church, Archdiocese of New Orleans, Archives, 1–9v.

8. *Adelle v Beauregard*, 1 Mart. (o.s.) 183 (La. 1810), SCLA.

9. Frederic Bancroft, *Slave Trading in the Old South* (Baltimore: J. H. Furst, 1931), 312–38.

10. Ingersoll, "Slave Trade and the Ethnic Diversity of Louisiana's Slave Community," 159.

11. "Estimates of the Value of Slaves, 1815," *AHR* 19 (1914): 835.

12. Ibid., 828, 835.

13. John S. Kendall, "The Huntsmen of Black Ivory," *LHQ* 24 (1941): 9–34; Gene A. Smith, "U.S. Navy Gunboats and the Slave Trade in Louisiana Waters, 1801–1811," *Military History of the West* 23 (1993), 135–47.

14. Beverly Chew to William H. Crawford, 1, 30 Aug. 1817, *Annals of Congress*, 15th Cong., 1st sess. [1 Dec. 1817 to 20 Apr. 1818], 1790–95.

15. Bill of Sale by Pitot to Henri Dukeilus, 4 May 1810, NONA, Narcisse Broutin, 265–65v.

16. Bill of Sale by Lafitte to the Ursulines, 11 Feb. 1810, NONA, Narcisse Broutin, 73–73v.

17. James E. Alexander, *Transatlantic Sketches*, 2 vols. (London: R. Bentley, 1833), 2:26.

18. Conspicuous Cases and Synopses of Cases in the U.S. District Court of Louisiana, cases 1 to 3,000, 1806–1831, Survey of Federal Archives in Louisiana, Works Progress Administration of Louisiana, Louisiana Historical Center, Louisiana State Museum, New Orleans, cases 378 to 381 and 383 to 388 concerning the *Alerta*; cases 1183, 1221, and 1635 concerning the *Josefa Segunda*. The evidence and witnesses presented by Beluche suggest that he did not intend to sell the slaves in Louisiana. At least 124 slaves (and perhaps as many as 152) taken from the ship were sold at auction in New Orleans on 30 July 1818, many selling at $1,000 or more, with one eighteen-year-old man bringing the top price of $1,515. See cases 1728 to 1733 and 1778 to 1781 for the last important smuggling cases in this record. See case 1728 for a description of smuggling operations in 1821. See also Jane Lucas De Grummond, *Renato Beluche: Smuggler, Privateer, and Patriot, 1780–1860* (Baton Rouge, La., 1983), 160–70.

19. For discussions of this issue, see W. E. B. Du Bois, *The Suppression of the African Slave Trade to the United States of America, 1638–1870* (1896; reprint, Baton Rouge: Louisiana State Univ. Press, 1969), 109ff; Donnan, *Documents Illustrative*, 4:513 n. 1, 525 n. 6, 665; Joe G. Taylor, "The Foreign Slave Trade in Louisiana After 1808," *LH* 1 (1960): 36–43.

20. For the debate on social divisions in the slave community, see especially Genovese, *Roll, Jordan, Roll*, 327–98; and Paul D. Escott, *Slavery Remembered: A Record of Twentieth-Century Slave Narratives* (Chapel Hill: Univ. of North Carolina Press, 1979), 59–70.

21. Anonymous observer quoted in Gary A. Donaldson, "A Window on Slave Culture: Dances at Congo Square in New Orleans, 1800–1862," *JNH* 69 (1984): 66.

22. [J. G. Flügel], "Pages from a Journal of a Voyage down the Mississippi to New Orleans in 1817," ed. Felix Flügel, *LHQ* 7 (1924): 432.

23. Succession of Avart, 2 Feb. 1810, Orleans Parish, Old Inventories of Estate, Vol. A, 1807–1839, Louisiana Division, New Orleans Public Library, New Orleans.

24. Roger Bastide, *African Civilisations in the New World*, trans. Peter Green (New York: Harper, 1971) 145–49.

25. Recapitulation of Vital Statistics for 1809, *Moniteur de la Louisiane*, 24 Jan. 1810. Tally of Cuban Refugees, 24 Mar. 1810, ibid. Recapitulation of Vital Statistics of 1810, 12 Jan. 1811, ibid. Baptisms numbered 1,034 and mortalities, 1,046.

26. Latrobe, *Impressions Respecting New Orleans*, 75, see 74–80 for the whole discussion. See also Paul Wilhelm, Duke of Württemberg, *Travels in North America, 1822–1824*, trans. W. Robert Nitske, ed. Savoie Lottinville (1835; reprint, Norman: Univ. of Oklahoma Press, 1973), 33.

27. Affidavit of 20 Apr. 1818, Slavery in Louisiana Collection, 1785–1860, folder 9, Historic New Orleans Collection.

28. For evidence of the amazing variety of 135,000 of the people sold in New Orleans between 1804 and 1862, see Herman Freudenberger and Jonathan B. Pritchett, "The Domestic United States Slave Trade: New Evidence," *Journal of Interdisciplinary History* 21 (1991): 447–77.

29. The overland route has received much attention, but for the Mississippi River domestic slave trade, see Fearon, *Sketches of America*, 267–68.

30. Douglas R. Egerton, *Gabriel's Rebellion: The Virginia Slave Conspiracies of 1800 and 1802* (Chapel Hill: Univ. of North Carolina Press, 1993), 151, 178.

31. Mayor John Watkins to Secretary John Graham, 6 Sept. 1805, *TPO,* 500–504; Town Council Deliberations, CDV, vol. 1, no. 2, 97, 99, 106, 120–21. Given the high appraisal of Celestin and the fact that it is not mentioned again, Celestin may not have been freed.

32. Claiborne to Secretary of State 13 Feb. 1809, *Claiborne*, 4:316–17, on the "base faction in this City, composed principally of Burrites and Englishmen."

33. *L'Ami des Lois*, 8 Jan. 1811.

34. Ibid., 25 Dec. 1810.

35. There had also been a rash of mysterious crimes of arson in New Orleans. See *L'Ami des Lois*, 2 Oct. 1810.

36. *Louisiana Gazette*, 11 Jan. 1811.

37. See also Depositions of 20 and 25 Feb. 1811, in Conrad, *German Coast*, 106–8; Manuel Andry to Claiborne, 11 Jan. 1811, *TPO,* 915–16. *Moniteur de la Louisiane*, 17 Jan. 1811, for the report by Perret, including names of seven free blacks who should receive recognition for "zeal and courage"; Claiborne to Legislature, 25 Feb. 1811, *Claiborne,* 5:163, so recommending.

38. Hampton to Secretary of War, 16 Jan. 1811, *TPO,* 917–18.

39. *Moniteur de la Louisiane*, 24 Jan. 1811; Claiborne's reports begin with that to the Secretary of State, 7 Jan. 1811, *Claiborne,* 5:93–6, and *passim* to 227; "Summary of Trial Proceedings of Those Accused of Participating in the Slave Uprising of January 9, 1811," ed. Glenn R. Conrad, *LH* 28 (1977): 472–73; and Slave Trial of Jupiter, 20 Feb. 1811, Conrad, *German Coast*, 106. See Claiborne to Dr. Steele, 20 Jan. 1811, ibid., 5, 112–13; Hampton to Secretary of War, 17 Jan. 1811, *TPO,* 918, reported that fifteen to twenty slaves were killed in the final battle and many wounded. See Claiborne to Legislative Council and House of Representatives, 19, 25, 29 Apr. 1811, *Claiborne,* 5:214, 218–19, 227, requesting twenty-nine thousand dollars to compensate masters for loss of slaves, fifteen hundred dollars to reward those who apprehended the principal leaders, and twenty-five hundred dollars to pay the expenses of the militia; see *Acts Passed at the Second Session of the Third Legislature of the Territory of Orleans* (New Orleans: Thierry, 1811), 132, 190, for an appropriation act to compensate slaveowners for both slaves and other property destroyed in the uprising and aftermath; see *Acts*

Passed at the Third Session of the First Legislature of the State of Louisiana (New Orleans: Wagner, 1814), 18–20, for an act of 22 February 1814, requiring that henceforth slaves executed as rebels "shall be at the loss of the owner only." See Secretary of War to Claiborne, 30 Mar. 1811, *TPO,* 929, refusing to pay the militia bill Claiborne submitted. For an interesting case probably related to the rebellion, in which Claiborne pardoned (on the master's plea) a slave who had been condemned by a jury to hang, substituting the sentence of thirty lashes and confinement to the plantation for two years; see Claiborne Pardon, 1 Apr. 1811, *Claiborne,* 5:198–99. See also James H. Dormon, "The Persistent Specter: Slave Rebellion in Territorial Louisiana," *LH* 18 (1977): 389–400; Thomas M. Thompson, "National Newspaper and Legislative Reactions to Louisiana's Deslondes Slave Revolt of 1811," *LH* 33 (1992); and Herbert Aptheker, *American Negro Slave Revolts* (New York: Columbia Univ. Press, 1943), 249–51.

40. Claiborne to Legislative Body, 29 Jan. 1811, *Claiborne,* 5:121–26; Claiborne to John Ballinger, 20 Jan. 1811, *Claiborne,* 5:108–9; *L'Ami des Lois,* 16 Feb. 1811.

41. *Louisiana Gazette,* 17 Jan. 1811; Response of the Legislature, 29 Jan. 1811, *Claiborne,* 5:127–31; Claiborne to Secretary of War Eustis, 31 Aug. 1811, *Claiborne,* 5:348, requesting permission to form a regiment that could be easily filled by refugees from Cuba.

42. *L'Ami des Lois,* 19 Jan. 1811. See also Fearon, *Sketches of America,* 276–78.

43. Claiborne to Captain John Ballinger, 20 Jan. 1811, *Claiborne,* 5:109; Claiborne to Robert Smith, 14 Jan. 1811, *Claiborne,* 5:100.

44. Hampton to Claiborne, 12 Jan. 1811, *TPO,* 916–17. For a slackjawed description of Hampton's four hundred slaves and princely income, see Nuttall, *Journal of Travels,* 262.

45. Dormon, "Persistent Specter," 400–404.

46. *Moniteur de la Louisiane,* 19 Jan. 1811.

47. *Louisiana Gazette,* 12 Sept. 1812.

48. Hampton to Secretary of War, 16 Jan. 1811, *TPO,* 917.

49. Legislative Council to Claiborne, *Claiborne,* 5:129–31.

50. Robert McColley, *Slavery and Jeffersonian Virginia,* 2d ed. (Urbana: Univ. of Illinois Press, 1973), 101–13.

51. Claiborne to Commanders, 24 Dec. 1811, *Claiborne,* 6:16–18; Claiborne to Paul Hamilton, 26 Dec. 1811, *Claiborne,* 6:20, declared the rumor unfounded.

52. William Byrd II to the Earl of Egmont, 12 July 1736, Donnan, *Documents Illustrative,* 4:132.

53. *Louisiana Gazette,* 12 Sept. 1812.

54. *State v Paul Macarty,* No. 2236, 2 *Mart.* (o.s.) 279 (New Orleans, Fall, 1812), SCLA. For a discussion of this affair that includes minor errors of fact because the author relies on a New York newspaper report, see Aptheker, *American Negro Slave Revolts,* 254.

55. Aptheker, *American Negro Slave Revolts,* 248–49.

56. Ibid., 282–83, 288.

57. Judith Kelleher Schafer, "The Immediate Impact of Nat Turner's Insurrection on New Orleans," *LH* 21 (1980): 361–76.

58. Eugene D. Genovese, *From Rebellion to Revolution: Afro-American Slave Revolts in the Making of the New World* (New York: Random House, 1979), 118.

59. A supplementary ordinance of 1814 adds an aural detail to this picture. The town

council angrily ordered that anyone using trumpets or drums to advertise their wares in the streets must have a permit signed by the mayor and must not make any racket after sunset. Violators who were free would pay up to fifteen dollars, slaves would get up to twenty-five stripes. Ordinance of 3 October 1814, New Orleans Municipal Papers: Police Records, folder 6, Manuscripts Section, Special Collections Division, Howard-Tilton Memorial Library, Tulane Univ., New Orleans.

60. Ordinances of 10 Jan. 1811 by Order of Town Council, 19 Feb. 1812, *Télégraphe Louisianais and Mercantile Advertiser.*

61. Depositions by Guinault, Casimir Bourcier, and Jean Paris before Mayor James Mather, 14 Feb. 1812, box 8, folder C, part 1, item 3, Charles F. Heartman Collection of Manuscripts Relating to the Negro and Slavery (hereafter cited as CFHC), Special Collections, Xavier Univ. Library.

62. Deposition by Edouard Cardinaud, 14 Feb. 1812, box 2, folder D, item 5, CFHC.

63. For the most unusual of all cases involving a disease, a great classic in the judicial history of slavery, see *Saulet v Loiseau,* No. 300, 6 *Mart.* (o.s.) 512 (La. 1819), SCLA. For other instructive cases, see *Dewees v Morgan,* No. 2351, 1 *Mart.* (o.s.) 1 (La. 1809), SCLA; *St. Romès v Pore,* No. 583, 10 *Mart.* (o.s.) 30, 203 (La. 1821), SCLA.

64. For one example, see *Macarty v Bagnières,* No. 2320, 1 *Mart.* (o.s.) 149 (New Orleans, Fall, 1810), SCLA, on a habitual maroon, in which the court found for Macarty by apparently arbitrary logic even though Macarty had purchased the slave straight out of jail, where he had languished 5 months for marronage. See *Watkins v McDonough,* 2 *Mart.* (o.s.) 154 (New Orleans, Spring, 1812), SCLA, for a more concise but still contradictory definition of the court's guidelines.

65. Judgment of 8 Oct. 1808, Conrad, *German Coast,* 69–71.

66. *Andry et al. v Foy,* No. 342, 6 *Mart.* (o.s.) 689 (New Orleans, June 1819), SCLA.

67. *Pierre Marigny's Executor v Heirs of Delabarre,* 23 Feb. 1805, case 71, box 3-98, RSTC.

68. See *Duncan v Cevallos' Executors,* No. 185, 4 *Mart.* (o.s.) 571 (New Orleans, Dec. 1817), SCLA. See also *Madame Leiba v Jean-Baptiste Ramonet,* 23 Nov. 1804, RSTC, box 3-98, in which the court refused to grant redhibition when a buyer's slave died of smallpox despite a verbal guarantee of having been vaccinated.

69. Police Jury Minutes, 26 June 1813, box 7, folder C, part 2, item 32, CFHC.

70. John James Audubon, *Delineations of American Scenery and Character,* intro. Francis Hobart Herrick (New York: G. A. Baker, 1926), 120–23.

71. Flügel, "Pages from a Journal of a Voyage," 439–40.

72. *L'Ami des Lois,* 10 Apr. 1810.

73. *Andry et al. v Foy,* 1819, in Martin, *Martin's Reports of Cases,* 3:364–70, 407–12. As is sometimes true, Judge Martin includes this detail in his published report, cited here, but it is not to be found in the extant manuscript documentation of the case.

74. *Mitchell v Comyns,* 1 *Mart.* (o.s.) 133 (New Orleans, Spring 1810), SCLA.

75. Runaway Advertisement by William Gillespie, *Louisiana Gazette,* 3 Jan. 1809.

76. Jailor's Advertisement, 18 Nov. 1814, *Louisiana Courrier.* The jailbreak actually occurred on 4 September.

77. *Charles Jefferys v Blas Puche,* 20 July 1813, reel 1, case 229, OPCR; *Forsyth et al. v Nash,* No. 150, 4 *Mart.* (o.s.) 385 (New Orleans, June 1816), SCLA. The Dred Scott case had a long prehistory.

78. *Moniteur de la Louisiane*, 11 Sept. 1802, 24 Sept. 1803, 15 Oct. 1803, 11 Feb. 1804.

79. Runaway Advertisement, *Louisiana Courrier*, 18 Nov. 1814.

80. *Dossat v Guillotte*, No. 81, 4 *Mart.* (o.s.) 203 (New Orleans, Mar. 1816), SCLA.

81. *L'Ami des Lois*, 4 Sept. 1810.

82. Boze to Henri Ste-Gême, 20 Apr. 1818, Ste-Gême Papers.

83. Edouard de Montulé, *Travels in America, 1816–1817*, trans. Edward D. Seeber (Bloomington: Indiana Univ. Press, 1951), 89.

84. Ibid.

85. *Feriet v Seguin*, 10 Jan. 1814, reel 2, case 251, OPCR.

86. *Jourdan v Patton*, No. 304, 5 *Mart.* (o.s.) 615 (New Orleans, July 1818), SCLA.

87. *Bayon v Prévot*, No. 115, 4 *Mart.* (o.s.) 58 (New Orleans, Dec. 1815), SCLA. In this, and in the similar case of *Palfrey v Rivas*, No. 381, 7 *Mart.* (o.s.) 371 (New Orleans, Jan. 1820), SCLA, the court found for the neighbor undertaking the "kindly office."

88. Boze to Henri de Ste-Gême, 10, 22 Oct., 1 Nov. 1818, Ste-Gême Papers.

89. *Delery v Mornet*, No. 616, 11 *Mart.* 4 (New Orleans, Feb. 1822), SCLA.

90. Barbara Bush, *Slave Women in Caribbean Society, 1650–1838* (Bloomington: Indiana Univ. Press, 1990), 83–108.

91. Gutman, *Black Family in Slavery and Freedom*.

92. White, *Ar'n't I A Woman?* 158.

93. Boze to Henri Ste-Gême, 26 Jan. 1819, Ste-Gême Papers. See also Gutman, *Black Family in Slavery and Freedom*, 80–82.

94. Boze to Henri Ste-Gême, 11 Mar. 1820, Ste-Gême Papers. See also Boze to Henri Ste-Gême, 21 July 1819, Ste-Gême Papers.

95. Boze to Henri Ste-Gême, 28 May 1820, Ste-Gême Papers.

96. Ann Patton Malone, *Sweet Chariot: Slave Family and Household Structure in Nineteenth-Century Louisiana* (Chapel Hill: Univ. of North Carolina Press, 1992), 13–25.

97. Ibid., 54–6.

98. *New Orleans in 1805: A Directory and a Census*.

99. Gutman, *Black Family in Slavery and Freedom*, 222–24.

100. Derby, *Journal of a Tour in America*, 252–58.

101. Ibid., 254.

102. Ibid., 255.

103. Ibid., 255–56.

104. Ibid., 256.

105. Ibid., 263.

106. Ibid., 257–58.

107. Genovese, *Roll, Jordan, Roll*, 144.

108. Derby, *Journal of a Tour in America*, 246.

109. Stuart, *Three Years in North America*, 2:206.

110. John S. Kendall, "Notes on the Criminal History of New Orleans," *LHQ* 34 (1951): 149.

111. *Sives v Delogny*, 16 July 1812, box 3373-3454, RSTC.

112. *Marie Louise v Francois Bernoudy*, 17 July 1813, OPCR.

113. *Marie Zabeth v Pierre Lafitte*, 17 Dec. 1805, box 100-209, RSTC.

114. Amendment to the Criminal Code, Section 6, *Acts Passed at the First Session of the Fourth Legislature of the State of Louisiana* (New Orleans: J. C. de St. Romes, 1819), 64.

115. Ibid., 62–64, secs. 4 and 5.

116. *Jacob v Antoine Demarchy*, 31 May 1805, folder (some cases in this group are in individual folders rather than boxes), RSTC.

117. *Augustine et al. v Caillau Lafontaine*, 18 May 1814, case 407, OPCR.

118. *Delphine v Devèze*, No. 996, 2 *Mart.* (n.s.) 650 (New Orleans, June 1824), SCLA.

119. *Lunsford v Coquillon*, No. 815, 2 *Mart.* (n.s.) 401 (New Orleans, June 1824), SCLA.

120. See, for example, New Orleans' "First Directory, 1807," transcript by Mrs. Fred O. James, Louisiana State Museum, New Orleans, in which no blacks are identified.

121. Carter G. Woodson, *Free Negro Heads of Families in the United States in 1830* (Washington, D.C.: Association for the Study of Negro Life and History, 1925), 31–38; Patricia Brady, "Black Artists in Antebellum New Orleans," *LH* 32 (1991): 5–28; Charles E. O'Neill, "Fine Arts and Literature: Nineteenth-Century Louisiana Black Artists and Authors," in *Louisiana's Black Heritage*, ed. Macdonald, Kemp, and Haas, 63–84; Sterkx, *Free Negro in Ante-Bellum Louisiana*, 240–84.

122. David C. Rankin, "The Politics of Caste: Free Colored Leadership in New Orleans During the Civil War," in *Louisiana's Black Heritage*, ed. Robert R. Macdonald, John R. Kemp, and Edward F. Haas (New Orleans: Louisiana State Museum, 1979) 139–46.

123. Loren Schweninger, "Antebellum Free Persons of Color in Postbellum Louisiana," *LH* 30 (1989): 363.

124. On this, see James Roark and Michael Johnson, "Strategies of Survival: Free Negro Families and the Problem of Slavery," in Carol Bleser, ed., *In Joy and in Sorrow: Women, Family, and Marriage in the Victorian South, 1830–1900* (New York: Oxford Univ. Press, 1991), 88–102, who argue that free blacks' social vulnerability created special pressure on them to be slaveowners.

125. Emancipation of Angelique, 29 Mar. 1806, NONA, Narcisse Broutin, 135–36. See also Sterkx, *Free Negro in Ante-Bellum Louisiana*, 200–39, on planters.

126. Deposition by Piron, 13 Feb. 1816, in CFHC, Xavier Univ. Library, Special Collections, box 8, folder D, part 2.

127. *New Orleans in 1805: A Directory and a Census.* To establish these figures, it was assumed that any residence with an adult white householder present was a white-headed household, whereas the presence of any free black adult in the absence of a white adult indicated a black-headed household.

128. Robert C. Reinders, "The Free Negro in the New Orleans Economy, 1850–1860," *LH* 6 (1965): 274.

129. Lachance, "Intermarriage and French Cultural Persistence," 60–63.

130. Ashworth, *Slavery, Capitalism, and Politics*, 1:13–15.

CHAPTER 11. BLACK MANON IN THE CAPITAL CITY OF THE SLAVE SOUTH

1. Hirsch and Logsdon, Preface to *Creole New Orleans*, xi.

2. The view that a particular planter class must be studied within the context of its cultural or national origins, a refurbished version of the Tannenbaum thesis, is most eloquently argued by Eugene D. Genovese, notably in "The Comparative Focus in Latin American History," in *In Red and Black*, and in "Materialism and Idealism in the History of Negro Slavery," 371–94. The argument that Louisiana slaves experienced "massive re-Africanization" between the 1770s and the 1810s, which added

significantly to their ability to resist the regime, is found in Gwendolyn Midlo Hall, "The Formation of Afro-Creole Culture," in *Creole New Orleans*, ed. Hirsch and Logsdon, 58–87. The view that the Upper and Lower South were distinguished by the higher status of free blacks in the latter is presented by Berlin in *Slaves Without Masters*.

3. Darby, *Geographical Description*, 76.
4. "Six Dollars Reward," *L'Ami des Lois*, 4 Sept. 1818.
5. Regulations of Laborers, 19 May 1804, CDV, vol. 1, no. 1, 96–98; Market Regulations, 19 Sept. 1804, ibid., 182–83; Regulations of Laborers, 6 Aug. 1806, CDV, vol. 1, no. 3, 100.
6. *Louisiana Gazette*, 17 June 1817.
7. Eugene D. Genovese, "The Treatment of Slaves in Different Countries: Problems in the Applications of the Comparative Method," in *In Red and Black*, 158–72.
8. Even the best evidence for the Tannenbaum thesis is weak, like the laconic remark by Dutch-born, English-bred Bernard Romans in 1775, when he wrote that "Negroes in general are used with more lenity there [in Mississippi] than in Carolina." See *A Concise Natural History of East and West Florida*, facs., intro. Rembert W. Patrick (1775; reprint, Gainesville: Univ. Presses of Florida, 1962), 111.
9. Judith Kelleher Schafer, "New Orleans Slavery in 1850 in Advertisements," *Journal of Southern History* 47 (1981): 56.
10. David C. Rankin, "The Tannenbaum Thesis Reconsidered: Slavery and Race Relations in Antebellum Louisiana," *Southern Studies* 18 (1979): 31.
11. Berquin-Duvallon, *Vue de la colonie espagnole du Mississipi*, 210, 262–74. Another vengeful settler, who addressed an impassioned plea to Jefferson to seize Louisiana, attacked the local planters as grinding great profit from their slaves. See Alliot, "Historical and Political Reflections on Louisiana," 1:61–63, 67–69, 118–23.
12. Latrobe, *Impressions Respecting New Orleans*, 47.
13. Ibid.
14. Nuttall, *Journal of Travels*, 268.
15. Roderick A. McDonald, "Independent Economic Production by Slaves on Antebellum Louisiana Sugar Plantations," *Slavery and Abolition* 12 (1991): 182–208.
16. According to Latrobe, it was "a very unprofitable mode of dealing [because of] the infidelity of the peddlars, their ignorance or forgetfulness of prices . . . [and] the slow sales." See Latrobe, *Impressions Respecting New Orleans*, 101.
17. See, for example, Betty Wood, *Women's Work, Men's Work: The Informal Slave Economies of Low Country Georgia* (Athens: Univ. of Georgia Press, 1995); Loren Schweninger, "The Underside of Slavery: The Internal Economy, Self-Hire, and Quasi-Freedom in Virginia, 1780–1865," *Slavery and Abolition* 12 (1991): 1–22; and Joseph P. Reidy, *From Slavery to Agrarian Capitalism in the Cotton Plantation South: Central Georgia, 1800–1880* (Chapel Hill: Univ. of North Carolina Press, 1992), 60–62, 67–73, 101–6. Reidy asserts (102–3) that independent production was a source of conflict in the American South but not in South America or the Caribbean, but he cites no evidence for the latter regions.
18. Latrobe, *Impressions Respecting New Orleans*, 102.
19. Ibid. Martin's work has been mostly ignored here because it is of no scholarly value,

although it has been reprinted as *The History of Louisiana from the Earliest Period* (1827; reprint, New Orleans: Pelican, 1963).

20. Latrobe, *Impressions Respecting New Orleans*, 102. See also 53–54.

21. Stoddard, *Sketches, Historical and Descriptive*, 333.

22. Ibid., 336.

23. Harriet Martineau, *Retrospect of Western Travel*, 2 vols. (1838; reprint, New York: Haskell House, 1969), 1:276.

24. Baptism of "Maria Delfina," 26 Dec. 1993, in Woods and Nolan, *Sacramental Records*, 4:252; Marriage of Macarty and Ramon Lopez y Angulo, 11 June 1800, Libro de matrimonios celebrados en esta Iglesia parroq.l de San Luis de Nueva Orleans, 1784–1806, Archives, Archdiocese of New Orleans, 129.

25. Martineau, *Retrospect of Western Travel*, 1:263–67. For further details by an outsider, Armand Saillard, who claimed to have witnessed the incident, see *Les aventures du consul de France de New Orleans à Carthagène*, eds. Max Dorian and Dixie Reynolds (La Rochelle: Editions Navarre, 1981), 101–3. Saillard reported that the mob destroyed the interior of her house, in a rage because authorities refused to prosecute her. He also reported she had been denounced to authority earlier by a "parent" but her sworn denial got the charge dismissed. See also Fred R. Darkis Jr., "Madame Lalurie of New Orleans," *LH* 23 (1982): 383–99.

26. William Fogel and Stanley L. Engerman, *Time on the Cross: The Econometrics of American Negro Slavery* (Boston: Little, Brown, 1974); Paul A. David et al., *Reckoning with Slavery: A Critical Study in the Quantitative History of American Negro Slavery* (New York: Oxford Univ. Press, 1976.)

27. Louis Moreau-Lislet, comp., "Black Code," in *A General Digest of the Acts of the Legislature of Louisiana Passed from the Year 1804, to 1827 Inclusive*, 2 vols. (New Orleans: Benjamin Levy, 1828), 1:100–29. Compare to the one passed by planters on 15 Dec. 1803, Laussat Papers.

28. Latrobe, *Impressions Respecting New Orleans*, 57; see 55–57.

29. *Dominique Bouligny and Belizire LeBlanc v François Bernoudy*, 19 Nov. 1813, case 194, OPCR.

30. "Crimes and Offenses, and Supplementary Acts," in Moreau-Lislet, *General Digest of the Acts of the Legislature of Louisiana*, 1:112–29.

31. *Laverty v Duplessis*, 3 *Mart.* (o.s.) 42 (New Orleans, May 1813), SCLA. The case concerns an Irish alien ordered to remove inland as a security measure at the beginning of the War of 1812.

32. *The Laws of Las Siete Partidas Which Are Still in Force in the State of Louisiana*, trans. Louis Moreau-Lislet and Henry Carleton, 2 vols. (1820; reprint, Baton Rouge: Claitor's Publishing, 1978).

33. Ibid., 1:584.

34. For other relevant laws, see ibid., 30–31, 112–13, 298, 378–79, 386–88, 578–79, 583–85. All can be traced to conditions in Spain in the thirteenth century.

35. Judith Kelleher Schafer, *Slavery, the Civil Law, and the Supreme Court of Louisiana* (Baton Rouge: Louisiana State Univ. Press, 1994), 63.

36. Derby, *Journal of a Tour in America*, 262.

37. Genovese, "Treatment of Slaves in Different Countries," 159.

38. Norrece T. Jones Jr., *Born a Child of Freedom, Yet A Slave: Mechanisms of Control and Strategies*

of *Resistance in Antebellum South Carolina* (Hanover, N.H.: Wesleyan Univ. Press, 1990), 37–63; Brenda Stevenson, "Distress and Discord in Virginia Slave Families, 1830–1860," in *In Joy and in Sorrow*, ed. Bleser, 103–24.

39. Bill of Sale, 19 Jan. 1811, NONA, François Broutin, 17v–18v. Bill of Sale, 3 July 1813, NONA, Pierre Pedesclaux, 261.

40. Exposé by Bergé, n.d., Brown Papers, 5:921.

41. Fogel and Engerman, *Time on the Cross*, 124; see 110–33 for the whole discussion. For critics, see Herbert Gutman and Richard Sutch, "The Slave Family: Protected Agent of Capitalist Masters or Victims of the Slave Trade?" in *Reckoning with Slavery: A Critical Study in the Quantitative History of American Negro Slavery*, ed. David et al., 112–33; and Michael Tadman, *Speculators and Slaves: Masters, Traders, and Slaves in the Old South* (Madison: Univ. of Wisconsin Press, 1989), 133–78.

42. Laurence J. Kotlikoff, "The Structure of Slave Prices in New Orleans, 1804 to 1862," *Economic Inquiry* 17 (1979): 512–14.

43. The priest most likely to have had the influence to make a difference was Father Sedella. But nowhere in the records is there any sign he did. His surviving correspondence is concerned almost exclusively with political matters, like his quarrel with authorities about the Inquisition in 1790, his quarrel with Father Patrick Walsh about his pastorate, and his reports to Spanish authorities about the activities of Spanish American revolutionaries in New Orleans. See the Sedella Collection.

44. St. Louis Parish Schedule of Fees by Father Luis de Quintanilla, 29 Nov. 1792, Misc. 1: 6, Various Documents, 1791–1793, Archives, Archdiocese of New Orleans.

45. Timothy F. Reilly, "Slavery and the Southwestern Evangelist in New Orleans, 1800–1861," *Journal of Mississippi History* 41 (1979): 301.

46. Genovese, "Materialism and Idealism in the History of Negro Slavery," 37–48.

47. Herbert Klein's study of Cuba in this regard has been refuted by Kenneth F. Kiple, who finds that the rate of freedom purchase was low there in the nineteenth century: most slaves had no hope of being manumitted. See *Blacks in Colonial Cuba, 1774–1899* (Gainesville: Univ. Presses of Florida, 1976), 41–42.

48. For the legal degradation of free blacks, see especially Moreau-Lislet, *General Digest of the Acts of the Legislature of Louisiana*, 1:112ff. See also Annie Lee West Stahl, "The Free Negro in Ante-Bellum Louisiana," *LHQ* 25 (1942): 312–35; Taylor, *Negro Slavery in Louisiana*, 153–54, 195–96; and John Lofton, *Insurrection in South Carolina: The Turbulent World of Denmark Vesey* (Yellow Springs, Ohio: Antioch Press, 1964), 75–95.

49. A feverish deposition by one free black in 1806 that most free blacks were plotting a rebellion in concert with the Spanish, entailing the emancipation of all slaves who joined them, was not taken seriously by Claiborne. See "Statement of Stephen, A Free Negro, to Governor Claiborne," 23 Jan. 1806, *TPQ* 575–76; and Claiborne to Madison, 24 Jan. 1806, *Claiborne*, 3:248. Claiborne exploited the story as an excuse to order all Spanish officials out of the territory, as he had long yearned to do. See Claiborne to Col. José Martinez, 25 Jan. 1806, *Claiborne*, 3:248–49.

50. *Louisiana Courrier*, 18 Nov. 1814.

51. Deposition by Mazureau before the Mayor, 18 Dec. 1813, Charles Francis Heartman Collection, Special Collections, Xavier Univ. Library, box 8, folder C, item 41. Isolated signs of resistance like this one, when examined in context, do not support the

sweeping argument that "control over the Negro population was, in short, virtually nonexistent in New Orleans." See Roger A. Fischer, "Racial Segregation in Ante Bellum New Orleans," *AHR* 74 (1969): 930.

52. See also Robin, *Voyage*, 251–52. He pointed to the Spartans and Romans as examples of slave systems that lasted for centuries because freedmen were not stigmatized. He was also referring, of course, to the provocation of the free blacks of Saint Domingue by whites in the years before the Haitian Revolution.

53. Moreau-Lislet, *General Digest of the Acts of the Legislature of Louisiana*, 1:454.

54. For key cases in which the court denied appeals by slaves to enforce coartación agreements, see *Victoire v Dussuau*, No. 103, 4 Mart. (o.s.) 212 (New Orleans, Mar. 1816), SCLA; *Trudeau's Executor v Robinette*, No. 184, 4 Mart. (o.s.) 577 (New Orleans, Jan. 1817), SCLA; *Cuffy v Castillon*, No. 255, 5 Mart. (o.s.) 494 (New Orleans, May 1818), SCLA; *Marie v Avart*, No. 352, 6 Mart. (o.s.) 731 (New Orleans, June 1819), and No. 488, 8 Mart. (o.s.) 512 (New Orleans, Jan. 1820), SCLA; *Julien v Langlish*, No. 492, 9 Mart. (o.s.) 205 (New Orleans, Jan. 1821), SCLA.

55. Moreau-Lislet, *General Digest of the Acts of the Legislature of Louisiana*, 1:454–56. In 1827, the law was changed to allow emancipations of slaves under thiry if the police jury allowed the exception. See *ibid.*, 456–57. See also Claiborne to Jeffereson, 10 Apr., 1806, *Claiborne*, 3:288–89.

56. In the following year the police jury was given the authority to make exceptions, but it was a severe discouragement to emancipations. See *Digest of the Laws Relative to Slaves and Free People of Color in the State of Louisiana* (New Orleans: Louisiana Constitutional and Anti-Fanatical Society, 1835), 19, 27.

57. Petition to Laussat, 2 Dec. 1803, CDV, vol. 1, no. 1, 4; Petition to Claiborne, 25 Feb. 1804, CDV, vol. 1, no. 1, 47; Claiborne to Madison, 13 Apr. and 8 May 1804, *Claiborne*, 2:95–6, 134; Governor's Authority to Inspect Slave Ships, 25 Apr. 1804, CDV, vol. 1, no. 1, 82–83, and *passim*; CDV Petition to Claiborne, 30 June 1804, CDV, vol. 1, no. 1, 126–128. "An Act to Prevent the introduction of Free People of Colour, from Hispaniola and the other French islands of America, into the Territory of Orleans," 7 June 1806, and "An Act to Prevent the emigration if Free Negroes and Mulattoes into the Territory of Orleans," 14 Apr. 1807, in Moreau-Lislet, *General Digest of the Acts of the Legislature of Louisiana*, 1:498–99. See also Lachance, "Politics of Fear," 164–67.

58. *Digest of the Laws Relative to Slaves and Free People of Color in the State of Louisiana*, 17–18.

59. Ibid., 27.

60. Moreau-Lislet, *General Digest of the Acts of the Legislature of Louisiana*, 2:5. See also *Girod v Lewis*, 1819, No. 35, 6 Mart. (o.s.) 559 (New Orleans, May 1819), SCLA, ruling that marriage of slaves has no civil effects after manumission.

61. *Adelle v Beauregard*, 1 Mart. (o.s.) 183 (La. 1810), SCLA.

62. See, for example, *Scott v Williams*, 1828, in Helen Tunicliff Catterall, ed. and comp., *Judicial Cases Concerning American Slavery and the Negro*, 5 vols. (Washington, D.C.: Carnegie Institution, 1926), 2:54. See also Tushnet, *American Law of Slavery*, 145.

63. "An Act to prescribe certain formalities respecting Free Persons of Color," 31 Mar. 1808, in Moreau-Lislet, *General Digest of the Acts of the Legislature of Louisiana*, 1:499–500. The purpose was not "to prevent light-skinned freemen from eluding these carefully drawn rules of racial deportment by fading into Louisiana's swarthy French

and Spanish creole population," as argued by Berlin, *Slaves Without Masters*, 123. The white population was not swarthy, and there had always been a recording system to keep free blacks legally separate from whites. This innovation was a refinement of the existing system because a number of free "blacks" were becoming "completely" morphologically white.

64. William Waller Hening, *The Statutes at Large* (Richmond, Va., 1812), 3:252.

65. Jefferson to Francis C. Gray, 4 Mar. 1815, cited in Brodie, *Thomas Jefferson*, 586. This would help to explain why the free black population of the upper South remained so much blacker than in the Lower South (because its racial escape hatch was more open). On passing in other states, in a discussion that does not give much attention to either law or custom, see Jordan, *White over Black*, 171–74.

66. Marriage of Celestin Lachapelle and Aimé Lachaise, 30 Oct. 1803, St. Louis Cathedral Marriages, 1806–1821, 126.

67. Marriage of Gabriel Girodeau and Félicité Pomet, 3 July 1817, ibid., 195.

68. "Leaves from a Slave's Journal of Life," in *Slave Testimony: Two Centuries of Letters, Speeches, Interviews, and Autobiographies*, ed. John W. Blassingame (Baton Rouge: Louisiana State Univ. Press, 1977), 153.

69. Gutman, *Black Family in Slavery and Freedom*, 230–56.

70. Holmes, *Account of the United States of America*, 333.

71. Virginia R. Dominguez, *White by Definition: Social Classification in Creole Louisiana* (New Brunswick: Rutgers Univ. Press, 1986), 267.

72. To the Public, 13 Dec. 1811, *Télégraphe Louisianais and Mercantile Advertiser.*

73. *John Cauchoix v Jean Dupuy et al.*, No. 2125, 3 La. (Louisiana Reports) 206 (New Orleans, Dec. 1831), SCLA.

74. Whitelaw Reid, *After the War: A Tour of the Southern States, 1865–1866*, ed. C. Vann Woodward (1866; reprint, New York: Harper and Row, 1965), 243.

75. While we must not minimize the suffering inflicted on slave women by masters who exploited them sexually, Richard H. Steckel has pointed out that slaves could impose significant costs on an offending slaveowner for excessive behavior, which undermined his profits and authority. See his "Miscegenation and the American Slave Schedules," *Journal of Interdisciplinary History* 11 (1980): 254–55.

76. *Joanna Dessales Danicant v Louis Darby Danicant*, 2 Feb. 1805, box 100-209, RSTC; *Baschemin v Dessalles*, 22 Apr. 1805, boxes 303-437 and 438-572, RSTC. Marie Darby's will is a study in misrepresentation, showing that we must exercise caution in using such instruments as a guide to reality. Not only does she ignore the fact that Louis had a wife and child while itemizing carefully the members of the "good" son's family, she also states flatly that Pierre had no children. See Testament of Widow Darby, 25 Apr. 1805, NONA, Narcisse Broutin.

77. *Marie Corbin (Baschemin Darby) v François Darby et al.*, 9 June 1804, box 438-572, RSTC.

78. *François Darby et al. v Marie Baschemin Darby*, 22 June 1805, box 303-437, RSC. Judgment of 19 Nov. 1806.

79. On this point, it is hard to agree with those who interpret the laws of Virginia to the contrary, most recently Kathleen M. Brown in her *Good Wives, Nasty Wenches, & Anxious Patriarchs: Gender, Race, and Power in Colonial Virginia* (Chapel Hill: Univ. of North Carolina Press, 1996), 194–201. It is true that a law of 1662 laid fines for acts of

interracial "fornication." But it is clear from both the judicial application of the law and from the law of 1691 that reaffirmed and broadened the law of 1662 that what was outlawed was the conception and birth of children by racially mixed couples, and the marriage of the latter. Neither Brown nor any other scholar has ever provided a single example of a white person being punished for committing a mere sexual act with a person of color of the opposite sex. The isolated case of Hugh Davis in 1630, cited by Brown (195) and many others, concerning a white man who was whipped for having sex with a "negro," obviously concerns a homosexual act, for the specific language of the decree and the nature of the punishment is totally different from every other judicial finding concerning heterosexuals in the record of this and every other colony and state.

80. For this very widespread assumption, see, for example, Berlin, *Slaves Without Masters*, 109. A related notion is that the French of all classes were more inclined to mingle with black women, marry them, and legitimize their offspring, whereas in Anglo-American slave society only people from the lower classes mixed with slaves. See Carter G. Woodson, "The Beginnings of the Miscegenation of the Whites and Blacks," *JNH* 3 (1918): 339.

81. Libro Primero de Patrimonios de Negros y Mulatos de la Parroquia de Sn Luis de esta Ciudad de la Nueva-Orleans, 20 Jan. 1777 to 29 July 1830, Archives, Archdiocese of New Orleans, New Orleans. This does not include an important number of stable domestic households that came under the sacrament of marriage only later in the record. Like some whites, some free blacks seem to have preferred to live without the sacrament until one spouse was dying, when they applied to the priest to wed them.

82. Tannenbaum, *Slave and Citizen*, 123, 124.

83. *Patton v Patton*, 1831, in Catterall, *Judicial Cases Concerning American Slavery and the Negro*, 1:318.

84. Gary Mills, "Miscegenation and the Free Negro in Antebellum 'Anglo' Alabama: A Reexamination of Southern Race Relations," *Journal of American History* 68 (1981): 39. The "Anglo" parishes are also the focus of attention in Malone, *Sweet Chariot*, 218–24.

85. Anne Royall, *Sketches of History, Life, and Manners in the United States, By a Traveler* (New Haven, Conn.: Author, 1826), 100–101. For one sensible discussion of the subject in the antebellum South outside Louisiana, see Orville Vernon Burton, *In My Father's House Are Many Mansions: Family and Community in Edgefield, South Carolina* (Chapel Hill: Univ. of North Carolina Press, 1985), 138–40, 145–47, 185–90. Burton emphasizes the paucity of serious studies of this question.

86. Frances Trollope, *Domestic Manners of the Americans,* ed. Donald Smalley (1832; reprint, New York: Alfred A. Knopf, 1949), 13; Arfwedson, *United States and Canada,* 2:60–61.

87. Trollope, *Domestic Manners of the Americans,* 13–14. Barbara Bush elaborates on the theme of interracial sexual desire and jealousy with sensitivity. See "White 'Ladies,' Coloured 'Favourites' and Black 'Wenches': Some Considerations on Sex, Race and Class Factors in Social Relations in White Creole Society in the British Caribbean," *Slavery and Abolition* 2 (1981): 259.

88. See, for example, Foner, "Free People of Color in Louisiana and St. Domingue," 411. For the most detailed and tasteless version, see Harnett T. Kane, *Queen New Orleans: City By the River* (New York: William Morrow, 1949), 183–98.

89. Stahl, "Free Negro in Ante-Bellum Louisiana," 301–96.

90. Thomas Ashe, *Travels in America, Performed in 1806, For the Purpose of Exploring the Rivers Alleghany, Monongahela, Ohio, and Mississippi* (Newburyport: E. M. Blount, 1808), 344–46. See Iain McCalman, *Radical Underworld: Prophets, Revolutionaries and Pornographers in London, 1795–1840* (Oxford: Clarendon Press, 1993), 162–65, 226. Ashe's autobiography is a fantastic potpourri of improbable adventures, but it is notable that he does not mention New Orleans, and he was probably never in Louisiana. See *Memoirs and Confessions of Captain Ashe*, 3 vols. (London: Henry Colburn, 1815). Ashe's work and others presumably furnished the raw material for Theophilus Moore's description of interracial *plaçage* (at a standard rate of fifty dollars per month), in *Marriage Customs and Modes of Courtship of the Various Nations of the Universe*, 2d ed. (London: John Bumpus, 1820), 286–90.

91. Stuart, *Three Years in North America*, 2:204.

92. Henry A. Kmen situates this relatively minor phenomenon in the context of the town's ballroom culture. See "The Music of New Orleans," in *The Past As Prelude*, ed. Carter et al., 211–14.

93. Karl Bernhard, Duke of Saxe-Weimar, *Travels through North America during the Years 1825 and 1826*, 2 vols. (Philadelphia: Carey, Lea and Cary, 1828), 2:58.

94. For descriptions of drunken brawling, see ibid., 70–1.

95. Ibid., 62.

96. Ibid.

97. Wilhelm, *Travels in North America*, 35.

98. Ibid., 118.

99. See, for example, John F. Schermerhorn and Samuel J. Mills, *A Correct View of that Part of the United States which Lies West of the Allegany Mountains, With Regard to Religion and Morals* (Hartford, Conn.: Peter B. Gleason, 1814), 34–35.

100. Flint, *Recollections of the Last Ten Years*, 245.

101. Arfwedson, *United States and Canada*, 2:62.

102. According to Francis Tuckett, nonetheless, an observer who arrived in New Orleans not long after Trollope, outsiders had let their imaginations run wild about sex in that city. No less morally upright than Trollope, he saw prostitution as a normal urban phenomenon. "The females of repute conduct themselves with propriety," he thought, "and this vice prevails everywhere in proportion to the number of strangers frequenting any place and therefore the stigma is improperly attached to the inhabitants." See *A Journey in the United States in the Years 1829 and 1830*, ed. Hubert C. Fox (Plymouth, Eng.: St. Nicholas Books, 1976), 72.

103. Richard Tansey, "Prostitution and Politics in Antebellum New Orleans," *Southern Studies* 18 (1979): 448–79. See also Phil Johnson, "Good Time Town," in *The Past As Prelude*, ed. Carter et al., 233–57.

104. It is true that the inclination of free black women to marry was in some cases weak. Just as Suzanne Lebsock found in her study of Petersburg, Virginia, an important

minority of New Orleans women of color resisted yielding autonomy to a formal spouse, preferring to cohabit with a free black man and marry him only at death's door. But that is a separate issue. See *Free Women of Petersburg*, 104–11.

105. The minority who did is represented by Jean-Joseph Carrel, who, although legitimately married, had no children by his white wife and acknowledged a colored son. In fact, Carrel was probably a refugee from Haiti, and these refugees (white and black) had a pronounced tendency to write wills in which they indicated misalliances, suggesting that either these were more acceptable (openly acknowledged) in Saint Domingue or that for some reason the refugees were more likely to be involved in them. See Testament of Carrel, 26 Oct. 1816, NONA, Pierre and Philippe Pedesclaux No. 73, 626v–27v.

106. Will of Perou, 20 Mar. 1810, NONA, Narcisse Broutin, 245v–46.

107. Testament of Picou, 12 Oct. 1812, NONA, Pedesclaux, 436–37.

108. Testament of Roux, 30 Oct. 1813, NONA, Pedesclaux, 451–52.

109. Will of Macarty, 21 Nov. 1808, NONA, Narcisse Broutin, 491v–92.

110. Will of Moquin, 31 Aug. 1807, NONA, B. Van Pradelles, 114v–16v.

111. Will of Hassett, 19 Apr. and Codicil of 20 Apr. 1804, NONA, Narcisse Broutin, 317–21v.

112. Testament of Dubreuil, 25 Apr. 1811, NONA, N. Broutin, 271v–74. His white friend Pierre Colson was to enjoy the usufruct of the estate for three years before Manette could inherit.

113. Testament of Bauré, 13 Nov. 1810, NONA, Stephen de Quiñones, 511v–13. Finally, it should be mentioned that illicit liaisons were not exclusively interracial. Pierre Ambroise Cuvillier left a legitimate wife and children, but he not only left one third of his estate to a natural daughter born in England, he requested that his wife look after her, "which I have discussed with her several times." See Testament of Cuvillier, 24 July 1811, NONA, N. Broutin, 286–87v.

114. Kotlikoff, "Structure of Slave Prices in New Orleans," 515–17.

115. Testament of Delery Desillet, 25 Feb. 1814, NONA, Pedesclaux, 75–76.

116. Testament of Ferrer, 15 Nov. 1817, NONA, Philippe Pedesclaux, 787–88.

117. Allan, *Life and Work of John McDonogh*, 20–21; Leon Huhner, *The Life of Judah Touro, 1775–1854* (Philadelphia: Jewish Publication Society of America, 1946), 62–72, 104–7.

118. This is a point argued well by Sterkx, *Free Negro in Ante-Bellum Louisiana*, 253–54.

119. White, *Ar'n't I a Woman?* 27–36. The battle was somewhat more prolonged and complex in New Orleans: particular rules about the color line were long established since the eighteenth century by planters in the Anglo-American states. By some fine tuning, the legislature and courts made it next to impossible for a black concubine or natural children of mixed race to make claims on a white master's estate. See *Adèle v Beauregard*, 1 *Mart.* (o.s.) 183 (New Orleans, Fall, 1810), SCLA; *Tonnelier v Maurin's Executor*, 2 *Mart.* (o.s.) 206 (New Orleans, Spring 1812), SCLA; *Boré's Executor v Quierry's Executor*, No. 189, 4 *Mart.* (o.s.) 545 (New Orleans, Dec. 1816), SCLA. *Carrel's Heirs v Magdalen Cabaret*, No. 391, 7 *Mart.* (o.s.) 375 (New Orleans, Jan. 1820), SCLA, is a classic case in the same collection, in which a man's longtime mulatto concubine won the right to inherit against the odds by great persistence. In one classic case,

when three white minors sued their widower father for alimony to live on their own to protect their reputation rather than live with him and his free black concubine, as he insisted they do, the judges angrily ordered the man "to do that, which nature and duty both require he should perform, without being urged to it." See *George Heno et al. v Heno*, No. 510, 9 *Mart.* (o.s.) 205 (New Orleans, May 1821), SCLA. For a general discussion, see Judith K. Schafer, "'Open and Notorious Concubinage': The Emancipation of Slave Mistresses by Will and the Supreme Court in Antebellum Louisiana," *LH* 28 (1987): 165–82.

120. For a different view, see Virginia Gould, "In Defense of their Creole Culture: The Free Creoles of Color of New Orleans, Mobile, and Pensacola," *Gulf Coast Historical Review* 9 (1993): 37. This is not to deny that in the rural areas outside New Orleans, where free blacks were dispersed, relations of clientage with whites could be important, as emphasized by Barbara J. Fields in *Slavery and Freedom on the Middle Ground: Maryland during the Nineteenth Century* (New Haven: Yale Univ. Press, 1985), 85–86.

121. Reuter, *Mulatto in the United States*, 174–82.

122. Berlin, *Slaves Without Masters*, 137. On the development of the free black community after 1819, see Caryn Cossé Bell, *Revolution, Romanticism, and the Afro-Creole Protest Tradition in Louisiana, 1718–1868* (Baton Rouge: Louisiana State Univ. Press, 1997), chaps. 4–7.

123. Berlin, *Slaves Without Masters*, 197.

124. Ibid., 198.

125. Michael P. Johnson and James L. Roark, *Black Masters: A Free Family of Color in the Old South* (New York: W. W. Norton, 1984), 160–73.

126. Ibid., 192.

127. Sterkx, *Free Negro in Ante-Bellum Louisiana*, 285–315.

128. Stephen Small, "Racial Group Boundaries and Identities: People of 'Mixed Race' in Slavery across the Americas," *Slavery and Abolition* 15 (1994): 17–37.

129. Paul F. Lachance, "The Formation of a Three-Caste Society: Evidence from Wills in Antebellum New Orleans," *Social Science History* 18 (1994): 211–42. Lachance's further argument is that there was a "convergence in American and Gallic racial attitudes" by which a former "racial openness" was abandoned (233). To whatever degree that racial openness existed, I would argue, it was merely the practice of a minority of individuals for specific local reasons.

130. Carl J. Ekberg and William E. Foley, eds., Carl J. Ekberg, trans., *An Account of Upper Louisiana* (Columbia: Univ. of Missouri Press, 1989), 109.

131. An Act to Incorporate the City of New Orleans, in *Acts Passed at the First Session of the Legislative Council of the Territory of Orleans*, 58–60, requiring voters to be free white males resident in the town one year and owning property worth at least five hundred dollars, or paying rent of at least one hundred dollars; An Act to Determine [Elections and Police], in *Acts Passed at the First Session of the First General Assembly of the State of Louisiana* (New Orleans: Thierry, 1812), 26. See *Journal of the House of Representatives during the First Session of the First Legislature of the State of Louisiana*, 25–26, for the protest by "respectable electors." A related tactic was to condemn officially the black republic: any white man suspected of having aided the wrong side in the Haitian Revolution

was an outcast in New Orleans society. The legal profession tried to disbar a white attorney who was suspected of having abetted the Haitian Revolution; see *Derbigny v Pierre Dormenon*, 1810, in Martin, *Martin's Reports of Cases*, 1:70–72.

132. *Acts Passed at the First Session of the Legislative Council of the Territory of Orleans*, 156, requiring jurors to be free white householders resident one year.

133. Claiborne to the Mayor, 8 July 1806, *Claiborne*, 3:357.

134. Recommendations of the Health Committee, 12 Sept. 1804, CDV, vol. 1, no. 1, 174.

135. Interrogation of Regnier, 9 July 1804, CDV, vol. 1, no. 1, 132–33, who was made a police inspector by way of compensation; Petition to the Mayor, 30 Apr. 1808, CDV, vol. 2, no. 1, 183–84.

136. *Louisiana Gazette*, 27 Aug. 1805.

137. Moreau-Lislet, *General Digest of the Acts of the Legislature of Louisiana*, 1:104.

138. Ibid., 498.

139. Ordinance of 17 Dec. 1814, CDV, vol. 2. no. 5, 24–25.

140. Moreau-Lislet, *General Digest of the Acts of the Legislature of Louisiana*, 1:129, 362.

141. Ibid., 103, 115, 127.

142. Albert Voorhies, *A Treatise on the Criminal Jurisprudence of Louisiana*, 2 vols. (New Orleans: Bloomfield and Steel, 1860), 1:613–14.

143. Moreau-Lislet, *General Digest of the Acts of the Legislature of Louisiana*, 1:112.

144. Ibid., 127.

145. Betty Porter, "The History of Negro Education in Louisiana," *LHQ* 25 (1942): 735.

146. *Digest of the Laws Relative to Slaves and Free People of Color in the State of Louisiana*, 18–19.

147. Ibid., 25–26. Finally, specific free blacks who overstepped boundaries were targeted. In the Tchoupitoulas district, the white neighbors of the Bachus family moved to evict them from their land to punish them for showing insufficient deference. See Order of Slave Auction, 3 Mar. 1804, CDV, vol. 1, no. 1, 50; Order of Arrest and Imprisonment of Nicholas Bachus, 11, 18 Apr. 1804, CDV, vol. 1, no. 1, 76, 79, for "lack of respect for his neighborhood syndic." Old contracts with free blacks were violated with impunity. In one key jury trial, the Ursuline Nuns despoiled the heirs of their longtime free black overseer of the little farm the nuns had given him in return for his services. See *Jacob et al. v Ursulines*, 1812, 2 Mart. (o.s.) 269 (New Orleans, Fall, 1812), SCLA.

148. Timothy Flint, quoted in [Woodson?], "Observations on the Negroes of Louisiana," 177. Testimonials to their industry and respectability, like the remarkable description by none other than Charles Gayarré, went unpublished and ignored. See ibid., 181–84.

149. Curry, *Free Black in Urban America*, 40, 268.

150. Robert C. Reinders, "The Free Negro in the New Orleans Economy, 1850–1860," *LH* 6 (1965): 273–85. See Isabelle Dubroca, "A Study of Negro Emancipation in Louisiana, 1803–1865" (Ph.D. diss., Tulane Univ., 1924), on the declining fortunes of free blacks after 1803; see especially 106–22 for her suggestion that whites' attitudes were shaped by northern antislavery agitation and the opposition by white mechanics to the employment of black labor.

151. Voorhies, *Treatise on the Criminal Jurisprudence of Louisiana*, 1:623–24.

152. Claiborne to Madison, 12 July 1804, *Claiborne*, 2:244–46; see also Berlin, *Slaves Without Masters*, 81–85.

153. Allan, *Life and Work of John McDonogh*, 42–43.

154. Stuart, *Three Years in North America*, 2:211.

155. Berlin, *Slaves Without Masters*, 89–90, 54–55, 63–65; see also Tate, *Negro in Eighteenth-Century Williamsburg*, 222–33. For the results in cities outside Louisiana, see Curry, *Free Black in Urban America*.

156. Berlin, *Slaves Without Masters*, 89–107, for an earlier view.

157. Davis, *Problem of Slavery in Western Culture*, 288.

EPILOGUE

1. Latrobe, *Impressions Respecting New Orleans*, 103.

2. George C. Groce and David H. Wallace, *The New York Historical Society's Dictionary of Artists in America, 1564–1860* (New Haven: Yale Univ. Press, 1957), 508; Chris Petteys, *Dictionary of Women Artists: An International Dictionary of Women Artists Born before 1900* (Boston: G. K. Hall, 1985), 567. The latter gives her dates of birth (in France) and death (in Philadelphia) as 1778 and 1853. According to the former, she painted *The Treaty of Ghent* in Washington and first displayed it there in 1817.

3. Latrobe, *Impressions Respecting New Orleans*, 103.

4. Ibid., 103, 104.

5. Edgar Faure, *La banqueroute de Law, 17 juillet 1720* (Paris: Gallimard, 1977), 488ff.

6. J. David Harden, "Liberty Caps and Liberty Trees," *Past and Present* 146 (1995): 73–74, 88, 100.

7. Richard Slotkin, *Regeneration through Violence: The Mythology of the American Frontier, 1600–1860* (Middletown, Conn.: Wesleyan Univ. Press, 1973), 241.

8. *The Oxford Classical Dictionary*, ed. Simon Hornblower and Antony Spawforth, 3d ed. (Oxford: Oxford Univ. Press, 1996), 688, 962, 984.

Bibliography

MANUSCRIPT SOURCES

Archdiocese of New Orleans, Archives. New Orleans.

    Baptêmes des personnes de couleur libres et des esclaves, St. Marie Church, 1805–44.

    Libro de matrimonios celebrados en esta Iglesia parroq.l de San Luis de Nueva Orleans, 1784–1806.

    Libro primero de matrimonios de negros y mulatos de la parroquia de Sn Luis de esta Ciudad de la Nueva-Orleans, Jan. 20, 1777 to July 29, 1830.

    Miscellaneous Manuscripts. 1:6, Various Documents, 1791–93.

    St. Louis Cathedral Baptisms, 1731–33.

    St. Louis Cathedral Baptisms, 1744–53.

    St. Louis Cathedral Baptisms, 1753–59.

    St. Louis Cathedral Baptisms, 1767–71.

    St. Louis Cathedral Baptisms, 1772–76.

    St. Louis Cathedral Baptisms, 1777–86.

    St. Louis Cathedral Baptisms, 1786–96.

    St. Louis Cathedral Baptisms, 1796–1802.

    St. Louis Cathedral Baptisms, 1802–6.

    St. Louis Cathedral Baptisms, 1809–11.

    St. Louis Cathedral Baptisms, 1811–15.

    St. Louis Cathedral Baptisms and Marriages, 1759–62.

    St. Louis Cathedral Baptisms and Marriages, 1763–66.

    St. Louis Cathedral Baptisms of Slaves and Free Persons of Color, 1801–4.

    St. Louis Cathedral Funerals, 1803–15.

    St. Louis Cathedral Funerals of Slaves and Free Persons of Color, 1806–10.

    St. Louis Cathedral Funerals of Slaves and Free Persons of Color, 1810–15.

    St. Louis Cathedral Marriages, 1720–30.

    St. Louis Cathedral Marriages, 1764–74.

    St. Louis Cathedral Marriages, 1777–84.

    St. Louis Cathedral Marriages, 1806–21.

Archives Nationales, Paris.
> Archives des Colonies. Séries A, B, C8, C13, C14, D2, F1-5. (Microfilm copies also used in the Historic New Orleans Collection and the National Archives, Ottawa, Canada.)
> Archives de la Bastille. Série 10600–72.

Archivo Histórico Nacional, Madrid.
> Consejos. Legajos 20925, 20981.
> Estado. Legajos 3451, 3888, 3891, 3898–3901.

Biblioteca Nacional, Manuscritos, Madrid.
> Legajos 3178, 19247, 19248, 19508, 19509.

Historical Society of Pennsylvania, Philadelphia.
> An Exact Collection of the Facts Relating to the Cession of Louisiana to the Spaniards. c. 1770.
> Gilpin Family Papers.
> Josiah Stoddard Johnston Papers, 1821–39.

The Historic New Orleans Collection.
> Archivo General de Indias.
>> Sección 5, Audiencia de Santo Domingo. Microfilm Copy.
>> Papeles Procedentes de la Isla de Cuba. Roscoe Hill Collection. Library of Congress. Microfilm Copy.
> Laussat Papers.
> Miscellaneous Manuscripts.
> Ste-Gême Family Papers.

Howard-Tilton Memorial Library. Special Collections Division, Manuscripts Section. Tulane Univ.
> Antonio Sedella Collection, 1787–1815.
> Despatches of the Spanish Governors. Translations by Works Progress Administration of Louisiana, 1767–96.
> Favrot Family Papers, 1669–1803.
> John McDonogh Papers, 1800–52.
> John Minor Wisdom Collection. General Manuscripts, 1810–15.
> New Orleans Municipal Papers: Police Records, 1808–32.
> Pontalba Family Papers, 1796–1914.
> Rosemonde E. and Emile Kuntz Collection, 1665–1768.

Library of Congress, Manuscript Division.
> James Brown Papers, 1765–1867. 5 vols.

Louisiana State Museum. Louisiana Historical Center, New Orleans.
> Black Books, summaries of documents in the Louisiana Historical Collection.

Conspicuous Cases and Synopses of Cases in the U.S. District Court of Louisiana, Cases 1 to 3,000, 1806–31. Works Progress Administration of Louisiana. Transcripts. Louisiana Historical Collection.

New Orleans' First Directory, 1807. Transcript.

Louisiana State Univ. Library.
Pintado Collection of Land Surveys.

National Archives, Washington, D.C.
Despatches from United States Consuls in New Orleans, Mar. 17, 1798, to Feb. 6, 1807. Microfilm Copy.

Newberry Library, Chicago. Edward E. Ayer Collection of Americana and American Indians. Manuscript Division.
Archivo Nacional de Cuba. Collection of Transcripts of Documents, 1770–1830. 11 vols.
France, Colonies, 1702–50. 4 vols.
Relation de la Louisiane, c. 1721.

New Orleans Notarial Archive. Civil District Courts Building, New Orleans.
Notarial acts of
Almonester, Andres, 1771–79, 1782.
Armas, Michel, 1810.
Bermudez, Francisco, 1801–2.
Broutin, François, 1791–99.
Broutin, Narcisse, 1799–1810.
Brown, Henry, 1804–6.
Fernandez, Joseph [with Andres Almonester], 1768–70.
Fitch, Eliphalet, 1805–10.
Garic, Jean-Baptiste, 1765–79.
Godefroy, P. F. S. [with Michel Armas], 1808–9.
Hernandez, Firmin, 1770–91.
Lynd, John, 1805–10.
Mazange, Leonard, 1780–83.
Miscellaneous Records, 1732–1869.
Pedesclaux, Pierre, 1788–1810.
Perdomo, Rafael, 1782–90.
Quiñones, Estevan, 1805–10.
Rodriguez, Fernando, 1783–87.
Successions, 1731–92.
Testaments, 1807–80.
Von Pradelles, Bernard, 1806–10.
Ximenes, Carlos, 1790–94.

New Orleans Public Library. Louisiana Division.

Conseil de Ville: Proceedings of Council Meetings. Vols. 1–3. Translations by Works
    Progress Administration of Louisiana.
Copia Fiel de las Actas del Cabildo de Nueva Orléans. 4 vols. of transcriptions.
New Orleans City Council: Petitions, Decrees, and Letters of the Cabildo, 1789–1803.
New Orleans Parish Indentures [*Engagements*], 1809–18.
Orleans Parish Court Records, 1813–15.
Orleans Parish, Old Inventories of Estate. Vol. A, 1807–1839.
Records of the City Council of New Orleans, 1794–1803. Book 4087. Translations by
    Works Progress Administration of Louisiana.
Records of the City Court of Appeals, 1807, 1813.
Records of the Superior Court, 1804–13.

Univ. of California at Berkeley. Bancroft Library.
    Documentos Relativos a la Luisiana, 1767–1816.

Univ. of New Orleans. Earl K. Long Library. Archives, Manuscripts, and Special Collections.
    Supreme Court of Louisiana. Collection of Legal Archives.

Univ. of Texas at Austin Library. Humanities Research Center.
    Census of Louisiana in 1785. Parsons Collection.

Xavier Univ. Library. Special Collections. New Orleans.
    Charles F. Heartman Collection of Manuscript Material Relating to the Negro and
    Slavery.

PUBLISHED PRIMARY SOURCES

American State Papers: Documents, Legislative and Executive, of the Congress of the United States, Class X,
    Miscellaneous. Vol. 1. Edited by Walter Lowrie and Walter S. Franklin. Washington D.C.:
    Gales and Seaton, 1834.
Bouligny, Francisco. *Louisiana in 1776: A Memoria of Francisco Bouligny.* Edited by Gilbert C. Din.
    New Orleans: Jack D. L. Holmes, 1977.
Brasseaux, Carl A., ed. and trans. *A Comparative View of French Louisiana, 1699 and 1762: The Journals
    of Pierre Le Moyne d'Iberville and Jean-Jacques-Blaise d'Abbadie.* 2d ed. 1979. Reprint, Lafayette:
    Center for Louisiana Studies, Univ. of Southwestern Louisiana, 1981.
Carter, Clarence E., ed. and comp. *The Territorial Papers of the United States.* Vol. 9, *The Territory of
    Orleans, 1803–1812.* Washington D.C.: GPO, 1940.
Claiborne, W. C. C. *Official Letter Books of W. C. C. Claiborne, 1801–1816.* Edited by Dunbar Rowland.
    6 vols. Jackson, Miss.: State Dept. of Archives and History, 1917.
*Code noir ou loi municipale: entrepris par délibération du cabildo en vertu des ordres du roi, que Dieu garde,
    consignés dans sa lettre faite à Aranjuez le 14 de mai, 1777.* New Orleans: L'Imprimerie d'Antoine
    Boudousquie, 1778.
Conrad, Glenn R., trans. and comp. *The First Families of Louisiana.* 2 vols. Baton Rouge: Claitor's,
    1970.]
Cruzat, Heloise H., and G. Lugano, eds. and trans. "Index to the Records of the Superior
    Council." *LHQ* 1–26 (1917–43).

Dart, Henry P., ed. "Bienville's Lands." *LHQ* 10 (1927): 6–24, 161–175, 364–80, 538–61; 11 (1928): 87–110, 209–32, 463–65.

Du Pratz, Antoine-Simon Le Page. *The History of Louisiana, Or of the Western Parts of Virginia and Carolina.* Edited by Joseph G. Tregle Jr. 1774. Reprint, Baton Rouge: Louisiana State Univ. Press, 1975.

French, Benjamin F., ed. *Historical Memoirs of Louisiana, From the First Settlement of the Colony to the Departure of Governor O'Reilly in 1770.* 5 vols. 1853. Reprint, New York: AMS Press, 1976.

Journals of the Louisiana Senate and House of Representatives. New Orleans: Official Printers, 1812–20.

Kinnaird, Lawrence, ed. *Spain in the Mississippi Valley, 1765–1794.* Part 1, *The Revolutionary Period, 1765–1781.* Part 2, *Post-War Decade, 1782–1791.* Part 3, *Problems of Frontier Defense, 1792–1794.* Annual Report of the American Historical Association for the Year 1945, vols. 2–4. Washington, D.C.: GPO, 1946–49.

Latrobe, Benjamin H. B. *Impressions Respecting New Orleans: Diary and Sketches, 1818–1820.* Edited by Samuel Wilson Jr. New York: Columbia Univ. Press, 1951.

Laussat, Pierre-Clément de. *Memoirs of My Life, to my Son during the Years 1803 and After . . .* Edited by Robert D. Bush. Translated by Agnès-Joséphine Pastwa. Baton Rouge: Louisiana State Univ. Press for the Historic New Orleans Collection, 1978.

Le Gac, Charles. *Immigration and War: Louisiana, 1718–1721.* Edited and translated by Glenn R. Conrad. Lafayette: Center for Louisiana Studies, Univ. of Southwestern Louisiana, 1970.

Martin, François-Xavier. *Martin's Reports of Cases Argued and Determined in the Superior Court of the Territory of Orleans, 1809–12, and in the Supreme Court of the State of Louisiana, 1813–30.* Edited by Thomas Morgan. 12 vols., n.s. New Orleans: Samuel M. Stewart, 1846–53.

Meneray, Wilbur E., ed. *The Rebellion of 1768: Documents from the Favrot Family Papers and the Rosamonde E. and Emile Kuntz Collection.* Translated by Philippe Seiler. New Orleans: Howard-Tilton Memorial Library of Tulane Univ., 1995.

Mettas, Jean, comp. *Répertoire des expéditions négrières au XVIIIe siècle.* Vol. 2, *Ports autres que Nantes.* Edited by Serge Daget and Michèle Daget. Paris: Société Française d'Histoire d'Outre-Mer, 1984.

Moreau-Lislet, Louis, comp. *A General Digest of the Acts of the Legislature Louisiana of Passed from the Year 1804, to 1827 Inclusive.* 2 vols. New Orleans: Benjamin Levy, 1828.

Nasatir, Abraham P., and James R. Mills, eds. *Commerce and Contraband in New Orleans During the French and Indian War: A Documentary Study of the Texel and Three Brothers Affairs.* Cincinnati: Hebrew Union College–Jewish Institute of Religion, 1968.

New Orleans in 1805: A Directory and a Census. Edited by Charles Thompson. New Orleans: Pelican Gallery, 1936.

Padgett, James A., ed. "'A Decree for Louisiana,' June 1, 1795." *LHQ* 20 (1937): 590–605.

———. "The Difficulties of Andrew Jackson in New Orleans, including His Later Dispute with Fulwar Skipworth, as Shown by the Documents." *LHQ* 21 (1938): 367–419.

Pitot, James. *Observations on the Colony of Louisiana from 1796 to 1802.* Translated by Henry C. Pitot. Baton Rouge: Louisiana State Univ. Press for the Historic New Orleans Collection, 1979.

Porteous, Laura, ed. and trans. "Index to the Spanish Judicial Records of Louisiana." *LHQ* 6 to 31 (1923–48).

Pradel, Jean-Charles de. *Le Chevalier de Pradel: vie d'un colon français en Louisiane au XVIIIe siècle d'après sa correspondance et celle de sa famille.* Edited by A. Baillardel and A. Prioult. Paris: Librairie Orientale et Américaine, 1928.

Recueils de réglemens, édits, déclarations at arrêts, concernant le commerce, l'administration de la justice, & la police des colonies françaises de l'Amérique, & les engagés. Avec le code noir et l'addition audit code. 2d ed. 2 vols. in 1. Paris: Les Libraires Associés, 1765.

Robertson, James A., ed. Louisiana under the Rule of Spain, France, and the United States, 1785–1807. 2 vols. Cleveland: Arthur H. Clark, 1911.

Robin, Claude-Cézar. Voyage to Louisiana, 1803–1805. Translated and abridged by Stuart O. Landry Jr. 1807. Reprint, New Orleans: Pelican, 1966.

Voorhies, Jacqueline K., trans. and comp. Some Late Eighteenth-Century Louisianians: Census Records of the Colony, 1758–1796. Lafayette: Univ. of Southwestern Louisiana, 1973.

Woods, Rev. Mgr. Earl C., and Charles E. Nolan, eds. Sacramental Records of the Roman Catholic Church of the Archdiocese of New Orleans. 10 vols. (New Orleans: Archdiocese of New Orleans, 1987–95.

NEWSPAPERS

Ami des Lois. 1810–15.
Courier de la Louisiane. 1810–14.
Louisiana Gazette. 1804–19.
Moniteur de Louisiane. 1802–11.
Telegraphe et le Commercial Advertiser. 1803–12.
Union, Orleans Advertiser and Price Current. 1804.

BIBLIOGRAPHICAL, ARCHIVAL, AND OTHER GUIDES

Astorquia, Madeleine. Guide des sources de l'histoire des États-Unis dans les archives françaises. Paris: France Expansion, 1976.

Beers Henry P. French and Spanish Records of Louisiana: A Bibliographical Guide to Archive and Manuscript Sources. Baton Rouge: Louisiana State Univ. Press, 1989.

Boimare, A. L. "Notes bibliographiques et raisonnés sur les principaux ouvrages publiés sur la Floride et l'ancienne Louisiane . . ." LHQ 1, no. 2 (1917–18): 9–78.

Conrad, Glenn, and Carl A. Brasseaux. A Selected Bibliography of Scholarly Literature on Colonial Louisiana and New France. Lafayette: Center for Louisiana Studies, Univ. of Southwestern Louisiana, 1982.

Cummins, Light T., and Glen Jeansonne. A Guide to the History of Louisiana. Westport, Conn.: Greenwood Press, 1982.

Favier, Jean, ed. Guide des sources de l'histoire de l'Amérique latine et des Antilles dans les archives françaises. Paris: Archives Nationales, 1984.

Haas, Edward F. Louisiana, A Dissertation Bibliography. Ann Arbor: UMI Press, 1978.

Kukla, John, ed. A Guide to the Papers of Pierre Clément Laussat, Napoleon's Prefect for the Colony of Louisiana and General Claude Perrin Victor at the Historic New Orleans Collection. New Orleans: Historic New Orleans Collection, 1993.

Menier, Marie-Antoinette, Étienne Taillemite, and Gilberte de Forges. Inventaire des archives coloniales: correspondence à l'arrivée en provenance de la Louisiane. 2 vols. Paris: Archives Nationales, 1976.

Peña y Camara, José de la, Ernest J. Burrus, S.J., Charles E. O'Neill, S.J., and Maria Teresa

Garcia Fernandez, eds. *Catálogo de documentos del Archivo General de Indias, sección V, Gobierno, Audiencia de Santo Domingo sobre la época española de Luisiana.* 2 vols. Seville: G. E. H. A., 1968.

Surrey, N. M. Miller, ed. *Calendar of Manuscripts in Paris Archives and Libraries Relating to the History of the Mississippi Valley to 1803.* 2 vols. Washington, D.C.: Carnegie Institution, 1926–28.

SECONDARY WORKS

Arnold, Morris, S. *Unequal Laws unto a Savage Race: European Legal Traditions in Arkansas, 1686–1836.* Fayetteville: Univ. of Arkansas Press, 1985.

Burson, Caroline M. *The Stewardship of Don Esteban Miró, 1782–1792.* New Orleans: American Printing, 1940.

Carter, Hodding, et al., eds. *The Past as Prelude: New Orleans, 1718–1968.* New Orleans: Pelican, 1968.

Caughey, John W. *Bernardo de Gálvez in Louisiana, 1776–1783.* 1934. Reprint, Gretna, La.: Pelican, 1972.

Clark, John G. *New Orleans, 1718–1812: An Economic History.* Baton Rouge: Louisiana State Univ. Press, 1970.

Coker, William S., and Robert R. Rea, eds. *Anglo-Spanish Confrontation on the Gulf Coast during the American Revolution.* Pensacola, Fla.: Gulf Coast History and Humanities Conference, 1982.

Conrad, Glenn R., ed. *Cross, Crucible and Crozier: A Volume Celebrating the Bicentennial of a Catholic Diocese in Louisiana.* Lafayette: Archdiocese of New Orleans and Center for Louisiana Studies, 1993.

Dart, Henry P. "The Career of Dubreuil in French Louisiana." *LHQ* 18 (1935): 267–331.

———. *Courts and Law in Colonial Louisiana.* New Orleans: Montgomery-Andree, 1921.

Debien, Gabriel. *Les esclaves aux Antilles françaises, XVIIe–XVIIIe siècles.* Basse-Terre and Fort de France: Sociétés d'Histoires de la Guadeloupe et Martinique, 1974.

DeConde, Alexander. *This Affair of Louisiana.* New York: Charles Scribner's Sons, 1976.

Delanglez, Jean, S.J. *The French Jesuits in Lower Louisiana, 1700–1763.* Washington D.C.: Catholic Univ. of America, 1935.

De Villiers du Terrage, Marc. "The History of the Foundation of New Orleans, 1717–1722." *LHQ* 3 (1920): 157–251.

———. *The Last Years of French Louisiana.* Translated by Hosea Phillips and edited by Carl A. Brasseaux and Glenn R. Conrad. Lafayette: Center for Louisiana Studies, Univ. of Southwestern Louisiana, 1982.

Din, Gilbert C. *Francisco Bouligny: A Bourbon Soldier in Spanish Louisiana.* Baton Rouge: Louisiana State Univ. Press, 1993.

Din, Gilbert C., and John E. Harkins. *The New Orleans Cabildo: Colonial Louisiana's First City Government, 1769–1803.* Baton Rouge: Louisiana State Univ. Press, 1996.

Frégault, Guy. *Le grand marquis: Pierre de Rigaud de Vaudreuil et la Louisiane.* Montréal: Fides, 1952.

Galloway, Patricia K., ed. *La Salle and His Legacy: Frenchmen and Indians in the Lower Mississippi Valley.* Jackson: Univ. Press of Mississippi, 1982.

Gautier, Arlette. *Les soeurs de solitude: la condition féminine dans l'esclavage aux Antilles du XVIIe siècle.* Paris: Éditions Caribéenes, 1985.

Gayarré, Charles. *A History of Louisiana.* 5th ed. 4 vols. Gretna, La.: Pelican, 1965.

Giraud, Marcel. *A History of French Louisiana.* Vol. 1, *The Reign of Louis XIV, 1698–1715.* Translated by Joseph C. Lambert. Vol. 2, *Années de transition, 1715–1717.* Vol. 3, *L'Époque de John Law, 1717–1720.* Vol. 4, *La Louisiane après le système de Law, 1721–1723.* Vol 5, *The Company of the Indies, 1723–1731.* Translated by Brian Pearce. Vols. 2–4: Paris: Presses Universitaires de France, 1958–74; Vols. 1 and 5: Baton Rouge: Louisiana State Univ. Press, 1974 and 1991.

Haas, Edward F., and Robert R. McDonald, eds. *Louisiana's Legal Heritage.* Pensacola, Fla.: Perdido Bay Press, 1983.

Hall, Gwendolyn Midlo. *Africans in Colonial Louisiana: The Development of Afro-Creole Culture in the Eighteenth Century.* Baton Rouge: Louisiana State Univ. Press, 1992.

Hanger, Kimberly. *Bounded Lives, Bounded Places: Free Black Society in Colonial New Orleans, 1769–1803.* Durham, N.C.: Duke Univ. Press, 1997.

Heaney, Sister Jane Frances. *A Century of Pioneering: A History of the Ursuline Nuns in New Orleans, 1727–1827.* Edited by Mary Ethel Booker Siefken. Chelsea, Mich.: Bookcrafters, 1993.

Hirsch, Arnold R., and Joseph Logsdon, eds. *Creole New Orleans: Race and Americanization.* Baton Rouge: Louisiana State Univ. Press, 1992.

Holmes, Jack D. L. *Gayoso: The Life of a Spanish Governor in the Mississippi Valley, 1789–1799.* Baton Rouge: Louisiana State Univ. Press, 1965.

Ingersoll, Thomas N. "Free Blacks in a Slave Society, 1718–1812." *William and Mary Quarterly,* 3d ser., 48 (1991): 173–200.

———. "Slave Codes and Judicial Practice in New Orleans, 1718–1807." *Law and History Review* 13 (1995): 23–62.

———. "The Slave Trade and the Ethnic Diversity of Louisiana's Slave Community." *LH* 37 (1996): 133–61.

Korn, Bertram W. *The Early Jews of New Orleans.* Waltham, Mass.: American Jewish Historical Society, 1969.

Lachance, Paul F. "The 1809 Immigration of Saint-Domingue Refugees to New Orleans: Reception, Integration, and Impact." *Louisiana History* 29 (1988): 109–41.

———. "L'effet du déséquilibre des sexes sur la comportement matrimonial: comparaison entre la Nouvelle France, Saint-Domingue et la Nouvelle-Orléans." *Revue d'histoire de l'Amérique française* 39 (1985): 211–31.

———. "The Formation of a Three-Caste Society: Evidence from Wills in Antebellum New Orleans." *Social Science History* 18 (1994): 211–42.

———. "Intermarriage and French Cultural Persistence in Late Spanish and Early American New Orleans." *Histoire Sociale–Social History* 15 (1982): 47–81.

———. "The Politics of Fear: French Louisianians and the Slave Trade, 1786–1809." *Plantation Societies in the Americas* 1 (1979): 162–97.

McConnell, Roland C. *Negro Troops of Antebellum Louisiana: A History of the Battalion of Free Men of Color.* Baton Rouge: Louisiana State Univ. Press, 1968.

McDermott, John F., ed. *The French in the Mississippi Valley.* Urbana: Univ. of Illinois Press, 1965.
———. *Frenchmen and French Ways in the Mississippi Valley.* Urbana: Univ. of Illinois Press, 1969.
———. *The Spanish in the Mississippi Valley, 1762–1804.* Urbana: Univ. of Illinois Press, 1974.

McGowan, James T. "Planters Without Slaves: Origins of a New World Labor System." *Southern Studies* 16 (1977): 5–26.

Malone, Ann Patton. *Sweet Chariot: Slave Family and Household Structure in Nineteenth-Century Louisiana.* Chapel Hill: Univ. of North Carolina Press, 1992.

Matas, Rudolph. *History of Medicine in Louisiana from the Earliest Period*, vol. 1. Edited by John Duffy. Baton Rouge: Louisiana State Univ. Press, 1958.

Moore, John P. *Revolt in Louisiana: The Spanish Occupation, 1766–1770*. Baton Rouge: Louisiana State Univ. Press, 1976.

O'Neill, Charles E., S.J. *Church and State in French Colonial Louisiana: Policy and Politics to 1732*. New Haven: Yale Univ. Press, 1966.

————. "'A Quarter Marked by Sundry Peculiarities': New Orleans, Lay Trustees, and Père Antoine." *Catholic Historical Review* 76 (1990): 235–77.

Price, Jacob M. *France and the Chesapeake: A History of the French Tobacco Monopoly, 1674–1791, and of Its Relationship to the British and American Tobacco Traders*. 2 vols. Ann Arbor: Univ. of Michigan Press, 1973.

Rankin, David C. "The Tannenbaum Thesis Reconsidered: Slavery and Race Relations in Antebellum Louisiana." *Southern Studies* 18 (1979): 5–31.

Schafer, Judith K. *Slavery, the Civil Law, and the Supreme Court of Louisiana*. Baton Rouge: Louisiana State Univ. Press, 1994.

Sterkx, H. E. *The Free Negro in Ante-Bellum Louisiana*. Rutherford: Fairleigh Dickinson Univ. Press, 1972.

Surrey, Nancy M. Miller. *The Commerce of Louisiana during the French Regime, 1699–1763*. New York: AMS Press, 1968.

Tannenbaum, Frank. *Slave and Citizen*. Introduction by Franklin W. Knight. Boston: Beacon Press, 1992.

Taylor, Joe G. *Negro Slavery in Louisiana*. New York: Negro Universities Press, 1969.

Texada, David K. *Alejandro O'Reilly and the New Orleans Rebels*. Lafayette: Univ. of Southwestern Louisiana Press, 1970.

Tregle, Joseph G., Jr. "Early New Orleans: A Reappraisal." *Journal of Southern History* 18 (1952): 20–36.

————. "Louisiana and the Tariff, 1816–1846." *LHQ* 25 (1942): 24–148.

Usner, Daniel. *Indians, Settlers, and Slaves in a Frontier Exchange Economy: The Lower Mississippi Valley before 1803*. Chapel Hill: Univ. of North Carolina Press, 1992.

Wilson, Samuel, Jr. *The Architecture of Colonial Louisiana: Collected Essays of Samuel Wilson, Jr., F. A. I. A.* Compiled and edited by Jean M. Farnsworth and Ann M. Masson. Lafayette: Univ. of Southwestern Louisiana Press, 1987.

Woods, Patricia D. *French-Indian Relations on the Southern Frontier, 1699–1762*. Ann Arbor: UMI Research Press, 1979.

Index

St. Malo (slave rebel), 200-201, 209

St. Marie Church, 263

St. Martin, Miss. 57

St. Pé (planter), 175

St. Philip Street Ballroom, 338-39

Ste.-Gême, Henri de and wife, 303

Ste.-Hermine, Marie-Louise, 44

Salmon, Edme-Gatien, 40, 55, 67, 76, 141

Saly, Marie-Louise (slave), 224

Sam (slave), 299

Samson, 87

Sanitté (slave), 324

Sauvagin, Euphrozine, 263

Saxe-Weimar, Karl Berhard, duke of, 338

Schafer, Judith Kelleher, 319, 323

Schools. See Children

Schwarz, Philip J., 85

Scipio (slave), 99

Sedella, Francisco-Antonio-Ildefonso ("Père Antoine"), 154, 252, 253, 261-63, 267, 457n.4, 369-70, 457n.43

Seguin, Justine, 301

Semonville-Canet concession, 37

Sex. See Gender, Racial intermixture, Sex distribution, Women

Sex distribution, 5, 47, 72, 80, 258-59

"Showboat," 333

Silver, 185

Simson, Thomas, 263

Sives, Betsy and daughter, 308

Slave children, 81-82, 85, 94-95, 96, 225-26, 274

Slave codes. See Black Code of 1806; Code Noir, Code of June 1, 1795, Codigo Negro, *Loi Municipale*, Regulations of 1751

Slave community, 70-76, 91, 95-96, 115, 117-18, 186-93, 202-3, 288-91, 304-5; and free blacks, 207; independent production and marketing, 105-7, 220, 232, 239, 320. *See also* Plantations, Slave family, Slave hire

Slave culture, xxii-xxiii, 285-86; African influence, 69-70, 72, 80, 94, 189-90, 285, 288, 306, 316-17, 325-26; dance and music, 192-93, 285, 306; language, 134, 299, 333,

388n.2; names, 142-43; religion, 114, 142, 289, 325, 382n.18. *See also* Rice production, Sugar production, Tobacco production, Wood production

Slave family, 80-83, 95, 192, 302-5. *See also* Marriage, Slave children

Slave hire, 98, 295

Slave manumission, 78-79, 215-17, 220-34, 326-28. *See also* Free blacks

Slave marronage, 85-92, 131-32, 196-202, 298-301. *See also* Slave resistance

Slave mortality, 68, 127-28, 185, 194-95. *See also* Diseases

Slave population, 17-18, 95-96, 155, 184-85, 284. *See also* Slave trade

Slave rebellion, xvi-xvii, 68, 74-77, 95, 186, 201, 203, 208-9, 291-95. *See also* Haiti

Slave resistance, 83-85, 97-103, 195-96, 202-5. *See also* Slave marronage, Slave rebellion

Slave society, xix, 96-97, 101, 159-60, 211-12, 315-17, 351-52. *See also* Free blacks, Nonslaveholders, Slave community, Slaveholding class

Slave trade: African, 68, 73, 74, 125-27, 130, 133-34, 181, 184-86, 194-95, 221-22, 230-31, 244-45, 281, 286-88; domestic, 290-91, 293, 324-25

Slave treatment, 127, 134-37, 181-84, 200-203, 212, 295-97, 305-7, 317-26. *See also* Racial intermixture, Slave family, Slave marronage, Slave resistance

Slaveholding class, xvi, xxii-xxiii, 4, 11-12, 41-45, 50, 59-61, 125, 143-44, 151, 158, 160, 170-74, 178-80, 244-47, 254-61, 263, 274-81, 317-18. *See also* individual slaveholders

Small, Stephen, 344

Smith (fiancée), 332

Smith, Julia Floyd, 129

Soldiers, 14-16, 177-78, 360n.59, 361n.69

Soler, Francisco, 216

Soto, Hernando de, 4, 20

Soulande, Marie-Louise, 50-51, 64

South Carolina, 6, 24, 53, 73, 92, 108, 132, 129, 159, 198-99, 287, 344

Spain, 24, 148, 157, 164, 256

Spanish America, 158, 176, 184, 212-13, 228. *See also* Trinidad

Sparks, William, 260

Stampp, Kenneth, 182

Stevenson, Brenda, 324

Stoddard, Amos, 219, 252, 262, 315, 320

Stuart, James, 338

Sugar production, 127-28, 173, 184, 193-95, 202, 211, 275, 279-80, 283, 304-5; U.S. tariff, 279-80

Sujuire (slave), 287

Superior Council, 39-40, 62, 79, 103, 116, 132, 136-37, 148-49

Supreme Court of Louisiana, 267, 269

Tannenbaum, Frank, xviii-xix, 120, 122, 221, 231, 233, 318, 321, 336, 395n.3, 454n.2

Tanesse, Jacques, 246

Tany (free grif), 215

Tarascon, Jacques, 190

Tate, Thad W., 134

Temba (slave), 195

Terrebonne, Jacques, 217

Tixerant, Louis, 59; and Marie Arlut, 57; plantation, 207

Tobacco production, 23, 366n.109

Tonti, Henri de, 4

Touro, Judah, 342

Tousard, Anne-Louis, 245

Toutant, Marguerite (slave), 206

Tregle, Joseph G. Jr., 246, 258, 260

Tremé, Claude, 239

Trinidad, 231

Trollope, Frances, 337-38

Trudeau, François, 79

Trudeau, Jean-Louis, 215

Turner (slaveowner), 298

Turner, Nat, 295, 344

Tushnet, Mark, 101

Ulloa, Antonio de, 92, 213, 214

United States, 244; cities and states, 254, 299, 311, 349. *See also* American Revolution, Civil War, Crash of 1819, Kentucky, South Carolina, Upper South, Virginia, War of 1812, Washington City

Unzaga, Luís, 157, 161, 169, 172

Upper South, 316-17

Ursuline Nuns, 32, 43, 51, 55-56, 108-9, 265-66, 287

Usner, Daniel H. Jr., xx, 19

Valère (slave), 300-1

Vanon, Simon, 77

Vaudreuil (free black), 214

Vaudreuil, Pierre, marquis de, 14, 40, 53, 93, 104

Vaugine de Nuisement, Captain, 35

Vénus, 68

Vénus (free black), 191

Verteuil (plantation director), 61

Victoria (slave), 216

Vielle, Bernard-Alexandre, 98

Villars, Joseph Dubreuil, 169, 172-74

Villeneuve, Jean, 178-79

Villeré, Jacques, 251, 279

Virginia, 6, 9, 12, 23, 24, 33, 62, 63, 65, 85, 134, 138, 204, 214, 247, 254, 264, 291, 294, 295, 316, 329, 337, 339, 343, 344

Vulcain (slave), 88

Walsh, Patrick, 261-62

War of 1812, 281, 294

Washington, George, 214, 245

Washington City, 349, 351

Watts, Margaret, 192

Weir, James, 260

West Florida, 8, 156, 225, 290

White, Deborah Gray, 303, 343

Wilkinson, James, 246

Women, black, 72, 80, 220-21; white: management and entrepreneurship, 48-49, 166-67, 265; prostitution, 339, 461n.102; racial attitudes, 167-68, 334-35, 337-39, 342; status, literacy, education and manners, 46-47, 49, 52, 54-56, 160-61, 264-66. *See also* Gender, Marriage, Slave family

Mammon and Manon in Early New Orleans was designed and typeset on a Macintosh computer system using PageMaker software. The text and titles are set in Centaur. This book was designed and composed by Angela Stanton and manufactured by Thomson-Shore, Inc. The recycled paper used in this book is designed for an effective life of at least three hundred years.